D1623121

SOMETHING ABOUT THE AUTHOR®

Something about
the Author *was named
an* **"Outstanding
Reference Source,"**
*the highest honor given
by the American
Library Association
Reference and Adult
Services Division.*

ISSN 0276-816X

SOMETHING ABOUT THE AUTHOR®

**Facts and Pictures about Authors
and Illustrators of Books for Young People**

volume 165

THOMSON

GALE

Detroit • New York • San Francisco • San Diego • New Haven, Conn. • Waterville, Maine • London • Munich

THOMSON

⁎

GALE ™

Something About the Author, Volume 165

Project Editor
Lisa Kumar

Editorial
Michelle Kazensky, Joshua Kondek, Tracey
Matthews, Julie Mellors, Mary Ruby, Mark
Rzeszutek, Maikue Vang

Permissions
Lori Hines, Shalice Shah-Caldwell, Kim Smilay

Imaging and Multimedia
Leitha Etheridge-Sims, Lezlie Light

Composition and Electronic Capture
Carolyn Roney

Manufacturing
Drew Kalasky

Product Manager
Chris Nasso

LIBRARY OF CONGRESS CATALOG CARD NUMBER 62-52046

ISBN 0-7876-8789-8
ISSN 0276-816X

This title is also available as an e-book.
ISBN 1-4144-1066-2
Contact your Thomson Gale sales representative for ordering information.

Printed in the United States of America
10 9 8 7 6 5 4 3 2 1

Contents

Authors in Forthcoming Volumes

Below are some of the authors and illustrators that will be featured in upcoming volumes of *SATA*. These include new entries on the swiftly rising stars of the field, as well as completely revised and updated entries (indicated with *) on some of the most notable and best-loved creators of books for children.

*Roch Carrier ▌ One of Canada's most esteemed novelists, Carrier has also penned a classic for children in his book *The Hockey Sweater*, and has sought to promote the history and traditions of his native French Canada in books such as *The Flying Canoe*.

Jean Gralley ▌ Writer/illustrator Gralley was a staff artist at the popular *Cricket* magazine for more than a dozen years. With her first book, *Hogula, Dread Pig of Night*, she began sharing her quirky sense of humor in a fun-filled story as well, and has also been exploring the digital future of the picture-book medium.

Leigh Hobbs ▌ He is scraggly, he is grouchy, and he is usually battered from a recent fight. He is the furball-ridden Old Tom, canine star of a series of darkly humorous books by Australian author/illustrator Leigh Hobbs that critics have compared to the works of Quentin Blake due to Hobbs' sketchy but captivating illustrations.

*Roger Ingpen ▌ The first Australian to be awarded the Hans Christian Andersen Medal for Illustration, Ingpen has coauthored numerous works in addition to illustrating new editions of classic books by such writers as Mark Twain and Robert Louis Stevenson. One of the hallmarks of Ingpen's finely detailed art, his fascination with technology, can be seen in *A Robert Ingpen Compendium* and *Pictures Telling Stories: The Art of Robert Ingpen*.

David Levithan ▌ The editorial director of Scholastic's PUSH imprint for new young-adult authors, Levithan is also a published novelist in his own right. In addition to his television and movie tie-in novels, his books *Boy Meets Boy* and *The Realm of Possibility* explore the complex relationships of modern teens.

Nerissa Nields ▌ Part of The Nields, a New England-based folk-singing group started by Nields and her sister, Nerissa is also a writer whose first novel, *Plastic Angel*, includes a music CD. She also conducts writing retreats and the "Writing It up in the Garden" workshop from her home in western Massachusetts.

Carl Norac ▌ A former French teacher and journalist, Norac has become a popular picture-book author in his native Belgium, where his works have been paired with art from several different illustrators. His books, which have reached English-speaking audiences via *I Love You So Much*, *My Daddy is a Giant*, and *I Love to Cuddle*, have engaged children around the world, and have been published in eighteen languages.

*Chris Riddell ▌ Riddell is an illustrator, and Paul Stewart is a writer. Their meeting—the result of the fact that their children attended the same school—has proved serendipitous: their collaborations in the "Edge Chronicles" series of fantasy novels have catapulted the pair into popularity, with Riddell's pen-and-ink art bringing the authors' fantasy world to vivid life.

Coleen Salley ▌ A born storyteller who has been sharing her gift with children in her native New Orleans, Salley has also created picture books featuring alligators, nutrias, and armadillos rather than puppies, kittens, and bears. Among her books, *Epossumondas* and *Why Epossumondas Has No Hair on His Tail* feature Salley's warm-hearted view of life.

Chris Wooding ▌ Wooding achieved success as an author at a young age, and his debut novel, *Crashing*, was in print by the time its author was in college. His more recent novel, the supernatural thriller *The Haunting of Alaizabel Cray*, has earned Wooding the Smarties Book Prize, a prestigious honor in his native England.

Introduction

Something about the Author (*SATA*) is an ongoing reference series that examines the lives and works of authors and illustrators of books for children. *SATA* includes not only well-known writers and artists but also less prominent individuals whose works are just coming to be recognized. This series is often the only readily available information source on emerging authors and illustrators. You'll find *SATA* informative and entertaining, whether you are a student, a librarian, an English teacher, a parent, or simply an adult who enjoys children's literature.

What's Inside *SATA*

SATA provides detailed information about authors and illustrators who span the full time range of children's literature, from early figures like John Newbery and L. Frank Baum to contemporary figures like Judy Blume and Richard Peck. Authors in the series represent primarily English-speaking countries, particularly the United States, Canada, and the United Kingdom. Also included, however, are authors from around the world whose works are available in English translation. The writings represented in *SATA* include those created intentionally for children and young adults as well as those written for a general audience and known to interest younger readers. These writings cover the entire spectrum of children's literature, including picture books, humor, folk and fairy tales, animal stories, mystery and adventure, science fiction and fantasy, historical fiction, poetry and nonsense verse, drama, biography, and nonfiction. Obituaries are also included in *SATA* and are intended not only as death notices but also as concise overviews of people's lives and work. Additionally, each edition features newly revised and updated entries for a selection of *SATA* listees who remain of interest to today's readers and who have been active enough to require extensive revisions of their earlier biographies.

Autobiography Feature

Beginning with Volume 103, *SATA* features one or more specially commissioned autobiographical essays in each volume. These unique essays, averaging about ten thousand words in length and illustrated with an abundance of personal photos, present an entertaining and informative first-person perspective on the lives and careers of prominent authors and illustrators profiled in *SATA*.

Two Convenient Indexes

In response to suggestions from librarians, *SATA* indexes no longer appear in every volume but are included in alternate (odd-numbered) volumes of the series, beginning with Volume 57.

SATA continues to include two indexes that cumulate with each alternate volume: the Illustrations Index, arranged by the name of the illustrator, gives the number of the volume and page where the illustrator's work appears in the current volume as well as all preceding volumes in the series; the Author Index gives the number of the volume in which a person's biographical sketch, autobiographical essay, or obituary appears in the current volume as well as all preceding volumes in the series.

These indexes also include references to authors and illustrators who appear in *Gale's Yesterday's Authors of Books for Children, Children's Literature Review,* and *Something about the Author Autobiography Series.*

Easy-to-Use Entry Format

Whether you're already familiar with the *SATA* series or just getting acquainted, you will want to be aware of the kind of information that an entry provides. In every *SATA* entry the editors attempt to give as complete a picture of the person's life and work as possible. A typical entry in *SATA* includes the following clearly labeled information sections:

PERSONAL: date and place of birth and death, parents' names and occupations, name of spouse, date of marriage, names of children, educational institutions attended, degrees received, religious and political affiliations, hobbies and other interests.

ADDRESSES: complete home, office, electronic mail, and agent addresses, whenever available.

CAREER: name of employer, position, and dates for each career post; art exhibitions; military service; memberships and offices held in professional and civic organizations.

MEMBER: professional, civic, and other association memberships and any official posts held.

AWARDS, HONORS: literary and professional awards received.

WRITINGS: title-by-title chronological bibliography of books written and/or illustrated, listed by genre when known; lists of other notable publications, such as plays, screenplays, and periodical contributions.

ADAPTATIONS: a list of films, television programs, plays, CD-ROMs, recordings, and other media presentations that have been adapted from the author's work.

WORK IN PROGRESS: description of projects in progress.

SIDELIGHTS: a biographical portrait of the author or illustrator's development, either directly from the biographee—and often written specifically for the *SATA* entry—or gathered from diaries, letters, interviews, or other published sources.

BIOGRAPHICAL AND CRITICAL SOURCES: cites sources quoted in "Sidelights" along with references for further reading.

EXTENSIVE ILLUSTRATIONS: photographs, movie stills, book illustrations, and other interesting visual materials supplement the text.

How a *SATA* Entry Is Compiled

A *SATA* entry progresses through a series of steps. If the biographee is living, the *SATA* editors try to secure information directly from him or her through a questionnaire. From the information that the biographee supplies, the editors prepare an entry, filling in any essential missing details with research and/or telephone interviews. If possible, the author or illustrator is sent a copy of the entry to check for accuracy and completeness.

If the biographee is deceased or cannot be reached by questionnaire, the *SATA* editors examine a wide variety of published sources to gather information for an entry. Biographical and bibliographic sources are consulted, as are book reviews, feature articles, published interviews, and material sometimes obtained from the biographee's family, publishers, agent, or other associates.

Entries that have not been verified by the biographees or their representatives are marked with an asterisk (*).

Contact the Editor

We encourage our readers to examine the entire *SATA* series. Please write and tell us if we can make *SATA* even more helpful to you. Give your comments and suggestions to the editor:

Editor
Something about the Author
Thomson Gale
27500 Drake Rd.
Farmington Hills MI 48331-3535

Toll-free: 800-877-GALE
Fax: 248-699-8070

Something about the Author Product Advisory Board

The editors of *Something about the Author* are dedicated to maintaining a high standard of excellence by publishing comprehensive, accurate, and highly readable entries on a wide array of writers for children and young adults. In addition to the quality of the content, the editors take pride in the graphic design of the series, which is intended to be orderly yet inviting, allowing readers to utilize the pages of *SATA* easily and with efficiency. Despite the longevity of the *SATA* print series, and the success of its format, we are mindful that the vitality of a literary reference product is dependent on its ability to serve its users over time. As literature, and attitudes about literature, constantly evolve, so do the reference needs of students, teachers, scholars, journalists, researchers, and book club members. To be certain that we continue to keep pace with the expectations of our customers, the editors of *SATA* listen carefully to their comments regarding the value, utility, and quality of the series. Librarians, who have firsthand knowledge of the needs of library users, are a valuable resource for us. The *Something about the Author* Product Advisory Board, made up of school, public, and academic librarians, is a forum to promote focused feedback about *SATA* on a regular basis. The nine-member advisory board includes the following individuals, whom the editors wish to thank for sharing their expertise:

Eva M. Davis
Youth Department Manager,
Ann Arbor District Library,
Ann Arbor, Michigan

Joan B. Eisenberg
Lower School Librarian,
Milton Academy,
Milton, Massachusetts

Francisca Goldsmith
Teen Services Librarian,
Berkeley Public Library,
Berkeley, California

Susan Dove Lempke
Children's Services Supervisor,
Niles Public Library District,
Niles, Illinois

Robyn Lupa
Head of Children's Services,
Jefferson County Public Library,
Lakewood, Colorado

Victor L. Schill
Assistant Branch Librarian/Children's Librarian,
Harris County Public Library/Fairbanks Branch,
Houston, Texas

Caryn Sipos
Community Librarian,
Three Creeks Community Library,
Vancouver, Washington

Steven Weiner
Director,
Maynard Public Library,
Maynard, Massachusetts

Acknowledgments

Grateful acknowledgment is made to the following publishers, authors, and artists whose works appear in this volume.

AHLBERG, ALLAN ▮ Howard, Paul, illustrator. From an illustration in *The Bravest Ever Bear,* by Allan Ahlberg. Text copyright © 1999 Allan Ahlberg. Illustrations Copyright © 1999 Paul Howard. Reproduced by permission of the publisher Candlewick Press, Inc., Cambridge, MA., on behalf of Walker Books Ltd., London.

ARMSTRONG, JENNIFER ▮ Van Fleet, John, illustrator. From a cover of *The Keepers of the Flame,* by Jennifer Armstrong and Nancy Butcher. HarperCollins Publishers, 2002. Cover art © 2002 by John Van Fleet. Used by permission HarperCollins Publishers./ Van Fleet, John, illustrator. From a cover of *The Kindling,* by Jennifer Armstrong and Nancy Butcher. HarperCollins Publishers, 2002. Cover art © 2002 by John Van Fleet. Used by permission HarperCollins Publishers./ Armstrong, Jennifer, photograph. Reproduced by permission of Jennifer Armstrong.

ASARO, CATHERINE ANN ▮ Asaro, Catherine Ann, photograph by John Cannizzo. Reproduced by permission./ Royo, illustrator. From a cover of *The Moon's Shadow,* by Catherine Asaro. Tom Doherty Associates, LLC, 2003. Reproduced by permission./ Bell, Julie, illustrator. From a cover of *The Quantum Rose,* by Catherine Asaro. Tom Doherty Associates, LLC, 2000. Reproduced by permission.

BIAL, RAYMOND ▮ Bial, Raymond, photograph by Sarah Bial. Reproduced by permission./ Leutz, Emanuel, illustrator. From an illustration in *Where Washington Walked,* by Raymond Bial. Walker &Company, 2004. Reproduced by permission./ Bial, Raymond. From an illustration in *Tenement: Immigrant Life on the Lower East Side,* by Raymond Bial. Houghton Mifflin Company, 2002. Illustration, Allen Street, Third-Story Front: Group of Children on Fire-Escape, August 4, 1916. Gift of the Tenement House Department, 31.93.14. Copyright © Museum of the City of New York. Reproduced by permission.

CADNUM, MICHAEL ▮ Cadnum, Michael, photograph by Richard Mewton. © Richard Mewton. Reproduced by permission./ Thorkelson, Gregg, illustrator. From a cover of *The Book of the Lion,* by Michael Cadnum. Speak, 2000. Cover copyright © 2000 by Gregg Thorkelson. All rights reserved. Used by permission of Viking Children's Books, a division of Penguin Young Readers Group (USA) Inc./ Thorkelson, Gregg, illustrator. From a cover of *The Dragon Throne,* by Michael Cadnum. Viking, 2005. Cover copyright © 2005 Gregg Thorkelson. All rights reserved. Used by permission of Viking Children's Books, a division of Penguin Young Readers Group, a member of Penguin Group (USA) Inc.

CHOYCE, LESLEY ▮ Choyce, Lesley, photograph by Jason McGroarty. Reproduced by permission of Lesley Choyce./ From a cover of *Smoke and Mirrors,* by Lesley Choyce. A Boardwalk Book, 2004. © Nancy R. Cohen/Getty Images.

CROSS, GILLIAN ▮ Cross, Gillian, photograph by Bob Jesson. Reproduced by permission of Gillian Cross and Bob Jesson.

CROSSLEY-HOLLAND, KEVIN ▮ Crossley-Holland, Kevin, photograph by Oenone Crossley-Holland. Reproduced by permission of Kevin Crossley-Holland./ Alcorn, Stephen, illustrator. From a cover of *King of the Middle March,* by Kevin Crossley-Holland. Arthur A. Levine Books, 2003. Jacket illustration copyright © 2003 by Scholastic Inc. Reprinted by permission of Scholastic Inc./ Call, Greg, illustrator. From a cover of the paperback edition of *The Seeing Stone,* by Kevin Crossley-Holland. Scholastic Inc., 2000. Reprinted by permission of Scholastic Inc.

DeFELICE, CYNTHIA ▮ DeFelice, Cynthia. From a cover of *Lostman's River,* by Cynthia DeFelice. Avon Camelot Books, 1995. Reproduced by permission./ DeFelice, Cynthia, photograph by Neil Sjoblom. Reproduced by permission of Cynthia DeFelice./ Bowers, David, illustrator. From a cover of *The Ghost and Mrs. Hobbs,* by Cynthia DeFelice. HarperTrophy, 2001. Cover art © 2003 by David Bowers. Used by permission HarperCollins Publishers.

d'LACEY, CHRIS ▮ Rinaldi, Angelo, illustrator. From a cover of *The Fire Within,* by Chris d'Lacey. Orchard Books, 2001. Jacket illustration copyright © 2001 by Angelo Rinaldi. Reprinted by permission of Orchard Books, an imprint of Scholastic Inc./ d'Lacey, Chris, photograph. Photo courtesy of Chris d'Lacey.

DOYLE, DEBRA ▮ Romas, illustrator. From a cover of *A Working of Stars,* by Debra Doyle. Tom Doherty Associates, LLC, 2002. Reproduced by permission./ Doyle, Debra. From a cover of *Gene Roddenbury's Earth: Final Conflict-Requiem for Boone,* by Debra Doyle. Tom Doherty Associates, LLC, 2000. Reproduced by permission.

DOYLE, MALACHY ▮ Doyle, Malachy, photograph. Reproduced by permission of Malachy Doyle./ Cneut, Carll, illustrator. From an illustration in *Antonio on the Other Side of the World, Getting Smaller* by Malachy Doyle. Candlewick Press, 2003. Text copyright © Malachy Doyle. Illustrations copyright © 2003 by Carll Cneut. Reproduced by permission of the publisher Candlewick Press, Inc., Cambridge, MA., on behalf of Walker Books Ltd., London./ Rinaldi, Angelo, illustrator. From an illustration in *Cow,* by Malachy Doyle. Margaret K. McElderry Books, 2002. Illustrations copyright © 2002 by Angelo Rinaldi. Reprinted with the permission of Margaret K. McElderry Books, an imprint of Simon &Schuster Children's Publishing Division.

DURANT, ALAN ▮ Boon, Debbie, illustrator. From an illustration of *If You Go Walking in Tiger Wood,* by Alan Durant. HarperCollins Children's Books, 2004. Text copyright © Alan Durant 2004. Illustrations copyright © Debbie Boon 2004. Reproduced by permission HarperCollins Publishers Ltd.

EISNER, WILL ▮ Eisner, Will, illustrator. From an illustration in *The Spirit No. 64,* by Will Eisner. Kitchen Sink Press, 1990.Copyright

court Brace & Company, 1996. Copyright © Debra Doyle and James D. Macdonald. Jacket illustration copyright © 1996 by Cliff Nielsen. Reprinted by permission of Harcourt, Inc.

MAYO, MARGARET ∎ Mayo, Margaret, photograph. Reproduced by permission of Margaret Mayo.

MUTH, JOHN J. ∎ From an illustration in *Zen Shorts,* by Jon J. Muth. Scholastic Press, 2005. Copyright © 2005 by Jon J. Muth. Reprinted by permission of Scholastic Inc.

NOVAK, MATT ∎ Novak, Matt. From an illustration in *Flip Flop Bop,* by Matt Novak. Roaring Brook Press, 2005. Copyright © 2005 by Matt Novak. Reproduced by permission of the author./ Novak, Matt. From an illustration in *No Zombies Allowed,* by Matt Novak. Atheneum Books, 2002. Copyright © 2002 Matt Novak. Reprinted with the permission of Atheneum Books for Young Readers, an imprint of Simon &Schuster Children's Publishing Division.

PAUSEWANG, GUDRUN ∎ Pausewang, Gudrun, photograph. © Ravensburger Buchverlag. Reproduced by permission.

PERRY, MARIE FRITZ ∎ Perry, Marie Fritz, illustrator. From an illustration in *A Gift for Sadia,* from Marie Fritz Perry. Buttonweed Press, 2004. Copyright © 2004 text and illustrations by Marie Fritz Perry. Reproduced by permission.

REID BANKS, LYNNE ∎ Reid Banks, Lynne, photograph. © Jerry Bauer. Reproduced by permission./ Harrison, Mark, illustrator. From an illustration in *The Dungeon,* by Lynne Reid Banks. HarperCollins Publishers, 2002. Copyright © 2002 Mark Harrison. Used by permission HarperCollins Publishers./ Elliott, Mark, illustrator. From a cover of *Alice-by-Accident,* by Lynne Reid Banks. HarperTrophy, 2000. Cover art © 2002 by Mark Elliott. Used by permission HarperCollins Publishers.

SENDAK, MAURICE ∎ Sendak, Maurice, photograph. Getty Images.

SHULEVITZ, URI ∎ Shulevitz, Uri. From an illustration in *Snow,* by Uri Shulevitz. Farrar, Straus and Giroux, 1998. Copyright © 1998 by Uri Shulevitz. Reprinted by permission of Farrar, Straus and Giroux, LLC./ Shulevitz, Uri, photograph by Mel Adelglass. © Mel Adelglass. Reproduced by permission./ Shulevitz, Uri. From an illustration in *The Travels of Benjamin of Tudela,* by Uri Shulevitz. Farrar, Straus and Giroux, 2005. Copyright © 2005 by Uri Shulevitz. Reprinted by permission of Farrar, Straus and Giroux, LLC.

SILVERMAN, ERICA ∎ Gerstein, Mordicai, illustrator. From an illustration in *Sholom's Treasure: How Sholom Aleichem Became a Writer,* by Erica Silverman. Farrar, Straus and Giroux, 2005. Illustrations copyright © 2005 by Mordicai Gerstein. Reprinted by permission of Farrar, Straus and Giroux, LLC./ Trueman, Matthew, illustrator. From an illustration in *When the Chickens Went on Strike,* by Erica Silverman. Dutton Children's Books, 2003. Illustrations copyright © 2003 by Matthew Trueman. All rights reserved. Used by permission of Dutton Children's Books, a division of Penguin Young Readers Group, a member of Penguin Group (USA) Inc.

STINE, CATHERINE ∎ McGillivray, Kim, illustrator. From a cover of *Refugees,* by Catherine Stine. Delacorte Press, 2005. Jacket illustration Copyright © by Kim McGillivray. Used by permission of Random House Children's Books, a division of Random House, Inc./ Stine, Catherine, photograph. Photo courtesy of Catherine Stine.

STROUD, BETTYE ∎ Stroud, Bettye, photograph by Sharon Jackson. Reproduced by permission of Bettye Stroud./ Bennett, Susanne, illustrator. From an illustration in *The Patchwork Path,* by Bettye Stroud. Candlewick Press, 2005. Illustrations copyright © 2005 by Erin Susanne Bennett. Reproduced by permission of the publisher Candlewick Press, Inc., Cambridge, MA.

TOEWS, MIRIAM ∎ Toews, Miriam. From a cover of *A Complicated Kindness,* by Miriam Toews. Counterpoint, 2004. Copyright © 2004 by Miriam Toews. Reprinted by permission of Counterpoint, a member of Perseus Books, LLC./ Gullung, Charles, photographer. From a cover of *Swing Low: A Life,* by Miriam Toews. Jacket design by Charlotte Strick. Arcade Publishing, New York, New York, 2001. Copyright © 2000 by Arcade Publishing. Reprinted by permission.

TOMLINSON, TERESA ∎ Tomlinson, Theresa, photograph. Reproduced by permission. Browne, Jane, illustrator. From an illustration in *Little Stowaway,* by Theresa Tomlinson. Julia MacRae Books, 1997. Illustrations copyright © 1997 A. E. T. Browne &Partners. Reproduced by permission of The Random House Ltd.

van GENECHTEN, GUIDO ∎ Van Genechten, Guido. From a jacket of *The Cuddle Book,* by Guido van Genechten. HarperCollins Publishers, 2003. Jacket Art © 2003 Uitgeverij Clavis, Amsterdam-Hasselt. Used by permission HarperCollins Publishers.

WALKER, KATE ∎ Yamazaki, Masakatsu/Photonicay, top photo. Bottom photo by Shinichiro Okajima/Photonica. From a cover of *Peter,* by Kate Walker. Houghton Mifflin Company, 1991. Reproduced by permission of Houghton Mifflin Company.

WHITE, RUTH ∎ Monks, Julie, illustrator. From a cover of *Memories of Summer,* by Ruth White. Farrar Straus and Giroux, 2000. Jacket art copyright © 2000 by Julie Monks. Reprinted by permission of Farrar Straus and Giroux, LLC./ Carpenter, Nancy, illustrator. From a cover of *Buttermilk Hill,* by Ruth White. Farrar, Straus and Giroux, 2004. Jacket art copyright © 2004 by Nancy Carpenter. Reprinted by permission of Farrar, Straus and Giroux, LLC./ Garns, Allen, illustrator. From a cover of *The Search for Belle Prater,* by Ruth White. Farrar, Straus and Giroux, 2005. Jacket art copyright © 2005 by Allen Garns. Reprinted by permission of Farrar, Straus and Giroux, LLC./ Kachik, John, illustrator. From a cover of *Belle Prater's Boy,* by Ruth White. Dell Yearling Book, 1996. Used by permission of Random House Children's Books, a division of Random House, Inc.

WINCH, JOHN ∎ Winch, John. From an illustration in *Two by Two,* by John Winch. Holiday House, 2004. Text and illustrations copyright © 2004 by John Winch. Reproduced by permission of Holiday House, Inc.

WINDAWI, THURA-al ∎ Windawi, Thura-al. From an illustration in *Thura's Diary: My Life in Wartime Iraq,* by Thura al-Windawi. Translated by Robin Bray. Viking, 2004. Copyright © 2004 by Thura al-Windawi. All rights reserved. Used by permission of Viking Children's Books, a division of Penguin Young Readers Group, a member of Penguin Group (USA) Inc.

WOLFE, GENE ∎ Wolfe, Gene. From a cover of *On Blue's Waters,* by Gene Wolfe. Tom Doherty Associates, LLC, 1999. Reproduced by permission./ Wolfe, Gene. From a cover of *Innocents Aboard,* by Gene Wolfe. Tom Doherty Associates, 2004. Cover art © 2003 C. Herscovici, Brussels/Artists Rights Society (ARS), New York. Reproduced by permission./ Manchess, Gregory, illustrator. From a cover of *The Knight,* by Gene Wolfe. Tom Doherty Associates, LLC, 2004. Illustrations copyright © 2004 by Gregory Manchess. Reproduced by permission.

SOMETHING ABOUT THE AUTHOR

ADAMS, Nicholas
  See DOYLE, Debra

* * *

ADAMS, Nicholas
  See MACDONALD, James D.

* * *

AHLBERG, Allan 1938-

Personal

Born June 5, 1938, in England; married Janet Hall (an illustrator), July, 1969 (died 1994); children: Jessica. *Education:* Sunderland College of Education, certificate in education, 1966.

Addresses

Home and office—20 Nether Hall Ln., Birstall, Leicester LE4 4DT, England. *Agent*—c/o Author Mail, Walker Books, 87 Vauxhall Walk, London SE11 5HJ, England.

Career

Children's book author. Worked variously as a letter carrier, grave digger, soldier, plumber's helper, and teacher; full-time writer, beginning 1975.

Awards, Honors

Commendation, British Library Association (BLA), 1977, for *Burglar Bill;* Kate Greenaway Medal, BLA, 1979, citation, Notable Children's Book Committee of the Association for Library Service to Children, 1979, and citation on honor list for illustration in Great Britain, International Board on Books for Young People, 1980, all for *Each Peach Pear Plum;* Other Award, Children's Rights Workshop, 1980, for *Mrs. Plug the Plumber;* Best Books of the Year designation, *School Library Journal,* 1981, and Silver Paint Brush award (Holland), 1988, both for *Funnybones;* citation, Notable Children's Book Committee of the Association for Library Service to Children, 1981, and Best Book for Babies award, *Parents* magazine, 1985, both for *Peek-a-Boo!;* BLA commendation, 1982, and Best Books of the Year designation, *School Library Journal,* Children's Books of the Year award, Library of Congress, Teacher's Choice award, National Council of Teachers of English, and citation, Notable Children's Book Committee of the Association for Library Service to Children, all 1983, all for *The Baby's Catalogue;* Emil/Kurt Mashler Award, British Book Trust, BLA commendation, and award, Federation of Children's Book Groups, all 1986, Golden Key (Holland), 1988, and Prix du Livre pour la Jeunesse, all for *The Jolly Postman; or, Other People's Letters;* Signal Poetry Award, 1990, for *Heard It in the Playground;* Kate Greenaway Medal, 1991, for *The Jolly Christmas Postman;* runner-up, British Book Awards, 1989, 1991; Blue Peter Book Award, 2001, and shortlist, 2002, 2004.

1

Writings

FOR CHILDREN

Ten in a Bed, illustrated by André Amstutz, Granada (London, England), 1983.

Please, Mrs Butler (verse; also see below), illustrated by Fritz Wegner, Viking Kestrel (New York, NY), 1983.

Woof!, illustrated by Fritz Wegner, Viking Kestrel (New York, NY), 1986.

The Mighty Slide (verse), illustrated by Charlotte Voake, Viking Kestrel (New York, NY), 1988.

Heard It in the Playground (verse; also see below), Viking Kestrel (New York, NY), 1989.

Mrs Butler Song Book (based on poems from *Please, Mrs. Butler* and *Heard It on the Playground*), music by Colin Matthews, illustrated by Fritz Wegner, Viking (New York, NY), 1992.

The Giant Baby, illustrated by Fritz Wegner, Viking (New York, NY), 1994.

The Better Brown Stories, illustrated by Fritz Wegner, Viking (New York, NY), 1995.

The Mysteries of Zigomar, illustrated by John Lawrence, Walker (London, England), 1997.

Monkey Do!, illustrated by André Amstutz, 1997.

Mockingbird, illustrated by Paul Howard, Walker (London, England), 1998.

The Bravest Ever Bear, illustrated by Paul Howard, Walker (London, England), 1999.

The Snail House, illustrated by Gillian Tyler, Candlewick Press (Cambridge, MA), 2000.

My Brother's Ghost, illustrated by Fritz Wegner, Viking (New York, NY), 2001.

The Man Who Wore All His Clothes, illustrated by Katherine McEwen, Candlewick Press (Cambridge, MA), 2001.

The Adventures of Bert, illustrated by Raymond Briggs, Farrar Straus (New York, NY), 2001.

Treasure Hunt, illustrated by Gillian Tyler, Candlewick Press (Cambridge, MA), 2002.

The Woman Who Won Things, illustrated by Katherine McEwen, Candlewick Press (Cambridge, MA), 2002.

Meow!: A Lift-the-Cat-Flap Book, illustrated by André Amstutz, Candlewick Press (Cambridge, MA) 2002.

A Bit More Bert, illustrated by Raymond Briggs, Farrar, Straus (New York, NY), 2002.

The Cat Who Got Away, illustrated by Katharine McEwen, Candlewick Press (Cambridge, MA), 2003.

The Little Cat Baby, illustrated by Fritz Wegner, Dial (New York, NY), 2004.

The Improbable Cat, illustrated by Peter Bailey, Delacorte (New York, NY), 2004.

Half a Pig, illustrated by daughter, Jessica Ahlberg, Candlewick Press (Cambridge, MA), 2004.

The Boy, the Wolf, the Sheep, and the Lettuce, illustrated by Jessica Ahlberg, Puffin (London, England), 2004.

The Shopping Expedition, illustrated by André Amstutz, Candlewick Press (Cambridge, MA), 2005.

The Children Who Smelled a Rat, illustrated by Katharine McEwen, Candlewick Press (Cambridge, MA), 2005.

FOR CHILDREN; WITH WIFE, JANET AHLBERG

Here Are the Brick Street Boys ("Brick Street Boys" series), Collins (London, England), 1975.

A Place to Play ("Brick Street Boys" series), Collins (London, England), 1975.

Sam the Referee ("Brick Street Boys" series), Collins (London, England), 1975.

Fred's Dream ("Brick Street Boys" series), Collins (London, England), 1976.

The Great Marathon Football Match ("Brick Street Boys" series), Collins (London, England), 1976.

The Old Joke Book, Kestrel Books (Harmondsworth, England), 1976, Viking (New York, NY), 1977.

The Vanishment of Thomas Tull, Scribner (New York, NY), 1977.

Burglar Bill, Greenwillow (New York, NY), 1977.

Jeremiah in the Dark Woods, Kestrel Books (Harmondsworth, England), 1977, Viking (New York, NY), 1978.

Cops and Robbers (verse), Greenwillow (New York, NY), 1978.

Each Peach Pear Plum: An "I Spy" Story (verse), Kestrel Books (Harmondsworth, England), 1978, Viking (New York, NY), 1979.

The One and Only Two Heads, Collins (London, England), 1979.

Two Wheels, Two Heads, Collins (London, England), 1979.

Son of a Gun, Heinemann (London, England), 1979.

The Little Worm Book, Granada (London, England), 1979, Viking (New York, NY), 1980.

Funnybones, Greenwillow (New York, NY), 1980.

Peek-a-Boo! (verse), Viking (New York, NY), 1981, published as *Peepo!*, Kestrel Books (Harmondsworth, England), 1981.

The Ha Ha Bonk Book, Penguin (London, England), 1982.

The Baby's Catalogue, Little, Brown (Boston, MA), 1982.

Yum Yum (part of "Slot Book" series), Viking Kestrel (London, England), 1984, Viking Kestrel (New York, NY), 1985.

Playmates (part of "Slot Book" series), Viking Kestrel (London, England), 1984, Viking Kestrel (New York, NY), 1985.

The Jolly Postman; or, Other People's Letters, Little, Brown (Boston, MA), 1986.

The Cinderella Show, Viking Kestrel (New York, NY), 1986.

The Clothes Horse and Other Stories, Viking Kestrel (London, England), 1987, Viking Kestrel (New York, NY), 1988.

Starting School, Viking Kestrel (New York, NY), 1988.

Bye-Bye, Baby: A Sad Story with a Happy Ending, Little, Brown (Boston, MA), 1989, published as *Bye-Bye, Baby: A Baby without a Mommy in Search of One*, 1990.

The Jolly Christmas Postman, Little, Brown (Boston, MA), 1991.

The Bear Nobody Wanted, Viking (New York, NY), 1992.

It Was a Dark and Stormy Night, Viking (New York, NY), 1993.

The Jolly Pocket Postman, Little, Brown (Boston, MA), 1995.

See the Rabbit, Doll and Teddy, Baby Sleeps, and *Blue Pram* (board books adapted from *The Baby's Catalogue*), Little Brown (Boston, MA), 1998.

"HAPPY FAMILIES" SERIES

Mr Biff the Boxer, illustrated by Janet Ahlberg, Puffin (London, England), 1980, published in "Wacky Families" series, Golden Press (New York, NY), 1982.

Mr Cosmo the Conjuror, illustrated by Joe Wright, Puffin (London, England), 1980.

Miss Jump the Jockey, illustrated by André Amstutz, Puffin (London, England), 1980.

Master Salt the Sailor's Son, illustrated by André Amstutz, Puffin (London, England), 1980, published in "Wacky Families" series, Golden Press (New York, NY), 1982.

Mrs Plug the Plumber, illustrated by Joe Wright, Puffin (London, England), 1980, published in "Wacky Families" series, Golden Press (New York, NY), 1982.

Mrs Wobble the Waitress, illustrated by Janet Ahlberg, Puffin (London, England), 1980, published in "Wacky Families" series, Golden Press (New York, NY), 1982.

Miss Brick the Builder's Baby, illustrated by Colin McNaughton, Puffin (London, England), 1981, published in "Wacky Families" series, Golden Press (New York, NY), 1982.

Mr Buzz the Beeman, illustrated by Faith Jaques, Puffin (London, England), 1981, published in "Wacky Families" series, Golden Press (New York, NY), 1982.

Mr and Mrs Hay the Horse, illustrated by Colin McNaughton, Puffin (London, England), 1981, published in "Wacky Families" series, Golden Press (New York, NY), 1982.

Mr Tick the Teacher, illustrated by Faith Jaques, Puffin (London, England), 1981.

Mrs Lather's Laundry, illustrated by André Amstutz, Puffin (London, England), 1981, published in "Wacky Families" series, Golden Press (New York, NY), 1982.

Master Money the Millionaire, illustrated by André Amstutz, Puffin (London, England), 1981.

Master Bun the Baker's Boy, illustrated by Fritz Wegner, Puffin (London, England), 1988.

Miss Dose the Doctor's Daughter, illustrated by Fritz Wegner, Puffin (London, England), 1988.

Mr Creep the Crook, illustrated by André Amstutz, Puffin (London, England), 1988.

Mrs Jolly's Joke Shop, illustrated by Colin McNaughton, Viking Kestrel (New York, NY), 1988.

Miss Dust the Dustman's Daughter, illustrated by Tony Ross, Viking (New York, NY), 1996.

Mrs Vole the Vet, illustrated by Emma Chichester-Clark, Viking (New York, NY), 1996.

Ms Cliff the Climber, illustrated by Fritz Wegner, Viking (New York, NY), 1997.

Master Track's Train, illustrated by André Amstutz, Viking (New York, NY), 1997.

"HELP YOUR CHILD TO READ" SERIES

Bad Bear (also see below), illustrated by Eric Hill, Granada (London, England), 1982.

Double Ducks (also see below), illustrated by Eric Hill, Granada (London, England), 1982.

Fast Frog (also see below), illustrated by Eric Hill, Granada (London, England), 1982.

Poorly Pig (also see below), illustrated by Eric Hill, Granada (London, England), 1982, Rand McNally (Chicago, IL), 1984.

Rubber Rabbit (also see below), illustrated by Eric Hill, Granada (London, England), 1982.

Silly Sheep (also see below), illustrated by Eric Hill, Granada (London, England), 1982.

Hip-Hippo-Ray, illustrated by André Amstutz, Granada (London, England), 1983, Rand McNally, 1984.

King Kangaroo, illustrated by André Amstutz, Granada (London, England), 1983.

Mister Wolf, illustrated by André Amstutz, Granada (London, England), 1983.

Spider Spy, illustrated by André Amstutz, Granada (London, England), 1983.

Tell-Tale-Tiger, illustrated by André Amstutz, Granada (London, England), 1983.

Travelling Moose, illustrated by André Amstutz, Granada (London, England), 1983.

Fast Frog and Friends: Help Your Child to Read Collection (first six volumes of series), illustrated by Eric Hill, Dragon, 1984.

"DAISYCHAINS" VERSE SERIES

Ready Teddy Go, illustrated by Janet Ahlberg, Heinemann (London, England), 1983.

Summer Snowmen, illustrated by Janet Ahlberg, Heinemann (London, England), 1983.

That's My Baby!, illustrated by Janet Ahlberg, Heinemann (London, England), 1983.

Which Witch, illustrated by Janet Ahlberg, Heinemann (London, England), 1983.

Monster Munch, illustrated by André Amstutz, Heinemann (London, England), 1984.

The Good Old Dolls, illustrated by André Amstutz, Heinemann (London, England), 1984.

Rent-a-Robot, illustrated by André Amstutz, Heinemann (London, England), 1984.

Clowning About, illustrated by André Amstutz, Heinemann (London, England), 1984.

One True Santa, illustrated by Janet Ahlberg, Heinemann (London, England), 1985.

"FOLDAWAYS" SERIES

Families, illustrated by Colin McNaughton, Granada (London, England), 1984.

Monsters, illustrated by Colin McNaughton, Granada (London, England), 1984.

Zoo, illustrated by Colin McNaughton, Granada (London, England), 1984.

Circus, illustrated by Colin McNaughton, Granada (London, England), 1984.

"RED NOSE READERS" SERIES

Jumping, illustrated by Colin McNaughton, Walker (London, England), 1985.

So Can I, illustrated by Colin McNaughton, Walker (London, England), 1985.

Big Bad Pig, illustrated by Colin McNaughton, Random House (New York, NY), 1985.

Bear's Birthday, illustrated by Colin McNaughton, Walker (London, England), 1985.

Help!, illustrated by Colin McNaughton, Random House (New York, NY), 1985.

Fee Fi Fo Fum, illustrated by Colin McNaughton, Random House (New York, NY), 1985.

Happy Worm, illustrated by Colin McNaughton, Random House (New York, NY), 1985.

Make a Face, illustrated by Colin McNaughton, Walker (London, England), 1985.

One Two Flea!, illustrated by Colin McNaughton, Walker (London, England), 1986.

Tell Us a Story, illustrated by Colin McNaughton, Walker (London, England), 1986.

Blow Me Down, illustrated by Colin McNaughton, Walker (London, England), 1986.

Look out for the Seals!, illustrated by Colin McNaughton, Walker (London, England), 1986.

Shirley Shops, illustrated by Colin McNaughton, Random House (New York, NY), 1986.

Me and My Friend, illustrated by Colin McNaughton, Random House (New York, NY), 1986.

Crash, Bang, Wallop!, illustrated by Colin McNaughton, Random House (New York, NY), 1986.

Push the Dog, illustrated by Colin McNaughton, Random House (New York, NY), 1986.

Who Stole the Pie, illustrated by Colin McNaughton, Walker (London, England), 1996.

Put on a Show!, illustrated by Colin McNaughton, Walker (London, England), 1996.

"FUNNYBONES" SERIES

The Pet Shop, illustrated by André Amstutz, Greenwillow (New York, NY), 1990.

The Black Cat, illustrated by André Amstutz, Greenwillow (New York, NY), 1990.

Mystery Tour, illustrated by André Amstutz, Greenwillow (New York, NY), 1991.

Dinosaur Dreams, illustrated by André Amstutz, Greenwillow (New York, NY), 1991.

Bumps in the Night, illustrated by André Amstutz, Greenwillow (New York, NY), 1991.

Give the Dog a Bone, illustrated by André Amstutz, Greenwillow (New York, NY), 1991.

Skeleton Crew, illustrated by André Amstutz, Greenwillow (New York, NY), 1992.

The Ghost Train, illustrated by André Amstutz, Greenwillow (New York, NY), 1992.

"FAST FOX, SLOW DOG" SERIES

Chicken, Chips, and Peas, illustrated by André Amstutz, Viking (New York, NY), 1999.

Fast Fox Goes Crazy, illustrated by André Amstutz, Viking (New York, NY), 1999.

The Hen House, illustrated by André Amstutz, Viking (New York, NY), 1999.

Slow Dog Falling, illustrated by André Amstutz, Viking (New York, NY), 1999.

Slow Dog's Nose, illustrated by André Amstutz, Viking (New York, NY), 2000.

OTHER

(With John Lawrence) *The History of a Pair of Sinners: Forgetting Not Their Ma Who Was One Also* (verse), Granada (London, England), 1980.

Janet's Last Book: Janet Ahlberg 1944-1994 (biography), Penguin (London, England), 1997.

Also author of the stage play *The Giant's Baby*.

Adaptations

A number of Allan and Janet Ahlberg's books were adapted for audiocassette, including *A Place to Play, Fred's Dream,* and *Each Peach Pear Plum.*

Sidelights

An award-winning British writer of children's stories, verse, picture books, and short novels, Allan Ahlberg is known for his irreverent wit and unfailing ability to make the commonplace seem extraordinary. From the mid-1970s until her death in 1994, wife Janet Alhberg served as both illustrator and co-designer, working with Ahlberg to produce highly regarded picture books, comic tales, and rhyming stories. The Ahlbergs were known for creating whimsical tales such as *The Jolly Postman, Each Peach Pear Plum,* and *The Bear Nobody Wanted,* books that continue to delight young audiences while also earning their creators such top awards as the prestigious Kate Greenaway Medal. Since his wife's death, Ahlberg has continued to blend his sardonic humor and often-times wacky world view with illustrations by a wide range of talented artists. In series such as the "Red Nose Readers," "Funnybones," and the ever-popular and zany "Happy Families," he incorporates nonsense rhymes into easy-to-tackle texts for budding readers, and his tongue-in-cheek humor keeps kids turning the pages.

Born in 1938, Ahlberg was educated at Sunderland Teacher Training College in England where he met his future wife, Janet Hall. In 1969 the two married and Ahlberg went on to work at a variety of jobs, including teaching, while his wife pursued a career in the graphic arts. By the mid-1970s they had set up a collaborative effort producing picture books, a joint effort that took flight with the "Brick Street Boys" series. Part of the couple's success, according to Aidan Chambers in *Horn Book,* came from the sense of unity in their work: "Their books certainly possess that integrated relationship between words and pictures usually achieved only when writer and illustrator are the same—one person," Chambers noted.

The Ahlbergs' beginning readers combine lighthearted fun, clear morals, and happy endings; good triumph over evil, and when adversity strikes, it is never overwhelming. In *Burglar Bill,* for instance, Bill steals commonplace items, such as a toothbrush and a can of beans. When he is finally robbed himself, he realizes how unpleasant it is to have things stolen and subsequently changes his ways. In picture books such as *The Baby's Catalogue, Each Peach Pear Plum,* and *Peek-a-Boo!* the couple focus on the simplicity of common objects and the security of everyday life, entertaining as well as reassuring young preschoolers. As Eric Hadley noted in *Twentieth-Century Children's Writers,* an Ahlberg book is "wholesome and decent" and does not "present a troubled world or set out to disturb."

One notable Ahlberg convention is to include classic fairy-tale characters like the three bears and Little Red Riding Hood in some of their stories. In *Each Peach Pear Plum* preschoolers can scan the vibrant, detailed illustrations to find such celebrated figures as Jack and Jill, Little Bo Peep, Tom Thumb, and Robin Hood. The boy detective in *Jeremiah in the Dark Woods* embarks on a journey that introduces him to three bears and takes him past a field of giant beanstalks. And *The Jolly Postman* features a postman delivering mail to famous

In **The Bravest Bear Ever** *Ahlberg serves up a supremely silly fairy-tale stew when the main character, a wooly bear, takes over the story; saving Little Red Riding Hood and thwarting a dragon, he ends the tale as a celebrated hero. (Illustration by Paul Howard.)*

characters like Cinderella, the Big Bad Wolf, and Gold-ilocks. *The Jolly Postman* was especially popular with readers and critics alike; as Chris Powling commented in *Books for Keeps,* "Once in a while a picture-book arrives that's so brilliant, so broad in its appeal, it seems to be a summation of the state-of-the-art. For me, *The Jolly Postman* is just such a book. As a matching of word and image it's a virtuoso performance; as a feat of design it's without a flaw."

On his own since Janet's death, Ahlberg has paired with talented illustrators such as André Amstutz, Katherine McEwen, and even his own daughter, Jessica Ahlberg, to produce numerous picture books that reflect his whimsical take on life. *Ten in a Bed* focuses on a little girl who finds a different fairy tale character in her bed each night: the Three Bears, the Big Bad Wolf, and the Cat from "Hey Diddle, Diddle," among others. Each time, the girl is able to get rid of the intruder by telling her own version of the fairy tale they inhabit. Critiquing this title in *Books for Your Children,* J. Tweedie commented that Ahlberg's "stories are ideal for children at the stage when fantasy and reality are still interchangeable," and predicted that the "racy and humorous" tales are "bound to become familiar favourites."

In *The Snail House* illustrations by Gillian Tyler enhance Ahlberg's story-within-a-story that finds siblings Michaeland Hannah, and their infant brother shrinking so small that they can live in a snail's snug shell. The adventures of the trio in their new garden home are narrated by their imaginative grandmother as the three children—all still human-sized—sit nestled in the woman's lap. *The Snail House* "will surely set young imaginations loose," noted a *Publishers Weekly* critic, adding that the story book "may well color the way readers view diminutive garden dwellers." In *Horn Book* Joanna Rudge Long noted of Ahlberg's story that "the enchantment of a world observed from the perspective of the smallest creatures is developed here with unusual felicity," while in *School Library Journal* Tina Hudak proclaimed that the book's "story and artwork together kindle the magic for anyone who has ever dreamed of unseen worlds with secret doors."

Other books for preschoolers and young children include *The Adventures of Bert, Treasure Hunt,* and *Half a Pig.* In *The Adventures of Bert* a day in the life of a somewhat clumsy young protagonist is set forth in a series of very short chapters. Introduced to readers first thing in the morning, Ahlberg's smiling, round-headed hero stumbles good-naturedly through his day, inadvertently waking up the family's baby, getting tangled in his shirt while dressing, fleeing from a giant sausage during a walk down the road, and diving into a chilly river to save a puppy. A *Horn Book* reviewer praised the gentle-hearted picture book as "chock full of pratfalls and slapstick humor" designed to "score a direct hit on five-year-old funnybones." Noting the comic-book elements introduced in Raymond Briggs's illustrations, a *Publishers Weekly* critic added that "both author

and illustrator invite audience conversation with their amiable hero." Bert reappears in *A Bit More Bert,* in which the amiable youngster goes dog-walking, gets a rather strange haircut, and then hopes to hunt for his lost pooch in a town where everybody, animal and human, is named Bert. "Ahlberg's poker-faced text is ready with wit," noted a *Kirkus* contributor, while in *Horn Book* Martha V. Parravano called Briggs's illustrations "sublime," adding: "a bit more Bert is not enough."

A book designed to "celebrate the playful games that deepen family ties," according to a *Kirkus* reviewer, *Treasure Hunt* finds a toddler named Tilly indulging in her love of discovery with the help of her loving parents. All day long things are deliberately hidden and joyously discovered: a delicious banana, a fuzzy toy bunny, the family cat. Finally, near bedtime, Tilly hides a special treasure for her parents: herself! In his simple tale Ahlberg creates "effervescent vignettes [that] convey a keen sense of humor," noted a *Publishers Weekly* contributor, while in *Horn Book* Christine M. Heppermann dubbed *Treasure Hunt* a story full of "joyous" discoveries about a family that "exhibits the happy disorganization that comes from having a young child around."

Continuing a family tradition, Ahlberg joins with his daughter, illustrator Jessica Ahlberg, in creating the picture book *Half a Pig.* Noting that the illustrations "call to mind the simple line and soft pastel shadings" of the late Janet Ahlberg's art, a *Publishers Weekly* writer called the father-daughter collaboration "high-spirited." In *Half a Pig* the duo tell a story about a pig named Esmeralda, whose secure life is shattered after her two owners, Mrs. Harbottle and her evil ex-husband, do battle over custodianship of the novel's porcine protagonist. The sausage-loving Mr. Harbottle has something other than Esmeralda's best intentions in mind, and when possible plans for her future involve rump roast and pork loin, the roly poly pet takes to the hills in a book that "positively squeals for some parent and child sharing," according to *Horn Book* reviewer Roger Sutton.

Ahlberg has a knack for capturing the attention of beginning readers with his simply worded texts which feature likeable characters and lively plots. His "Happy Families" series follows the antics of a variety of families from *Mr. Biff the Boxer* to *Ms. Cliff the Climber.* "To the uninitiated," remarked Jeff Hynds in *Books for Keeps,* "they might seem like simple stories in simple language, but those who think like this are missing the parody and underestimating the linguistic tricks that Ahlberg plays continually with his readers." While equally captivating, several of Ahlberg's stories hint at complex themes, such as the competing needs of work and family after divorce breaks up a home in *Mrs. Vole the Vet.* Reviewing *Master Bun the Baker's Boy* and *Miss Dose the Doctor's Daughter, Growing Point* contributor Margery Fisher concluded, "Simple jokes and expressive, dramatically active coloured pictures should confirm the popularity of a favourite series, conducted with the utmost expertise in word and line." Also appraising multiple titles in the series, a *Books for Keeps* reviewer commented on Ahlberg's casting of a "resourceful and ambitious" female protagonist who capably saves her entire town in *Miss Dose the Doctor's Daughter.*

Featuring illustrations by Colin McNaughton, Ahlberg's popular "Red Nose Readers" series was hailed by *Books for Keeps* contributor Pat Triggs as a "brilliant . . . collaboration," while other critics noted its significant comic appeal. "Funnybones," a series that stars a cast of boney skeletons in Ahlberg's trademark silly plots, also drew significant praise. Reviewing the first two series titles, *The Black Cat* and *The Pet Shop, School Library Journal* critic Ruth Smithof noted the books' "cartoonlike layout, repetitive language, and situational humor" and dubbed them a "good choice for beginning readers." Reviewing *Dinosaur Dreams* and *Mystery Tour* in the same periodical, Leslie Barban remarked that Ahlberg's "crazy and wacky" stories are "more funnier-than-spooky entries for an audience often looking for good material in this genre." A *Books for Keeps* contributor also praised the series, noting that "few beginning readers can resist the sheer silliness of these stories, . . . which are full of repetition, so easy to read and yet are quirky, witty and original."

In a multi-chapter book that features what a *Publishers Weekly* reviewer described as "an appealing madcap plot, dialogue that verges on slapstick, and sprightly pictures," Ahlberg introduces the Gaskitt family: Mr. and Mrs. Gaskitt and nine-year-old twins Gloria and Gus. *The Man Who Wore All His Clothes* finds Mr. Gaskitt dressing for work; in fact, he seems to be OVER-dressing, as he dons layer after layer of clothing until his closet is almost empty. While this mystery percolates in young readers' minds, Mrs. Gaskitt races off in her taxi-cab, and her first fare appears to be a bank-robber fleeing from a heist. The robber races from taxi to school bus, where he takes the Gaskitt twins and their fellow passengers on a merry chase until Ahlberg's confabulation neatly sorts itself out. A *Kirkus Reviews* writer dubbed *The Man Who Wore All His Clothes* as a "tilt-a-whirl tale" and praised the "bright, comic cartoon scenes" brought to life by illustrator Katharine McEwen, while in *School Library Journal* a reviewer cited the book's "numerous funny touches . . . and surprise ending."

The Gaskitts have appeared in several more books by Ahlberg, including *The Woman Who Won Things,* which finds Mrs. Gaskitt on a winning streak while the twins' substitute teacher seems more than a bit shifty; *The Cat Who Got Carried Away,* in which the disappearance of the twins' classroom mascot, a rat, is followed by the disappearance of family cat Horace; and *The Children Who Smelled a Rat,* wherein a series of mysterious occurrences leave each member of the Gaskitt family in a quandary. Dubbing *The Children Who Smelled a Rat* "unputdownable," *School Library Journal* reviewer Jodi Kearns called Ahlsberg's easy-to-read chapterbook text "funny, riveting, [and] absorbing." The book is "part graphic novel, part breathless action-packed soap opera," explained a *Kirkus Reviews* writer, while in the same periodical Kathleen Kelly Macmillan predicted that in *The Woman Who Won Things* Ahlberg's "clever use of language will delight new readers."

Writing for middle-grade readers, Ahlberg has turned his humorous talents to novels with *Woof!* and *The Giant Baby,* and to short stories with both *The Better Brown Stories* and *The Bravest Bear Ever.* In *Woof!* Ahlberg creates a Kafka-esque scenario when young Eric Banks suddenly transforms into a Norfolk terrier. Eric gets a dog's eye view of things until he becomes Eric once more, but he never knows when this change will occur again. With *The Giant Baby* Ahlberg again pushes the bounds of reality when a giant infant unexpectedly arrives on Alice's doorstep. Though the young girl longs for a baby brother, the new arrival is rather too much for poor Alice. Soon, however, Alice and her parents become attached to the large infant and they get into all sorts of predicaments trying to keep the foundling from being taken away to a foster family. "Fast-paced, tightly plotted, and packed with excitement and humor, this tale is destined to take its place with the very best novels for this age group," wrote Ruth Semrau in a *School Library Journal* review of *The Giant Baby.* Comparing Ahlberg's prose to that of British writer Roald Dahl, Semrau added that Ahlberg's "wry wit makes his book as appealing to adults as to children."

Ahlberg presents characters who rebel against their creator in both *The Better Brown Stories* and *The Bravest Bear Ever.* Miffed with the stories that are mapping out their day-to-day lives and leaving them little time for their own devices, the members of the Brown family seek out the writer responsible and give him a piece of their communal mind in *The Better Brown Stories.* Another frustrated bear, with aspirations of being a story-book hero, takes over writing duties altogether in *The Bravest Bear Ever.* First Baby Bear concocts a heroic exploit, featuring trolls, dragons, a princess, a penguin, and even a sausage; then each character in turn retells the tale in a way that puts their part in the spotlight. Christina Dorr, writing in *School Library Journal,* called *The Better Brown Stories* a "clever collection of short stories that's sure to be a hit." *Booklist* critic Hazel Rochman concluded that if American readers do not quite get the British references in the story, "everyone will enjoy the mischief and the wry characters that suddenly move from the mundane to the marvelous." Praising *The Bravest Bear Ever* as chock-full of "hilarious non sequiturs and inventive plot twists," *Booklist* contributor Shelle Rosenfeld also noted that a subtext rife with smart-alecky banter creates "lively, chaotic scenarios" out of what would otherwise be straightforward tales. As a *Books for Keeps* critic remarked of *The Bet-*

ter Brown Stories, "Picking up a book by Allan Ahlberg is always exciting, for children and adults. There is a feeling that one is going to be both entertained and challenged, and this new title certainly lives up to that expectation."

Moving his attention to somewhat older readers, Ahlberg penned the novel *My Brother's Ghost,* which takes place in 1956. Part of an ill-fated blue-collar British family in which both parents are dead, ten-year-old Tom Fogarty dies when he is struck by a milk float, but reappears to his nine-year-old sister, Frances, and little brother Harry as they mourn his death at his funeral. Taking on the role of guardian angel, Tom helps Frances cope with the hard-hearted aunts now raising the Fogarty children, and also face a bully at school. When Frances takes Harry and runs away to escape her unhappy home life, Tom is there to avert a third family tragedy. Timothy Capehart, reviewing *My Brother's Ghost* in *School Library Journal,* found the writing excellent and the period evocatively described, but added that the book's "intended audience is difficult to define" because the tale reads as "a ghost story that isn't scary and an affecting family tale that centers on the supernatural."

Whether producing whimsical series readers or stand-alone stories full of tongue-in-cheek witticisms, Ahlberg has become popular with children on both side of the Atlantic. Surprising, given the numerous awards and praise that he has received during his long career, he remains understated about his achievement. "It's play," he once told Victoria Neumark in the *Times Literary Supplement* in describing his work. The reason for his success? "It's farce, it's the neatness of the plot."

Biographical and Critical Sources

BOOKS

Carpenter, Humphrey, and Mari Prichard, *The Oxford Companion to Children's Literature,* Oxford University Press (Oxford, England), 1984.

Children's Literature Review, Volume 18, Thomson Gale (Detroit, MI), 1989.

Hobson, Margaret, Jennifer Madden, and Ray Prytherch, *Children's Fiction Sourcebook,* Ashgate Publishing (Brookfield, VT), 1992.

Martin, Douglas, *The Telling Line: Essays on Fifteen Contemporary Book Illustrators,* Julia MacRae Books, 1989, Doubleday (New York, NY), 1990.

Pendergast, Sara, and Tom Pendergast, editors, *St. James Guide to Children's Writers,* 5th edition, St. James Press (Detroit, MI), 1999.

Silvey, Anita, editor, *Children's Books and Their Creators,* Houghton Mifflin (Boston, MA), 1995.

Twentieth-Century Children's Writers, 2nd edition, St. James Press (Detroit, MI), 1983.

Ward, Martha E., and others, *Authors of Books for Young People,* 3rd edition, Scarecrow Press (Metuchen, NJ), 1990.

PERIODICALS

Booklist, May 1, 1994, p. 1606; January 1, 1996, Hazel Rochman, review of *The Better Brown Stories,* p. 832; December 1, 1997, GraceAnne A. DeCandido, review of *The Mysteries of Zigomar: Poems and Stories,* p. 61; April, 1998, Linda Perkins, review of *Monkey Do!,* p. 1328; September 15, 1998, Carolyn Phelan, review of *Mockingbird,* p. 228; January 1, 1999, p. 784; May 15, 2000, Shelle Rosenfeld, review of *The Bravest Bear Ever,* p. 175; July, 2001, Carolyn Phelan, review of *The Snail House,* p. 2016; September 1, 2001, Ilene Cooper, review of *The Adventures of Bert,* p. 112; March 15, 2002, Michael Cart, review of *Treasure Hunt,* p. 1261; November 1, 2002, Julie Cummins, review of *A Bit More Bert,* p. 502; May 15, 2004, Ilene Cooper, review of *The Little Cat Baby,* p. 1624; August, 2004, Diane Foote, review of *Half a Pig,* p. 1932.

Books for Keeps, January, 1987, Chris Powling, review of *The Jolly Postman,* pp. 4-5; January, 1988, p. 3; January, 1988, review of *Woof!,* p. 17; May, 1988, review of *One Two Flea!,* p. 12; September, 1988, review of *Miss Dose the Doctor's Daughter,* p. 8; March, 1993, review of *Mystery Tour,* p. 10; July, 1996, review of *The Giant Baby,* p. 12; November, 1996, Jeff Hynds, "Master Allan the Ahlberg," pp. 4-5, Liz Waterland, review of "Happy Families," p. 5, and review of *Who Stole the Pie?,* p. 8; January, 1997, review of *The Better Brown Stories,* p. 23; September, 1997, Jill Bennett, review of *Master Track's Train,* p. 21; January, 1998, Annabel Gibb, review of *The Mysteries of Zigomar,* p. 19; January, 1999, Valerie Coghlan, review of *Mockingbird,* p. 18.

Books for Your Children, spring, 1991, J. Tweedie, review of *Ten in a Bed,* p. 17.

Bulletin of the Center for Children's Books, April, 1998, Pat Mathews, review of *Monkey Do!,* pp. 272-273; October, 1998, Janice M. Del Negro, review of *Mockingbird,* p. 51.

Carousel, summer, 2000, Pat Tate, review of *My Brother's Ghost,* p. 25.

Commonweal, November 11, 1977.

Growing Point, September, 1988, Margery Fisher, review of *Master Bun the Baker's Boy* and *Miss Dose the Doctor's Daughter,* p. 5049; January, 1990, Margery Fisher, review of *Heard It in the Playground,* p. 5283.

Horn Book, December, 1982, Aidan Chambers, "Letter from England: Two in-One," pp. 686-690; July-August, 1993, p. 456; September-October, 1996, pp. 590-591; May-June, 1999, review of *The Better Brown Stories,* p. 354; March, 2000, review of *The Bravest Ever Bear,* p. 180; May, 2001, review of *The Snail House,* p. 307; July, 2001, review of *The Adventures of Bert,* p. 437; May-June, 2002, Christine M. Heppermann, review of *Treasure Hunt,* p. 311; September-October, 2002, Martha V. Parravano, review of *A Bit More Bert,* p. 548; July-August, 2004, Roger Sutton, review of *Half a Pig,* p. 433; July-August, 2005, Joanna Rudge Long, review of *The Shopping Expedition,* p. 447.

Junior Bookshelf, December, 1979; August, 1987, review of *One Two Flea,* p. 158; April, 1996, review of *Who Stole the Pie?,* pp. 64-65.

Kirkus Reviews, September 15, 2001, review of *The Man Who Wore All His Clothes,* p. 1352; March 1, 2002, review of *Treasure Hunt,* p. 328; April 15, 2002, review of *The Woman Who Won Things,* p. 560; September 1, 2002, review of *A Bit More Bert,* p. 1300; April 15, 2004, review of *Half a Pig,* p. 389; June 1, 2004, review of *The Little Cat Baby,* p. 533; July 1, 2004, review of *The Improbable Cat,* p. 625; May 15, 2005, review of *The Shopping Expedition,* p. 583; September 1, 2005, review of *The Children Who Smelled a Rat,* p. 967.

Listener, November 8, 1979.

Los Angeles Times Book Review, May 31, 1981.

Magpies, May, 1998, review of *Monkey Do!,* p. 5.

New Statesman, November 28, 1975; November 21, 1980; December 4, 1981; December 3, 1982.

New York Times Book Review, April 10, 1977; April 22, 1979; April 29, 1979; May 20, 1979; March 1, 1981; June 17, 2001, Marigny Dupuy, review of *The Snail House,* p. 25.

Observer (London, England), July 19, 1981; December 6, 1981; December 7, 1997, p. 17.

Publishers Weekly, November 2, 1990, p. 73; August 9, 1991, p. 56; January 25, 1993, p. 87; February 28, 1994, p. 88; November 27, 1995, p. 70; October 13, 1997, review of *The Mysteries of Zigomar,* p. 75; January 31, 2000, review of *The Bravest Ever Bear,* p. 106; February 19, 2001, review of *The Snail House,* p. 91; June 25, 2001, review of *The Adventures of Bert,* p. 71; September 10, 2001, review of *The Man Who Wore All His Clothes,* p. 93; March 25, 2001, review of *Treasure Hunt,* p. 63; February 2001, review of *The Snail House,* p. 91; June 25, 2001, review of *The Adventures of Bert,* p. 71; April 26, 2004, review of *The Little Cat Baby* and *Half a Pig,* p. 65; August 9, 2004, review of *The Improbable Cat,* p. 251.

Punch, November 17, 1982.

Saturday Review, May 28, 1977; May 26, 1979.

School Library Journal, September, 1981; April, 1986, Louise L. Sherman, review of *Big Bad Pig,* p. 67; February, 1987, Kathleen Brachman, review of *Woof!,* p. 76; March, 1991, Ruth Smith, review of *The Black Cat,* p. 166; July, 1991, Leslie Barban, review of *Dinosaur Dreams,* p. 52; July, 1995, Ruth Semrau, review of *The Giant Baby,* p. 76; February, 1996, Christina Dorr, review of *The Better Brown Stories,* p. 100; November, 1997, John Sigwald, review of *The Mysteries of Zigomar,* p. 76; June, 1998, Christine A. Moesch, review of *Monkey Do!,* p. 94; October, 1998, Paula A. Kiely, review of *Mockingbird,* p. 119; June, 2000, Marlene Gawron, review of *The Bravest Ever Bear,* p. 100; March, 2001, Tina Hudak, review of *The Snail House,* p. 192; July, 2001, Timothy Capehart, review of *My Brother's Ghost,* p. 102; August, 2001, Grace Oliff, review of *The Adventures of Bert,* p. 142; October, 2001, review of *The Man Who Wore All His Clothes,* p. 62; April, 2002, Gay Lynn Van Vleck, review of *Treasure Hunt,* p. 100; June, 2002, Kathleen Kelly MacMillan, review of *The Woman Who Won Things,* p. 80; November, 2002, Teri Markson, review of *A Bit More Bert,* p. 110; September, 2003, Liza Graybill, review of *The Cat Who Got Carried Away,* p. 166; August, 2004, Phyllis M. Simon, review of *Half a Pig,* p. 82, and Susan Hepler, review of *The Improbable Cat,* p. 115; October, 2004, Marianne Saccardi, review of *The Little Cat Baby,* p. 108; August, 2005, Robin L. Gibson, review of *The Shopping Expedition,* p. 84; October, 2005, Jodi Kearns, review of *The Children Who Smelled a Rat,* p. 102.

Spectator, July 16, 1977.

Teacher Librarian, November, 1998, pp. 42, 44; June 2000, Shirley Lewis, review of *The Bravest Ever Bear,* p. 49.

Times (London, England), March 5, 1980.

Times Educational Supplement, November 23, 1979; January 18, 1980; March 7, 1980; June 20, 1980; November 21, 1980; January 2, 1981; July 24, 1981; November 20, 1981; November 19, 1982; March 11, 1983; June 3, 1983; September 30, 1983; March 21, 1997, Elaine Williams, "More than Words" (interview), p. B8; November 7, 1997, p. 2; December 5, 1997, p. 17; January 2, 1998, p. 23; November 20, 1998, p. 10; March 19, 1999, p. 25.

Times Literary Supplement, March 25, 1977; December 1, 1978; March 28, 1980; June 20, 1980, Victoria Neumark, "A Marriage of Words and Pictures," p. 42; November 21, 1980; September 18, 1981; March 26, 1982; November 26, 1982; July 22, 1983; November 30, 1984.

Washington Post Book World, February 11, 1979.*

*　　*　　*

al-WINDAWI, Thura
See WINDAWI, Thura al-

*　　*　　*

APPLETON, Victor
See DOYLE, Debra

*　　*　　*

APPLETON, Victor
See MACDONALD, James D.

*　　*　　*

ARMSTRONG, Jennifer 1961-
(Julia Winfield)

Personal

Born May 12, 1961, in Waltham, MA; daughter of John (a physicist) and Elizabeth (a master gardener; maiden name, Saunders) Armstrong. *Education:* Smith College, B.A., 1983. *Hobbies and other interests:* Gardening, teaching, music, reading.

Addresses

Agent—Susan Cohen, Writers House, 21 W. 26th St., New York, NY 10010.

Career

Cloverdale Press, New York, NY, assistant editor, 1983-85; freelance writer, 1985—; teacher. Girl Scout leader, 1987-89; Smith College, Northampton, MA, recruiter, 1990-95; leader of writing workshops. Literacy Volunteers of Saratoga, board president, 1991-93; puppy raiser for Guiding Eyes for the Blind. President and cofounder of Children's Literature Connection, Inc., 1997—.

Awards, Honors

Best Book Award, American Library Association (ALA), and Golden Kite Honor Book Award, Society of Children's Book Writers and Illustrators, both 1992, and Teacher's Choice Award, International Reading Association (IRA), 1993, all for *Steal Away;* Notable Book citations, ALA, 1992, for *Steal Away* and *Hugh Can Do;* IRA/Children's Book Council (CBC) Children's Choice designation, 1995, for *That Terrible Baby;* Blue Ribbon Book designation, *Bulletin of the Center for Children's Books,* 1996, and Children's Books of Distinction designation, *Hungry Mind Review,* both 1997, both for *The Dreams of Mairhe Mehan; Smithsonian* Notable Books for Children citation, 1998, for *Pockets;* Children's Books of Distinction Award, *Riverbank Review,* 1998, for *Mary Mehan Awake;* Children's Books of Distinction Award, *Riverbank Review,* Orbis Pictus Award, National Council of Teachers of English, and *Boston Globe/Horn Book* Honor designation, all 1999, all for *Shipwreck at the Bottom of the World: The Extraordinary True Story of Shackleton and the Endurance;* Cuffies Award for Best Autobiography, Children's Booksellers, 1999, and Anisfeld-Wolf Book Award, and Children's Book of Distinction Award, *Riverbank Review,* both 2000, all for *In My Hands;* Best Children's Book of the Year Award, Bank Street College, 2001, for *Spirit of Endurance;* National Science Foundation artists and writers in the Antarctic grant, 2002.

Writings

Steal Away (novel), Orchard (New York, NY), 1992.
Hugh Can Do (picture book), illustrated by Kimberly Root, Crown (New York, NY), 1992.
Chin Yu Min and the Ginger Cat (picture book), illustrated by Mary GrandPre, Crown (New York, NY), 1993.
That Terrible Baby (picture book), illustrated by Susan Meddaugh, Tambourine Books (New York, NY), 1994.
Little Salt Lick and the Sun King (picture book), illustrated by Jon Goodell, Crown (New York, NY), 1994.
The Whittler's Tale (picture book), illustrated by Valery Vasiliev, Tambourine Books (New York, NY), 1994.
King Crow (picture book), illustrated by Eric Rohman, Crown (New York, NY), 1995.

Wan Hu Is in the Stars (picture book), illustrated by Barry Root, Tambourine Books (New York, NY), 1995.
Black-eyed Susan, illustrated by Emily Martindale, Crown (New York, NY), 1995.
The Dreams of Mairhe Mehan (young-adult novel; also see below), Knopf (New York, NY), 1996.
The Snowball, illustrated by Jean Pidgin, Random House (New York, NY), 1996.
Patrick Doyle Is Full of Blarney, illustrated by Krista Brauckmann-Towns, Random House (New York, NY), 1996.
Mary Mehan Awake (young adult novel; also see below), Knopf (New York, NY), 1996.
Sunshine, Moonshine, Random House (New York, NY), 1997.
Foolish Gretel, illustrated by Bill Dodge, Random House (New York, NY), 1997.
Lili the Brave, illustrated by Uldis Klavins, Random House (New York, NY), 1997.
Pockets (picture book), illustrated by Mary GrandPre, Crown (New York, NY), 1998.
Pierre's Dream (picture book), illustrated by Susan Gaber, Dial (New York, NY), 1999.
Theodore Roosevelt: Letters from a Young Coal Miner ("Dear Mr. President" series), Winslow Press (Delray Beach, FL), 2000.
Thomas Jefferson: Letters from a Philadelphia Bookworm ("Dear Mr. President" series), Winslow Press (Delray Beach, FL), 2000.
Becoming Mary Mehan: Two Novels (includes *The Dreams of Mairhe Mehan* and *Mary Mehan Awake*), Random House (New York, NY), 2002.
The Snowball, illustrated by Jean Pidgeon, Random House (New York, NY), 2003.
Once upon a Banana, illustrated by David Small, Simon & Schuster (New York, NY), 2006.
Magnus at the Fire, illustrated by Owen Smith, Simon & Schuster (New York, NY), 2005.

MIDDLE GRADE FICTION; "PETS, INC." SERIES

The Puppy Project, Bantam (New York, NY), 1990.
Too Many Pets, Bantam (New York, NY), 1990.
Hillary to the Rescue, Bantam (New York, NY), 1990.
That Champion Chimp, Bantam (New York, NY), 1990.

YOUNG ADULT FICTION; UNDER PSEUDONYM JULIA WINFIELD

Only Make Believe (part of "Sweet Dreams" series), Bantam (New York, NY), 1987.
Private Eyes (part of "Sweet Dreams" series), Bantam (New York, NY), 1989.
Partners in Crime (part of "Private Eyes" series), Bantam (New York, NY), 1989.
Tug of Hearts (part of "Private Eyes" series), Bantam (New York, NY), 1989.
On Dangerous Ground (part of "Private Eyes" series), Bantam (New York, NY), 1989.

JUVENILE FICTION; "WILD ROSE INN" SERIES

Bridie of the Wild Rose Inn, Bantam (New York, NY), 1994.

Ann of the Wild Rose Inn, Bantam (New York, NY), 1994.

Emily of the Wild Rose Inn, Bantam (New York, NY), 1994.

Laura of the Wild Rose Inn, Bantam (New York, NY), 1994.

Claire of the Wild Rose Inn, Bantam (New York, NY), 1994.

Grace of the Wild Rose Inn, Bantam (New York, NY), 1994.

"FIRE-US" TRILOGY; WITH NANCY BUTCHER

The Kindling, HarperCollins (New York, NY), 2002.

The Keepers of the Flame, HarperCollins (New York, NY), 2002.

The Kiln, HarperCollins (New York, NY), 2003.

NONFICTION

Shipwreck at the Bottom of the World: The Extraordinary True Story of Shackleton and the Endurance, Crown (New York, NY), 1998.

(With Irene Gut Opdyke) *In My Hands: Memories of a Holocaust Rescuer,* Knopf (New York, NY), 1999.

(With Peter Jennings and Todd Brewster) *The Century for Young People,* Doubleday (New York, NY), 1999.

Spirit of Endurance, illustrated by William Maughan, Crown (New York, NY), 2000.

(Editor) *Shattered: Stories of Children and War,* Knopf (New York, NY), 2002.

A Three-Minute Speech: Lincoln's Remarks at Gettysburg, illustrated by Albert Lorenz, Aladdin (New York, NY), 2003.

Audubon: Painter of Birds in the Wild Frontier, Abrams (New York, NY), 2003.

(Editor) *What a Song Can Do: Twelve Riffs on the Power of Music,* Knopf (New York, NY), 2004.

Photo by Brady: A Picture of the Civil War, Atheneum (New York, NY), 2005.

The American Story: 100 True Tales from American History, illustrated by Roger Roth, Knopf (New York, NY), 2006.

Sidelights

Jennifer Armstrong is a versatile writer of young-adult novels, middle-grade fiction, chapter books, picture books, and series books for both young and older readers. Some of her best writing is in the genre of historical fiction, such as the award-winning *Steal Away,* about a runaway slave and the white girl who accompanies her, and the U.S. Civil War *The Dreams of Mairhe Mehan* and its sequel, *Mary Mehan Awake.* Armstrong asks large questions in such novels and takes risks as a writer. She has also been lauded for her picture books, such as *Hugh Can Do,* and for such historical series as

"Wild Rose Inn," documenting the fictional lives of several generations of young girls whose families all inhabit the same Massachusetts tavern. Along with the number of works credited to her under her real name and under the pseudonym Julia Winfield, Armstrong has ghost-written over fifty titles in the "Sweet Valley High" series, and its spin-off, "Sweet Valley Kids."

After graduating from college, Armstrong worked as an assistant editor at Cloverdale Press in New York City. Although she quickly discovered that this entry-level position was more of a secretarial posting than an editorial one, after a learning period she was entrusted with her own projects. She also began writing for the "Sweet Valley High" series as well as for its spin-off "Sweet Valley Kids" chapter books for younger readers, viewing this work as a writing apprenticeship. "I learned scene and dialogue," Armstrong explained in *Something about the Author Autobiography Series (SAAS),* "I learned pacing, I learned plot and chapter structure, and most of all, I learned to write fast. Not infrequently I had to write a one-hundred-and-thirty-page book in four weeks. It was like being trained on a daily newspaper. I also lost all fear of 'writing a book.' I could write books at the drop of a hat."

Writing under the pseudonym Julia Winfield, Armstrong penned five series books of her own, two for the "Sweet Dreams" series and three more for the "Private Eyes" series as a tip of the hat to Nancy Drew and the Hardy Boys. The second "Sweet Dreams" title, *Private Eyes,* was the inspiration for the detective series. Reviewing *Partners in Crime,* the first novel in the "Private Eyes" series, a *Publishers Weekly* contributor noted that it "blends romance with a fairly complicated mystery, providing light entertainment." Such easy reading was exactly Armstrong's intent with these books, as well as her middle-grade series "Pets, Inc.," about girls who take care of neighborhood pets.

The first novel to bear Armstrong's name, *Steal Away* is a mix of adventure story, memoir, and coming-of-age tale that explores friendship, the nature of courage, race relations, and the history of slavery. Taking structural inspiration from Wallace Stegner's *Angle of Repose,* Armstrong moves her story back and forth across time by employing three fictional voices. Two of these voices are those of the young girls involved in the adventure; the third is that of one of the protagonist's granddaughters, who responds forty years later to the story her grandmother tells her. Young Susannah, abolitionist-minded, is orphaned in Vermont and sent to relatives in Virginia where she is given her own slave, Bethlehem. These two girls become friends and run away together to the north. Well received by critics and readers alike, *Steal Away* ultimately won a Golden Kite award. Reviewing the novel in *School Library Journal,* Ann Welton noted that "the issues explored in this book run deep" and the book "will go a long way toward explicating the damage done by slavery."

Taking place in the near future, this 2002 novel follows seven children as they fight to stay alive in a harsh new world after all the adults on Earth fall prey to a fatal virus. (Cover illustration by John Van Fleet.)

Published the same year, Armstrong's first picture book, *Hugh Can Do,* blends a poetic structure with a folktale-like story, creating what *School Library Journal* reviewer Kate McClelland deemed "an especially nice balance of dramatic tension, droll humor, and positive philosophy." Several more picture books have followed, including the award-winning *Chin Yu Min and the Ginger Cat.*

The critical success of *Steal Away* allowed Armstrong to find a market for her next project: a six-book series of historical romances. Based on the tales of six girls living in a family-run tavern in Marblehead, Massachusetts, the stories span three centuries. "Keeping to the same family, the same house, and the same town, while changing historical periods, was an interesting writing job," Armstrong noted in *SAAS.* The series begins in 1695 with *Bridie of the Wild Rose Inn,* in which sixteen-year-old Bridie immigrates to North America from Scotland, to be reunited with the family that had arrived a decade earlier. Now prospering as owners of Marblehead's Wild Rose Inn, Bridie's family has conformed to

the Puritan faith and culture of the Massachusetts colony, and the Scottish teen quickly discovers that she must as well. Trouble ensues when she is attracted to young Will Handy and is subsequently declared a witch after going to local Indians for an herbal cure for her sick brother. *Booklist* critic Sheilamae O'Hara called *Bridie of the Wild Rose Inn* a "promising beginning to a series of historical novels that can be read for diversion or as an adjunct to an American history unit." Writing in *Wilson Library Bulletin,* Cathi Dunn MacRae declared that "Armstrong's vivid language paints a striking picture of a harsh land and somber folk." Reviewing the second novel in the series, *Ann of the Wild Rose Inn,* set in 1774, MacRae went on to note that this "dramatic tale of Crown versus Colony telescopes the dawn of the American Revolution into one young girl's view."

Armstrong has also incorporated history into several of her fictional chapter books. Basing stories of immigrants to the United States on a July 4th motif, Armstrong sets her stories on or around Independence Day. She also weaves into these tales elements of well-known folktales, myths, or legends from the country of origin of each protagonist. Thus in *Lili the Brave,* the young Norwegian protagonist must become something of a Viking heroine, while *Patrick Boyle Is Full of Blarney* finds a young Irish immigrant growing up in New York's Hell's Kitchen re-enacting St. Patrick's feat of driving the snakes from Ireland. In this latter tale, the legend is replayed as the defeat of a street gang known as the Copperheads. Charlyn Lyons, reviewing *Patrick Boyle Is Full of Blarney* for *School Library Journal,* dubbed it a "beginning chapter book that's sure to be a hit." For *Foolish Gretel,* Armstrong adapts a Grimm's fairy tale, setting her version of the story in Galveston, Texas, in 1854. "World folklore and mythology are full of stories," Armstrong noted in *SAAS,* "and reading them in conjunction with the immigration history of different nationalities almost gives me these stories ready-made. It is a delight to write them."

In her books for middle graders and older teens Armstrong also explores the past. *Black-eyed Susan* is about the geography of the prairie and how that bleak environment can either lift or crush the human spirit. Susie, the novel's protagonist, is a pioneer girl who loves her South Dakota home, but for Susie's mother the prairie is a desert compared with the tree-filled landscape of the woman's native Ohio. Susie ultimately helps her mother break through her depression when she encounters an Icelandic family on their way west to homestead. Set within a twenty-four-hour span, *Black-eyed Susan* explores the extent of family relationships and the spirit of the settlers in the American frontier. "Armstrong writes in a simple but quite literary style," a *Kirkus Reviews* contributor observed, and Margaret B. Rafferty noted in *School Library Journal* that the author's "elegant, spare prose is readable and evocatively recreates the time and place."

Armstrong's 1996 novel, *The Dreams of Mairhe Mehan,* "proved to be the most challenging one I have yet written," as the author noted in *SAAS*. Young Mairhe Mehan, an Irish barmaid working in the Swampoodle district of Washington, D.C., during the U.S. Civil War, has allegiances to two countries. In some ways she is still Irish; in others very much American. When her older brother, Mike, decides to fight for the Union the young man's decision breaks the heart of his Irish father, and Mairhe finds herself caught in the middle of the conflict. Noted American poet Walt Whitman plays a role in this story, serving as Mairhe's inspiration to work as a nurse in army hospitals. A critic in *Kirkus Reviews* deemed the novel a "haunting, eloquent story," citing Armstrong's "breathtaking virtuosity" in blending "vision and reality." *Booklist* contributor Linda Perkins felt that "this grim, gritty, working-class view of the Civil War provides a unique perspective and could be valuable in a curriculum." Armstrong is never one for formulaic happy endings, and with the death of Mike, part of Mairhe's world dies as well.

Mairhe returns in *Mary Mehan Awake,* and the young Irish girl now spells her name in the American fashion. In the wake of Mike's death, she is persuaded by Whitman to leave Washington for the more therapeutic climes of upstate New York where she is employed as a naturalist's assistant by Jasper and Diana Dorset. Mary's journey north provides salvation for her, as she begins to recover at the Dorsets', partly as a result of their kindness, partly through interaction with a veteran made deaf by the war who is working as gardener at the Dorsets' home. Anne O'Malley concluded in *Booklist* that while lacking the "lively action" of the first novel, *Mary Mehan Awake* contains "beautiful writing [that] captures personalities deftly, and fully evokes Mary's internal suffering and quietude." Jennifer M. Brabander, writing in *Horn Book,* likened the novel to "*The Secret Garden* for an older audience, with friendship and nature gratifyingly providing healing and wholeness."

Armstrong moves to nonfiction with her 1998 book, *Shipwreck at the Bottom of the World*. This depiction of British explorer Ernest Shackleton's 1914 expedition and his heroic and ultimately tragic efforts to cross Antarctica by foot is crafted into "an unforgettable story of true heroism and the triumph of the human spirit," according to Edward Sullivan writing in *School Library Journal*. Sullivan concluded that Armstrong's book "will capture the attention and imagination of any reader," while Christine Hepperman noted in *Riverbank Review* that *Shipwreck at the Bottom of the World* is one "to finish in one breathless sitting, then dream about all night long." Armstrong retells the same story for younger readers in *Spirit of Endurance*. On her home page she explained her reason for moving from fiction-writing to tell of Shackleton's exploits: "I always thought it was one of the greatest adventures I had ever heard about. At the time, nobody had written a book about the voyage for kids, so when I decided I'd like to try writing nonfiction I picked this story to write." *Spirit of Endurance,* which describes the travails encountered by Shackleton's ship, *Endurance,* and her crew in

Five years after the events recounted in **The Kindling,** *the family of children discover a group of adults, but their initial sense of security vanishes when they realize that something about these grown-ups is horribly wrong. (Cover illustration by John Van Fleet.)*

picture-book format, "masterfully foreshortens the key events" of the Antarctica expedition, according to a *Publishers Weekly* reviewer. Patricia Manning, writing in *School Library Journal,* felt the book offers "a good picture of human survival."

Armstrong's experience with nonfiction has grown beyond her two books on Shackleton, to encompass *In My Hands: Memories of a Holocaust Rescuer,* a memoir written in collaboration with Irene Gut Opdyke, a woman who sheltered Jews during the Holocaust; a picture-book biography of John James Audubon titled *Audubon: Painter of Birds in the Wild Frontier;* and a volume discussing how Matthew Brady's photographs affected the U.S. Civil War titled *Photo by Brady: A Picture of the Civil War.* In her youth, Opdyke worked at an officers' dining room, and she used her position to begin hiding Jews. Kristi Beavin wrote in a review of *In My Hands* for *Horn Book* that "the power of this tale lies as much in the text's matter-of-fact narration of events as it does in the cumulative courage" of Opdyke. *Audubon* follows the noted naturalist and artist on his travels between 1804 and 1812, and features artwork by both illustrator Joe A. Smith and by Audubon himself. "Armstrong and Smith make a great team in this immensely likeable biographical portrait," wrote a critic for *Kirkus Reviews,* describing the book as "an excellent example of what picture-book biography can be." *Photo by Brady* 'gives youngsters a double exposure of the Civil War," explained Betty Carter in *Horn Book,* the critic describing how the four sections of the book provide both facts and an overview about the war itself, as well as information about how print photography affected the public's understanding of the war.

As an editor, Armstrong has produced two collections of stories and essays. *Shattered: Stories of Children and War* collects short stories from authors including M.E. Kerr and David Lubar that focus on the effects of war on the lives of the young people living through them. "The stories are remarkable not only for their depth, but also for how much they avoid cliché," wrote a critic for *Kirkus Reviews. What a Song Can Do: Twelve Riffs on the Power of Music* collects essays from authors describing the impact music had on their lives. The essays "show the power of both words and music to express the turbulent emotions of growing up," Jennifer Mattson wrote in *Booklist.*

In 2002, Armstrong published *The Kindling,* the first volume in the "Fire-Us" series coauthored with Nancy Butcher. The two authors planned the outline together, and Armstrong wrote the even chapters for each book in the series while Butcher wrote the odd chapters. The series takes place in a futuristic, post-apocalyptic world in which almost all of the adult population has been wiped out. The surviving children and teens of a small U.S. town band together and form a new type of family unit suitable for the new world they now live. Older teens Mommy, Teacher, and Hunter, as well as young ones Teddy Bear, Baby, and Doll. The children have grown into the roles they are named after and have all but forgotten life before the virus wiped out everything they had known. Their lives are changed again when a teen called Angerman draws them, along with two feral young ones called Puppy and Kitty, into his quest to find the president and figure out how a deadly virus could have killed so many. Paula Rohrlick, writing in *Kliatt,* called *The Kindling* "a riveting, powerful tale, with underpinnings of religion." Trish Anderson noted in *School Library Journal* that while the first book lacks a solid conclusion, "the cliff-hanger ending will leave [readers] interested to see what happens next."

In *Keepers of the Flame* the children find a groups of adults who have survived the plague and have taken up residence in an abandoned shopping mall. At first glad to be taken care of, they soon realize that in trade, they give up their own power to make decisions. They soon realize that something sinister lurks beneath the surface pleasantness the adults offer, and they flee. "The kids

relationships and their desperate struggle to help one another survive make mesmerizing reading," noted Sally Estes in her *Booklist* review. Paula Rohrlick stated in *Kliatt:* "The action is fast and furious and the suspense never lets up in this powerful series. The second book doesn't disappoint."

In the final book of the "Fire-Us" series, *The Kiln,* the teens and their charges take refuge in a hold for the elderly that was somehow spared from the virus, then continue their quest to find the resident, only to discover that the truth is worse than they suspected. "This adventure is jam-packed with thrills, narrow escapes, and grief, and the answers will satisfy fans," commented a *Kirkus Reviews* contributor. Paula Rohrlick in *Kliatt* considered the book a good conclusion: "The suspense runs high . . . and all the loose ends from the other books are neatly wrapped up."

History and dreams are sometimes interchangeable in Armstrong's work. "I wanted to write about how we understand history, how we tell it," she noted in *SAAS,* "how hearing an adventure forty years old can change our lives today, how storytelling is an active, dynamic process rather than a passive, static one." While Armstrong wrote these words about her inspiration for her first non-series novel, *Steal Away,* they could apply to much of the rest of her work also.

Biographical and Critical Sources

BOOKS

Something about the Author Autobiography Series, Volume 110, Thomson Gale (Detroit, MI), 1997, pp. 1-15.

PERIODICALS

Audubon, December, 2003, David Seideman, review of *Audubon: Painter of Birds in the Wild Frontier,* p. 98.
Booklist, February 15, 1993, p. 1065; March 15, 1994, Sheilamae O'Hara, review of *Birdie of the Wild Rose Inn,* p. 1341; April 1, 1994, p. 1457; June 1, 1994, p. 1801; September 1, 1994, p. 47; June 1, 1995, p. 1781; July, 1995, p. 1882; May 1, 1996, p. 1505; December 1, 1997, Anne O'Malley, review of *Mary Mehan Awake,* p. 615; January 1, 1997, Linda Perkins, review of *The Dreams of Mairhe Mehan,* p. 842; August, 1998, p. 2012; April 1, 2000, Stephanie Zvirin, review of *In My Hands: Memories of a Holocaust Rescuer,* p. 1430; June, 2000, Ted Hipple, review of *In My Hands,* p. 1921; July, 2000, Karen Harris, review of *In My Hands,* p. 2052; September 15, 2000, Stephanie Zvirin, review of *Spirit of Endurance,* p. 233; March 1, 2001, Kay Weisman, review of *Theodore Roosevelt: Letters from a Young Coal Miner,* p. 1275; May 15, 2001, Randy Meyer, review of *Thomas Jefferson: Letters from a Philadelphia Bookworm,*

p. 1749; August, 2002, Sally Estes, review of *The Keepers of the Flame,* p. 1962; January 1, 2003, review of *The Kindling,* p. 795; April 1, 2003, Carolyn Phelan, review of *Audubon,* p. 1391; April 15, 2003, Sally Estes, review of *The Kiln,* p. 1464; September 1, 2003, Carolyn Phelan, review of *A Three-Minute Speech: Lincoln's Remarks at Gettysburg,* p. 117; August, 2004, Jennifer Mattson, review of *What a Song Can Do: Twelve Riffs on the Power of Music,* p. 1921; March 15, 2005, Stephanie Zvirin, review of *Photo by Brady: A Picture of the Civil War,* p. 1283.

Bulletin of the Center for Children's Books, May, 1995, p. 299; July-August, 1995, p. 376; October, 1995, p. 45; April, 1996, p. 256; December, 1997, pp. 116-117.

Horn Book, March-April, 1996, p. 193; November-December, 1997, Jennifer M. Brabander, review of *Mary Mehan Awake,* pp. 675-676; July-August, 1999, pp. 478-479; January, 2000, review of *Shipwreck at the Bottom of the World,* p. 50; May, 2000, Kristi Beavin, reviews of *Shipwreck at the Bottom of the World* and *In My Hands,* pp. 342-341; September, 2000, Jennifer Armstrong, "Blood from a Stone," p. 611; May-June, 2002, Peter D. Sieruta, review of *Shattered,* p. 323; November-December, 2003, Kristi Elle Jemtegaard, review of *Thomas Jefferson: Letters from a Philadelphia Bookworm,* p. 773; May-June, 2005, Betty Carter, review of *Photo by Brady,* p. 344.

Kirkus Reviews, February 15, 1993; April 15, 1994; October 15, 1994, p. 1404; August 15, 1995, review of *Black-eyed Susan,* p. 1184; September 1, 1996, review of *The Dreams of Mairhe Mehan,* pp. 1318-1319; May 1, 1999, p. 718; June 15, 1999, pp. 968-969; December 1, 2001, review of *Shattered: Stories of Children and War,* p. 1681; March 1, 2002, review of *The Kindling,* p. 329; October 15, 2002, review of *The Keepers of the Flame,* p. 1526; March 1, 2003, review of *The Kiln,* p. 379; March 15, 2003, review of *Audubon,* p. 458; June 1, 2004, review of *What a Song Can Do,* p. 533; January 15, 2005, review of *Photo by Brady,* p. 115; April 15, 2005, review of *Magnus at the Fire,* p. 468.

Kliatt, March, 2002, Paula Rohrlick, review of *The Kindling,* p. 6; November, 2002, Paula Rohrlick, review of *The Keepers of the Flame,* p. 5; March, 2003, Paula Rohrlick, review of *The Kiln,* p. 5; May, 2003, Paula Rohrlick, review of *The Kindling,* p. 23; May, 2004, Paula Rohrlick, review of *The Kiln,* p. 26, and Olivia Durant, review of *Shattered,* p. 31.

Publishers Weekly, March 24, 1989, review of *Partners in Crime,* p. 73; July 13, 1990, p. 55; March 14, 1994, p. 71; November 7, 1994, p. 78; April 17, 1995, p. 59; October 19, 1998, p. 78; June 14, 1999, pp. 22-23; July 17, 2000, review of *Spirit of Endurance,* p. 196.

Riverbank Review, spring, 1999, Christine Hepperman, review of *Shipwreck at the Bottom of the World,* p. 41.

School Library Journal, July, 1990, p. 74; February, 1992, Ann Welton, review of *Steal Away,* p. 85; October, 1992, Kate McClelland, review of *Hugh Can Do,* p. 78; July, 1993, p. 84; October, 1995, Margaret A. Rafferty, review of *Black-eyed Susan,* p. 132; August, 1996, Charlyn Lyons, review of *Patrick Doyle Is Full of Blarney,* p. 115; August, 1997, p. 128; January, 1998, p. 108; October, 1998, p. 86; April, 1999, Edward Sullivan, review of *Shipwreck at the Bottom of the World,* p. 144; June, 1999, p. 85; October, 2000, Patricia Manning, review of *Spirit of Endurance,* p. 177; April, 2001, Janie Schomberg, review of *Theodore Roosevelt,* p. 138; June, 2001, Janet Gillen, review of *Thomas Jefferson,* p. 142; January, 2002, Saleena L. Davidson, review of *Shattered,* p. 131; October, 2002, Trish Anderson, review of *The Kindling,* p. 154; December, 2002, Mara Alpert, review of *The Keepers of the Flame,* p 132; May, 2003, Robyn Walker, review of *Audubon,* p. 134, and Mara Alpert, review of *The Kiln,* p. 144; September, 2003, review of *A Three-Minute Speech,* p. 224; May, 2004, Vicki Reutter, review of *Shipwreck at the Bottom of the World,* p. 64; July, 2004, Renee Steinberg, review of *What a Song Can Do,* p. 98; March, 2005, Kathleen T. Isaacs, review of *Shattered,* p. 69, and Jodi Kearns, review of *Photo by Brady,* p. 223.

Voice of Youth Advocates, August, 1992, p. 165; February, 1994, p. 363; August, 1994, pp. 141-142.

Wilson Library Bulletin, May, 1994, Cathi Dunn MacRae, "The Young Adult Perplex," p. 100.

ONLINE

Jennifer Armstrong Home Page, http://www.jennifer-armstrong.com (November 5, 2005).

* * *

ASARO, Catherine Ann 1955-

Personal

Born November 6, 1955, in Oakland, CA; daughter of Frank and Lucille Marie (Lavezo) Asaro; married John Kendall Cannizzo (an astrophysicist), August 9, 1986; children: Catherine Kendall. *Education:* University of California, Los Angeles, B.S., 1978; Harvard University, A.M., 1983, Ph.D., 1985; postdoctoral study at University of Toronto, 1985-87. *Hobbies and other interests:* Classical piano, ballet dancing, choir

Addresses

Home—MD. *Office*—c/o Molecudyne Research, P.O. Box 1302, Laurel, MD 20725. *E-mail*—asaro@sff.net.

Career

Kenyon College, Gambier, OH, assistant professor of physics, 1987-90, affiliated scholar, 1990-91; Molecudyne Research, MD, president, 1990—; writer. Consultant to Lawrence Livermore Laboratory, 1978-83, Biodesign, 1987, and Harvard-Smithsonian Center for Astrophysics, 1991. Visiting scientist at Max Planck Institute for Astrophysics, 1991-92. Teacher at Caryl Maxwell Classical Ballet Maryland.

Catherine Ann Asaro

Member

Science Fiction and Fantasy Writers of America (past president), American Association of Physics Teachers, American Physicists Society, Mathematical Association of America, National Council of Teachres of Mathematics, Tau Beta Pi, Sigma Xi, Romance Writers of America.

Awards, Honors

Sapphire Award, 1997, and UTC Award for Best Science Fiction Novel of 1997, both for *Catch the Lightning;* nominations for Hugo and Nebula Awards for Best Novella, both 1999, both for "Aurora in Four Voices"; nominated for best novel, Nebula Award, 1999, for *The Last Hawk;* Nebula Award in novel category, 2001, for *The Quantum Rose;* nominated for Hugo Award and Nebula Award for Best Novella, for "A Roll of the Dice," and 2004, for "Walk in Silence"; three-time winner of Best Science Fiction Novel Award, Romantic Times Book Club.

Writings

The Veiled Web, Bantam (New York, NY), 1999.
The Phoenix Code, Bantam (New York, NY), 2000.
With Mercedes Lackey and Rachel Lee, *Charmed Destines* (includes novella "Moonglow"), Silhouette (New York, NY), 2003.
The Charmed Sphere, Luna (New York, NY), 2004.

Sunrise Alley, Baen (Riverdale, NY), 2004.
(Editor and contributor) *Irresistible Forces* (includes "Stained Glass Heart"), New American Library (New York, NY), 2004.
The Misted Cliffs, Luna (New York, NY), 2005.
The Dawn Star, Luna (New York, NY), 2006.
Alpha, Baen (New York, NY), 2006.

Contributor of short fiction to anthologies, including *Christmas Forever,* Tor, 1993; *Sextopia,* Circlet Press; *Redshift and Fantasy: The Year's Best,* 2001; *Flights: Extreme Visions of Fantasy,* 2004; *The Journey Home,* Imajinn, 2005; and *Down These Dark Spaceways,* Science Fiction Book Club, 2005. Contributor to periodicals, including *Analog, Bulletin of the Science Fiction and Fantasy Writers of America, New York Review of Science Fiction, Pirate Writings,* and *Science Fiction Age.* Contributor of scholarly articles to refereed journals, including *American Journal of Physics, International Journal of Quantitative Chemistry, Journal of Chemical Physics,* and *Physical Review Letters.* Columnist, *Tangent.* Editor and publisher, *Mindsparks: The Magazine of Science and Science Fiction,* 1993-96, and *Mindsparks Review,* 1997—.

"SAGA OF THE SKOLIAN EMPIRE" SERIES

Primary Inversion, Tor (New York, NY), 1995.
Catch the Lightning, Tor (New York, NY), 1996.
The Last Hawk, Tor (New York, NY), 1997.
The Radiant Seas, Tor (New York, NY), 1998.
Ascendant Sun, Tor (New York, NY), 2000.
The Quantum Rose, Tor (New York, NY), 2000.
Spherical Harmonic, Tor (New York, NY), 2001.
Moon's Shadow, Tor (New York, NY), 2003.
Skyfall, Tor (New York, NY), 2003.
Schism (book one of "Triad" series), Tor (New York, NY), 2004.
The Final Key (book two of "Triad" series), Tor (New York, NY), 2005.

Sidelights

Catherine Ann Asaro is both a distinguished astrophysicist and a science-fiction writer. She earned her doctorate from Harvard University in 1985 and taught at Kenyon College from 1987 to 1990, subsequently serving as an affiliated scholar there while assuming the presidency of Molecudyne Research, which she founded in Maryland in 1990. As a novelist, Asaro has penned a series of books comprising the "Saga of the Skolian Empire." The saga includes *Primary Inversion, Catch the Lightning,* and *The Quantum Rose,* the last which garnered Asaro the prestigious Nebula Award in 2001. While her novels have a YA appeal, Asaro once told *SATA* that she believes the romantic scenes in many of her novels may be "a bit mature" for young-adult readers. "The scenes are tastefully done," she noted, "but they are perhaps better suited for an adult audience. As she has expanded her "Saga of the Skolian Empire" and delved into the pasts of her main characters, the teen appeal of her novels has grown: the "Triad" sub series, beginning with *Schism,* features one of the heroes of an earlier novel during her teen years.

As a girl, Asaro loved reading fantasy and science fiction. "My dad is a scientist, so we were always exposed to science in my family, and I suspect that's why I tend to go more toward science fiction," she told J. Alexander Harman in an interview for *StrangeHorizons.com.* She began writing tales at an early age. "The first time I tried to write was when I was eight," she told Harman. "For as long as I can remember, from the time I could form thoughts in my head, I was always making up stories. . . . I didn't really start writing seriously until graduate school; I put away the book when I was eight and didn't write another one until I was in college. By that time I knew how to do research. I do spend a lot of time researching details, even those which may hardly show up in the book at all."

Primary Inversion the first of Asaro's science-fiction "Saga of the Skolian Empire," is a futuristic tale in which three galactic empires vie for domination of the galaxy. Inhabitants of Earth have ties to both the other empires, the Skolians and their enemies, the Traders. In the story, Skolian princess and star fighter pilot Sauscony Valdoria becomes attracted to Jaibriol Qox, son of the Trader emperor. Valdoria's sensory capabilities enable her to discover that Jaibriol, despite his ancestry, is her soul mate. However, she also discerns that Jaibriol has been genetically contrived to overpower her fellow Skolians. *Booklist* reviewer Carl Hays called *Primary Inversion* "an unusually masterful first novel," adding that "Asaro innovatively blends computer technology and telepathy into the electrifying, action-rich drama she creates." A *Publishers Weekly* commentator asserted that Asaro "manages to anchor her story with thoughtful, engaging characters and an intriguing vision of the future—and she leaves the door open for a sequel."

Asaro followed *Primary Inversion* with *Catch the Lightning,* which relates more conflicts between the Skolians and the Traders. In *Catch the Lightning,* Skolian Jagernaut Althor, destined to rule Skolia, lands his sabotaged space vehicle on an alternative Earth and befriends Tina Pulivok, a psychic teenager from 1980s Los Angeles. Inquisitive scientists, meanwhile, are conducting investigations into the capabilities of Althor's craft. Althor, with the help of Tina and her friends, determines to recover his ship and return to his own world. Although it was honored with the 1997 Sapphire Award for the year's best romantic science fiction, several reviewers maintained that *Catch the Lightning* falls short of the expectations set by her debut novel. A *Kirkus Reviews* critic called it "an unexciting but solidly crafted, and at times absorbing narrative" yet added that too many technical details and a slow plot weaken the book. A *Publishers Weekly* reviewer noted that the novel "fails to cohere and to deliver the vibrant reading experience that [Asaro's] first novel offered," but nonetheless stated

that the book contains good characterization and "many fine passages." However, Melinda Helfer, writing in the *Romantic Times,* found value in the sequel, writing, "Asaro's Skolian Empire is a truly masterful accomplishment in world-building, an example of consummate craftsmanship and an impeccable feel for the technical and social possibilities that lie ahead of us."

Asaro recounts another adventure featuring a Skolian hero in 1997's *The Last Hawk,* and returns to the lives of her beloved Sauscony and Jaibriol in *The Radiant Seas.* In *The Last Hawk,* Imperial Heir Prince Kelric is stranded and held captive on a female-ruled planet. Taken in as a slave, he grows to love his captors. "The fate of a man on such a planet has usually been handled didactically, disastrously, or sometimes both ways," noted *Booklist* reviewer Roland Green, "but Asaro avoids most of the pitfalls, giving us an intelligent action story, with strong overtones of the better sort of romance." A *Publishers Weekly* critic maintained that with this third Skolian story, Asaro "has settled into a smoothly absorbing space-opera formula that mixes high-tech gimmickry with galactic politics and plenty of romance." In *The Radiant Seas,* Sauscony and Jaibriol have faked their own deaths and stolen away to a secluded planet to raise their children. They are drawn back into the conflict between their respective empires, however, and Sauscony must attempt her husband's rescue. Jackie Cassada, reviewing *The Radiant Seas* for *Library Journal,* praised the author's "mix of romantic intrigue" and "large-scale dynastic" science fiction.

Taking place directly after the events of *The Last Hawk, Ascendant Sun* tells how Kelric escapes from his captors to reclaim his place in the Skolian Empire. As a refugee, he has no proof of his identity, and he must travel through dangerous Aristo territory to make his way home. Injured and deprived of some of his cybernetic skills, he is also aware that his brother has been captured by the Aristos. Working under a false name, Kelric is also taken hostage. Roland Green wrote in *Booklist* that the novel is "one of the better treatments of the lone-male-on-a-woman-ruled-planet gambit," while a *Publishers Weekly* critic commented that "series veterans will find this to be yet another fast-paced and pleasing saga."

Both *The Quantum Rose* and *Spherical Harmonic* take place in the same universe Asaro created for *Primary Inversion,* but each novel features a new cast of characters. The heroine of *The Quantum Rose* is Kamoj, the young governor of a province on a backwater planet. Kamoj is set to marry a fellow governor of a much more important province when she is swept off her feet by the wandering Skolian Vyrl. Together she and Vyrl eventually travel back to his home planet to fight for its independence. Originally published as a serial for *Analog* and later expanded to its novel form, the story also deals with an abusive relationship; Asaro, who has worked as a sexual harassment counselor, wanted to portray a woman stuck in an abusive situation who could not see her way out of it. "I wanted to show that people can have difficult situations and still recover," Asaro told Harman in the *Strange Horizons* online interview; "I guess that's a theme in all of my books." *The Quantum Rose* provides what Green in *Booklist* termed "the requisite happy ending." A *Publishers Weekly* critic commented that Kamoj is "as brainy as she is beautiful," and called the novel "a freestanding page-turner as a romance."

In *Spherical Harmonic* beautiful telepath Dyhianna Selei recovers from a case of amnesia only to discover that her husband and son have disappeared and the empire is now thrust into chaos as a result of a political coup. After the events of *The Radiant Seas,* Dyhianna had escaped, with her son, into an alternate universe, and her amnesia is, in part, a result of her return to her native universe. "A small amount of the text in the book is actually in the form of simple spherical harmonic wave functions," Asaro told Harman. *Booklist* contributor Diane Tixier Herald added that "fans of

In Asaro's futuristic romance, Kamoj Argali's wedding to a wealthy but brutal man is put on hold when a suitor from another planet lays his claim to her hand . . . and her provincial kingdom. (Cover illustration by Julie Bell.)

Asaro's 'Saga of the Skolian Empire' will not want to miss" *Spherical Harmonic.*

Following *Spherical Harmonic* with the titles *The Moon's Shadow* and *Skyfall,* Asaro continued the series by bringing the Skolians and Aristo Traders closer to peace, as well as by taking a look at the beginning of the saga. In *The Moon's Shadow* teen Aristo ruler Jaibriol must hide the secret that he is a telepath or be forced into slavery by his own people. While Jaibriol realizes that his uncle Corbal Xir might know his secret, Xir has a secret of his own: he seeks to restore the psiberweb, which was destroyed in the war but once provided instant communication to the galaxy. A *Kirkus Reviews* contributor complained about the layers of the plot, calling the novel "Tedious, confusing, [and] pointlessly self-referential." Green, writing in *Booklist,* however, felt that *The Moon's Shadow* "just raises the stakes higher than usual in an Asaro book," while a *Publishers Weekly* contributor considered the work a "mesmerizing, passionate novel," commenting: "Asaro skillfully shows the hesitant sprouting of loyalty, trust, and even love."

Skyfall, which takes place before any of the other books in the "Saga of the Skolian Empire," tells the story of Roca Skolia and a powerful telepath named Eldrinson Althor Valdoria. Roca is the widow of the Skolian imperator and the heir to the Ruby Dynasty. Her son Kurj manipulates his mother as he quests to destroy the threat of the Aristo Traders. When Roca escapes her son's power, she finds herself on the backwater planet of *Skyfall* as well as in the arms of Eldrinson. Their love blooms, but is threatened when Kurj comes to reclaim his mother from the backwater planet. "*Skyfall* pleases like its predecessors," noted Roland Green in *Booklist,* while a *Publishers Weekly* reviewer wrote that although Asaro's science-fiction fans "may be disappointed to find so little of the physics" usually found in Asaro's novels, "romance readers will have no cause to complain."

Asaro's "Skolian" novels in the "Triad" sub-series follow Sauscony Valdoria (called Soz) through her teen years, beginning when she applies to become an Imperial Jagernaut at age seventeen, much to her father's dismay. Her world is at war and her brother, already a Jagernaut, goes to battle; meanwhile, Soz herself faces sexual harassment and scandals at the military academy. Whether she can succeed at the training and reconcile with her father is already known to readers of the series, but here it is experienced first hand. In *Booklist,* Green comparing *Schism,* the first book of the series, to a cross between Georgette Heyer's romances and Frank Herbert's science fiction, called the story "the best of large-scale romance interleaved with the best of space-operatic saga." Though feeling that *The Final Key,* the second book in the sub-series, lacks focus, a reviewer for *Publishers Weekly* praised Asaro's portrayal of Soz, noting that the character "seizes the book's spotlight with her combination of vulnerability and bravery."

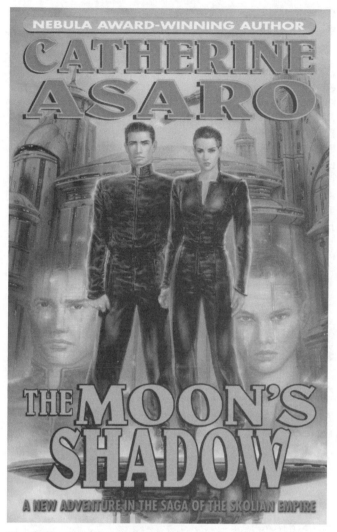

The eighth volume in the "Skolian Empire" series follows Jai Qox, a young man of noble blood, as he attempts to regain his birthright while averting a war that threatens the entire galaxy. (Cover illustration by Royo.)

In addition to novels about the Skolian and Trader empires, Asaro has written some books that take place outside her fictional world. Notable among these is *The Veiled Web,* featuring a Latina-American heroine who is drawn to the Moroccan inventor of a new internet technology. *The Veiled Web* was praised by some critics for its cultural sensitivity; for instance, a *Publishers Weekly* reviewer cited Asaro's "sensuous and respectful evocation of Islamic culture" as one of the novel's best features. Noting that Asaro also includes creativity, virtual reality, and the question of a soul in the novel, Charles De Lint wrote in his *Magazine of Fantasy and Science Fiction* review that she "has combined these elements, along with the pacing of a thriller and a dash of romance, to great effect."

Stand-alone novel *Sunrise Alley* also features a cross-cultural relationship, this one between biotech engineer Samantha and Turner, a cyborg who believes he is a human who was killed and reborn in a technologically enhanced body. The pair team up to try to undo the plans of rogue scientist Charon while also solving the mystery of Sunrise Alley, a harbor for artificial intelligences who have evolved their own self-awareness. The novel was recommended for a high-school audience by Christine C. Menefee in *School Library Journal,* who noted: "The plot is an epic chase across a near-future landscape, enlivened by twists, complicated puzzles to solve, plenty of intriguing technology, and a strong element of romance." *Sunrise Alley* "reinforces [Asaro's] reputation for combining high tech adventure and romance," stated Regina Schroeder in her *Booklist* review.

Frequently praised for her ability to blend romance and hard science in her novels and short stories, Asaro stated in an interview with Terry Hickman for *The Market List* that she "made a conscious decision not to downplay the romantic elements. I like them." "A great deal of good romantic literature exists," she added. "So I decided to talk about that as well as the other aspects of the books. That is the only way to counteract negative stereotypes." Discussing her fiction's crossover value with a *Locus* interviewer, Asaro noted: "The amount of romance varies from book to book, but I'm happy to have that crossover. I don't play to it, though. I actually held back at first, because a part of me wondered how much of a love story I should involve in a science fiction book. But I found out my fans really enjoyed it."

Regarding advice to beginning writers, Asaro noted in her *StrangeHorizons.com* interview: "Don't take rejection personally. No matter how good you are, chances are you'll get a lot of rejections. I certainly got my share of them. And if you are one of the lucky ones, and the first thing you ever write is published by a major house and they pay you two million dollars, try not to let your head get swollen."

Biographical and Critical Sources

PERIODICALS

Analog, July-August, 1999, Jay Kay Klein, "Biolog," pp. 224-225.

Booklist, February 15, 1995, Carl Hays, review of *Primary Inversion,* p. 1064; November 1, 1997, Roland Green, review of *The Last Hawk,* p. 456; February 1, 2000, Roland Green, review of *Ascendant Sun,* p. 1010; December 1, 2000, Roland Green, review of *The Quantum Rose,* p. 698; November 1, 2001, Diane Tixier Herald, review of *Spherical Harmonic*; February 15, 2002, Whitney Scott, review of *The Last Hawk,* p. 1039; April 15, 2002, Whitney Scott, review of *The Radiant Seas,* p. 1422; February 15, 2003, Roland Green, review of *The Moon's Shadow,* p. 1058; September 1, 2003, Roland Green, review of *Skyfall,* p. 73; August, 2004, Regina Schroeder, review of *Sunrise Alley,* p. 1912; January 1, 2005, Roland Green, review of *Schism,* p. 833

Kirkus Reviews, October 15, 1996, review of *Catch the Lightning,* p. 1500; September 15, 2001, review of *Spherical Harmonic,* p. 1329; March 1, 2003, review of *The Moon's Shadow,* p. 352.

Kliatt, March, 2002, Bette D. Ammon, review of *The Last Hawk,* p. 50.

Library Journal, February 15, 1995, p. 186; November 15, 1996, p. 92; December, 1998, Jackie Cassada, review of *The Radiant Seas,* p. 162; November 15, 2000, Jackie Cassada, review of *The Quantum Rose,* p. 101; December, 2000, Jackie Cassada, review of *The Phoenix Code,* p. 197; November 15, 2001, Jackie Cassada, review of *Spherical Harmonic.*

Locus, November, 1999, interview with Catherine Asaro.

Magazine of Fantasy and Science Fiction, April, 2000, Charles De Lint, review of *The Veiled Web,* p. 34.

Publishers Weekly, January 16, 1995, review of *Primary Inversion,* p. 442; November 18, 1996, review of *Catch the Lightning,* p. 66; October 27, 1997, review of *The Last Hawk,* p. 57; November 8, 1999, review of *The Veiled Web,* p. 65; January 17, 2000, review of *Ascendant Sun,* p. 48; November 27, 2000, review of *The Quantum Rose,* p. 60; November 12, 2001, review of *Spherical Harmonic,* p. 41; November 27, 2002, review of *Spherical Harmonic,* p. 41; February 3, 2003, review of *The Moon's Shadow,* p. 59; August 18, 2003, review of *Skyfall,* p. 62; December 6, 2004, review of *Schism,* p. 48; October 17, 2005, review of *The Final Key,* p. 44.

Romantic Times, December, 1996, Melinda Helfer, review of *Catch the Lightning,* p. 92.

School Library Journal, January, 2005, Christine C. Menefee, review of *Sunrise Alley,* p. 158.

Wilson Library Bulletin, June, 1995, p. 96.

ONLINE

Catherine Asaro Home Page, http://www.sff.net/people/asaro (August 21, 2005).

MarketList.com, http://www.marketlist.com/ (November 3, 2005), interview with Asaro.

ParaNormal Romance Paraphernalia Web site, http://www.writerspace.com/ParanormalRomance/ (October, 2001), interview with Asaro.

StrangeHorizons.com, http://www.strangehorizons.com/ (October 2, 2000), J. Alexander Harman, interview with Asaro.

*   *   *

AXELSEN, Stephen 1953-

Personal

Born 1953, in Sydney, New South Wales, Australia; married; children.

Addresses

Home—New South Wales, Australia. *Agent*—c/o Author Mail, Random House Australia, 20 Alfred St., Milsons Point, Sydney, New South Wales 2061, Australia.

Career

Writer and illustrator.

Awards, Honors

Children's Book Council of Australia (CBCA) Book of the Year Awards, 1979, for *The Oath of Bad Brown Bill;* Critici in Erba award, Bologna Book Fair, 1985, for *The Racing Car Driver's Moustache* by Trevor Todd; Eve Pownall Award for Information Books notable book designation, 2003, for *Weird! Amazing Inventions and Wacky Science,* by Simon Torok; Aurealis Award finalist for Children's Short Stories, 2004, for *The Very Messy Inspection;* KOALA Awards shortlist, for *Cocky Colin.*

Writings

SELF-ILLUSTRATED

The Oath of Bad Brown Bill, Thomas Nelson (West Melbourne, Victoria, Australia), 1978.

Eucalyptus Christmas, Hodder & Stoughton (Sydney, New South Wales, Australia), 1983.

The Very Messy Inspection ("Piccolo and Anabelle" series), Random House Australia (Milsons Point, New South Wales, Australia), 2004.

The Disastrous Party ("Piccolo and Anabelle" series), Random House Australia (Milsons Point, New South Wales, Australia), 2005.

ILLUSTRATOR

Cliff Green, *The Incredible Steam-driven Adventures of Riverboat Bill,* Hodder & Stoughton (Sydney, New South Wales, Australia), 1975.

Dorothy Wall, *Blinky Bill and the Guest House: Based on The Complete Adventures of Blinky Bill,* Angus & Robertson (London, England), 1975.

Anne-Marie Willis, *Blinky Bill and the Pelicans,* Angus & Robertson (London, England), 1976.

Vince Jones, *Eli's Camel,* Rigby (Adelaide, Australia), 1978.

Dorothy Wall, *Blinky Bill and Nutsy Have Fun,* Angus & Robertson (Sydney, New South Wales, Australia), 1978.

Lorraine Wilson, *And the Teacher Got Mad,* Thomas Nelson Australia (West Melbourne, Victoria, Australia), 1979.

Lorraine Wilson, *La Festa in Costume,* Thomas Nelson Australia (West Melbourne, Victoria, Australia), 1979.

Lorraine Wilson, *The Fancy Dress Parade,* Thomas Nelson Australia (West Melbourne, Victoria, Australia), 1979.

Lorraine Wilson, *Teachers at Our School,* Thomas Nelson Australia (West Melbourne, Victoria, Australia), 1979.

Lorraine Wilson, *The New School,* Thomas Nelson Australia (West Melbourne, Victoria, Australia), 1980.

Lorraine Wilson, *Pet Day at School,* Thomas Nelson (West Melbourne, Victoria, Australia), 1980.

Lorraine Wilson, *Seeing the School Doctor,* Thomas Nelson (West Melbourne, Victoria, Australia), 1980.

Leslie Wilson, *Sunburn,* Thomas Nelson (West Melbourne, Victoria, Australia), 1980.

Lorraine Wilson, *Billy Card Day,* Nelson (West Melbourne, Victoria, Australia), 1980.

Lorraine Wilson, *Doing the Dishes,* Thomas Nelson (West Melbourne, Victoria, Australia), 1980.

Joan Dalgleish, *The Latchkey Dog,* Hodder & Stoughton (Lane Cove, New South Wales, Australia), 1980.

Cliff Green, *The Further Adventures of Riverboat Bill,* Hodder & Stoughton (Sydney, New South Wales, Australia), 1981.

Trevor Todd, *The Racing-Car Driver's Moustache,* Hodder & Stoughton (Sydney, New South Wales, Australia), 1984.

Cliff Green, *Riverboat Bill Steams Again,* Hodder & Stoughton (Sydney, New South Wales, Australia), 1985.

Libby Hathorn, *All about Anna—and Harriet and Christopher and Me,* Methuen (North Ryde, New South Wales, Australia), 1986.

Maurice Saxby and Glenys Smith, compilers, *What If?,* Methuen (North Ryde, New South Wales, Australia), 1987.

(With Jenny Axelsen) *Little Sisters,* Hodder & Stoughton (Sydney, New South Wales, Australia), 1988.

The Big Book of Australian Funny Poems, Macmillan (South Melbourne, Victoria, Australia), 1989.

Joan Dalgleish, *Dog on a Diet,* Hodder & Stoughton (Sydney, New South Wales, Australia), 1989.

Denise Ryan and David Drew, compilers, *Nobody Likes Me, Everybody Hates Me,* Oxford University Press (Melbourne, Victoria, Australia), 1990.

Denise Ryan and David Drew, compilers, *That's Impossible!,* Oxford University Press (Melbourne, Victoria, Australia), 1990.

Denise Ryan and David Drew, compilers, *What's So Funny?,* Oxford University Press (Melbourne, Victoria, Australia), 1990.

Roger Morgan, *I Thought I Saw a Dinosaur,* Murdoch Books (Sydney, New South Wales, Australia), 1990.

Melissa Hamilton and Margaret Hamilton, compilers, *The Recycled Joke Book: The Environment-friendly Collection,* Margaret Hamilton Books (Sydney, New South Wales, Australia), 1991.

Moira Cochrane, *The Wombat Who Wanted to Fly,* Jacaranda (Milton, Queensland, Australia), 1992.

Max Dann, *Jason Prince,* Puffin Books (Camberwell, Victoria, Australia), 1992.

Garry Hurle, *The Second-Hand Tongue, and Other Hilarious Stories,* Margaret Hamilton Books (Sydney, New South Wales, Australia), 1993.

David Drew, *Looney Tools: Inventing Technology,* Rigby Heinemann (Port Melbourne, Victoria, Australia), 1993.

Tom Bradley, *Crowded House,* Angus & Robertson (Pymble, New South Wales, Australia), 1995.

Tom Bradley, *Double Dilemma,* Angus & Robertson (Pymble, New South Wales, Australia), 1995.

Tom Bradley, *Fair Weather,* Angus & Robertson (Pymble, New South Wales, Australia), 1995.

Tom Bradley, *Father Daze,* Angus & Robertson (Pymble, New South Wales, Australia), 1995.

Tom Bradley, *Nine Lives,* Angus & Robertson (Pymble, New South Wales, Australia), 1995.

Tom Bradley, *Trading Spaces,* Angus & Robertson (Pymble, New South Wales, Australia), 1995.

Stephen Gard, *O, Susanna,* Ashton Scholastic (Sydney, New South Wales, Australia), 1995.

Peter McFalane, *Rebecca the Wrecker,* Angus & Robertson (Pymble, New South Wales, Australia), 1995.

Colleen Barton, *Murder Most Fowl: More of I Findem,* Scholastic (Sydney, New South Wales, Australia), 1996.

Ellen Frances, *Undercover!,* Longman Australia (Melbourne, Victoria, Australia), 1996.

Peter McFarlane, *Betty the Balloon Buster,* Angus & Robertson (Pymble, New South Wales, Australia), 1996.

Peter McFarlane, *Bruce the Goose,* Angus & Robertson (Pymble, New South Wales, Australia), 1996.

Red Hot Jokes for Kool Kids, ABC Books for the Australian Broadcasting (Sydney, New South Wales, Australia), 1997.

Dianne Bates, *Desert Dan the Dunny Man,* Hodder Children's Books Australia (Rydalmere, New South Wales, Australia), 1997.

Dianne Bates, *Hairy Hannah and the Grandad Gang,* Hodder Headline Australia (Sydney, New South Wales, Australia), 1997.

Peter McFarlane, *Max the Man Mountain,* HarperCollins (Pymble, New South Wales, Australia), 1997.

Peter McFarlane, *Soula the Ruler,* Angus & Robertson (Pymble, New South Wales, Australia), 1997.

Pat Long and John Phemister, editors, *Why? Scientists Answer Children's Questions,* ABC Books for the Australian Broadcasting Corporation (Sydney, New South Wales, Australia), 1998.

Rose Inserra, *Albert Spells Trouble,* Nelson ITP (South Melbourne, Victoria, Australia), 1998.

Andy Jones, compiler, *Sizzling Hot Jokes for Kool Kids,* ABC Books for the Australian Broadcasting Corporation (Sydney, New South Wales, Australia), 1998.

Rose Inserra, *The Missing Teeth,* Rigby Heinemann (Port Melbourne, Victoria, Australia), 1998.

Margaret Mahy, *Down in the Dump with Dinsmore,* Puffin Books (Ringwood, Victoria, Australia), 1998.

Peter McFarlane, *Barnaby the Barbarian,* HarperCollins (Pymble, New South Wales, Australia), 1998.

Teri McLauchlan, *Warped William; Watch out William,* Nelson ITP (South Melbourne, Victoria, Australia), 1998.

Jen McVeity, *Joe Cocker Spaniel,* Longman (South Melbourne, Victoria, Australia), 1998.

Duncan Ball, *Quentin's Lunch,* ABC Books for the Australian Broadcasting Corporation (Sydney, New South Wales, Australia), 1999.

Paul Holper and Simon Torok, *Wow! Amazing Science Facts and Trivia* (also see below), ABC Books for the Australian Broadcasting Corporation (Sydney, New South Wales, Australia), 1999.

Peter McFarlane, *Michaela the Whaler,* HarperCollins (Pymble, New South Wales, Australia), 1999.

Bob Ryan, *The Mad Murkins' Holiday,* ABC Books for the Australian Broadcasting Corporation (Sydney, New South Wales, Australia), 1999.

John Heffernan, *The Adventures of Pete Paddock Basher: Six Stories,* Margaret Hamilton Books (Sydney, New South Wales, Australia), 1999.

Richard Tulloch, *Cocky Colin,* Omnibus Books (Norwood, South Australia, Australia), 1999.

Michelle Atkins, *Marion and the Mudpies; Marion's Big Secret,* Nelson ITP (South Melbourne, Victoria, Australia), 2000.

Max Dann, *Teacher's Pest,* Puffin Books (Ringwood, Victoria, Australia), 2000.

Max Fatchen, *Terrible Troy,* ABC Books for the Australian Broadcasting Corporation (Sydney, New South Wales, Australia), 2000.

Cynthia Maxwell, *Wild Things,* Omnibus Books (Norwood, South Australia, Australia), 2000.

Terri McLauchlan, *William Loses His Memory; William Can Read Minds,* Nelson ITP (South Melbourne, Victoria, Australia), 2000.

Debra Oswald, *Frank and the Emergency Joke,* Penguin (Ringwood, Victoria, Australia), 2000.

Emily Rodda, *Gobbleguts,* ABC Books for the Australian Broadcasting Corporation (Sydney, New South Wales, Australia), 2000.

Simon Torok and Paul Holper, *Whiz! Amazing Maths and Science Puzzles* (also see below), ABC Books for the Australian Broadcasting Corporation (Sydney, New South Wales, Australia), 2000.

Richard Tulloch, *Lucke's Amazing Smell,* ABC Books for the Australian Broadcasting Corporation (Sydney, New South Wales, Australia), 2000.

Cedric Axelsen, *Yeast: The Elixir of Life* (memoir), Halstead Press (Rushcutters Bay, New South Wales, Australia), 2001.

Phil Cummings, *Sid and the Slimeballs,* Heinemann Library (Port Melbourne, Victoria, Australia), 2001.

Max Dann, *Bernice Knows Best,* Penguin (Ringwood, Victoria, Australia), 2001.

Paul N. Holper and Simon Torok, *Zap! Amazing Science Experiments* (also see below), ABC Books for the Australian Broadcasting Corporation (Sydney, New South Wales, Australia), 2001.

Katrina Nannestad, *Bungaloo Creek,* ABC Books for the Australian Broadcasting Corporation (Sydney, New South Wales, Australia), 2001.

Andy Jones, compiler, *Bumper Book of Hot Jokes for Kool Kids Volume Two,* ABC Books for the Australian Broadcasting Corporation (Sydney, New South Wales, Australia), 2002.

Kathy Hoopman, *Race of Fear,* Word Weavers Press (Bulimba, Queensland, Australia), 2002.

Sherryl Clark, *Susie the Lifesaver,* Penguin Books (Camberwell, Victoria, Australia), 2003.

Paul N. Holper and Simon Torok, *101 Great Solar System Facts and Trivia,* ABC Books for the Australian Broadcasting Corporation (Sydney, New South Wales, Australia), 2004.

Max Dann, *One Night at Lottie's House,* Puffin Books (Camberwell, Victoria, Australia), 2004.

Glenda Millard, *Mrs Wiggins' Wartymelons,* ABC Books for the Australian Broadcasting Corporation (Sydney, New South Wales, Australia), 2004.

Angela Moore, *Dizzy and Me: A Hairy, Holiday Adventure,* ABC Books for the Australian Broadcasting Corporation (Sydney, New South Wales, Australia), 2004.

The Stinky Cheese Gypsies, Random House Australia (Milsons Point, New South Wales, Australia), 2005.

Cassandra Golds, *The Mostly True Story of Matthew and Trim,* Puffin (Melbourne, Victoria, Australia), 2005.

Simon Torok and Paul Holper, *Amazing Science! Weird! Inventions and Wacky Science; Whiz! Maths and Science Puzzles; Zap! Science Experiments; Wow! Science Facts and Trivia,* ABC Books for the Australian Broadcasting Corporation (Sydney, New South Wales, Australia), 2005.

Also illustrator of *Out of Read!* (training kit), for New South Wales Department of Education and Training, 2002.

Adaptations

The Oath of Bad Brown Bill was adapted as a musical, music by Barry Conyngham, libretto by Murray Copland, produced in Melbourne, Victoria, Australia, 1985.

Work in Progress

Writing and illustrating more books in the "Piccolo and Annabelle" series.

Biographical and Critical Sources

PERIODICALS

Byron Shire Echo (Byron Bay, New South Wales, Australia), December 14, 2004, Micael McDonald, "Axelsen's Bumbling Angel Takes Wing," p. 17.

Magpies, March, 2005, Jane Connolly, review of *The Very Messy Inspection,* p. 33.

ONLINE

Aussie Reviews Online, http://www.aussiereviews.com/ (October 5, 2005), Sally Murphy, review of *Mrs Wiggins' Wartymelons.*

Lateral Learning Web site, http://www.laterallearning.com/ (October 5, 2005), "Stephen Axelsen."

Penguin Books Australia Web site, http://www.penguin.com.au/ (October 5, 2005).*

*   *   *

AXTON, David
See KOONTZ, Dean R.

BIAL, Raymond 1948-

Personal

Born November 5, 1948, in Danville, IL; son of Marion (a U.S. Air Force officer) and Catherine (a medical secretary) Bial; married Linda LaPuma (a librarian), August 25, 1979; children: Anna, Sarah, Luke. *Education:* University of Illinois, B.S. (with honors), 1970, M.S., 1979. *Politics:* "Independent." *Religion:* Roman Catholic. *Hobbies and other interests:* Gardening, fishing, hiking, travel.

Addresses

Home—Urbana, IL. *Home and office*—First Light Photography, P.O. Box 593, Urbana, IL 61801. *E-mail*—info@raybial.com.

Career

Photographer, librarian, and writer. Parkland College Library, Champaign, IL, librarian, 1980-c. 2004.

Member

Children's Reading Roundtable, Society of Children's Book Writers and Illustrators.

Awards, Honors

Best Publicity commendation, Library Public Relations Council, 1984, 1986; Historian of the Year, Champaign County, IL, 1984; Award of Superior Achievement, Illinois State Historical Society, 1985; staff development award, Parkland College, 1985, 1990; Certificate of Commendation, American Association for State and Local History, 1986; Writer's Choice selection, National Endowment for the Arts/Pushcart Foundation, 1986, for *First Frost;* Outstanding Science Trade Book for Children designation, 1991, for *Corn Belt Harvest;* Parents' Choice Foundation Choice designation, and American Library Association Notable Children's Book designation, both 1994, both for *Amish Home;* Ohio Farm Burea Children's Literature Award, 1995, for *Portrait of a Family Farm;* Black History Month 25 Top Picks includee, 1996, for *The Underground Railroad;* Spur Award selections for Best Children's Books about the American West, for *Ghost Towns of the American West* and *The Pueblo;* John Burroughs Award for best environmental books for children, for *A Handful of Dirt;* Orbis Pictus honor books for nonfiction, for *With Needle and Thread* and *Tenement: Immigrant Life on the Lower East Side;* numerous selections as Notable Social Studies Trade Book for Young People, Children's Book Council.

Writings

FICTION; FOR CHILDREN

The Fresh Grave and Other Ghostly Stories, illustrated by daughter, Anna Bial, Face to Face Books, 1997.

Raymond Bial

The Ghost of Honeymoon Creek, illustrated by Anna Bial, Face to Face Books, 1999.
Shadow Island (novel), Face to Face Books, 2000.

NONFICTION FOR CHILDREN; AND PHOTOGRAPHER

Corn Belt Harvest, Houghton (Boston, MA), 1991.
County Fair, Houghton (Boston, MA), 1992.
Amish Home, Houghton (Boston, MA), 1993.
Frontier Home, Houghton (Boston, MA), 1993.
Shaker Home, Houghton (Boston, MA), 1994.
Portrait of a Farm Family, Houghton (Boston, MA), 1995.
The Underground Railroad, Houghton (Boston, MA), 1995.
With Needle and Thread: A Book about Quilts, Houghton (Boston, MA), 1996.
Mist over the Mountains: Appalachia and Its People, Houghton (Boston, MA), 1997.
The Strength of These Arms: Life in the Slave Quarters, Houghton (Boston, MA), 1997.
Where Lincoln Walked, Walker, 1997.
Cajun Home, Houghton (Boston, MA), 1998.
One-Room School, Houghton (Boston, MA), 1999.
A Handful of Dirt, Walker (New York, NY), 2000.
Ghost Towns of the American West, Houghton (Boston, MA), 2001.
(And photographer) *A Book Comes Together: From Idea to Library,* Bound to Stay Bound Books (Jacksonville, IL), 2002.

Tenement: Immigrant Life on the Lower East Side, Houghton (Boston, MA), 2002.
The Long Walk: The Story of Navajo Captivity, Benchmark Books (New York, NY), 2003.
Where Washington Walked, Walker (New York, NY), 2004.
Nauvoo: Mormon City on the Mississippi River, Houghton Mifflin (Boston, MA), 2006.

NONFICTION; "LIFEWAYS" SERIES

The Navajo, Benchmark Books (New York, NY), 1999.
The Cherokee, Benchmark Books (New York, NY), 1999.
The Iroquois, Benchmark Books (New York, NY), 1999.
The Sioux, Benchmark Books (New York, NY), 1999.
The Ojibwe, Benchmark Books (New York, NY), 2000.
The Pueblo, Benchmark Books (New York, NY), 2000.
The Seminole, Benchmark Books (New York, NY), 2000.
The Comanche, Benchmark Books (New York, NY), 2000.
The Apache, Benchmark Books (New York, NY), 2001.
The Huron, Benchmark Books (New York, NY), 2001.
The Haida, Benchmark Books (New York, NY), 2001.
The Cheyenne, Benchmark Books (New York, NY), 2001.
The Inuit, Benchmark Books (New York, NY), 2002.
The Shoshone, Benchmark Books (New York, NY), 2002.
The Powhatan, Benchmark Books (New York, NY), 2002.
The Nez Perce, Benchmark Books (New York, NY), 2002.
The Blackfeet, Benchmark Books (New York, NY), 2003.
The Tlingit, Benchmark Books (New York, NY), 2003.
The Mandan, Benchmark Books (New York, NY), 2003.
The Choctaw, Benchmark Books (New York, NY), 2003.
The Delaware, Benchmark Books (New York, NY), 2004.
The Chumash, Benchmark Books (New York, NY), 2004.
The Arapaho, Benchmark Books (New York, NY), 2004.
The Wampanoag, Benchmark Books (New York, NY), 2004.
The Shawnee, Benchmark Books (New York, NY), 2004.
The Menominee, Benchmark Books (New York, NY), 2005.
The Crow, Benchmark Books (New York, NY), 2005.
The Cree, Benchmark Books (New York, NY), 2005.

NONFICTION; "BUILDING AMERICA" SERIES

The Mills, Benchmark Books (New York, NY), 2002.
The Houses, Benchmark Books (New York, NY), 2002.
The Forts, Benchmark Books (New York, NY), 2002.
The Farms, Benchmark Books (New York, NY), 2002.
The Canals, Benchmark Books (New York, NY), 2002.

NONFICTION; "AMERICAN COMMUNITY" SERIES

Missions and Presidios, Children's Press (New York, NY), 2004.
Longhouses, Children's Press (New York, NY), 2004.
Frontier Settlements, Children's Press (New York, NY), 2004.
Early American Villages, Children's Press (New York, NY), 2004.
Cow Towns, Children's Press (New York, NY), 2004.

OTHER

Ivesdale: A Photographic Essay, Champaign County Historical Archives, 1982.
(Photographer and calligrapher) *Upon a Quiet Landscape: The Photographs of Frank Sadorus,* Champaign County Historical Museum, 1983.
(Editor) *In All My Years: Portraits of Older Blacks in Champaign-Urbana,* Champaign County Historical Museum, 1983, revised edition, 1985.
There Is a Season, Champaign County Nursing Home, 1984.
(With Kathryn Kerr) *First Frost,* Stormline Press, 1985.
Common Ground: Photographs of Rural and Small Town Life, Stormline Press, 1986.
Stopping By: Portraits from Small Towns, University of Illinois Press, 1988.
(With wife, Linda LaPuma Bial) *The Carnegie Library in Illinois,* University of Illinois Press, 1988.
(Author of introduction) Gary Irving, photographer, *Beneath an Open Sky,* University of Illinois Press (Champaign, IL), 1990.
From the Heart of the Country: Photographs of the Midwestern Sky, Sagamore Publishing, 1991.
Looking Good: A Guide to Photographing Your Library, American Library Association, 1991.
Champaign: A Pictorial History, Bradley Publishing, 1993.
(Photographer) *Marcia Adams Heirloom Recipes,* Clarkson Potter (New York, NY, 1994.
Visit to Amish Country, Phoenix Publishing, 1995.
Zoom Lens Photography, Amherst Media, 1996.

Contributor of photo-essay to *Townships,* University of Iowa Press, 1992. Contributor of photographers to periodicals.

Sidelights

Raymond Bial has blended a love of photography and writing with a special feeling for rural and small-town America to create numerous illustrated books looking at subjects from harvesting corn to rural architecture to one-room schools. His books on the many cultures of America—from Cajun to Native American to Appalachian—also introduce young readers to a type of living history that makes dry facts come alive. Other texts by Bial present historical topics, such as slavery, tenement life, the growth of the Shaker community, the treatment of Native Americans, and the life of U.S. presidents George Washington and Abraham Lincoln. His contributions to the "Building America" series, which include such titles as *The Canals, The Mills,* and *The Forts,* were cited by *Booklist* contributor Susan Dove Lempke for their "strong research, clear writing, good organization," and Bial's "handsome color photographs." In addition, Bial has produced several works of juvenile fiction, among them *The Fresh Grave and Other Ghostly Stories* and the novel *Shadow Island.*

Born in Illinois, Bial grew up in the same rural, small-town community he portrays in books such as *Corn Belt Harvest, Cow Towns,* and *Early American Villages.*

As the author/photographer once told *SATA:* "When I was growing up in the 1950s I spent several of the most joyous years of my young life in a small town in Indiana. With my friends, I bicycled around the neighborhood, went swimming at the municipal pool, stopped for ice cream at the local hotspot, and frequently visited our Carnegie public library. Some people might think that such memories are simply nostalgic, but I know that our little town was pleasant, comfortable, and safe—and I will always cherish those years.

"Later, our family moved to a farm in southern Michigan. Although I missed my old friends, as well as the charming atmosphere of my old 'hometown,' I enjoyed taking care of our livestock and running free through the woods, marsh, and fields around our new home. The moment I walked out of the house, I was truly outside. The marsh, in particular, was bursting forth with wildlife—turtles, frogs, muskrats, ducks—and I delighted in my explorations and discoveries." While his family had the usual ups and downs, as Bial recalled, "I was simply thrilled to be alive, directly experiencing the world around me, especially when I could be out of doors in the light and weather."

During childhood, Bial was also interested in social and cultural history, and he continued this interest in college. After training as a librarian, he worked in that field for over three decades; his wife, Linda, is a professor of library science, and the couple has produced several volumes of local history. Although Bial knew as a child that he wanted to become an author, during his twenties he discovered photography. "I never consciously decided to become a photographer," he once explained; "I simply loved the experience of making photographs. I've never received any formal training or education in the art form. Rather, I have relied upon my own instincts in making photographs which matter to me personally." While developing his skills in 35mm and large-format photography, in 1991 Bial fulfilled his childhood dream, combining his talents in writing and photography in his first book for children, *Corn Belt Harvest.*

Blending photographs and a straightforward, sometimes lyrical, text, *Corn Belt Harvest* describes the planting, harvesting, storage, and marketing methods of Midwest corn growers. Well received by critics, the book also received an Outstanding Science Trade Book for Children citation. Reviewing the title in *Booklist,* Hazel Rochman called *Corn Belt Harvest* an "informative photoessay" that features "clear color photographs" depicting the corn-growing and-harvesting process. The author/photographer "communicates a sense of process and connection in machines and nature," concluded Rochman, while a *Kirkus Reviews* critic noted that both text and photos are "commendably clear and informative." Writing in *School Library Journal,* Joyce Adams Burner noted the book's "big, beautiful color photographs," and further remarked that "Bial writes in a smooth, pre-

cise manner, yet conveys his love for the region." Burner concluded: "Overall, this is a jewel of a book, well suited for reports."

Other photo essays by Bial include *County Fair, Portrait of a Farm Family,* and *A Handful of Dirt. County Fair* traces a fair from set-up through opening day to the break-down of the tents. "Bial captures the sense of anticipation that swirls around a fair, as well as offering an insightful look at what goes on behind the scenes," noted *Booklist* contributor Ilene Cooper. Focusing on everything from livestock barns to homemade pies to and rides and other amusements, the book features "Attractive color photos [that] . . . stand out on the pages," according to Cooper.

Dairy farming is the subject of 1995's *Portrait of a Farm Family.* Mary Harris Veeder, writing in *Booklist,* noted that the author's profile of the "everyday world" of the Steidinger family "fits its subject neatly into an excellent discussion of family-farm based agriculture in the U.S. economy." *Horn Book* contributor Elizabeth S. Watson praised the work, noting that Bial's "fine photoessay radiates the warmth of a close ten-member family engaged in hard work toward a common goal—the survival of the family farm." Moving from the farm directly down to the land itself, *A Handful of Dirt* introduces readers to the many creatures—from bacteria to bugs and worms to shakes and gophers—that live on and in the soil. Noting the inclusion of photographs taken with an electron microscope, *Book* contributor Kathleen Odean predicted that Bial's "fine photo-essay will change how children view everyday dirt."

With *Amish Home* Bial struck on a winning formula: introducing America's diverse culture through domestic artifacts. His focus on things rather than people was a necessity in his first book of this type; the Amish people do not wish to be photographed. In more recent volumes, however, such as *Frontier Home, Cajun Home,* artifacts take on almost totemic values, introducing readers to the language, culture, food, and even history of the groups described. *Frontier Home* conjures up a bygone life through photos taken at pioneer villages and sites, pairing them with the letters of actual pioneers, while in *Cajun Home,* Bial profiles the ethnic group which originally came from France, settled in Canada, and later moved on to Louisiana.

Reviewing *Amish Home* for *Booklist,* Kay Weisman praised the work as "haunting" and noted that Bial's work "will be welcomed by libraries everywhere." Alexandra Marris, reviewing *Amish Home* for *School Library Journal,* called the work "attractive and compelling," adding that "Bial clearly demonstrates his deep respect for these people and their complex system of values." *Booklist* critic Carolyn Phelan commented of *Frontier Homes* that "Bial's photography gives the book a look of integrity as well as a window into the lives of the pioneers," while Judith Constantinides, reviewing *Cajun Home* in *School Library Journal,* remarked on

Bial's "stunning full-color pictures of little things" by means of which he "meticulously builds a portrait of a fascinating people."

Tenement: Immigrant Life on the Lower East Side stands in contrast to much of Bial's works because, while it presents a look backward to a historic time and place, it takes readers far from its author's rural roots. Inspired by the author's visit to New York City's Lower East Side Tenement Museum and the writings and photographs of turn-of-the-twentieth-century social reformer Jacob Riis, *Tenement* weaves together many threads, including what *School Library Journal* reviewer Diane S. Marton praised as a "finely written, spare text" and the author's "beautifully composed, stunning" photographs, to depict a harsh life of cramped, unsanitary living conditions, brutal poverty, and debilitating work. Praising the book as a "substantial historic overview," a *Kirkus Reviews* critic noted that Bial's "out-of-towner" status aided in his work: "his picture is a clearer one, especially for non-New Yorkers," than other books on the subject, the critic explained. With an eye toward the book's audience, *Booklist* reviewer Ilene Cooper wrote that *Tenement* "will certainly be an eye-opener to many young people who are used to their own space."

The people of Appalachia received the Bial treatment in *Mist over the Mountains: Appalachia and Its People.* As much a culture as a place, this region of small farms

The substandard and often unhealthy living conditions endured by New York City's immigrant populations during the late nineteenth- and early twentieth centuries are brought to life by Bial in his well-illustrated Tenement: Immigrant Life on the Lower East Side.

and folk arts is rich in culture and history, both of which Bial illuminates in text and photos. A *Kirkus Reviews* contributor called Bial's book a "superb photo-essay," while *Booklist* writer Phelan concluded that "this handsome book casts its beam of light with care and respect." A popular American handicraft forms the focus of *With Needle and Thread: A Book about Quilts,* a survey of patch-fabric stitchery from pioneer days through the era of the AIDS quilt. "With quiet prose and clear, lovely full-color photographs, Bial has stitched together a 'sampler' about people and the quilts they sew," commented *Booklist* contributor Hazel Rochman in her review of this title.

The lives of American presidents have also come into clearer focus through Bial's work. *Where Lincoln Walked* traces the career of the man who guided the nation through a civil war from his humble log-cabin beginnings to his years in Washington, D.C. Interspersed with the text are photos of places associated with Abraham Lincoln, including his homes and offices, as well as contemporary mid-nineteenth-century images, such as paintings and engravings. Eunice Weech, writing in *School Library Journal,* called this book "another of Bial's beautifully executed photo-essays," while a *Kirkus Reviews* writer dubbed it an "extraordinarily honest, if brief, pictorial portrayal."

Where Washington Walked is a similar work that follows the revolutionary general and first president on his path through the country's early history, pairing what *School Library Journal* contributor Elaine Fort Weischedel dubbed an "interesting" text with prints, paintings, and Bial's photographs of historic landmarks in Washington's life. From the first president's boyhood home of Ferry Farm to Mount Vernon and the sites now contained in Colonial Williamsburg, Bial's "sharply focused, well-composed" color photographs were cited by *Booklist* contributor Phelan, along with the book's "clearly written biographical account." *Where Washington Walked* comprises a "unusually vivid photographic record" of its subject's life and accomplishments, concluded Phelan.

Beginning the "Lifeways" series in 1999, Bial has completed fact-based histories of over two dozen Native American tribes, profiling "the history, culture, and social traditions" of each people "in clear, respectful language," according to Linda Greengrass in her *School Library Journal* review of *The Inuit.* Each volume contains an example of tribal folklore as well as a discussion of the ceremonies, geography, language, history, way of life, crafts, and community organization that make each group unique. Not surprisingly, these histories also have a special feature: what *School Library Journal* reviewer Sue Morgan characterized as "elegant full-color photography" of both tribal landmarks and existing artifacts. Also containing the author's photographs, a related volume, *The Long Walk: The Story of Navajo Captivity* focuses on the 300-mile march endured by the Navajo to a U.S. government reservation

Using original art as well as contemporary photographs, Bial traces the path of America's first president in **Where Washington Walked,** *which follows George Washington from his parents' farm through battlefields and political office to his final years at Mount Vernon.* (*Painting by Emanuel Leutz.*)

in southeastern New Mexico during the late 1800s, an imprisonment policy that was later overturned. Bial also includes an overview of Navajo history in this well-illustrated work.

Biographical and Critical Sources

PERIODICALS

Book, March, 2001, Kathleen Odean, review of *A Handful of Dirt,* p. 86.

Booklist, December 15, 1991, Hazel Rochman, review of *Corn Belt Harvest,* p. 761; February 1, 1992, Ilene Cooper, review of *County Fair,* p. 1023; February 15, 1993, Kay Weisman, review of *Amish Home,* p. 1055; November 1, 1993, Carolyn Phelan, review of *Frontier Home,* p. 516; April 1, 1995, Hazel Rochman, review of *The Underground Railroad,* p. 1390; September 1, 1995, Mary Harris Veeder, review of *Portrait of a Farm Family,* p. 73; March 1, 1996, Hazel Rochman, review of *With Needle and Thread,* p. 1175; March 1, 1997, Carolyn Phelan, review of *Mist over the Mountains,* p. 1156; September 15, 1997, p. 224; March 1, 1998, p. 1125; March 15, 1998, Ilene Cooper, review of *Cajun Home,* p. 1236; March 1, 2002, Susan Dove Lempke, review of *The Canals* and *The*

Houses, p. 1132; October 15, 2002, Ilene Cooper, review of *Tenement: Immigrant Life on the Lower East Side,* p. 406; December 15, 2004, Carolyn Phelan, review of *Where Washington Walked,* p. 739.

Horn Book, May-June, 1994, Ellen Fader, review of *Shaker Home,* p. 332; July-August, 1995, p. 474; November-December, 1995, Elizabeth S. Watson, review of *Portrait of a Farm Family,* pp. 759-760; May-June, 1998, p. 355; November-December, 2002, Susan P. Bloom, review of *Tenement,* p. 773.

Kirkus Reviews, December 1, 1991, review of *Corn Belt Harvest,* p. 1529; February 1, 1993, review of *Amish Home,* p. 142; July 15, 1993, p. 930; July 15, 1995, p. 1021; January 1, 1996, p. 64; February 15, 1997, review of *Mist over the Mountains,* p. 297; November 15, 1997, review of *Where Lincoln Walked,* p. 1704; February 15, 1998, p. 264; July 1, 2002, review of *Tenement,* p. 949; December 15, 2004, review of *Where Washington Walked,* p. 1198.

Publishers Weekly, March 22, 1993, p. 80; January 16, 1995, review of *The Underground Railroad,* p. 455; December 15, 1997, p. 59; July 20, 2002, review of *Tenement,* p. 73.

School Library Journal, February, 1992, Joyce Adams Burner, review of *Corn Belt Harvest,* p. 92; May, 1993, Alexandra Marris, review of *Amish Home,* p. 112; March, 1994, pp. 225-226; April, 1995, p. 140; December, 1995, p. 112; June, 1996, p. 134; May, 1997, p. 142; November, 1997, p. 125; December, 1997, p. 120; February, 1998, Eunice Weech, review of *Where Lincoln Walked,* p. 94; May, 1998, Judith Constantinides, review of *Cajun Home,* p. 150; February, 1999, p. 39; February, 2002, Marlene Gawron, review of *The Canals,* p. 140; April, 2002, Linda Greengrass, review of *The Inuit,* p. 163; September, 2002, Diane S. Marton, review of *Tenement,* p. 240; March, 2003, Ginny Gustin, review of *The Long Walk,* p. 246; June, 2003, S. K. Joiner, review of *The Mandan,* p. 155; May, 2004, Sue Morgan, review of *The Chumash* and *The Wampanoag,* p. 162; January, 2005, Joyce Adams Burner, review of *Cow Towns,* p. 107; February, 2005, Elaine Fort Weischedel, review of *Where Washington Walked,* p. 114.

ONLINE

Raymond Bial Home Page, http://www.raybial.com (October 20, 2005).

*   *   *

BOWEN, Rhys
See QUIN-HARKIN, Janet

C

CADNUM, Michael 1949-

Personal
Born May 3, 1949, in Orange, CA; married; wife's name, Sherina. *Education:* Attended University of California, Berkeley, and San Francisco State University.

Addresses
Home—Albany, CA. *Agent*—Katharine Kidde, Kidde, Hoyt, and Picard, 335 E. 51st St., New York, NY 10022.

Career
Writer. Worked for a suicide prevention help-line.

Awards, Honors
Creative writing fellowship, National Endowment for the Arts; Helen Bullis Prize, *Poetry Northwest;* Owl Creek Book Award; finalist, *Los Angeles Times* Book Award; finalist, National Book Award, 2000, for *The Book of the Lion.*

Writings

YOUNG-ADULT NOVELS

Saint Peter's Wolf, Carroll and Graf (New York, NY), 1991.
Calling Home, Viking (New York, NY), 1991.
Breaking the Fall, Viking (New York, NY), 1992.
Taking It, Viking (New York, NY), 1995.
In a Dark Wood, Orchard (New York, NY), 1998.
Heat, Viking (New York, NY), 1998.
Raven of the Waves, Orchard (New York, NY), 2000.
The Book of the Lion, Viking (New York, NY), 2000.
Forbidden Forest: The Story of Little John and Robin Hood, Orchard (New York, NY), 2002.
The Leopard Sword (sequel to *The Book of the Lion*), Viking (New York, NY) 2002.

Michael Cadnum

Daughter of the Wind, Orchard (New York, NY), 2003.
Ship of Fire, Viking (New York, NY), 2003.
Starfall: Phaeton and the Chariot of the Sun, Orchard (New York, NY), 2004.
Blood Gold, Viking (New York, NY), 2004.
The Dragon Throne (sequel to *The Leopard Sword*), Viking (New York, NY), 2005.
Nightsong, Viking (New York, NY), 2006.

FOR CHILDREN

The Lost and Found House, illustrated by Steve Johnson and Lou Fancher, Viking (New York, NY), 1997.

FOR ADULTS

Nightlight, St. Martin's Press (New York, NY), 1990.
Sleepwalker, St. Martin's Press (New York, NY), 1991.
Ghostwright, Carroll and Graf (New York, NY), 1992.
The Horses of the Night, Carroll and Graf (New York, NY), 1993.
Skyscape, Carroll and Graf (New York, NY), 1994.
The Judas Glass, Carroll and Graf (New York, NY), 1996.
Zero at the Bone, Viking (New York, NY), 1996.
Edge, Viking (New York, NY), 1997.
Rundown, Viking (New York, NY), 1999.
Redhanded, Viking (New York, NY), 2000.

POETRY

The Morning of the Massacre (chapbook), Bieler Press, 1982.
Wrecking the Cactus (chapbook), Salt Lick Press, 1985.
Invisible Mirror (chapbook), Ommation Press, 1986.
Foreign Springs (chapbook), Amelia Press (Bakersfield, CA), 1987.
By Evening, Owl Creek Press (Seattle, WA), 1992.
The Cities We Will Never See, Singular Speech Press (Canton, CT), 1993.
The Woman Who Discovered Math, Red Booth Chapbooks, 2001.
Illicit (chapbook), Frank Cat Press, 2001.

Also author of *Day by Day* (e-book), Mudlark, 2003.

OTHER

Ella and the Canary Prince (fiction chapbook), Subterranean Press, 1999.
Together Again: The True Story of Humpty Dumpty (fiction chapbook), Subterranean Press, 2001.
Can't Catch Me (short stories), Tachyon Publications, 2006.

Contributor to anthologies, including *Mystery Writer's Annual, Mystery Scene, Poet and Critic,* and *Second Sight: Stories for a New Millennium,* Putnam, 1999. Contributor to periodicals, including *America, Antioch Review, Beloit Fiction Journal, Beloit Poetry Journal, Commonweal,* and *Rolling Stone.* Contributor to "Read This" (column), *New York Review of Science Fiction.*

Work in Progress

Crimson Voyage: The Story of Jason and Medea, for Orchard.

Sidelights

Known as a poet during the 1980s, Michael Cadnum has since gained a reputation for his adult suspense novels as well as his many young-adult novels based on history, myth, and legend. Horror and suspense novels such as *Ghostwright, Sleepwalker,* and *The Judas Glass* have a broad appeal to adults and teens who enjoy stories featuring ghosts, werewolves, and vampires, while his psychological thrillers address many of the serious problems experienced by adolescents. In more recent years, teen novels such as *Ship of Fire,* National Book Award finalist *The Book of the Lion,* and *The Dragon Throne* have presented new twists on traditional stories, by featuring exciting storylines, compelling characters, and realistic settings that bring to life everything from the voyage of Sir Francis Drake to the crusades of Richard the Lionhearted to Ovid's Metamorphoses. Reviewing *Ship of Fire,* a story about Drake's raid on Spanish ships at Cadiz in 1597, *Booklist* critic John Peters cited Cadnum's reputation "for rousing historical adventures set against gruesomely naturalistic backdrops." In a contrast that shows the author's versatility, Cadnum's retelling of portions of Ovid's ancient tales in *Starfall: Phaeton and the Chariot of the Sun* was praised by a *Publishers Weekly* contributor as "a trilogy of enchanting tales" in which the storyteller succeeds in "humanizing classical figures and transforming lofty language into accessible, lyrical prose."

Cadnum grew up near the beaches of Southern California, and while he enjoyed watching television like most teens, he derived even greater pleasure from reading. "I have always felt our lives are too small, too thin and insubstantial," he explained in an interview with *Authors and Artists for Young Adults* (*AAYA*). "When we watch television—and I have always watched a lot of television—we are powerfully distracted from our routines, but only through reading are we really nourished." A voracious reader, he dipped into everything from pulp fiction to philosophy, and in books he discovered much about the world. "Books, like so much in the real world, give, and ask nothing in return," Cadnum explained.

After graduating from high school, Cadnum attended college, taking classes at both the University of California at Berkeley and San Francisco State University, and earning a National Endowment for the Arts fellowship for his poetry. His first published book, *The Morning of the Massacre,* was published in 1982, and was followed by several other verse collections. While poetry continued to be his main focus through the 1980s, Cadnum was dabbling with prose as early as the 1970s, when he began the copious research on the historical novel that would be published, decades later, as *Ship of Fire.*

In addition to his writing, Cadnum also worked for a suicide help-line, which brought him into contact with people who exist on the margins of life, such as successful professionals harboring unfulfilled desires or hidden demons and troubled teenagers coping with dysfunctional families. His first published novel, 1990's *Nightlight,* features a man who is haunted by a recurring nightmare that ultimately morphs into real-life terror during his search for a missing relative. An archaeologist who is haunted by dreams of his dead wife finds his own tendency to sleepwalk shared by an eighth-century Norse corpse that he and his crew discover while excavating a Yorkshire bog in *Sleepwalker,* while *Saint Peter's Wolf* finds a San Francisco psychologist and art collector with marital problems becoming obsessed by werewolves after discovering a set of antique silver fangs. *Saint Peter's Wolf,* which was Cadnum's first book to attract a young-adult audience, retells the werewolf myth with a twist: after the psychologist begins to morph into a violent beast, he finds the freedom and power of his creature-self attractive and ultimately attempts to cast off his human side. Writing in *Voice of Youth Advocates,* Delia A. Culberson praised *Saint Peter's Wolf* as "a spellbinding *tour de force* in a rare blend of fantasy, horror, adventure, suspense, and passionate love. . . . A superb, fascinating book that subtly evokes that ancient, primal yearning in all living, breathing things for total, exhilarating freedom."

Although it was written for an adult audience, *Calling Home* was Cadnum's first book published specifically for young adults. The novel focuses on Peter, a teen-aged alcoholic who accidentally kills his best friend, Mead, in a moment of drunken anger. To cover up the act, Peter impersonates Mead in phone calls to the boy's worried parents, making them think that Mead has run away. Ultimately, his guilt overcomes his alcoholic haze, and Peter confesses to another friend.

Reviewing *Calling Home* for the *Wilson Library Journal,* Cathi Dunn MacRae noted that Cadnum "skillfully shapes suspense through masterful control of language," taking readers "so completely inside this disconnected boy, . . . they will never forget the experience." *Horn Book* critic Patty Campbell dubbed the novel an "exquisitely crafted work, a prose poem of devastating impact," adding that, "not since the debut of Robert Cormier with *The Chocolate War* . . . has such a major talent emerged in adolescent literature." Roger Sutton observed in the *Bulletin of the Children's Center for Books* that *Calling Home* offers "probably the truest portrait of a teenaged alcoholic we've had in YA fiction."

Like *Calling Home, Breaking the Fall* focuses on a troubled teenager. In this case, high school sophomore Stanley North has difficulty coping with his parents' crumbling marriage and his grades are suffering. While his savvy girlfriend Sky encourages him to turn to sports as a way of dealing with his stress, Stanley's self-destructive friend Jared has a stronger lure: the thrill of breaking into houses. Praising the author's engrossing, suspenseful plot and his ability to create sympathetic characters, *Horn Book* contributor Maeve Visser Knoth wrote that in *Breaking the Fall* Cadnum "writes truthfully about the seductive nature of power and friendships, recognizing the lengths to which young people will go in order to prove themselves." Susan L. Rogers noted as a caveat in *School Library Journal* that "some readers may be disturbed by this story, although mature teens may find it a more realistic reflection of a troubled world."

After aiding Richard's failed effort to claim the city of Jerusalem, Edmund returns to England, only to find his country in upheaval and his safety threatened by Prince John's henchmen in the concluding volume in Candum's fast-paced trilogy. (Cover illustration by Gregg Thorkelson.)

Other teen thrillers followed, including *Taking It, Zero to the Bone,* and *Edge.* In *Taking It,* Cadnum traces the psychological deterioration of Anna Charles, a seventeen-year-old kleptomaniac and the daughter of wealthy, divorced parents, as her compulsion to shoplift causes her to withdraw from family and friends and ultimately put herself in danger. *Zero at the Bone* is narrated by Cray Buchanan, a high-school senior whose sister, Anita, has disappeared, sending the Buchanan family into an emotional tailspin. Family tragedy is also the subject of *Edge,* which focuses on high-school dropout Zachary Madison. After his successful father, a writer, is permanently paralyzed by a car-jacker, Zach decides to seek justice after the man accused of attacking his father is set free. Praising Cadnum's "tight, beautiful prose" and his "finesse" in handling Anna's problems, *Booklist* reviewer Merri Monks concluded that *Taking It* "should not be missed." A *Publishers Weekly* commentator was similarly impressed, declaring that Cadnum writes with "subtlety and tremendous insight" and "keeps readers on the edge of their seats with this taut psychological portrait."

In the late 1990s Cadnum shifted his focus once again, this time moving from contemporary suspense to more time-bound novels. An interest in fairy tales inspired *In a Dark Wood* while *Forbidden Forest: The Story of Little John and Robin Hood* is a retelling of the Robin Hood legend. "I did a tremendous amount of research for *In a Dark Wood*," Cadnum recalled, "but I didn't know I was doing research. I thought I was reading about Robin Hood and traveling to Crusader castles in the Middle East and monasteries in France. I was just doing what I loved, and I turned out to know enough after a while to write a novel." In the first novel the classic story is told from the point of view of the Sheriff of Nottingham, usually cast as the villain of the piece. In Cadnum's version, the sheriff and his teenaged assistant must deal with the chaos caused by the wily thief known only as Robin Hood. In *Forbidden Forest* the story of Robin's slow-witted sidekick Little John is recounted, from the man's flight into the woods to avoid the wrath of a vicious nobleman to his efforts to right a wrong done to a beautiful young woman that has won his heart. "Cadnum succeeds admirably in capturing the squalor and casual brutality of the times," noted a *Kirkus Reviews* critic in reviewing *Forbidden Forest,* while in *Kliatt* Paula Rohrlick deemed the novel a "stirring story that imaginatively elaborates on the legend of the forest outlaws."

Continuing his focus on medieval history, Cadnum spins a three-part story of the Crusades in *The Book of the Lion, The Leopard Sword,* and *The Dragon Throne.* As the trilogy opens, Edmund finds himself fleeing for his life after his master, a moneyer who mints coins for the king, is found to be dishonest. Captured and imprisoned, the boy is taken on as squire to Sir Nigel, a knight on his way to Rome to fight for the cross in the Third Crusade. The pair meet up with Sir Rannulf and his squire, Hubert. Traveling together, they join the armies of King Richard and other Christian kings to fight in the bloody Siege of Acre, during which Muslim commander Saladin and his army ultimately manage to withstand the crusading armies for almost two years before surrendering.

Narrated by eighteen-year-old Hubert, *The Leopard Sword* finds the knights and their retinue surviving shipwrecks, storms, and Roman thieves before making the treacherous journey back to England. Once at home, the war-weary group encounters a kingdom in tatters due to Prince John's efforts to usurp the throne from his brother, Richard, as well as more personal difficulties. While noting the violence throughout the series, Rorhlick wrote in *Kliatt* that the books "offer . . . a new perspective on knights and the Crusades." Praising *The Leopard Sword,* Rohrlick described the novel as a "stirring, violent tale of life in the Middle Ages" in which "Cadnum continues his exploration of 'the call that war has on young people.'" In *School Library Journal* Renee Steinberg praised the book's "exciting climax," noting that Cadnum has "skillfully woven" a wealth of historical facts into his fictional tale.

An act of courage on the part of Hubert results in knighthood for both squires, and in *The Dragon Throne* Edmund and Hubert once again find themselves on the road to Rome. While hunted by Prince John due to their continued allegiance to King Richard, the pair are also escorting Ester de Laci on a pilgrimage to the holy city so that she can pray for her injured father. "During this journey through Europe, the dangers and unrest of the time period come alive," Denise Moore noted in *School Library Journal,* describing the third volume in the series, while in *Kirkus Reviews* a critic note that *The Dragon Throne* will, "like its predecessors, . . . leave readers pondering . . . 'the terrible paradox—that caring, responsible individuals can engage in acts of brutality.'"

In addition to his poetry and novels for older readers, Cadnum has also authored several collections of short stories as well as the picture book *The Lost and Found House,* which describes the excitement of moving to a

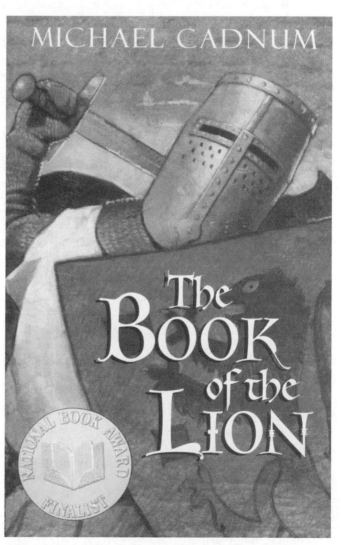

In the first part of Cadnum's trilogy about the twelfth-century Crusades, seventeen-year-old Edmund avoids a harsh and unfair punishment by serving as squire to a knight bound for the Holy Land and service to Richard the Lionhearted. (Cover illustration by Gregg Thorkelson.)

new home. In this work the author's poetic text is complemented with paintings by Steven Johnson and Lou Fancher that portray the experience through the eyes of an unnamed small boy. "My family moved several times during my childhood," Cadnum explained in his *AAYA* interview, "much like the family in *The Lost and Found House.*"

In his *AAYA* interview Cadnum described his wider purpose in creating fiction: "I want to give a voice to characters who ordinarily never have one. So few people tell the story of a family that never discovers the truth about a missing child, as in *Zero at the Bone,*" he asserted. "Few people have seen the Robin Hood story through the eyes of the Sheriff of Nottingham, as I do in *In a Dark Wood.* I want to tell the secrets that are not told, and to see the world through new eyes." Finally, Cadnum is motivated by the ultimate challenge to a writer: "I want to experience the joys and fears of people whom I never really meet."

Biographical and Critical Sources

BOOKS

Authors and Artists for Young Adults, Volume 23, Thomson Gale (Detroit, MI), 1998.

St. James Guide to Young-Adult Writers, second edition, St. James Press (Detroit, MI), 1999.

PERIODICALS

America, October 28, 1995, p. 27.

Booklist, July, 1991; November 15, 1992; July, 1995, Merri Monks, review of *Taking It,* p. 1879; August, 1996, p. 1094; December 1, 1997, p. 639; March 1, 1998, p. 1124; September 15, 1999, p. 252; August, 2002, Carolyn Phelan, review of *The Leopard Sword,* p. 1945; September 15, 2003, John Peters, review of *Ship of Fire,* p. 229; November 15, 2003, Linda Perkins, review of *Daughter of the Wind,* p. 591; January 1, 2004, Patricia Austin, review of *The Book of the Lion,* p. 892; May 15, 2004, Ed Sullivan, review of *Blood Gold,* p. 1628; October 1, 2004, Gillian Engberg, review of *Starfall: Phaeton and the Chariot of the Sun,* p. 321.

Bulletin of the Center for Children's Books, May, 1991, Roger Sutton, review of *Calling Home,* p. 212; July-August, 1997, Deborah Stevenson, review of *Edge.*

Childhood Education, fall, 2002, John McAndrew, review of *Forbidden Forest,* p. 51.

Georgia Review, fall, 1990, pp. 503-505.

Horn Book, November-December, 1992, Maeve Visser Knoth, review of *Breaking the Fall,* p. 726; March-April, 1994, Patrick Jones, "People Are Talking about . . . Michael Cadnum," pp. 177-180; May-June, 1994, Patty Campbell, review of *Calling Home;* January-February, 1996, p. 77; September-October, 1996,

p. 602; July-August, 1997, Amy E. Chamberlain, review of *Edge,* p. 452; March-April, 1998, p. 219; March, 2000, p. 192; July-August, 2002, Joanna Rudge Long, review of *Forbidden Forest,* p. 453; July-August, 2004, Betty Carter, review of *Blood Gold,* p. 448.

Kirkus Reviews, May 1, 1991; May 15, 1992; June 1, 1993, review of *Horses of the Night,* p. 674; May 1, 2002, review of *Forbidden Forest,* p. 650; August 15, 2002, review of *The Leopard Sword,* p. 1219; April 2, 2004, review of *Blood Gold,* p. 325; September 1, 2004, review of *Starfall,* p. 861; April 15, 2005, review of *The Dragon Throne,* p. 469.

Kliatt, March, 1994, Larry W. Prater, review of *Ghostwright,* p. 14; March, 2002, Paula Rohrlick, review of *Forbidden Forest,* p. 6, and *The Book of the Lion,* p. 14; September, 2002, Paula Rohrlick, review of *The Leopard Sword,* p. 8; September, 2003, Paula Rohrlick, review of *Ship of Fire,* p. 6; November, 2003, Claire Rosser, review of *Daughter of the Wind,* p. 5; January, 2004, Sherri F. Ginsberg, review of *The Book of the Lion,* p. 44; May, 2004, Paula Rohrlick, review of *Blood Gold,* p. 6, and Janet Julian, review of *The Leopard Stone,* p. 52; September, 2004, Paula Rohrlick, review of *Starfall,* p. 6; May, 2005, Paula Rohrlick, review of *The Dragon Throne,* p. 8.

Library Journal, February 15, 1991, Eric W. Johnson, review of *Sleepwalker,* p. 219; July, 1992, Marylaine Block, review of *Ghostwright,* pp. 119-120; July, 1993; September 1, 1994, Robert C. Moore, review of *Skyscape,* p. 213.

Locus, June, 1990, Edward Bryant, review of *Nightlight,* p. 23; June, 1990, Scott Winnett, review of *Nightlight,* p. 31; December, 1990, pp. 23-24; July, 1993, Scott Winnett, review of *Horses of the Night,* p. 33.

Los Angeles Times Book Review, July 21, 1991, Don G. Campbell, review of *Saint Peter's Wolf,* p. 6.

New York Times Book Review, March 31, 1991, Ed Weiner, review of *Sleepwalker,* p. 16.

Publishers Weekly, January 19, 1990, p. 98; May 3, 1991, p. 62; May 10, 1991; June 1, 1992, review of *Ghostwright;* November 16, 1992; June 21, 1993; August 22, 1994, review of *Skyscape,* p. 43; July 10, 1995, review of *Taking It,* p. 59; January 8, 1996, review of *The Judas Glass,* p. 59; June 17, 1996, review of *Zero at the Bone,* p. 66; June 2, 1997, p. 72; October 13, 1997 p. 74; January 26, 1998, p. 92; July 6, 1998, p. 62; June 21, 1999, p. 69; February 21, 2000, p. 88; July 14, 2003, review of *Daughter of the Wind,* p. 78; October 18, 2004, review of *Starfall,* p. 64.

School Library Journal, February, 1992, p. 121; September, 1992, Susan L. Rogers, review of *Breaking the Fall,* p. 274; June, 2002, Starr E. Smith, review of *Forbidden Forest,* p. 130; October, 2002, Renee Steinberg, review of *The Leopard Sword,* p. 160; October, 2003, Karen T. Bilton, review of *Ship of Fire,* p. 162; December, 2003, Barbara Scotto, review of *Daughter of the Wind,* p. 144; June, 2004, Kimberly Monaghan, review of *Blood Gold,* p. 136; October, 2004, Patricia D. Lothrop, review of *Starfall,* p. 158; June, 2005, Denise Moore, review of *The Dragon Throne,* p. 152.

Voice of Youth Advocates, October, 1990, Mary Lee Tiernan, review of *Nightlight,* p. 225; August, 1991, Jane

Chandra, review of *Calling Home,* p. 168; December, 1991, Delia A. Culberson, review of *Saint Peter's Wolf;* February, 1996, Becky Kornman, review of *Taking It,* pp. 368-369; December, 1996, Rachelle M. Blitz, review of *The Judas Glass,* p. 276; February, 1997, Carla A. Tripp, review of *Zero at the Bone,* p. 326.

Wilson Library Journal, April, 1992, Cathi Dunn MacRae, review of *Calling Home,* p. 98.

ONLINE

Michael Cadnum Web site, http://www.michaelcadnum. com (November 15, 2005).*

* * *

CATT, Louis
See FRENCH, Vivian

* * *

CHOYCE, Lesley 1951-

Personal
Born March 21, 1951, in Riverside, NJ; son of George (a mechanic) and Norma (a homemaker; maiden name, Willis) Choyce; children: Sunyata, Pamela. *Education:* Rutgers University, B.A., 1972; Montclair State College, M.A. (American literature), 1974; City University of New York, M.A. (English literature), 1983. *Hobbies and other interests:* Surfing, transcendental woodsplitting.

Addresses
Home—83 Leslie Rd., East Lawrencetown, Nova Scotia B2Z 1P8, Canada. *Office*—Pottersfield Press, 83 Leslie Rd., East Lawrencetown, Nova Scotia B2Z 1PG, Canada.

Career
Writer, publisher, educator, musician, and television host. Referrals Workshop, Denville, NJ, rehabilitation counselor, 1973-74; Bloomfield College, Bloomfield, NJ, coordinator of writing tutorial program, 1974; Montclair State College, Upper Montclair, NJ, instructor in English, 1974-78; Alternate Energy Consultants, Halifax, Nova Scotia, Canada, writer and consultant to Energy, Mines and Resources Canada, 1979-80; Dalhousie University, Halifax, 1981—, began as instructor, became professor of English. Founder of Pottersfield Press. Creative writing instructor, City of Halifax continuing education program, 1978-83; instructor at St. Mary's University, 1978-82, Nova Scotia College of Art and Design, 1981, and Mount St. Vincent University, 1982. Participant in creative writing workshops; public

Lesley Choyce

reader and lecturer. Freelance broadcaster, beginning 1972; host of television talk show *Choyce Words,* beginning 1985; musician/poet performing with Surf Poets. Worked variously as a freight hauler, corn farmer, janitor, journalist, newspaper delivery person, and well digger.

Member
International PEN, Atlantic Publishers Association, Association of Canadian Publishers, Literary Press Group, Canadian Poetry Association, Canadian Writers' Foundation (member of board), Writers' Union of Canada, Writers Federation of Nova Scotia.

Awards, Honors
Canadian Science Fiction and Fantasy Award finalist, 1981; recipient, Order of St. John Award of Merit, 1986; Stephen Leacock Medal shortlist, 1987; Dartmouth Book Award, 1990, and 1995, for *The Republic of Nothing; Event* magazine creative nonfiction winner, 1990; Ann Connor Brimer Award for Children's Literature, 1994, and 2003, for *Shoulder the Sky;* Manitoba Young Reader's Choice Award finalist, 1994; Authors Award (co-recipient), Foundation for the Advancement of Canadian Letters, 1995; Canadian Surfing Championships first place, 1995; Hackmatack Children's Book Award finalist, 2000; Landmark East Literacy Award, 2000; poet laureate, Peter Gzowski Invitational Golf Tournament, 2000; Young Adult Canadian Book Award finalist, 2003, for *Shoulder the Sky;* White Pine Award finalist, 2004.

Writings

FOR CHILDREN AND YOUNG ADULTS

Skateboard Shakedown, Formac Publishing (Halifax, Nova Scotia, Canada), 1989.

Hungry Lizards, Collier-Macmillan (Toronto, Ontario, Canada), 1990.

Wave Watch, Formac Publishing (Halifax, Nova Scotia, Canada), 1990.

Some Kind of Hero, Maxwell-Macmillan (Toronto, Ontario, Canada), 1991.

Wrong Time, Wrong Place, Formac Publishing (Halifax, Nova Scotia, Canada), 1991.

Clearcut Danger, Formac Publishing (Halifax, Nova Scotia, Canada), 1992.

Full Tilt, Maxwell-Macmillan (Toronto, Ontario, Canada), 1993.

Good Idea Gone Bad, Formac Publishing (Halifax, Nova Scotia, Canada), 1993.

Dark End of Dream Street, Formac Publishing (Halifax, Nova Scotia, Canada), 1994.

Big Burn, Thistledown, 1995.

Falling through the Cracks, Formac Publishing (Halifax, Nova Scotia, Canada), 1996.

Go for It, Carrie (chapter book), Formac Publishing (Halifax, Nova Scotia, Canada), 1997.

Famous at Last, illustrated by Jill Quinn, Pottersfield Press (East Laurencetown, Nova Scotia, Canada), 1998.

Carrie's Crowd (chapter book), illustrated by Mark Thurman, Formac Publishing (Halifax, Nova Scotia, Canada), 1998.

Roid Rage, Harbour Publishing (Madeira Park, British Columbia, Canada), 1999.

The Summer of Apartment X, Goose Lane Editions (Fredericton, New Brunswick, Canada), 1999.

Far Enough Island, illustrated by Jill Quinn, Pottersfield Press (Lawrencetown Beach, Nova Scotia, Canada), 2000.

Carrie's Camping Adventure (chapter book), illustrated by Mark Thurman, Formac Publishing (Halifax, Nova Scotia, Canada), 2001.

Shoulder the Sky, Dundurn Press (Toronto, Ontario, Canada), 2002.

Refuge Cove, Orca Book (Victoria, British Columbia, Canada), 2002.

Smoke and Mirrors, Boardwalk Books (Toronto, Ontario, Canada), 2004.

Thunderbowl, Orca Soundings (Victoria, British Columbia, Canada), 2004.

Sudden Impact, Orca Soundings (Victoria, British Columbia, Canada), 2005.

FICTION; FOR ADULTS

Eastern Sure, Nimbus Publishing, 1981.

Billy Botzweiler's Last Dance (stories), Blewointment Press, 1984.

Downwind, Creative Publishers, 1984.

Conventional Emotions (stories), Creative Publishers, 1985.

Coming up for Air, Creative Publishers, 1988.

The Second Season of Jonas MacPherson, Thistledown Press (Saskatoon, Saskatchewan, Canada), 1989.

Magnificent Obsessions (photo-novel), Quarry Press, 1991.

The Ecstasy Conspiracy, Nuage Editions, 1992.

Margin of Error (stories), Borealis Press, 1992.

The Republic of Nothing, Goose Lane Editions (Fredericton, New Brunswick, Canada), 1994.

Dance the Rocks Ashore, Goose Lane Editions (Fredericton, New Brunswick, Canada), 1997.

World Enough, Goose Lane Editions (Fredericton, New Brunswick, Canada), 1998.

Cold Clear Morning, Porcepic Books (Vancouver, British Columbia, Canada), 2002.

Sea of Tranquility, Simon & Pierre (Tonawanda, NY), 2003.

Contributor to more than one hundred magazines and anthologies.

SCIENCE FICTION

The Dream Auditor, Ragweed Press, 1986.

The Trap Door to Heaven, Quarry Press, 1996.

NONFICTION

Edible Wild Plants of the Maritimes, Wooden Anchor Press, 1977.

An Avalanche of Ocean (autobiography), Goose Lane Editions (Fredericton, New Brunswick, Canada), 1987.

December Six/The Halifax Solution, Pottersfield Press (East Laurencetown, Nova Scotia, Canada), 1988.

Transcendental Anarchy: Confessions of a Metaphysical Tourist (autobiography), Quarry Press, 1993.

Nova Scotia: Shaped by the Sea, Penguin (Toronto, Ontario, Canada), 1996.

The Coasts of Canada: A History, Goose Lane Editions (Fredericton, New Brunswick, Canada), 2002.

POETRY

Reinventing the Wheel, Fiddle Head Poetry Books, 1980.

Fast Living, Fiddle Head Poetry Books, 1982.

The End of Ice, Fiddle Head Poetry Books, 1982.

The Top of the Heart, Thistledown Press, 1986.

The Man Who Borrowed the Bay of Fundy, Brandon University, 1988.

The Coastline of Forgetting, Pottersfield Press (East Laurencetown, Nova Scotia, Canada), 1995.

Beautiful Sadness, Ekstasis Editions (Victoria, British Columbia, Canada), 1998.

Caution to the Wind, Ekstasis Editions (Victoria, British Columbia, Canada), 2000.

Typographical Eras, Gaspereau Press (Kentville, Nova Scotia, Canada), 2003.

Revenge of the Optimist, Ekstasis Editions (Victoria, British Columbia, Canada), 2004.

Contributor of lyrics and music to poetry/music recordings, including *Sea Level,* Pottersfield Press, 1999; *Long Lost Planet,* 1999.

EDITOR

The Pottersfield Portfolio, Volumes 1-7, Pottersfield Press (East Lawrencetown, Nova Scotia, Canada), 1971–85.
Alternating Current: Renewable Energy for Atlantic Canada, Wooden Anchor Press, 1977.
Chezzetocook (fiction and poetry), Wooden Anchor Press, 1977.
(With Phil Thompson) *ACCESS,* Pottersfield Press (East Lawrencetown, Nova Scotia, Canada), 1979.
(With John Bell) *Visions from the Edge,* Pottersfield Press (East Lawrencetown, Nova Scotia, Canada), 1981.
The Cape Breton Collection, 2 volumes, Pottersfield Press (East Lawrencetown, Nova Scotia, Canada), 1984–89.
(With Andy Wainwright) Charles Bruce, *The Mulgrave Road,* Pottersfield Press (East Lawrencetown, Nova Scotia, Canada), 1985.
Ark of Ice: Canadian Futurefiction, Pottersfield Press (East Lawrencetown, Nova Scotia, Canada), 1985.
(With Rita Joe) *The Mi'kmaq Anthology,* Pottersfield Press (East Lawrencetown, Nova Scotia, Canada), 1997.
(And contributor) *Atlantica: Stories from the Maritimes and Newfoundland,* Goose Lane Editions (Fredericton, New Brunswick, Canada), 2001.
Pottersfield Nation: East of Canada, Pottersfield Press (East Lawrencetown, Nova Scotia, Canada), 2004.
Nova Scotia: A Traveller's Companion: Over 300 Years of Travel Writing, Pottersfield Press (East Lawrencetown, Nova Scotia, Canada), 2005.

Adaptations

The Republic of Nothing was optioned for film.

Sidelights

American-born Canadian author, educator, publisher, editor, musician, and champion surfer Lesley Choyce has written numerous works of fiction for both adults and young adults, as well as nonfiction, science fiction, and poetry. He works some of his many interests—including nature and the environment, surfing, skateboarding, and music—into his novels for young adults, which include *Hungry Lizards, Wrong Time, Wrong Place, Roid Rage,* and *Smoke and Mirrors.* Choyce's teen novels feature high-interest story lines and accessible vocabulary, making them popular among reluctant readers. "Choyce's talent for portraying quirky, if troubled, idealists" as lead characters has also made him popular with teens, according to *Resource Links* contributor Nadine d'Entremont in a positive review of *Smoke and Mirrors.*

In Choyce's first book, 1989's *Skateboard Shakedown,* a skateboarder, his girlfriend, and a group of friends take on a corrupt mayor who wants to turn their favorite skateboard site into a shopping mall. Skateboarding

After a skateboarding accident leaves Simon more "out of it" than he was before, his budding friendship with an invisible girl named Andrea seems totally normal in this 2004 novel. (Cover photograph by Nancy R. Cohen/Getty Images.)

is also the focus of *Smoke and Mirrors,* which focuses on a sixteen-year-old boy whose skateboarding injury caused the brain damage that he suspects is causing him to see and speak with a strange classmate that seems too good—and too mysterious—to be real. Reviewing *Skateboard Shakedown* for *Quill & Quire,* Norene Smiley noted that Choyce's "fast-paced novel marks the entrance of a new and refreshing voice for young readers." A sport of another sort is central to *Roid Rage,* which focuses on the use of steroids in athletic competition. Ray's use of performance-enhancing drugs is of growing concern to best buddy Craig, who watches Ray's skills on the football field increase as his wellbeing declines. In *Quill & Quire* Paul Challen praised the book's "snappy junior-jock dialogue and realistic game-action description," adding that *Roid Rage* portrays "the kind of teen peer pressure" that causes teen steroid use. Adolescent "pressure to perform above expectations is enormous," added a *Resource Links* reviewer, "and Choyce develops this theme in fine style."

Rock music takes center stage in several of Choyce's novels, including *Hungry Lizards* and *Thunderbowl.* In *Hungry Lizards* a sixteen-year-old rock band leader finds the advantages of winning a performing contract at a local club outweighed by the realities of the entertainment business, the conflicting time demands of school and work, and the temptations of a questionable lifestyle. *Thunderbowl* finds talented teen guitarist Jeremy winning a band playoff; the prize is a chance to perform at a popular bar called the Dungeon. The opportunity forces the teen to weigh the importance of his obligations to his family and finishing his education over following his dream of being a professional musician, and his ultimate choice is prompted by some harsh lessons about the life he has chosen. Commenting on *Hungry Lizards,* Kenneth Oppel concluded in *Quill & Quire* that Choyce's "tempered view of teenage street life and the rock 'n' roll underworld should appeal to young readers." Reviewing *Thunderbowl* in *Resource Links,* Maria Forte noted that the voice of Choyce's young protagonist "rings true" and that Jeremy's story "deals with teenage angst without being corny or superficial."

Wrong Time, Wrong Place explores racial tensions and social injustice through the story of Corey, a young man with one parent who is black and one who is white. Corey first becomes aware of the disadvantages of being biracial when he is branded as a troublemaker and rebel and begins to notice how both students and faculty treat lighter-skinned students differently. Through his uncle Larry's positive example and the man's stories of a black community in Halifax called Africville, Corey begins to identify with his black forebears. As *Canadian Children's Literature* reviewer Heidi Petersen noted, Corey "realises that he must face injustices himself, and embraces a form of social activism which begins by keeping the past, the truth, alive."

Coping with the loss of a parent and the many feelings that result is the subject of *Shoulder the Sky,* Choyce's award-winning 2002 novel. Seemingly untroubled and thus encouraged by his father to explore his emotions by writing, sixteen-year-old Martin Emerson divides himself into three different personas: the average, everyday, schoolgoing teen; the outgoing, egocentric Emerso, who comes into being on Martin's personal Web site; and the nameless guy who sometimes blacks out and cannot remember things that have just happened. In between the precocious Internet rants of Emerso, Martin details his day-to-day life before and after his mother's death, including his efforts at rebellion, his unrequited love for a classmate, and his friendship with fellow nerd Darrell. Ultimately, a family road trip to Alaska causes the teen to confront his mother's death and begin the process of reworking his fractured self into whole cloth. Praising the colorful secondary characters introduced in the novel, *Canadian Review of Materials* contributor Dave Jenkinson predicted that Choyce's protagonist will be "quite interesting to the adolescent reader" despite the fact that Martin's character "unfolds slowly." Dubbing Martin "a sweet funny kid," *Quill & Quire* contributor Teresa Toten added that in *Shoulder the Sky* the author "expertly infuses his characters with an engaging combination of muscle and

poetry" and creates a lead character that young readers will "root for."

In addition to fiction for older readers, Choyce has produced several chapter books for early elementary-graders, many published by his own Pottersfield Press. As part of Pottersfield's illustrated series of readers, Choyce penned *Famous at Last,* which focuses on a nine year old who turns a role in a local television bean commercial into a chance at superstardom—even though he really hates beans. "When his career path takes him from beans to Brussels sprouts to stewed tomatoes, Fred draws the line," explained *Quill & Quire* reviewer Maureen Garvie, noting the boy's late-dawning conscience. In *Quill & Quire* Ann Abel deemed *Famous at Last* "fast-paced" and "hilarious."

Other beginning readers written by Choyce include several volumes in Formac's "First Novel" series, all of which feature a high-spirited and likeable ten year old named Carrie. In *Go for It, Carrie* the desire to learn how to roller skate prompts the girl to find a creative way to get skates she can afford and overcome her frustration while working to master the sport, while a camping trip with friends introduces the city girl to more wildlife than she really wants to handle in *Carrie's Camping Adventure.* In *Carrie's Crowd,* which a *Resource Links* reviewer called a "brisk story," Carrie plans her strategy to become part of the popular clique until she realizes that the loss of her old friends will come at too high a cost. In each of the "Carrie" books Choyce highlights the young girl's resourcefulness; as Gillian Richardson noted in a review of *Carrie's Camping Adventure* for *Canadian Review of Materials,* elementary-aged girls in particular will likely "enjoy the obvious superiority in competence" of the girls featured in the story.

Describing his growth as a writer, Choyce once told *SATA:* "As a kid, I had a fairly minute ego; no one within earshot was ready to persuade me that my opinions and insights were of much value in the world I lived in. So later, when I grew into my skin as a writer, I pretended for awhile that *what I had to say* really was of importance. After a time, I started believing in the myth, and this convinced me to abandon fiction for awhile and get autobiographical.

"Since my life story would be exceedingly boring, I was forced to edit my personal history ruthlessly until there was something left worth sharing. My first fragmented history of the self came out as *An Avalanche of Ocean,* and I almost thought that I was done with autobiography. What more could I possibly say once I'd written about winter surfing, transcendental wood-splitting, and getting strip-searched for cod tongues in a Labrador airport?

"But then something happened to me that I can't quite explain. *Avalanche* set off something in me: a kind of manic, magical couple of years where I felt like I was living on the edge of some important breakthrough. It was a time of greater compressed euphoria and despair than I'd ever felt before. Stuff was happening to me, images of the past were flooding through the doors, and I needed to get it all down. Some of it was funny, some of it was not. Dead writers were hovering over my shoulder, saying, 'Dig deep; follow it through. Don't let any of it go.' And I didn't.

"So again I have the audacity to say that these things that happened to me are worth your attention. Like Wordsworth, I am a man 'pleased with my own volitions.' Like Whitman, I find myself saying to readers, 'to you, endless announcements.'

"Write about what makes you feel the most uncomfortable, a voice in my head told me. So I tackled fear and my own male anger and my biggest failures. And, even more dangerous, I tried writing about the most ordinary of things: a morning in Woolco, an unexceptional day, the thread of things that keeps a life together.

"Throughout it all, there is, I hope, a record of a search for love and meaning fraught with failure and recovery. Maybe I've developed a basic mistrust of the rational, logical conclusions. I've only had the briefest glimpses beyond the surface, but I've seen enough to know that sometimes facts are not enough. There are times to make the leap, to get metaphysical, and suppose that we all live larger lives than appearances would suggest."

Biographical and Critical Sources

PERIODICALS

Books in Canada, October, 1995, pp. 49-50.
Canadian Book Review Annual, 1998, review of *Carrie's Crowd,* p. 497; 1999, review of *World Enough,* p. 162, review of *Roid Rage,* p. 488; 2000, review of *The Summer of Apartment X,* p. 140.
Canadian Children's Literature (annual), 1991, pp. 86-88; 1994, Heidi Petersen, review of *Wrong Time, Wrong Place,* pp. 72-76.
Canadian Review of Materials, January, 1991, p. 34; May, 1992, p. 165; October 18, 1996, Jennifer Sullivan, review of *Big Burn;* January 31, 1997, Irene Gordon, review of *Falling through the Cracks;* September 19, 1997, Irene Gordon, review of *Go for It, Carrie;* November 2, 2001, Gillian Richardson, review of *Carrie's Camping Adventure;* November 29, 2002, Dave Jenkinson, review of *Shoulder the Sky.*
Kliatt, January, 2003, review of *Refuge Cove,* p. 18.
Maclean's, August 15, 1994, p. 44.
Publishers Weekly, June 28, 1999, review of *World Enough,* p. 56.
Quill & Quire, March, 1990, Norene Smiley, review of *Skateboard Shakedown,* p. 22; August, 1990, Kenneth Oppel, review of *The Hungry Lizards,* p. 15; April, 1991, p. 18; May, 1993, Patty Lawlor, review of *Clearcut Danger,* pp. 33-34; March, 1995, Fred Boer, review of *Dark End of Dream Street,* p. 79; May, 1995, Maureen Garvie, review of *Big Burn,* pp. 46-47; May, 1998, Maureen Garvie, review of *Famous at Last,* p. 35; July, 1999, review of *The Summer of Apartment X,* p. 42; August, 1999, Paul Challen, review of *Roid Rage,* p. 39; February, 2003, Teresa Toten, review of *Shoulder the Sky.*
Resource Links, April, 1999, Ann Abel, review of *Famous at Last,* p. 9; June, 1999, review of *Carrie's Crowd,* p. 10; October, 1999, review of *Roid Rage,* p. 25; October, 2001, Mavis Holder, review of *Carrie's Camping Adventure,* p. 12; June, 2004, Maria Forte, review of *Thunderbowl,* p. 24; April, 2005, Nadine d'Entremont, review of *Smoke and Mirrors,* p. 29.
School Library Journal, August, 1999, Cheryl Cufari, review of *Carrie's Crowd,* p. 124.

ONLINE

Lesley Choyce Home Page, http://www.lesleychoyce.com/ (October 20, 2005).
Writers' Federation of Nova Scotia Web site, http://www.writers.ns.ca/Writers/ (August 15, 2005).
Writers Union of Canada Web site, http://www.writers union.ca/ (October 20, 2005), "Lesley Choyce."

*   *   *

COFFEY, Brian
See KOONTZ, Dean R.

*   *   *

COLQUHOUN, Glenn 1964-

Personal

Born 1964, in South Auckland, New Zealand. *Education:* Trained for the ministry; University of Auckland, degree (English); earned M.D.

Addresses

Home—Waikawa Beach, New Zealand. *Agent*—c/o Author Mail, Steele Roberts Publishing, Box 9321, Wellington, New Zealand.

Career

Physician and author. Worked variously as a builder and cook; Whangarei Hospital, doctor; Waikato Hospital, doctor. *New Zealand Post* Children's Book Awards, judge, 2002.

Awards, Honors

Jessie Mackay NZSA Best First Book Award for Poetry, Montata New Zealand Book Awards, 2000, for *The Art of Walking Upright;* Montana New Zealand Book Award in poetry, and Readers Choice Award, both 2003, both for *Playing God;* Prize in Modern Letters (New Zealand), 2004.

Writings

FOR CHILDREN

Uncle Glenn and Me, illustrated by Kevin Wildman, Reed (Auckland, New Zealand), 1999.
Uncle Glenn and Me Too, illustrated by Kevin Wildman, Reed (Auckland, New Zealand), 2004.
Mr Short, Mr Thin, Mr Bald and Mr Dog, illustrated by Nicky Slade-Robinson, Stede Roberts (Auckland, New Zealand), 2005.

POETRY

The Art of Walking Upright, Steele Roberts Publishing (Wellington, New Zealand), 1999.
Playing God, Steele Roberts (Wellington, New Zealand), 2002.
Jumping Ship, Four Winds Press (Wellington, New Zealand), 2004.

Biographical and Critical Sources

PERIODICALS

Landfall, May, 2004, Claire Hero, review of *Playing God,* p. 200.
M2 Best Books, March 16, 2004, "Poet Doctor Wins New Zealand's Prize in Modern Letters."
Magpies, May, 2005, review of *Uncle Glenn and Me Too,* p. 6.

ONLINE

New Zealand Book Council Web site, http://www.bookcouncil.org/nz/ (October 20, 2005), "Glenn Colquhoun."
New Zealand Electronic Poetry Centre Web site, http://www.nzepc.auckland.ac.nz/ (August 1, 2003), "Glenn Colquhoun."

*   *   *

CROSS, Gillian 1945-
(Gillian Clare Cross)

Personal

Born December 24, 1945, in London, England; daughter of (James) Eric (a scientist and musician) and Joan (an English teacher; maiden name, Manton) Arnold;

Gillian Cross

married Martin Cross (an educational consultant), May 10, 1967; children: Jonathan George, Elizabeth Jane, Colman Anthony Richard, Katherine Clare. *Education:* Somerville College, Oxford, England, B.A. (with first-class honors), 1969, M.A., 1972; University of Sussex, D.Phil., 1974. *Hobbies and other interests:* Playing the piano, orienteering.

Addresses

Agent—c/o Author Mail, Oxford Children's Books, Oxford University Press, Great Clarendon St., Oxford OX2 6DP, England. *E-mail*—gillian@gilliancross.co.uk.

Career

Author of juvenile and young-adult books. Also worked as teacher, assistant to old-style village baker, office clerical assistant, and assistant to member of British Parliament.

Member

British Society of Authors.

Awards, Honors

The Dark behind the Curtain was a Carnegie highly commended book, 1982, and a *Guardian* Award runner-up, 1983; American Library Association (ALA) best books for young adults designation, and Whitbread Award runner-up, both 1984, ALA notable books of the year, 1985, and Edgar Allan Poe Award runner-up, Mystery Writers of America, 1986, all for *On the Edge;* Carnegie commended book, 1986, and ALA best books for young adults designation, 1987, both for *Chartbreaker;* ALA notable books of the year designation, 1987, for *Roscoe's Leap;* Carnegie commendation, 1988, for *A Map of Nowhere;* Carnegie Medal, 1990, and Parents' Choice award, 1991, both for *Wolf;* Smarties Grand Prix award, and Whitbread Children's Novel Award, both 1992, both for *The Great Elephant Chase.*

Writings

The Runaway, illustrations by Reginald Gray, Methuen (London, England), 1979.
The Iron Way, illustrations by Tony Morris, Oxford University Press (Oxford, England), 1979.
Revolt at Ratcliffe's Rags, illustrations by Tony Morris, Oxford University Press (Oxford, England), 1980.
Save Our School, illustrations by Gareth Floyd, Methuen (London, England), 1981.
A Whisper of Lace, Oxford University Press (Oxford, England), 1981.
The Dark behind the Curtain, illustrations by David Parkins, Oxford University Press (Oxford, England), 1982.
The Mintyglo Kid, illustrations by Gareth Floyd, Methuen (London, England), 1983.
Born of the Sun, illustrations by Mark Edwards, Holiday House (New York, NY), 1984.
On the Edge, Oxford University Press (Oxford, England), 1984, Holiday House (New York, NY), 1985.
Swimathon!, illustrations by Gareth Floyd, Methuen (London, England), 1986.
Chartbreak, Oxford University Press (Oxford, England), 1986, published as *Chartbreaker,* Holiday House (New York, NY), 1987.
Roscoe's Leap, Holiday House (New York, NY), 1987.
A Map of Nowhere, Oxford University Press (Oxford, England), 1988, Holiday House (New York, NY), 1989.
Rescuing Gloria, illustrated by Gareth Floyd, Methuen (London, England), 1989.
Twin and Super-Twin, illustrations by Maureen Bradley, Holiday House (New York, NY), 1990.
The Monster from Underground, illustrated by Peter Firmin, Heinemann (London, England), 1990, illustrated by Chris Priestley, 2002.
Gobbo the Great, illustrated by Philippe Dupasquier, Methuen (London, England), 1991.
Rent-a-Genius, illustrated by Glenys Ambrus, Hamish Hamilton (London, England), 1991.
Wolf, Holiday House (New York, NY), 1991.
Beware Olga!, illustrated by Arthur Robins, Walker (London, England), 1993.
The Furry Maccaloo, illustrated by Madeleine Baker, Heinemann (London, England), 1993.
The Great American Elephant Chase, Holiday House (New York, NY), 1993, published as *The Great Elephant Chase,* Methuen (London, England), 1993.
The Tree House, illustrated by Paul Howard, Methuen (London, England), 1994.

What Will Emily Do?, illustrated by Paul Howard, Methuen (London, England), 1994.
The Crazy Shoe Shuffle, Methuen (London, England), 1995.
Posh Watson, Walker (London, England), 1995.
New World, Holiday House (New York, NY), 1995.
The Roman Beanfest, illustrated by Linzi Henry, Hamish Hamilton (London, England), 1996.
Pictures in the Dark, Holiday House (New York, NY), 1996.
The Goose Girl, Scholastic (New York, NY), 1998.
Tightrope, Holiday House (New York, NY), 1999.
Down with the Dirty Danes!, HarperCollins (New York, NY), 2000.
The Treasure in the Mud, Oxford University Press (Oxford, England, 2001.
Phoning a Dead Man, Holiday House (New York, NY), 2002, published as *Calling a Dead Man,* Oxford University Press (Oxford, England), 2002.

"DEMON HEADMASTER" SERIES; FOR CHILDREN

The Demon Headmaster (also see below), illustrations by Gary Rees, Oxford University Press (Oxford, England), 1982.
The Prime Minister's Brain (sequel to *The Demon Headmaster*), Oxford University Press (Oxford, England), 1985.
Hunky Parker Is Watching You, illustrated by Maureen Bradley, Oxford University Press (Oxford, England), 1994, published as *The Revenge of the Demon Headmaster,* Puffin (New York, NY),1995.
The Demon Headmaster Strikes Again, Puffin (New York, NY), 1997.
The Demon Headmaster Takes Over, Puffin (New York, NY), 1998.
Beware of the Demon Headmaster, Oxford University Press (Oxford, England), 2002.
Facing the Demon Headmaster, illustrated by Kevin Lyles, Oxford University Press (Oxford, England) 2002.

"DARK GROUND" TRILOGY; FOR CHILDREN

The Dark Ground, Dutton's Children's Books (New York, NY), 2004.
The Black Room, Oxford University Press (Oxford, England), 2004, Dutton Children's Books (New York, NY), 2006.

Adaptations

The "Demon Headmaster" series was adapted for British television, and was adapted as a musical published by Samuel French, 2003. Many of Cross's books have been adapted as audiobooks.

Sidelights

In novels such as *The Dark behind the Curtain, Wolf,* and *Calling a Dead Man,* as well as in her "Demon Headmaster" series, about a sinister school principal whose ambitions include controlling both his students and the world, British writer Gillian Cross blends suspense, history, adventure, and social concerns. Not one to shy away from the darker aspects of the world, such as violence, terrorism, and political intrigue, Cross weaves such themes into her fiction for older readers, while her books for middle graders features more light-hearted fare. A versatile author, she has also written across genres, from historical and Gothic fiction and school stories to comic novels, realistic fiction, and psychological thrillers. While her protagonists are often loners or misfits, these young men and women generally learn through experience and interaction, and grow as a result of contact—both positive and negative—with an adult world. One of England's most respected writers for children and young adults, Cross has won both the prestigious Carnegie Medal and the Whitbread Children's Novel Award.

Cross was born on Christmas Eve, 1945, in London, England. Her father held a doctorate in chemistry and managed a paint company, and her mother worked as an English teacher. Growing up in postwar England in a home filled with books, Cross early on learned to love stories and storytelling, and also gained an early love of writing. Known to her friends as a teller of tales, she regaled her classmates with imaginative tales on their daily trek to and from North London Collegiate School for Girls, a respected day school.

After graduation from secondary school, Cross worked as a volunteer teacher for teenagers in inner-city London, an experience that introduced her to a world totally different from the protected suburban one in which she had been raised. She then went to Oxford University, studying English literature at Somerville College. Still a student, she married and left her studies behind for a time to have her first child. She graduated with honors in 1969, earned a master's degree in 1972, and then a Ph.D. in 1974 from the University of Sussex.

It was the writing of her doctoral thesis that convinced Cross she had the stamina to write novels. "What really made me into a writer was finishing my doctoral thesis," she once commented. "Suddenly, I was no longer a student. For the first time in my life I had lots of free time and no 'official' writing to do. And I was up to my knees in stories. I had two children by then, and I was always making up stories for them and making them small, illustrated books. I'd also helped to start a children's book group in Lewes, the small town where I was living by then. So I decided it was time I had a go at some proper writing. Thanks to my thesis I knew how to handle something long and, very tentatively, I began my first real book. It has never been published (quite rightly!), but by the time I'd finished it I was hooked and I went straight on to the next one. Four years later, when I had five finished books and a whole host of rejection slips, two of my books were accepted simultaneously, by two different publishers."

Cross's first two novels revealed her ability to tackle a range of subjects and settings. *The Iron Way* is an historical novel set in Victorian England that focuses on the effects brought about by the arrival of the railroad and its strict timetables in a small Sussex village. In her contemporary novel *The Runaway* two urban children of vastly different social backgrounds hide away together in an abandoned house. Although different, these two books demonstrate Cross's interest in history as well as the things that surface when individuals are forced to confront social, political, and ethnic differences. Reviewing *The Iron Way* in *Booklist,* Marilyn Kaye called the novel a "gripping story" about "hostility, friendship, and loyalty."

With *Save Our School,* Cross turned her talents to the school story, a genre that has comprised a large part of her work for middle-grade readers. In this comic novel she introduces the characters Barny, Spag, and Clipper, who make return appearances in *The Mintyglo Kid, Swimathon!,* and *Gobbo the Great.* Kathy Piehl, writing in the *Dictionary of Literary Biography,* commented that this series "is notable for the camaraderie it depicts across ethnic and gender lines." Clipper, a West Indian girl, is easily a match for the two English boys who are her buddies. Employing slapstick humor, Cross sets her young protagonists to Herculean tasks, from saving the honor of Bennett Junior High School in *Save Our School* to organizing a swimming competition in *Swimathon!* Lots of action, plus a "familiar setting and school slang help carry even less-than-eager readers through the novels," Piehl noted. Reviewing *Save Our School* in the *Times Literary Supplement,* Anne Carter commented: "Racy, frequently vulgar and abounding in character, Barny, Spag and Clipper . . . are as real and recognizable as the streets among which they live." More humor for young readers can be found in *Rescuing Gloria, Rent-a-Genius,* and *Down with the Dirty Danes!*

Cross hatched her most popular character in 1982 when her middle-grade novel *The Demon Headmaster* was published. Focusing on an adult figure that has been cast as the villain for centuries, the novel was a spin-off of her books about Barny, Spag, and Clipper. The demonic headmaster began life as the subject of an essay penned by Clipper for a school writing competition, and when Cross's young daughter heard the story, she encouraged her mother to expand the idea into a book. In *The Demon Headmaster* a villainous headmaster hypnotizes everyone in his school, but his dastardly plan to control minds is ultimately foiled by a group of nonconformist kids, led by foster-child Dinah Glass, who form the Society for the Protection of Our Lives Against Them, or SPLAT. Immediately popular with readers, Cross's villain was unstoppable; he has returned to hatch maniacal plans in several other novels, including *The Prime Minister's Brain, The Revenge of the Demon Headmaster, The Demon Headmaster Takes Over,* and *Beware of the Demon Headmaster.* "A rattling good yarn" is the way Ann Martin described the first "Demon Headmaster" novel in the *Times Literary Supplement,* and her sentiments were somewhat echoed by *Booklist* critic Ilene Cooper who noted that the book "has plenty of creepy moments."

In *The Prime Minister's Brain* the megalomaniacal educator is out to brainwash students who are part of a national computer competition, and once again it is up to Dinah and her SPLAT team to stop him. In *Revenge of the Demon Headmaster,* he tries to pass on subliminal messages via a popular television show, while *The Demon Headmaster Strikes Again* finds him making plans to genetically re-engineer the world. In his fifth outing, *The Demon Headmaster Takes Over,* the evil one schemes to control the Hyperbrain, a worldwide smart computer, while in *Facing the Demon Headmaster* he seems to have some involvement with a popular new musical club and its mysterious masked DJ. In every case, Dinah and SPLAT do battle and save the world, winning praise from reviewers such as a *Books for Keeps* critic who dubbed *The Demon Headmaster Takes Over* a "fast moving and very readable thriller."

In addition to her quirky thrillers for younger readers, Cross has also proved herself a master of the suspense novel in books such as *Whisper of Lace, The Dark behind the Curtain, On the Edge,* and the award-winning *Wolf.* In these novels she blends history, psychology, social and moral issues, and come up with page-turning tales. In *A Whisper of Lace* she focuses on inter-family intrigue against an historical setting, with smuggling as a narrative hook. "Layer and layer of observation and manipulation add to the plot's suspense," according to Piehl. Neil Philip, reviewing the title in the *Times Educational Supplement,* felt that Cross "brilliantly puts the stagy conventions of costume fiction . . . at the service of a real sense of history's complexity."

In *The Dark behind the Curtain,* a school production of the musical *Sweeney Todd* calls forth a group of ghostly children who once suffered under a cruel master. Writing in the *Times Literary Supplement,* Geoffrey Trease maintained that "Cross has a practiced icy hand at producing a delicious frisson," while Dorothy Nimmo, writing in *School Librarian,* found the novel "gripping." In *On the Edge* a modern-day London teen is kidnapped by terrorists who want to abolish the family unit. As a hostage, Tug Shakespeare is held by the terrorist group at a remote cottage, but when Jinny Slattery, who lives nearby, becomes suspicious, her controlling father ridicules her concerns. With its focus on themes of freedom and individuality, *On the Edge* was a runner-up for both the Whitbread and Edgar Allan Poe awards. In *Horn Book,* Mary M. Burns called the novel "a tense, compelling adventure-mystery in which the lives of two adolescents move on convergent tracks to a chilling denouement."

Virtual reality games are at the heart of *New World,* and as with many plots of the "Demon Headmaster" series, youthful protagonists must battle the hidden agenda of programmers. A *Publishers Weekly* contributor noted in

a review of the book that "the pace never slackens, the characters are subtly developed and suspense is delivered in wholesale quantities." With *Pictures in the Dark,* Cross creates "a spellbinding novel of emotional suspense, spiked with a highly British sort of magical realism," according to a *Publishers Weekly* reviewer. A chance photograph brings young Charlie into the lives of classmate Jennifer and her secretive younger brother, leading him to mysteries and the supernatural. Deborah Stevenson, reviewing the novel for the *Bulletin of the Center for Children's Books,* described *Pictures in the Dark* as "very, very chilling."

In *The Great American Elephant Chase,* set in 1881, young Tad, an orphan, eagerly takes a job with a travelling salesman who uses an elephant to help sell his elixir. When the salesman dies in a train accident, Tad aids the man's daughter in attempting to get the animal to safety in Nebraska, one step ahead of a group of people attempting to steal the imperiled pachyderm. A *Kirkus Reviews* critic noted that Cross, an "author of splendidly complex, challenging thrillers, sets a picaresque adventure in 19th-century America" with this tale, concluding of the Smarties Prize-winning novel that the trip into the past is "grand, old-fashioned fun." Writing in *Booklist,* Emily Melton called the novel "a heartwarming story of courage and perseverance," while in *School Library Journal* Sally Margolis described *The Great American Elephant Chase* as part "showboat melodrama, part Dickensian squalor, part Barnum hype, and all adventure."

Moving from past to present, Cross plumbs emotional depths in *Tightrope,* which finds a teenager shouldering the burden of caring for her disabled mother in a run-down urban neighborhood. A serious, highly conscientious girl, Ashley struggles to handle the responsibilities that have been heaped on her: too many responsibilities. To cope with the lack of a childhood, she develops an alter-ego, Cindy, a graffiti artist who eventually takes up with members of a local gang. Martha V. Parravano, reviewing *Tightrope* for *Horn Book,* deemed the novel a "riveting psychological thriller" with a "satisfying, catch-your-breath ending," while a *Publishers Weekly* critic praised its "impeccable plotting" and "complex characterizations."

Moving from stark reality to fantasy, Cross began her "Dark Ground Trilogy" in 2004 with *The Dark Ground.* Setting the stage for her fantasy tale, she introduces Robert, a teen flying home from a trip with his family. After a strange vision in a mirror, he falls into unconsciousness, and awakens to find himself naked and alone in a vast forest full of gigantic plants and creatures. As the story continues, Robert learns to view his world from a new perspective; he has shrunk in size to mouse-like proportions and must now join other tiny creatures in their quest to stay alive. Describing *The Dark Ground* as "creative, mysterious fantasy bookend[ing] . . . a woodland survival story," a *Kirkus Reviews* critic praised Robert's determined quest to reunite with his family as "heart-stoppingly dangerous." While noting that the novel leaves many questions for subsequent series installments, *Horn Book* contributor Roger Sutton praised Cross for her skill in "evoking the change in scale and all the difficulties in survival it would entail." The series continues in *The Black Room,* as Robert escapes the woodland world and now hopes to rescue Lorn, a girl he fears is becoming drawn into a sinister underground world.

In young-adult novels such as *Tightrope, The Dark behind the Curtain,* and *The Dark Room,* Cross portrays the harsh, even malevolent, side of human nature, and this tendency has contributed to her popularity among teen readers. Writing about the underside of life in a realistic manner reflects her philosophy that elements such as violence belong in children's literature. Noting the violence that surfaces in age-old fairy and folk tales, she observed in *School Librarian* that "Death and danger and injury are hard, definite, dramatic things. Human life is taxing and fulfilling and—absolute," and "the old dramatic virtues and vices standing out sharply. Love. Hate. The struggle for power. Irrevocable choices. Physical damage. And I've thought, 'So the stories didn't exaggerate after all. It's all there. As absolute, as heroic in its dimensions as anything in Tolkien—or Shakespeare.'"

Despite being salted with the darker aspects of life, Cross's writing for older teens is never depressing. She believes individuals are capable of confronting difficult problems, making decisions, and living happier, more informed existences as a result. "I like to write for children and young people because then I feel free to write about important things: love, death, moral decisions," Cross once noted. "I find a lot of adult fiction is cynical and despairing, concerned with illustrating the powerlessness and unimportance of ordinary people. I believe that ordinary people *are* important and that everyone has the power to influence his own life. I think the young know that too."

Biographical and Critical Sources

BOOKS

Authors and Artists for Young Adults, Volume 24, Thomson Gale (Detroit, MI), 1998.

Beacham's Guide to Literature for Young Adults, Volume 9, Beacham Publishing (Osprey, FL), 1999.

Carter, Humphrey, and Mari Prichard, *The Oxford Companion to Children's Literature,* Oxford University Press (New York, NY), 1984.

Children's Literature Review, Volume 28, Thomson Gale (Detroit, MI), 1992.

Hunt, Caroline C., editor, *Dictionary of Literary Biography,* Volume 161: *British Children's Writers since 1960,* Thomson Gale (Detroit, MI), 1996.

Pendergast, Tom, and Sarah Pendergast, editors, *St. James Guide to Young-Adult Writers,* 2nd edition, St. James Press (Detroit, MI), 1999.

Reginald, Robert, *Science Fiction and Fantasy Literature, 1975-1991,* Thomson Gale (Detroit, MI), 1992.

Silvey, Anita, editor, *Children's Books and Their Creators,* Houghton Mifflin (Boston, MA), 1995.

Twentieth-Century Children's Writers, third edition, St. James Press (Detroit, MI), 1989.

PERIODICALS

Booklist, January 1, 1980, Marilyn Kaye, review of *The Iron Way,* p. 666; June 15, 1983, Ilene Cooper, review of *The Demon Headmaster,* pp. 1336-1337; January 15, 1991, Hazel Rochman, review of *Wolf,* pp. 1052-1053; March 15, 1992, Emily Melton, review of *The Great American Elephant Chase,* p. 1320; February 1, 1995, p. 999; January 1, 1997, Susan Dove Lempke, review of *Pictures in the Dark,* p. 858; September 15, 1999, Roger Leslie, review of *Tightrope,* p. 247; September 1, 2004, Sally Estes, review of *The Dark Ground,* p. 106.

Books for Keeps, May, 1998, review of *The Demon Headmaster Takes Over,* p. 27.

Books for Your Children, summer, 1984, Gillian Cross, "How I Started Writing for Children," pp. 15-16.

Bulletin of the Center for Children's Books, September, 1983; March, 1985; June, 1985; July-August, 1986; March, 1987; January, 1988; June 1993, p. 312; June, 1995, pp. 340-341; January, 1997, Deborah Stevenson, review of *Pictures in the Dark,* pp. 161-162.

Growing Point, January, 1984, Margery Fisher, review of *Born to the Sun,* p. 4189.

Horn Book, November-December, 1980, Ann A. Flowers, review of *Revolt at Ratcliffe's Rags,* p. 647; July-August, 1985, Mary M. Burns, review of *On the Edge,* p. 453; January-February, 1989, Claudia Lepman-Logan, "Books in the Classroom: Moral Choices in Literature," p. 110; May-June, 1989, Mary M. Burns, review of *A Map of Nowhere,* p. 375; September-October, 1993, p. 596; July-August, 1995, p. 465; January-February, 1997, Maeve Visser Knoth, review of *Pictures in the Dark,* p. 54; January, 2000, Martha V. Parravano, review of *Tightrope,* p. 74; July-August, 2002, Lauren Adams, review of *Phoning a Dead Man,* p. 457; September-October, 2004, Roger Sutton, review of *The Dark Ground,* p. 579.

Junior Literary Guild, October, 1987-March, 1988.

Kirkus Reviews, March 1, 1989, review of *A Map of Nowhere,* pp. 375-376; March 15, 1993, review of *The Great American Elephant Chase,* p. 368; August 15, 1999, p. 1309; August 1, 2004, review of *Kirkus Reviews,* p. 739.

Publishers Weekly, March 13, 1995, review of *A New World,* p. 70; September 23, 1996, review of *Pictures in the Dark,* p. 77; August 23, 1999, review of *Tightrope,* p. 60; March 4, 2002, review of *Phoning a Dead Man,* p. 81; July 1, 2002, Kit Allerdice, "The British Invasion," p. 26; November 1, 2004, review of *The Dark Ground,* p. 52.

School Librarian, December, 1982, Dorothy Nimmo, review of *The Dark behind the Curtain,* p. 358; May, 1991, Gillian Cross, "Twenty Things I Don't Believe about Children's Books," pp. 44-46; winter, 2001, review of *Calling a Dead Man,* p. 210; May, 2002, Kim Carlson, review of *Phoning a Dead Man,* p. 147.

School Library Journal, April, 1987, Jack Forman, review of *Chartbreaker,* p. 108; January, 1993, p. 65; May, 1993, Sally Margolis, review of *The Great American Elephant Chase,* p. 104; December, 1993, p. 24; March, 1995, p. 222; November, 1996, p. 40; September, 1997, p. 130; May, 1998, p. 50; October 1999, Francisca Goldsmith, review of *Tightrope,* p. 148; January, 2002, Maren Ostergard, review of *Gobbo the Great* (audiobook), p. 75; September, 2004, Susan L. Rogers, review of *The Dark Ground,* p. 202.

Times Educational Supplement, April 9, 1982, Neil Philip, "Blackmail and Old Lace," p. 29.

Times Literary Supplement, March 27, 1981, Anne Carter, "Encouraging Stories," p. 340; July 23, 1982, Geoffrey Trease, "Curdling the Blood," p. 788; September 17, 1982, Ann Martin, "Forms of Believability," p. 1002; September 30, 1983, Sarah Hayes, review of *Born of the Sun.*

Voice of Youth Advocates, October, 1993, p. 215; December, 1995, p. 313; June, 1996, p. 86; June, 1998, p. 102; June 2002, review of *Phoning a Dead Man,* p. 115.

ONLINE

Gillian Cross Web site, http://www.gillian-cross.co.uk (November 17, 2005).*

*   *   *

CROSS, Gillian Clare
See CROSS, Gillian

*   *   *

CROSSLEY-HOLLAND, Kevin 1941-
(Kevin John William Crossley-Holland)

Personal

Born February 7, 1941, in Mursley, Buckinghamshire, England; son of Peter Charles (a composer and musicologist) and Joan Mary (a potter and gallery director; maiden name, Cowper) Crossley-Holland; married Caroline Fendall Thompson, 1963 (marriage ended); married Ruth Marris, 1972 (marriage ended); married Gillian Cook, 1982 (marriage ended); married Linda Washew, 1999; children: (first marriage) Kieran, Dominic; (third marriage) Oenone, Eleanor. *Education:* St. Edmund Hall, Oxford, M.A. (with honors), 1962. *Hobbies and other interests:* Music, archaeology, travel, walking, wine, the company of friends.

Kevin Crossley-Holland

Addresses

Office—Clare Cottage, Burnham Market, Norfolk PE31 8HE, England. *Agent*—c/o Author Mail, Orion Publishing Group, Orion House, 5 Upper Saint Martin's Lane, London WC2H 9EA, England.

Career

Writer and translator. Macmillan & Co. (publishers), London, England, editor, 1962-69; Victor Gollancz Ltd. (publisher), London, editorial director, 1972-77; Boydell & Brewer (publisher), Woodbridge, Suffolk, England, editorial consultant, 1983-91. Tufts-in-London program, lecturer in English, 1967-78; University of Leeds, Gregory fellow in poetry, 1969-72; University of Regensburg, English lecturer, 1978-80; Winchester School of Art, Arts Council fellow in writing, 1983-84; St. Olaf College, Northfield, MN, visiting professor of English and Fulbright scholar-in-residence, 1987-88; St. Thomas College, MN, professor and endowed chair of humanities, 1991-95; visiting lecturer for British Council in Germany, Iceland, India, Slovakia, and Yugoslavia. BBC, London, talks producer, 1972; contributor to radio, television, and musical works.

Member

Eastern Arts Association (chairman, literature panel, 1986-89), Friends of Wingfield College (trustee and chairman, 1989—), Royal Society of Literature (fellow), Poetry-next-the-Sea (cofounder and chair, 1997—).

Awards, Honors

Arts Council awards for best book for children, 1968, for *The Green Children,* 1977, and 1978; poetry award, 1972, for *The Rain-Giver;* Poetry Book Society Choice, 1976, for *The Dream-House;* Francis Williams Award, 1977, for *The Wildman;* Carnegie Medal, 1985, for *Storm;* Nestlé Smarties Prize bronze medal, Youth Libraries Group, 2000, and *Guardian* Award for Children's Fiction, and Tir na n-Og Award, Welsh Books Council, both 2001, all for *Arthur: The Seeing Stone;* St. Edmund Hall, Oxford, honorary fellow.

Writings

FOR CHILDREN AND YOUNG ADULTS

Havelok the Dane, illustrated by Brian Wildsmith, Macmillan (London, England), 1964, Dutton (New York, NY), 1965.

King Horn, illustrated by Charles Keeping, Macmillan (London, England), 1965, Dutton (New York, NY), 1966.

(Reteller) *The Green Children* (also see below), illustrated by Margaret Gordon, Macmillan (London, England), 1966, Seabury Press (New York, NY), 1968, revised edition, illustrated by Alan Marks, Oxford University Press (Oxford, England), 1994.

(Editor) *Winter's Tales for Children: No. 3,* Macmillan (London, England), 1967, St. Martin's Press (New York, NY), 1968.

(Reteller) *The Callow Pit Coffer,* illustrated by Margaret Gordon, Macmillan (London, England), 1968, Seabury Press (New York, NY), 1969.

(With Jill Paton Walsh) *Wordhoard: Anglo-Saxon Stories,* Farrar, Straus (New York, NY), 1969.

(Translator) *Storm and Other Old English Riddles* (verse), illustrated by Miles Thistlethwaite, Farrar, Straus (New York, NY), 1970.

(Reteller) *The Pedlar of Swaffham,* illustrated by Margaret Gordon, Macmillan (London, England), 1971, Seabury Press (New York, NY), 1972.

The Sea-Stranger (first volume of "Wulf" series), illustrated by Joanna Troughton, Heinemann (London, England), 1973, Seabury Press (New York, NY), 1974.

The Fire-Brother (second volume of "Wulf" series), illustrated by Joanna Troughton, Seabury Press (New York, NY), 1975.

Green Blades Rising: The Anglo-Saxons, Deutsch (London, England), 1975, Seabury Press (New York, NY), 1976.

The Earth-Father (third volume of "Wulf" series), illustrated by Joanna Troughton, Heinemann (London, England), 1976.

The Wildman (also see below), illustrated by Charles Keeping, Deutsch (London, England), 1976.

(Editor) *The Faber Book of Northern Legends,* illustrated by Alan Howard, Faber (London, England), 1977.

(Editor) *The Faber Book of Northern Folk-Tales,* illustrated by Alan Howard, Faber (London, England), 1980.

(Editor) *The Riddle Book,* illustrated by Bernard Handelsman, Macmillan (London, England), 1982.

(Reteller) *The Dead Moon and Other Tales from East Anglia and the Fen Country,* illustrated by Shirley Felts, Deutsch (London, England), 1982.

(Reteller) *Beowulf,* illustrated by Charles Keeping, Oxford University Press (Oxford, England), 1982, reprinted, 1999.

(Reteller with Gwyn Thomas) *Tales from the Mabinogion,* illustrated by Margaret Jones, Gollancz (London, England), 1984, Overlook Press (New York, NY), 1985.

(Reteller) *Axe-Age, Wolf-Age: A Selection from the Norse Myths,* illustrated by Hannah Firmin, Deutsch (London, England), 1985.

Storm, illustrated by Alan Marks, Heinemann (London, England), 1985, Barron's (Hauppage, NY), 1989.

(Reteller) *The Fox and the Cat: Animal Tales from Grimm,* illustrated by Susan Varley, Andersen Press (London, England), 1985, Lothrop (New York, NY), 1986.

(Reteller) *Northern Lights: Legends, Sagas, and Folk-Tales,* illustrated by Alan Howard, Faber (London, England), 1987.

(Reteller) *British Folk Tales: New Versions,* Orchard (New York, NY), 1987, published in four volumes as *Boo!, Dathera Dad, Piper and Pooka,* and *Small-Tooth Dog,* illustrated by Peter Melnyczuk, Orchard (London, England), 1988.

(Reteller with Gwyn Thomas) *The Quest for Olwen,* illustrated by Margaret Jones, Lutterworth Press (Cambridge, England), 1988.

(Reteller) *Wulf,* Faber & Faber (London, England), 1988.

(Reteller) *Under the Sun and over the Moon* (poetry), illustrated by Ian Penney, Putnam (New York, NY), 1989.

(Reteller) *Sleeping Nanna,* illustrated by Peter Melnyczuk, Orchard (London, England), 1989, Ideals (New York, NY), 1990.

(Reteller) *Sea Tongue,* illustrated by Clare Challice, BBC/Longman (London, England), 1991.

(Reteller) *Tales from Europe,* BBC (London, England), 1991.

(Reteller with Gwyn Thomas) *The Tale of Taliesin,* illustrated by Margaret Jones, Gollancz (London, England), 1992.

(Reteller) *Long Tom and the Dead Hand,* illustrated by Shirley Felts, Deutsch (London, England), 1992.

The Labours of Herakles, illustrated by Peter Utton, Orion (London, England), 1993.

(Reteller) *The Old Stories: Folk Tales from East Anglia and the Fen Country,* illustrated by John Lawrence, Colt (Cambridge, England), 1997.

Short! A Book of Very Short Stories, Oxford University Press (Oxford, England), 1998.

The King Who Was and Will Be: The World of King Arthur and His Knights, illustrated by Peter Malone, Orion (London, England), 1998, published as *The World of King Arthur and His Court: People, Places, Legend, and Lore,* Dutton (New York, NY), 1999.

(Editor) *Young Oxford Book of Folk Tales,* Oxford University Press (New York, NY), 1998.

(Reteller) *Enchantment: Fairy Tales, Ghost Stories, and Tales of Wonder,* illustrated by Emma Chichester Clark, Allen & Unwin (London, England), 2000.

Arthur: The Seeing Stone (first volume of "Arthur Trilogy"), Orion (London, England), 2000, Arthur A. Levine (New York, NY), 2001.

(Reteller) Hans Christian Andersen, *The Ugly Duckling,* illustrated by Meilo So, Knopf (New York, NY), 2001.

Arthur: At the Crossing-Places, (second volume of "Arthur Trilogy"), Orion (London, England), 2001, Arthur A. Levine (New York, NY), 2002.

The Magic Lands, Orion (London, England), 2001.

King of the Middle March (third volume of "Arthur Trilogy"), Orion (London, England), 2003, Arthur A. Levine (New York, NY), 2004.

How Many Miles to Bethlehem?, illustrated by Peter Malone, Arthur A. Levine (New York, NY), 2004.

(Editor and author of foreword) *Once upon a Poem: Favorite Poems That Tell Stories,* illustrated by Peter Bailey and others, Scholastic (New York, NY), 2004.

POETRY; FOR ADULTS

On Approval, Outposts (London, England), 1961.

My Son, Turret (London, England), 1966.

Alderney: The Nunnery, Turret (London, England), 1968.

Confessional, Sceptre Press (Frensham, Surrey, England), 1969.

Norfolk Poems, Academy (London, England), 1970.

A Dream of a Meeting, Sceptre Press (Frensham, Surrey, England), 1970.

More than I Am, Steam Press (London, England), 1971.

The Wake, Keepsake Press (Richmond, Surrey, England), 1972.

The Rain-Giver, Deutsch (London, England), 1972.

Petal and Stone, Sceptre Press (Knotting, Bedfordshire, England), 1975.

The Dream-House, Deutsch (London, England), 1976.

Between My Father and My Son, Black Willow Press (Minneapolis, MN), 1982.

Time's Oriel, Hutchinson (London, England), 1983.

Waterslain and Other Poems, Hutchinson (London, England), 1986.

The Painting-Room and Other Poems, Hutchinson (London, England), 1988.

East Anglian Poems, Jardine (Colchester, England), 1988.

Oenone in January, Old Stile Press (Llandogo, Wales), 1988.

New and Selected Poems: 1965-1990, Hutchinson (London, England), 1990.

Eleanor's Advent, Old Stile Press (Llandogo, Wales), 1992.

The Language of Yes, Enitharmon (London, England), 1996.

Poems from East Anglia, Enitharmon (London, England), 1997.

Selected Poems, Enitharmon (London, England), 2001.

EDITOR; FOR ADULTS

Running to Paradise: An Introductory Selection of the Poems of W.B. Yeats, Macmillan (London, England), 1967, Macmillan (New York, NY), 1968.

Winter's Tales 14, Macmillan (London, England), 1968.

(With Patricia Beer) *New Poetry 2,* Arts Council of Great Britain (London, England), 1976.

The Norse Myths: A Retelling, Deutsch (London, England), 1981, Pantheon (New York, NY), 1982.

(And translator) *The Anglo-Saxon World: An Anthology,* Boydell Press (Woodbridge, Suffolk), 1982, Barnes & Noble (New York, NY), 1983, reprinted, Oxford University Press (New York, NY), 1999.

Folk Tales of the British Isles, Folio Society (London, England), 1985, Pantheon (New York, NY), 1988.

The Oxford Book of Travel Verse, Oxford University Press (New York, NY), 1986.

Medieval Lovers: A Book of Days, Weidenfeld & Nicolson (New York, NY), 1988.

Medieval Gardens: A Book of Days, Rizzoli (New York, NY), 1990.

(Editor, with Lawrence Sail) *The New Exeter Book of Riddles,* illustrated by Simon Drew, Enitharmon (London, England), 1999.

General editor, "Mirror of Britain" series, Deutsch (London, England), 1975-80.

TRANSLATOR; FOR ADULTS

Bruce Mitchell, editor, *The Battle of Maldon and Other Old English Poems,* St. Martin's Press (New York, NY), 1965.

Beowulf, Farrar Straus (New York, NY), 1968, published with *The Fight at Finnsburh,* edited by Heather o'Donoghue, Oxford University Press (New York, NY), 1999.

The Exeter Riddle Book, Folio Society (London, England), 1978, revised as *The Exeter Book of Riddles,* Penguin (London, England), 1979, revised edition, Penguin (New York, NY) 1993.

The Wanderer, Jardine (Colchester, England), 1986.

The Old English Elegies, Folio Society (London, England), 1988.

OTHER

Pieces of Land: Journeys to Eight Islands, Gollancz (London, England), 1972.

The Stones Remain: Megalithic Sites of Britain, photographs by Andrew Rafferty, Rider (London, England), 1989.

(Author of libretto) *The Green Children* (two-act opera; based on his work of the same title), music by Nicola LeFanu, Novello (London, England), 1990.

(Author of libretto) *The Wildman* (opera; based on his work of the same title), Boydell & Brewer (Woodbridge, England), 1995.

Different—but Oh How Like! (booklet), Daylight Press (London, England), 1998.

Contributor to periodicals, including *Books for Your Children.*

Crossley-Holland's poetry notebooks are housed in the Brotherton Collection, University of Leeds; manuscripts for children's books are housed at the Lillian H. Smith and Osborne Collections, Toronto Public Library, Toronto, Ontario, Canada, and the Brotherton Collection, University of Leeds; the Kerlan Collection, University of Minnesota, Minneapolis, houses material relating to *Under the Sun and over the Moon.*

Adaptations

Crossley-Holland's *Exeter Book of Riddles* was adapted as the musical work *Riddles: For Six Solo Voices, SATB Chorus, Bells, and Piano* by William Mathias, 1991.

Sidelights

A poet. translator, and editor, Kevin Crossley-Holland is an acknowledged authority on European history and literature. However, the British writer is most familiar to younger readers for his retellings of British and Norse folktales, as well as for his well-received translations of the Anglo-Saxon epic *Beowulf* and historical fiction such as his "Wulf" and "Arthur" novel trilogies. Praised for his preservation of traditional literature, as well as for his ability to bring the past to life for modern readers, Crossley-Holland has often referred to the folk tales, legends, and poetry of the Anglo-Saxons as the main influences on his work. Marcus Crouch, writing in the *Junior Bookshelf,* called Crossley-Holland a "leading interpreter of the Dark Ages and an eloquent writer too."

As a writer for children and young people, Crossley-Holland draws upon sources similar to those that inform his literature for adults. Most of his books for the young are retellings; for example, he has produced volumes taken from Norse and Greek myths and medieval romances, as well as from the folktales of East Anglia. In addition, he has collaborated with Gwyn Thomas on retellings of the Mabinogion, a Welsh cycle of hero tales, and with Susanne Lugert on a collection of animal stories originally written by the Brothers Grimm. While he has been consistently praised for these retellings, Crossley-Holland is also well regarded for his historical fiction. His "Wulf" trilogy of young-adult novels—*The Sea Stranger, The Fire-Brother,* and *The Earth-Father*—describe how an artistic, fatherless boy in seventh-century England becomes a monk after he gets to know the Northumbrian missionary Cedd, a real figure who brought Christianity to the East Saxons. Taking place in the thirteenth century, the "Arthur" trilogy follows young Arthur de Caldicot who, bearing the name of the famous king, leads a parallel life in which he encounters Merlin, trains as a squire, and joins Lord Stephen on a crusade to the Holy Land, all the while following the stories of the ancient king and his knights of the Round Table via a seeing stone given him by Merlin. *Storm,* Crossley-Holland's Carnegie Medal-winning story for younger readers, features a young girl who saves the life of her older sister with the help of a farmer's ghost.

Born in Mursley, Buckinghamshire, England, Crossley-Holland grew up in an intellectual family heavily involved in music and the arts. In addition to music, the Crossley-Holland household was filled with stories, and at bedtime his father, musicologist Peter Crossley-Holland, "sometimes came with his Welsh harp and sat by our bunk beds, and said-and-sang (as the Anglo-Saxons called it) folktales," as the author recalled in *Something about the Author Autobiography Series* (*SAAS*). "In the gloom," he added, "I saw pookas and pipers, changelings, and the Banshee, dark horsemen, Tam Lin, and (my father's favourite), the bewitching lady who walked out of the lake up the mountain of Fan Fach. I haven't the slightest doubt that the seeds of my lifelong interest in folktale, legend, and myth were sown there, in the blue hour between day and night, waking and sleep."

As a boy, Crossley-Holland often accompanied his father on walking tours of archeological sites. "[F]rom that day to this," the author wrote, "I don't suppose I've walked past a molehill without kicking it over." Father and son found several artifacts from the Iron Age and medieval times, including two pieces of a Romano-British cooking pot that fit together. When they discovered a Roman coin with the head of the emperor Constantine on it, Crossley-Holland recalled, "I was electrified. . . . That was the place and moment at which I was first fully conscious of the presence of the past: that mysterious, challenging, enriching, shared dimension which has underpinned so much of my writing for adults and children." At the age of nine the boy became something of an expert; a letter he submitted on the subject of ancient coins was printed in the London *Times,* and the makeshift "museum" he created in a small garden shed to house all of his treasures actually attracted visitors. Crossley-Holland's mother, meanwhile, arranged dancing, riding, golf, and cricket lessons and also paid for instruction in tennis.

Crossley-Holland went to Swanbourne House, a preparatory boarding school, at the age of nine and a half. At Swanbourne, a Latin teacher, "Floppy" Wright, inspired the young student in a lifelong interest in Romance languages. Although not an avid reader, Crossley-Holland was also inspired by the book *Our Island Story,* an account of key episodes in British history. "Fired by this patriotic and highly coloured book, and nothing if not ambitious, I decided at the age of eleven to embark on a major literary enterprise of my own," he recalled in *SAAS,* "a History of the World which, somewhat later, and rather reluctantly, I scaled down to a History of Britain! I resumed work at the beginning of each holiday, and managed quite a number of chapters before eventually losing heart." At age fourteen he decided to become a priest, a vocation that he sustained until he entered Oxford University.

At Oxford University Crossley-Holland studied English literature, and became drawn to old Anglo-Saxon poems like *Beowulf* and *The Battle of Maldon,* works he would eventually retell or translate. He also wrote poetry, and published his first book, the short pamphlet *On Approval,* in 1961. He supplemented his academic experiences with travel, and at age seventeen hitchhiked through Belgium, Germany, Denmark, Sweden, and Finland; before he was twenty, he had visited nearly every country in western Europe. Crossley-Holland would eventually travel India and Russia, lived and worked in Bavaria, and spent five years in Minnesota.

In 1962 Crossley-Holland graduated from Oxford with a B.A. with honors. His first job was in the publicity department of the London publishing house of Macmillan, and he stayed with the company for nine years, eventually rising to the position of editor. He also became associated with "The Group," a gathering of English poets—Martin Bell, Peter Porter, Alan Brownjohn, Fleur Adcock, George MacBeth, and others—who met regularly to discuss each other's work. In 1963, Crossley-Holland married his first wife, Caroline Fendall Thompson, with whom he would have two sons, Kieran and Dominic. The following year he produced his first book for children and young people, the retelling *Havelok the Dane,* and embarked on his new career: author.

Havelok the Dane was inspired by a Middle English romance that captured Crossley-Holland's attention. In his retelling, young Havelok, the rightful king of Denmark, is forced to flee his homeland to escape death at the hand of his evil regent, Lord Godard. Havelok goes to England, where he meets Princess Goldborough, the rightful queen of England; like Havelok, the princess has been deposed by her regent. Forced to marry as an indignity, Havelok and Goldborough fall in love and set about regaining their respective thrones. Havelok returns to Denmark and defeats Godard; he then returns to England and reinstates Goldborough. The king and queen live alternate years in Denmark and England and have fifteen children. Praising the illustrations by Brian Wildsmith, Ethna Sheehan observed in the *New York Times Book Review* that Crossley-Holland retells *Havelok the Dane* "with drama, horror, and fun," bringing to the fore "Havelok's likable personality and Goldborough's spirited nature." Writing in *Horn Book.* Ethel L. Heins concluded that "this is a tale of ambition, bloody murder, loyalty, love, and the triumph of freedom over tyranny . . . retold . . . in a colorful, vigorous manner."

Havelok the Dane was followed by other books about the Anglo-Saxon world. *Wordhoard: Anglo-Saxon Stories,* written with Jill Paton Walsh, paints a vivid picture of that ancient culture, while *Tales from the Mabinogion, The Quest for Olwen,* and *The Tale of Taliesin,* the last co-authored with Gwyn Thomas, are simple, lyrical retellings of Welsh hero tales. *The Dead Moon* collects ghostly tales inhabited by bogarts, will-o'-the-wykes, witches, dead hands, and green children, woven into tales salted with a hint of East Anglian dialect. Several of the stories included in his anthologies, such as those in *The Dead Moon* and *British Folk Tales: New Versions,* have been more recently reissued as picture books. One of these retellings, published as *Small-*

Tooth Dog, recounts the story of a curious dog who saves the life of a man only to demand the man's only daughter as payment.

A major focus of Crossley-Holland's young adult-work has been the folktales of his native East Anglia, England. *The Green Children,* a retelling of a twelfth-century English legend, is one of his best known works for the young. In this book, Crossley-Holland describes how two siblings, a boy and a girl with green skin, are found in a chalk pit. The children do not speak English, eat only green vegetables, and are blinded by the sun. The boy dies of homesickness, but the girl adapts to her new life and learns to speak; she is able to tell the tale of how she and her brother strayed from their subterranean world. Although the girl gradually turns fairer and even marries, she never stops looking for the entrance to her lost home. As a testament to Crossley-Holland's ability to bring these age-old stories to life, Charles Causley commented in *Twentieth-Century Children's Writers* that in *The Green Children* "mind and imagination are continuously stimulated and fed as the tales are resolved."

Other books that draw from Anglo-Saxon history include *Green Blades Rising: The Anglo-Saxons,* an informational book for young adults that describes the daily lives, beliefs, practices, art, and literature of the culture, as well as its influence on modern times. *The Wildman,* a retelling of an East Anglian story, is considered among Crossley-Holland's most memorable—and disturbing—works. The Wildman of the title is a merman who tells of his capture, imprisonment, and torture during the reign of England's King Henry II. Through the narrator's eyes, readers learn his impressions of human behavior. Finally, the Wildman becomes alienated from life on sea as well as on land. while Nicholas Tucker, reviewing *The Wildman* for the *Times Literary Supplement,* questioned the book's appeal to children, *Junior Bookshelf* critic Marcus Crouch cited it as "a most moving experience" for readers young and old, while Donna R. White wrote in the *Dictionary of Literary Biography* that the book "is a moody, evocative piece, both haunting and sad." Crossley-Holland also wrote the libretto for an operatic version of *The Wildman* by Nicola LeFanu, which premiered at the Aldeburgh Festival in 1995.

In 1972, Crossley-Holland produced the first of his "Wulf" series of historical novels. The first of a trilogy set in Northumberland in eastern England during the seventh century, *The Sea Stranger* centers on Wulf, a boy who is more interested in making carvings in wood and bone than he is in battles. When Cedd, a Christian missionary, spends the night with the boy's family, Wulf is intrigued by the charismatic man and his message. Cedd leaves, but returns in the spring to build a cathedral on land granted by King Ethelwald. At the end of the novel, Wulf is baptized, becomes Cedd's student, and decides to join his teacher's order of monks. As A.R. Williams wrote in *Junior Bookshelf,* the novel fo-

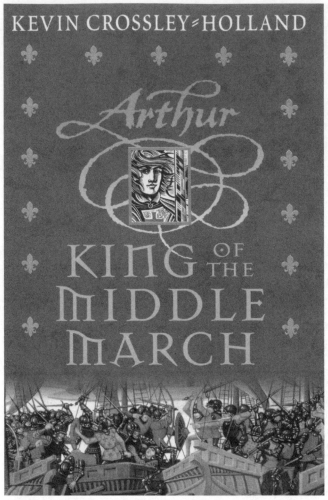

Crossley-Holland closes his trilogy as Arthur, now a knight, finds himself in Venice at the start of the fourth Crusade and must make a choice regarding his own destiny. (Cover illustration by Stephen Alcorn.)

cuses on "the attitudes of contemporary rulers and their subjects to the largely welcome ideas of Christianity." Writing in *Horn Book,* Paul Heins noted that "Wulf, the other members of his family, and Cedd are well-drawn, and the simple narrative is rich with historical, literary, and archeological details."

The second volume of the series, *The Fire-Brother,* takes place a year after the conclusion of *The Sea Stranger.* When their harvest is bad, some of the farmers blame the Christian monks for convincing them not to sacrifice to their traditional goddess, Freya. In retaliation, Wulf's brother Oswald sets the monastery on fire before running away. Wulf, who is torn between the love for his family and his devotion to Cedd's teachings, is sent by Cedd—now a bishop—to find Oswald with a message of forgiveness and a plea to return home. In *Horn Book,* Heins noted that in this novel Crossley-Holland maintains "a nice balance . . . between the presentation of the purposeful, hopeful activities of monastic life and worship and the labors and tribulations of primitive land-cultivators." The final volume of the trilogy, *The Earth-Father,* finds Wulf the

sole survivor after a plague kills all of the brothers in his monastery. In an attempt to reunite with Cedd, Wulf travels to the bishop's side, risking disease himself. Cedd and Wulf are finally reunited; after Cedd's death, Wulf resolves to carry on the older man's work. In 1988 Crossley-Holland rewrote the "Wulf" trilogy and published it in a single volume, *Wulf.*

With his interest in ancient British literature, it was only natural that Crossley-Holland eventually bring his attention to one of the most classic pieces of Anglo-Saxon writing. In addition to producing a complete translation of *Beowulf* for adults, he has also created a picture-book version of the poem for older children. Illustrated by noted artist Charles Keeping, the story outlines how Beowulf the Geat travels to Denmark to destroy the evil monster Grendel, who has been harassing his father's friends. After Beowulf kills Grendel, the monster's mother, an old sea-wolf, seeks revenge. Beowulf kills her and takes her head back to the king of the Danes. He rules over the Geats for fifty years and dies while courageously fighting a dragon; after his death, Beowulf is celebrated by his subjects. Although the retelling is considered especially graphic, it has been credited with making the legend understandable to modern children due to Crossley-Holland's strong prose and use of modern idioms. Margery Fisher, writing in *Growing Point,* calling *Beowulf* "a remarkable new presentation of a hero-tale basic to our culture," while in *School Library Journal* Bonnie Saunders concluded that Crossley-Holland's "retelling of the classic epic maintains much of the ancient storytelling tradition in its richly tapestried prose."

Many of Crossley-Holland's books are geared for young children and beginning readers. The picture book *The Labours of Herakles* recounts the twelve labors performed by the Greek hero for the king of Argos, while in *The Ugly Duckling* Crossley-Holland retells Hans Christian Andersen's classic tale in an abridged text that was judged "sprightlier than the original" by *Booklist* contributor Ilene Cooper. One of the author's most popular stories for elementary-aged readers is *Storm.* This story (not to be confused with Crossley-Holland's riddle book of the same name) features a girl named Annie, who lives with her family in an isolated part of the East Anglian marsh. When her pregnant older sister goes into labor during a bad storm, it is up to Annie to help her. While Annie is apprehensive about fetching help because of the ghost rider who haunts her village, she conquers her fears and heads into the storm. Fortunately, she meets a silent man on horseback who helps her get to the home of the village doctor, and when she attempts to thank this good Samaritan it turns out that the fellow may not have been human after all. Writing in the *Junior Bookshelf,* A.R. Williams commented that "a great deal of convincing drama is packed into so few pages without limiting character to cardboard cut-out." *Storm* was awarded the Carnegie Medal in 1985.

Crossley-Holland has mined more than Anglo-Saxon lore in his story collections, and books such as *Folk Tales of the British Isles* established him as an authority in the myths and legends of the many people who have inhabited the British Isles. *British Folk Tales: New Versions* draws fifty-five stories and ballads from that work and presents them in versions compelling to modern children. The book includes hero tales, ghost stories, trickster tales, and works featuring fairies, goblins, selkies, and other supernatural creatures that have long inhabited the imagination of the residents of England, Ireland, Wales, and Scotland. Familiar favorites such as "Jack and the Beanstalk," "Goldilocks and the Three Bears," and "Tam Lin" appear alongside tales and verse that are less well known. Avoiding a strict retelling, Crossley-Holland plays with his original sources, combining some tales and reframing others, shifting points of view, and turning narratives into poems. Calling the author "a fine story-teller with a poet's ear," Jennifer Westwood wrote in the *Times Literary Supplement* that *British Folk Tales* "is the most representative by a modern reteller." Writing in the *Bulletin of the Center for Children's Books,* Betsy Hearne noted that, "in its revealing and revitalizing of the traditional," the book "makes a long-lasting contribution to readers and storytellers alike." Viewing *British Folk Tales* as one of the major accomplishments of his career, Crossley-Holland has adapted several of the tales as picture books illustrated by Peter Melnyczuk.

The legend of King Arthur and the Knights of the Round Table figure prominently in Crossley-Holland's work. His *The King Who Was and Will Be: The World of King Arthur and His Court*—published in the United States as *The World of King Arthur and His Court: People, Places, Legend, and Lore*—contains not only stories of Arthur, Lancelot, Merlin, and Guinevere but also what Carolyn Phelan described in *Booklist* as "a veritable collage of materials related to King Arthur." Containing a wealth of facts, quotes from Chaucer and other ancient texts, maps of Briton, and discussions of heraldry, jousting, castle life, art, and other aspects of everyday life during the time of Camelot, the beautifully illustrated volume "will delight young readers with a taste for history," according to a reviewer for *Publishers Weekly.* "If ever a book could ignite a passion for Camelot," the reviewer concluded of *The World of King Arthur and His Court,* "this is it."

The golden age of Camelot is also the focus of *The Seeing Stone, At the Crossing-Places,* and *King of the Middle March,* which together comprise Crossley-Holland's "Arthur" trilogy. These novels focus on the life of the legendary king by linking it with that of twelve-year-old Arthur de Caldicot, who lives, in the twelfth century, hundreds of years after Arthur's death. The two stories—the trials of an ancient king and the coming of age of a young man—reflect each other, beginning with Arthur de Caldicot's receipt of a gift: a mysterious piece of black obsidian given him by an old

Readers meet Arthur de Caldicot, a young boy who is given a talisman that connects him with his namesake, King Arthur, in this award-winning novel. (Cover illustration by Greg Call.)

friend of his father named Merlin. *The Seeing Stone* won several awards, including Great Britain's *Guardian* Children's Award for Fiction in 2001.

The Seeing Stone takes place in 1199, and the next two novels in the trilogy follow Arthur to 1203, when he has reached eighteen. *At the Crossing Places* finds the now-fourteen year old determined to make a new life for himself after discovering that his real parents are not the honorable folk who have raised him. Taken on as a squire by Lord Stephen de Holt, Arthur gains in experience through his training as well as through the visions from the seeing stone, and soon finds himself on his way to Jerusalem. As he follows his dream of joining his lord on a holy crusade, his actions are paralleled by the stone's revelations about the ancient knights' quest for the Holy Grail. While several critics noted that the volume does not stand well on its own, *Horn Book* contributor Joanna Rudge Long noted that Crossley-Holland "once again evokes a rich and credible panoply and circumstances and characters"; while "much is left open," the sequel will make clear "the true design of this absorbing and carefully wrought trilogy."

Concluding the "Arthur" trilogy, *King of the Middle March* does indeed reveal the "true design" of Crossley-Holland's epic tale. Arthur and Lord Stephen are by now in Venice where, with thousands of other Christian knights from throughout Europe, they yearn to travel to Jerusalem to capture the holy city. However, in exchange for the money to buy ships to transport them, these knights become mercenaries for a local monarch, and ravage the city of Zara, Christian killing Christian. As the Crusades dissolve into brutal bloodshed and greed the stone reveals the tragic end of King Arthur's own history, and "the questions . . . [Arthur de Caldicot] raises about religion, morality, and war resonate," both in his world and that of the ancient king, as well as "in our own," as Phelan noted in *Booklist*. "Superb writing, prodigious research, [and] a wealth of detail" characterize the entire trilogy, noted a *Kirkus Reviews* writer, while in *Horn Book* Martha V. Parravano called *King of the Middle March* "a novel of extraordinary richness, packed with event and color and texture."

Crossley-Holland's many books reflect his abiding interests: the sea, Anglo-Saxons, and East Anglia. Asked to describe the basis of his work, he once commented that it was lodged in "roots, the sense of past embodied in present, [and] the relationship of person to place." While he has also published poetry and other works for adults, and has served as a university professor, librettist, translator, radio and television commentator, and editor, it has been his work for children that many view as his greatest accomplishment.

Biographical and Critical Sources

BOOKS

Children's Literature Review, Volume 47, Thomson Gale (Detroit, MI), 1998, pp. 18-50.

De Montreville, Doris, and Elizabeth D. Crawford, editors, *Fourth Book of Junior Authors and Illustrators,* H.W. Wilson (Bronx, NY), 1979.

Dictionary of Literary Biography, Thomson Gale (Detroit, MI), Volume 40: *Poets of Great Britain and Ireland since 1940,* 1985, Volume 161: *British Children's Writers since 1960,* 1996, pp. 103-108.

St. James Guide to Young-Adult Writers, 2nd edition, edited by Tom Pendergast and Sara Pendergast, St. James Press (Detroit, MI), 1999, pp. 34-36.

Something about the Author Autobiography Series, Volume 30, Thomson Gale (Detroit, MI), 1995, pp. 125-140.

Twentieth-Century Children's Writers, 3rd edition, St. James Press (Detroit, MI), 1989.

PERIODICALS

Best Sellers, May, 1976, Mary Columba, review of *Green Blades Rising: The Anglo-Saxons,* p. 60.

Booklist, May 15, 1999, GraceAnne A. DeCandido, review of *The Young Oxford Book of Folk Tales,* p. 1694; November 15, 1999, Carolyn Phelan, review of *The World of King Arthur and His Court,* p. 617; July, 2001, Ilene Cooper, review of *The Ugly Duckling,* p. 2012; November, 1, 2002, Carolyn Phelan, review of *At the Crossing Places,* p. 494; September 1, 2004, Carolyn Phelan, review of *King of the Middle March,* p. 122; October 1, 2004, Carolyn Phelan, review of *How Many Miles to Bethlehem?,* p. 331.

Books for Keeps, November, 1990, Kevin Crossley-Holland, "Restraints and Possibilities," pp. 18-19; November, 1997, p. 24.

Bulletin of the Center for Children's Books, January, 1988, Betsy Hearne, review of *British Folk Tales: New Versions,* pp. 86-87; February, 2005, Timnah Card, review of *King of the Middle March,* p. 248.

Children's Literature, Volume 3, 1974, Alexander Taylor, review of *Storm,* pp. 199-200.

Encounter, September, 1971, Elizabeth Maslen, "Riddles," pp. 81-82.

Folklore, April, 2000, Ruth Glass, review of *Different—but Oh How Like!,* p. 146.

Growing Point, November, 1966, Margery Fisher, review of *The Green Children,* p. 791; January, 1983, Margery Fisher, review of *Beowulf,* pp. 3998-3999; March, 1989, Margery Fisher, review of *Wulf,* p. 5116.

Guardian (London, England), September 29, 2001, Claire Armitstead, interview with Crossley-Holland.

Horn Book, February, 1966, Ethel L. Heins, review of *Havelok the Dane,* p. 51; December, 1969, Paul Heins, review of *Wordhoard: Anglo-Saxon Stories,* p. 680; June, 1974, Paul Heins, review of *The Sea Stranger,* pp. 280-281; December, 1975, Paul Heins, review of *The Fire-Brother,* p. 591; November-December, 2002, Joanna Rudge Long, review of *At the Crossing Places,* p. 752; November-December, 2004, Jennifer M. Brabander, review of *How Many Miles to Bethlehem?,* p. 658; January-February, 2005, Martha V. Parravano, review of *King of the Middle March,* p. 91.

Junior Bookshelf, November, 1964, review of *Havelok the Dane,* pp. 307-308; October, 1969, review of *Wordhoard: Anglo-Saxon Stories,* p. 321; April, 1974, A.R. Williams, review of *The Sea Stranger,* p. 110; March, 1977, Marcus Crouch, review of *The Wildman,* p. 39; April, 1983, G. Bott, review of *Beowulf;* December, 1984, Marcus Crouch, review of *Tales from the Mabinogion,* p. 359; December, 1988, D.A. Young, review of *Wulf,* pp. 288-89; October, 1985, A.R. Williams, review of *Storm,* p. 215.

Kirkus Reviews, February 1, 1976, review of *Green Blades Rising,* p. 140; September 1, 2002, review of *At the Crossing Places,* p. 1307; September 15, 2004, review of *King of the Middle March,* p. 912; November 1, 2004, review of *How Many Miles to Bethlehem?,* p. 1048; December 15, 2004, review of *Once upon a Poem,* p. 1199.

Kliatt, November, 2002, Claire Rosser, review of *At the Crossing Places,* p. 6; September, 2004, Janis Flint-Ferguson, review of *King of the Middle March,* p. 6.

Listener, November 14, 1968.

Magpies, July, 1991, Kevin Crossley-Holland, "The Flying Word, the Word of Life: Approaches to Norse Myth and British Folktale, Pt. II"; March, 1999, p. 44.

New Leader, May 4, 1987, Phoebe Pettingell, review of *The Oxford Book of Travel Verse,* p. 9.

New York Times Book Review, November 14, 1965, Ethna Sheehan, review of *Havelok the Dane,* pp. 66-67; May 5, 1968, Alice Low, review of *The Green Children,* p. 47.

Observer Review (London, England), February 26, 1970.

Publishers Weekly, October 18, 1999, review of *The World of King Arthur and His Court,* p. 85; November 1, 1999, p. 58; July 16, 2001, review of *The Ugly Duckling,* p. 180; September 27, 2004, review of *How Many Miles to Bethlehem?,* p. 62.

Punch, October 23, 1968.

Saturday Review, March 15, 1969.

School Librarian, spring, 1998, pp. 23-24; autumn, 1998, p. 136.

School Library Journal, February, 1970, Bruce L. MacDuffie, review of *Wordhoard: Anglo-Saxon Stories,* pp. 91-92; April, 1985, Bonnie Saunders, review of *Beowulf,* pp. 84-85; April, 1991, Ruth K. MacDonald, review of *Sleeping Nanna,* p. 91; October, 1999, Grace Oliff, review of *The Young Oxford Book of Folk Tales,* p. 166; January, 2000, Connie C. Rockman, review of *The World of King Arthur and His Court,* p. 140; April, 2003, Cindy Lombardo, review of *At the Crossing Places,* p. 89; November, 2004, Cheri Dobbs, review of *King of the Middle March,* p. 139; January, 2005, Cris Riedel, review of *Once upon a Poem: Favorite Poems That Tell a Story,* p. 108.

Spectator, December 10, 1988, Juliet Townsend, review of *Wulf,* pp. 37-38.

Teacher Librarian, June, 2000, Jessica Higgs, review of *The King Who Was and Will Be,* p. 54.

Times Educational Supplement, January 19, 1990, John Mole, review of *Under the Sun and over the Moon,* p. 29; November 29, 1991, James Riordan, review of *Tales from Europe,* p. 27; May 15, 1992, James Riordan, review of *Long Tom and the Dead Hand,* p. S13; May 29, 1992, Gillian Clarke, review of *The Tale of Taliesin,* p. 30; November 12, 1993, Charles Causley, review of *The Labours of Herakles,* p. R2; March 24, 1994, John Mole, review of *The Green Children,* p. R7.

Times Literary Supplement, December 10, 1976, Nicholas Tucker, "A Picture of Ugliness," p. 1550; November 13-18, 1987, Jennifer Westwood, "Tales within Tales," p. 1264; December 16-22, 1988, Heather O'Donoghue, "Actually Anglo-Saxon," p. 1406; March 30, 1990, Gerald Mangan, review of *Under the Sun and over the Moon,* p. 356; June 21, 1991, Virginia Rounding, *New and Selected Poems,* p. 18.

Young Reader's Review, January, 1967; June, 1968; October, 1969.

ONLINE

Achuka Web site, http://www.achuka.co.uk/ (August 29, 2001), "Kevin Crossley-Holland."

Allen & Unwin Web site, http://www.allenandunwin.com/ (August 29, 2001), "Kevin Crossley-Holland."*

* * *

CROSSLEY-HOLLAND, Kevin John William
   See CROSSLEY-HOLLAND, Kevin

D

DAVID, Lawrence 1963-

Personal

Born January 20, 1963, in Boston, MA; son of Barry S. (in business) and Elizabeth (a social worker) David. *Education:* Bennington College, B.A., 1985; New York University, M.F.A., 1987.

Addresses

Home—New York, NY. *Agent*—Cynthia Cannell, Janklow & Nesbit, 598 Madison Ave., New York, NY 10022.

Career

Teacher's assistant at a school in New York, NY, 1991-92; Bantam, Doubleday, Dell Books for Young Readers, New York, NY, assistant to the publisher, 1992-93; freelance writer, beginning 1993.

Writings

FOR CHILDREN

The Good Little Girl, illustrated by Clement Oubrerie, Doubleday (New York, NY), 1998.

Beetle Boy, illustrated by Delphine Durand, Doubleday (New York, NY), 1999.

Peter Claus and the Naughty List, Doubleday (New York, NY), 1999.

The Land of the Hungry Armadillos, illustrated by Frédérique Bertrand, Doubleday (New York, NY), 2000.

Superhero Max, illustrated by Tara Calahan King, Doubleday (New York, NY), 2001.

Full Moon, illustrated by Brian Wilcox, Random House (New York, NY), 2001.

Pickle & Penguin, illustrated by Scott Nash, Dutton (New York, NY), 2004.

"CUPCAKED CRUSADER" SERIES; FOR CHILDREN

Horace Splattly: The Cupcaked Crusader, illustrated by Barry Gott, Dutton (New York, NY), 2002.

When Second Graders Attack, illustrated by Barry Gott, Dutton (New York, NY), 2002.

The Terror of the Pink Dodo Balloons, illustrated by Barry Gott, Dutton (New York, NY), 2003.

To Catch a Clownosaurus, illustrated by Barry Gott, Puffin (New York, NY), 2003.

The Most Evil, Friendly Villain Ever, illustrated by Barry Gott, Dutton (New York, NY), 2004.

The Invasion of the Shag Carpet Creature, illustrated by Barry Gott, Dutton (New York, NY), 2004.

OTHER

Family Values (adult novel), Simon & Schuster (New York, NY), 1993.

Need (adult novel), Random House (New York, NY), 1994.

Sidelights

After penning two novels for adults that explore the intricacies of human relationships, Lawrence David turned his attention to books for younger readers, with much success. His books *The Good Little Girl* and *Beetle Boy,* are both tales of metamorphosis in which children adapt to their distracted parents. Miranda, the young protagonist of *The Good Little Girl,* cheerfully puts up with the strain induced by having two working parents. She dutifully listens to her parents continually make promises of "tomorrow," but when they fail to produce the much-anticipated "Saturday Family Waffle Breakfast," enough is enough, and Miranda turns into her nasty alter ego, mean-and-green Lucretia. At first, Lucretia wrangles from Miranda everything she wants, but gets out of hand when she demands that Miranda's mother stick pencils up her nose and sing "Polly Wolly Doodle." Good-natured Miranda is ultimately able to take charge again and all seems well, until Lucretia rears her head one last time to remind the parents not to ignore Miranda. A *Kirkus Reviews* critic wrote that "Lucretia will appeal to every child who has ever succumbed to vague parental procrastinations," and a *Publishers Weekly* reviewer stated that "David . . .

effectively depicts how disappointment upsets even the best-natured child."

David readily admits that his second book for children, *Beetle Boy,* was inspired by Franz Kafka's *Metamorphosis,* which a *Kirkus Reviews* critic said "translates splendidly into a story for younger audiences." Like the adult character in Kafka's novel, second-grader Gregory Sampson wakes up one morning and realizes he has become an insect. Distressed that no one but his best friend, Michael, sees his hard exoskeleton and six legs, Gregory finally shouts out, "Look at me. I'm a giant beetle." After his exclamation, his father replies: "And I'm a hippo." After finding Gregory on the ceiling of his room, sobbing, the family has to admit that the boy has indeed turne into a beetle, but no matter: they love him just the same and their affirmations ultimately help return the boy to human form.

The picture book *Superhero Max* is the story of Max's attempts to fit in at a new school. On Halloween, he wows his classmates with his Caped Crusader costume, so he decides to wear it to school every day. This plan leads Max's classmates to think he is even stranger, however, and Max's dad finally helps the boy learn that it is okay to just be himself. *School Library Journal* critic Wendy Lukehart commented on the book's "realistic, yet ultimately positive, treatment of what it's like to be or have a new kid in class."

David's other picture books feature everything from a talking pickle who is also a talk-show host in *Pickle and Penguin* to a boy who has to rescue his sister from a strange world ruled by a large orange monster in *The Land of Hungry Armadillos.* More fun is dished up in his Christmas-time picture-book offering, *Peter Claus and the Naughty List,* which finds Santa's son Peter given responsibility for tracking the world's naughty children. Because Peter is often included on the naughty roster himself, the younger Claus is determined to get Santa to give naughty kids a second chance. Ilene Cooper, writing in *Booklist,* called *Peter Claus and the Naughty List* "a delightful mix of message, moral, and merry holiday fun."

Along with his picture books, David is the author of the adventures of Horace Splattly, which he sets forth in the "Cupcaked Crusader" series. In the series opener, *Horace Splattly: The Cupcaked Crusader,* Horace's genius-rated younger sister bakes some mysterious cupcakes, which, amazingly, give the boy super powers. Now Horace must defeat a man-eating guinea pig. Designed to entertain reluctant readers, the chapter books feature such villains as a brainwashing chef, hair-eating hairclips that threaten to turn an entire town bald, and a clownasaurus. In *School Library Journal,* Christina F. Renaud praised the "quick pace and silly characters" featured in each of David's stories. "Watch out, Captain Underpants, there's a new superhero on the scene," a critic for *Kirkus Reviews* exclaimed, comparing David's series to a similar series of superhero chapter books by

Dav Pilkey. In a review of *When Second Graders Attack,* book two of the series, Sharon R. Pearce noted in *School Library Journal* that David's "text provides plenty of creative twists, danger, and excitement to keep readers turning pages."

Biographical and Critical Sources

PERIODICALS

Booklist, August, 1994, p. 2021; September 15, 2001, Ilene Cooper, review of *Peter Claus and the Naughty List,* p. 236; November 1, 2002, Todd Morning, review of *Superhero Max,* p. 507.
Kirkus Reviews, May 1, 1993, pp. 545-546; June 15, 1994, p. 790; January 15, 1999, review of *Beetle Boy,* p. 172; September 15, 1998, review of *The Good Little Girl,* p. 1382; April 15, 2002, review of *Horace Splattly,* p. 565; August 1, 2002, review of *Superhero Max,* p. 1125; December 1, 2002, review of *The Terror of the Pink Dodo Balloons,* p. 1767; October 15, 2004, review of *Pickle and Penguin,* p. 1003.
Library Journal, December, 1998, p. 82; March, 1999, p. 173.
Publishers Weekly, April 26, 1993, p. 55; June 4, 1994, p. 53; November 2, 1998, review of *The Good Little Girl,* p. 82; January 25, 1999, review of *Beetle Boy,* p. 95; May 8, 2000, review of *The Good Little Girl,* p. 223; June 12, 2000, review of *The Land of Hungry Armadillos,* p. 73; May 7, 2001, review of *Full Moon,* p. 245; September 24, 2001, review of *Peter Claus and the Naughty List,* p. 54; July 15, 2002, review of *Superhero Max,* p. 73; December 13, 2004, review of *Pickle and Penguin,* p. 67.
School Library Journal, March, 1999, Kimberlie Monteforte, review of *Beetle Boy,* p. 173; July, 2000, Steven Engelfried, review of *The Land of Hungry Armadillos,* p. 70; June, 2001, Margaret Bush, review of *Full Moon,* p. 132; October, 2001, A.C., review of *Peter Claus and the Naughty List,* p. 64, and Christina F. Renaud, review of *Horace Splattly,* p. 113; July, 2002, Sharon R. Pearce, review of *When Second Graders Attack,* p. 88; November, 2002, Wendy Lukehart, review of *Superhero Max,* p. 121; December 1, 2002, Elaine E. Knight, review of *The Terror of the Pink Dodo Balloons,* p. 104; January, 2004, Pat Leach, review of *To Catch a Clownosaurus,* p. 96; January, 2005, Debbie Stewart, review of *Pickle and Penguin,* p. 90.

ONLINE

Penguin Group Web site, http://www.penguinputnam.com/ (November 5, 2005), "Lawrence David."*

*   *   *

DeFELICE, Cynthia 1951- (Cynthia C. DeFelice)

Personal

Born December 28, 1951, in Philadelphia, PA; daughter of William (a psychiatrist) and Ann (an English teacher

Cynthia DeFelice

and homemaker; maiden name, Baldwin) Carter; married Ralph DeFelice (a dentist), February 16, 1974; stepchildren: Michelle, Ralph. *Education:* William Smith College, B.A., 1973; Syracuse University, M.L.S., 1980. *Hobbies and other interests:* Quilt making, dulcimer playing, hiking, backpacking, bird watching, fishing, reading, watching films.

Addresses

Home—Geneva, NY. *Agent*—c/o Author Mail, Farrar, Straus & Giroux, Inc., 19 Union Square West, New York, NY 10003.

Career

Storyteller and writer. Worked variously as a barn painter, day-care provider, and advertising layout artist; Newark public schools, Newark, NY, elementary school media specialist, 1980-87. Co-founder of Wild Washerwomen Storytellers, 1980.

Member

Authors Guild, Authors League of America, Society of Children's Book Writers and Illustrators, National Storytelling Association, Audubon Society, Nature Conservancy, Wilderness Society, Seneca Lake Pure Waters Association.

Awards, Honors

Notable Children's Trade Book for Language Arts designation, National Council of Teachers of English, and Teacher's Choice Award, International Reading Association (IRA), both 1989, both for *The Strange Night Writing of Jessamine Colter;* Best Children's Books of the Year designation, Library of Congress, Best Illustrated Children's Books of the Year designation, *New York Times,* and Reading Magic Award, *Parenting,* all 1989, all for *The Dancing Skeleton;* Best Books designation, *School Library Journal,* Notable Children's Book designation, American Library Association (ALA), Notable Children's Trade Book in the Field of Social Studies designation, National Council for the Social Studies/Children's Book Council (NCSS/CBC), and IRA/CBC Young-Adult Choice Award, all 1990, Hodge-Podger Society Award for Fiction, 1992, and Sequoyah, and South Carolina children's book awards, all for *Weasel;* Best Book designation, New York Public Library, 1994, for *Mule Eggs;* listed among Books for the Teen Age, New York Public Library, 1995, for *Lostman's River;* Best Book designation, New York Public Library, 1995, and Anne Izard Storytellers' Choice Award, 1996, for *Three Perfect Peaches;* South Dakota Prairie Pasque Children's Book Award, and Sunshine State Young Reader's Award, both 1995, both for *Devil's Bridge;* Best Book designation, *School Library Journal,* 1996, and NCSS/CBC Notable Children's Trade Book in the Field of Social Studies designation, 1997, ALA Notable Children's Book designation, Judy Lopez Memorial Award, International Honor Book designation, Society of School Librarians, and Books for the Teen Age selection, New York Public Library, all for *The Apprenticeship of Lucas Whitaker;* New York State Knickerbocker Award, 1998, for body of work; NCSS/CBC Notable Children's Trade Book in the Field of Social Studies designation, 1999, for *Nowhere to Call Home;* Texas Bluebonnet Award, and Iowa Children's Choice Award, both 2002, both for *The Ghost of Fossil Glen.*

Writings

JUVENILE NOVELS

The Strange Night Writing of Jessamine Colter, calligraphy by Leah Palmer Preiss, Macmillan (New York, NY), 1988.

Weasel, Macmillan (New York, NY), 1990.

Devil's Bridge, Macmillan (New York, NY), 1992.

The Light on Hogback Hill, Macmillan (New York, NY), 1993.

Lostman's River, Macmillan (New York, NY), 1994.

The Apprenticeship of Lucas Whitaker, Farrar, Straus & Giroux (New York, NY), 1996.

The Ghost of Fossil Glen, Farrar, Straus & Giroux (New York, NY), 1998.

Nowhere to Call Home, Farrar, Straus & Giroux (New York, NY), 1999.

Death at Devil's Bridge, Farrar, Straus & Giroux (New York, NY), 2000.

The Ghost and Mrs. Hobbs, Farrar, Straus & Giroux (New York, NY), 2001.

Under the Same Sky, Farrar, Straus & Giroux (New York, NY), 2003.

The Ghost of Cutler Creek, Farrar, Straus & Giroux (New York, NY), 2004.

The Missing Manatee, Farrar, Straus & Giroux (New York, NY), 2005.

Bringing Ezra Back, Farrar, Straus & Giroux (New York, NY), 2006.

PICTURE BOOKS

The Dancing Skeleton, illustrated by Robert Andrew Parker, Macmillan (New York, NY), 1989.

When Grampa Kissed His Elbow, illustrated by Karl Swanson, Macmillan (New York, NY), 1992.

Mule Eggs, illustrated by Mike Shenon, Orchard (New York, NY), 1994.

(Reteller, with Mary DeMarsh and others) *Three Perfect Peaches: A French Folktale,* illustrated by Irene Trivas, Orchard (New York, NY), 1995.

Casey in the Bath, illustrated by Chris L. Demarest, Farrar, Straus & Giroux (New York, NY), 1996.

Willy's Silly Grandma, illustrated by Shelley Jackson, Orchard (New York, NY), 1997.

Clever Crow, illustrated by S.D. Schindler, Atheneum (New York, NY), 1998.

Cold Feet, illustrated by Robert Andrew Parker, DK Ink (New York, NY), 2000.

The Real, True Dulcie Campbell, illustrated by R.W. Alley, Farrar, Straus & Giroux (New York, NY), 2002.

Old Granny and the Bean Thief, illustrated by Cat Bowman Smith, Farrar, Straus & Giroux (New York, NY), 2003.

One Potato, Two Potato, illustrated by Andrea U'Ren, Farrar, Straus & Giroux (New York, NY), 2006.

Sidelights

Praised for her talent as a storyteller as well as her writing skills, Cynthia DeFelice creates children's stories that are drawn from the folk tradition, American history, and contemporary society. Her books feature young people thrust into situations that require them to make vital decisions and assume responsibilities far beyond their years. In her picture books and novels, DeFelice mixes the elements of suspense, drama, and humor into "crackling good storytelling," as a *Publishers Weekly* reviewer described her efforts. Whether illuminating a past way of life for twenty-first-century readers in historical novels such as the award-winning *Weasel* and *The Apprenticeship of Lucas Whittaker* or highlighting the threats to Earth's ecosystem in *Lostman's River* and *Devil's Bridge,* DeFelice has as her primary concern the telling of a compelling story. "DeFelice knows how to make history come alive by providing characters who readers will find both realistic and sympathetic," maintained *Voice of Youth Advocates* contributor Cindy Lombardo, recommending titles by DeFelice that showcase epochs from nineteenth-and early-twentieth-century American history.

With his parents while they hide from the law in the Florida Everglades, Tyler learns to respect, and ultimately defend, the fragile ecosystem thanks to the Seminole people who live nearby in DeFelice's suspenseful novel, which takes place in 1905.

Born in Philadelphia, Pennsylvania, in 1951, DeFelice was raised in a Philadelphia suburb where she enjoyed a secure upbringing and inherited a strong storytelling tradition. As she once recalled, "my two brothers, my sister, and I would snuggle in Mom's lap while she read to us. She was a great storyteller and had this terrific sense of rhythm and timing. It was in that big, tan chair where we all used to curl up together that I learned to love stories and to feel their magic." DeFelice recalled her childhood as "pretty idyllic," with time spent either playing with her brothers or curled up in a chair somewhere, lost in a good book. Her psychiatrist father was also supportive of his daughter's interests. "You could tell him anything. So my early years were very nourishing."

Graduating from high school, DeFelice enrolled at William Smith College, located about forty miles southeast of Rochester, New York. She immediately fell in love with the region, and has lived there ever since. After graduating in 1973, she worked briefly as a barn painter; a year later she was married, and her two young stepchildren became her priority. Once her children were older, DeFelice enrolled at Syracuse University and earned an advanced degree in library science. Her job as a school librarian in Newark, New York ultimately sparked her interest in both storytelling and writing children's books.

DeFelice teamed up with music teacher Mary DeMarsh in a storytelling venture called the Wild Washerwomen, in which the two women told stories in schools throughout upstate New York. After these sessions, intrigued listeners often requested written versions of her tales. When DeFelice set about fulfilling this request, her career as a children's-book author began, and her first book, *The Strange Night Writing of Jessamine Colter,* was published in 1988.

The inspiration for her first novel came from a nightmare DeFelice had, in which, as she recalled, "I dreamed I saw my hand floating through space, come to rest at my desk, and then pen in perfect calligraphy, 'You are going to die tomorrow night at ten o'clock.'" In DeFelice's novel, a calligrapher named Jessie, who writes out the important notices for her small town, suddenly discovers that she has the ability to foretell the future through her writing. When she foretells her own death, Jessie passes on her knowledge of calligraphy and her strength to her young apprentice. Reviewing *The Strange Night Writing of Jessamine Colter*, a *Voice of Youth Advocates* critic called the novel "a simple, loving story," while in *Publishers Weekly* a reviewer noted the story's "wistful mood and . . . gently unwinding pace," adding that readers "will revel in its poetic language." Roger Sutton, writing in the *Bulletin of the Center for Children's Books,* dubbed the story "sentimental in the best sense."

Encouraged by the success of her first book, DeFelice left library work and embarked on a career as a full-time writer, continuing to alternate novels for older readers with picture books for the younger set. Her second novel, set in Ohio during the 1830s, benefited from the increased time DeFelice had to research. In *Weasel* readers meet Nathan, part of a pioneering family, who wakes one night to learn that a deranged former Indian hunter named Weasel has wounded Nathan's father. Vowing to avenge his father's attack, Nathan hunts down the violent and disturbed man, but when the opportunity to strike arises, he realizes that such violence would make him no better than the assailant he has been hunting.

Weasel earned both praise and commendations. Calling DeFelice's young protagonist "unforgettable," *School Library Journal* contributor Yvonne Frey praised the author for addressing race relations in a new way, by turning "the results of hate back on the white race itself." *Weasel* "makes a positive contribution to a world caught up with killing and revenge," Kathryn Hackler added in her *Voice of Youth Advocates* review, while a contributor to *Publishers Weekly* praised the author's "fast-paced" tale which "effectively conveys the battle

between good and evil." Nathan's story continues in *Bringing Ezra Back,* as the young man goes on a journey that teaches him a great deal about the measure of men.

Devil's Bridge takes place off the coast of Massachusetts in Martha's Vineyard. Twelve-year-old Ben Daggett hears two men scheming to cheat their way to the ten-thousand-dollar prize in the annual striped bass fishing derby by injecting an illegally caught fish with mercury to increase its weight. Before he perished in a hurricane the year before, Ben's fisherman father had set the record for the largest bass ever caught, and Ben does not want his father's accomplishments overshadowed by dishonest efforts. Since no one will listen to him when he attempts to divulge the men's scheme, Ben determines to catch the biggest fish himself. While he manages to hook the winning fish, Ben lets the creature go free at the last minute because he is unwilling to take its life. Praising the novel, *School Library Journal* contributor Louise L. Sherman dubbed it a "fast paced and involving" adventure yarn, while *Booklist* critic Janice Del Negro called Ben "an appealing main character." The novel's protagonist also appears in *Death at Devil's Bridge,* in which the thirteen-year-old Ben takes a job as first-mate on a fishing boat, only to find himself enmeshed in the illegal drug trade and possibly even murder. *School Library Journal* reviewer Renee Steinberg wrote that the "lively prose style, a plot that keeps readers wondering, and generally fleshed-out characters create a selection that will hook its target audience to the end."

A desire for justice is also the focus of *The Missing Manatee,* which takes place in coastal Florida, where eleven-year-old Skeet Waters discovers a huge manatee shot dead, its body beached on the rocks near the boy's fishing spot. When the body of the animal is secretly removed, Skeet dedicates himself to finding the killer of the endangered creature; Although he had planned to spend his time fishing, investigating the crime is a way of taking his mind off his parents' crumbling marriage. A few hours spent with Deadbeat Dan, his fishing-guide father's fishing buddy, soon provides the boy with clues as to the culprit. Noting that Skeet's narration "rings true," Allison Grant added in *School Library Journal* that in *The Missing Manatee* "DeFelice offers a realistic story that is fast paced and full of drama." In *Booklist* Todd Morning predicted that the author's focus on fly fishing "will grab young lovers of outdoor adventure," while in *Kliatt* Janis Flint-Ferguson noted the story's coming-of-age element, writing that Skeet ultimately learns "that growing up means learning to cope with things as they are and not as you want them to be."

Inspired by an newspaper article pointed out to DeFelice by her husband, *The Apprenticeship of Lucas Whitaker* concerns a young boy who goes to work for a local physician after his entire family dies of tuberculosis (TB). Once commonly known as "consumption," TB was a major cause of death prior to the turn of the twentieth century. Because of the wasting characteristics of the disease, some communities believed that the illness was transmitted by the newly dead, who, like vampires, spread the disease through entire households. Set in Connecticut during the mid-1800s, the novel finds twelve-year-old Lucas working for the town doctor. As he gains in medical knowledge, the boy is freed from a secret guilt: the folk remedy he failed to perform—digging up the body of the first member of his family to die of consumption, removing the heart, and burning it—would not have saved lives. Praising the novel's likeable main characters and its description of the harsh realities of farm life during the nineteenth century, *School Library Journal* contributor Jane Gardner Connor noted that "readers will experience a period when even a doctor's knowledge was very limited, and . . . will come to realize how fear and desperation can make people willing to try almost anything." In her *Horn Book* review of *The Apprenticeship of Lucas Whitaker*, Elizabeth S. Watson added that the novel's plot moves swiftly "in spite of a wealth of detail" about "health, hygiene, and witchcraft."

The loss of both parents is also a motivating factor in the life of twelve-year-old Frances Barrow in DeFelice's *Nowhere to Call Home.* When her father loses his Philadelphia-based business—as well as everything else—during the stock market crash of 1929, he commits suicide, leaving Frances an orphan. Determined to make her own way rather than live with a distant aunt, Frances disguises herself as a boy and travels west by jumping trains. "The dialogue rings true," *Voice of Youth Advocates* critic Cindy Lombardo noted, adding that the story's "fast pace . . . will keep readers turning pages until the poignant resolution." While setting her story in the past, DeFelice bridges the gap between her young protagonist and modern-day readers, according to *Horn Book* reviewer Margaret A. Bush. "The story is a good adventure," Bush maintained, "presenting readers with insights into homelessness quite relevant to our own time."

Basing her setting on the Finger Lakes region near her home in central New York, DeFelice brings a supernatural twist to a trio of novels featuring Allie Nichols, friend Dub, and canine companion Hoover. In *The Ghost of Fossil Glen*, while roaming the lands near her home Allie hears a ghostly whisper, and soon becomes haunted by the voice of Lucy, a girl who was murdered in that area four years earlier. Although Dub questions her sanity, Allie is determined to bring justice to the now-departed Lucy. *The Ghost and Mrs. Hobbs* picks up the action, as Allie attracts the attentions of a second spectre. The ghost this time around is a good-looking young man who gets Allie to help him seek what she thinks is justice; actually, she discovers almost too late that it is really vengeance this ghost is after. A local pet store becomes the focus of *The Ghost of Cutler Creek*, as Allie and Dub join Hoover in investigating mysterious goings on in their community, while also following their curiosity over a new boy in town. Praising *The*

Ghost of Fossil Glen as a "beautifully crafted thriller," *Booklist* contributor Lauren Peterson added that DeFelice creates an "expertly paced, dynamic page-turner that never gives readers the chance to become distracted or lose interest." "There's more than enough suspense in this well-told story," noted Sharon McNeil in a *School Library Journal* review of *The Ghost and Mrs. Hobbs,* adding that "Allie is a strong, likeable, believable character." A *Horn Book* critic deemed *The Ghost of Cutler Creek* "a gripping, suspenseful story," while in *School Library Journal* a reviewer again praised Allie and Dub as likeable protagonists, adding: "Mystery fans will not be disappointed."

While continuing to pen novels for middle-grade readers, DeFelice has also produced picture books, once explaining: "I enjoy doing both kinds of books. . . . But with picture books, every word has to count. It is more like writing poetry." Her first picture book, *The Dancing Skeleton,* focuses on the difficulties a widow faces when her deceased husband refuses to stay dead; he comes back to dance about when the widow's new suitor—a fiddler—comes a'courting. Like several of her

In this page-turning novel ghosthunter Allie tries to help the spirit of a murdered girl, only to find herself in hot water with her friend and in far greater danger from someone else . . . but who? (Cover illustration by David Bowers.)

picture books, *The Dancing Skeleton* is a retelling of a traditional folk tale. "These stories never get old for me," DeFelice once noted. "Even if I tell them a hundred times, I find something new in them, and looking at the faces in the audience is so much fun. The kids are like my editors: I know immediately when something works or doesn't." In praise of *The Dancing Skeleton*, Ellen D. Warwick wrote in *School Library Journal* that DeFelice's "rhythmic prose captures the vocabulary, tone, the very cadences of the oral tradition."

Other picture books by DeFelice include *Mule Eggs, Willy's Silly Grandma, Cold Feet,* and *The Real, True Dulcie Campbell.* In *Mule Eggs* a city slicker named Patrick moves to the country where, in addition to the challenges posed by farm life, has to contend with a local practical joker. *Willy's Silly Grandma* finds that grandmother's folk cures prove not to be as silly as people thought, and in *Cold Feet* a Scottish bagpiper takes the boots off a dead man in the forest one wintry night, only to have the feet snap off with them. Later, to avenge a slight, he places the thawed-out feet under a farmer's cow to make it appear the beast has eaten him. "DeFelice pitches this deliciously eerie tale in the kind of cadence and language that make for a grand read-aloud," wrote a *Publishers Weekly* reviewer, while *Horn Book* critic Robert Strang dubbed *Cold Feet* a "good choice for cold winter nights as well as Halloween." In another illustrated offering, an imaginative young farm girl's dreams of being a princess last only so long as the sun is out in *The Real, True Dulcie Campbell,* which a *Publishers Weekly* critic praised as "a smartly told story with a gentle moral."

Whether creating picture books or novels, DeFelice has the same basic goals. "I want to write a story to entertain, to engage the minds, hearts, and senses of young readers," she once stated. "I really think that kids are the most challenging audience to write for. They demand a satisfying story. They will not sit through something that does not please them." "I want my readers to come away from my books with a memory worth having," she also noted, "something that will enrich their lives and something that they might not otherwise have the chance to experience. But I don't like to tie up all the loose ends. I respect my readers and figure they will become part of the process if I don't answer all the questions for them. After all, life isn't like that. We can't know everything in real life. Why should we expect to in fiction?"

Biographical and Critical Sources

BOOKS

Authors and Artists for Young Adults, Volume 36, Thomson Gale (Detroit, MI), 2000.

PERIODICALS

Booklist, March 15, 1992, Karen Hutt, review of *When Grampa Kissed His Elbow,* pp. 1386-1387; December 1, 1992, Janice Del Negro, review of *Devil's Bridge,* p. 669; March 15, 1998, Lauren Peterson, review of *The Ghost of Fossil Glen,* p. 1243; August, 2000, Gillian Engberg, review of *Death at Devil's Bridge,* p. 2131; September 1, 2000, p. 112; December 1, 2000, p. 740; September 1, 2001, p. 103; March 1, 2005, Todd Morning, review of *The Missing Manatee,* p. 1193.

Book Report, September-October 1999, Catherine M. Andronik, review of *Nowhere to Call Home,* p. 59.

Bulletin of the Center for Children's Books, September, 1988, Roger Sutton, review of *The Strange Night Writing of Jessamine Colter,* p. 5; November, 1992, pp. 70-71; December, 1993, p. 79; June, 1994, p. 317; October, 1996, pp. 54-55; March, 1998, p. 240; May, 2003, review of *Under the Same Sky,* p. 358.

Horn Book, January-February, 1990, Elizabeth S. Watson, review of *The Dancing Skeleton,* pp. 75-76; March-April, 1994; January-February, 1997, Elizabeth S. Watson, review of *The Apprenticeship of Lucas Whitaker,* p. 55; March-April, 1999, Margaret A. Bush, review of *Nowhere to Call Home,* p. 207; September-October, 2000, Robert Strang, review of *Cold Feet,* p. 585; March-April, 2004, review of *The Ghost of Cutler Creek.*

Journal of Adolescent and Adult Literacy, May, 2000, Barbara Powell, review of *Nowhere to Call Home,* p. 778.

Kirkus Reviews, July 15, 1988, p. 1055; November 1, 1992, p. 1374; April 15, 2005, review of *The Missing Manatee,* p. 471.

Kliatt, March, 2005, Janis Flint-Ferguson, review of *The Missing Manatee,* p. 9; May, 2005, Paula Rohrlick, review of *Under the Same Sky,* p. 22.

Publishers Weekly, August 12, 1988, review of *The Strange Night Writing of Jessamine Colter,* pp. 460-61; April 27, 1990, review of *Weasel,* p. 62; September 7, 1992, review of *Devil's Bridge,* pp. 96-97; May 4, 1998, review of *Clever Crow,* p. 211; April 26, 1999, p. 84; September 4, 2000, review of *Cold Feet,* p. 108; July 16, 2001, p. 183; July 15, 2002, review of *The Real, True Dulcie Campbell,* p. 73; March 10, 2003, review of *Under the Same Sky,* p. 72.

School Library Journal, September, 1989, Ellen D. Warwick, review of *The Dancing Skeleton,* p. 239; May, 1990, Yvonne Frey, review of *Weasel,* pp. 103-104; August, 1992, p. 134; November, 1992, Louise L. Sherman, review of *Devil's Bridge,* pp. 88-89; August, 1996, Jane Gardner Connor, review of *The Apprenticeship of Lucas Whitaker,* p. 142; July, 1998, pp. 92-93; April, 1999, p. 113; September, 2000, Renee Steinberg, review of *Death at Devil's Bridge,* p. 228; September, 2000, p. 193; August, 2001, Sharon McNeil, review of *The Ghost and Mrs. Hobbs;* September, 2002, Ruth Semrau, review of *The Real, True Dulcie Campbell,* p. 183; March, 2003, Gerry Larson, review of *Under the Same Sky,* p. 232; August, 2003, Kathy Piehl, review of *Lostman's River,* p. 115; March, 2004, review of *The Ghost of Cutler Creek;*

June, 2005, Allison Grant, review of *The Missing Manatee,* p. 154.

Voice of Youth Advocates, April, 1989, review of *The Strange Night Writing of Jessamine Colter,* p. 26; June, 1990, Kathryn Hackler, review of *Weasel,* pp. 101-2; October, 1999, Cindy Lombardo, review of *Nowhere to Call Home,* p. 256; April, 2003, review of *Under the Same Sky,* p. 47; June, 2005, Barbara Johnston, review of *The Missing Manatee,* p. 126.

ONLINE

Cynthia DeFelice Home Page, http://www.cynthiadefelice.com (November 15, 2005).*

* * *

DeFELICE, Cynthia C.
See DeFELICE, Cynthia

* * *

DeLRIO, Martin
See DOYLE, Debra

* * *

DeLRIO, Martin
See MacDONALD, James D.

* * *

d'LACEY, Chris 1954-

Personal
Born December, 1954, in Valetta, Malta; married; wife's name, Jay. *Hobbies and other interests:* Playing electric guitar, writing songs.

Addresses
Home—Leicester, East Midlands, England. *Agent*—c/o Author Mail, Scholastic, Inc., 557 Broadway, New York, NY 10012. *E-mail*—ldc@le.ac.uk.

Career
Writer; Leicester University, Leicester, England, began as histologist, 1978, currently confocal microscopist.

Awards, Honors
Carnegie Medal nomination, 1999, for *Fly Cherokee Fly;* Rotherham Children's Book Award, for *The Fire Within;* honorary doctor of letters, University of Leicester, 2002; Leicester Book of the Year Award shortlist, 2005, for *Icefire;* Bolton Book of the Year Award shortlist, 2005, for *Horace.*

Chris d'Lacey

Writings

FOR CHILDREN

A Hole at the Pole, illustrated by Joanna Carey, Heinemann (London, England), 1994.

Juggling with Jeremy, illustrated by Gus Clarke, Heinemann (London, England), 1996.

Henry Spaloosh!, illustrated by Philip Reeve, Little Hippo (London, England), 1997.

Fly, Cherokee, Fly, Corgi (London, England), 1998.

A Break in the Chain, illustrated by Joanna Carey, Mammoth (London, England), 1998, Crabtree (New York, NY), 2002.

The Table Football League, illustrated by Philip Reeve, Little Hippo (London, England), 1998.

Snail Patrol, illustrated by Philip Reeve, Little Hippo (London, England), 1998.

Bubble and Float, illustrated by Nick Sharratt, Little Hippo (London, England), 1999.

Riverside United, illustrated by Mick Reid, Corgi (London, England), 1999.

Lofty, illustrated by Anna C. Leplar, Orchard (London, England), 1999.

Dexter's Journey, illustrated by David Roberts, Mammoth (London, England), 2000, Crabtree (New York, NY), 2002.

Scupper Hargreaves, Football Genie!, illustrated by Michael London, Corgi (London, England), 2000.

(With Linda Newbery) *From E to You,* Scholastic (London, England), 2000.

The Salt Pirates of Skegness, Orchard (London, England), 2001.

Pawnee Warrior, Yearling (London, England), 2002.

Falling 4 Mandy, Corgi (London, England), 2003.

The Prompter, illustrated by Ella Okstad, Young Corgi (London, England), 2003.

Franklin's Bear, illustrated by Thomas Taylor, Egmont (London, England), 2003, Crabtree (New York, NY), 2005.

Horace: A Teddy Bear Story, Corgi (London, England), 2004.

Shrinking Ralph Perfect, Orchard Books (London, England), 2005.

"DRAGON" SERIES

The Fire Within, Orchard (London, England), 2001, Orchard (New York, NY), 2005.

Icefire, Orchard (London, England), 2003, Orchard (New York, NY), 2005.

Fire Star, Orchard (London, England), 2005.

Short stories published in anthologies, including *Nice One, Santa: A Football Anthology,* Scholastic (London, England), 1998; and *On Me 'Ead, Santa,* Scholastic (London, England), 1999.

Author's works have been translated into German, Finnish, Italian, Japanese, Spanish, Greek, and Thai.

Sidelights

British writer Chris d'Lacey never intended to become a writer. In fact, as he recalled of his elementary-school experience on his home page, "my English teacher once told me that I didn't have a creative thought in my head." As a teenager, he dreamed of being a rock star, but he focused on science during college and eventually got a job in that field, working with microscopy at Leicester University. It was not until age thirty-two that d'Lacey wrote his first children's story; seven years later, he entered a competition in writing for young people. Although he did not win the prize, his story was accepted by a publisher and became the book *A Hole at the Pole.* D'Lacey has been writing for children ever since.

Many of d'Lacey's picture books and chapter books for young readers feature animals, although a plea from a young reader prompted him to also focus on human topics. During a visit to a primary school, "a young lad, not noted for his fascination with literature, pointed out forcefully that if only Chris wrote about football, he might just read it," Stewart Peterson explained during an awards presentation speech transcribed on the *Leicester University Web site.* Noting that all of his books have a humorous slant, d'Lacey commented on the *Leicester Writers Club Web site* that he writes about "polar bears, pigeons, squirrels, and, erm . . . snails."

When he discovers a collection of clay dragons that come to life, college student David becomes involved in a mystery that only he can solve in this 2001 fantasy. (Cover illustration by Angelo Rinaldi.)

D'Lacey's first novel for young readers is based on his experience rescuing an injured pigeon from a local park. He took the injured creature to a local veterinarian and, when the vet said there was no hope for the bird, d'Lacey kept the pigeon anyway, and nursed it back to health. *Fly, Cherokee, Fly* tells the story of a boy named Darryl, who finds an injured racing pigeon. Darryl wants the bird to get better and hopes he will be able to return it to its rightful owner. However, when the boy discovers that the owner might kill the bird if it is unable to race, he decides to keep the pigeon himself, and consequently finds himself in a peck of trouble. *Fly, Cherokee, Fly* was nominated for the Carnegie Medal, Britain's most prominent prize for juvenile fiction. *Pawnee Warrior* continues Darryl's story, and finds the boy determined to protect a baby pigeon.

From E to You, a novel written entirely in e-mail format, is a collaboration between d'Lacey and writer Linda Newbery. In the story Guy and Annabelle are encouraged by their fathers to write to each other, even though they have never met. In a twist from similar boy-girl collaborations, Newbery writes in the voice of teenager Guy while d'Lacey narrates events from the perspective of Annabelle. In the resulting story, despite their initial grumbling, the two teens begin to form a solid friendship and ultimately help each other deal with the struggles in their lives. According to a reviewer for *Publishers Weekly,* the authors "have shaped two very distinct and likable characters and a cleverly composite tale."

Some of d'Lacey's most popular titles are in his "Dragon" series, which begins with *The Fire Within.* David Rain, a college student, finds lodging with Mrs. Pennykettle, who makes ceramic dragons, and the woman's daughter, Lucy. Though David does not intend to become involved with the family, Lucy convinces the new lodger to aid her in a quest to find and help an injured squirrel. Their quest leads David to some interesting discoveries about the Pennykettle family and about their mysterious pets—dragons! "D'Lacey mixes up a lovely bag of dragons, squirrels, and a strangely appropriate adult protagonist," reported a contributor to *Kirkus Reviews.*

David's adventures with dragons continue in *Icefire,* in which he must travel to the Arctic and the local polar-bear population in order to discover an important secret about the dragons and also about the evil sibyl who wishes the creatures harm. The series concludes with *Fire Star,* in which David and the Pennykettles face the sibyl, hoping to prevent the evil creature from bringing a real dragon to life.

When not writing books or working as a university-based scientist, d'Lacey makes school visits as a way of getting to know his readers. He explained on his Web site, "I think this is one of the best things about being an author. It's really brilliant to see [children in the classes I visit] all getting excited about making up stories. It makes me feel I am doing a good job."

Biographical and Critical Sources

PERIODICALS

Kirkus Reviews, May 1, 2005, review of *The Fire Within,* p. 537.

Publishers Weekly, June 25, 2001, review of *From E to You,* p. 73.

Resource Links, April, 2002, review of *Dexter's Journey,* p. 13; February, 2003, review of *A Break in the Chain,* p. 21.

School Librarian, summer, 1999, review of *The Table Football League,* p. 80; spring, 2000, review of *Riverside United,* p. 23; autumn, 2000, review of *From E to You,* p. 156; summer, 2002, review of *The Fire Within,* p. 79, and review of *Pawnee Warrior,* p. 100; autumn, 2002, review of *The Salt Pirates of Skegness,* p. 136; autumn, 2003, review of *Falling 4 Mandy,* p. 154; winter, 2003, review of *Icefire,* p. 209; summer, 2004, Cliff Moon, review of *The Prompter,* p. 80; winter, 2004, Nansi Taylor, review of *Horace,* p. 214.

School Library Journal, August, 2002, Kathleen Simonetta, review of *Dexter's Journey,* p. 146.

Voice of Youth Advocates, December, 2001, review of *From E to You,* p. 351.

ONLINE

Canadian Review of Materials, http://www.umanitoba.ca/cm/ (November 1, 2002), review of *Dexter's Journey.*

Chris d'Lacey Home Page, http://www.chris.dlacey.btinternet.co.uk (October 26, 2005).

Egmont Publisher Web site, http://www.egmont.co.uk/ (October 26, 2005).

Leicester Writers' Club Web site, http://www.leicesterwriter.org.uk/ (October 26, 2005).

University of Leicester Web site, http://www.le.ac.uk/ (October 26, 2005), "Chris d'Lacey."

*   *   *

DOYLE, Debra 1952-
(Nicholas Adams, a joint pseudonym, Victor Appleton, a joint pseudonym, Martin Delrio, a joint pseudonym, Douglas Morgan, a joint pseudonym, Robyn Tallis, a joint pseudonym)

Personal

Born 1952, in FL; married James D. Macdonald (a writer and former navy officer), August 5, 1978; children: Katherine, Brendan, Peregrine, Alexander. *Education:* University of Pennsylvania, Ph.D. (English literature); also educated in Florida, Texas, and Arkansas.

Addresses

Home—127 Main St., Colebrook, NH 03576. *Agent*—Valerie Smith, 1746 Rte, 44-55, Modena, NY 12548. *E-mail*—doylemacdonald@sff.net.

Career

Writer. Computer-assisted Learning Center, teacher of fiction writing.

Awards, Honors

Mythopoeic Society Aslan Award for young-adult literature, 1992, and Books for the Teen Age selection, New York Public Library, 1993, both for *Knight's Wyrd;* Best Young-Adult Science Fiction Award, *Science Fiction Chronicle,* 1997, for *Groogleman.*

Writings

NOVELS, UNLESS OTHERWISE NOTED; WITH HUSBAND JAMES D. MACDONALD

(Under pseudonym Robyn Tallis) *Night of Ghosts and Lightning* ("Planet Builders" series), Ivy, 1989.

(Under pseudonym Robyn Tallis) *Zero-Sum Games* ("Planet Builders" series), Ivy, 1989.

(Under pseudonym Nicholas Adams) *Pep Rally* ("Horror High" series), Harper (New York, NY), 1991.

(Under pseudonym Victor Appleton) *Monster Machine* ("Tom Swift" series), Pocket Books (New York, NY), 1991.

(Under pseudonym Victor Appleton) *Aquatech Warriors* ("Tom Swift" series), Pocket Books (New York, NY), 1991.

Timecrime, Inc. ("Robert Silverberg's 'Time Tours'" series), Harper (New York, NY), 1991.

Night of the Living Rat ("Daniel Pinkwater's 'Melvinge of the Megaverse'" series), Ace Books (New York, NY), 1992.

Knight's Wyrd, Harcourt, Brace (New York, NY), 1992.

Groogleman, Harcourt, Brace (New York, NY), 1996.

Requiem for Boone (based on the television series *Gene Roddenberry's Earth—Final Conflict*), Tor (New York, NY), 2000.

(As Douglas Morgan) *Tiger Cruise,* Forge (New York, NY), 2001.

(As Douglas Morgan) *What Do You with a Drunken Sailor?* (nonfiction), Swordsmith, 2002.

NOVELS; "CIRCLE OF MAGIC" SERIES; WITH JAMES D. MACDONALD

School of Wizardry, Troll (Metuchen, NJ), 1990.

Tournament and Tower, Troll (Metuchen, NJ), 1990.

City by the Sea, Troll (Metuchen, NJ), 1990.

The Prince's Players, Troll (Metuchen, NJ), 1990.

The Prisoners of Bell Castle, Troll (Metuchen, NJ), 1990.

The High King's Daughter, Troll (Metuchen, NJ), 1990.

Several "Circle of Magic" books have been translated into Spanish.

NOVELS; "MAGEWORLD" SERIES; WITH JAMES D. MACDONALD

The Price of the Stars, Tor Books (New York, NY), 1992.

Starpilot's Grave, Tor (New York, NY), 1993.

By Honor Betray'd, Tor (New York, NY), 1994.

The Gathering Flame, Tor (New York, NY), 1995.

The Long Hunt, Tor (New York, NY) 1996.

The Stars Asunder, Tor (New York, NY) 1999.

A Working of Stars, Tor (New York, NY), 2002.

NOVELS; "BAD BLOOD" SERIES; WITH JAMES D. MACDONALD

Bad Blood, Berkley (New York, NY), 1993.

Hunters' Moon, Berkley (New York, NY), 1994.

Judgment Night, Berkley (New York, NY), 1995.

UNDER JOINT PSEUDONYM MARTIN DELRIO; WITH JAMES D. MACDONALD

Mortal Kombat (movie novelization), Tor (New York, NY), 1995.

Midnight Justice ("Spider-Man Super-Thriller" series), Byron Preiss (New York, NY), 1996.

Global War ("Spider-Man Super-Thriller" series), Byron Press (New York, NY), 1996.

Harold R. Foster's Prince Valiant (movie novelization), Avon (New York, NY), 1998.

The Loch Ness Monster (nonfiction), Rosen Publishing (New York, NY), 2002.

A Silence in the Heavens (novel; "MechWarrior: Dark Age" series), Roc (New York, NY), 2003.

Truth and Shadows (novel; "MechWarrior: Dark Age" series), Roc (New York, NY), 2003.

Service for the Dead (novel; "MechWarrior: Dark Age" series), Roc (New York, NY), 2003.

OTHER

Contributor (with James D. Macdonald) of short stories to anthologies, including *Werewolves,* edited by Jane Yolen and Martin Greenberg, Harper Junior Books, 1988; *Vampires,* edited by Yolen and Greenberg, HarperCollins, 1991; *Newer York,* edited by Lawrence Watt-Evans, Roc, 1991; *Alternate Kennedys,* edited by Mike Resnick and Greenberg, Tor, 1992; *Bruce Coville's Book of Monsters,* edited by Coville, Scholastic, 1993; *Swashbuckling Editor Stories,* edited by John Betancourt, Wildside Press, 1993; *Bruce Coville's Book of Ghosts,* edited by Coville, Scholastic, 1994; *A Wizard's Dozen,* edited by Michael Stearns, Harcourt, Brace, 1995; *A Starfarer's Dozen,* edited by Stearns, Harcourt, Brace, 1995; *Witch Fantastic,* edited by Mike Resnick and Greenberg, DAW Books, 1995; *Camelot,* edited by Yolen, Philomel, 1995; *The Book of Kings,* edited by Richard Gilliam and Greenberg, Roc, 1995; *Tales of the Knights Templar,* edited by Katherine Kurtz, Warner, 1995; *Otherwere,* edited by Laura Anne Gilman and Keith R.A. DeCandido, Berkley/Ace, 1996; *A Nightmare's Dozen,* edited by Stearns, Harcourt, Brace, 1996; *Bruce Coville's Book of Spine Tinglers,* edited by Coville, Scholastic, 1996; *High-Tech Wars #2,* edited by Jerry Pournelle and John F. Carr; *On Crusade: More Tales of the Knights Templar,* edited by Katherine Kurz, Warner, 1998; *Not of Woman Born,* edited by Constance Ash, Roc, 1999; *The First Heroes: New Tales of the Bronze Age,* edited by Harry Turtledove, Tor, 2004; *Murder by Magic,* edit by Rosemary Edghill, Warner, 2004; *New Magics,* edited by Patrick Nielsen Hayden, 2004; and *Cosmic Tales: Adventures in Far Futures,* edited by T.K.F. Weisskopf, Baen Books, 2005. Contributor to *Timewalker* comic-book series, Valiant Comics, 1995.

Sidelights

Together with her husband, writer James D. Macdonald, Debra Doyle has become known for such award-winning science fiction as *Knight's Wyrd* as well as for the long-running sci-fi/fantasy series "Mageworld," which features the novels *The Price of the Stars, The Long Hunt,* and *A Working of Stars.* Dedicated to their craft, the couple produced six young-adult fantasy nov-

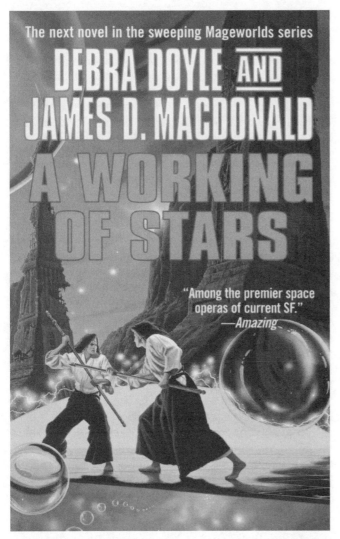

One of many novels Doyle has written in collaboration with her husband, this work finds Arekhon traveling home to repair relations with his brother, only to discover ongoing preparations for galactic war. (Cover illustration by Romus.)

els for their "Circle of Magic" series during 1990 alone, and they have published under a variety of pseudonyms as well as their own names. Praising the continuing work of what he dubbed "the prolific Doyle-Macdonald collaboration," *Booklist* reviewer Roland Green praised the "Mageworld" novel *A Working of Stars* as part of a series that comprises "imaginative, intelligent, fast-paced space opera, in the positive sense of the term."

Raised in Florida, Doyle eventually earned her doctorate in Old English literature at the University of Pennsylvania. While living and studying in Philadelphia, she met her future husband, who was then serving in the U.S. Navy, where he rose in rank from enlisted man to officer during a fifteen-year career. During Macdonald's military career, the couple traveled to Virginia, California, and Panama, eventually settling to raise their four children in a nineteenth-century Victorian house in New Hampshire.

Macdonald once described the unique working arrangement he and Doyle have devised to aid their effective collaboration, telling *SATA:* "Years ago, before we started writing together, Doyle and I noticed that we had some characteristic weaknesses. Doyle's prose style is very good, but her plotting is straight-line predictable. I do pretty decent plots, but my prose is deepest purple. So we got together, and now I plot while Doyle proses. My outlines . . . are about eighty percent of the length of the eventual finished work. They read like someone telling about a movie. Fast, slangy, self-referential, with the characters and backgrounds lightly sketched in. Doyle takes this and fleshes it out, adding additional dialog, fuller descriptions, transition scenes, and so on. Then I take her output, add missing parts, trim and move other scenes, and otherwise mess with the structure. By the time we're done, usually a fourth or fifth draft, we're handing individual sheets of paper back and forth between us, scribbling, drawing arrows, and coming to some kind of consensus. We don't argue about things: Doyle has the final say on words, I have the final say on plot."

Using this back-and-forth arrangement, the couple have produced dozens of stories and novels for adults, young adults, and children during their long career. Sometimes using pseudonyms such as Douglas Morgan, Robyn Tallis, or Martin Delrio, they have contributed to fantasy and science-fiction novel series, produced novelizations of films, television series, computer games, and comic books, and authored books within series created by other writers, namely Robert Silverberg and Daniel Pinkwater.

The "Circle of Magic" chronicles the story of Randal, who hopes to become a wizard. In *School of Wizardry* twelve-year-old Randal becomes an apprentice into the famous Schola Sorceriae (School of Wizardry), but must conquer numerous enemies on his way to becoming a master wizard. *Tournament and Tower* Randal graduates but, prohibited from using his magic powers, becomes a squire to his cousin Walter. When Walter sustains life-threatening injuries during a tournament, Randal must work to retain his magic power to help his friend. In *City by the Sea* Randal makes a promise to a dying man that sends him on a quest, while in *The Prince's Players* Randal and friend encounter a master wizard with diabolical plans. *The High King's Daughter* finishes up the series, as Randal and his friends journey into Elfland to rescue Diamante, the High King's daughter, and restore her to her rightful throne.

Like the "Circle of Magic" books, many of Doyle and Macdonald's other books appeal to teen readers. Noteworthy among their fiction works are two young-adult novels that the couple wrote as solo projects unconnected to any series. *Knight's Wyrd,* published in 1992, is a knights-in-armor fantasy involving magic, while *Groogleman* focuses on a teen living in a quasi-medieval future culture that develops in a post-apocalypse Earth. In *Knight's Wyrd* young Will Odosson must find his wyrd—his fate. When he discovers that his destiny is doom, Will journeys bravely to meet it, with complex and adventurous results. The New York Public Library listed this novel as one of its Books for the Teen Age in 1993, and the novel also won a Mythopoeic fantasy award. A *Kirkus Reviews* critic commended *Knight's Wyrd* for its "strong sense of time, place, and code of honor," while *Voice of Youth Advocates* contributor Jennifer A. Long asserted: "Strong main characters and a smoothly written plot make this a hard book to put down."

Groogleman takes place in some unspecified future that follows the technological collapse of civilization as we know it. Young hero Dan Henchard possesses weller's blood, an inherited immunity to the plague that is claiming the lives of many. A stranger named Joshua eventually joins Dan at his farm, and the two, along with another "weller," Leezie, travel to a nearby village to help plague victims in need of assistance. Upon arrival they find that the area has been terrorized by the mysterious grooglemen, and these creatures ultimately kidnap Leezie. Joshua claims to know which way the grooglemen have traveled, and he leads Dan on a arduous search to recover his friend. Reviewing the novel for *School Library Journal,* Susan L. Rogers called it a "successful" example of its genre, explaining that "Dan and Joshua quickly become sympathetic and interesting characters on a desperate journey through a foreboding landscape." Janice M. Del Negro, writing in the *Bulletin of the Center for Children's Books,* admired Doyle and Macdonald's ability to convey the sensory qualities of the setting and dubbed Dan "a believable adolescent in a grimly dangerous situation." Commending the way in which the authors created a vivid, convincing alternate culture in *Groogleman,* Del Negro stated that "This intriguing novel suggests more than it reveals and could provoke some thoughtful group discussion."

Doyle and Macdonald's popular "Mageworld" series, begun in 1992 with *The Price of the Stars,* focuses on a centuries-long conflict between the Republic, with its human population, and the mysterious Mageworld. Shocked by the murder of her famous mother, Beka Rosselin-Metadi gains strength from her family's strong legacy of courage and leadership. After she vows to bring the assassin to justice, Beka takes command of her father's starship, *Warhammer,* and, adopting a new identity, begins her conquest of the dangerous enemies of the galaxy. Her search continues through out other novels in the series, including *Starpilot's Grave,* which reveals the threat posed by the Magelords as they breach the Republic's stronghold. While the Magelords leave the Republic floundering in *By Honor Betray'd,* Beka rebuilds what she can from the wreckage of her world.

Beka's parents' contributions to the battle against the Magelords is the focus of *The Gathering Flame,* which takes readers back in time to the growing battle between the kingdoms on both sides of the interstellar void called the Sundering. Drawing readers further back in time, Doyle and Macdonald present another "prequel" with *The Stars Asunder,* which focuses on the origins of the war between rival mages five centuries before Beka's birth, as the competition between two apprentice mages, Garrod, and Rekhe, is sparked after their shared universe and Mage Circle is fractured and each finds himself a leader of a competing world. The history of these competing cultures continues in *A Working of Stars,* as the fragmented Mage Circle shows signs of being reformed through the efforts of its strong-willed mage Arekhon to complete the unfinished cycle known as the Great Working, which will rejoin Mageworld and the Republic. Writing in *Locus,* Carolyn Cushman called the "Mageworld" series "a space opera with unusual depth, and some wonderful characters." While noting that the series is difficult to penetrate due to the lengthy names and long cast of characters, *Bookloons* online contributor Wesley Williamson praised the "Mageworld" sequence during a review of *A Working of Stars,* writing that Doyle and Macdonald "have an interesting and exciting tale to tell and the tell it very well indeed."

Based on a television series, this novel delves into the past of William Boone, whose position as confident to the alien Taelons during their takeover of Earth covers his true role as a leader of the human Resistance. (Cover illustration by Cliff Nielson.)

Biographical and Critical Sources

PERIODICALS

Analog Science Fiction and Fact, February, 1999, Tom Easton, review of *The Stars Asunder,* p. 132; October, 2002, Tom Easton, review of *A Working of Stars,* p. 311.
Booklist, November 15, 1992, pp. 589-590; August, 2000, Roland Green, review of *Requiem for Boone,* p. 2124; April 15, 2002, Roland Green, review of *A Working of Stars,* p. 1387.
Bulletin of the Center for Children's Books, February, 1993, pp. 173-174; December, 1996, Janice M. Del Negro, review of *Groogleman,* p. 132.
Horn Book, January-February, 1993, review of *Knight's Wyrd,* pp. 89-90; March-April, 1996, p. 202.
Kirkus Reviews, October 1, 1992, review of *Knight's Wyrd,* p. 1253; March 1, 2002, review of *A Working of Stars,* p. 297.
Library Journal, June 15, 1999, Jackie Cassada, review of *The Stars Asunder,* p. 112; April 15, 2002, Jackie Cassada, review of *A Working of Stars,* p. 127.
Locus, August, 1995.
Publishers Weekly, May 31, 2000, review of *The Stars Asunder,* p. 72; August 7, 2000, review of *Requiem for Boone,* p. 80; March 11, 2002, review of *A Working of Stars,* p. 56.
Realms of Fantasy, April, 1997, review of *Groogleman.*
School Library Journal, November, 1992, p. 90; December, 1996, Susan L. Rogers, review of *Groogleman,* pp. 120, 122; April 2002, Paul M. Kienlen, review of *School of Wizardry,* p. 63; November, 2002, review of *A Working of Stars,* p. 194.
Science Fiction Chronicle, April-May, 1997, review of *Groogleman.*
Voice of Youth Advocates, June, 1993, Jennifer A. Long, review of *Knight's Wyrd,* p. 102; June, 2001, review of *Requiem of Boone,* p. 132.

ONLINE

BookLoons, http://www.bookloons.com/ (October 20, 2005), Wesley Williamson, review of *A Working of Stars.*
Doyle and Macdonald Home Page, http://www.sff.net/people/doylemacdonald (October 20, 2005).
SFSite, http://www.sfsite.com/ (October 20, 2005), Rich Horton, review of *The Stars Asunder.**

*   *   *

DOYLE, Malachy 1954-

Personal

Born June 30, 1954, in Carrickfergus, County Antrim, Northern Ireland; son of Conan Doyle (a sales representative) and Eileen (Dempsey) Doyle; married Liz Townsend-Rose (an artist), August 6, 1977; children:

Malachy Doyle

Naomi, Hannah, Liam. *Education:* Bolton Institute of Technology, B.A. (with honors), 1975; Shenstone New College, postgraduate certificate in education, 1976. *Hobbies and other interests:* Walking, cycling, reading, theater and music.

Addresses

Agent—Celia Catchpole Ltd., 56 Gilpin Ave., East Sheen, London SW14 8QY, England. *E-mail*—malachy@malachy.plus.com.

Career

Rowntree Mackintosh, York, England, media controller, 1976-81; General Foods, Banbury, England, media controller, 1981-84; Highmead Special School, Llanybydder, Wales, care assistant, 1984-91; Aran Hall School, Dolgellau, Wales, deputy head, 1991-94; Coleg Powys, Newtown, Wales, lecturer in sociology and psychology, 1994-96; Coleg Ceredigion, Aberystwyth, Wales, lecturer in sociology, 1994-97; writer of children's books, 1994—.

Member

Welsh Academy.

Awards, Honors

Arts Council of Northern Ireland Literature Award, 1997; shortlisted, Children's Book Award, and shortlisted, Tir na n-Og Award, both 2001, both for *Owen and the Mountin;* Parents' Choice Gold Award, and Bisto Award shortlist, both 2001, and Anne Izard Storytellers' Choice Award, 2003, all for *Tales from Old Ireland;* shortlisted, Lancashire Children's Book Award, shortlisted, Angus Award, and Tir na n-Og Award, all 2002, all for *Georgie;* English Association Award for Nonfiction, 2002, for *Cow;* shortlisted, Bisto Award, and shortlisted, South Lanarkshire Book Award, both 2003, both for *Who Is Jesse Flood?;* shortlisted, Tir na n-Og Award, 2003, for *Lake of Shadows;* shortlisted, Nestlé Children's Book Award, 2005, for *The Dancing Tiger.*

Writings

The Children of Nuala, illustrated by Amanda Harvey, Faber (London, England), 1998.

Farewell to Ireland: A Tale of Emigration to America, illustrated by Greg Gormley, Franklin Watts (London, England), 1998.

The Great Hunger: A Tale of Famine in Ireland, illustrated by Greg Gormley, Franklin Watts (London, England), 1998.

Little People, Big People, illustrated by Jac Jones, Faber (London, England), 1998.

The Changeling, illustrated by Jac Jones, Pont Readalone (Llandysul, Wales), 1999.

The Great Castle of Marshmangle, illustrated by Paul Hess, Andersen Press (London, England), 1999.

Jody's Beans, illustrated by Judith Allibone, Candlewick (Cambridge, MA), 1999.

12,000 Miles from Home, illustrated by Greg Gormley, Franklin Watts (London, England), 1999.

Well, a Crocodile Can!, illustrated by Britta Teckentrup, Frances Lincoln (London, England), 1999, Millbrook Press (Minneapolis, MN), 2000.

Tales from Old Ireland, illustrated by Niamh Sharkey, Barefoot Books (Cambridge, MA), 2000.

Hungry! Hungry! Hungry!, illustrated by Paul Hess, Andersen Press (London, England), 2000, Peachtree (Atlanta, GA), 2001.

Owen and the Mountain, illustrated by Giles Greenfield, Bloomsbury (London, England), 2000.

Carrot Thompson, Record Breaker, illustrated by Leonard O'Grady, Poolbeg (Dublin, Ireland), 2000.

Just-the-Same Jamie, illustrated by Shane O'Meara, Poolbeg (Dublin, Ireland), 2000.

Hero, Toffer, and Wallaby, illustrated by Jan Nesbitt, Pont Books (Llandysul, Wales), 2000.

Tales from Old Ireland, illustrated by Niamh Sharkey, Barefoot Books (Cambridge, MA), 2000.

Joe's Bike Race, illustrated by Michelle Conway, Poolbeg (Dublin, Ireland), 2001.

The Bold Boy, illustrated by Jane Ray, Candlewick (Cambridge, MA), 2001.

Georgie, Bloomsbury (New York, NY), 2001.

Baby See, Baby Do!, illustrated by Britta Teckentrup, Penguin Putnam (New York, NY), 2001.

Billy and the Bees, illustrated by Sandra Elsweiler, Poolbeg (Dublin, Ireland), 2002.

Lake of Shadows, illustrated by Jac Jones, Pont Books (Llandysul, Wales), 2002.

Storm Cats, illustrated by Stuart Trotter, Margaret K. McElderry (New York, NY), 2002.

Sleepy Pendoodle, illustrated by Julie Vivas, Candlewick (Cambridge, MA), 2002.

Riley, Kylie, and Smiley, illustrated by Fran Evans, Pont Books (Llandysul, Wales), 2002.

Cow, illustrated by Angelo Rinaldi, Margaret K. McElderry (New York, NY), 2002.

Who Is Jesse Flood?, Bloomsbury (New York, NY), 2002.

Antonio on the Other Side of the World, Getting Smaller, illustrated by Carll Cneut, Candlewick (Cambridge, MA), 2003.

The Ugly Great Giant, illustrated by David Lucas, Orchard (London, England), 2003.

Long Grey Norris, illustrated by Sholto Walker, Egmont (London, England), 2003.

Una and the Sea-Cloak, illustrated by Alison Jay, Frances Lincoln (London, England), 2004.

One, Two, Three O'Leary, illustrated by Will Hillenbrand, Margaret K. McElderry (New York, NY), 2004.

Splash, Joshua, Splash!, illustrated by Ken Wison-Max, Bloomsbury (New York, NY), 2004.

Teddybear Blue, illustrated by Christina Bretschneider, Frances Lincoln (London, England), 2004.

Amadans, Orchard (London, England), 2004.

Amadans Alert, Orchard (London, England), 2005.

The Dancing Tiger, illustrated by Steve Johnson and Lou Fancher, Viking (New York, NY), 2005.

The Barefoot Book of Fairy Tales, illustrated by Nicoletta Ceccoli, Barefoot Books (Cambridge, MA), 2005.

Doyle's works have been translated into Scottish Gaelic, French, Italian, Greek, German, Dutch, Finnish, Danish, Korean, Spanish, Catalan, Japanese, Swedish, Portuguese, and Welsh.

Sidelights

Since launching his career as a children's author in the 1990s, Malachy Doyle has enjoyed success in both the United Kingdom and the United States. His early works included some instructive, entertaining presentations of Irish and British colonial history, while many of his more recent books adapt Irish legends in a fresh retelling. Doyle once recounted to *SATA* his path to becoming a writer: "I was born in Carrickfergus, Northern Ireland, in 1954. My parents had recently moved up from Dublin and named me, their seventh child, after a local saint. We lived in Whitehead, a small town at the mouth of Belfast Lough, all my childhood. I went to secondary school (St. Malachy's College) in Belfast, and then to Bolton, Lancashire, to take a degree in psychology.

"I taught in Leeds for a year, followed by six months packing Polo Mints. I then worked for seven long years in advertising, firstly for Rowntree Mackintosh in York and later for General Foods in Banbury, before buying a smallholding in West Wales. To feed my wife, Liz, our three young children, Naomi, Hannah, and Liam, and numerous goats, pigs and chickens, I took a job as a care assistant in a local residential special school. For the next seven years I darned socks, patched jeans and generally looked after the children there, before being offered the post of deputy head at another special school. We moved to Machynlleth, a small town on the edge of the Snowdonia National Park, and three years later I began to write for children.

"It took me forty years to become a writer. Forty years of growing up, selling coffee, teaching, raising children, goats and pigs. From Ireland, through England, to Wales. I'm finally doing it—writing.

"I didn't know I was a writer. I knew I loved words, loved books. I knew I could tell stories, write the occasional soppy love poem, ramble on in long letters to my Dad back home in Ireland.

"But then, back in 1994, for want of a better way to while away the long Welsh winter, I enrolled in a creative writing evening class. 'Write about your childhood,' said Anna. 'Remember how it felt, how it smelt . . .' So I wrote a piece about my mother's button box. I brought it in the next week and read it out loud. Anna seemed to like it.

"'Okay,' I thought. 'That's what I'll do. I'll pack in this teaching lark and become a writer, a writer for children.' And here I am.

"I write about things that matter to me. About relationships—children, parents, grandparents. About animals. I try to recapture some of the joy, the freedom, the curiosity, imagination, and humour of my early childhood. I often draw on folk tale because it's part of me—I was brought up on it."

Doyle spends a lot of time editing his work, sometimes rewriting a piece more than a hundred times. When his first book was bought by a publisher, he was incredibly excited. As he recalled on his home page, "When I sold *Owen and the Mountain,* my first picture book story, to Bloomsbury, I was delighted. I ran up to the top of the hill behind my house and did a little dance. Then I came back down and counted the number of times I'd rewritten the story—I'd kept all the print-outs off the computer. It's only 800 words long and I'd written it 187 times! It's become a habit now—every time I sell a new story, I always have to run up the nearest hill and do a little dance."

In 1998, Doyle's retelling of a classic Irish folk tale appeared. Titled *The Children of Nuala,* the story is one of misfortune: a stepfather finds a way to make his

A little boy's visit to a grandmother living far, far away is cut short when he begins to shrink in the imaginative picture book Antonio on the Other Side of the World, Getting Smaller. *(Illustration by Carll Cneut.)*

wife's children disappear, but then feels remorseful. His wife still loves him, however, and in the end the children return. "Although this is a melancholy tale it is well-written and contains a strong message without preaching," wrote Annette Dale-Meiklejohn in *Magpies.*

Doyle has authored other tales inspired by Welsh and Irish folklore, including *Sleepy Pendoodle, Antonio on the Other Side of the World, Getting Smaller,* and *One, Two Three O'Leary.* In *Sleepy Pendoodle* a little girl is frustrated when her puppy will not open his eyes. Her grandfather gives her a rhyme to repeat to help the puppy wake up, but she manages to get it wrong in increasingly silly attempts. The book is "chock full of warm sentiment and playful language," according to a *Kirkus Reviews* contributor. "The straightforward story line is leavened by playful language and silly endearments," making it "pure pleasure to read aloud," wrote Carol Ann Wilson in *School Library Journal,* while *Booklist* contributor Connie Fletcher dubbed *Sleepy Pendoodle* "a laugh-inducing tale."

Young Antonio is the star of *Antonio on the Other Side of the World, Getting Smaller.* Though he loves visiting his grandmother, during his visit he begins to shrink.

She explains that this is happening because he misses his mother and sends him home—but he continues to get smaller along the way, causing several adventures until his mother sees him and feeds him back up to normal size. "With a straight face and even tone, Doyle . . . unspools an outlandishly picaresque plot," wrote a *Publishers Weekly* contributor. Abby Nolan, writing for *Booklist*, complimented Doyle's "bright, silly storytelling" while *School Library Journal* reviewer Catherine Threadgill noted that, "in the end, the story is all about perspective, and how the world can look pretty big through the eyes of a small child."

One, Two, Three O'Leary is a bedtime story told entirely in nonsense words drawn from traditional Irish rhymes. After each rhyme, one of the ten O'Leary children spills out of bed and onto the floor, until their parents finally come up, join the fun, and then put them all to bed. "In spite of the high energy, this has a comfortable feel," wrote a contributor to *Kirkus Reviews,* while a *Publishers Weekly* reviewer called the book a "dandy collection of ditties." Noting that it makes for a "boisterous bedtime story," Wanda Meyers-Hines of *School Library Journal* advised parents that "the tongue-twisting text will have kids laughing out loud." Doyle has also collected folktales into collections, such as *Tales from Old Ireland* and the *Barefoot Book of Fairy Tales. Tales from Old Ireland* features seven folk tales retold by Doyle and combined into an "excellent and enthusiastically recommended" collection, according to a reviewer for *Children's Bookwatch.*

Among Doyle's books that are not based on legend, *Jody's Beans* has a universal appeal. The story begins when Jody's grandfather visits, and together the two plant scarlet runner beans in the garden. Over the summer growing season, the two meet regularly, or speak on the phone about their project. To answer Jody's sometimes anxious inquiries, the grandfather likes to remind her, "Wait and see." Doyle manages to provide basic gardening lessons through this format, and when the beans are harvested, some cooking tips are provided as well. A *Publishers Weekly* review commended "Doyle's winningly spare narration," and other reviewers remarked upon the nice parallel plot concerning Jody's mother, who is expecting a baby. "The cozy tale of everyday events . . . is very satisfying," remarked *Horn Book* reviewer Margaret A. Bush. Another original offering, *Cow,* is less a story book than a description of what life is like for a cow. Though the cow thinks its existence is hard, one will be in on the joke of how little the cow has to do. "Doyle is plainly envious, as will be readers when they meander through these pages," commented a *Kirkus Reviews* contributor. Gillian Engberg, calling the text "poetic," noted in *Booklist* that Doyle uses "just a few words per spread" to capture the life of the cow. According to *School Library Journal* reviewer Carolyn Janssen, "this is a book not to be missed."

Storm Cats is a tale of two cats, and their owners, neighbors who never meet until a storm frightens the cats.

The two children who care for the cats go out after the storm has ended, looking for their lost pets. They eventually find their cats sheltering together in a storm drain, having been trapped inside by a fallen tree. The result of the adventure is a new friendship—and surprise several months later. Doyle "reflects a genius in offering a simply rhythmic, rhyming text," noted a *Kirkus Reviews* contributor. Jody McCoy of *School Library Journal* called the book "a reassuring tale of budding friendship with a four-kitten conclusion." A *Publishers Weekly* critic summed up the moral to the story: "When it comes to community-building, proximity sometimes needs a nudge from serendipity."

In 2001 Doyle expanded his writing beyond picture books by publishing his first novel for teens, *Georgie.* A mentally ill teenager who was orphaned by his mother's murder, Georgie is transferred to a residence home in Wales. Shannon, another mentally ill teen, and Georgie's kind teacher seem to understand the boy, and eventually their friendships help bring him out of his anger and help him begin to speak again. Told mostly from Georgie's perspective, *Georgie* is a tale about mental illness, but also about the power of friendship. Doyle's "uplifting story demonstrates what a few people who genuinely care can do for another human being," wrote a reviewer for *Publishers Weekly.* "The novel brilliantly takes readers inside a damaged psyche," described Faith Brautigam in her *School Library Journal* review, the critic added that, "on the whole this book is exceptionally well crafted, from its gripping opening to its hopeful conclusion." *Booklist* reviewer Jean Franklin praised Doyle's portrayal of mental illness, writing that "Georgie's voice is utterly real, and his recovery is realistically gradual."

Doyle's second novel, *Who Is Jesse Flood?,* tells the story of a very different teen: a boy who labels himself "different" by choice. Bored with his town and frustrated with the constant arguing of his parents, Jesse looks to stories and folktales to provide some meaning in his life. Full of humorous and sometimes embarrassing stories of Jesse's exploits, *Who Is Jesse Flood?* is a coming-of-age story about a boy looking for a purpose in his life. While a *Publishers Weekly* reviewer warned that the slow pacing of the novel may not suit all readers, other reviewers found much to commend in the book. A *Kirkus Reviews* contributor noted that while the story covers territory mined in other teen books, "its delivery and the originality of Jesse's voice will resonate with readers." Crystal Faris, writing for *School Library Journal,* felt that "Jesse's voice comes through with poignant tellings of embarrassing situations and with a wonderful sense of humor." The book is "a very episodic but occasionally stunningly crafted first-person glimpse of an anxious, insecure adolescent," noted *Booklist* contributor Anne O'Malley.

As Doyle once told *SATA:* "I'm passionate about books, about stories. I love going into schools, meeting children, encouraging them to read, encouraging them to

Young readers imagine what it would be like to spend a leisurely day as a cow, where tail-swishing and standing in a milk shed are the highlights in Doyle's imaginative Cow. *(Illustration by Angelo Rinaldi.)*

write. Don't wait till you're forty, I say. Do it. Do it now!" On his home page, Doyle told readers that he and his wife "now live in Aberdyfl, with our cats Bracken and Milo, in a big old house overlooking the sea. And on days when I'm not visiting schools or walking in the mountains, that's where you'll find me, sitting in my study, looking at the view, and, hopefully, writing."

Biographical and Critical Sources

PERIODICALS

Booklist, April 15, 2002, Connie Fletcher, review of *Sleepy Pendoodle,* p. 1407; June 1, 2002, Gillian Engberg, review of *Cow,* p. 1734; September 1, 2002, Jean Franklin, review of *Georgie,* p. 114; October 1, 2002, Anne O'Malley, review of *Who Is Jesse Flood?,*
p. 312; October 15, 2003, Abby Nolan, review of *Antonio on the Other Side of the World, Getting Smaller,* p. 417; August, 2004, Karin Snelson, review of *Splash, Joshua, Splash!,* p. 1941.

Bookseller, June 16, 2000, review of *Tales from Old Ireland.*

Books for Keeps, May, 1999, George Hunt, review of *The Great Castle of Marshmangle;* September, 1999, Roy Blatchford, review of *Jody's Beans,* and Elizabeth Schlenther, review of *The Changeling.*

Books Ireland, September, 2000, review of *Carrot Thompson, Record Breaker.*

Bulletin of the Center for Children's Books, November, 2002, review of *Georgie,* p. 103; December, 2002, review of *Who Is Jesse Flood?,* p. 152; November, 2004, Karen Coates, review of *Splash, Joshua, Splash!,* p. 119.

Cambrian News, July 2, 1998, reviews of *The Great Hunger* and *Farewell to Ireland;* November 12, 1998, reviews of *The Children of Nuala* and *Little People, Big People;* May 20, 1999, review of *The Changeling.*

Cambriensis, December, 1999, Lynne Walsh, review of *The Changeling.*

Carousel, September, 1999, Michael Thorn, reviews of *The Great Castle of Marshmangle* and *Jody's Beans,* and Jan Mark, review of *The Changeling.*

Children's Books in Ireland, June, 1999, Bronagh Naughton, review of *Little People, Big People.*

Children's Bookseller, March 19, 1999, reviews of *The Great Castle of Marshmangle* and *Jody's Beans;* September 8, 2000, review of *Tales from Old Ireland.*

Children's Bookwatch, August, 2004, review of *Tales from Old Ireland,* p. 4.

Early Years Educator, November, 1999, review of *Well, A Crocodile Can!*

Guardian (London, England), May 25, 1999, Vivian French, review of *Jody's Beans.*

Horn Book, March, 1999, Margaret A. Bush, review of *Jody's Beans,* p. 187; January-February, 2005, Susan Dove Lempke, review of *One, Two, Three O'Leary,* p. 76.

Irish Examiner, June 10, 2000, Brendan Malone, review of *Carrot Thompson, Record Breaker.*

Irish Times, May 22, 1999, Geraldine Whelan, reviews of *The Great Castle of Marshmangle* and *Jody's Beans.*

Kirkus Reviews, March 15, 1999, review of *Jody's Beans;* January 1, 2002, reviews of *Owen and the Mountain* and *Sleepy Pendoodle,* p. 44; January 15, 2002, review of *Baby See, Baby Do!,* p. 103; June 1, 2002, review of *Cow,* p. 804; August 1, 2002, review of *Who Is Jesse Flood?* p. 126; October 1, 2002, review of *Storm Cats,* p. 1467; June 1, 2004, review of *Splash, Joshua, Splash!,* p. 535; August 1, 2004, review of *One, Two, Three O'Leary,* p. 740; October 15, 2004, review of *The Great Castle of Marshmangle,* p. 1004; April 15, 2005, review of *The Dancing Tiger,* p. 472.

Kliatt, November, 2004, Stephanie Squicciarini, review of *Who Is Jesse Flood?,* p. 15.

London Parent's Guide (England), November, 1999, review of *Jody's Beans.*

Magpies, February, 1999, John Zahnleiter, review of *Jody's Beans;* March, 1999, Annette Dale-Meiklejohn, review of *Little People, Big People* and *The Children of Nuala,* p. 32.

Publishers Weekly, May 3, 1999, review of *Jody's Beans,* p. 74; April 29, 2002, review of *Georgie,* p. 71; May 27, 2002, review of *Cow,* p. 59; July 29, 2002, review of *Who Is Jesse Flood?,* p. 73; October 21, 2002, review of *Storm Cats,* p. 74; September 29, 2003, review of *Antonio on the Other Side of the World, Getting Smaller,* p. 64; October 4, 2004, review of *One, Two, Three O'Leary,* p. 86.

School Librarian, June, 1999, Teresa Scragg, review of *The Children of Nuala;* September, 1999, Carolyn Boyd, review of *Jody's Beans;* December, 1999, Ann Jenkin, review of *The Changeling.*

School Library Journal, June, 1999, Carolyn Jenks, review of *Jody's Beans,* pp. 92-93; March, 2000, Christine A. Moesch, review of *Well, a Crocodile Can!;* January, 2002, Debbie Stewart, review of *The Bold Boy,* p. 97; March, 2002, Carol Ann Wilson, review of *Sleepy Pendoodle,* p. 176; July, 2002, Carolyn Janssen, review of *Cow,* p. 88, and Faith Brautigam, review of

Georgie, p. 119; October, 2002, Jody McCoy, review of *Storm Cats,* p. 103, and Crystal Faris, review of *Who Is Jesse Flood?,* p. 162; December, 2003, Catherine Threadgill, review of *Antonio on the Other Side of the World, Getting Smaller,* p. 112; September, 2004, Maryann H. Owen, review of *Splash, Joshua, Splash!,* p. 158; November, 2004, Wanda Meyers-Hines, review of *One, Two, Three O'Leary,* p. 97.

South China Morning Post, September 25, 1999, Katherine Forestier, review of *Jody's Beans.*

Sunday Tribune (Dublin, Ireland), March 28, 1999, Mary Arrigan, review of *The Great Castle of Marshmangle;* May 2, 1999, Mary Arrigan, review of *Jody's Beans;* August 1, 1999, Mary Arrigan, review of *Well, a Crocodile Can!*

ONLINE

Malachy Doyle Home Page, http://www.malachydoyle. co.uk (November 4, 2005).

*   *   *

DREWERY, Melanie 1970-

Personal

Born February 4, 1970, in Palmerston North, New Zealand; married; children: two daughters, two step-daughters. *Education:* Nelson Polytechnic, certificate (craft and design), 1989; New Zealand Institute of Business, diploma (freelance journalism), 1998. *Hobbies and other interests:* Riding horses, reading books, listening to music, painting.

Addresses

Home—Ruby Bay, Nelson, New Zealand. *Agent*—c/o Author Mail, Reed Books, 39 Rawene Rd..Birkenhead, Auckland, New Zealand.

Career

Writer, illustrator, and artist. Worked variously as a children's librarian, potter, freelance journalist, and pre-school teacher. New Zealand Book Council Books-in-Schools program, participant. *Exhibitions:* Has exhibited paintings and sculptures in Mapua, Nelson, Riversdale, and Christchurch, New Zealand.

Writings

FOR CHILDREN

Nanny Mihi and the Rainbow, illustrated by Tracy Duncan, Reed (Auckland, New Zealand), 2001.

Nanny Mihi's Garden, illustrated by Tracy Duncan, Reed (Auckland, New Zealand), 2002.

The Treasure, illustrated by Bruce Potter, Reed (Auckland, New Zealand), 2003.

Nanny Mihi's Birthday Surprise, illustrated by Tracy Duncan, Reed (Auckland, New Zealand), 2003.

Matariki, illustrated by Bruce Potter, Reed (Auckland, New Zealand), 2003.

Child of Aotearoa, illustrated by Bruce Potter, Reed (Auckland, New Zealand), 2004.

Koro's Medicine, illustrated by Sabrina Malcolm, Huia (Wellington, New Zealand), 2004.

Nanny Mihi's Treasure Hunt, illustrated by Tracy Duncan, Reed (Auckland, New Zealand), 2004.

Nanny Mihi's Christmas, Reed (Auckland, New Zealand), 2005.

Author's books have been translated into Maori.

ILLUSTRATOR

Joan Lees, *The Camping Trip,* Rainbow Reading Programme (Nelson, New Zealand), 1995.

Maria Beard, *Just a Kid,* Rainbow Reading Programme (Nelson, New Zealand), 1995.

Sidelights

Melanie Drewery told *SATA:* "I write for children because I love it. I sent my first story away when I was seven years old. It was rejected, but I didn't give up. Every year I sent some stories away, and I kept trying to learn how to write a better story. Finally, after a very long time and lots of perseverance, a publisher said 'Yes.' That was in 2000, and the book was called *Nanny Mihi and the Rainbow.* It was my reward for thirteen years of trying.

"My advice to anyone who wants to be a writer is, 'Keep trying, keep learning, read lots, and never give up.'"

Biographical and Critical Sources

PERIODICALS

Magpies, November, 2002, review of *Nanny Mihi's Garden,* p. 6; September, 2003, review of *Nanny Mihi's Birthday Surprise,* p. 6; November, 2004, Raymond Huber, review of *Nanny Mihi's Treasure Hunt,* p. 6.

ONLINE

Artists in Schools Web site, http://www.artistsinschools.ac. nz/ (October 5, 2005), "Melanie Drewery, Ceramics."

Christchurch City Libraries Web site, http://www.library. christchurch.org.nz/ (July 13, 2005), interview with Drewery.

New Zealand Book Council Web site, http://www.book council.org/nz/ (July 13, 2005), "Melanie Drewery."

DUFFY, Carol Ann 1955-

Personal

Born December 23, 1955, in Glasgow, Scotland; daughter of Francis (an engineer) and Mary (Black) Duffy; partner of Jackie Kay (a poet), beginning 1999; children: Ella. *Education:* University of Liverpool, B.A. (with honors), 1977.

Addresses

Home—Manchester, England. *Office*—Department of English, Manchester Metropolitan University, Goffrey Manton Building, Rosamond St. W., off Oxford Rd., Manchester M15 6LL, England. *Agent*—Penny Tackaberry, Tessa Sayle Agency, 11 Jubilee Pl., London SW3 3TE, England.

Career

Writer, 1977—. Poetry editor of *Ambit* magazine, beginning 1983; visiting fellow at North Riding College, 1985; writer-in-residence, Southern Arts, Thamesdown, 1987-88; Manchester Metropolitan University, Manchester, England, professor.

Member

Society of Authors (panel member), Poetry Society (vice president), Royal Society of Literature (fellow).

Awards, Honors

C. Day Lewis fellow of poetry for Greater London Arts Association, 1982-84; first prize, British Broadcasting Corporation National Poetry Competition, 1983, for "Whoever She Was"; Eric Gregory Award, British Society of Authors, 1984; Scottish Arts Council award, 1986, for *Standing Female Nude,* 1990, for *The Other Country,* 1993, for *Mean Time;* first prize, Poems about Painting competition, Peterloo Poets, 1986, for "The Virgin Punishing the Infant"; Somerset Maugham Award, 1988, for *Selling Manhattan;* Dylan Thomas Award, 1989; Cholmondeley Award, 1992; *Forward* Poetry Prize for Best Poetry Collection of a Year, and Whitbread Poetry Award, both 1993, both for *Mean Time;* Lannan Literary Award for Poetry, 1995; named to Order of the British Empire, 1995, named commander, 2001; Signal Poetry Award, 1997, for *Stopping for Death;* Whitbread Children's Book Award shortlist, 2000, for *Meeting Midnight,* honorary doctorates from University of Hull, University of Warwick, and Keele University; National Endowment for Science, Technology, and the Arts grant, 2000.

Writings

FOR YOUNG PEOPLE

(Editor and contributor) *I Wouldn't Thank You for a Valentine: Anthology of Women's Poetry,* illustrated by Trisha Rafferty, Viking (New York, NY), 1992, published as *I Wouldn't Thank You for a Valentine: Poems for Young Feminists,* Holt (New York, NY), 1993.

(Adaptor) Jacob Grimm and Wilhelm Grimm, *Grimm Tales* (plays), dramatized by Tim Supple, Faber & Faber (London, England), 1996.

(Editor) *Stopping for Death: Poems of Death and Loss,* illustrated by Trisha Rafferty, Holt (New York, NY), 1996.

(Adaptor) Jacob and Wilhelm Grimm, *More Grimm Tales,* Faber & Faber (London, England), 1997.

(Editor) *Meeting Midnight,* illustrated by Eileen Cooper, Faber & Faber (London, England), 1999.

(Reteller) *Rumpelstiltskin and Other Grimm Tales,* illustrated by Marketa Prachaticka, Faber & Faber (London, England) 1999.

(With others) *Five Finger-Piglets: Poems,* illustrated by Peter Bailey, Macmillan Children's (London, England), 1999.

The Oldest Girl in the World, illustrated by Marketa Prachaticka, Faber & Faber (London, England), 2000.

Underwater Farmyard, illustrated by Joel Stewart, Macmillan Children's (London, England), 2002.

Queen Munch and Queen Nibble, illustrated by Lydia Monks, Macmillan Children's (London, England), 2002.

(Editor) *Overhead on a Saltmarsh: Poets' Favourite Poems,* Young Picador (London, England), 2003.

The Skipping-Rope Snake, illustrated by Lydia Monks, Macmillan Children's (London, England), 2003.

The Good Child's Guide to Rock 'n' Roll, Faber & Faber (London, England), 2003.

The Stolen Childhood and Other Dark Fairy Tales, illustrated by Jane Ray, Puffin (London, England), 2003.

Beasts and Beauties: Eight Tales from Europe, dramatized by Tim Supple and Melly Still, Faber & Faber (London, England), 2004.

Doris the Giant, illustrated by Annabel Hudson, Puffin (London, England), 2004.

Moon Zoo, illustrated by Joel Stewart, Macmillan Children's (London, England), 2005.

POETRY COLLECTIONS

Fleshweathercock, and Other Poems, Outposts, 1973.

Fifth Last Song, Headland, 1982.

Standing Female Nude, Anvil Press Poetry, 1985, new edition, 1998.

Thrown Voices, Turret Books, 1986.

Selling Manhattan, Anvil Press Poetry (London, England), 1987.

(Editor) *Home and Away,* 1988.

The Other Country, Anvil Press Poetry (London, England), 1990.

Mean Time, Anvil Press Poetry (London, England), 1993.

Selected Poems, Penguin/Anvil Press Poetry (London, England), 1994.

The Pamphlet, Anvil Press Poetry (London, England), 1998.

(Editor) *Time's Tidings: Greetings the Twenty-first Century: An Anthology,* Anvil Press Poetry (London, England), 1999.

The World's Wife, Anvil Press Poetry (London, England), 1999, Faber & Faber (New York, NY), 2000.

The Salmon Carol Ann Duffy: Poems Selected and New 1985-1999, Salmon Publishing (Knockeven, County Clare, Ireland), 2000.

Selected Poems, notes by Michael J. Woods, Longman (Harlow, England), 2001.

(Editor) *Hand in Hand: An Anthology of Love Poems,* Picador (London, England), 2001.

Feminine Gospels, Picador (London, England), 2002, Faber & Faber (New York, NY), 2003.

New Selected Poems, Picador (London, England), 2004.

(Editor) *Out of Fashion: An Anthology of Poems,* Faber & Faber (London, England), 2004.

Rapture, Picador (London, England), 2005.

Contributor to *Penguin Modern Poets,* Volume 2: *Carol Ann Duffy, Vicki Feaver, Eavan Boland,* Penguin (London, England), 1995.

PLAYS

Take My Husband (two-act), produced in Liverpool, England, 1982.

Cavern of Dreams (two-act), produced in Liverpool, England, 1984.

Loss (one-act), broadcast by BBC-Radio, 1986.

Little Women, Big Boys (one-act), produced in London, England, 1986.

Adaptations

Several poems by Duffy were set to music by Aaron Jay Kernis as *Valentines,* Associated Music Publishers, 2000.

Sidelights

"In the world of British poetry, Carol Ann Duffy is a superstar," proclaimed Katharine Viner in a London *Guardian* review of Duffy's award-winning and best-selling verse collection *The World's Wife.* Duffy, who writes and edits numerous poetry collections and was a strong collector for British poet laureate after the 1998 death of Ted Hughes, has also penned a number of books for younger readers, including several illustrated adaptations of stories by the Brothers Grimm as well as original picture books such as *Queen Much and Queen Nibble, The Stolen Childhood,* and *Moon Zoo.*

Drawing on the stories originally collected by seventeenth-century German folklorists Wilhelm and Jacob Grimm, Duffy joined playwright Tim Supple in creating stageable adaptations stories such as "Hansel and Gretel" and "The Golden Goose" in *Grimm Tales* and *More Grimm Tales.* Employing "a poet's vigor and economy" and "combining traditions of style with direct, colloquial dialogue," according to Vida Conway in *School Librarian,* the play collections are intended for older children and young adults to use in drama and English classes. While other European tales such as "Bluebeard" and "Beauty and the Beast" are also recast as dramas for teens in *Beasts and Beauties: Eight Tales from Europe,* Duffy returns to the Grimms' stories with an eye toward younger readers to produce *Rumpelstiltskin and Other Grimm Tales,* which features illustrations by Marketa Prachaticka.

According to many critics, works such as *Moon Zoo, The Stolen Childhood, and Other Dark Fairy Tales,* and the beginning chapter book *Doris the Giant* have enriched British literature due to Duffy's skill with language. In reviewing *Moon Zoo* for *Reviewer's Bookwatch,* Ann Skea noted that the author's "humour, her empathy with small children, and her versatility as a poet provide exactly the right words to stir the imagination." *Moon Zoo* introduces a lunar landscape full of magical, Earth-like creatures—everything from polar bears and penguins to baboons and hippos—that float in zero-gravity and dine on delicacies such as Neptune salad and a slice of Pluto pie served up by an eight-armed alien zookeeper. *The Stolen Childhood* contains a selection of short stories featuring haunting and sometimes macabre elements that, reflecting the darker side of human nature, will resonate equally with children and adults. Citing Duffy's "brief and delicate" verse, London *Guardian* contributor Julia Eccleshare called *Moon Zoo* a verbal "feast that inspires close attention," while in *Writeaway Online* Bridget Carrington praised *The Stolen Childhood,* noting that Duffy's "miniature tales . . . deserve to enter the genre as classics." Another *Writeaway* contributor, Sarah Mears, cited *Doris the Giant* as a "lively story" about an lonely giant who ultimately finds a loving companion, adding that the "vividly illustrated" beginning reader contains "some rather sweet jokes."

Among Duffy's edited poetry anthologies, several have been deemed particularly appropriate for young-adult readers. *I Wouldn't Thank You for a Valentine: Poems for Young Feminists* features nearly seventy female poets, including such celebrated American writers as Maya Angelou, Alice Walker, and Nikki Giovanni, although British poets dominate the collection. The eighty-five poems collected here are grouped according to theme. Each grouping is approached from such a broad range of viewpoints "that young adults will find suitably subversive . . . and surprisingly traditional" treatments placed side by side in what *Bulletin of the Center for Children's Books* reviewer Betsy Hearne dubbed a "generous anthology." Nancy Vasilakis, writing in *Horn Book,* also highlighted the collection's diversity, noting that it "capture[s] the joys and burdens of womanhood in expressions that are by turns wistful, angry, turbulent, sad, funny, and wise." While a *Kirkus Reviews* critic wrote that "the whine of victimization is audible in several" poems, Doris Telford commented in *School Librarian* that *I Wouldn't Thank You for a Valentine* is a collection "most girls and women will enjoy."

Another anthology suitable for teen readers, *Stopping for Death: Poems of Death and Loss* collects verses that span four centuries and draw from many cultures in capturing "the mystery, grief, fear, and occasional gal-lows humor that surround death," as a *Kirkus Reviews* critic observed. Though the collection emphasizes variety, the poems selected by Duffy share a common "vision," as Sharon Korbeck noted in *School Library Journal,* giving "readers a deeper understanding of the impact of loss." As with the poet's earlier anthology, critics praised Duffy for her ability to assemble a range of poetic styles, viewpoints, approaches, and cultural and historical origins. In the *Bulletin of the Center for Children's Books* Hearne deemed *Stopping for Death* "an anthology so full and richly representative of both famous and lesser-known poets that any library . . . would be the better for it," while Hazel Rochman wrote in *Booklist* that the assembled poems "lift the spirit with their truthful feeling and words that sing."

Biographical and Critical Sources

BOOKS

Contemporary Women Poets, edited by Pamela Kester-Shelton, St. James Press (Detroit, MI), 1996.
Rees-Jones, Deryn, *Carol Ann Duffy,* 2nd edition, North-cote House, 2002.

PERIODICALS

Booklist, March 1, 1994, p. 1260; August, 1996, Hazel Rochman, review of *Stopping for Death: Poems of Death and Loss,* p. 1893.
Book Report, September, 1994, p. 49.
Bulletin of the Center for Children's Books, February, 1994, Betsy Hearne, review of *I Wouldn't Thank You for a Valentine: Poems for Young Feminists,* pp. 184-185; September, 1996, Betsy Hearne, review of *Stopping for Death,* pp. 9-10.
Guardian (London, England), September 25, 1999, Katharine Viner, "Meter Maid," pp. 20, 26; February 26, 2005, Julia Eccleshare, review of *Moon Zoo;* October 9, 2005, Kate Kellaway, review of *Rapture.*
Horn Book, May, 1994, Nancy Vasilakis, review of *I Wouldn't Thank You for a Valentine,* p. 329.
Kirkus Reviews, January 1, 1994, review of *I Wouldn't Thank You for a Valentine,* p. 66; June 15, 1996, review of *Stopping for Death,* p. 897; August, 1996, Sharon Korbeck, review of *Stopping for Death,* p. 168.
Reviewer's Bookwatch, May, 2004, Ann Skea, review of *Moon Zoo.*
School Librarian, November, 1992, Doris Telford, review of *I Wouldn't Thank You for a Valentine,* p. 154; May, 1996, Vida Conway, review of *Grimm Tales,* p. 70; summer, 2003, review of *Queen Munch and Queen Nibble,* p. 74; winter, 2003, review of *Overheard on a Saltmarsh,* p. 206; summer, 1999, review of *Five Finger-Piglets,* p. 96; summer, 2000, review of *Rumpelstiltskin and Other Grimm Tales,* p. 24; spring, 2004, Marie Imeson, review of *The Good Child's Guide to Rock 'n' Roll,* p. 39.

School Library Journal, January, 1994, p. 66.

Times Literary Supplement, March 3, 1995, p. 24; July 7, 1995, p. 32.

Voice of Youth Advocates, April, 1994, p. 48; October, 1996, review of *Stopping for Death,* p. 238.

ONLINE

Contemporary Writers Online, http://www.contemporary writers.com/ (October 20, 2005), "Carol Ann Duffy."

Knitting Circle Web site, http://www.myweb.lsbu.ac.uk/~stafflag/ (October 20, 2005), "Carol Ann Duffy."

Writeaway, http://www.improbability.ultralab.net/writeaway/ (October 20, 2005), Sarah Mears, review of *Doris the Giant,* and Bridget Carrington, *The Stolen Childhood.**

*　　*　　*

DURANT, Alan 1958-

Personal

Born September 6, 1958, in Sutton, Surrey, England; son of Christopher (a sales manager) and Joy (Simpson) Durant; married Jinny Johnson (a primary-school teacher), May 25, 1985; children: Amy, Kit, Josie. *Education:* Keble College, Oxford, B.A. (English language and literature). *Politics:* "Leftish." *Religion:* "Christian."

Addresses

Home—46 Poplar Grove, New Malden, Surrey KT3 3DE, England. *E-mail*—alan@durant1234.fsnet.co.uk.

Career

Writer. Former publicist for Spastics Society (charity; now SCOPE); Walker Books, London, England, senior copywriter, beginning 1986; full-time writer. National Reading Campaign reading champion; lecturer and workshop presenter.

Awards, Honors

Two-time winner, Kingston Borough/Waterstone's Poetry Competition; Red House Children's Book Award shortlist, 2004, for *Dear Tooth Fairy;* Kate Greenaway Medal shortlist, 2004, for *Always and Forever,* illustrated by Debi Gliori; Nottingham and Portsmouth children's book awards, 2004, for *Game Boy.*

Writings

Hamlet, Bananas, and All That Jazz (young adult), Red Fox (London, England), 1991.

Jake's Magic (easy reader), Walker (London, England), 1991.

(Compiler) *Little Dracula's Fiendishly Funny Joke Book,* Walker (London, England), 1992, revised as *Little Dracula's Joke Book,* illustrated by Paul Tempest, 2000.

Blood (young adult), Red Fox (London, England), 1992.

Nightmare Rave (young adult), Fantail (London, England), 1994.

The Fantastic Football Fun Book, illustrated by Cathy Gale, Walker (London, England), 1994 published as *Football Fun,* 1999.

Snake Supper (picture book), illustrated by A. Parker, Walker (London, England), 1994, Western (New York, NY), 1995.

Mouse Party (picture book), illustrated by Sue Heap, Candlewick Press (Cambridge, MA), 1995.

The Good Book (young adult), Red Fox (London, England), 1995.

Creepe Hall (easy reader), illustrated by Hunt Emerson, Walker (London, England), 1995.

Prince Shufflebottom (picture book), illustrated by Nick Schon, Dutton (New York, NY), 1995.

Angus Rides the Goods Train (picture book), illustrated by Chris Riddell, Viking (London, England), 1996.

Spider McDrew (easy reader), illustrated by Martin Chatterton, HarperCollins, 1996, illustrated by Philip Hopman, 2002.

Big Fish, Little Fish (picture book), illustrated by A. Parker, Golden Books (New York, NY), 1996.

Hector Sylvester (picture book), illustrated by A. Parker, HarperCollins, 1996.

A Short Stay in Purgatory (young adult), Red Fox (London, England), 1997.

Happy Birthday, Spider McDrew (easy reader), illustrated by Martin Chatterton, HarperCollins, 1997, illustrated by Philip Hopman, 2004.

The Return to Creepe Hall (easy reader), illustrated by Hunt Emerson, Walker (London, England), 1997.

Publish or Die (young-adult mystery), Scholastic, 1998.

(Compiler) *The Kingfisher Book of Vampire and Werewolf Stories,* Kingfisher (New York, NY), 1998.

Little Troll (easy reader), illustrated by Julek Heller, HarperCollins, 1998.

Little Troll and the Big Present (easy reader), illustrated by Julek Heller, HarperCollins, 1999.

A Good Night's Sleep (picture book), Walker (London, England), 1999.

Star Quest: Voyage to the Greylon Galaxy (easy reader), illustrated by Mick Brownfield, Walker (London, England), 1999.

Creepe Hall for Ever! (easy reader), illustrations by Hunt Emerson, Walker (London, England), 1999.

(Compiler) *Sports Stories,* illustrated by David Kearney, Kingfisher (New York, NY), 2000.

Big Bad Bunny (picture book), illustrated by Guy Parker-Rees, Orchard (London, England), 2000, Dutton (New York, NY), 2001.

The Ring of Truth, Barrington Stoke (Edinburgh, Scotland), 2001.

Kicking Off (stories), Walker (London, England), 2001.

Leagues Apart (stories), Walker (London, England), 2001.

That's Not Right (easy reader), illustrated by Katharine McEwen, Red Fox (London, England) 2002, Crabtree Publishing (New York, NY), 2004.

Always and Forever (picture book), illustrated by Debi Gliori, David Fickling Books (Oxford, England), 2003, Harcourt (Orlando, FL), 2004.

Brown Bear Gets in Shape (easy reader), illustrated by Annabel Hudson, Kingfisher (London, England), 2003, Kingfisher (Boston, MA), 2004.

Game Boy (story collection), illustrated by Sue Mason, Barrington Stoke (Edinburgh, Scotland) 2003.

Dear Tooth Fairy (picture book), illustrated by Vanessa Cabban, Walker Books (London, England), 2003, Candlewick Press (Cambridge, MA), 2004.

If You Go Walking in Tiger Wood (picture book), illustrated by Debbie Boon, HarperCollins (London, England), 2004.

Doing the Double (young adult), Evans (London, England), 2004.

(Compiler) *Vampire Stories,* illustrated by Nick Hardcastle, Kingfisher (Boston, MA), 2004.

Dear Santa Claus (picture book), illustrated by Vanessa Cabban, Candlewich Press (Cambridge, MA), 2005, published as *Dear Father Christmas,* Walker (London, England), 2005.

Jumping Jack Rabbit (picture book), illustrated by Ant Parker, Scholastic (New York, NY), 2005.

Bird Flies South (picture book), illustrated by Kath Lucas, Gingham Dog Press (Columbus, OH), 2005.

Burger Boy (picture book), illustrated by Mei Matsouka, Anderson Press (London, England), 2005, Clarion Books (New York, NY), 2006.

Night of the Dragon (easy reader), illustrated by David Lupton, Ginn (Oxford, England), 2005.

Game Boy Reloaded (story collection), illustrated by Sue Mason, Barrington Stoke (Edinburgh, Scotland), 2005.

Stat Man (fact/fiction), illustrated by Brett Hudson, Barrington Stoke (Edinburgh, Scotland), 2005.

Contributor of stories to *Toddler Time, Centuries of Stories,* for HarperCollins; *Same Difference,* for Egmont; *Gary Lineker's Favourite Football Stories, Princess Stories,* and *More of Gary Lineker's Favourite Football Stories,* for Macmillan; *Football Shorts* and *The Animals' Bedtime Storybook,* for Orion; *Nice One, Santa, On Me 'Ead, Santa,* and *Thirteen Murder Mysteries,* for Scholastic; *The Walker Treasury of First Stories; Stories for Me!,* for Candlewick; and *Lines in the Sand,* for Frances Lincoln. Also author of poetry.

Durant's work has been translated into Danish, Norwegian, Finnish, French, German, Greek, Italian, Spanish, Dutch, Welsh, Korean, Chinese, and Japanese.

"LEGGS UNITED" SERIES

The Phantom Footballer, illustrated by Chris Smedley, Macmillan (London, England), 1998.

Fair Play or Foul, illustrated by Chris Smedley, Macmillan (London, England), 1998.

Up for the Cup, illustrated by Chris Smedley, Macmillan (London, England), 1998.

Spot the Ball, illustrated by Chris Smedley, Macmillan (London, England), 1998.

Red Card for the Ref, illustrated by Chris Smedley, Macmillan (London, England), 1998.

Team on Tour, illustrated by Chris Smedley, Macmillan (London, England), 1998.

Sick as a Parrot, illustrated by Chris Smedley, Macmillan (London, England), 1999.

Super Sub, illustrated by Chris Smedley, Macmillan (London, England), 1999.

"BAD BOYZ" SERIES

Barmy Army, Walker (London, England), 2002.
K.O. Kings, Walker (London, England), 2002.

Adaptations

Several of Durant's books have been adapted as audiobooks by Chivers North America, including *Creepe Hall for Ever!,* 2001, and *Spider McDrew,* 2003.

Work in Progress

Dear Mermaid, The Diary of a Trainee Tooth Fairy, the young-adult novel *Flesh and Bones,* and the picture books *Football Feever, I Love You Little Monkey,* and *Billy Monster's Daymare.*

Sidelights

English writer Alan Durant began his writing career penning teen novels such as *Hamlet, Bananas, and All That Jazz* and *Blood,* but while raising his own three children he expanded into picture books, chapter books for young readers, and short stories for children and young adults. "I'm a versatile writer," Durant once told *SATA:* "As a professional publishing copywriter for many years I had to be; and I like turning my hands to different forms of book[s]. Also, when I first started writing books, they were very much for me, but since I've had children their preoccupations have come to the fore. They are my inspiration." This inspiration has produced such popular picture books as *Mouse Party, Snake Supper,* and *If You Go Walking in Tiger Wood,* as well as easy readers and juvenile novels such as *Jake's Magic, That's Not Right!,* and the "Creepe Hall" and "Leggs United" series.

Born in Surrey, in southern England, Durant was educated at Trinity School in Croydon, which later became the model for the school in his first novel, *Hamlet, Bananas, and All That Jazz.* "I started writing seriously at the age of fourteen," he explained, "because that was the only way I could express myself. The book that had the most influence on me was J.D. Salinger's *The Catcher in the Rye.* Reading that book was so inspiring. My first books were novels about the trauma of adolescence and were, I guess, a kind of catharsis. I really didn't enjoy being a teenager at all."

Durant graduated from Keble College, Oxford, with a degree in English. He then lived in Paris for several years, working at a school for spontaneous expression "run by one of the shortest, fattest, most volatile couples the world has seen," as he told *SATA*. Returning to England, Durant worked as a writer and publicist for the Spastics Society (now SCOPE), married, and in 1986 became a copywriter for Walker Books in London until becoming a full-time writer in 2004.

In 1991 Durant's first novel and his first book for young readers, *Jake's Magic,* both appeared. In *Jake's Magic* a young boy desperately wants to keep the stray cat he has found, despite all the logical arguments against the idea, and he finally devises a means to do so. Pam Harwood, reviewing the title in *Books for Keeps,* called it a "delightfully gentle story" that is "sensitively written." Readers "share Jake's dilemma right up to the unexpected ending," the critic added. In *School Librarian,* Ann G. Hay wrote that the story's "language is simple enough for the newly independent reader," making *Jake's Magic* worthy of a "welcome place" in the libraries of beginning readers.

Other beginning readers by Durant include the popular "Creepe Hall" series, as well as the books *That's Not Right!, Spider McDrew,* and *Star Quest.* In *Creepe Hall,* when young Oliver is sent to stay with distant relatives, he discovers that these relatives are ghosts and mummies straight out of a horror film. Calling the characters "chilling monsters of the cinema screen," Julia Marriage wrote in *School Librarian* that Durant's ghouls are "also friendly characters who can scare the villains of the story when necessary." Oliver soon finds himself allied with the servant, "Mummy," an ancient Egyptian mummy, to save Creepe Hall from poachers. As his new family weans Oliver off television, he in turn gently nudges them into late-twentieth-century technology. Marriage commented that the story "moves rapidly" and that the characters "are larger than life but never improbable or unbelievable," and further noted that this "fun" and "decidedly lively" read will appeal to those children who "do not find reading an enjoyable process." *Magpies* reviewer Russ Merrin called *Creepe Hall* "lightweight, but . . . also lots of fun!" Durant conjures up Oliver and the creature inhabitants of Creepe Hall in two further installments: *Return to Creepe Hall* and *Creepe Hall for Ever!*

In *That's Not Right!* a little girl named Ellie gets a lesson in viewpoint when she writes a story about a lowly bug that gets stepped on, and then hears the same story from a chatty bug's perspective as well as a third version, told by the shoe that did the actually stepping. Another young protagonist appears in the "Spider McDrew" books, which feature what *School Library Journal* critic Cynthia Grabke described as the most "lovable loser . . . since Charlie Brown." In *Spider McDrew* a young boy bumbles goodheartedly through life, forgetting his lines in the school play, inviting friends to a party on the wrong day, and makes a series of other minor muddles that many young readers can identify with, only to prove himself a winner at story's end.

Picture books from Durant include *Snake Supper, Mouse Party, Angus Rides the Goods Train,* and the playful *If You Go Walking in Tiger Wood.* In *Snake Supper* a hungry snake slithers through the forest, swallowing up all the animals in its path until it is stymied by an ingenious elephant. After the snake's undoing, all the animals he has swallowed survive unharmed, and the snake himself slithers away, happily unrepentant. Also featuring a jungle setting, *If You Go Walking in Tiger Wood* finds two children creeping through a dark forest alive with a unusual assortment of baboons, deer, and other creatures, while forest's tiger population trail behind the unaware children with a mysterious—and ultimately good-hearted—purpose. Writing in *Books for Keeps,* Liz Waterland called *Snake Supper* an "entertaining tale" and a "simple and enjoyable book with amusing illustrations," while in *Publishers Weekly* a reviewer predicted that young readers "will likely applaud the solution achieved by an ingenious elephant." Noting the sense of fun in *If You Go Walking in Tiger Wood,* a *Kirkus Reviews* writer concluded that Durant's playful picture book will lead storytimers on an adventurous "outing with a toddler-pleasing combination of danger and safety."

Mouse Party tells the story of a mouse who moves into a deserted house and invites all his friends to a party: there is the Owl with a towel and the Hare with a chair, among others. Then an unexpected arrival—the elephant who lives in the house and is returning from vacation—surprises Mouse. "The text will delight those who are doing their first reading," commented a contributor for *Kirkus Reviews,* the critic adding that Durant's tale is "laced with humor and incident," and gives "new meaning to the phrase 'party animal.'" *Booklist* reviewer Ilene Cooper found the simple text "clever" and the illustrations full of "visual excitement," dubbing *Mouse Party* an "energetic offering that has Party! written all over it."

Angus Rides the Goods Train tells of a dream train that chugs across the bedclothes after little Angus falls asleep. Entering this dream, the boy is frustrated that the train's driver refuses to stop for hungry people along the train route, and ultimately takes matters into his own small hands. A *Junior Bookshelf* reviewer called *Angus Rides the Goods Train* "an unusual picture book," while George Hunt, writing in *Books for Keeps,* remarked how "refreshing it is to find an imaginatively undidactic picture book . . . which vigorously and unashamedly celebrates that antiquated notion, the redistribution of wealth."

Durant often shares his love of sports—particularly soccer, which the British call football—with middle-grade readers in books such as *The Fantastic Football Fun Book, The Kingfisher Book of Sports Stories,* the eight-book series "Leggs United," and the "Bad Boyz" series of readers. "I believe in writing about things you know about," he explained, "and, even more, things that you are passionate about. I'm passionate about sport—and

Surprises lurk on every page in Durant's interactive 2004 peep-hole picture-book adventure, **If You Go Walking in Tiger Wood.** *(Illustration by Debbie Boone.)*

soccer in particular. Like it or loathe it, sport plays a massive role in many children's lives. It's a great subject for fiction, too, because you can address many different issues through it—bullying, self-confidence, friendship, justice."

Among Durant's novels and story collections for young-adult readers are *The Good Book, A Short Stay in Purgatory,* and *Publish or Die.* In *The Good Book* Durant portrays a fifteen-year-old gang leader named Ross who follows his local football team and with his gang members participates in all manner of hooliganism. Ironically, Ross takes inspiration from the Old Testament and also has his own ideas about serious issues ranging from the Gulf War to redemption. Enter a Youth Peace Mission and one of its members, Morgan, to whom Ross is romantically drawn. The teen begins to leave his violent life behind, until his drunken and cruel father returns and ratchets up the violence once more. Steve Rosson, reviewing the novel in *Books for Keeps,* called *The Good Book* an "unrelentingly grim read."

The dozen stories collected in *A Short Stay in Purgatory* "focus on the special hell which only teenage years can bring," according to Val Randall in *Books for Keeps.* In these tales, Durant focuses on themes from first love to crime, and from homosexuality to an unwanted pregnancy. Randall went on to mention that the "writing is clear and well-focused." A mystery, *Publish or Die* deals with a new publisher's assistant, young Calico Dance, who is fresh out of school and now encounters the worst sort of writer: a threatening one. An anonymous writer sends chapters of a book with a note that warns, "publish or die." When the publisher refuses such blackmail conditions, it becomes clear that the writer is very serious. Then it is up to Calico to try to stop matters before they turn deadly. "The plot moves at a good pace with plenty of red herrings along the way," noted Felicity Wilkins in *School Librarian.* Wilkins concluded that *Publish or Die* "is bound to be enjoyed by . . . fans in the secondary school."

In addition to writing, Durant is a frequent speaker in schools as a National Reading Campaign reading champion, and also gives writing workshops. Inspired by his love of sports and interest in young people, much of Durant's personal motivation stems from his personal spiritual beliefs. "Religion has been a preoccupation throughout my writing life," the author once told *SATA*. "I don't come from a religious background, but I started singing in a church choir at the age of nine or ten and most of my closest friends as a teenager were connected with the youth group attached to a number of churches in the area where I grew up. I've always believed in God, but my faith has fluctuated in intensity over the years. Whether or not there's an afterlife and what form it might take is the most persistent thorn in my flesh. There's barely a day goes by without me worrying about it. Given this, it's maybe surprising that I don't write about religion more; death, though, pops up quite regularly."

Biographical and Critical Sources

PERIODICALS

Booklist, September 1, 1995, Ilene Cooper, review of *Mouse Party,* p. 84; January 1, 1999, p. 857; May 1, 2001, Connie Fletcher, review of *Big Bad Bunny,* p. 370; July, 2004, Gillian Engberg, review of *Always and Forever,* p. 1847.

Books for Keeps, March, 1993, Pam Harwood, review of *Jake's Magic,* p. 9; March, 1995, Liz Waterland, review of *Snake Supper,* p. 9; March, 1996, Steve Rosson, review of *The Good Book,* p. 13; July, 1996, p. 6; January, 1997, George Hunt, review of *Angus Rides the Goods Train,* p. 20; September, 1997, Val Randall, review of *A Short Stay in Purgatory,* p. 29.

Junior Bookshelf, August, 1995, p. 134; December, 1996, review of *Angus Rides the Goods Train,* p. 230.

Kirkus Reviews, August 1, 1995, review of *Mouse Party,* p. 1108; June 1, 2005, review of *If You Go Walking in Tiger Wood,* p. 635.

Magpies, September, 1995, Russ Merrin, review of *Creepe Hall,* p. 29; March, 1996, p. 27; July, 1996, p. 45; March, 1999, Margaret Phillips, review of *Little Troll,* pp. 28-29.

Observer (London, England), July 23, 1995, p. 12.

Publishers Weekly, April 24, 1995, review of *Snake Supper,* p. 70; July 10, 1995, review of *Mouse Party,* p. 57; February 5, 1996, p. 90; January 26, 2004, review of *Dear Tooth Fairy,* p. 253.

School Librarian, February, 1992, Ann G. Hay, review of *Jake's Magic,* p. 19; August, 1995, Julia Marriage, review of *Creepe Hall,* p. 108; March, 1998, Felicity Wilkins, review of *Publish or Die,* p. 156; spring, 2001, review of *Sports Stories,* p. 46; summer, 2002, review of *Leagues Apart* and *Kicking Off,* p. 80.

School Library Journal, September, 1995, Alexandra Marris, review of *Snake Supper,* p. 169; August, 1998, p. 146; November, 1999, p. 67; November, 2000, Michael McCullough, review of *Sports Stories,* p. 154; February, 2001, Sue Sherif, review of *Big Bad Bunny,* p. 99; August, 2001, Nicole A. Cooke, review of *Creepe Hall for Ever!* (audiobook), p. 89; June, 2004, Rachel G. Payne, review of *Always and Forever,* p. 106; August, 2004, Christine E. Carr, review of *That's Not Right!,* p. 85, and Anne Knickerbocker, review of *Brown Bear Gets in Shape,* p. 86.

Times Educational Supplement, January 29, 1993, p. 10; May 27, 1994, p. 12; March 8, 1996, p. 4158; May 29, 1998, p. 857.

ONLINE

Alan Durant Home Page, http://www.alandurant.co.uk (October 20, 2005).

Jubilee Books Web site, http://www.jubileebooks.co.uk/ (May, 2003) interview with Durant.

*   *   *

DWYER, Deanna
See KOONTZ, Dean R.

*   *   *

DWYER, K.R.
See KOONTZ, Dean R.

E-F

EGOFF, Sheila A. 1918-2005

OBITUARY NOTICE—See index for *SATA* sketch: Born January 20, 1918, in Auburn, ME; died May 22, 2005, in Vancouver, British Columbia, Canada. Librarian, educator, and author. Egoff was a widely respected authority on, and advocate of, children's literature, and was often credited as a profound influence in making the study of children's literature a respected scholarly discipline. Although she was born in Maine, she grew up in Ontario, Canada, and attended the University of Toronto, where she received a diploma in library science in 1938. After working as a children's librarian at the Galt Public Library for five years, she joined the Toronto Public Library in 1942, becoming its reference librarian from 1952 to 1957. During these years, she completed a B.A. at the University of Toronto in 1948, and the next year earned another library science diploma at the University of London in England. After working for several years as an editor for the Canadian Library Association, Egoff joined the University of British Columbia faculty in 1961, becoming a professor of librarianship and the first tenured professor in children's literature before retiring in 1983. Egoff spearheaded many initiatives to increase the quality of children's literature in Canada and abroad. While in Toronto, she helped establish the British Osborne Collection of Early Children's Books at the Toronto Public Library. At the University of Toronto, furthermore, she established a master's program in children's literature. In addition, she was the first Canadian to be a judge on the Hans Christian Andersen Awards committee, and, in 1994, was the first professor of children's literature to be named an Officer of the Order of Canada. As a scholar, she insisted that only books of the highest quality were good enough for children, inspiring many authors to excel in the genre, including protégés Sarah Ellis and Kit Pearson. Many of her books are considered standards in the field, including *The Republic of Childhood: A Critical Guide to Canadian Children's Literature* (1967) and *Worlds Within: Children's Fantasy from the Middle Ages to Today* (1988). Among Egoff's many honors for her contributions to the study of children's literature are the Ralph R. Shaw Award from the American Library Association in 1982, an Outstanding Public Library Service Award from the Canadian Association of Public Libraries in 1992, the 2004 Anne Devereaux Jordan Award from the Children's Literature Association, and induction into the Waterloo Hall of Fame and Cambridge Hall of Fame. Egoff also received several honorary degrees and had an award from the British Columbia Book Prizes named after her. Among her other publications are *Thursday's Child: Trends and Patterns in Contemporary Children's Literature* (1981) and *Once upon a Time: My Life with Children's Books* (2005), which was her last book.

OBITUARIES AND OTHER SOURCES:

BOOKS

Egoff, Sheila, *Once upon a Time: My Life with Children's Books,* Orca (Port Townsend, WA), 2005.

PERIODICALS

Chronicle of Higher Education, July 22, 2005, p. A30.

ONLINE

Canadian Children's Book Centre Web site, http://www.bookcentre.ca/ (August 10, 2005).

*   *   *

EISNER, Will 1917-2005
(William Erwin Eisner, Will Erwin, Willis Rensie)

Personal

Born March 6, 1917, in New York, NY; died January 3, 2005, in Fort Lauderdale, FL; son of Samuel (a furrier) and Fannie (Ingber) Eisner; married Ann Louise Wein-

Will Eisner

garten (a director of volunteer hospital services), June 15, 1950; children: John David, Alice Carol. *Education:* Attended Art Students League (New York, NY), 1935.

Career

Author, cartoonist, and publisher. *New York American,* New York, NY, staff artist, 1936; Eisner & Iger, New York, NY, founder and partner, 1937-40; Eisner-Arnold Comic Group, New York, NY, founder and publisher, 1940-46; author and cartoonist of syndicated newspaper feature, "The Spirit," 1940-52; American Visuals Corp., founder and president, beginning 1949; Bell McClure North American Newspaper Alliance, president, 1962-64; Koster-Dana Corp., executive vice president, 1962-64; Educational Supplements Corp., president, 1965-72; School of Visual Arts, New York, NY, member of faculty, beginning 1973. President of IPD Publishing Co., Inc.; chair of the board, Croft Educational Services Corp., 1972-73; member of board of directors, Westchester Philharmonic. *Military service:* U.S. Army, Ordnance, 1942-45.

Member

Princeton Club (New York, NY).

Awards, Honors

Comic book artist of the year designation, National Cartoonists Society, 1967; best artist award, National Cartoonists Society, 1968-69; award for quality of art in comic books, Society of Comic Art Research, 1968; In-

ternational Cartoonist Award, 1974; named to Hall of Fame of the Comic Book Academy; Eisner Award for Best Archival Collection, 2001, for *The Spirit Archives;* Eisner Award for Best New Graphic Novel, 2002, for *The Name of the Game.*

Writings

SELF-ILLUSTRATED

A Pictorial Arsenal of America's Combat Weapons, Sterling (New York, NY), 1960.

America's Space Vehicles: A Pictorial Review, edited by Charles Kramer, Sterling (New York, NY), 1962.

A Contract with God, and Other Tenement Stories, Baronet (New York, NY), 1978.

(With P. R. Garriock and others) *Masters of Comic Book Art,* Images Graphiques (New York, NY), 1978.

Odd Facts, Ace Books (New York, NY), 1978.

Dating and Hanging Out (for young adults), Baronet (New York, NY), 1979.

Funny Jokes and Foxy Riddles, Baronet (New York, NY), 1979.

Ghostly Jokes and Ghastly Riddles, Baronet (New York, NY), 1979.

One Hundred and One Half Wild and Crazy Jokes, Baronet (New York, NY), 1979.

Spaced-out Jokes, Baronet (New York, NY), 1979.

The City (narrative portfolio), Hollygraphic, 1981.

Life on Another Planet (graphic novel), Kitchen Sink (Princeton, WI), 1981.

Signal from Space, Kitchen Sink (Princeton, WI), 1981.

Will Eisner Color Treasury, text by Catherine Yronwode, Kitchen Sink (Princeton, WI), 1981.

Spirit: Color Album, Kitchen Sink (Princeton, WI), 1981–83.

(Catherine Yronwode, with Denis Kitchen) *The Art of Will Eisner,* introduction by Jules Feiffer, Kitchen Sink (Princeton, WI), 1982.

(Coauthor, with Jules Feiffer and Wallace Wood) *Outer Space Spirit, 1952,* edited by Denis Kitchen, Kitchen Sink (Princeton, WI), 1983.

Will Eisner's Quarterly, Kitchen Sink (Princeton, WI), 1983–86.

Will Eisner's 3-D Classics Featuring . . . , Kitchen Sink (Princeton, WI), 1985.

Comics and Sequential Art, Poorhouse (Tamarac, FL), 1985.

Will Eisner's Hawks of the Seas, 1936-1938, edited by Dave Schreiner, Kitchen Sink (Princeton, WI), 1986.

Will Eisner's New York, the Big City, Kitchen Sink (Princeton, WI), 1986.

Will Eisner's The Dreamer, Kitchen Sink (Princeton, WI), 1986.

The Building, Kitchen Sink (Princeton, WI), 1987.

A Life Force, Kitchen Sink (Princeton, WI), 1988.

City People Notebook, Kitchen Sink (Princeton, WI), 1989.

Will Eisner's Spirit Casebook, Kitchen Sink (Princeton, WI), 1990–98.

Will Eisner Reader: Seven Graphic Stories by a Comics Master, Kitchen Sink (Princeton, WI), 1991.

To the Heart of the Storm, Kitchen Sink (Princeton, WI), 1991.

The White Whale: An Introduction to Moby-Dick, Story Shop (Tamarac, FL), 1991.

The Spirit: The Origin Years, Kitchen Sink (Princeton, WI), 1992.

Invisible People, Kitchen Sink (Northampton, MA), 1993.

The Christmas Spirit, Kitchen Sink (Northampton, MA), 1994.

Sketchbook, Kitchen Sink (Northampton, MA), 1995.

Dropsie Avenue: The Neighborhood, Kitchen Sink (Northampton, MA), 1995.

Graphic Storytelling, Poorhouse (Tamarac, FL), 1996.

(Adapter) *Moby Dick by Herman Melville,* NBM (New York, NY), 1998.

A Family Matter, Kitchen Sink (Northampton, MA), 1998.

(Reteller) *The Princess and the Frog by the Grimm Brothers,* NBM (New York, NY), 1999.

Minor Miracles: Long Ago and Once upon a Time, Back When Uncles Were Heroic, Cousins Were Clever, and Miracles Happened on Every Block, DC Comics (New York, NY), 2000.

The Last Knight: An Introduction to Don Quixote by Miguel de Cervantes, NBM (New York, NY), 2000.

Last Day in Vietnam: A Memory, Dark Horse (Milwaukie, OR), 2000.

Will Eisner's The Spirit Archives, multiple volumes, DC Comics (New York, NY), 2000—.

The Name of the Game, DC Comics (New York, NY), 2001.

Will Eisner's Shop Talk, Dark Horse (Milwaukie, OR), 2001.

(With Dick French, Bill Woolfolk, and others) *The Blackhawk Archives,* DC Comics (New York, NY), 2001.

Fagin the Jew, Doubleday (New York, NY), 2003.

(Adapter) *Sundiata: A Legend of Africa,* NMB (New York, NY), 2003.

The Plot: The Secret Story of The Protocols of the Elders of Zion (nonfiction), Norton (New York, NY), 2005.

For U.S. Department of Defense, creator of comic-strip instructional aid, *P.S.* magazine, 1950; for U.S. Department of Labor, creator of career guidance series of comic booklets, *Job Scene,* 1967. Creator of comic strips, sometimes under pseudonyms Will Erwin and Willis Rensie, including "Uncle Sam," "Muss 'em up Donovan," "Sheena," "The Three Brothers," "Blackhawk," "K-51," and "Hawk of the Seas." Author of newspaper feature, "Odd Facts." Contributor to *Artwork for "9-11 Emergency Relief,"* Alternative Comics, 2001.

Sidelights

A giant in his field, cartoonist Will Eisner "virtually invented the comic-book anti-hero (and by extension, the underground comic)," maintained Steven Heller in *Print* magazine. Introducing his groundbreaking comic "The Spirit" in 1940, Eisner proved himself an innovator, and in his fifty-plus-year career, the comic-book characters he created were influential with Americans, whether guiding teens in choosing a career, instructing military personnel, or for their overarching purpose: simply to entertain. During a career that began in the 1930s with the sale of his first comic feature, "Scott Dalton," to *Wow!* magazine, Eisner worked for New York publishers as well as the U.S. government, and he also produced a series of comic-book-style training manuals sponsored by the Agency for International Development and the United Nations that help teach modern farming techniques to people living in developing nations.

Eisner's comic strip "The Spirit," a weekly adventure series published as a sixteen-page insert in Sunday papers from 1940 to 1951, features Denny Colt, a private investigator who is seriously injured and presumed dead after an explosion in the laboratory of evil scientist Dr. Cobra. Once Colt recovers, he vows to exploit his new anonymity to enhance his ability to bring hardened criminals to justice. Renowned for its sarcasm, social satire and its status as the first mainstream comic to feature a black character, "The Spirit" gained legions of new fans after being re-issued in multi-volume graphic-novel form beginning in 2001.

Interested in cartooning from a young age, the New York City-born Eisner's work was first published in his Bronx high school newspaper; his first professional success was a strip published in *Wow! What a Magazine* in 1936, when he was nineteen years old. Although he had attended the Art Students League in New York City in 1935 to study painting and anatomy, Eisner was largely self-taught, and his first regular job was working as a staff artist for the *New York American,* which he started in 1936. Within a year the ambitious artist had co-founded Eisner & Iger, a comic-book publishing company that, along with Eisner and Jerry Iger, included "Batman" creator Bob Kane. Eisner ran the company until 1940, when he founded the Eisner-Arnold Comic Group.

Nineteen-forty was also the year "The Spirit," made its debut. The title character of the strip was unique at the time because, unlike such characters as Superman, he possessed no superpowers. Instead, Eisner created a complex, hard-edged character who had seemingly been brought back mysteriously from death in order to help victims of crime. His work on "The Spirit" was interrupted by World War II, when he was drafted into the U.S. Army. There he designed safety posters and used cartoon-strip techniques to simplify a military training manual for equipment maintenance. Returning to civilian life in 1946, he continued to write and illustrate "The Spirit," making his characters and stories even more complex. Discontinuing the strip in 1952, he then founded the American Visuals Corporation, to produce comic books for schools and businesses. In 1967 he was hired by the U.S. Department of Labor to create a comic-book series geared for potential school dropouts. The "Job Scene" booklet series introduces career choices to young people ambivalent about their educa-

Eisner's **The Spirit,** *which was syndicated for newspaper publication from 1940 through the early 1950s, has been made available to new fans through its many graphic-novel incarnations.*

tion, and it proved so successful that several national publishers issued similar series.

In another highly influential move, Eisner was hired by the Department of Defense to develop an instructional manual to replace the dry, prose-heavy technical manuals then used for military training. Regarding his *P.S.* magazine, he wrote in a *Library Journal* essay that, along with comic-book-style sequential art, the manual "employed the soldier's argot, rendering militarese into common language. The magazine said 'Clean away the crud from the flywheel' instead of 'All foreign matter should be removed from the surface of the flywheel and the rubber belt which it supports.'" From one hundred words of dense prose to a three-panel sequence which quickly presented the necessary instruction, Eisner's distillation anticipated the needs of the reluctant readers of future generations.

While Eisner believed that the simple language and visual impact of comics made them desirable in a variety of educational settings, critics were quick to complain that a teacher's task is to instill a healthy respect for proper language, and comic books violate every rule of grammar. In *Publishers Weekly,* Eisner once responded: "This is an understandable criticism, but it is based on the assumption that cartoons are designed primarily to

teach language. *Comics are a message in themselves!* . . . To readers living in the ghetto and playing in the street and school yard, comic books, with their inventive language, argot, and slang, serve as no other literature does."

Although Eisner had abandoned his storytelling in favor of vocation-based comics in the early 1950s, two decades later he was inspired by the innovative work of artists such as Robert Crumb to renew his interest in narrative comics. In 1975 he began work on what he called a "graphic novel," published three years later as *A Contract with God and Other Tenement Stories.* Unlike his earlier adventure comics, *A Contract with God* presents a serious treatment of religious faith, sexual betrayal, prejudice and similar themes, through the story of Jewish immigrant slumlord Frimme Hersh. He also used this innovative graphic-novel format to tell the story of Jewish immigrants in America in books such as *Life on Another Planet, Big City, A Life Force, Minor Miracles,* and the award-winning *The Name of the Game. The Name of the Game,* a multi-generational saga following the Arnheim family as they expand their businesses from corset manufacturing to stock brokering, was described as melodramatic and predictable by *Booklist* reviewer Gordon Flagg, although the critic appreciated Eisner's "expressive" artwork and noted that the book reflects "a sensibility somehow appropriate to the period and subject."

Geared for younger readers, the graphic novel, *Sundiata: A Legend of Africa* is an adaptation of a thirteenth-century African tale about the death of the Mali king and the resulting conquest of the leaderless tribe by a tyrant claiming to control the elements. *Booklist* contributor Carlos Orellana felt that, although the tale's ending is disappointing, in Eisner's retelling "the plot flows smoothly; the telling never feels rushed; and the sequential art, which is full of movement and expression, gives the familiar good-versus-evil theme extra depth." Noting the book's intended audience, Steve Raiteri predicted in *Library Journal* that teens and adults would also "appreciate Eisner's concise and clear storytelling and his dramatic artwork, distinctively colored in grays and earth tones."

Eisner combines biography and fiction in *Fagin the Jew,* which finds the pivotal character from nineteenth-century British writer Charles Dickens' *Oliver Twist* telling his personal story. Published in 2003 when its author was in his eighties, *Fagin the Jew* reveals its leading character in a much more flattering light than did Dickens' classic novel. As told by Eisner, Fagin was virtually forced into crime as a youth because of circumstances, not the least of which was the general prejudice against his family, all Ashkenazi Jews. The graphic novel includes a foreword explaining the probable historical antecedents of the tale and how they related to Dickens' portrayal of Jews. While noting that Eisner's depiction of Victorian London is "wholly convincing," a *Publishers Weekly* reviewer wrote that "the story errs on the side of extreme coincidence and melodrama." Francisca Goldsmith, writing in *School Library Journal,* noted that while the book's greatest appeal would be to readers looking for another view of the Dickens classic, it would serve as is a useful resource "for those concerned with media influence on stereotypes and the history of immigration issues."

In other explorations of the literary classics, Eisner created graphic-novel versions of Miguel de Cervantes's *Don Quixote* and Herman Melville's *Moby-Dick,* as well as fairy tales by the Brothers Grimm. Although this approach, taken up by new generations of artists such as P. Craig Russell, has since found favor with critics, these early projects were sometimes viewed with trepidation. Susan Weitz, reviewing *Moby Dick* for *School Library Journal,* considered Eisner's version of the American classic "simplistic" and disappointing, although in *Booklist* Goldsmith found it highly successful in conveying the basic plot, characterizations, and mood of the original. Similarly, in an appraisal of Eisner's *The Last Knight: An Introduction to Don Quixote by Miguel de Cervantes.* Marian Drabkin commented in *School Library Journal* that the complex character Don Quixote is distilled into a "clownish madman whose escapades are slapstick and pointless." *Booklist* critic Roger Leslie, on the other hand, found Eisner's book to be "faithful to the spirit of the original" and an excellent introduction to the great classic.

While his place in the Golden Age of Comics remains secure due to his work on "The Spirit," Eisner was also phenomenally influential within his field. During his later years he devoted much of his time to sharing his insight into the comic-book medium with new generations of artists, and from 1973 to 1995 taught an influential course in sequential art at New York's School of Visual Arts. Honored by Comic-Con International in 1988 when the Eisner Awards were named in his honor, the celebrated artist also became a successful contender for this prestigious honor: in 2001 he won an Eisner for best archival collection for *The Spirit Archives* and in 2002 he won for best new graphic novel for *The Name of the Game.* At his death in 2005, Eisner was remembered as a legend in his field, and as a man dedicated to his craft. Reported to have been working until the day of his death, Eisner's final book, the nonfiction graphic novel *The Plot: The Secret Story of The Protocols of the Elders of Zion,* was published posthumously. Recounting the history of a forged document dating from 1898 that purporting to set forth a plan by Jewish leaders to take over the world, Eisner's book "provides a great service to the truth," noted *Library Journal* contributor Steve Raiteri, while in *Publishers Weekly* a reviewer praised the books pen-and-ink art as examples of Eisner's "most exquisite work."

Biographical and Critical Sources

BOOKS

Couch, N.C. Christopher, and Stephen Weiner, *The Will Eisner Companion,* DC Comics (New York, NY), 2004.

PERIODICALS

Booklist, August, 1998, Gordon Flagg, review of *A Family Matter,* p. 1948; December 15, 1999, Stephanie Zvirin, review of *The Princess and the Frog by the Grimm Brothers,* p. 780; June 1, 2000, Roger Leslie, review of *The Last Knight: An Introduction to Don Quixote by Miguel de Cervantes,* p. 1884; August, 2000, Gordon Flagg, review of *The Spirit Archives,* p. 2094; September 15, 2000, Gordon Flagg, review of *Minor Miracles,* p. 200; November 15, 2001, Francisca Goldsmith, review of *Moby Dick by Herman Melville,* p. 568, and "Sequential Art Meets the White Whale," p. 569; February 1, 2002, Gordon Flagg, review of *The Name of the Game,* p. 914; February 1, 2003, Carlos Orellana, review of *Sundiata: A Legend of Africa,* p. 984; September 1, 2003, Gordon Flagg, review of *Fagin the Jew,* p. 76; August, 2004, Gordon Flagg, review of *The Spirit Archives,* Volume 13, p. 1916; October 15, 2004, Gordon Flagg, review of *The Spirit Archives,* Volume 14, p. 396.
College English, February, 1995, George Dardess, review of *Comics and Sequential Art,* p. 213.

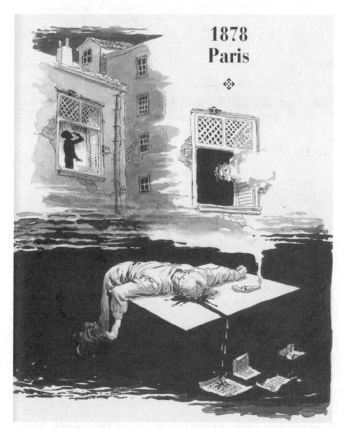

Eisner's final work, The Plot: The Secret Story of The Protocols of the Elders of Zion, *follows the history of a fabricated conspiracy implicating Jewish leaders in designs on world domination.*

Library Journal, October 15, 1974, Will Eisner, "Comic Books in the Library"; June 1, 1991, Keith R.A. De-Candido, review of *To the Heart of the Storm,* p. 134; October 15, 1974; September 15, 2000, Stephen Weiner, review of *Minor Miracles,* p. 66; November 1, 2002, Steve Raiteri, review of *The Name of the Game,* p. 68; March 1, 2003, Steve Raiteri, review of *Sundiata: A Legend of Africa,* p. 74; September 1, 2003, Steve Raiteri, review of *The Spirit Archives,* p. 140; November 1, 2003, Steve Raiteri, review of *Fagin the Jew,* p. 60; May 15, 2005, Steve Raiteri, review of *The Plot: The Secret Story of The Protocols of the Elders of Zion,* p. 98.

New York Review of Books, June 21, 2001, David Hajdu, "The Spirit of the Spirit," p. 48.

Philadelphia, August, 1984, Jack Curtin, "Signals from Space," p. 70.

Publishers Weekly, October 4, 1985, review of *Comics and Sequential Art,* p. 75; March 25, 1988, review of *A Life Force,* p. 61; March 22, 1991, review of *To the Heart of the Storm,* p. 76; June 21, 1991, review of *Will Eisner Reader: Seven Graphic Stories by a Comics Master,* p. 58; May 8, 1995, review of *Dropsie Avenue: The Neighborhood,* p. 293; January 3, 2000, review of *The Princess and the Frog,* p. 78; November 17, 2003, review of *Fagin the Jew,* p. 46; April 18, 2005, review of *The Plot,* p. 45.

School Arts, April, 2002, Ken Marantz, review of *Comics and Sequential Art,* p. 58.

School Library Journal, July, 2000, Marian Drabkin, review of *The Last Knight,* p. 115; January, 2002, Susan Weitz, review of *Moby Dick by Herman Melville,* p. 138; February, 2003, John Peters, review of *Sundiata,* p. 129; January, 2004, Francisca Goldsmith, review of *Fagin the Jew,* p. 166.

Variety, September 28, 1988, "Comic Book Confidential," p. 30.

Whole Earth, spring, 1998, review of *The Spirit,* p. 25.

ONLINE

Will Eisner Web site, http://www.willeisner.tripod.com (October 15, 2005).

OBITUARIES

PERIODICALS

Chicago Tribune, January 5, 2005, section 3, p. 11.
Los Angeles Times, January 5, 2005, p. B8.
New York Times, January 5, 2005, p. C14.
Print, March-April, 2005, p. 37.
School Library Journal, February, 2005, p. 22.
Times (London, England), January 13, 2005, p. 68.*

*   *   *

EISNER, William Erwin
See EISNER, Will

ERWIN, Will
See EISNER, Will

*   *   *

FARLEY, Terri

Personal

Born in Los Angeles, CA; married (husband a journalist); children: two. *Education:* San Jose State University, B.A. (secondary teaching credential in English); University of Nevada, Reno, M.A. (journalism).

Addresses

Home—Verdi, NV. *Agent*—Karen Solem, Spencerhill Agency, 24 Park Row, P.O. Box. 374, Chatham, NY 12037. *E-mail*—farleyterri@aol.com.

Career

Writer. Formerly worked as a waitress and journalist; teacher of remedial reading in Los Angeles, CA; instructor in college English in Reno, NV; participant in writing workshops.

Member

International Reading Association, National Council of Teachers of English, National Education Association.

Writings

Seven Tears into the Sea (young-adult novel), Simon Pulse (New York, NY), 2005.

NOVELS; "PHANTOM STALLION" SERIES

The Wild One, Avon Books (New York, NY), 2002.
Mustang Moon, Avon Books (New York, NY), 2002.
Dark Sunshine, Avon Books (New York, NY), 2002.
The Challenger, Avon Books (New York, NY), 2003.
The Renegade, Avon Books (New York, NY), 2003.
Desert Dancer, Avon Books (New York, NY), 2003.
Golden Ghost, Avon Books (New York, NY), 2003.
Gift Horse, Avon Books (New York, NY), 2003.
Free Again, Avon Books (New York, NY), 2003.
Untamed, Avon Books (New York, NY), 2004.
Rain Dance, Avon Books (New York, NY), 2004.
Heartbreak Bronco, Avon Books (New York, NY), 2004.
Moonrise, Avon Books (New York, NY), 2005.
Kidnapped Colt, Avon Books (New York, NY), 2005.

Sidelights

Growing up in the suburbs of southern California, Terri Farley was frustrated in her love affair with horses, but although she was not able to ride the range or keep a pony in her back yard, she learned to ride at local stables and sustained herself on books about horses. After she and her family moved to the foothills of the Sierra Nevada mountains, an opportunity to go on a cattle drive rekindled Farley's love for horses. She was able to pursue her dreams of making horses a major part of her life when she and her family moved to the foothills of the Sierra Nevada mountains. Leaving work as a teacher to devote herself to writing, Farley shares her passion for all things equine in her "Phantom Stallion" novel series, which follow the adventures of friends Samantha and Jake, as well as an elusive gray stallion known as the Phantom, in novels such as *Desert Dancer, Mustang Moon,* and *The Wild One.* In a *Booklist* review of *The Wild One,* Kelly Milner Halls praised Samantha for her "infectious, independent spirit," and added that Farley "proves herself to be an able storyteller," while in *School Library Journal* Carol Schene predicted that the novel's action-packed plot will make the novel an "entertaining read for fans of [the] . . . genre."

In addition to her "Phantom Stallion" books, Farley is the author of the young-adult novel *Seven Tears into the Sea.* Based on the Celtic myth of the selkie, the book introduces readers to seventeen-year-old Gwen Cooke. When Gwen was ten years old she had an unusual experience: Prone to sleepwalking, she ended up on the beach one night and encountered a strange young boy . . . or was it all a dream? Now returned to her family's seaside home to help her grandmother run the family inn, Gwen becomes haunted by this memory, and her meeting with a young man named Jesse makes her realize that, along with her childhood memories, there are other things she may have wanted to forget. Noting the fairy-tale quality of Farley's story, *School Library Journal* reviewer Ginny Collier added that *Seven Tears into the Sea* contains enough "romance and mystery" to keep teens "reading until the very end."

In an interview for the *Lazy Lion Books* Web site, Farley commented: "I've loved reading as long as I can remember and when my mother gave me her electric typewriter, I immediately started writing." "Writing fulfills my wildest dreams," she added. "I get to go anywhere I want and do what I want. . . . It's the perfect intersection of all my goals—writer, teacher and mother—when I hear from readers who can't put the book down or who talk about my characters (human and equine) as if they're real."

Biographical and Critical Sources

PERIODICALS

Booklist, September 1, 2002, Kelly Milner Halls, review of *The Wild One,* p. 123.
School Library Journal, December, 2002, Carol Schene, review of *The Wild One,* p. 137; June, 2005, Ginny Collier, review of *Seven Tears into the Sea,* p. 156.

Tribune Books (Chicago, IL), August 24, 2003, review of *Phantom Stallion,* p. 6.
Voice of Youth Advocates, June, 2005, Christina Fairman, review of *Seven Tears into the Sea,* p. 145.

ONLINE

Lazy Lion Books Web site, http://www.lazylionbooks.com/ (July 13, 2005), interview with Farley.
Phantom Stallion Web site, http://www.phantomstallion. com/ (July 13, 2005).
Terri Farley Home Page, http://www.terrifarley.com (November 20, 2005).

*   *   *

FARRAR, Jill
See MORRIS, Jill

*   *   *

FORRESTAL, Elaine 1941-

Personal

Born October 9, 1941, in Perth, Western Australia, Australia; daughter of Russell Alfred (a bank officer) and Emily Annie "Bonnie" (a secretary; maiden name, Ives) Chandler; married Barry Edmonds, November 17, 1962 (marriage ended February 28, 1980); married Peter Forrestal (a wine and food writer), January 10, 1981; children: Lee Anne Beet, Carmel Jane Keylock. *Education:* Earned degree in early childhood education. *Hobbies and other interests:* Swimming, traveling, reading, walking, gardening.

Addresses

Home—1 Cobb St., Scarborough 6019, Western Australia, Australia. *E-mail*—eforrie@iinet.net.au, or forrie@ attglobal.net.

Career

Bank of New South Wales, secretary, 1958-62; Education Department of Western Australia, teacher, 1970-81, early childhood specialist, 1984-99. Lecturer; speaker at festivals and conferences; writer-in-residence at libraries and schools throughout Australia and in Northern Ireland.

Member

Australian Society of Authors, Children's Book Council of Australia (Western Australia Branch).

Awards, Honors

Western Australian Premier's Book Award shortlist for children's book, 1991, and Australian Children's Book Council (CBC) Notable Book designation, 1992, both

Elaine Forrestal

for *The Watching Lake;* Highly Commended designation, National Association for Special Education Children's Book Award, 1997, Book of the Year, CBC, and Western Australia Young Readers Award (WAYRA) Hoffman Award in Younger Readers category, both 1998, and Young Australia Best Book Award shortlist, 1999 and 2000, all for *Someone like Me;* Western Australian Premier's Book Awards shortlist, 1999, for *Straggler's Reef;* CBC Book of the Year for Younger Readers shortlist, 2000, for *Graffiti on the Fence;* WAYRA for Young Readers shortlist, 2003, for *Winning;* Western Australia Premier's Book Award shortlist for children's book, 2003, for *Deep Water,* and 2005, for *Black Earth;* CBC Notable Book designation, 2004, for *Deep Water.*

Writings

FOR CHILDREN

The Watching Lake, Puffin (Melbourne, Australia), 1991.
Someone like Me, Puffin (Melbourne, Australia), 1996.
Straggler's Reef, Fremantle Arts Centre Press (Fremantle, Western Australia, Australia), 1999.
Graffiti on the Fence, Puffin (Melbourne, Australia), 1999.
Leaving No Footprints, Puffin (Ringwood, Victoria, Australia), 2001.
Winning, Puffin (Camberwell, Victoria, Australia), 2002.
A Glassful of Giggles (stories), illustrated by Sharon Thompson, Fremantle Arts Centre Press (Fremantle, Western Australia, Australia), 2002.
Rainbow Jackets (stories), illustrated by Sharon Thompson, Fremantle Arts Centre Press (North Fremantle, Western Australia, Australia), 2003.

Stories have appeared on Australian television program *Mulligrubs.* Contributor to periodicals, including *Highlights for Children;* contributor to anthologies, including *Creepy-Crawly Stories,* edited by Barbara Ireson, Century Hutchinson (London, England), 1986, and *Stories to Share,* edited by Jean Chapman, Hodder and Stoughton (Sydney, New South Wales, Australia), 1983.

Author's works have been translated into Italian and Slovenian.

FOR CHILDREN; "EDEN GLASSIE MYSTERY" SERIES

Deep Water, Puffin (Camberwell, Victoria, Australia), 2003.
Stone Circle, Puffin (Camberwell, Victoria, Australia), 2004.
Black Earth, Puffin (Camberwell, Victoria, Australia), 2004.
Wild Wind, Puffin (Camberwell, Victoria, Australia), 2005.

Sidelights

Elaine Forrestal is an Australian writer who has produced middle-grade novels such as the award-winning *Straggler's Reef, Someone like Me,* and *Winning,* as well as the collections of simple, short read-aloud tales published as *A Glassful of Giggles* and *Rainbow Jackets.* Her "Eden Glassie" mystery novels, which take place during the holiday season on a working Australian vineyard, focus on Tori, Maddie, Brontë, and Morgan, four cousins who encounter a host of interesting people as well as adventures that sometimes lead them into a parallel world where fairies, pirates, or ghosts can cross their path. In a *Magpies* profile, Alison Gregg praised Forrestal's writing for possessing "realistic child characters in realistic settings," a "sure-sense of dialogue," and action-packed plots that contain an "exploration of issues that are meaningful to children now."

Working as a preschool teacher in Perth, Australia, for many years, Forrestal began her writing career by writing down several of the stories she told her students and submitting them for publication in anthologies and periodicals. Her first novel, *The Watching Lake,* was inspired by a local legend about a ghost that haunted Herdman's Lake, near Forrestal's suburban home. The novel presents readers with a mystery as well as an inherent warning about the ecological damage that may result from tampering with nature, and was shortlisted for the Western Australia Premier's Book Award in 1991.

In Forrestal's novel *Someone like Me,* the life of an ordinary sixth-grade boy is changed in many ways when he discovers that his family's neighbor has a troubling mystery in her past. The recipient of several honors, *Someone like Me* is "bursting with lovely images of the Australian countryside and lifestyle," according to reviewer Cecile Grumelart in *Magpies.*

Curious about her family's past, Karri finds her questions leading to a dangerous reef where treasure as well as danger may await her in Forrestal's 1999 novel. (Cover illustration by Marion Duke.)

In *Straggler's Reef* the past surfaces in the present as young Australians Karri and Jarrad are stranded on a reef while sailing with their father off the coast of western Australia. Karrie passes the time reading her grandmother's journal when Carrie, a ghostly figure from the past, appears on the yacht deck and announces that the boat is stranded directly overtop a sunken treasure. Forrestal's "recount of events in the 1840s is engrossing and evocative," wrote *Australian Book Review* writer Pam Mcintyre, while *Magpies* critic Fran Knight called *Straggler's Reef* "a gripping tale." Although Forrestal's emphasis on action appeals to middle-grader readers, in the novel she weaves in issues such as "how [language] has changed, family history, children's roles in their families and expectations of how boys and girls should behave," according to Kylie Williams in a review of *Straggler's Reef* for *REACT*.

Other novels by Forrestal include *Leaving No Footprint*, *Winning,* and her ongoing "Eden Glassie Mystery" series, focusing on friends Henny and Kip and Kip's dog Stranger. Part of the "Eden Glassie" series, *Leaving No Footprints* follows the teens as they first

meet during a summer holiday when Henny's family go to their vacation home on Dog Beach. At first fellow beach dweller Kip seems reserved and moody, but the two soon become friends, and when their boat is endangered during a storm Henny finally learns the reasons for Kip's need for emotional distance.

Focusing on the rivalries that can sometimes occur even in the closest friendships, *Winning* introduces middle-graders Pearce and Yosef. Always a natural at sports, Pearce is also a natural leader among his schoolmates, and when Yosef begins to show a talent for running Pearce feels threatened by this unfamiliar competition. A series of local robberies also prove cause for concern among the group of boys when it coincides with Pearce's seemingly sudden change in behavior. Suspicions grow among his friends, who do not know their friend's secret: that Pearce is also dealing with a violent father.

Forrestal once told *SATA:* "Children are not as easily fooled as some people seem to think. They will not tolerate anything but the highest degree of honesty and transparency from their authors. And they demand rel-

In addition to novels, Aussie writer Forrestal has also authored short stories for younger readers, such as the five tales in this 2003 collection. (Cover illustration by Sharon Thompson.)

evance in what they read, which means that the children's author must keep up to date with what kids are watching on TV, the games they are playing, and the music they are listening to. In this regard, access to kids in a school playground is a very useful thing.

"Until recently, teaching and writing have been complementary careers for me. I began writing stories to use with my class when I became frustrated with the lack of suitable commercially available material. And many of my stories are based on incidents or characters I have encountered at school."

Biographical and Critical Sources

PERIODICALS

Australian Book Review, July, 1999, Pam Macintyre, review of *Straggler's Reef,* p. 43.
Books for Keeps, May, 1998, Juliana Oliver, review of *Someone like Me,* p. 18.
Magpies, July, 1992, p. 20; March, 1997, Cecile Grumelart, review of *Someone like Me,* p. 33; July, 1999, Fran Knight, review of *Straggler's Reef;* March, 2002, review of *Leaving No Footprints,* p. 33; May, 2002, review of *Winning,* p. 33, and Alison Gregg, "Know the Author: Elaine Forrestal"; November, 2003, review of *Deep Water,* p. 34.
REACT, Volume 99, number 4, Kylie Williams, review of *Straggler's Reef,* p. 3.
Reading Time, Volume 43, number 4.

ONLINE

Aussie Reviews Online, http://www.aussiereviews.com/ (October 20, 2005), Sally Murphy, review of *A Glassful of Giggles* and *Rainbow Jackets.*
Penguin Books Australia Web site, http://www.penguin.com.au/ (May 4, 2005), "Elaine Forrestal."

*   *   *

FRENCH, Vivian
(Louis Catt)

Personal

Children: four daughters. *Hobbies and other interests:* Live music, traveling.

Addresses

Home—Edinburgh, Scotland. *Agent*—Fraser Ross, 6 Wellington Place, Leith EH6 7EQ, England.

Career

Writer and storyteller. Visiting lecturer, University of the West of England. Previously worked in theater as an actor and writer, and National Book League; writer-in-residence at various schools; former reviewer for *Guardian,* London, England.

Awards, Honors

Emil/Kurt Maschler Award shortlist, 1993, for *Caterpillar, Caterpillar;* Smarties Book Prize shortlist, 1995, for *A Song for Little Toad;* Sheffield Children's Book Award; numerous Parents' Honor awards.

Writings

Tottie Pig's Noisy Christmas, illustrated by Clive Scruton, Walker (London, England), 1990.
Tottie Pig's Special Birthday, illustrated by Clive Scruton, Walker (London, England), 1990.
Doctor Elsie, illustrated by Rowan Barnes-Murphy, Walker (London, England), 1991.
Baker Ben, illustrated by Rowan Barnes-Murphy, Walker (London, England), 1991.
One Ballerina Two, illustrated by Jan Ormerod, Walker (London, England), 1991.
It's a Go to the Park Day, illustrated by Clive Scruton, Walker (London, England), 1991, Simon & Schuster (New York, NY), 1992.
Christmas Mouse, illustrated by Chris Fisher, Walker (London, England), 1992, Candlewick (Cambridge, MA), 1995.
(Abridger) Charles Dickens, *A Christmas Carol,* illustrated by Patrick Benson, Walker (London, England), 1992, Candlewick (Cambridge, MA), 1993.
Tillie McGillie's Fantastical Chair, illustrated by Sue Heap, Walker (London, England), 1992.
Caterpillar, Caterpillar, illustrated by Charlotte Voake, Walker (London, England), 1993, Candlewick (Cambridge, MA), 1995.
Under the Moon, illustrated by Chris Fisher, Walker (London, England), 1993, Candlewick (Cambridge, MA), 1994.
Kim and the Sooper Glooper Torch, illustrated by Chris Fisher, Young Lions (London, England), 1993.
Kevin and the Invisible Safety Pin, illustrated by Chris Fisher, Young Lions (London, England), 1993.
Mary Poggs and the Sunshine, illustrated by Colin West, Walker (London, England), 1993.
Mandy and the Purple Spotted Hanky, illustrated by Chris Fisher, Young Lions (London, England), 1993.
Hedgehogs Don't Eat Hamburgers, illustrated by Chris Fisher, Puffin (London, England), 1993.
Why the Sea Is Salt, illustrated by Patrice Aggs, Candlewick (Cambridge, MA), 1993.
Ian and the Stripy Bath Plug, illustrated by Chris Fisher, Young Lions (London, England), 1993.
Jackson's Juniors, illustrated by Thelma Lambert, Walker (London, England), 1993.
Once upon a Time, illustrated by John Prater, Candlewick (Cambridge, MA), 1993.
Little Tiger Goes Shopping, illustrated by Andy Cooke, Candlewick (Cambridge, MA), 1994.
Little Ghost, illustrated by John Prater, Candlewick (Cambridge, MA), 1994.
Spider Watching, illustrated by Alison Wisenfeld, Walker (London, England), 1994, Candlewick (Cambridge, MA), 1995.

The Little Red Hen and the Sly Fox, illustrated by Sally Hobson, ABC (London, England), 1994, published as *Red Hen and Sly Fox,* Simon & Schuster (New York, NY), 1995.

Robbie and the Amazing Presents, illustrated by Selina Young, Orchard (London, England), 1994.

Princess Primrose, illustrated by Chris Fisher, Walker (London, England), 1994.

Mervyn and the Hopping Hat, illustrated by Chris Fisher, Young Lions (London, England), 1994.

The Hedgehogs and the Big Bag, illustrated by Chris Fisher, Puffin (London, England), 1994.

Fat Ginger and the Awful Aliens, illustrated by Chris Fisher, Young Lions (London, England), 1994.

Warren and the Flying Football, illustrated by Chris Fisher, Young Lions (London, England), 1994.

Buster and the Bike Burglar, illustrated by Chris Fisher, Young Lions (London, England), 1994.

Please, Princess Primrose, illustrated by Chris Fisher, Walker (London, England), 1994.

The Apple Trees, illustrated by Terry Milne, Walker (London, England), 1994.

(Reteller) *Lazy Jack,* illustrated by Russell Ayto, Walker (London, England), 1995.

Jolly Roger and the Underwater Treasure, illustrated by Chris Fisher, Hodder (London, England), 1995.

First Mate Mutt and the Wind Machine Mutiny, illustrated by Chris Fisher, Hodder (London, England), 1995.

Captain Jennifer Jellyfish Jones, illustrated by Chris Fisher, Hodder (London, England), 1995.

Morris in the Apple Tree, illustrated by Guy Parker-Rees, Collins (London, England), 1995.

Morris the Mouse Hunter, illustrated by Guy Parker-Rees, Collins (London, England), 1995.

Oliver's Vegetables, illustrated by Alison Bartlett, Orchard (New York, NY), 1995.

Sea Dog Williams and the Frozen North, illustrated by Chris Fisher, Hodder (London, England), 1995.

A Walker Treasury: Magical Stories, Walker (London, England), 1995, published as *The Walker Book of Magical Stories,* Walker (London, England), 2000.

The Thistle Princess and Other Stories (also see below), illustrated by Chris Fisher, Walker (London, England), 1995.

A Song for Little Toad, illustrated by Barbara Firth, Candlewick (Cambridge, MA), 1995.

Painter Bear, illustrated by Chris Fisher, Candlewick (Cambridge, MA), 1995.

Molly in the Middle, illustrated by Venice Shone, Candlewick (Cambridge, MA), 1996.

Little Tiger Finds a Friend, illustrated by Andy Cooke, Candlewick (Cambridge, MA), 1996.

Bob the Dog, illustrated by Alison Bartlett, Hodder (London, England), 1996.

Squeaky Cleaners in a Tip!, illustrated by Anna Currey, Hodder (London, England), 1996.

Squeaky Cleaners in a Stew!, illustrated by Anna Currey, Hodder (London, England), 1996.

Squeaky Cleaners in a Muddle!, illustrated by Anna Currey, Hodder (London, England), 1996.

Once upon a Picnic, illustrated by John Prater, Candlewick (Cambridge, MA), 1996.

Squeaky Cleaners in a Hole!, illustrated by Anna Currey, Hodder (London, England), 1996.

Morris and the Cat Flap, illustrated by Olivia Villet, Collins (London, England), 1996.

The Christmas Kitten, illustrated by Chris Fisher, Candlewick (Cambridge, MA), 1996.

(Reteller) *Aesop's Funky Fables,* illustrated by Korky Paul, Hamilton (London, England), 1997, Viking (New York, NY), 1998.

Guinea Pigs on the Go, illustrated by Clive Scruton, Collins (London, England), 1997.

Kelly and the Crime Club, illustrated by Lesley Harker, Hodder (London, England), 1997.

Zenobia and Mouse, illustrated by Duncan Smith, Walker (London, England), 1997.

Peter and the Ghost, illustrated by Lesley Harker, Hodder (London, England), 1997.

Oh No Anna!, illustrated by Alex Ayliffe, Peachtree (Atlanta, GA), 1997.

A Christmas Star Called Hannah, illustrated by Anne Yvonne Gilbert, Candlewick (Cambridge, MA), 1997.

The Thistle Princess, illustrated by Elizabeth Harbour, Candlewick (Cambridge, MA), 1998.

Iggy Pig's Skippy Day, illustrated by David Melling, Hodder (London, England), 1998.

Kick Back, illustrated by Jake Abrams, Barrington Stoke (Edinburgh, Scotland), 1998.

Oliver's Fruit Salad, illustrated by Alison Bartlett, Orchard (New York, NY), 1998.

The Boy Who Walked on Water, and Other Stories, Walker (London, England), 1998.

I Spy ABC, illustrated by Sally Holmes, Walker (London, England), 1998.

Iggy Pig's Party, illustrated by David Melling, Hodder (London, England), 1998.

(With Ross Collins) *Write around the World: The Story of How and Why We Learnt to Write,* Zero to Ten (New York, NY), 1998 published as *Write around the World,* Zero to Ten (Slough, England), 1999.

Whale Journey, illustrated by Lisa Flather, Zero to Ten (New York, NY), 1998.

Not Again, Anna!, illustrated by Alex Ayliffe, Levinson (London, England), 1998.

Lullaby Lion, Candlewick (Cambridge, MA), 1998.

Iggy Pig's Big Bad Wolf Trouble, illustrated by David Melling, Scholastic (New York, NY), 1998.

The Story of Christmas, illustrated by Jane Chapman, Candlewick (Cambridge, MA), 1999.

Iggy Pig at the Seaside, illustrated by David Melling, Hodder (London, England), 1999.

Iggy Pig's Dark Night, illustrated by David Melling, Hodder (London, England), 1999.

Mrs Hippo's Pizza Parlour, illustrated by Clive Scruton, Kingfisher (London, England), 1999, published as *Mrs. Hippo's Pizza Parlor,,* Kingfisher (Boston, MA), 2004.

Iggy Pig's Shopping Day, illustrated by David Melling, Hodder (London, England), 1999.

Iggy Pig's Snow Day, illustrated by David Melling, Hodder (London, England), 1999.

The Snow Dragon, illustrated by Chris Fisher, Doubleday (London, England), 1999.

(With Rebecca Elgar) *Tiger and the New Baby,* Kingfisher (New York, NY), 1999.

Rainbow House, illustrated by Biz Hull, Tamarind (Camberley, England), 1999.

Space Dog Finds Treasure, illustrated by Sue Heap, Hodder (London, England), 1999.

(With Jan Lewis) *Big Fat Hen and the Hairy Goat,* David & Charles (London, England), 1999.

(With Jan Lewis) *Big Fat Hen and the Red Rooster,* David & Charles (London, England), 1999.

Space Dog Meets Space Cat, illustrated by Sue Heap, Hodder (London, England), 1999.

Space Dog to the Rescue, illustrated by Sue Heap, Hodder (London, England), 1999.

Space Dog Visits Planet Earth, illustrated by Sue Heap, Hodder (London, England), 1999.

(With Rebecca Elgar) *Tiger and the Temper Tantrum,* Kingfisher (New York, NY), 1999.

(Adapter) Michael Rosen, *We're Going on a Bear Hunt* (play), Walker (London, England), 2000.

Growing Frogs, illustrated by Alison Bartlett, Candlewick (Cambridge, MA), 2000.

The Gingerbread Boy, illustrated by John Prater, Walker (London, England), 2000.

(Reteller) *Funky Tales,* illustrated by Korky Paul, Hamish Hamilton (London, England), 2000.

(Reteller) *The Three Billy Goats Gruff* (play), illustrated by Arthur Robins, Walker (London, England), 2000.

(Adapter) Martin Waddell, *Farmer Duck* (play), Walker (London, England), 2000.

Falling Awake, illustrated by Roy Petrie, Barrington Stoke (Edinburgh, Scotland), 2000.

(Adapter) Sarah Hayes, *This Is the Bear* (play), Walker (London, England), 2000.

Space Dog, illustrated by Sue Heap, Hodder (London, England), 2000.

(Reteller) *Noah's Ark, and Other Bible Stories,* illustrated by Jane Chapman, Early Learning Centre (Swindon, England), 2000.

(Reteller) Michael Rosen, *Little Rabbit Foo Foo,* illustrated by Arthur Robins, Walker (London, England), 2000.

Let's Go, Anna!, illustrated by Alex Ayliffe, David & Charles (London, England), 2000.

Space Dog Goes to Planet Purrgo, illustrated by Sue Heap, Hodder (London, England), 2000.

Swallow Journey, illustrated by Karin Littlewood, Zero to Ten (Slough, England), 2000.

Space Dog and the Space Egg, illustrated by Sue Heap, Hodder (London, England), 2000.

(Reteller) *The Kingfisher Book of Fairy Tales,* illustrated by Peter Malone, Kingfisher (New York, NY), 2000.

From Zero to Ten: The Story of Numbers, Oxford University Press (New York, NY), 2000.

Ladybird, Ladybird, illustrated by Selina Young, Orion (London, England), 2001.

Oliver's Milk Shake, illustrated by Alison Bartlett, Orchard (New York, NY), 2001.

(Reteller) *The Tiger and the Jackal: A Traditional Indian Tale,* illustrated by Alison Bartlett, Walker (London, England), 2001.

Big Bad Bug, illustrated by Emily Bolam, Walker (London, England), 2001.

Mean Green Machine, illustrated by Ana Martín Larraníaga, Walker (London, England), 2001.

Singing to the Sun and Other Magical Tales, illustrated by Chris Fisher, Walker (London, England), 2001.

Guinea Pigs Go to Sea, illustrated by Clive Scruton, Collins (London, England), 2001.

(Reteller) *Jack and the Beanstalk* (play), illustrated by Harry Horse, Walker (London, England), 2001.

(Reteller) *The Three Little Pigs* (play), illustrated by Liz Million, Walker (London, England), 2001.

Five Little Ducks, illustrated by Paul Dowling, Walker (London, England), 2001.

One Fat Cat (play), illustrated by Liz Million, Walker (London, England), 2001.

To Mum, with Love, illustrated by Dana Kubick, Walker (London, England), 2002.

(Editor) *Survivor, and Other Stories,* Walker (London, England), 2002.

(Editor) *Paying for It, and Other Stories,* Walker (London, England), 2002.

Baby Baby, Barrington Stoke (Edinburgh, Scotland), 2002.

A Present for Mom, illustrated by Dana Kubick, Candlewick (Cambridge, MA), 2002.

Wicked Chickens, illustrated by John Bradley, Macmillan (London, England), 2003.

(Reteller) *The Kingfisher Book of Nursery Tales,* illustrated by Stephen Lambert, Kingfisher (Boston, MA), 2003.

Morris the Mouse Hunter, illustrated by Olivia Villet, Collins (London, England), 2003.

T. Rex, illustrated by Alison Bartlett, Candlewick (Cambridge, MA), 2004.

I Love You, Grandpa, illustrated by Dana Kubick, Candlewick (Cambridge, MA), 2004.

Bert and the Burglar, illustrated by Ed Boxall, Walker (London, England), 2004.

Bill Bird's New Boots, illustrated by Alison Bartlett, Egmont Books (London, England), 2004.

Detective Dan, illustrated by Alison Bartlett, A. & C. Black (London, England), 2004.

I Wish I Was an Alien, illustrated by Lisa Williams, Evans (London, England), 2005, published as *I Wish I Were an Alien,* Gingham Dog (Columbus, OH), 2005.

Brian the Giant, illustrated by Sue Heap, Walker (London, England), 2005.

Buck and His Truck, illustrated by Julie Lacome, Walker (London, England), 2005.

The Cat in the Coat, illustrated by Alison Bartlett, Evans (London, England) 2005.

Pig in Love, illustrated by Tim Archbold, Gingham Dog (Columbus, OH), 2005.

Meet the Mammoth!, illustrated by Lisa Williams, Gingham Dog (Columbus, OH), 2005.

A Cat in a Coat, illustrated by Alison Bartlett, Gingham Dog (Columbus, OH), 2005.

Sharp Sheep, illustrated by John Bradley, Macmillan (London, England), 2005.

The Magic Bedtime Storybook, illustrated by Emily Bolam, Orion (London, England), 2005.

Princess Charlotte and the Birthday Ball, illustrated by Sarah Gibb, Orchard (London, England), 2005, HarperColllins (New York, NY), 2007.

Princess Katie and the Silver Pony, illustrated by Sarah Gibb, Orchard (London, England) 2005, HarperCollins (New York, NY), 2007.

Princess Daisy and the Dazzling Dragon, illustrated by Sarah Gibb, Orchard (London, England), 2005, HarperCollins (New York, NY), 2007.

Princess Alice and the Magical Mirror, illustrated by Sarah Gibb, Orchard (London, England), 2005, HarperCollins (New York, NY), 2007.

Princess Sophia and the Sparkling Surprise, illustrated by Sarah Gibb, Orchard (London, England) 2005, HarperCollins (New York, NY), 2007.

Princess Emily and theBeautiful Fairy, illustrated by Sarah Gibb, Orchard (London, England), 2005, HarperCollins (New York, NY), 2007.

Henny Penny, illustrated by Sophie Windham, Bloomsbury (New York, NY), 2006.

Ellie and Elvis, illustrated by Michael Terry, Bloomsbury (London, England), 2006.

Princess Charlotte and the Enchanted Rose, illustrated by Sarah Gibb, Orchard (London England), 2006.

French's books have been translated into more than thirty languages.

"SLEEPOVER CLUB" SERIES; UNDER NAME LOUIS CATT

Sleepover on Friday the Thirteenth (also see below), Collins (London, England), 1998.

Sleepover Girls Go Detective, Collins (London, England), 1999.

(With Fiona Cummings) *Sleepover on Friday the Thirteenth; Sleepover Girls Go Camping; Sleepover Girls at Camp* ("Mega Sleepover Club" series), Collins (London, England), 2002.

Work in Progress

The books *Princess Katie and the Dancing Broomstick, Princess Daisy and the Magical Merry go Round, Princess Alice and the Crystal Slipper, Princess Sophia and the Prince's Party,* and *Princess Emily and the Wishing Star,* all for Harper Collins.

Sidelights

Vivian French is a professional storyteller and the prolific author of picture books, plays, and novels for children and young adults. French has created such memorable characters as Iggy Pig, Space Dog, the Staple

While Grandpa has his limitations, a little boy realizes that his older relative can be counted on for the most important things in **I Love You, Grandpa.** *(Illustration by Dana Kubick.)*

Street Gang, the Squeaky Cleaners, and Tottie Pig. Her retellings of folk and fairy tales have been published in her native England in story collections and as plays for young performers. As Louis Catt—a pen name inspired by the author's cat, Louis—French also contributed novels to Rose Impey's "Sleepover Club" series, based on a popular British television series.

French has been interested in stories since childhood, when she read all the fairy tales she could find. "I especially remember a copy of *Grimm's Fairy Tales* belonging to my grandfather," she told a *Jubilee Books* online interviewer. "It had really crude woodcut pictures, and it gave me nightmares—but I kept going back and reading it again and again."

Publishing her first three children's books in 1990, French has gone on to produce more than one hundred titles, most of them picture books for young readers. Some of these, including *Little Tiger Goes Shopping*, focus on teamwork. Little Tiger and Big Tiger want to bake a cake, but they have no eggs. They head out to the store only to discover that many other animals are also headed that way to pick up various ingredients. When the animals arrive at the store, however, it is closed, and they decide to pool their resources to make a cake everyone can enjoy. "Kids (and cooks) will identify with this all-too-frequent culinary predicament," wrote Deborah Abbott in her review for *Booklist*. Little Tiger appears again as the hero of *Little Tiger Finds a Friend*, while a different young tiger stars in *Tiger and the New Baby* and *Tiger and the Temper Tantrum*, the last which *Booklist* reviewer Ilene Cooper deemed "on target for the audience."

French's "Oliver" stories all feature a young protagonist who likes foods such as french fries but absolutely detests vegetables. In *Oliver's Vegetables*, the boy's grandfather convinces Oliver that certain vegetables might be worth trying. Julie Corsaro wrote in *Booklist* that "this breezy story" is suitable "as the centerpiece in a preschool story time . . . or just for plain old fun." While noting that some adults may question whether a child would find beet salad to be "very, very, very good," in the opinion of a *Publishers Weekly* reviewer "agreeable readers will accept her try-it-you'll-like-it approach." Oliver's second adventure with food takes place in *Oliver's Fruit Salad*. When the boy is hesitant to eat canned fruit, his mother thinks the remedy is a trip to the grocery store. Fortunately, memories of his grandfather's garden help Oliver enjoy the fresh fruit his mother soon sets before him. Stephanie Zvirin considered the title "great for lap sharing or use with small groups." Food is central to another incident from Oliver's life, as the boy and his cousin take a trip to the dairy farm in *Oliver's Milk Shake*. As DeAnn Tabuchi noted in a review of the series for *School Library Journal*, "Oliver is a charmer."

Stanley, the youngest of his siblings, cannot figure out what he should get his mother for Mother's Day in *A Present for Mom*. When he tries to copy older family members the gift does not seem right; finally, his older sister helps Stanley figure out just the right present. French's "simple tale rings true for little ones," according to a *Kirkus Reviews* critic. "Children will identify with Stanley, his quest, and his ultimate triumph," assured Heather E. Miller in her *School Library Journal* review. A *Publishers Weekly* reviewer felt that "French's use of detail gives her story its individuality," and *Booklist* contributor Hazel Rochman suspected that readers "will enjoy [Stanley's] . . . bumbling, messy failures as much as the final triumphant encircling embrace."

Stanley returns in *I Love You, Grandpa,* as both Stanley and Grandpa realize they cannot keep up with the activities of Stanley's older siblings. However, after a nap and a song, the boy and older man discover an activity they both enjoy: swinging at the playground. Ilene Cooper, in a *Booklist* review of *I Love You, Grandpa*, noted that "the special bond between young and old plays out sweetly in this happy picture book," while a *Kirkus Reviews* contributor recommended the book as a "wonderful selection for the littlest one in any family and for the grandpa that is special in his or her life." Andrea Tarr, writing in *School Library Journal*, considered the title "a delightful choice for reading aloud or for family sharing."

Some of French's picture books focus on nature-related topics. For example, in *Spider Watching* three cousins study the spiders living in a garden shed. While two of the children are enthusiastic, the third is initially afraid of the spiders, but she eventually gets over her fear as she watches the fascinating creatures. *Whale Journey* follows a pod of whales on their migration from Baja California to the Arctic. "French's text keeps the story moving, offering information and action to capture children's attention," Carolyn Phelan wrote of the title in her *Booklist* review. *Growing Frogs* describes the life-cycle of a frog from tadpole to adult, showing readers that many types of frogs are endangered. Jody McCoy, writing in *School Library Journal*, considered the book, illustrated by Alison Bartlett, "a hopping good collaboration," while a *Horn Book* reviewer pointed out that "French provides enough step-by-step guidance so that readers can gather and observe their own frog spawn."

Like *Whale Journey,* both *Caribou Journey* and *Swallow Journey* focus on animal migration. For both, "French writes in the present tense with a quiet immediacy," according to *Booklist* reviewer Hazel Rochman. While *Whale Journey* and *Caribou Journey* both focus on a mother animal and her new baby, *Swallow Journey* shows the journey of a whole flock on their voyage from England, through Spain and France, as they cross the Sahara, until they finally end their trip in southern Africa.

Dinosaurs, particularly the tyrannosaurus rex, are the focus of *T. Rex.* Focusing on dino-facts and discussing how paleontologists piece together information about

In T. Rex *readers can join a boy and his grandfather as they tour a natural-history museum and learn about the giant dinosaur that walked the earth millions of years ago. (Illustration by Alison Bartlett.)*

the prehistoric creatures, the story is told from the perspective of a grandfather and a young boy who are touring a science museum together. "This brief tale simply and succinctly sums up how much is still unknowable in the scientific world, while also acknowledging how much can be proven through study," commented a *Publishers Weekly* critic. Karin Snelson, writing for *Booklist,* considered *T. Rex* to be "a sprightly picture book that's as much about the mysteries of science as it is about dinosaurs." Noting that French suggests that young readers may be the ones to grow up and discover more about dinosaurs, a *Kirkus Reviews* contributor commented that such suggestions serve as "an energizing idea for young dinosaur fans." Marge Loch-Wouters commented in *School Library Journal* that "young dinosaur lovers will enjoy the story and return to the book often."

French's retellings of folk tales are perhaps her most popular titles. In *Red Hen and Sly Fox* the traditional story of the gullible hen eventually outsmarting a wily fox "is given new life by French's fresh text," according to *Booklist* critic Lauren Peterson. "This energetic book is as fresh as it is classic," a *Publishers Weekly* contributor commented, while Mary M. Burns, in her review for *Horn Book,* praised French's use of language, noting: "The dialogue is pithy and concrete—attuned to the sensibilities of young audiences."

Lazy Jack is a retelling of the traditional story about a lackadasical boy who keeps losing the pay he receives from his various jobs. French "nicely tweaks the traditional ending to show redemption on Jack's part without losing the comedic tone," a *Publishers Weekly* contributor noted. Hazel Rochman, writing in *Booklist,* commented that "any child who's messed up with the best intentions will love the disaster tale and will relish Jack's sweet revenge."

Not all of French's folk tales are traditional; the story in *The Thistle Princess* is a fairy tale of French's own creation. A king and queen want a daughter, and a thistle tells the royal couple how they can have a child. Soon, a little thistle girl appears, and the parents are at first over protective, but when they allow the princess to play outside, she truly thrives. "Readers with a strong taste for . . . nostalgic and happily-ever-after endings will take to this one from the start," predicted a reviewer for *Publishers Weekly.*

Along with picture books, French is also the author of several collections of short fiction, some retellings of traditional tales and some original stories. In *Under the Moon,* she presents three stories: one a folktale from Eastern Europe and the others original stories. "All the stories exhibit a folkloric style, with a timelessness that should make for broad appeal," wrote Kay Weisman in *Booklist.* French takes a new approach to an old favorite in *Aesop's Funky Fables,* using plenty of sound-words to encourage acting-out storytelling. The author's "impressive range of voice reveals a keen ear for dialogue and description," noted a critic for *Publishers Weekly.*

French assembles seven of her favorite fairy tales in *The Kingfisher Book of Fairy Tales.* Retelling and shortening such stories as "Cinderella," "Jack and the Beanstalk," and "Rumplestiltskin" for a younger audience, she does not shy away from the darker aspects of some of these tales, and works to retain the traditional "fairy" elements, as she notes in her introduction to the collection. *School Library Journal* reviewer Barbara Buckley considered the work to be "a well-executed anthology."

In working on *The Kingfisher Book of Fairy Tales,* "it was exciting to revisit all my old favourites," French explained on the *Jubilee Books* Web site. Continuing to re-explore the stories of childhood, she has also produced *The Kingfisher Book of Nursery Tales,* a related anthology of retellings that "playfully retells eight . . . best-known fairy tales," according to a *Publishers Weekly* critic. Carolyn Janssen dubbed French's work on this second anthology "well done," in her review for *School Library Journal.*

In her *Jubilee Books* interview, French recommended the following advice to young writers: "Talk a lot, read a lot, listen, watch people and be around people. . . . Don't EVER let the fact that you can't spell or write neatly put you off writing stories—use a tape recorder, tell the story to a friend, draw it out in pictures—it's the story that matters, not the packaging."

Biographical and Critical Sources

PERIODICALS

Booklist, February 1, 1994, Deborah Abbott, review of *Little Tiger Goes Shopping,* p. 1009; March 15, 1994, Kay Weisman, review of *Under the Moon,* p. 1365; March 1, 1995, Carolyn Phelan, review of *Spider Watching,* p. 1247; May 1, 1995, Lauren Peterson, review of *Red Hen and Sly Fox,* p. 1579; September 1, 1995, Hazel Rochman, review of *Lazy Jack,* p. 73; September 15, 1995, Julie Corsaro, review of *Oliver's Vegetables,* p. 175; November 1, 1997, Ilene Cooper, review of *A Christmas Star Called Hannah,* p. 480; October 15, 1998, Stephanie Zvirin, review of *Oliver's Fruit Salad,* p. 426; January 1, 1999, Carolyn Phelan, review of *Whale Journey,* p. 887; January 1, 1999, Kathleen Squires, review of *Not Again, Anna!,* p. 887; May 1, 1999, Ilene Cooper, review of *Tiger and the New Baby* and *Tiger and the Temper Tantrum,* p. 1598; May 1, 2000, Susan Dove Lempke, review of *Growing Frogs,* p. 1672; August, 2001, Shelley Townsend-Hudson, review of *Oliver's Milk Shake,* p. 2129; January 1, 2002, Hazel Rochman, review of *Swallow Journey,* p. 861; May 1, 2002, Hazel Rochman, review of *A Present for Mom,* p. 1532; November 1, 2004, Ilene Cooper, review of *I Love You, Grandpa,* p. 488; December 1, 2004, Karin Snelson, review of *T. Rex,* p. 672; December 15, 2004, Hazel Rochman, review of *Mrs. Hippo's Pizza Parlor,* p. 746.

Five Owls, March, 1995, review of *Spider Watching,* p. 87.

Horn Book, July-August, 1995, Mary M. Burns, review of *Red Hen and Sly Fox,* p. 469; May, 2000, review of *Growing Frogs,* p. 332; November-December, 2004, Danielle J. Ford, review of *T. Rex,* p. 726.

Kirkus Reviews, March 1, 2002, review of *A Present for Mom,* p. 334; September 1, 2004, review of *I Love You, Grandpa,* p. 864; October 15, 2004, review of *T. Rex,* p. 1005.

Publishers Weekly, May 8, 1995, review of *Red Hen and Sly Fox,* p. 295; July 10, 1995, review of *Lazy Jack,* p. 57; July 31, 1995, review of *A Song for Little Toad,*

p. 80; October 9, 1995, review of *Oliver's Vegetables,* p. 84; October 6, 1997, review of *A Christmas Star Called Hannah,* p. 55; February 9, 1998, review of *Aesop's Funky Fables,* p. 95; October 19, 1998, review of *The Thistle Princess,* p. 80; May 22, 2000, "Many Happy Returns," p. 95; March 11, 2002, review of *A Present for Mom,* p. 71; November 24, 2003, "Enduring Favorites," p. 66; November 29, 2004, review of *T. Rex,* p. 39.

School Library Journal, June, 1994, Susan Helper, review of *Under the Moon,* p. 98; May, 2000, Jody McCoy, review of *Growing Frogs,* p. 161; December, 2000, review of *Growing Frogs,* p. 53; January, 2001, Barbara Buckley, review of *The Kingfisher Book of Fairy Tales,* p. 116; March, 2001, Martha Link, review of *Let's Go, Anna!,* p. 208; June, 2001, DeAnn Tabuchi, review of *Oliver's Milk Shake,* p. 114; December, 2001, Sally Bates Goodroe, review of *Caribou Journey,* p. 158; May, 2002, Heather E. Miller, review of *A Present for Mom,* p. 114; January, 2004, Carolyn Janssen, review of *The Kingfisher Book of Nursery Tales,* p. 114; October, 2004, Andrea Tarr, review of *I Love You, Grandpa,* p. 113; December, 2004, Marge Loch-Wouters, review of *T. Rex,* p. 108.

ONLINE

Jubilee Books Web site, http://www.jubileebooks.co.uk/ (October 31, 2005), interview with French.

Walker Books Web site, http://www.walkerbooks.co.uk/ (October 31, 2005), "Vivian French."*

G-H

GEISERT, Bonnie 1942-

Personal
Born November 17, 1942, in Hartley, IA; daughter of Anton (a farmer) and Leona (Johnson) Meier; married Arthur Geisert (an author and illustrator), June 1, 1963; children: Noah. *Education:* Concordia College (Seward, NE), B.S., 1963; Concordia University (River Forest, IL), M.A., 1968.

Addresses
Home—P.O. Box 3, Galena, IL 61036. *E-mail*—geisert@galenalink.net.

Career
Writer and photographer. Has worked as a teacher. *Freeport Journal-Standard,* Freeport, IL, feature writer and columnist, 1991-95. *Exhibitions:* Photographs have appeared in group shows at Dubuque Museum of Art, Eagle Ridge Inn and Resort, Freeport Art Museum, Galena City Hall, Galena Art Festival, 1995, and Group Photography Show-Galena, 1996 and 1997.

Awards, Honors
Children's Honor Book Award, Nebraska Center for the Book, 2003, for *Prairie Summer.*

Writings

Haystack, illustrated by husband, Arthur Geisert, Houghton (Boston, MA), 1995.
Prairie Town, illustrated by Arthur Geisert, Houghton (Boston, MA), 1998.
River Town, illustrated by Arthur Geisert, Houghton (Boston, MA), 1999.
Mountain Town, illustrated by Arthur Geisert, Houghton (Boston, MA), 2000.
Desert Town, illustrated by Arthur Geisert, Houghton (Boston, MA), 2001.
Prairie Summer (novel), illustrated by Arthur Geisert, Houghton (Boston, MA), 2002.
Lessons (novel), illustrated by Arthur Geisert, Houghton (Boston, MA), 2005.

Monthly columnist for *Journal Standard* (Freeport, IL). Contributor of poetry and articles to *Lutheran, Cobblestone, Galenian,* and *Julien's Journal.* Poetry has been featured in annual poetry anthology, *Gallery,* Dubuque, IA.

Work in Progress
A third novel for Houghton.

Sidelights
Bonnie Geisert is the writer of picture books and novels for young readers, all illustrated by her husband, Arthur Geisert. Their teamwork debuted in 1995 with the picture book *Haystack,* which describes the life cycle of a haystack and reveals the purpose it served in early farms. Called "a quiet tribute to a bygone era" by a reviewer for *Publishers Weekly,* the book shows readers what farm life was in earlier years. Leone McDermott, writing for *Booklist,* noted that "readers will gain not only knowledge about haystacks, but also a sense of the atmosphere of farm life." *Horn Book* critic Margaret A. Bush wrote that Geissert's "simple exercise in ingenuity is a satisfying tale."

The Geiserts followed *Haystack* with a series of books about life in a small town. Beginning with *Prairie Town,* the Geiserts described in simple text and detailed art what life is like in a small Midwestern town. Kay Weisman, writing in *Booklist,* called *Prairie Town* "a sure bet for primary social studies classes as well as browsers." In her review for *Horn Book,* Joanna Rudge Long found the text to be "clear and uncondescending . . . making the book suitable for use with older readers." The author and illustrator team followed with *River*

Town, portraying life in a town that depends on a nearby river for its economy. "Children will easily absorb the deceptively straightforward information about river town industry and economy," noted a *Publishers Weekly* reviewer. The book "is sure to serve well in primary-school units on community life and on the value of natural resources," explained Ellen Mandel in *Booklist. Mountain Town,* which describes life in a small town in the mountains, was complimented by Carol Ann Wilson for its collaboration of image and words: "The present-tense text occasionally provides helpful explanations for the already-informative pictures," Wilson wrote in her *School Library Journal* review although she noted at times that the text only reiterates what readers already notice in the pictures. Susan Dove Lempke, writing in *Booklist,* felt that "the text is brief, just one or two lines per page, and pleasant." *Desert Town* transports readers to the American Southwest. "The Geiserts let readers explore this town inside and out, from the minutest detail to the grandest view," wrote Nina Lindsay of *School Library Journal. Booklist* contributor GraceAnne A. DeCandido called the picture books "an absolutely engaging series."

In 2002 Geisert published her first novel for young readers, which featured some small line drawings by her husband. Titled *Prairie Summer,* the book tells the story of Rachel, a fifth grader on a South Dakota farm in 1954. Rachel does not like farm work and manages to make plenty of mistakes, but when she is able to come through for the family when her mother goes into early labor, she saves the day. "The Geiserts here expand their repertoire with fiction in the same thematic vein," commented a *Publishers Weekly* reviewer, who favorably compared the novel to the Geiserts' picture books. Though noting that the slow pace might not appeal to some readers, *Booklist* reviewer John Peters praised Geisert's "carefully detailed picture of everyday life on the farm." *School Library Journal* critic Carolyn Janssen wrote that the author "skillfully uses the plot and the setting to reveal the relationships and develop the characters."

Lessons, the sequel to *Prairie Summer,* delves into deeper issues of family, religion, and healing, all from the past. Rachel's father can't stand to be around her new baby brother, and her mother explains to her that the first child Rachel's parents had was a boy who died before he could be baptized. Because of this, their minister told them the child could not have a proper burial or go to heaven. Rachel's mother does not believe it, but her father still suffers from guilt. Rachel makes it her mission to help her father heal, if only so that he can grow to love his new son. "Geisert's quiet, simple style gives the details immediacy and interest," com-

A collaboration between author Bonnie Geisert and her husband (and illustrator) Arthur Geisert, **Haystack** *has received several awards, both for its illustrations and its story, which opens a window onto life in the rural Midwest.*

Life in a small town in the Rocky Mountains, where snow still falls in July and change occurs at a slower pace is profiled in Mountain Town, *part of the Geisert's picture-book paean to small-town America. (Illustration by Arthur Geisert.)*

mented *Horn Book* reviewer Roger Sutton, who compared the novel to the "Little House" books by Laura Ingalls Wilder. A *Kirkus Reviews* critic noted that while *Lessons* "isn't for every reader," it would appeal to "children like Rachel, who care deeply about matters of the heart and soul."

Though all of her books are illustrated by her husband, Geisert once shared with *SATA* her own interest in art: "I find that the camera is a powerful tool in exploring the world around me—whether I'm taking photos of Galena architecture, rolling hills, people, animals, or flowers. My interest in photography started in 1991 while writing feature stories for the *Freeport Journal-Standard*. I could count on my fingers the times I held a camera before I started stringing for the *Journal-Standard*. Jim Quick was a great help in getting me started with equipment and fundamentals. Recently I've been shooting butterflies and other insects with a macro lens, and that has lured me into abstract photography."

Biographical and Critical Sources

PERIODICALS

Booklist, September 15, 1995, Leone McDermott, review of *Haystack*, p. 165; April, 1998, Kay Weisman, review of *Prairie Town*, p. 1326; July, 1999, Ellen Mandel, review of *River Town*, p. 1948; March 15, 2000, Susan Dove Lempke, review of *Mountain Town*, p. 1386; March 1, 2002, John Peters, review of *Prairie Summer*, p. 1136.

Bulletin of the Center for Children's Books, October, 1995, review of *Haystack*, p. 54.

Horn Book, November, 1995, Margaret A. Bush, review of *Haystack*, p. 756; May-June, 1998, Joanna Rudge Long, review of *Prairie Town*, p. 332; March, 2001, Joanne Rudge Long, review of *Desert Town*, p. 229; March-April, 2005, Roger Sutton, review of *Lessons*, p. 201.

Kirkus Reviews, July 15, 1995, review of *Haystack*, p. 1023; March 15, 2005, review of *Lessons*, p. 351.

New York Times Book Review, January 28, 1996, p. 27.

Publishers Weekly, August 28, 1995, review of *Haystack*, p. 112; April 19, 1999, review of *River Town*, p. 72; March 4, 2002, review of *Prairie Summer*, p. 80.

School Library Journal, September, 1995, review of *Haystack*, p. 193; April, 2000, Carol Ann Wilson, review of *Mountain Town*, p. 104; March, 2001, Nina Lindsay, review of *Desert Town*, p. 208; May, 2002, Carolyn Janssen, review of *Prairie Summer*, p. 114; May, 2005, Laura Scott, review of *Lessons*, p. 126.

Time, December 11, 1995, p. 77.

ONLINE

Kids Reads Web site, http://www.kidsreads.com/ (November 4, 2005), Norah Piehl, review of *Lessons.*
Society of Children's Book Writers and Illustrators, Illinois Web site, http://www.scbwi-illinois.org/ (November 4, 2005).*

*   *   *

HASKINS, James S. 1941-2005
(Jim Haskins)

OBITUARY NOTICE—See index for *CA* sketch: Born September 19, 1941, in Demopolis, AL; died of complications from emphysema, July 6, 2005, in New York, NY. Educator and author. Haskins was a prolific author of nonfiction works for children, many of which focused on drawing attention to black history and biography. After being expelled from Alabama State University because he participated in student protests supporting civil rights, he completed a B.A. in psychology at Georgetown University in 1960. Haskins went on to earn a B.S. in history from Alabama State University in 1962 and a master's degree in social psychology from the University of New Mexico in 1963. Moving to New York City, he worked as a stock trader and reporter for a time before becoming a teacher in 1966. While working at Public School 92, Haskins became discouraged by the deplorable conditions of the school buildings and the family problems his students were suffering through that distracted them from learning. He began to write his thoughts down in a diary that was later published as *Diary of a Harlem School Teacher* (1969; second edition, 1979), which also brought public attention to the problems that school bureaucracies bring to education. After the release of this book, Haskins was approached by publishers who asked him if he could write for children and young adults. Unable to pass up the opportunity, Haskins went on a mission to write books for young readers that would make them aware of the many accomplishments and contributions made by African Americans. Over the decades, he published dozens of these books, many of them earning awards, such as the Coretta Scott King Award for *The Story of Stevie Wonder* (1976) and the Carter G. Woodson Award for *Black Music in America: A History through Its People* (1987). In addition to his biographies, Haskins wrote books on historical and cultural subjects, such as his *The Cotton Club* (1977; revised edition, 1994), which inspired the 1984 Francis Ford Coppola film. While pursuing his successful writing career, Haskins continued to teach. He was a visiting lecturer for two years at the New School for Social Research in the early 1970s, and from 1970 to 1977 was an associate professor at Staten Island Community College. In 1977, he joined the faculty at the University of Florida at Gainesville, where he was an English professor, but he often returned to New York City while also living in Florida. Haskins published about three dozen juvenile biographies in his lifetime, as well as numerous nonfiction titles for young readers and adults alike, including more recent titles such as *African Beginnings* (1995), *One Love, One Heart: A History of Reggae* (2001), and *Champion: The Story of Muhammad Ali* (2001).

OBITUARIES AND OTHER SOURCES:

PERIODICALS

Chicago Tribune, July 13, 2005, Section 3, p. 10.
Los Angeles Times, July 17, 2005, p. B14.
New York Times, July 11, 2005, p. A19.
Washington Post, July 18, 2005, p. B5.

*   *   *

HASKINS, Jim
See HASKINS, James S.

*   *   *

HAWKE, Rosanne 1953-

Personal

Born October 6, 1953, in Penola, South Australia, Australia; daughter of Lenard (a farmer and grazier) and Doreen Joyce (a bank teller and secretary; maiden name, Bedford) Trevilyan; married Gary Wayne Hawke (a master plumber), June 8, 1974; children: Lenore Penner, Michael, Emma. *Education:* Salisbury College of Advanced Education, teaching diploma, 1975; Moody Bible College, diploma, 1985; University of South Australia, English as a second language graduate diploma, 1988, information studies graduate diploma, 2000; University of Adelaide, B.A. (with honors), 2001, Ph.D., 2005. *Hobbies and other interests:* Cornish studies, music, history, walking, reading.

Addresses

Home—P.O. Box 417, Kapunda, South Australia 5373, Australia. *Agent*—Jacinta di Mase Management, 342 St. Geroges Rd., North Gitzroy, Victoria 3068, Australia. *E-mail*—hawknest@roseannehawke.com.

Career

Writer and educator. Junior primary teacher in South Australia, Pakistan, and United Arab Emirates, beginning 1975; English-as-a-second-language teacher trainer, Pakistan, 1986-91, acting principal, 1988, 1990; special-needs teacher in South Australia, 1993-96; creative-writing teacher in South Australia, beginning 1993; writer, 1994—. Also worked as a music teacher, house parent, English resource position, all through The Evangelical Alliance Mission (TEAM) in Pakistan and United Arab Emirates. Residency at Tyndale Christian School; Asialink Literature residency in Packistan, 2006; currently teaches creative writing at Adelaide TAFE and at Tabor Adelaide. Has also volunteered as a newsletter editor and writing competition judge.

Member

Australian Society of Authors, Children's Book Council of South Australia, Ekidnas: South Australian Published Children's Authors, Writers' Centre of South Australia, Cornish Society of South Australia.

Awards, Honors

ArtSA emerging artist grant, 1996, 1999; Children Rate Outstanding Writers Awards shortlist, and Notable Book designation, Children's Book Council of South Australia, both 1996, both for *Re-entry;* Christian School Book Awards shortlist, 1999, for *Jihad;* Varuna Writers' Retreat fellowship, 2000; Australian Children's Book Council (CBC) Notable Book designation, and Kanga Award shortlist, both 2003, both for *Sailmaker;* Aurealis Awards shortlist, 2003, and CBCA Notable Book designation, KANGA Awards nomination, and Cornish Holyer an Gof award commendation, all 2004, all for *Wolfchild;* May Gibb Literature fellowship, 2004; Cornish Holyer an Gof award, 2004, for *Across the Creek;* Kanga Award nomination, CBC Awards shortlist, and Victorian Premier's Literary Awards commendation, all 2005, all for *Soraya the Storyteller.*

Writings

Re-Entry, Albatross Books (Sutherland, New South Wales, Australia), 1995.

Jihad: A Girl's Quest to Settle the Past—and Say Goodbye, Albatross Books (Sutherland, New South Wales, Australia), 1996.

The Keeper, Lothian Books (Port Melbourne, Victoria, Australia), 2000.

A Kiss in Every Wave, Lothian (Port Melbourne, Victoria, Australia), 2001.

Zenna Dare, Lothian (South Melbourne, Victoria, Australia), 2002.

Sailmaker, Lothian (South Melbourne, Victoria, Australia), 2002.

Wolfchild, Lothian (South Melbourne, Victoria, Australia), 2003.

Borderland, Lothian (South Melbourne, Victoria, Australia), 2002.

The Collector, Lothian (South Melbourne, Victoria, Australia), 2004.

Across the Creek, Lothian (South Melbourne, Victoria, Australia), 2004.

Soraya the Storyteller, Lothian (South Melbourne, Victoria, Australia), 2004.

Yardil, Benchmark Publications (Montrose, Victoria, Australia), 2004.

Mustara, Lothian (South Melbourne, Victoria, Australia), 2006.

The Last Virgin in Year Ten, Lothian (South Melbourne, Victoria, Australia), 2006.

Contributor to periodicals, including *Reading Time;* contributor to anthologies, including *Forked Tongues,* Wakefield Press, 2002, and *Exile and Homecoming,* edited by P. O'Neil, University of Sydney (Sydney, New South Wales), 2005.

Sidelights

Even while growing up on a sheep farm in rural Penola, South Australia, Rosanne Hawke had a fascination with words and writing. Encouraged by her mother, she built her storytelling skills, and had her first short story published while still a teen. As college inspired more practical concerns, Hawke trained as a teacher, then spent ten years in the Middle East and Pakistan as a teacher of English as a second language. Her experiences with her young students, as well her introduction to Islamic culture inspired Hawke to return to writing, and with her award-winning 1994 young-adult novel *Re-Entry* she began her second career, as an author. Among Hawke's other novels for young readers are *Soraya the Storyteller, A Kiss in Every Wave,* and *Zenna Dare.*

A storyteller even as a child, Hawke was inspired to begin her writing career by her children. As she once explained to *SATA:* "When my fourteen-year-old was home on holidays, she asked for our story game where she would think up the characters, plot, and setting and I would tell the story. She wanted sixteen-year-old friends, kidnaping, freedom fighters, the Khyber Pass, and Afghanistan! One of our acquaintances had just been kidnaped and with his possible fate in mind I told the story. My daughter liked it so much she wanted it written up for her birthday. After that she wanted it typed so she could have a book of her own. And you've guessed it—after this she wanted it sent to a publisher."

As is sometimes the case, Hawke's first novel, *Jihad: A Girl's Quest to Settle the Past and Say Goodbye*, was not her first book to be published. That honor went to *Re-entry*, a prequel to *Jihad* that focuses on the concerns of most teens: worries about fitting in, peer pressure, developing one's unique identity, and budding romance. Hawke mixes these elements with a plot concerning an Australian teen whose family returns Down Under after living in Pakistan for ten years. Jaime feels like an outsider in her new school in Adelaide, and as a way to deal with her longing to return to the Middle East she creates Suneel, a Pakistani boy she pretends to have left behind, and she writes of him in her diary. As Jaime starts to see beneath the seemingly anarchistic surface of Australian teen culture, she also begins to view the realities of life in Pakistan with more objectivity. Describing *Re-entry* as a book "written from the perspective of a thoughtful girl who after learning to fit into an alien society has to go through the same process in her own," H. Nowicka dubbed the novel "fascinating" in a *Reading Time* review. Other critics noted Hawke's effective multicultural moral, while also adding praise for the novel's likable protagonist.

Published in 1996, *Jihad* finds Jaime back in Pakistan during school holiday. While visiting her friends there, the teen attempts to make emotional sense of the turbulent year she just spent at her new Australian high school. Self-exploration is put on the back burner, however, after Jaime and her friends are kidnaped by jihad freedom fighters. Hawke spins "a real page-turner that grabs you by the scruff of the neck and drags you through the action," according to Kate Graham in *Youth Express.*

Designed for middle-grade readers, *The Keeper* finds twelve-year-old Joel being raised by his grandmother during his parents' long absence. Joel has trouble controlling his emotions when provoked by bullies at school and, his frustration over his difficulty with some school subjects makes matters worse. "Hawke displays an unerring touch with the thoughts and feelings of a troubled youngster who knows only fisticuffs and foul words to grapple with confronting situations," remarked Cynthia Anthony in *Magpies*. Joel feels he needs a father figure and out of desperation he advertises for one. His stipulations that the candidate be tough and know all about fishing are amply met by Dev, a tattooed biker with a ponytail whose role as a new friend Joel decides to keep a secret. In addition to fishing expertise, Dev is successful at managing his own anger, and he helps the boy manage his emotional life. Immersed in his friendship with Dev, Joel hardly notices the arrival of a stranger in town who appears to know Joel's Gran. The mystery of this unknown woman's identity, as well as the subsequent arrival of a dangerous individual, adds an element of suspense to *The Keeper.*

Reviewing *The Keeper,* several critics focused on Hawke's ability to evoke a preteen's emotional ups and downs: the author "is excellent at conveying the turbulence that takes over Joel's mind and the impotent anger which makes him lash out, as well as the strategies quiet Dev is able to give him to channel his aggression into calmer and more constructive responses," Katharine England wrote in the Adelaide *Advertiser.* Critics also lauded Hawke for successfully incorporating a suspense/mystery into the second half of her story, building up to an exciting and satisfying conclusion that should hold the attention of even reluctant readers.

Other young-adult novels by Hawke include *Zenna Dare,* which moves across a century of Australian history through its main characters, modern teen Jenefer and the nineteenth-century singer known as Zenna Dare, who may be Jenefer's great-great-great-grandmother. Helping the teen solve this haunting family mystery is

Caleb, an aboriginal classmate at Jenefer's new school whose strong ancestral ties Jenefer envies. In the Adelaide *Advertiser* Katherine England praised *Zenna Dare* as a "richly textured tale of family relationships and changing morality across two centuries," while in *Viewpoint* a critic cited Hawke for her "relaxed, natural voice" and "cast of engaging and well-drawn characters."

Also for middle-grade readers, *Soraya the Storyteller* focuses on a twelve-year-old girl who flees with her family from their native Afghanistan after the repressive Taliban take power and imprison her father. Moving from Pakistan to Australia, they now live in a refugee camp on a temporary visa, fearing the time when they will be forced to return. Inspired by dreams of a winged, black horse, the young refugee turns to storytelling to deal with the fears and worry brought about by the upheaval, as well as to recall fond memories of her peaceful life in Afghanistan before the terrorist government took power. As the author noted on her home page, "I was first inspired to write *Soraya* when I heard about innocent children kept in detention centres in Australia. At first I didn't believe it, or take much notice—I thought there was a mistake. When I realized it was true and the people detained were not hardened criminals but people just asking for help, I felt compelled to write their story."

"My purpose in writing is always to entertain, to take people away," Hawke once explained to *SATA;* "to enter someone else's world for a while. While doing that I sometimes want to show what it may be like in that world and so foster understanding and acceptance for someone who may be different or have some difficulty. Much of my work has a multicultural theme as in *Reentry* and *Jihad.* Even *Zenna Dare* deals with ethnic identity. My books aren't only for readers—I find that the characters in my books teach me about life as they are materialising on the page.

"Sometimes I get excited about what I see while writing and would like others to see it too. But I try to write in such a way that if young people are interested only in a story that's what they'll get, yet if they want something deeper they can find that too. *The Keeper* is a story like this—on the surface, a simple adventure/mystery about a boy who wants a dad, but underneath there's a boy trying so hard to deal with a stallion-sized problem in his life: that of Attention Deficit Disorder. No one listens if you tell them things. Manning Clark once said that if you want people to learn anything at all, tell them a story.

"I love history and how the things that have gone before can solve some puzzle in the present. I like the mysteriousness of secrets and how one thing leads to another. I'm most probably an idealist, although I'm wary of such labels—I would like people to be able to accept themselves and each other, to love, to be able to live in peace."

Discussing her working conditions as a writer, Hawke explained: "I like to write drafts and plan outside. As a young person, I wrote my best stories out in the paddock or by the creek. I write a lot in my head as well while I'm out walking or swimming. Going to the symphony may suddenly give me an amazing idea just as the cymbals crash or the whole group of first violinists are lifting off their chairs in excitement. I enjoy historical surroundings too. I live in an 1860s country homestead in the mid-north of South Australia near Australia's oldest mining town, Kapunda. My husband is restoring the house and I have an underground writing room (it was built by the Cornish). It is very quiet out here and if I am not on tour visiting schools I can get a lot done. On a good day I can write 3-4,000 workds—they may not be the best and final words but once the draft is done I can play with those words as much as I like. If I get "stuck' I go for a walk or write in my journal about the project. I read at night. I also write to music—it helps keep me on the chair."

"Advice I give to young writers is write from the heart," Hawke added: "do it with all your passion and energy and courage. If you really want to write, then think of it as the most important thing you can do, like a mission you've been sent on, or a race you have to finish but not necessarily win. For most of us who want to write, writing is as necessary as breathing, so learn to breathe properly. I show young people that first of all they have to start, and read lots as well. And once started, writing is 3D: determination, drive, and darn hard work."

Biographical and Critical Sources

PERIODICALS

Advertiser (Adelaide, Australia), March 11, 2000, Katherine England, review of *The Keeper,* p. 19; September, 14, 2002, Katherine England, review of *Zenna Dare;* February 25, 2004, p. 28.

Australian Book Review, April, 2000, Pam Macintyre, review of *The Keeper,* p. 56; September, 2003, Karen Brooks, "Wonderworks," p. 61; October, 2004, Sherryl Clark, "Animals, Boats, and Shacks,"pp. 61-62.

Bookbird, Volume 37, number 2, 1999, John and Heather Foster, "Caught in the Crack: Stereotypes of South Asians in Australian Children's and Adolescent Literature."

Church Scene, August, 1995, Fiona Prentice, review of *Re-entry,* p. 8.

Courier Mail, March 28, 2000, Millan Richards, review of *The Keeper,* Books section, p. 2.

Lollipops, What's on for Kids, July-August, 1995, Cecile Ferguson, review of *Re-entry,* p. 18; May-June, 1996, Cecile Ferguson, "Meet Rosanne Hawke," p. 20; May-June, 1996, Cecile Ferguson, review of *Jihad,* p. 21; April-May, 2000, Cecile Ferguson, review of *The Keeper,* p. 18.

Magpies, July, 1995, review of *Re-Entry,* p. 25; May, 2000, Cynthia Anthony, review of *The Keeper,* p. 34; March, 2002, review of *A Kiss in Every Wave,* p. 33; May, 2002, review of *Zenna Dare,* p. 40; July, 2003, review of *Borderland,* p. 41; July, 2003, review of *Wolfchild,* p. 34.

Reading Time, August, 1995, H. Nowicka, review of *Re-entry,* p. 34; Volume 44, number 2, 2000, Jane Gibian, review of *The Keeper,* p. 25.

School Librarian, spring, 2001, review of *The Keeper,* p. 33; summer, 2003, review of *A Kiss in Every Wave,* p. 99; spring, 2005, Mary Medlicott, review of *Soraya the Storyteller,* p. 34.

Viewpoint, summer, 1995, review of *Re-entry,* p. 44; winter, 2000, Rosemary Worssam, review of *The Keeper,* p. 43; spring, 2003, review of *Zenna Dare,* pp. 38-39.

Youth Express, spring, 1995, Jennifer Micallef, review of *Re-entry,* p. 25; spring, 1996, Kate Graham, review of *Jihad,* p. 22.

ONLINE

Rosanne Hawke Home Page, http://www.rosannehawke. com (July 13, 2005).

* * *

HICKS, Barbara Jean 1953-

Personal

Born July 21, 1953, in Bellingham, WA. *Education:* Los Angeles Baptist College, B.A. (English); Oregon College of Education, secondary teaching certificate (language arts). *Hobbies and other interests:* Sailing, travel.

Addresses

Home—Ventura, CA; Seattle, WA. *Agent*—c/o Author Mail, Farrar, Straus & Giroux, 19 Union Square W., New York, NY 10001. *E-mail*—bjhicks@ix.netcom. com.

Career

Writer, editor, and educator. Educational consultant; worked variously as a nanny, waitress, bank teller, and shop clerk.

Awards, Honors

Awards and award nominations for adult fiction; "Best of" awards for children's fiction.

Writings

FOR CHILDREN

Jitterbug Jam, illustrated by Alexis Deacon, Farrar, Straus & Giroux (New York, NY), 2005.

I Like Black and White, illustrated by Lila Prap, Tiger Tales (Wilton, CT), 2006.

I Like Colors, illustrated by Lila Prap, Tiger Tales (Wilton, CT), 2006.

FOR ADULTS

(With Lorena McCourtney and Karen M. Ball) *Mistletoe,* Palisades (Sisters, OR), 1996.

Coming Home, Palisades (Sisters, OR), 1996.

Snow Swan, Palisades (Sisters, OR), 1997.

Hearts Delight, Palisades (Sisters, OR), 1998.

China Doll, Palisades (Sisters, OR), 1998.

An Unlikely Prince, WaterBrook Press (Colorado Springs, CO), 1998.

All That Glitters: A Romantic Comedy, WaterBrook Press (Colorado Springs, CO), 1998.

Loves Me, Loves Me Not, WaterBrook Press (Colorado Springs, CO), 2000.

Restoration and Romance: For the Love of an Old House, WaterBrook Press (Colorado Springs, CO), 2001.

Sidelights

Born and raised in the Pacific Northwest, Barbara Jean Hicks began writing in fourth grade and eventually turned her childhood hobby into a career. After penning more than a dozen novels for adult readers, she turned to a younger audience with her picture book *Jitterbug Jam: A Monster Tale.* Referred to by a *Children's Bookwatch* critic as "a charming and wonderful story about how new friends could be just around the corner," *Jitterbug Jam* offers kids a fun twist to a much-told tale in its story about a young monster who is afraid there is a boy lurking under his bed. Despite reassurances from his grandpa and criticism from his brother, Bobo the monster must ultimately find the courage to take the dreaded look under the bed for himself. Praising Alexis Deacon's "slightly surreal, dreamy" illustrations, a *Publishers Weekly* contributor compared Hicks' story to Mercer Mayer's classic *There's a Monster in My Closet,* while in *Kirkus Reviews* a critic praised the author's use of "colorful turns of phrase" and predicted that the book would find an eager audience among "young readers, timorous or otherwise." Jennifer Mattson wrote in *Booklist* that Hicks' "folksy, slightly off-kilter language, full of fractured grammar and quirky aphorisms, keeps the sense of an exotic, alternate reality watertight," and dubbed *Jitterbug Jam* a "charming visit to the other side of the closet wall."

Discussing the art of writing on her home page, Hicks wrote: "I know this is going to be hard to believe . . . but everything I know about writing I learned from my cat." The lesson Hicks learned? Look, leap, and learn. "First, you look around for ideas," Hicks explained. "Then, before you have any real idea where you're going, you leap. You jump right into the writing. You might start out with a curious bit of dialogue, or a vivid description, or a word or phrase that tickles your funny bone. Then you let the writing take you wherever it wants to go."

Then comes the rewriting, according to the author, who suggests that writers read their work aloud at this point. "And you reread and rewrite and reread and rewrite. . . .

"Get the picture? You learn as you go. . . . Look. Leap. Learn."

Biographical and Critical Sources

PERIODICALS

Booklist, January 1, 1998, John Mort, review of *Heart's Delight,* p. 772; August, 1998, review of *An Unlikely Prince,* p. 1965; March 1, 2000, John Mort, review of *Loves Me, Loves Me Not,* p. 1196; March 1, 2005, Jennifer Mattson, review of *Jitterbug Jam: A Monster Tale,* p. 1194.

Children's Bookwatch, April, 2005, review of *Jitterbug Jam.*

Kirkus Reviews, February 1, 2005, review of *Jitterbug Jam,* p. 177.

Library Journal, June 1, 1996, Henry Carrigan, Jr., review of *Coming Home,* p. 92; September 1, 1998, Melissa Hudak, review of *China Doll,* p. 164; February 1, 2000, Melanie C. Duncan, review of *Loves Me, Loves Me Not,* p. 68.

Publishers Weekly, March 14, 2005, review of *Jitterbug Jam,* p. 66.

School Librarian, spring, 2005, Liz Baynton-Clarke, review of *Jitterbug Jam,* p. 22.

ONLINE

Barbara Jean Hicks Home Page, http://www.barbarajean-hicks.com (October 5, 2005).

*   *   *

HILL, John
See KOONTZ, Dean R.

*   *   *

HOLUBITSKY, Katherine 1955-

Personal

Surname is pronounced Hall-oo-*bit*-skee; born June 25, 1955, in Toronto, Ontario, Canada; daughter of F. Donald (an aeronautical drafter) and Marion B. (a teacher; maiden name, Buchanan) James; married Jeffrey M. Holubitsky (a journalist and newspaper editor), March 20, 1976; children: Maxwell James, Paul Jeffrey. *Education:* Attended Simon Fraser University, 1973-75; Grant MacEwan College, graduated (library and information technology), 1992.

Katherine Holubitsky

Addresses

Agent—c/o Author Mail, Orca Book Publishers, Box 5626, Station B, Victoria, British Columbia V8R 6S4, Canada.

Career

Edmonton Public School Board, Edmonton, Alberta, library technician, 1992—.

Member

Young Alberta Book Society.

Awards, Honors

Pick of the Lists designation, American Booksellers Association, and Young Adult Book of the Year, Canadian Library Association (CLA), both 1999, and Best Books for Young Adults designation, American Library Association, Books for the Teen Age citation, New York Public Library, I.O.D.E. Violet Downey Award, Ruth Schwartz Children's Literature Award finalist, and Red Maple Award finalist, Ontario Library Association, all 2000, all for *Alone at Ninety Foot;* Arthur Ellis Award nomination, and CLA Young Adult Book of the Year nomination, both 2005, and Manitoba Young Readers' Choice Award nomination, 2006, all for *The Hippie House.*

Writings

Alone at Ninety Foot, Orca (Custer, WA), 1999.
Last Summer in Agatha, Orca (Custer, WA), 2001.

The Hippie House, Orca (Custer, WA), 2004.
The Mountains That Walked, Orca (Custer, WA), 2005.

Sidelights

When Katherine Holubitsky's first published novel won the Canadian Library Association's 1999 Young Adult Book Award, perhaps no one was more surprised than the author herself. The book, *Alone at Ninety Foot,* started out as a short story Holubitsky wrote in her free time while working in a city high-school library in western Canada. More awards rolled in the following year, encouraging the writer who has since penned several more well-received novels for teen readers, including *Last Summer in Agatha, The Hippie House,* and *The Mountain That Walked.*

Alone at Ninety Foot focuses on fourteen-year-old Pamela Collins, who is trying to cope while everything around her seems to be turn into tragedy. After her baby sister dies of Sudden Infant Death syndrome, Pam's grieving and guilt-stricken mother kills herself. Now her father is starting to date again, bringing more upheaval into the teen's life when all Pamela wants is to be looked upon as normal. Fortunately, good friends, a budding romantic interest, and a special place to go to find peace and sunshine give the teen the wherewithal to navigate the other problems every adolescent encounters. Praising the book as an "accomplished first novel," Maureen Garvie wrote in *Quill and Quire* that Holubitsky "has a Salinger-like ear for adolescent speech," and that her protagonist's "observations of teen dynamics are astute." Garvie predicted that *Alone at Ninety Foot* "will engage a wide readership," while in the *Canadian Review of Materials* Joan Marshall described the novel as "a funny, touching, compelling book that will appeal to middle school students who love to read about tragic lives."

A small town in Alberta, Canada is the setting for *Last Summer in Agatha,* which finds sixteen-year-old Rachel Bennett strongly attracted to older teen Michael during her summer stay with her aunt and uncle. While Michael returns her attentions, Rachel soon realizes that something about him is just not right. As Michael battles his emotional response to a favorite brother's death and the increasing aggression directed at him by some neighborhood teens, his behavior becomes more erratic, and soon Rachel realizes that Michael's problems are more than she can handle. In the *Canadian Review of Materials,* Joanne Peters dubbed *Last Summer in Agatha* "strong and powerfully written," with "unique" and "sharply drawn characters." While *Quill and Quire* critic Kenneth Oppel noted that the novel reminded him "how besotted teenagers are with the dramas of their lives," he praised Holubitsky's "vivid" writing and her ability to accurately portray her young characters. "Her dialogue has a refreshing humour in places," Oppel added, noting that the author "wisely intersperses her crisis scenes with ones of greater normalcy." In *School Library Journal* Jana R. Fine noted that the novel "captures the beauty" of the Canadian Midwest and "intertwines a convincing look at . . . teens' lives into a quietly understated drama about overcoming grief."

The Hippie House also deals with the way young people are affected by tragedy, although in this case the tragedy—the murder of a teenage girl—changes the lives of several young people. Taking place in rural Canada during the 1970s, the novel focuses on fifteen-year-old Emma and Emma's older brother Eric, who gathers together with a group of friends and relatives to play rock music in a nearby shed dubbed the "hippie house." When their gathering place becomes the setting of an assault and murder, the lives of Emma, Eric, and their friends drastically change. For some, fear curtails their ability to trust the hippie musicians and groupies they formerly mingled with at a local town hangout, while for Emma's cousin Megan the knowledge that death could come at any time "fuelled her 'seize the day' hunger for experience," noted Sherie Posesorski in *Quill and Quire.* Although commenting on the relative length and slow pace of the novel, Posesorski concluded that Holubitsky's "emotional perceptiveness, her graceful,

During Emma's fourteenth summer, the free and easy mood created by a group of laid-back hippie friends is suddenly shattered when the body of a murdered young woman is discovered at a favorite teen hang-out. (Cover illustration by Karel Doruyter.)

nuanced writing, her painfully true depictions of teen life . . . shine" in *The Hippie House.*

In her first work of historical fiction, *The Mountain That Walked,* Holubitsky combines information about the lives of immigrant "home boys" who were sent to Canada from Great Britain to provide help to farming families with a look back to life in a mining town at the turn of the twentieth century. The novel finds sixteen-year-old English-born Charlie Sutherland sent West to work on the Brooks farm in Alberta, British Columbia. When he discovers one of the owners murdered, Charlie flees, fearful that he will be a suspect. He travels west to a mining town at the foot of Turtle Mountain in the Canadian Rockies, where he finds a job, begins to feel part of a community, and ultimately witnesses a tragic landslide that devastates the small town. Noting that the novel is "fast-paced and full of adventure," *Resource Links* contributor Victoria Pennell added that *The Mountain That Walked* presents a fact-filled and accurate view of "the life of early settlers on the Canadian prairie," weaving a wealth of historic detail into a story that would be especially enjoyable to boys.

"I write about adolescent life because I really *like* young adults, Holubitsky once told *SATA,* and I have a lot of empathy for that age. I remember the extremes of emotion so well. Developing teens need to be reassured that what they are feeling is normal. As well as entertaining them, this is what I hope to accomplish in writing for teens. It was certainly the driving motive behind my first novel, *Alone at Ninety Foot.*"

While working on her first novel, Holubitsky was influenced by the journals of nineteenth-century Canadian artist Emily Carr, a painter strongly influenced by her love of nature, as well as her love of Lynn Canyon, where *Alone at Ninety Foot* takes place. "There have been a lot of YA novels written dealing with saving the environment and that kind of thing," Holubitsky explained to *Canadian Review of Materials* interviewer David Jenkinson, "but I wanted to put a little bit more into it by showing the spiritual relationship you can have with the environment. . . . Growing up in a rural community, I was in the woods all the time as a kid. . . . Consequently, I think my writing's just an extension of that spiritual and emotional satisfaction of relating to and being close to nature."

"I can never complain of being lonely when I write," Holubitsky also explained to *SATA:* "in fact, the room is often quite crowded. My Clumber spaniel discovered long ago that it's the perfect opportunity to get his head scratched, one of my Siamese cats loves the warmth of the monitor, and the other one makes himself comfortable in my lap. I know I become very single-minded when I am writing. I think of the story and the characters constantly. Luckily, my family has learned to ignore me when I become that intense!

"There are so many writers of fiction who have influenced me, and they are a very diverse group. Common

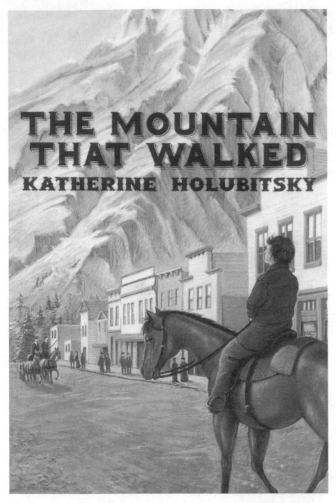

Taking place in 1903, Holubitsky's novel follows sixteen-year-old Char-lie as he witnesses a tragic landslide that engulfs part of a Rocky Mountain mining town. (Cover illustration by Leslie Elizabeth Watts.)

elements in the work of authors I return to, however, are strong characterization, terrific imagery, and wit. I think humor is a great equalizer, something every age understands.

"The one piece of advice I would give to aspiring writers is to read good literature, not just in the genre in which you are writing, but everything you can. You will soon learn to recognize bad writing when you pick it up and, hopefully, when you've typed it out. Then—persevere!"

Biographical and Critical Sources

PERIODICALS

Booklist, March 15, 2000, review of *Alone at Ninety Foot,* p. 1340.

Kliatt, July, 2004, Claire Rosser, review of *The Hippie House,* p. 8.

Prairie Books Now, summer, 2000, Irene D'Souza, "Alone at Any Age."

Publishers Weekly, September 13, 1999, review of *Alone at Ninety Foot,* p. 85.

Quill and Quire, August, 1999, Maureen Garvie, review of *Alone at Ninety Foot;* May, 2001, Kenneth Oppel, review of *Last Summer in Agatha,* p. 33; July, 2004, Sherie Posesorski, review of *The Hippie House.*

Resource Links, October, 1999, review of *Alone at Ninety Foot,* p. 28; October, 2001, Margaret Mackey, review of *Last Summer in Agatha,* p. 38; April, 2005, Victoria Pennell, review of *The Mountain That Walked,* p. 12.

School Library Journal, December, 2001, Jana R. Fine, review of *Last Summer in Agatha,* p. 138.

ONLINE

Canadian Review of Materials Online, http://www.umanitoba.ca/cm/ (March 3, 2000), Joan Marshall, review of *Alone at Ninety Foot;* July 25, 2000) Dave Jenkinson, "Katherine Holubitsky"; October 5, 2001, Joanne Peters, review of *Last Summer in Agatha.*

Childrenslit.com, http://www.childrenslit.com/ (October 20, 2005), "Katherine Holubitsky."

Orca Book Publishers Web site, http://www.orcabook.com/ (October 20, 2005).*

*　　　*　　　*

HOPKINS, Cathy 1953-
(C.M. Hopkins, Cathy M. Hopkins)

Personal

Born January, 23, 1953, in Manchester, England; married; husband's name Steve. *Education:* Attended art college; received degree in comparative religion.

Addresses

Home—North London, England. *Agent*—c/o Author Mail, Piccadilly Press Ltd., 5 Castle Rd., Kentish Town, London NW1 8PR, England. *E-mail*—cathy@cathyhopkins.com.

Career

Writer, 1987—. Worked previously as a rock-and-roll singer with Driving Rock and the Rockettes, as an occupational therapist in a mental hospital, as a teacher of meditation, as an aromatherapist, as a comedy-script reader for the BBC, and as a newspaper reviewer.

Writings

"MATES, DATES" SERIES

Mates, Dates, and Inflatable Bras (also see below), Piccadilly (London, England), 2001, Simon Pulse (New York, NY), 2003.

Mates, Dates, and Cosmic Kisses (also see below), Piccadilly (London, England), 2001, Simon Pulse (New York, NY), 2003.

Mates, Dates, and Portobello Princesses (also see below), Piccadilly (London, England), 2001, published as *Mates, Dates, and Designer Divas,* Simon Pulse (New York, NY), 2003.

Mates, Dates, and Sleepover Secrets (also see below), Piccadilly (London, England), 2002, Simon Pulse (New York, NY), 2003.

Mates, Dates, and Sole Survivors, Piccadilly (London, England), 2002, Simon Pulse (New York, NY), 2004.

Mates, Dates, and Mad Mistakes, Piccadilly (London, England), 2003, Simon Pulse (New York, NY), 2004.

Mates, Dates, and Pulling Power, Piccadilly (London, England), 2003, published as *Mates, Dates, and Sequin Smiles,* Simon Pulse (New York, NY), 2004.

Mates, Dates, and Tempting Trouble, Piccadilly (London, England), 2004, Simon Pulse (New York, NY), 2005.

Mates, Dates, and Great Escapes, Piccadilly (London, England), 2004, Simon Pulse (New York, NY), 2005.

Mates, Dates, and Chocolate Cheats, Piccadilly (London, England), 2005, Simon Pulse (New York, NY), 2006.

Mates, Dates, and Diamond Destiny, Piccadilly (London, England), 2005, Simon Pulse (New York, NY), 2006.

Mates, Dates Guide to Life, Piccadilly (London, England), 2005, published as *Mates, Dates Guide to Life, Love, and Looking Luscious,* Simon Pulse (New York, NY), 2005.

Mates, Dates, and Sizzling Summers, Piccadilly (London, England), 2006.

Mates, Dates Simply Fabulous: Books 1-4 (contains *Mates, Dates, and Inflatable Bras; Mates, Dates, and Cosmic Kisses; Mates, Dates, and Designer Divas;* and *Mates, Dates, and Sleepover Secrets*), Simon Pulse (New York, NY), 2006.

"TRUTH OR DARE" SERIES

White Lies and Barefaced Truths, Piccadilly (London, England), 2002, Simon Pulse (New York, NY), 2004.

Pop Princess, Piccadilly (London, England), 2002, published as *The Princess of Pop,* Simon Pulse (New York, NY), 2004.

Teen Queens and Has-beens, Piccadilly (London, England), 2003, Simon Pulse (New York, NY), 2004.

Starstruck, Piccadilly (London, England), 2003, Simon Pulse (New York, NY), 2005.

Double Dare, Piccadilly (London, England), 2005, Simon Pulse (New York, NY), 2006.

Midsummer Meltdown, Piccadilly (London, England), 2006.

Love Lottery, Piccadilly (London, England), 2006.

All Mates Together, Piccadilly (London, England), 2006.

OTHER

Girl Chasing: How to Improve Your Game, Angus & Robertson (London, England), 1989.

Sixty-nine Things to Do When You're Not Busy Doing It, Fontana (London, England), 1991.

The Joy of Aromatherapy, Angus & Robertson (London, England), 1991.

Revenge of the Essex Girls, Robson (London, England), 1992.

Keeping It Up!: How to Make Your Love Affair Last Forever, Fontana (London, England), 1993.

Blooming Pregnant!: The Real Facts about Having a Baby, Robson (London, England), 1993.

Divorce for Beginners: How to Get Unhitched without the Hitches, HarperCollins (London, England), 1995.

The World's Best Light-Bulb Jokes, HarperCollins (London, England), 1995.

Thorsons Principles of Aromatherapy, Thorsons (London, England), 1996.

101 Shortcuts to Relaxation, Bloomsbury (London, England), 1997.

The Wisdom of the Master Cat, Michael O'Mara (London, England), 1998.

Holy Moley, I'm a Dead Dude, Chicken House (Frome, Somerset, England), 2006.

Dead Dudes on Holiday, Chicken House (Frome, Somerset, England), 2006.

Adaptations

Film rights to *Holy Moley, I'm a Dead Dude* were optioned by Nickelodeon.

Sidelights

Cathy Hopkins began her writing career in 1987 with a series of humor books with cartoonist Gray Jolliffe. She continued work on nonfiction books about relationships and books on aromatherapy, but neither of these sated her writing bug. "In 2000, I met Brenda Gardner at Piccadilly Press who asked if I'd like to write for teenagers," Hopkins explained on her home page. "These last five years have been the best." Hopkins has written two series for teens: "Mates, Dates" and "Truth or Dare," and has begun the "Dude" series for middle-school readers. From trouble with relationships to friendship to ghosts, Hopkins has covered a wide variety of teen interests for readers both in the United Kingdom, where her books were first published, and the United States.

With *Mates, Dates, and Inflatable Bras* Hopkins introduced readers to best friends Lucy and Izzie, fourteen year olds who start having troubles in their friendship when Izzie befriends the new girl, Nesta, who is half-Jamaican. Lucy is jealous, but she is also confused about issues in her own life. A school assignment requiring Lucy to describe who she is and who she wants to be leads her to question her identity, and her crush on a new boy does not make things any better. With no cleavage in sight, and little self-confidence, Lucy feels doomed—until her Mum, a psychotherapist, helps her find her self-worth and Izzie and Nesta provide her with a beautiful inflatable bra. When Lucy begins to design new outfits to go with her new look, she finds a passion for design she had not before discovered. "Girls will eat this one up," wrote Janet Julian in a review for *Kliatt.*

Fourteen-year-old Lucy is happy the way things are between her and best-friend Izzie; she resents the intrusion of glam newbie Nesta until her eye catches a cute boy and she realizes Nesta may have wisdom to impart in Hopkins' teen romance. (Cover designed by Debbie Stetsios.)

Izzie is the one suffering from a crush—which becomes more like an obsession—in *Mates, Dates, and Cosmic Kisses.* Meanwhile, both Lucy and Nesta feel left out, but wait for their friend to come back to her sense. "Both novels fly along with pitch-perfect details and slapstick humor that is deepened by sharp insights into real issues," Gillian Engberg noted in a *Booklist* review of the first two titles in the "Mates, Dates" series. "The stories are fast paced and sassy," commented Angela M. Ottman in *School Library Journal,* who compared the books to Louise Rennison's series that began with *Angus, Thongs, and Full Frontal Snogging.* Sherri Forgash, writing in *Kliatt,* wrote of the characters that "they are hip, bright, and sassy teenagers," and commented that the series "should catch on like wildfire."

The "Mates, Dates" series continues, each book being narrated from the perspective of one of the three girls. When Nesta's family has financial trouble in *Mates, Dates, and Designer Divas,* she worries that a boy she

likes is out of her league until her friends convince her to be herself. Hopkins "nails the teenage dialogue and British slang," according to Sherri Forgash in her *Kliatt* review of the title. In *Mates, Dates, and Mad Mistakes* Izzy dates a bad boy, gets a bellybutton ring, and experiments with what it is like to be a "bad girl." "Izzie's mid-teen crisis and interactions with her mates, mother, and stepdad are authentic," complimented Linda L. Plevak in her *School Library Journal* review Nesta discovers that her friends think she is shallow in *Mates, Dates, and Sequin Smiles,* and when she has to get braces, her ideas of beauty are all called into question. "Hopkins creates a unique yet identifiable heroine in Nesta," wrote Lynne Pisano in *Kliatt.*

Unlike the North Londoners starring in the "Mates, Dates" series, the teens of the "Truth or Dare" books live in Cornwall and are a mix of boys and girls. *White Lies and Barefaced Truths* begins the series with a dare: Becca is too shy to talk to the object of her crush, Lia's brother, Ollie, so the girls dare Cat to talk to him on her behalf. Cat is dating Squidge, but when she follows up on the dare, she finds that she, like Becca, also has feelings for Lia's brother. She wants to tell Becca the truth but does not know how, and when she begins to keep track of how many lies she tells every day, Cat decides to tell only the truth. This puts Cat in the doghouse with Becca, as well as with her teachers, until she manages to find a balance between honesty and her friends' feelings.

In *The Princess of Pop* the friends (including Squidge and a boy named Mac) dare each other to audition for a reality show pop competition. Becca has just had a miserable audition for the school musical, but to her surprise, she finds herself as a real competitor for the title Princess of Pop. "This is primarily Becca's story," noted Steaphanie Squicciarini in *Kliatt,* "but readers get a sense of all the friends" from the series' second title. Squicciarini noted that while Hopkins uses British slang, "readers should have no trouble enjoying the universal humor, questions, and friendships explored." Catherine Ensley praised Hopkins's insight into the teen mind, writing in *School Library Journal* that "the stories are humorous and very hip; Hopkins clearly remembers exactly what it's like to be fourteen."

Taking some time out from teenage girls and focusing on a crowd-surfing rock star who dies—and becomes a ghost, Hopkins started the "Dude" series with *Holy Moley, I'm a Dead Dude!* As ex-rock star Dude is quick to find out, being a ghost is not all that bad, until you have to deal with ghost hunters like nerd Sid Wiper. Dude and his ghostly friends have to face off against the ghost hunter, or the whole ghost community will be wiped out! Dude's afterlife adventures continue in *Dead Dudes on Holiday.*

On her home page, Hopkins lists her top ten writing tips for young writers. Along with tips such as practicing writing and spending time reading, Hopkins pro-

Cat wrestles with totally serious moral issues while she tries to figure out the best way to break up with her soon-to-be ex in the first install-ment in the "Truth or Dare" series. (Cover designed by Debbie Stet-sios.)

vides the following advice: "Never give up. Persevere through rejection. Loads of famous novelists had their books rejected first time round but were successful be-cause they didn't give up."

Biographical and Critical Sources

PERIODICALS

Booklist, February 1, 2003, Gillian Engberg, review of *Mates, Dates, and Inflatable Bras* and *Mates, Dates, and Cosmic Kisses,* p. 981; March 1, 2005, Jean Hat-field, review of *Mates, Dates, and Inflatable Bras,* p. 1218.

Bookseller, March 21, 2003, "Covermounts for Hopkins," p. S6; February 18, 2005, review of *Mates, Dates, and Chocolate Treats,* and *Mates, Dates, and Dia-mond Destiny,* p. 38.

Kliatt, January, 2003, review of *Mates, Dates, and Inflat-able Bras,* p. 16; May, 2003, Sherri Forgash, review of *Mates, Dates, and Cosmic Kisses,* p. 17; Septem-ber, 2003, Sherri Forgash, review of *Mates, Dates, and Designer Divas,* p. 17; July, 2004, Stephanie Squicciarini, review of *White Lies and Barefaced Truths* and *The Princess of Pop,* pp. 19-20; January, 2005, Lynne Pisano, review of *Mates, Dates, and Se-quin Smile,* p. 14; May, 2005, Janet Julian, review of *Mates, Dates, and Inflatable Bras,* p. 58.

Publishers Weekly, December 9, 2002, review of *Mates, Dates, and Inflatable Bras* and *Mates, Dates, and Cos-mic Kisses,* p. 85; May 3, 2004, "The Latest Scoop," p. 194; December 13, 2004, "And Then What Hap-pened?," p. 70.

School Librarian, autumn, 2002, review of *White Lies and Barefaced Truths,* p. 155.

School Library Journal, April, 2003, Angela M. Ottman, review of *Mates, Dates, and Inflatable Bras* and *Mates, Dates, and Cosmic Kisses,* p. 164; July, 2003, Cathe-rine Ensley, review of *Mates, Dates, and Designer Di-vas,* p. 131; July, 2004, Catherine Ensley, review of *White Lies and Barefaced Truths* and *The Princess of Pop,* p. 106; September, 2004, Michele Capozzella, review of *Mates, Dates, and Sequin Smiles,* p. 209; October, 2004, Linda L. Plevak, review of *Mates, Dates, and Mad Mistakes,* p. 166.

Spectator, November 28, 1992, review of *Revenge of the Essex Girls,* p. 52.

Voice of Youth Advocates, April, 2003, review of *Mates, Dates, and Inflatable Bras* and *Mates, Dates, and Cos-mic Kisses,* p. 36.

ONLINE

Cathy Hopkins Home Page, http://www.cathyhopkins.com (November 2, 2005).

TeenReads, http://www.teenreads.com/ (November 2, 2005), interview with Hopkins.

*   *   *

HOPKINS, Cathy M.
See HOPKINS, Cathy

*   *   *

HOPKINS, C.M.
See HOPKINS, Cathy

*   *   *

HOWARD, Arthur 1948-
(Arthur Charles Howard)

Personal

Born January 26, 1948, in New York, NY; son of Ber-nard (an executive engineer and inventor) and Cora (an artist; maiden name Wisoff) Howard. *Education:* Reed College, B.A., 1970.

Addresses

Home—New York, NY. *Agent*—c/o Author Mail, Harcourt, 6277 Sea Harbor Dr., Orlando, FL 32887. *E-mail*—arthurhoward@earthlink.net.

Career

Writer and illustrator. Worked as a professional actor for twenty years, performing in theater productions on Broadway, off-Broadway, and in regional theater; in television commercials, and on *Square One,* Public Broadcasting Service.

Awards, Honors

ABC Children's Bestsellers Choice, for *Mr. Putter and Tabby Bake the Cake* by Cynthia Rylant; American Book Award (ABA) Pick of the Lists, ABC Children's Bestsellers Choice, and American Library Association (ALA) Notable Book designation, 1996, all for *Mr. Putter and Tabby Pick the Pears* by Rylant; ABA Pick of the Lists, Oppenheim Toy Portfolio Best Book Award, Crayola Kids Best Book of the Year, International Reading Association/Children's Book Council (IRA/CBC) Children's Choice Award, and Charlotte Award, New York State Reading Association, all 1998, all for *When I Was Five;* Reading Magic Award, *Parenting* magazine, for *Mr. Putter and Tabby Toot the Horn* by Rylant; Best Book of the Year citation, *School Library Journal,* 2001, Nevada Young Readers Award and Kentucky Bluegrass Award, both 2003, and Best of the Best citation, Bank Street College, and IRA-CBC Children's Choice Award, all for *Hoodwinked;* IRA Teacher's Choice, 2001, for *100th Day Worries*; Irma & James Black Award, Bank Street College, 2002, for *Bubba and Beau, Best Friends* by Kathie Appelt; ABA Pick of the Lists, IRA/CBC Children's Choice Award, Washington State Children's Choice Picture Book Award, 2002, and Tennessee Volunteer State Book Award, 2003, all for *Cosmos Zooms;* ABA Pick of the Lists and Oppenheim Toy Portfolio Platinum Award, both 2001, both for *Mr. Putter and Tabby Paint the Porch* by Rylant; Oppenheim Toy Portfolio Gold Award and Top Ten Easy Readers citation, *Booklist,* both 2004, both for *Mr. Putter and Tabby Stir the Soup* by Rylant; Oppenheim Toy Portfolio Platinum Award, 2005, for *Mr. Putter and Tabby Write the Book* by Rylant.

Writings

SELF-ILLUSTRATED

When I Was Five, Harcourt (San Diego, CA), 1996, published as *Now I Am Six,* Hazar (London, England), 1998.

Cosmos Zooms, Harcourt (San Diego, CA), 1999.
Hoodwinked, Harcourt (San Diego, CA), 2001.
Serious Trouble, Harcourt (San Diego, CA), 2003.
The Hubbub Above, Harcourt (Orlando, FL), 2005.

ILLUSTRATOR, "MR. PUTTER AND TABBY" SERIES BY CYNTHIA RYLANT

Mr. Putter and Tabby Pour the Tea, Harcourt (San Diego, CA), 1994.
Mr. Putter and Tabby Walk the Dog, Harcourt (San Diego, CA), 1994.
Mr. Putter and Tabby Bake a Cake, Harcourt (San Diego, CA), 1994.
Mr. Putter and Tabby Pick the Pears, Harcourt (San Diego, CA), 1995.
Mr. Putter and Tabby Fly the Plane, Harcourt (San Diego, CA), 1997.
Mr. Putter and Tabby Row the Boat, Harcourt (San Diego, CA), 1997.
Mr. Putter and Tabby Toot the Horn, Harcourt (San Diego, CA), 1998.
Mr. Putter and Tabby Take the Train, Harcourt (San Diego, CA), 1998.
Mr. Putter and Tabby Paint the Porch, Harcourt (San Diego, CA), 2000.
Mr. Putter and Tabby Feed the Fish, Harcourt (San Diego, CA), 2001.
Mr. Putter and Tabby Catch the Cold, Harcourt (San Diego, CA), 2002.
Mr. Putter and Tabby Stir the Soup, Harcourt (San Diego, CA), 2003.
Mr. Putter and Tabby Write the Book, Harcourt (Orlando, FL), 2004.
Mr. Putter and Tabby Make a Wish, Harcourt (Orlando, FL), 2005.
Mr. Putter and Tabby Spin the Yarn, Harcourt (Orlando, FL), 2006.

ILLUSTRATOR

Cynthia Rylant, *Gooseberry Park,* Harcourt (San Diego, CA), 1995.
Margery Cuyler, *The Battlefield Ghost,* Scholastic (New York, NY), 1999.
Margery Cuyler, *100th Day Worries,* Simon & Schuster (New York, NY), 2000.
Margery Cuyler, *Stop Drop and Roll,* Simon & Schuster (New York, NY), 2001.
Kathi Appelt, *Bubba and Beau, Best Friends,* Harcourt (San Diego, CA), 2002.
Kathi Appelt, *Bubba and Beau Go Night-Night,* Harcourt (San Diego, CA), 2003.
Kathi Appelt, *Bubba and Beau Meet the Relatives,* Harcourt (Orlando, FL), 2004.
Betsy Byars, Betsy Duffey, and Laurie Myers, *The SOS File,* Holt (New York, NY), 2004.

Co-author of humor column for *Glamour* magazine, "The World according to He & She," with Julie Logan, 1992-95, and a book of the same title. *The World ac-*

A city girl's quiet life high up in Ivory Towers is disrupted when a heavy-footed family of elephants moves in to the apartment upstairs in Howard's humorous **The Hubbub Above.**

cording to *He & She,* on which the column was based, has been translated into Chinese, Italian, French, German, Norwegian, and Brazilian Portuguese, and was printed as a column in the Brazilian magazine *Claudia.* Howard's children's books have been published in the United Kingdom, France, and Korea.

Work in Progress

Illustrations for future "Mr. Putter and Tabby" books, illustrations for a fourth "Bubba and Beau" book, and a novel cover for Eleanor Estes's *Miranda the Great.*

Sidelights

Arthur Howard began his career as an actor, working on stage and screen in everything from television commercials, Broadway and off-Broadway productions, and the Public Broadcasting Service television series *Square One.* After twenty years in theater, Howard began illustrating Cynthia Rylant's "Mr. Putter and Tabby" series, creating characters that children recognize on sight and enlivening Rylant's text of the adventures of the old man and his cat. In 1996 Howard took another step and began writing and illustrating his own books, including *When I Was Five, Serious Trouble,* and *The Hubbub Above.* Covering themes such as friendship, laughter, being a good neighbor, and judging people for their qualities not for their looks, Howard's books have been published around the world, including the United Kingdom, France, and Korea.

The "Mr. Putter and Tabby" series begins when elderly Mr. Putter decides that his loneliness can be cured if he gets a cat. When a trip to the pet store produces only kittens, Mr. Putter makes his way to the animal shelter and meets Tabby, a cat in just as much need of a friend as Mr. Putter. Tabby does succeed in keeping Mr. Putter company, and the pair accomplish tasks from travel to baking to recovering from illness. Linda Perkins of *Booklist* praised how Howard's illustrations "add character and sly humor" to Rylant's text. Diane Janoff commented of *Mr. Putter and Tabby Paint the Porch,* "The clearly rendered illustrations" make the book "a perfect choice for any weather." Anne Knickerbocker considered the illustrations in *Mr. Putter and Tabby Feed the Fish* "expressive." Stephanie Zvirin complimented Howard's "cozy, freewheeling artwork" in a *Booklist* review of *Mr. Putter and Tabby Stir the Soup.*

Howard's illustrations have also appeared in titles by Margery Cuyler and in Kathi Appelt's "Bubba and Beau" chapter-book series. In a review of *Stop, Drop, and Roll* by Cuyler, Annie Ayers commented that "Howard's quavering caricatures . . . are a hoot, adding to the general hilarity." In a *Booklist* review of *Bubba and Beau, Best Friends,* Kathy Broderick considered Howard's watercolors to be "familiar and comforting." A *Kirkus Reviews* critic said of the second title in the series, "Snappy pencil-and-watercolor illustrations feature the amusing cast of characters, providing honest down-home fun."

For his self-illustrated titles, Howard once described to *SATA* how he begins his books: "From time to time people ask me, which comes first, the story or the pictures, and I've always been quick to explain that definitely it's the story. But [with] . . . *The Hubbub Above* I've kind of changed my mind. I mean I do try to have a complete text finished before I work on the illustrations. But before I start writing a story, I have to have an idea—and my initial ideas for a story are always visual images."

Howard's first independent title, *When I Was Five,* tells the story of a six-year-old boy who remembers what it was like to be five, telling readers about the things that were important to him last year, and noting that while many of his favorite things have changed with advancing age, his best friend is still the same. "Few books this short and up beat are as involving and ultimately moving as this one," Carolyn Phelan wrote in *Booklist.* Lolly Robinson in *Horn Book* praised Howard for his ability to keep the perspective of a six year old, writing "Both text and art demonstrate the self-assurance acquired at this age, ringing true in every detail."

Howard's second self-illustrated picture book features Cosmo, a small black-and-white schnauzer who does not feel as though he is especially good at anything. All of the other pets in the story have unique talents, and it is not until Cosmo falls asleep on a skateboard that he finds his own talent. "The six canine characters (and single Siamese cat) exude personality," a reviewer for *Publishers Weekly* described. Kay Weisman, writing for *Booklist,* commented, "young children are sure to identify with Cosmo's insecurities and eventual success."

Hoodwinked tells a story of beauty, but not in the typical way. As Howard told *SATA, Hoodwinked* "began with a simple visual image. One day my nieces asked me to tell them a story. At the time they each had at least two Barbie dolls with them. I don't have anything against Barbie dolls, but I decided to tell them the most un-Barbie story I could think of; nothing about pretty clothes, or pretty hair, or pretty anything. So I began, 'Mitzi the witch liked creepy things. Creepy bedroom slippers. Creepy breakfast cereal.' The third line, 'Creepy relatives,' occurred to me later—right after Thanksgiving." Mitzi's dilemma in the story is a search for a pet. She wants a truly creepy pet, but the toad is boring and the bats do not pay attention to her. One night, a kitten appears at her door, and Mitzi allows it to stay, but just for one night, because she is not interested in a pet that cute. The kitten, however, has other ideas, and accompanies Mitzi on all of her witchy past times, until Mitzi realizes the kitten is just the pet for her, in spite of its non-creepy outward appearance. *Booklist* contributor Shelley Townsend-Hudson commented that "children will enjoy the preposterous fun

and hilarious illustrations" in *Hoodwinked*, while a *Publishers Weekly* critic noted the "cute-fierce characters and cobwebby settings" featured in the illustrations. (Mitzi, in spite of liking things to be creepy, is fairly cute herself.) "It's a satisfying story, illustrated with effective humorous line drawings," commented Martha V. Parravano in *Horn Book,* commenting on the "ghastly greens and putrid purples" of Howard's color choices. Ruth Semrau praised the book in her *School Library Journal* review, writing that "every page is a delight. Don't miss this one."

Howard's next solo effort, *Serious Trouble,* features young prince Ernest, who wants to be a jester, having to outsmart a dragon. Howard told *SATA:* "For *Serious Trouble,* the initial image was of a three-headed dragon that couldn't make up its minds. I pictured it tangled up with itself and arguing ferociously. The narrative grew from there. What would get the heads to stop bickering? Well, maybe they could all laugh at the same thing. But what would make them laugh? That's when Ernest the jester was born." Ernest makes a deal with the dragon: if he can get the dragon to laugh, the creature not eat him. "Children will giggle right up to the fitting conclusion of this lighthearted romp," wrote Marilyn Taniguchi in her *School Library Journal* review, while a *Kirkus Reviews* contributor noted that Howard tucks

A young witch is determined to prove her mettle by finding the creepiest of pets, until a decidedly un-creepy pet finds her in Hoodwinked.

"plenty of wordplay into the brief text to complement his playful, loosely drawn illustrations." Recommending the title for storytime groups, *Horn Book* contributor Kitty Flynn promised that Howard's "This crowd pleaser will tickle even a heckler's funny bone."

Howard related his inspiration for his next title to *SATA*: "The impulse to write *The Hubbub Above* was also little more than an image. I had a friend who often complained about her upstairs neighbors. One day she referred to them as 'the elephants upstairs.' I was immediately struck by the image of elephants dwelling in a small New York apartment. What would their home look like, I wondered. What kind of friends would they have? And the kitchen. I suppose it would be extremely well stocked . . . with peanuts. A book was born." Sydney, who lives on the fifty-second floor of the Ivory Towers, does not know that her upstairs neighbors are actually elephants. All she understands is how noisy they are, especially on Saturday nights when their friends come over for parties. One Saturday Sydney confronts her neighbors, only to discover the reason for the noise is because they and their guests are all wild animals. When the elephants realize they've caused Sydney aggravation, they promise they will try to be more quiet, and they invite her to come to all their parties. "Howard's sherbet-colored highly atmospheric art serves as the perfect setting" for the tale, according to a *Kirkus Reviews* contributor. Mary Elam, writing for *School Library Journal*, considered the story "a humorous tale with a subtle message of tolerance and cooperation." Kitty Flynn, writing in *Horn Book*, also noticed the message, calling it a "friendly conflict-resolution . . . accompanied by boisterous cartoon illustrations."

Summing up for *SATA* the debate on how he creates a story, Howard concluded, "So which comes first: the story or the pictures? Well, that's easy, it's, um, well. . . ."

Biographical and Critical Sources

PERIODICALS

Booklist, January 1, 1996, Linda Perkins, review of *Mr. Putter and Tabby Pick the Pears,* p. 850; November 1, 1999, Kay Weisman, review of *Cosmo Zooms,* p. 538; September 1, 2001, Shelly Townsend-Hudson, review of *Hoodwinked,* p. 120; September 15, 2001, Annie Ayers, review of *Stop, Drop, and Roll,* p. 230; April 1, 2002, Kathy Broderick, review of *Bubba and Beau, Best Friends,* p. 1331; November 1, 2002, Ilene Cooper, review of *Mr. Putter and Tabby Catch the Cold,* p. 509; July, 2003, Stephanie Zvirin, review of *Mr. Putter and Tabby Stir the Soup,* p. 1903.

Bulletin of the Center for Children's Books, September, 2001, review of *Hoodwinked,* p. 19.

Childhood Education, spring, 2004, Gina Hoagland, review of *Serious Trouble,* p. 161.

Horn Book, September-October, 1996, Lolly Robinson, review of *When I Was Five,* p. 579; January-February, 2002, Martha V. Parravano, review of *Hoodwinked,* p. 68; November-December, 2003, Kitty Flynn, review of *Serious Trouble,* p. 730; May-June, 2005, Kitty Flynn, review of *The Hubbub Above,* p. 309.

Instructor, April, 1998, review of *When I Was Five,* p. 26; May, 2000, review of *Cosmo Zooms,* p. 14.

Kirkus Reviews, October 15, 2002, review of *Mr. Putter and Tabby Catch the Cold,* p. 1538; March 1, 2003, review of *Bubba and Beau Go Night-Night,* p. 378; October 1, 2003, review of *Serious Trouble,* p. 1225; May 1, 2005, review of *The Hubbub Above,* p. 539.

Publishers Weekly, July 12, 1999, review of *Cosmo Zooms,* p. 93; August 16, 1999, review of *When I Was Five,* p. 87; September 24, 2001, review of *Hoodwinked,* p. 42; October 6, 2003, review of *Cosmos Zooms,* p. 87; November 3, 2003, review of *Serious Trouble,* p. 72.

Reading Teacher, October, 1997, review of *When I Was Five,* p. 132; October, 2000, review of *Cosmo Zooms,* p. 195.

School Librarian, spring, 2002, review of *Cosmo Zooms,* p. 19.

School Library Journal, May, 1996, Marianne Saccardi, review of *When I Was Five,* p. 92; September, 1999, Pat Leach, review of *Cosmo Zooms,* p. 184; July, 2000, Diane Janoff, review of *Mr. Putter and Tabby Paint the Porch,* p. 86; May, 2001, Anne Knickerbocker, review of *Mr. Putter and Tabby Feed the Fish,* p. 134; September, 2001, Ruth Semaru, review of *Hoodwinked,* p. 190; October, 2001, Roxanne Burg, review of *Stop, Drop, and Roll,* p. 46; November, 2003, Marilyn Taniguchi, review of *Serious Trouble,* p. 96; May, 2005, Mary Elam, review of *The Hubbub Above,* p. 86.*

*   *   *

HOWARD, Arthur Charles
See HOWARD, Arthur

I-J

ISADORA, Rachel 1953(?)-

Personal

Born c. 1953 in New York, NY; married Robert Maiorano (a ballet dancer and writer), September 7, 1977 (divorced, May, 1982); married James Turner; children: (second marriage) Gillian Heather. *Education:* Attended American School of Ballet.

Addresses

Home—New York, NY. *Agent*—c/o Author Mail, William Morrow and Co., 1350 Avenue of the Americas, New York, NY 10019.

Career

Dancer with Boston Ballet Company, Boston, MA; freelance author and illustrator of children's books.

Awards, Honors

Children's Book of the Year awards, Child Study Association, 1976, for *Max,* 1985, for *I Hear* and *I See,* and 1986, for *Flossie and the Fox* and *Cutlass in the Snow;* Children's Choice award, International Reading Association/Children's Book Council (CBC), 1976, Children's Book Showcase award, CBC, 1977, American Library Association (ALA) notable book citation, and Reading Rainbow selection, all for *Max;* ALA notable book citation, 1979, for *Seeing Is Believing; Boston Globe/Horn Book* honor book for illustration citation, 1979, Best Book for Spring designation, *School Library Journal,* 1979, and Caldecott Honor Book award, ALA, 1980, all for *Ben's Trumpet; A Little Interlude* included in American Institute of Graphic Arts Book Show, 1981; Best Book award, *School Library Journal,* and ALA notable book citation, both 1982, both for *The White Stallion;* Children's Book award, New York Public Library, 1983, for *City Seen from A to Z;* Outstanding Science Trade Book citation, National Science Teachers Association/CBC, 1985, for *I Touch; Horn Book* honor list citation, 1987, for *Flossie and the Fox;* ALA notable book, 1991, for *At the Crossroads.*

Writings

FOR CHILDREN; SELF-ILLUSTRATED

Max, Macmillan (New York, NY), 1976.
The Potters' Kitchen, Greenwillow (New York, NY), 1977.
Willaby, Macmillan (New York, NY), 1977.
(With Robert Maiorano) *Backstage,* Greenwillow (New York, NY), 1978.
Ben's Trumpet, Greenwillow (New York, NY), 1979.
My Ballet Class, Greenwillow (New York, NY), 1980.
No, Agatha!, Greenwillow (New York, NY), 1980.
Jesse and Abe, Greenwillow (New York, NY), 1981.
(Reteller) *The Nutcracker,* Macmillan (New York, NY), 1981.
City Seen from A to Z, Greenwillow (New York, NY), 1983.
Opening Night, Greenwillow (New York, NY), 1984.
I Hear, Greenwillow (New York, NY), 1985.
I See, Greenwillow (New York, NY), 1985.
I Touch, Greenwillow (New York, NY), 1985.
The Pirates of Bedford Street, Greenwillow (New York, NY), 1988.
(Adaptor) *The Princess and the Frog* (based on *The Frog King* and *Iron Heinrich* by Wilhelm and Jacob Grimm), Greenwillow (New York, NY), 1989.
(Adaptor) *Swan Lake: A Ballet Story* (based on the ballet *Swan Lake* by Pyotr Ilich Tchaikovsky), Putnam (New York, NY), 1989.
Friends, Greenwillow (New York, NY), 1990.
Babies, Greenwillow (New York, NY), 1990.
At the Crossroads, Greenwillow (New York, NY), 1991.
Over the Green Hills, Greenwillow (New York, NY), 1992.
Lili at Ballet, Greenwillow (New York, NY), 1993.
(Adaptor) *Firebird* (based on the ballet by Stravinsky), Putnam (New York, NY), 1994.
My Ballet Diary, Penguin Putnam (New York, NY), 1995.
Lili on Stage, Penguin Putnam (New York, NY), 1995.
(Adaptor) *The Steadfast Tin Soldier* (based on the story by Hans Christian Andersen), Penguin Putnam (New York, NY), 1996.

(Adaptor) *The Little Match Girl* (based on the story by Hans Christian Andersen), Penguin Putnam (New York, NY), 1996.

Lili Backstage, Penguin Putnam (New York, NY), 1997.

Young Mozart, Penguin (New York, NY), 1997.

(Adaptor) *The Little Mermaid* (based on the story by Hans Christian Andersen), Penguin Putnam (New York, NY), 1998.

Isadora Dances, Viking Penguin (New York, NY), 1998.

A South African Night, HarperCollins (New York, NY), 1998.

Caribbean Dreams, Putnam (New York, NY), 1998.

Listen to the City, Putnam (New York, NY), 1999.

ABC Pop!, Viking Penguin (New York, NY), 1999.

Sophie Skates, Penguin Putnam (New York, NY), 1999.

123 Pop!, Penguin Putnam (New York, NY), 2000.

Nick Plays Baseball, Penguin Putnam (New York, NY), 2001.

Bring on That Beat, Penguin Putnam (New York, NY), 2002.

Peekaboo Morning, Penguin Putnam (New York, NY), 2002.

Mr. Moon, Greenwillow (New York, NY), 2002.

On Your Toes: A Ballet ABC, Greenwillow (New York, NY), 2003.

Not Just Tutus, Putnam (New York, NY), 2003.

In the Beginning, Putnam (New York, NY), 2003.

What a Family, Putnam (New York, NY), 2005.

Luke Goes to Bat, Putnam (New York, NY), 2005.

Yo, Jo!,, Harcourt (Orlando, FL), 2007.

Also author of *Fulton Fish Market,* Putnam (New York, NY).

ILLUSTRATOR

Robert Maiorano, *Francisco,* Macmillan (New York, NY), 1978.

Elizabeth Shub, *Seeing Is Believing,* Greenwillow (New York, NY), 1979.

Robert Maiorano, *A Little Interlude,* Coward, McCann & Geoghegan (New York, NY), 1980.

Elizabeth Shub, *The White Stallion,* Greenwillow (New York, NY), 1982.

Elizabeth Shub, *Cutlass in the Snow,* Greenwillow (New York, NY), 1986.

Patricia C. McKissack, *Flossie and the Fox,* Dial (New York, NY), 1986.

Ruth Young, *Golden Bear,* Viking (New York, NY), 1990.

Sandol Stoddard, editor, *Prayers, Praises, and Thanksgivings,* Dial (New York, NY), 1992.

Reeve Lindbergh, *Grandfather's Lovesong,* Viking (New York, NY), 1993.

Jane Kurtz, *In the Small, Small Night,* Greenwillow (New York, NY), 2005.

Deborah Hopkinson, *Saving Strawberry Farm,* Greenwillow (New York, NY), 2005.

Adaptations

Ben's Trumpet was adapted for video and as a filmstrip with audiocassette.

Sidelights

After an injury forced her to abandon her first career as a professional dancer, Rachel Isadora turned to children's-book illustration and writing, and has produced a body of work notable both for its achievements and variety. Her books include award-winning titles such as *Max* and *Ben's Trumpet* as well as biographies, retellings of fairy tales and ballet stories, and her "Lili" series about a little girl's love affair with ballet. As an illustrator, Isadora brings her painterly eye and artist's perception to her work, producing art in a variety of mediums for both her own books and those of other writers. The recipient of a Caldecott Honor award, she peoples her books with characters of many cultures, nationalities, and ages. "Work like this is a dancer's fantasy," she once commented. "Because ballet is so demanding, dancers' stage careers are short. They can only dream of going on and on forever. With art, I can go on and on, and for me it's the only work that compares in intensity and joy."

Isadora began dancing as a toddler after wandering into her older sister's dance class, and by age eleven she was performing professionally and studying at the American School of Ballet on a scholarship. Despite the public nature of her art, she battled shyness as a girl, and in class would wait to be alone before practicing new movements. To deal with the pressures that came from training professionally, she also turned to drawing. "Ballet was very real to me: my world," she revealed to Elaine Edelman in a *Publishers Weekly* interview. "To escape it, I drew—so that became my fantasy world. I could express my thoughts in it, I could even express my anger. I couldn't do that as a dancer."

Seven years of study finally culminated in an offer to dance with the New York City Ballet; however, instead of accepting, Isadora broke down. "I went into my room," she told Edelman, "and didn't come out for three months." A few years later she joined the Boston Ballet Company, but a foot injury ended her brief career, and she was forced to establish herself in another vocation. So she loaded a paper bag with her sketches—all "odds and ends on bits of paper," she once commented—and took them to New York, hoping to obtain work as an illustrator. Her venture proved successful, for almost immediately she was assigned to work on her first book.

Both written and illustrated by Isadora, *Max* received considerable attention. Winner of the 1976 Child Study Association Children's Book of the Year award, the story revolves around the title character, a young baseball player who one day joins his sister at her ballet class. Clad in his uniform, the boy exercises along with the young ballerinas and decides to join the class when he realizes that ballet training will improve his athletic skills. Many reviewers praised Isadora for the nonsexist message in *Max:* that ballet can be enjoyed by all. Her black-and-white illustrations also drew praise as grace-

Through both text and illustrations, Isadora brings to life her story of a boy musician with a passion for jazz in her acclaimed 1979 picture book **Ben's Trumpet.**

ful, lively, and lifelike. The dancers in Max's class are "poised but fetchingly unpolished," decided a reviewer for *Publishers Weekly.*

Isadora incorporates music and dance in one of her best-known works, *Ben's Trumpet.* Winner of the 1980 Caldecott Honor award, the book is set during the 1920s Jazz Age and centers on Ben, a young boy who lives in the ghetto. Ben longs to play the lively music that emanates from a neighborhood club, but he cannot afford to buy a trumpet. His dream finally comes true when a seasoned jazz musician not only gives the youngster an instrument, but also teaches him to play. *Ben's Trumpet* is a "poignant, spare story," observed Marjorie Lewis in *School Library Journal.* Reviewers also lauded Isadora for the story's inventive artwork, which is appropriate reminiscent of the art deco style popular during the 1920s and 1930s. Bold outlines, dancing silhouettes, keyboards, and zigzag lines cover the pages of the book,

forming a pictorial image of the music. "Jazz rhythms visually interpreted in black and white fairly explode," proclaimed Mary M. Burns in a *Horn Book* review, while Linda Kauffman Peterson, writing in *Newbery and Caldecott Medal and Honor Books,* declared that Isadora's drawings possess a "swinging, throbbing beat."

Isadora shares her love of ballet in several of her books for children, drawing praise for her realistic portrayals of dancers' movements. In *Backstage,* which Isadora wrote with her first husband, ballet dancer Robert Maiorano, she describes a young girl's trek through the theater to meet her mother, who is rehearsing a part in the famous ballet *The Nutcracker. Opening Night* features a nervous and excited young dancer who is braving her first performance, and the story traces her steps from the time she walks backstage, to her first leap in front of the audience, to discovering roses in her dressing room following the production. Yet another book, *My Ballet Class,* portrays young ballerinas of all nationalities as they laugh together, clutter the dressing room floor, put on their tights and ballet slippers, stretch, and begin their practice. The dancers are sketched "with fluid agility," judged *Booklist* reviewer Barbara Elleman, adding that "facial expressions and body movements are surely and thoughtfully captured."

Focusing on younger dance-lovers, Isadora has created the poetry collection *Not Just Tutus,* which contains short verses that bring to life the dreams of determined young ballerinas alongside the author's "elegant pen-and-ink and watercolor illustrations [that] depict dancers of all shapes and sizes," according to *School Library Journal* contributor Joy Fleishhacker. The poems, which are divided into two sections, takes second stage to the art, according to some critics. In *On Your Toes: A Ballet ABC* brightly hued pastel drawings that corre-

spond to twenty-six words from Arabesque to Zipper "pulsate with the excitement of a grand jeté and a pas de chat," according to a *Kirkus Reviews* writer, while *School Library Journal* writer Carol Schene praised the work for presenting "a dreamy look at the world of ballet."

Introducing Isadora's "Lili" series, *Lili at Ballet* centers on one young girl who dreams of becoming a serious ballerina. Through Lili's experiences, young readers of a similar mindset learn about the practical aspects of ballet training, such as clothing, exercises, and some of the classic steps. A *Kirkus Reviews* contributor praised Isadora's illustrations for "nicely capturing [the dancers'] poise and grace." Deborah Stevenson, writing in the *Bulletin of the Center for Children's Books,* noted that "actual young dancers may want more sweat and less gossamer," but she also felt that *Lili at Ballet* "is a nice Nutcrackery treat for armchair Giselles." "Isadora's

A former ballerina, Isadora brings to life the excitement, worries, and hard work of a young dancer practicing for her first recital in **Not Just Tutus.**

own background in ballet is evident in the abundance and precision of her illustrations and in her understanding of the enthusiasm of the young dancer," concluded *Horn Book* reviewer Hanna B. Zeiger.

Readers meet the young dancer again in *Lili on Stage* and *Lili Backstage.* In *Lili on Stage* the girl performs the role of a party guest in act one of *The Nutcracker.* Returning home that evening, she dreams of her next performance. "The book's charm lies partly in the subject, but mainly in the simplicity and realism of both text and illustrations," wrote Carolyn Phelan in a *Booklist* review, while Zeiger noted in *Horn Book* that Isadora's "watercolor illustrations are like confections and will be a delightful reminder for children who have seen the ballet performed." Lili next leads readers to the excitement occurring behind the curtains in *Lili Backstage.* "For the stagestruck," *Booklist* contributor Hazel Rochman commented, "even the technical names will be magical, and they will pore over the graphic details of professionals at work."

In her writing and illustrating, Isadora has not confined herself to the performing arts. Her urban alphabet book, *City Seen from A to Z* is a collection of street scenes—all drawn in gray, black, and white—depicting the moods, settings, and ethnic diversity of metropolitan New York. Black, Asian, and Jewish people populate the pages, window shopping, relaxing in the sun, or just strolling through city streets. Isadora also incorporates an element of surprise into many of her scenes: "L," for example, points to the picture of a ferocious lion ironed onto the back of a young boy's T-shirt, while "Z" stands for the chalk-drawn zoo two children have sketched on the sidewalk. She also portrays elderly people sharing ice cream with their grandchildren or minding them at the beach. "Young and old people of different cultures and individual tastes all seem snugly at home," wrote Leonard S. Marcus in a review of the book for the *New York Times Book Review.* Beryl Lieff Benderly concluded in the *Washington Post Book World* that "Isadora's elegant, perceptive pictures capture small realities of city life."

The sounds of the city are evoked in *Listen to the City,* while its illustrations are rendered in pop art that captures "the sights and sounds of the city," according to a *Horn Book* reviewer. "In keeping with the Lichtenstein look, the text is limited to painted onomatopoeic words and brief utterances enclosed in dialogue bubbles," noted the same writer. Grace Oliff called *Listen to the City* an "exuberant picture book" in her review for *School Library Journal.* "The use of rich primary colors, coupled with the unique design of the pages, sometimes juxtaposing images in oddly angled segments, captures the energy of urban life," Oliff further observed.

With *ABC Pop!* and *123 Pop!* Isadora uses pop-art imagery to produce an alphabet and a counting book respectively. Reviewing the former title, *Horn Book* contributor Lolly Robinson noted that "Isadora has created a striking alphabet book in homage to the pop art she admired as a child. . . . But the pacing is pure Isadora, revealing a vitality that harks back to *Ben's Trumpet* and *City Seen from A to Z.*" Also reviewing *ABC Pop!,* In *Booklist* Michael Cart felt that the author/illustrator's "artfully energetic book will appeal to eyes of all ages." *Booklist* reviewer Gillian Engberg found *123 Pop!* to be a "sophisticated, playful introduction to numbers," while Robinson noted in another *Horn Book* review that the artist "manages to maintain her spontaneous style with vibrant gestural lines, surprising color choices, and unexpected whimsical touches."

South Africa is the subject of three picture books by Isadora: *At the Crossroads, Over the Green Hills,* and *A South African Night.* In the first title several South African children gather to welcome home their fathers, who have been away for several months working in the mines. *Over the Green Hills* "is a loving portrait of the Transkei and its people," according to a critic for *Junior Bookshelf,* while *A South African Night* is a "simply written picture book [that] focuses on the transition from day to night" in Kruger National Park, according to Gebregeorgis Yohannes in *School Library Journal.* Yohannes further observed that "Isadora's vibrant watercolor illustrations are evocative of both the human bustle and the wild untamed life force of the animals." More exotic locations are served up in *Caribbean Dream,* an "evocative" book, according to *Booklist* reviewer Ilene Cooper, and one that "captures the mood of an island and the spirit of children." A writer for *Publishers Weekly* called this same book a "simple, rhythmic paean to the Caribbean."

The Creation myth is celebrated in gentle watercolor in *In the Beginning,* which was described by *Booklist* contributor Ilene Cooper as a "small, ethereal picture book" that reflects the Biblical story from the Book of Genesis. In Isadora's newly formed heaven and Earth, "a host of angelic babies" await the arrival of each new creation, according to *School Library Journal* reviewer Linda L. Walkins, and the story closes as Adam and Eve walk along the shore at sunset, awaiting the birth of their first child. Noting that toddlers will enjoy the depictions of happiness, a *Publishers Weekly* contributor added that "Isadora's message of love is unmistakable."

Isadora turns to the baseball diamond for inspiration in *Nick Plays Baseball* and *Luke Goes to Bat.* In the first book, Nick plays on the Rockets, a boys-and-girls team that is involved in a championship game. The story relates in text and pictures the preparation for the game, playing the game, and the triumphant conclusion. "For all the ground the author covers," wrote a contributor for *Publishers Weekly,* the author's "presentation is simple and carefully pared down, keenly attuned to a picture book audience." The same reviewer concluded that *Nick Plays Baseball* is "just the ticket for aspiring sluggers." Little brother Luke gets his chance to play stickball in a neighborhood street team in *Luke Goes to Bat,* and after striking out on his turn at bat, he retains his enthusiasm for the game with the encouragement of his Grandma; after all, the boy understands, even local baseball hero Jackie Robinson strikes out sometimes at nearby Ebbets Field. Praising the nostalgic approach to the story, which takes place in early twentieth-century Brooklyn, *Booklist* reviewer Engberg added that Isadora's illustrations of African-American children "extend the sports action and reassuring emotions." Praising *Luke Goes to Bat* in *Kirkus Reviews,* a critic cited the author's "simple tale of love, baseball, and determination," dubbing Isadora's watercolor illustrations "warm" and "expressive."

Biographical and Critical Sources

BOOKS

Children's Literature Review, Volume 7, Thomson Gale (Detroit, MI), 1984, pp. 102-109.
Peterson, Linda Kauffman, and Marilyn Leathers Solt, *Newbery and Caldecott Medal and Honor Books: An Annotated Bibliography,* G.K. Hall (New York, NY), 1982, p. 372.
St. James Guide to Children's Writers, fifth edition, St. James Press (Detroit, MI), 1999.

PERIODICALS

Booklist, January 15, 1980, Barbara Elleman, review of *My Ballet Class,* p. 720; November 15, 1995, Carolyn Phelan, review of *Lili on Stage,* March 15, 1997, Hazel Rochman, review of *Lili Backstage,* p. 1247; May 1, 1997, Hazel Rochman, review of *Young Mozart,* p. 1500; February 15, 1998, p. 1019; March 15, 1998, Hazel Rochman, review of *Isadora Dances,* p. 1246; November 1, 1998, Ilene Cooper, review of *Caribbean Dreams,* p. 503; July, 1999, Michael Cart, review of *ABC Pop!,* p. 1949; December 1, 1999, Susan Dove Lempke, review of *Sophie Skates,* p. 711; May 1, 2000, Gillian Engberg, review of *123 Pop!,* p. 1672; June 1, 2000, p. 1909; September 1, 2000, p. 118; February 15, 2002, Ilene Cooper, review of *Bring on That Beat,* p. 1034; March 1, 2002, Gillian Engberg, review of *Peekaboo Morning,* p. 1142; January 1, 2003, Ilene Cooper, review of *Not Just Tutus,* p. 907; May 1, 2003, Ilene Cooper, review of *In the Beginning,* p. 1605; July, 2003, Carolyn Phelan, review of *On Your Toes: A Ballet ABC,* p. 1895; February 1, 2005, Gillian Engberg, review of *Luke Goes to Bat,* p. 978.
Bulletin of the Center for Children's Books, April, 1993, Deborah Stevenson, review of *Lili at Ballet,* p. 253; September, 1997, p. 14; April, 1998, p. 82; July, 1998, p. 386; June, 1999, p. 354; January, 2002, review of *Bring on That Beat,* p. 175; April, 2003, review of *Not Just Tutus,* p. 318; September, 2003, review of *On Your Toes,* p. 49.

Horn Book, June, 1979, Mary M. Burns, review of *Ben's Trumpet,* pp. 293-294; May-June, 1993, Hanna B. Zeiger, review of *Lili at Ballet,* p. 318; January-February, 1996, Hanna B. Zeiger, review of *Lili on Stage,* p. 98; July-August, 1997, p. 443; May-June, 1999, Lolly Robinson, review of *ABC Pop!,* p. 315; January-February, 2000, review of *Sophie Skates,* p. 66; March-April, 2000, review of *Listen to the City,* p. 186; May-June, 2000, Lolly Robinson, review of *123 Pop!,* p. 294.
Junior Bookshelf, August, 1993, review of *Over the Green Hills,* pp. 127-128.
Kirkus Reviews, May 15, 1991, p. 672; January 1, 1993, review of *Lili at Ballet,* p. 61; April 1, 1997, p. 558; January 15, 1998, p. 113; April 1, 1998, p. 496; October 1, 1998, p. 1460; May 1, 1999, p. 722; April 15, 2002, review of *Peekaboo Morning,* p. 570; February 15, 2003, review of *Not Just Tutus,* p. 309; March 1, 2003, review of *On Your Toes: A Ballet ABC,* p. 388; February 1, 2005, review of *Luke Goes to Bat,* p. 177.
New York Times Book Review, May 22, 1983, Leonard S. Marcus, review of *City Seen from A to Z,* p. 39; November 11, 1984, p. 55; January 15, 1995, p. 25; July 20, 1997, p. 22.
Publishers Weekly, August 2, 1976, review of *Max,* p. 114; February 27, 1981, Elaine Edelman, "Rachel Isadora and Robert Maiorano," pp. 66-67; October 10, 1994, p. 70; February 13, 1995, p. 79; March 31, 1997, review of *Young Mozart,* p. 73; March 2, 1998, review of *Isadora Dances,* p. 67; October 26, 1998, review of *Caribbean Dreams,* p. 65; October 11, 1999, review of *Sophie Skates,* p. 74; January 1, 2001, review of *Nick Plays Baseball,* p. 92; November 19, 2001, p. 70; December 10, 2001, review of *Bring on That Beat,* p. 69; April 15, 2002, review of *Peekaboo Morning,* p. 62; December 16, 2002, review of *Not Just Tutus,* p. 67; April, 2003, Joy Fleishhacker, review of *Not Just Tutus,* p. 122; August 4, 2003, review of *In the Beginning,* p. 76.
School Library Journal, February, 1979, Marjorie Lewis, review of *Ben's Trumpet,* p. 43; June, 1991, p. 80; March, 1998, p. 196; August, 1998, Gebregeorgis Yohannes, review of *A South African Night,* p. 140; April, 1999, p. 99; June, 1999, p. 116; August, 1999, p. 39; November, 1999, p. 143; May, 2000, Grace Oliff, review of *Listen to the City,* p. 144; June, 2000, p. 133; April, 2001, Adele Greenlee, review of *Nick Plays Baseball,* p. 131; January, 2002, Marianne Saccardi, review of *Bringon That Beat,* p. 102; July, 2002, Lisa Dennis, review of *Peekaboo Morning,* p. 93; June, 2003, Carol Schene, review of *On Your Toes: A Ballet ABC,* p. 129; August, 2003, Linda L. Walkins, review of *In the Beginning,* p. 135; February, 2005, Marilyn Taniguchi, review of *Luke Goes to Bat,* p. 103.
Teacher Librarian, May, 1999, p. 47.
Washington Post Book World, May 8, 1983, Beryl Lieff Benderly, "This Is the Way the World Works," pp. 16-17.

ONLINE

Harper Children's Web site, http://www.harperchildrens.com/ (November 21, 2005), "Rachel Isadora."*

JENNINGS, Paul 1943-

Personal

Born April 30, 1943, in Middlesex, England; immigrated to Australia, 1949; married; wife's name Claire; children: Tracy, Linda, Andrew, Sally, Bronson, Gemma. *Hobbies and other interests:* Racing historic cars, parties, Irish music, reading, walking.

Addresses

Home—Melbourne, Victoria, Australia; and Warambool, Victoria, Australia. *Agent*—c/o Author Mail, Penguin Group Australia, 250 Camberwell Rd., Camberwell, Victoria 3124, Australia.

Career

Writer. Teacher, 1963-68; Ministry of Education, Australia, speech pathologist, 1972-75; Burwood State College, lecturer in special education, 1976-78; Warambool Institute of Adult Education, senior lecturer in language and literature, 1979-88.

Awards, Honors

Young Australian Best Book Award, 1987, for *Unreal! Eight Surprising Stories,* 1988, for *Unbelievable! More Surprising Stories,* 1989, for *The Cabbage Patch Fib* and *Uncanny! Even More Surprising Stories,* 1990, for *The Paw Thing,* 1991, for *Round the Twist,* 1992, for *Quirky Tails! More Oddball Stories* and *Unmentionable! More Amazing Stories,* 1993, for *Unbearable! More Bizarre Stories,* 1994, for *Spooner or Later* and *Undone! More Mad Endings,* 1995, for *Duck for Cover* and *The Gizmo,* 1996, for *The Gizmo Again,* 1998, for *Wicked!,* and 2002, for *Tongue-tied;* Australian Writers' Guild Award for Best Adapted Screenplay for Children, 1990, and Prix Jeunesse Award, 1994, both for *Round the Twist* (television series); Gold Puffin Award, 1992, for selling one million books in Australia; Angus & Robertson Bookworld Award, 1993; Ashton Scholastic award (with Ted Greenwood and Terry Denton), 1993, for *Spooner or Later;* Victorian of the Year, Western Region, Australia Day (Victoria) Committee; Environment Award for Children's Literature, Wilderness Society, for *The Fisherman and the Theefyspray;* named member, General Division of the Order of Australia, 1995, for body of work; Dymocks Children's Choice Awards, 1998, for *Sink the Gizmo* and *Wicked!,* and voted Favourite Australian Author; Dromkeen Medal, 2001, for significant contributions to children's literature; numerous Australian child-selected awards, including Canberra's Own Outstanding List (COOL) award, West Australian Young Readers' Book Award, Kids Own Australian Literature (KOALA) award, Kids Reading Oz Choice (KROC) award, as well as Australian Publishers Association Book Industry award, Queensland Premier's Literary Award, Christian Schools' Book Award, Books I Like Best Yearly (BILBY) award, Australian Writers Guild award, and South Australian CROW award.

Writings

STORY COLLECTIONS

Unreal! Eight Surprising Stories (also see below), Penguin (Camberwell, Victoria, Australia), 1985, Viking (New York, NY), 1991.

Unbelievable! More Surprising Stories (also see below), Penguin (Camberwell, Victoria, Australia), 1986, Viking (New York, NY), 1995.

Quirky Tails! More Oddball Stories (also see below), Penguin (Camberwell, Victoria, Australia), 1987, Puffin (New York, NY), 1990.

Uncanny! Even More Surprising Stories (also see below), Penguin (Camberwell, Victoria, Australia), 1988, Viking (New York, NY), 1991.

Unbearable! More Bizarre Stories (also see below), Penguin (Camberwell, Victoria, Australia), 1990, Viking (New York, NY), 1995.

The Naked Ghost, Burp!, and Blue Jam, Longman Cheshire (Melbourne, Victoria, Australia), 1991.

Unmentionable! More Amazing Stories (also see below), Penguin (Camberwell, Victoria, Australia), 1991, Viking (New York, NY), 1993.

Undone! More Mad Endings, Penguin (Camberwell, Victoria, Australia), 1993, Viking (New York, NY), 1995.

Uncovered! Weird, Weird Stories, Penguin (Camberwell, Victoria, Australia), 1995, Viking (New York, NY), 1996.

Thirteen! Unpredictable Tales, Viking (New York, NY), 1996.

The Paul Jennings Superdiary, Puffin (Ringwood, Victoria, Australia), 1996.

Unseen!, Puffin (Ringwood, Victoria, Australia), 1998.

Uncollected: Every Story from Unreal!, Unbelievable!, and Quirky Tails, Viking (Ringwood, Victoria, Australia), 1998.

Uncollected: Volume Two: Every Story from Uncanny!, Unbearable!, and Unmentionable!, Penguin (Ringwood, Victoria, Australia), 1999.

Uncollected: Volume Three: Every Story from Undone!, Uncovered!, and Unseen!, Penguin (Ringwood, Victoria, Australia), 2000.

The Paul Jennings Superdiary 2002, Penguin (Ringwood, Victoria, Australia), 2001.

Tongue-tied!, Puffin (Camberwell, Victoria, Australia), 2002.

Uncooked!: Three Stories, Penguin (Melbourne, Victoria, Australia), 2005.

Paul Jennings' Funniest Stories, Penguin (Camberwell, Victoria, Australia), 2005.

NOVELS AND CHAPTER BOOKS

The Cabbage Patch Fib, illustrated by Craig Smith, Penguin (Camberwell, Victoria, Australia), 1988.

The Paw Thing, illustrated by Keith McEwan, Penguin (Camberwell, Victoria, Australia), 1989.

Round the Twist (also see below), Penguin (Camberwell, Victoria, Australia), 1990.

The Gizmo (also see below), illustrated by Keith McEwan, Penguin (Camberwell, Victoria, Australia), 1994.

The Gizmo Again (also see below), illustrated by Keith McEwan, Penguin (Camberwell, Victoria, Australia), 1995.

Sink the Gizmo (also see below), illustrated by Keith McEwan, Puffin (Ringwood, Victoria, Australia), 1997.

Singenpoo Strikes Again, illustrated by Keith McEwan, Puffin (Ringwood, Victoria, Australia), 1998.

Singenpoo Shoots Through, illustrated by Keith McEwan, Puffin (Ringwood, Victoria, Australia), 1999.

Sucked In, illustrated by Terry Denton, Penguin (Ringwood, Victoria, Australia), 2000.

Singenpoo's Secret Weapon, illustrated by Keith McEwan, Puffin (Ringwood, Victoria, Australia), 2001.

The Fantastic and Amazing Gizmo: All Four Stories in One (contains *The Gizmo, The Gizmo Again, Come Back Gizmo,* and *Sink the Gizmo*), Penguin (Camberwell, Victoria, Australia), 2002.

The Many Adventures of Singenpoo: All Four Stories in One (contains *The Paw Thing, Singenpoo Strikes Again, Singenpoo Shoots Through,* and *Singenpoo's Secret Weapon*), Puffin (Camberwell, Victoria, Australia), 2002.

The Cabbage Patch Pong, illustrated by Craig Smith, Puffin (Camberwell, Victoria, Australia), 2002.

Maggot, Nelson Thornes (Cheltenham, England), 2003.

The Cabbage Patch Curse, Puffin (Camberwell, Victoria, Australia), 2004.

How Hedley Hopkins Did a Dare, Robbed a Grave, Made a New Friend Who Might Not Have Really Been There at All, and While He Was at It Committed a Terrible Sin Which Everyone Was Doing Even Though He Didn't Know It, Puffin (Camberwell, Victoria, Australia), 2005.

PICTURE BOOKS

Teacher Eater, illustrated by Jeannette Rowe, Heinemann (London, England), 1991.

Grandad's Gifts, illustrated by Peter Gouldthorpe, Heinemann (London, England), 1991, Viking (New York, NY), 1993.

The Fisherman and the Theefyspray, illustrated by Jane Tanner, Penguin (Camberwell, Victoria, Australia), 1994.

The Spitting Rat, Penguin (Ringwood, Victoria, Australia), 1999.

Rascal the Dragon, illustrated by Bob Lea, Puffin (Camberwell, Victoria, Australia), 2004.

Rascal's Trick, illustrated by Bob Lea, Puffin (Camberwell, Victoria, Australia), 2004.

Rascal Takes Off, illustrated by Bob Lea, Puffin (Camberwell, Victoria, Australia), 2004.

Rascal in Trouble, illustrated by Bob Lea, Puffin (Camberwell, Victoria, Australia), 2004.

Rascal at the Show, illustrated by Bob Lea, Puffin (Camberwell, Victoria, Australia), 2004.

Rascal and the Hot Air Balloon, illustrated by Bob Lea, Puffin (Camberwell, Victoria, Australia), 2004.

Rascal and the Cheese, illustrated by Bob Lea, Puffin (Camberwell, Victoria, Australia), 2004.

Rascal and Little Flora, illustrated by Bob Lea, Puffin (Camberwell, Victoria, Australia), 2004.

GAME BOOKS; WITH TED GREENWOOD AND TERRY DENTON

Spooner or Later, Viking (New York, NY), 1992.

Duck for Cover, Penguin (Camberwell, Victoria, Australia), 1994.

Freeze a Crowd: Riddles, Puns, and Conundrums, Penguin (Ringwood, Victoria, Australia), 1999.

Spit It Out!, Puffing (Camberwell, Victoria, Australia), 2003.

"WICKED" SERIES; WITH MORRIS GLEITZMAN

The Slobberers (also see below), Puffin (Ringwood, Victoria, Australia), 1997.

Battering Rams (also see below), Puffin (Ringwood, Victoria, Australia), 1997.

Croaked (also see below), Puffin (Ringwood, Victoria, Australia), 1997.

Dead Ringer (also see below), Puffin (Ringwood, Victoria, Australia), 1997.

The Creeper (also see below), Puffin (Ringwood, Victoria, Australia), 1997.

Till Death Us Do Part (also see below), Puffin (Ringwood, Victoria, Australia), 1997.

Wicked! All Six Books in One (contains *The Slobberers, Battering Rams, Croaked, Dead Ringer, The Creeper,* and *Till Death Us Do Part*), Puffin (Ringwood, Victoria, Australia), 1998.

"DEADLY" SERIES; WITH MORRIS GLEITZMAN

Nude (also see below), Puffin (Camberwell, Victoria, Australia), 2000.

Brats (also see below), Puffin (Camberwell, Victoria, Australia), 2000.

Stiff (also see below), Puffin (Camberwell, Victoria, Australia), 2000.

Hunt (also see below), Puffin (Camberwell, Victoria, Australia), 2000.

Grope (also see below), Puffin (Camberwell, Victoria, Australia), 2000.

Pluck (also see below), Puffin (Camberwell, Victoria, Australia), 2000.

Deadly! All Six Books in One (contains *Nude, Brats, Stiff, Hunt, Grope,* and *Pluck*), Puffin (Camberwell, Victoria, Australia), 2001.

OTHER

Round the Twist (miniseries screenplay; based on his novel), Australian Children's Foundation, 1990.

The Reading Bug, and How You Can Help Your Child to Catch It (for adults), illustrated by Andrew Weldon, Penguin (Ringwood, Victoria, Australia), 2003.

Along with Uncanny!, Uncovered!, Unbearable!, *and* Unmentionable!, *Jennings' 1994 story collection has the same slapstick appeal as a "Three-Stooges" movie marathon.*

Jennings's books have been translated into Danish, Slovakian, German, French, Spanish, and Japanese.

Work in Progress

A script for a movie based on the "Gizmo" books.

Sidelights

In addition to possessing a vivid imagination and a mildly disgusting sense of humor, Australian author Paul Jennings can credit his son's absolute dislike for reading as the ingredient that fueled his own career as a popular children's author. If it were not for the fact that the boy turned up his nose at most of the books put on his literary plate, Jennings might never have decided to take pen in hand and begin concocting such appetizing tales as "Cow Dung Custard" and "Clear as Mud." "The strength of Jennings's writing lies in original precepts and unexpected plot twists," noted a reviewer in *Publishers Weekly*. That may be true from a scholarly point of view, but as far as the most reluctant of readers are

concerned, Jennings's appeal comes from his insistence upon digging around in places where parents and teachers always shout "hands-off," and constantly playing in the muck and mire of life.

Jennings introduces readers to his imaginative fiction with several collections of short stories, among them *Unreal! Eight Surprising Stories, Quirky Tails: More Oddball Stories, Unbelievable! More Surprising Stories,* and *Uncanny! Even More Surprising Stories.* Each of his tales concludes where the reader least expects it; surprise endings are concocted from a plotline that twists and turns like a cyclone. In "On the Bottom," a dying man cannot find peace even on his deathbed when his tattoos come to life and decide to find a new place to hang out. Brian's dog is determined to keep bringing home human bones that will not sit still in "Without a Shirt," while David ends up with super powers—and super problems—of his own in "Wonderpants." It is clear to young readers of *Unreal!, Unbelievable!,* and *Uncanny!* that, whether they are looking for haunted outhouses, a photocopy machine with an attitude, or piles of pig-poo, they will be sure to find it lurking somewhere in Jennings's unbelievable tales.

The subject matter of the stories in the fourth *Un*-book, *Unmentionable! More Amazing Stories,* came as no surprise to fans of Jennings's unbridled humor. Within the pages of *Unmentionable!* can be found "The Velvet Throne," which tells of the horrors of not only being locked in a public toilet, but having the graffiti scrawled upon the walls actually come true; and "Little Squirt," where a little boy triumphs over his brother in a contest that plays out in the school boys' room. In seven other stories, Jennings mines the same vein, not only mentioning the unmentionable but making it funny as well. *Unbearable! More Bizarre Stories* and *Undone! More Mad Endings,* following on the heels of *Unmentionable,* step more forcefully into the fantastic: In "Clear as Mud" the tables turn on a school bully after a bite he receives from a strange bug causes his skin to become as clear as cellophane. In "Noseweed," when Anthony only pretends to swallow the nasty cod liver oil-and-granola concoction his mother gives him, his cleverness backfires and the cereal starts sprouting. And in "What a Woman" a talented school athlete who also happens to be a girl gets her revenge against a group of taunting boys when she brings her aunt's toe in for show and tell.

Despite the bizarre elements, Jennings's tales "end with neat twists or telling questions that are more thoughtful than 'mad,'" according to reviewer John Peters in *School Library Journal.* Many of Jennings's short story collections have been combined into *Uncollected,* and he provides readers with an insight into his wildly off-kilter world with *The Paul Jennings Superdiary* and its sequel *The Paul Jennings Superdiary 2002.* Patricia Mahoney Brown, reviewing a Jennings collection for *School Library Journal,* felt that the stories featured in *Quirky Tails* are "imaginative, unusual, bizarre, and humor-

Running the gamut from a man who is trapped in a public restroom where graffiti comes true to a grandfather's search for the Waterholding Frog, the nine stories by Aussie author Jennings feature just the right mix of toilet humor and action. (Cover illustration by Keith McEwan.)

ous," and that readers "become immersed directly into the plot." In a review of *Thirteen! Unpredictable Tales,* also for *School Library Journal,* Brian E. Wilson commented that the assembled stories "show what a gifted storyteller Jennings is."

Along with stories of the gross and strange, Jennings has collaborated on two serials with fellow Aussie author Morris Gleitzman, dishing up icky tales about deadly slobber worms that can suck out people's insides in *The Slobberers,* the first book of the "Wicked" series. Before the story is over, the heroes of the tale have encountered killer frogs, white-haired spies, and way-too-near-death experiences. The pair collaborated on a second serial, collected in the volume *Deadly!,* which starts with Amy being kidnapped in a military vehicle by a bunch of bratty little kids and Sprocket, an amnesiac, alone in the bush, naked, and without food. Are the commandos really children, or is something sinister happening? Amy and Sprocket have to team together to find out.

Other books for pre-teen readers include the award-winning *The Cabbage Patch Fib, The Paw Thing, The Gizmo,* and *How Hedley Hopkins Did a Dare, Robbed a Grave, Made a New Friend Who Might Not Have Really Been There at All, and While He Was at It Committed a Terrible Sin Which Everyone Was Doing Even Though He Didn't Know It. The Cabbage Patch Fib* tells the story of Chris who, wondering where babies come from, manages to find a small green baby in a cabbage patch. The baby will only behave if Chris is there to take care of it. *The Paw Thing* is the first in a series of books about Singenpoo, a cat who can read. When the world is threatened by a plague of mice, led by a rat named Mac, it seems only Singenpoo can defeat them. In *The Gizmo* Stephen steals a device called the gizmo, only to realize that once he has taken it, he will not be able to get rid of the thing. Most unfortunately, the gizmo seems to have the ability to switch Stephen's clothing with that of any passing person. The gizmo continues to cause trouble over a course of four books, and all of the stories are collected in *The Fantastic and Amazing Gizmo: All Four Stories in One.*

Written for slightly older readers, the story of Hedly Hopkins has a somewhat autobiographical feel: like Jennings himself, Hedly and his family move from England to Australia in 1956. Lonely and desperate to fit in, Hedly accepts a dare from a local gang to remove a skull from an opened grave and deliver it to the gang's leader. Contrary to its long title, *How Hedley Hopkins Did a Dare, Robbed a Grave, Made a New Friend Who Might Not Have Really Been There at All, and While He Was at It Committed a Terrible Sin Which Everyone Was Doing Even Though He Didn't Know It* features extremely short chapters with short sentences, and sustains a very quick pace while dealing with some serious issues and keeping Jennings's typical sense of humor.

Along with novels and picture books, Jennings has also designed a game book, along with coauthors Ted Greenwood and Terry Denton, called *Spooner or Later,* which is filled to brimming with silly illustrations and their accompanying "spoonerisms," a form of wordplay where the beginning sound of a pair of words is reversed, making "read the book" into the nonsensical "bead the rook." Jennings has collaborated with Greenwood and Denton on other game books filled with riddles, tongue-twisters, and jokes. Also the author of award-winning picture books, he introduces a dragon called Rascal and his young friend Ben in a series of eight books that begin with *Rascal the Dragon.* The story is a "delight to share with young people," according to a reviewer for *Children's Bookwatch,* while Teresa Wittmann noted in *School Library Journal* that "Beginning readers will enjoy this simple story about a boy who loves dragons."

Although Jennings's stories might raise eyebrows among parents, critics have praised his efforts for getting kids to sit down and *read* in the first place. "Here's a man whose definition of a reluctant reader is 'a child for whom adults have not been able to find a good enough book,'" according to Karen Jameyson in *Horn Book.* Jameyson praised Jennings for his ability to craft "quirky, incredibly accessible, funny tales with unexpected twists and turns" that provide enough interest in reading to motivate a host of children who have difficulty mastering this important skill. Jennings's efforts to encourage reluctant readers have been rewarded with several child-selected best book awards in his native country. He is particularly proud of such honors, once telling *SATA:* "Some adults think I should write about the sorts of things that they think kids *should* read. I only want to write the sorts of things that I think kids *want* to read. Books are fantastic. That's what I want my readers to think."

Biographical and Critical Sources

BOOKS

Dwyer, Judy, *A Wizard Lit Master to Paul Jennings,* Wizard Books (Ballarat, Victoria, Australia), 2000.
Ricketson, Matthew, *Paul Jennings: The Boy in the Story Is Always Me,* 2000.

PERIODICALS

Booklist, October 15, 1988, p. 423; March 15, 1990, p. 1467; March 15, 1993, p. 1314; January 1, 1995, p. 816; June 1, 1997, Jeanette Larson, review of *Unreal!,* p. 1733.
Children's Bookwatch, February, 2005, review of *Rascal the Dragon.*
Horn Book, July-August, 1992, Karen Jameyson, "News from Down Under," pp. 497-500.
Junior Bookshelf, April, 1996, p. 78.
Kirkus Reviews, October 15, 1991, p. 1344; January 1, 1993, p. 62.
Magpies, November, 1997, review of *Wicked!,* p. 6, and *Sink the Gizmo,* p. 7; July, 1998, review of *Singenpoo Strikes Again,* p. 34; November, 1998, review of *Unseen!,* p. 6; May, 2002, review of *Tongue-tied,* p. 214; March, 2003, review of *The Cabbage Patch Pong,* p. 33; July, 2003, review of *The Reading Bug, and How You Can Help Your Child to Catch It,* p. 6.
Publishers Weekly, October 11, 1991, review of *Unreal! Eight Surprising Stories* and *Uncanny! Even More Surprising Stories,* p. 63.
School Librarian, November, 1995, p. 152; summer, 2001, review of *Sucked In,* p. 89, and review of *Unseen!* p. 102; winter, 2002, review of *Tongue-tied,* p. 214; autumn, 2004, Prue Goodwin, "The Reading Bug," p. 167.
School Library Journal, January, 1992, p. 113; January, 1995, John Peters, review of *Undone! More Mad Endings,* p. 108; August, 1998, review of *Unreal! Eight Surprising Stories,* p. 31; June, 2000, Patricia Mahoney Brown, review of *Quirky Tales,* p. 85; February, 2002, Brian E. Wilson, review of *Thirteen! Unpredictable Tales,* p. 74; March, 2004, Teresa Bateman, review of *Tongue-tied,* p. 88; January, 2005, Teresa Wittmann, review of *Rascal the Dragon,* p. 77.

ONLINE

Jubilee Books Web site, http://www.jubileebooks.co.uk/ (November 6, 2005), Paul Jennings, "The Writing Process" and interview.
Paul Jennings's Home Page, http://www.pauljennings. com.au (November 6, 2005).
Penguin Group Australia Web site, http://www.penguin. com.au/ (November 6, 2005), "Paul Jennings."*

* * *

JOHNS, Janetta
See QUIN-HARKIN, Janet

* * *

JUNGMAN, Ann

Personal

Born in London, England; married; husband a college professor (marriage ended). *Education:* Studied law at Exeter University; earned teaching credential. *Hobbies and other interests:* Reading, walking, cooking, the arts.

Addresses

Home—London, England. *Agent*—c/o Author Mail, Frances Lincoln, 4 Torriano Mews, Torriano Ave., London NW5 2RZ, England.

Career

Educator and author. Barn Owl Books (publisher), London, England, founder and owner, 1999—. Former researcher for television.

Writings

Vlad the Drac, Granada (London, England), 1982, reprinted, Barn Owl Books (London, England) 2002.
Lucy and the Big Bad Wolf, illustrated by Karin Littlewood, Dragon (London, England), 1986.
Max and the Moon Monsters, illustrated by Tony Kenyon, Macmillan Education (Basingstoke, England), 1986.
Fred and the Robot, Collins Educational (London, England), 1987.
Rundown on Robots, Collins Educational (London, England), 1987.
Big Max and the Satellite, Collins Educational (London, England), 1987.

Lucy and the Wolf in Sheep's Clothing, illustrated by Karin L. Dragon (London, England), 1987.

Big Max Goes to the Moon, Collins Educational (London, England), 1987.

Big Max and the Oil Rig, Collins Educational (London, England), 1987.

Robot Plays, Collins Educational (London, England), 1987.

I Don't Want to Live in a House, illustrated by Anni Axworthy, Picture Knight (London, England), 1988.

I Don't Want to Go to School, illustrated by Anni Axworthy, Picture Knight (London, England), 1988.

I Don't Want to Go in a Car, illustrated by Anni Axworthy, Hodder and Stoughton (London, England), 1989.

Lucky Keeps the Wolf from the Door, Young Lions (London, England), 1989.

The Little Dragon Steps Out, Young Corgi (London, England), 1989.

Count Boris Bolescu and the Black Pudding, Young Corgi (London, England), 1989.

Dracula Play, Collins Educational (London, England), 1989.

Count Dracula and the Monster, Collins Educational (London, England), 1989.

Count Dracula and the Victim, Collins Educational (London, England), 1989.

Count Dracula Meets His Match, Collins Educational (London, England), 1989.

The Day Teddy Didn't Tidy Up, Frances Lincoln/Windward (London, England), 1989.

Vlad the Drac down Under, Young Lions (London, England), 1989.

The Day Teddy Got Very Worried, Frances Lincoln/Windward (London, England), 1989.

The Day Teddy Made New Friends, Frances Lincoln/Windward (London, England), 1989.

The Day Teddy Wanted Grandad to Notice Him, Frances Lincoln/Windward (London, England), 1989.

Spine-Chiller, Collins Educational (London, England), 1989.

Count Dracula and the Ghost, Collins Educational (London, England), 1989.

Bold Bad Ben, illustrated by Cathy Wilcox, Collins Australia (Pymble, New South Wales, Australia), 1989.

Broomstick Services, illustrated by Jean Baylis, Scholastic (London, England), 1990.

The Little Dragon Falls Out, Young Corgi (London, England), 1991.

Leila's Magical Monster Party, Viking (London, England), 1991.

Count Boris Bolescu and the Transylvanian Tango, Young Corgi (London, England), 1991.

Septimouse, Supermouse, Viking (London, England), 1991.

There's a Troll at the Bottom of My Garden, illustrated by Doffy Weir, Viking (London, England), 1991.

Cinderella and the Hot Air Balloon, Frances Lincoln (London, England), 1992.

Rosie and the Royal Hunt, Young Corgi (London, England), 1992.

Roland and the Green Knight, Young Corgi (London, England), 1992.

Picnic for Tortoise, Ginn (Aylesbury, England), 1993.

Little Luis and the Bad Bandit, Walker (London, England), 1993.

The Little Dragon Nips Out, Young Corgi (London, England), 1993.

Septimouse, Big Cheese!, Viking (London, England), 1994.

Count Boris Balescu and the Midsummer Madness, Young Corgi (London, England), 1994.

Sally and the Booted Puss, and Other Stories, Longman (Harlow, England), 1994.

Pete and the Bully, pictures by Bucket, Collins Educational (London, England), 1995.

Count Dracula and the Vampire, Collins Educational (London, England), 1995.

Count Dracula and the Wedding, Collins Educational (London, England), 1995.

Count Dracula and the Witch, Collins Educational (London, England), 1995.

Count Dracula Gets a Shock, Collins Educational (London, England), 1995.

Pete and the Figs, pictures by Bucket, Collins Educational (London, England), 1995.

Pete and the New Girl, pictures by Bucket, Collins Educational (London, England), 1995.

Pete and the New Rucksack, pictures by Bucket, Collins Educational (London, England), 1995.

Homes (nonfiction), Collins Educational (London, England), 1995.

Schools Now and Then (nonfiction), Collins Educational (London, England), 1995.

Vlad the Drac Goes Travelling, Collins (London, England), 1996.

Count Draco down Under, illustrated by Toni Goffe, Hippo (London, England), 1996.

Sasha and the Wolfcub, illustrated by Cliff Wright, Collins Children's (London, England), 1996.

The Missing Monster, illustrated by Jan Smith, Orchard (London, England), 1996.

The Monster Idea, illustrated by Jan Smith, Orchard (London, England), 1996.

Frank N. Stein and the Monster in Love, illustrated by Jan Smith, Orchard (London, England), 1996.

Frank N. Stein and the Monster in Trouble, illustrated by Jan Smith, Orchard (London, England), 1996.

There's a Troll at the Bottom of Our Street, illustrated by Doffy Weir, Puffin (London, England), 1996.

School for Dragons, illustrated by John Eastwood, Hippo (London, England), 1997.

(With Cecilia Lenagh and Susan Gates) *The Big Wicked Witch Book,* Hippo (London, England), 1997.

(With Joan Lennon and Philippa Gregory) *The Big Book of Dragons,* Hippo (London, England), 1997.

There's a Troll at the Top of Our Tip, illustrated by Doffy Weir, Puffin (London, England), 1998.

Broomstick Baby, Scholastic (London, England), 1999.

Broomstick Removals, illustrated by Jan Lewis, Hippo (London, England), 1999.

Broomstick Rescues, illustrated by Lynne Chapman, Scholastic (London, England), 1999.

Sasha and the Wolf-Child, illustrated by Giles Greenfield, Collins (London, England), 1999.

Dracula Is Backula, illustrated by Doffy Weir, Anderson (London, England), 1999.

(Reteller) *A Pack of Wolf Tales,* illustrated by Vicki Yeates, Longman (Harlow), 2000.

(Reteller) *The Musicians of Bremen,* illustrated by James Marsh, Scholastic (London, England), 2001.

Resistance!, illustrated by Alan Marks, Barrington Stoke (Edinburgh, Scotland), 2002.

Twitta and the Ferocious Fever, illustrated by Mike Phillips, A. & C. Black (London, England), 2002.

Septimouse and the Cheese Party, illustrated by Kay Widdowson, Happy Cat Books (Bradfield, England), 2004.

The Most Magnificent Mosque, Frances Lincoln (London, England), 2004.

Also author of "Roman Quartet" series, including *Clottus and the Gladiator, Bacillus and the Beastly Bath, Tertius and the Horrible Hunt,* and *Twitta and the Ferocious Fever.*

Sidelights

It was while on a trip to Transylvania that English-born author and publisher Ann Jungman was inspired to write her first successful children's book, the beginning chapter book *Vlad the Drac,* about a baby vampire who is exported from Romania by two vacationing British children. Although Jungman's decision to take much of the bite out of her young undead hero by making him a vegetarian did much to make Vlad non-threatening to younger children, her story went the rounds of publishers for approximately five years before it was finally published. When *Vlad the Drac* proved that Jungman's take on elementary-aged children's reading tastes was on target, she expanded Vlad's adventures, and has also established herself as a prolific and popular writer whose other topics include dragons, wolves, ghosts, and other creatures. "Monsters are fun," the author noted on her home page. "You can do what you like with them, reality doesn't have to be taken into account. Anyway, all my monsters turn out to be really nice." Reviewing one "Vlad" story, *Vlad the Drac Goes Travelling,* for *Booklist,* Karen Harris called the humorous tale about the vampire who faints at the sight of blood "beautifully written and flawlessly narrated."

While many of Jungman's books present humorous stories with wildly imaginative plots and fantastic characters, *The Most Magnificent Mosque* undergirds its entertaining story with history and a message about religious and cultural tolerance. Based on a true story from the thirteenth century, the book recounts the story of three boys who become friends, despite having vastly different religions and beliefs. Rashid is Muslim, Samuel is Jewish, and Miguel is Christian, and all three live in Cordoba Spain, where these three faiths have crossed paths and sometimes created hostilities as they rubbed shoulders over the centuries. Best friends as children, the boys get into so much trouble with their hijinks that they are ordered by the caliph work together tending the garden of the city's mosque as punishment. Through this work taking care of the gardens, the boys each gain an appreciation of the beautiful old building and see it

In **Lucy and the Big Bad Wolf** *a wolf dreams of living out a popular fairy tale but soon realizes that docile grannies and gullible, red-hooded girls are not a part of modern life.* (Illustration by Karen Littlewood.)

as a symbol of the workings of God despite their differences of faith. The three come together again years later and inspire their multi-cultural and fragmented community to preserve their beloved mosque after Spain's conquering Christian king now orders that the religious building be torn to the ground. "This appealing story emphasizes the theme that when individuals work together, everyone wins," stated Margaret R. Tassia in a review of *The Most Magnificent Mosque* for *School Library Journal.*

Biographical and Critical Sources

PERIODICALS

Booklist, February 15, 1992, review of *Lucy and the Wolf in Sheep's Clothing,* p. 1119; September 1, 1993, Ilene Cooper, review of *When the People Are Away,* p. 69; January 15, 1995, Barbara Baskin, review of *Vlad the Drac Vampire,* p. 946; July, 1996, Karen Harris, review of *Vlad the Drac Goes Traveling* (audio version), p. 1838; November 1, 1996, Karen Harris, review of *Septimouse, Supermouse* and *Septi-*

Three boys who, despite their religious differences, come together as friends and ultimately unite the city of Cordoba during the early thirteenth century are the focus of Jungman's **The Most Magnificent Mosque.** *(Illustration by Selley Fowles.)*

mouse, Big Cheese, p. 522; February 15, 2001, Anna Rich, review of *Broomstick Rescues* and *Broomstick Baby,* p. 1165.

Magpies, July, 1992, review of *The Little Dragon Falls Out,* p. 29; July, 1993, review of *Cinderella and the Hot Air Balloon,* p. 30.

Publishers Weekly, March 29, 2004, review of *The Most Magnificent Mosque,* p. 60.

School Librarian, May, 1990, review of *Count Boris Bolescu and the Black Pudding,* p. 64; August, 1991, review of *Leila's Magical Monster Party,* p. 104; November, 1991, review of *The Little Dragon Falls Out,* p. 145; February, 1992, review of *There's a Troll at the Bottom of My Garden,* p. 20; August, 1992, review of *Roland and the Green Knight,* p. 103; February, 1993, review of *When the People Are Away,* p. 16; February 1993, review of *Cinderella and the Hot Air Balloon,* p. 16; spring, 2000, review of *Broomstick Rescues,* p. 33; spring, 2000, review of *Broomstick Baby,* p. 33; winter, 2001, review of *Dragon Disasters,* p. 201; summer, 2002, review of *Waiting for Elijah,* p. 94; autumn, 2002, review of *Resistance,* p. 145; spring, 2003, review of *Tertius and the Horrible Hunt,* p. 33.

School Library Journal, November, 1992, Priscilla Bennett, review of *Vlad the Drac,* p. 58; January, 1994, Elizabeth Hanson, review of *When the People Are Away,* p. 92; September, 2004, Margaret R. Tassia, review of *The Most Magnificent Mosque,* p. 170.

Washington Post Book World, April 11, 2004, Elizabeth Ward, review of *The Most Magnificent Mosque,* p. 11.

Wilson Library Bulletin, January, 1994, Donnarae MacCann and Olga Richard, review of *When the People Are Away,* p. 121.

ONLINE

Ann Jungman Home Page, http://homepage.ntlworld.com/alan.root/aj/bio.htm (July 13, 2005).

Children's Bookcase Online, http://www.thechildrensbookcase.com/ (October 5, 2005), review of *Vlad the Drac.*

Nancy Keane's Booktalks Online, http://www.nancykeane.com/booktalks/ (October 5, 2005), review of *The Most Magnificent Mosque.*

SocialStudiesforKids.com, http://www.socialstudiesforkids.com/ (October 5, 2005), review of *The Most Magnificent Mosque.**

K

KAY, Elizabeth 1949-

Personal

Born 1949, in London, England; married; children: two. *Education:* Nottingham Art School (now part of Nottingham Trent University), degree (fine art); Bath Spa, M.A. (creative writing). *Hobbies and other interests:* Traveling, watching wildlife.

Addresses

Home—Surrey, England. *Agent*—c/o Author Mail, The Chicken House, 2 Palmer St., Frome, Somerset BA11 1DS, England. *E-mail*—elizabethkay@hotmail.co.uk.

Career

Writer and illustrator. Formerly worked as an art and creative-writing teacher.

Awards, Honors

Cardiff International Poetry Competition winner; Canongate Prize; White Raven prize, Bologna Book Fair, 2004, and Stockton Children's Book of the Year, 2005, both for *The Divide.*

Writings

FOR CHILDREN

The Divide, Scholastic (New York, NY), 2003.
Back to the Divide, Scholastic (New York, NY), 2004.
The Jinx on the Divide, Scholastic (New York, NY), 2005.

Author's works have been translated into other languages.

OTHER

The Spirit Collection (poetry), Manifold (London, England), 2000.

Also illustrator of natural history books. Author of short stories and radio plays.

Sidelights

In addition to her work as an illustrator, playwright, and poet, Elizabeth Kay has penned the "Divide" trilogy for younger readers. Composed of *The Divide, Back to the Divide,* and *The Jinx on the Divide,* Kay's novel series draws readers into a fantasy world wherein a modern British teen is confronted by elves, dragons, and griffins as well as other creatures of a sinister nature. Evil forces threaten to destroy the boy's real world, as well as the parallel fantasy world connected by the Divide.

The first book in the trilogy, *The Divide* introduces thirteen-year-old Felix, who has a very dangerous heart condition. While visiting Costa Rica on a family vacation, Felix and his parents make a day trip to the continental divide, the point on the globe where the Atlantic meets the Pacific. Standing on this exact spot, Felix suddenly loses consciousness. Upon awaking, he suddenly realizes that he is no longer in the world he knows; rather, he finds himself in a strange place ripe with magic and filled with mythical beings. Befriended by an elf named Betony, Felix learns of the power of Snakeweed, a creature called a japegrin who is learned in the healing arts. He goes in search of this creature, who he is told may have a potion that will cure the heart condition that threatens his life.

The Divide was praised by *Kliatt* reviewer Paula Rohrlick as "an entertaining light read" containing "both suspense and humor," while *Booklist* critic Sally Estes dubbed it a "grand adventure." A *Publishers Weekly* reviewer had particular praise for the book's ending, commenting that Kay ends her tale "with a nicely constructed cliff-hanger, leaving those who enjoyed this odd journey hungry for the next."

While Felix safely returns to his own world in *The Divide,* it is clear to readers of *Back to the Divide* that he did not cross the portal back to modern-day Earth alone.

128

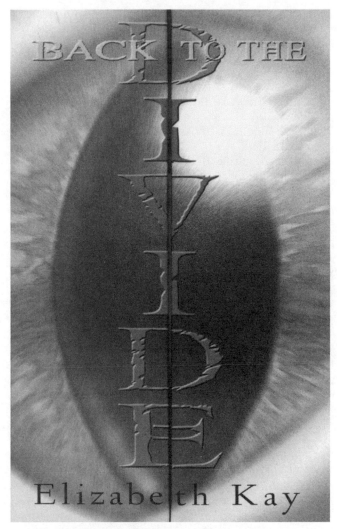

Part of Kay's ongoing series finds Felix forced to return to the world beyond the Divide after fiendish Snakeweed strikes Felix's parent with a contagious curse that threatens to destroy Earth. (Cover illustration by Ted Dewan.)

In Kay's second "Divide" installment she once again takes readers on a magical journey into a fantasy world, as Felix now attempts to locate the evil japegrin that turned his parents to stone. In fairy-tale fashion, Felix joins with both old friends and new to launch a crusade against the evil Snakeweed in hopes of restoring his parents to life. "Kay juggles several plot threads and a wide cast of characters without losing readers," commented *School Library Journal* reviewer Steven Engelfried of *Back to the Divide*. Felix and Betony's further adventures, which involve a forgotten genie, a vengeful school bully, and yet another journey across the Divide, are set forth in *The Jinx on the Divide*.

Biographical and Critical Sources

PERIODICALS

Booklist, June 1, 2003, Sally Estes, review of *The Divide,* p. 1762.

Bulletin of the Center for Children's Books, December, 2003, Janice Del Negro, review of *The Divide,* p. 154.
Kirkus Reviews, June 15, 2003, review of *The Divide,* p. 860; June 15, 2004, review of *Back to the Divide,* p. 578.
Kliatt, November, 2003, Paula Rohrlick, review of *The Divide,* p. 6.
Publishers Weekly, July 28, 2003, review of *The Divide,* p. 95.
School Librarian, winter, 2004, Rosemary Good, review of *Back to the Divide,* p. 202.
School Library Journal, September, 2003, Bruce Anne Shook, review of *The Divide,* p. 215; September, 2004, Steven Engelfried, review of *Back to the Divide,* p. 209.
Voice of Youth Advocates, August, 2003, review of *The Divide,* p. 237.

ONLINE

Chicken House Web site, http://www.doublecluck.com/ (October 5, 2005), "Elizabeth Kay."
Elizabeth Kay Home Page, http://www.elizabeth-kay.co.uk (October 5, 2005).

*　　*　　*

KAY, Jackie
See KAY, Jacqueline Margaret

*　　*　　*

KAY, Jacqueline Margaret 1961-
(Jackie Kay)

Personal

Born November 9, 1961, in Edinburgh, Scotland; partner of Carol Ann Duffy (a poet), since 1999; children: one son. *Education:* University of Stirling, B.A. (honors, English), 1983.

Addresses

Home—25 Macefin Ave., Manchester M21 7QQ, England. *Office*—School of English Literature, Language, and Linguistics, Percy Building, University of Newcastle upon Tyne, Newcastle upon Tyne NE1 7RU, England. *Agent*—Pat Kavanagh, Peters, Fraser & Dunlop, 503/4 The Chambers, Chelsea Harbour, London SW10 OXF, England. *E-mail*—jackie.kay@ncl.ac.uk.

Career

Poet and playwright. Writer-in-residence, Hammersmith, London, England, 1989-91; Wingfield Arts, Suffolk, England, poet-in-the-schools; University of Newcastle upon Tyne, Newcastle upon Tyne, England, instructor.

Jackie Kay

Awards, Honors

Eric Gregory Award, 1991; Scottish Arts Council Book Award, and Saltire First Book of the Year Award, both 1991, and *Forward* Prize, 1992, all for *The Adoption Papers;* Signal Poetry Award, 1993, for *Two's Company,* 1999, for *The Frog Who Dreamed She Was an Opera Singer;* Somerset Maugham Award, 1994, for *Other Lovers;* London *Guardian* Fiction Prize, 1998, and Authors' Club First Novel Award, and IMPAC Dublin Literary Award shortlist, both 2000, both for *Trumpet;* Cholmondeley Award, 2003.

Writings

FOR CHILDREN

Two's Company (poetry), illustrated by Shirley Tourret, Puffin (London, England), 1992.

Three Has Gone (poetry), illustrated by Jody Winger, Blackie Children's Books (London, England), 1994.

The Frog Who Dreamed She Was an Opera Singer, Bloomsbury Children's (London, England), 1998.

Strawgirl, Macmillan Children's (London, England), 2002.

Number Parade: Number Poems from 0-100, illustrated by Jo Brown, LDA, 2002.

ADULT POETRY

Chiaroscuro, Methuen (London, England), 1986.

The Adoption Papers, Bloodaxe Books (Newcastle upon Tyne, England), 1991.

That Distance Apart (chapbook), Turret (London, England), 1991.

Other Lovers, Bloodaxe Books (Newcastle upon Tyne, England), 1993.

Christian Sanderson: A Poem, illustrations by Peter Arkle, Prospero Poets (Alton, England), 1996.

Off Colour, Bloodaxe Books (Newcastle upon Tyne, England), 1998.

Sick Bag, Bloodaxe Books (Newcastle upon Tyne, England), 1998.

Life Mask, Bloodaxe Books (Newcastle upon Tyne, England), 2005.

OTHER

(Author of libretto) *Once through the Heart* (opera), produced by English National Opera, 1991.

Bessie Smith (biography), Absolute (Bath, England), 1997.

Trumpet (novel), Pantheon (New York, NY), 1998.

Why Don't You Stop Talking (short stories), Picador (London, England), 2002.

Also author of material for television and radio. Contributor of plays to anthologies, including *Lesbian Plays,* edited by Jill Davis, 1987; *Gay Sweatshop: Four Plays and a Company,* edited by Philip Osment, Methuen Drama (London, England), 1989; and *International Connections: New Plays for Young People,* Faber & Faber (London, England), 2003. Contributor of poems to anthologies, including *A Dangerous Knowing: Four Black Women Poets,* Sheba, 1983; and *Penguin Modern Poets,* Volume 8: *Jackie Kay, Merle Collins, Grace Nichols,* Penguin, 1996; and to periodicals *Artrage* and *Feminist Review.* Short stories included in anthologies *Everyday Matters 2,* 1984, and *Stepping Out,* 1986.

Sidelights

The writing of Scottish-born poet Jackie Kay has been praised for the unique qualities it gains due to the rich influences of Kay's background and life experiences. Kay, who writes in both the Scots dialect and in standard English, is also a black woman; she was adopted as a child by Caucasian parents and grew up in a predominantly white community. Kay's lesbianism also influences her work for adults, which consists of plays, fiction, and poetry. The award-winning poetry collection *The Adoption Papers,* for example, includes a ten-poem sequence describing Kay's search for her birth mother from three perspectives: that of the poet as a child, that of Kay's biological mother, and that of her adoptive mother.

Kay's highly praised poetry for children includes the collections *Two's Company, Three Has Gone,* and the award-winning *The Frog Who Dreamed She Was an Opera Singer.* In her works for younger readers she takes on serious topic such as racism, but filters these childhood experience through a gentle lens, tempering her characteristic thoughtful and meaningful approach with an uplifting view. In addition to her poetry and plays, Kay is the author of several works of fiction, including the adult novel *Trumpet,* a collection of short fiction, and the children's novel *Strawgirl.* Reflecting her love of blues music, she has also penned a well-received biography of American blues singer Bessie Smith. In 2003 Kay received the prestigious Cholmondeley Award.

Born in Edinburgh, Scotland, Kay grew up in the city of Glasgow; she discovered her love for poetry through the works of celebrated eighteenth-century Scots poet Robert Burns. After earning an honours degree in English at Stirling University, she moved to England and embarked upon a career as a writer for the theater as well as for television and radio. At a time of rising feminist consciousness, her plays were popular with women's theater groups, and she contributed poems and short stories to several anthologies and magazines. Discussing Kay's first published poetry collection, *The Adoption Papers, Booklist* reviewer Pat Monaghan claimed that the work "should become a feminist classic." The volume, which is noted for the poet's use of rhythm and sound, also includes poems about death, including dying of AIDS; about gay love; and about life in Great Britain under the government of Prime Minister Margaret Thatcher. Kay's second collection of poetry for adults, *Other Lovers,* was also praised for its use of language. In this work, Kay includes memories of the racism directed at her as a child, as well as a poem written from the perspective of a sixteen-year-old girl.

In her poetry collections for children Kay focuses on experiences important to her young audience and draws on many of the subjects and issues that she addresses in her adult works. Her writing for young people contains at its heart a sensitive child's developing perceptions of the people and society that exists around her. In her first collection for children, *Two's Company,* Kay uses blank verse to express a variety of childhood experiences, from the pain of divorce to the joys of travel. Imaginary friends are the subject of several poems, some of which are narrated by Carla, a girl whose parents have separated and who is trying to muster her customary spirit. *Two's Company* was praised as "a brilliant debut in writing for children" by Morag Styles in *Books for Keeps,* the critic adding: "There is plenty of fun, pain too, lyrical moments, compassion, but absolutely no sentimentality (the great fault of so many who attempt to write for the young)."

In *Three Have Gone* Kay's subjects range from a Gaelic dog who refuses to speak English to childhood betrayal and guilt and the joys and difficulties of living within a family. Writing in *Junior Bookshelf,* D.A. Young called the volume "an excellent successor to *Two's Company,* adding that Kay "continues to delight us with childhood memories crisply retold as if they had happened yesterday." "A spirited child with a lively imagination she must have been, and that spirit pervades her work," wrote Judith Nicholls, describing Kay in a review of

Three Has Gone for *Books for Keeps. The Frog Who Dreamed She Was an Opera Singer* is an imaginative collection that features droll characters such as Mr. and Mrs. Lilac, the Sulk Pod, Jimmy Mush, and, of course, the highly imaginative amphibian of the title.

In *Strawgirl* Kay spins a story about eleven-year-old Molly "Maybe" McPherson who lives in a rural Highland community where she is one of the few people of mixed race. Her innate feistiness when dealing with life—she earned her nickname because she never commits herself to answering a question with "yes" or "no"—and the local bullies is transformed into resilience and perseverance after Maybe's father is killed in a car accident and she must help her grieving mother run the farm and save the property from unscrupulous businessmen hoping to take advantage of the family's tragedy. At harvest time, when the girl's spirits start to sag, a magical doll called Strawgirl suddenly appears, helping Maybe harness her strengths and gain the confidence to deal with the challenges life has given her. Praising the novel's image-filled text in the London *Daily Telegraph,* Carole Mansur noted that with *Strawgirl* Kay crafts "a warm and comforting story in which

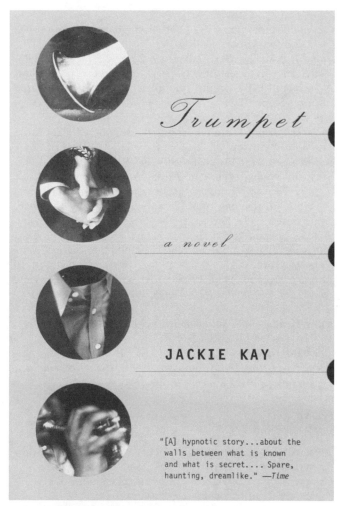

"[A] hypnotic story...about the walls between what is known and what is secret.... Spare, haunting, dreamlike." —*Time*

In addition to her poetry for both adults and children, Kay received acclaim for this 1998 novel, winner of the London Guardian *Fiction Prize.*

elements of traditional folk myths are yoked to a world recognisable to today's children."

Commenting on the difference between writing for children and adults, Kay told Jean Sprackland in *Poetry-Class.com:* "I don't like writing for children that is 'writing for children.' If it is any good, then adults will like it too. When I create a voice or character, I go through the same process. . . . When I am writing for children, my own childhood—my past—comes swimming back. I like to keep the conversation open between myself as an adult and myself as a child. When I am creating children's characters, the gap between childhood and adulthood doesn't seem that large."

Biographical and Critical Sources

BOOKS

Contemporary Poets, sixth edition, St. James Press (Detroit, MI), 1996, pp. 565-566.

PERIODICALS

Booklist, March 15, 1992, Pat Monaghan, review of *The Adoption Papers,* p. 1332.
Books for Keeps, November, 1992, p. 23; March, 1993, Morag Styles, review of *Two's Company,* p. 28; September, 1994, Judith Nicholls, review of *Three Has Gone,* pp. 20-21.
Books for Your Children, autumn, 1994, p. 28.
Daily Telegraph (London, England), July 12, 2002, Carole Mansur, review of *Strawgirl.*
Junior Bookshelf, August, 1994, p. 135; February, 1995, D.A. Young, review of *Three Has Gone,* pp. 21-21.
Library Journal, January, 1999, Lawrence Rungren, review of *Trumpet,* p. 152; July, 1999, Judy Clarence, review of *Off Colour,* p. 94; October 1, 1999, review of *Trumpet,* p. 51.
Publishers Weekly, December 21, 1998, review of *Trumpet,* p. 50.
School Librarian, May, 1994, p. 70; summer, 1999, review of *Off Colour,* p. 97; winter, 2002, review of *Strawgirl,* p. 192.
Times Educational Supplement, February 19, 1993, p. R2; November 11, 1994, p. R7.
Times Literary Supplement, May 22, 1992, p. 30.
World Literature Today, autumn, 1999, review of *Trumpet,* p. 736, and *Off Colour,* p. 743.

ONLINE

ContemporaryWriters.com, http://www.contemporary writers.com/ (July 31, 2005), "Jackie Kay."
PoetryClass.com, http://www.poetryclass.com/ (July 31, 2005), Jean Sprackland, interview with Kay.
Writing Scotland Web site, http://www.bbc.co.uk/scotland/ arts/writingscotland/ (July 13, 2005), "Jackie Kay."*

KEEHN, Sally M. 1947-

Personal

Born August 11, 1947, in London, England; daughter of Shirley (a naval officer) and Mary (a homemaker; maiden name, Giffen) Miller; married David C. Keehn (an attorney), December 30, 1972; children: Alison, Molly. *Education:* Hood College, B.A., 1969; Drexel University, M.L.S., 1972. *Religion:* Lutheran.

Addresses

Home—Allentown, PA. *Agent*—c/o Philomel Publicity, 345 Hudson St., New York, NY 10014. *E-mail*—sally-keehn@aol.com.

Career

Anne Arundel County Public Library, Annapolis, MD, young-adult librarian, 1972-75, part-time reference librarian, 1975-79; freelance writer, 1981—. Part-time and volunteer reference librarian, Parkland Community Library, 1980-91; part-time tour guide, Lehigh County Historical Society, 1985-86. Also worked for American Red Cross in Korea.

Member

Society of Children's Book Writers and Illustrators, Authors Guild, Inkweavers, Riverstone Writers, Bucks County Authors of Books for Children, Rutger's University Council on Children's Literature.

Awards, Honors

New York Public Library Reading and Sharing citation, and Notable Trade Book in the Field of Social Studies citation, both 1991, Carolyn W. Field Award, and Jefferson Cup Honor Book, both 1992, International Reading Association Young Adults' Choice citation, 1993, Favorite Paperback citation, and Hodge Podger Society Award, 1994, and Texas Lone Star Reading List includee, 1994-95, all for *I Am Regina;* New York Public Library Reading and Sharing citation, 1995, for *Moon of Two Dark Horses;* New York Public Library Reading and Sharing citation, 2005, for *Gnat Stokes and the Foggy Bottom Swamp Queen.*

Writings

(With husband, David C. Keehn) *Hexcursions: Daytripping in and around Pennsylvania's Dutch Country,* Hastings House (New York, NY), 1982.
I Am Regina (young-adult novel), Philomel (New York, NY), 1991.
Moon of Two Dark Horses (young-adult novel), Philomel (New York, NY), 1995.
The First Horse I See, Philomel (New York, NY), 1999.
Anna Sunday, Philomel (New York, NY), 2002.
Gnat Stokes and the Foggy Bottom Swamp Queen, Philomel (New York, NY), 2005.

Sally M. Keehn

I Am Regina was translated into Danish, Flemish, German, and Italian.

Work in Progress

Magpie Gabbard: The Quest for the Buried Moon.

Sidelights

Sally M. Keehn has always loved to read, and this passion led her to become a librarian for young adults. She never planned to be a fiction writer, but when she began writing a travel book with her husband, she discovered two stories that she had to tell. The result of this urge was the historical novels *I Am Regina* and *Moon of Two Dark Horses,* and they in turn opened Keehn to the possibility of becoming a writer for young adults. Several awards and novels later, she has written historical and contemporary fiction, and even voyaged into fantasy with her novel *Gnat Stokes and the Foggy Bottom Swamp Queen.*

I Am Regina is based on the true story of a ten-year-old girl who is captured by Indians during the French and Indian Wars. Renamed Tskinnak, she lives within a poor tribe for nine years, gradually losing the horrific memories of her capture and gradually bonding with the elderly woman who cares for her. Susan F. Marcus noted the educational value of the story, writing in her *School Library Journal* review that "Readers will hardly realize how much they're learning in the pleasure of the story." A *Kirkus Reviews* contributor called *I Am Regina* "a profoundly moving evocation of a terrible experience" that is "told with simplicity and compassion and

admirable restraint." Many critics noted that while Keehn clearly shows why white settlers were afraid of Indian raids, she makes Regina's ultimate acceptance of her captors believable.

Explaining the inspiration for *I Am Regina,* Keehn once told *SATA:* "The Native Americans say that a story stalks a writer and, if it finds you worthy, comes to live in your heart. The story of Regina Leininger . . . stalked me for nine years. Her story did come to live in my heart. It still does. I came upon the incident that gave rise to the story while researching a travel book on Pennsylvania's Dutch Country. . . . What I read started me on a journey that led from a few words in a program to a 237-page novel. Why? I was curious. I wanted to know why she was kidnapped. By whom? What was going on at the time? The French and Indian Wars? What were they? I wanted to know what life was like back then: for the Pennsylvania Germans with whom Regina lived for ten years; for the Native Americans with whom she lived nine. . . . I sifted through many secondary sources to find out about these things, but what truly inspired me to keep on going were the primary sources that detailed Regina's life. This story happened and I was fortunate to discover first-hand accounts that told about it. I call these accounts my 'voices from the past.' During the three years I worked on the novel, these voices stalked me. They told me, don't give up. This story's worth telling."

In *Moon of Two Dark Horses* Keehn recounts the story of two boys who must deal with the growing conflict between their people. Daniel is an American fighting for independence from Great Britain and Coshmoo is a member of the Delaware tribe who is trying to remain neutral in the conflict. With so much going on, how can the boys remain friends? The story is "well researched and lyrically written," according to Marilyn Long Graham in *School Library Journal,* while *Booklist* contributor Julie Yates Walton observed that "Keehn has produced an acutely insightful, complex, and deeply moving tale."

Encouraged by the successes of her first two books, Keehn decided to write a contemporary novel loosely based on her own childhood. In *The First Horse I See* Willo's dying mother has promised her daughter that she could have a horse. When Willo falls in love with an abused racehorse, her father will not let her keep the horse unless she can tame it. During the girl's efforts to calm the half-wild animal, she begins to deal with her mother's death and her father's alcoholism, both difficult issues drawn from the author's own life. "Coming to grips with the real depths of the story proved to be a heart-wrenching time for me," Keehn admitted to Debbi Michiko Florence on the interviewer's Web site.

With *Anna Sunday* Keehn returns to historical fiction and bases her novel on a little-known story about the U.S. Civil War and the song "Battle Hymn of the Republic." In the novel, Anna and Jed's father, a Union

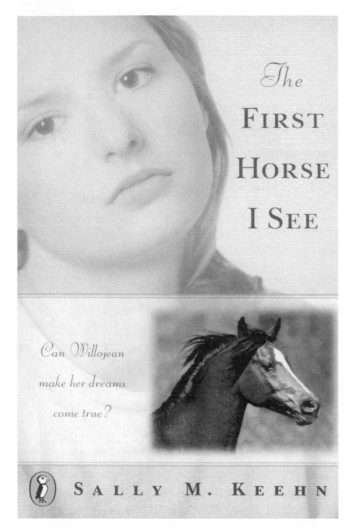

When Willo falls in love with a horse recently retired from the race-track, the work of retraining the high-spirited Tess may be more than she can handle alone in Keehn's 1999 novel.

Army soldier, is wounded and cared for by a Confederate woman. The children are determined to rescue their father, so Anna cuts her hair, disguises herself as a boy, and the pair and their horse leave their home in Pennsylvania and travel south into war-torn Virginia. "Facts about the war are interwoven and the often-fraught-with-peril journey concludes in a satisfying manner," commented a critic for *Kirkus Reviews.* Carolyn Phelan, reviewing *Anna Sunday* for *Booklist,* praised the book's "original, believable characters, whose idiosyncrasies add texture and occasional humor to the story."

In the fantastical novel *Gnat Stokes and the Foggy Bottom Swamp Queen* readers meet orphan Gnat Stokes, a twelve-year-old girl with a sense of adventure. Gnat decides to rescue friend Goodlow Pryce, who has fallen into the clutches of the Foggy Bottom Swamp Queen. Goodlow, trying to communicate with his true love Penelope, manages to send his beloved an enchanted locket. When Gnat intercepts the locket, the gift's magic causes the girl to fall in love with Goodlow as well. Armed now with magically inspired determination, Gnat undertakes the quest, only to discover more about her

parentage, and about love, than she had expected. "Keehn's tale is by turns creepy, laugh-aloud funny, touching, and utterly satisfying," observed Chris Sherman for *Booklist,* while a *Kirkus Reviews* contributor described *Gnat Stokes and the Foggy Bottom Swamp Queen* as a "warm, suspenseful, over-the-top adventure that bubbles up with swamp wisdom."

As Keehn explained to online interviewer Florence, before writing Gnat's story, "I'd always written books with a strong toe-hold on reality. . . . And then I came upon an old Scottish Ballad—'Tam Lin'—which grabbed my heart." At the suggestion of her editor, the author traveled through Appalachia, set the Scottish tale there, and Gnat Stokes was born.

On her home page, Keehn admitted: "Writing novels is a challenge for me, but I love the journey writing takes me on. I make such interesting discoveries about myself and about the world. I encourage everyone to read and write. There's a beautiful and intriguing world to be discovered—both inside and outside us."

In Keehn's coming-of-age novel, pre-teen Anna disguises herself as a boy and makes the dangerous trip across Confederate lines during the U.S. Civil War, determined to find her missing father. (Cover illustration by Howard Fine.)

Based on the Scottish ballad "Tam Lin," this 2005 novel finds a young Appalachian girl willing to brave the evil Swamp Queen while searching for a friend she is convinced is being held captive. (Cover illustration by Greg Swearingen.)

Biographical and Critical Sources

PERIODICALS

Booklist, July, 1991, review of *I Am Regina,* p. 2040; September 1, 1999, Linda Perkins, review of *The First Horse I See,* p. 133; June 1, 2002, Carolyn Phelan, review of *Anna Sunday,* p. 1723; March 1, 2005, Chris Sherman, review of *Gnat Stokes and the Foggy Bottom Swamp Queen,* p. 1197.

Book Report, March-April, 1996, Patti Sylvester Spencer, review of *Moon of Two Dark Horses,* p. 35.

Bulletin of the Center for Children's Books, April, 1991, review of *I Am Regina,* p. 198; October, 1995, review of *Moon of Two Dark Horses,* p. 59; September, 1999, review of *The First Horse I See,* p. 19; September, 2002, review of *Anna Sunday,* p. 23; March 1, 2005, review of *Gnat Stokes and the Foggy Bottom Swamp Queen,* p. 296.

Childhood Education, fall, 2002, Connie M. Fritch, review of *Anna Sunday,* p. 51.

Children's Book Review Service, June, 1991, review of *I Am Regina,* p. 131.

Emergency Librarian, March, 1996, review of *Moon of Two Dark Horses,* p. 43.

Journal of Reading, November, 1993, review of *I Am Regina,* p. 224.

Kirkus Reviews, June 1, 1991, review of *I Am Regina,* p. 730; September 1, 1995, review of *Moon of Two Dark Horses,* p. 1282; May 1, 2002, review of *Anna Sunday,* p. 658; March 1, 2005, review of *Gnat Stokes and the Foggy Bottom Swamp Queen,* p. 289.

Kliatt, November, 1997, review of *Moon of Two Dark Horses,* p. 8.

Library Talk, November, 1991, review of *I Am Regina,* p. 26.

Publishers Weekly, May 10, 1991, review of *I Am Regina,* p. 285; October 2, 1995, review of *Moon of Two Dark Horses,* p. 74; July 5, 1999, review of *The First Horse I See,* p. 71; December 17, 2001, review of *I Am Regina,* p. 94; June 17, 2002, review of *Anna Sunday,* p. 65.

School Library Journal, June, 1991, Susan F. Marcus, review of *I Am Regina,* p. 108; November, 1995, Marilyn Long Graham, review of *Moon of Two Dark Horses,* p. 120; July, 1999, review of *The First Horse I See,* p. 96; June, 2002, William McLoughlin, review of *Anna Sunday,* p. 140; April, 2005, Cindy Darling Codell, review of *Gnat Stokes and the Foggy Bottom Swamp Queen,* p. 135.

Social Education, April, 1992, review of *I Am Regina,* p. 263.

Voice of Youth Advocates, August, 1991, review of *I Am Regina,* p. 172; December, 1995, review of *Moon of Two Dark Horses,* p. 303; August, 2002, review of *Anna Sunday,* p. 193.

ONLINE

Debbi Michiko Florence Web site, http://debbimichiko florence.com/ (June, 2005), interview with Keehn.

Sally Keehn's Home Page, http://www.sallykeehn.com (November 7, 2005).

*   *   *

KHAN, Rukhsana 1962-

Personal

First name is pronounced "ruk-SA-na"; born March 13, 1962, in Lahore, Pakistan; immigrated to Canada, 1965; daughter of Muhammad Anwar (a tool-and-die maker) and Iftikhar Shahzadi (a homemaker) Khan; married Irfan Haseeb Alli (a production manager), March 31, 1979; children: three daughters, one son. *Education:* Seneca College of Applied Arts and Technology, earned degree as a biological-chemical technician; currently attends University of Toronto. *Religion:* Islam.

Addresses

Home—Toronto, Ontario, Canada. *Agent*—Charlotte Sheedy, Sterling Lord Literistic, 65 Bleecker St., New York, NY 10012. *E-mail*—rukhsana@rukhsanakhan. com.

Rukhsana Khan

Career

Writer and storyteller.

Member

Society of Children's Book Writers and Illustrators, Writer's Union of Canada, Canadian Society of Children's Authors, Illustrators, and Performers, Storytellers of Canada, Storytelling School of Toronto.

Awards, Honors

Honorary Janusz Korczak International Literature Award, Polish Section of International Board on Books for Young People, 1998, for *The Roses in My Carpets;* Writers' Reserve grant, Ontario Arts Council, 1998; Artists in Education grant, 1998-99; Ruth Schwartz Award shortlist, Canadian Booksellers Association/ Ontario Arts Council, and Red Maple Award shortlist, Ontario Library Association, both 2000, and Manitoba Young Reader's Choice Honour Award, Manitoba Library Association, 2001, all for *Dahling If You Luv Me Would You Please, Please Smile;* Hackmatack Award shortlist, and Canadian Children's Book Centre Choice designation, both 2001, both for *Muslim Child;* Toastmaster District 60 Communication and Leadership Award, 2004.

Writings

Bedtime Ba-a-a-lk (picture book), illustrated by Kristi Frost, Stoddart Kids (Toronto, Ontario, Canada), 1998.

The Roses in My Carpets (picture book), illustrated by Ronald Himler, Holiday House (New York, NY), 1998.

Dahling If You Luv Me, Would You Please, Please Smile (novel), Stoddart Kids (Toronto, Ontario, Canada), 1999.

Muslim Child: A Collection of Short Stories and Poems, illustrations by Patty Gallinger, Napoleon (Toronto, Ontario, Canada), 1999, published as *Muslim Child: Understanding Islam through Stories and Poems,* Albert Whitman (Morton Grove, IL), 2002.

King of the Skies, illustrations by Laura Fernandez and Rick Jacobson, North Winds Press (Markham, Ontario, Canada), 2001.

Ruler of the Courtyard, illustrated by R. Gregory Christie, Viking (New York, NY), 2003.

Silly Chicken, illustrated by Yunmee Kyong, Viking (New York, NY), 2005.

Contributor of short stories to magazines, including *Message International* and *Kahani;* contributor of songs to *Adam's World* children's videos, produced by Sound Vision.

Work in Progress

The Big Red Lollipop, for Viking Children's.

Sidelights

Pakistan-born Canadian writer and storyteller Rukhsana Khan draws on her experiences living within two very different cultures in her picture books for children. In *Bedtime Ba-a-a-lk, King of the Skies, Ruler of the Courtyard,* and *Silly Chicken* she introduces young children that cope with the universal problems of growing up while also living within a Muslim culture that is very different from that experienced by Khan's Canadian and American readers. While her picture books promote tolerance of such differences through gentle stories, her anthology *Muslim Child: Understanding Islam through Stories and Poems* takes a more direct route, collecting eight stories featuring young Muslims living in North America as well as Nigeria, and Pakistan. A *Kirkus Reviews* contributor praised the "earnest tone" Khan brings to her stories and poems, adding that readers' understanding of Islam will increase through the author's inclusion of passages from the Qu'ran, quotations by Muhammad, and sidebars that contains information about many aspects of the Muslim faith. While noting that Khan's motive is to educate Western readers, *School Library Journal* contributor Coop Renner wrote of *Muslim Child* that the book's "most avid audience . . . may be American Muslim children excited finally to find stories with characters to whom they can relate."

In her first picture book, *Bedtime Ba-a-a-lk,* Khan provides a twist on the usual scenario of a reluctant child counting sheep in order to be lulled to sleep. Here, a little girl conjures up a flock of imaginary sheep to aid in her efforts to go to sleep, but meets resistance from the wooly creatures on every front. First they require her to imagine more light on the far side of the fence so they can see what they are jumping into, then they get bored by the activity they have performed so many times before and demand entertainment instead. When the girl conjures up an imaginary carnival, however, the sheep become so entranced that they forget to jump at all. *Quill & Quire* reviewer Patty Lawlor praised Khan's soothing text, writing that *Bedtime Ba-a-a-lk* "opens almost poetically with lyrical language, phrasing and pacing, immediately creating an effective sleepytime mood." A reviewer for *Kirkus Reviews* praised the

book's illustrations and text for their "light touch": "A little bit of dream manipulation goes a long way in this lullaby tale," the reviewer stated.

Striking a decidedly different tone, *The Roses in My Carpets* recounts a day in the life of a young boy living in an Afghan refugee camp along with his mother and younger sister. Khan follows the boy as he rises early in the morning after a recurrent nightmare, prays at the mosque, eats, goes to school, prays again, then practices the craft of weaving. Learning to weave is the highlight of the boy's day; his work is the only beauti-

After bravely confronting a snake in the barn, young Saba gains the courage to stop running from her family's flock of pecking chickens in **Ruler of the Courtyard.** *(Illustration by R. Gregory Christie.)*

In Khan's realistic and timely picture book, a young Afghani displaced by war finds escape from his life in a dismal refugee camp through his job weaving beautiful, colorful carpets. (Illustration by Ronald Himler.)

ful thing he sees in the grim world of the camp and becoming proficient at a skill offers him hope that he will one day be able to support his family on his earnings from work. While at his weaving lesson, the boy learns his sister has been hit by a truck, though she will recover. That night he has a nightmare similar to the earlier ones, but this time he and his mother and sister take refuge on a bed of roses the size of the carpet he is learning to weave.

In *The Roses in My Carpets* "Khan hints at the boy's powerful emotions in spare prose, and handles her difficult subject matter sensitively," commented a reviewer in *Publishers Weekly. Booklist* critic Linda Perkins noted that while young children will likely need supplemental information on the Islamic religion and the war in Afghanistan, Khan's story nonetheless presents "a rare and welcome glimpse into a culture children usually don't see."

The disabled young boy who serves as the protagonist in Khan's *King of the Skies* is a native of Pakistan, and he shares his excitement at the approaching kite festival celebrated in the city of Lahore each spring. Showing the results of much practice, skill, and concentration, he navigates his own kite, the yellow Guddi Chore, among others in the festival as his siblings help clear fallen kites from the path of the boy's wheelchair. In *Canadian Review of Materials* a reviewer praised the book as "beautiful and satisfying," adding that Khan's "eloquence is matched by . . . luminous oil paintings" by illustrators Rick Jacobson and Laura Fernandez. *King of*

the Skies "is an excellent example of a story which carries the reader to another place," maintained *Resource Links* writer Kathryn McNaughton, the critic concluding that Khan's "fascinating" story, in addition to its multicultural elements, "may also spark conversations about children with diverse abilities."

Khan's first foray into teen fiction, *Dahling if You Luv Me, Would You Please, Please Smile* is a contemporary novel about Zainab, a young Muslim teen who is trying to fit in. The novel deals with mature themes of conformity, bullying, racism, and suicide. However, Khan feels that ultimately the novel is a look at the way people are manipulated: from the obvious sexual manipulation that Zainab's best friend Jenny faces, to the more subtle religious manipulation being perpetrated on Zainab. Reviewing the novel in the *Toronto Star,* Deirdre Baker wrote that the novel contains "wonderful warmth, humour and complexity."

Set in Pakistan, both *Ruler of the Courtyard* and *Silly Chicken* focus on chickens, although these birds of a feather do not share the same temperament. In *Ruler of the Courtyard* a young Pakistan girl named Saba lives in fear of a flock of sharp-beaked chickens that run unchecked through the courtyard of her rural home. The hold the dumb birds have over her is broken, however, when the girl gains self-confidence by bravely confronting a far more deadly threat. Sibling rivalry is the focus of the poignant *Silly Chicken,* in which a girl named Rani feels competition from a pet chicken named Bibi when the bird seems to take most of Rani's mother's attention. When Bibi meets an unfortunate end, however, the girl realizes her mistake and determines to be a loving guardian of the creature that will hatch from the egg Bibi leaves behind. Praising *Ruler of the Courtyard* as "perfectly paced," a *Kirkus Reviews* contributor added that the tale's exciting storyline and "positive message" combine to make Khan's book "a winner for reading aloud." In *Publishers Weekly* a critic cited the book's "message about self-reliance and courage," while in *Horn Book* Susan P. Bloom commented favorably about the tale's "wonderful energy and use of language." Noting the happy ending that concludes *Silly Chicken,* a *Kirkus Reviews* writer wrote that Khan's "language is conversational and spare and the [story's] pacing just right," while in *Booklist* reviewer Carolyn Phelan explained that the story "clearly depicts a child's jealousy" while sidestepping "the usual schmaltz."

"Growing up Muslim in North America was very difficult," Khan once recalled to *SATA,* explaining that "the release of each mega-blockbuster depicting Muslims as merciless bumbling terrorists or ignorant taxi drivers" as well as the *fatwa*—or death sentence—called by Muslim leaders against writer Salman Rushdie in 1989 made Muslims "look . . . like a bunch of barbaric idiots." Moving with her family to eastern Canada in the mid-1960s, Khan also carried childhood memories of the racial prejudice that was leveled at her family. "My father worked at a tool and die company, and his co-

Set in Pakistan, Silly Chicken *finds a young girl jealous over the attention her mother lavishes on Bibi, the family's pet chicken, until Bibi's sudden disappearance finds mother and daughter equally worried over the pet's safety. (Illustration by Yunmee Kyong.)*

workers used to call him 'black bastard' right to his face," she explained to *Canadian Review of Materials* interviewer Dave Jenkinson. "They hardly ever called him by his name, and he put up with it because he had four kids to feed. My father had chosen to live in Canada because he wanted to get away from those cultural influences which said girls are expendable. He also wanted to raise us as Muslims, and he wanted a good neighborhood."

Because Khan's family was one of only two Indian families living in their Ontario town, their differences were apparent to everyone. "Because we stuck out so much, we were persecuted from day one," the author continued to Jenkinson. "If it hadn't been for that negative treatment, I don't think I would have become a writer because my growing up was so horrible that I went to books to escape. Having no friends, I spent my

recesses among the trees. I used to think a lot, and that's when I really came to terms with what my beliefs are, who I am, and what my place is in the universe."

Even before Salman Rushdie's *The Satanic Verses* was published, Khan was striving to become an author. She wrote stories, began attending writing conferences and seminars, and did extensive reading. With the publication and ensuing uproar over Rushdie's book, she was all the more determined to provide a counter to Western misunderstandings of Islam. Khan's primary focus is to tell good stories, often set in Muslim culture, with the hope that these stories will help 'humanize' Muslims to unfamiliar readers.

At one particular conference held in Boston, Khan recalled, one of the speakers was a Western woman who had penned a novel about a Muslim child. "This was a case where this white lady had gotten the culture all wrong," Khan explained to *SATA*. "It was clear, almost from the beginning of the book, that a 'white feminist' had imposed her sensibilities on a girl who wouldn't have been exposed to them within the scope of the novel. There was some merit in the book, but unfortunately the book did perpetuate a lot of the prevalent Muslim stereotypes that so upset me." According to Khan, the author also wrote a sequel, which made matters even worse."

"At that moment," Khan continued, "what I really was up against fully hit me. Here I was, a Pakistani immigrant with quaint old-fashioned principles, trying to show this big amorphous blob of Western society that they'd pegged us 'Moslems' all wrong. How could I even aspire to such a lofty goal? Who did I think I was?

"What I eventually realized is that people, including Salman Rushdie, will write all kinds of garbage about Islam. In order to fight them, I'll have to be better.

"I'm working on it."

Biographical and Critical Sources

PERIODICALS

Booklist, November 15, 1998, Linda Perkins, review of *The Roses in My Carpets,* p. 596; February 15, 2002, John Green, review of *Muslim Child,* p. 1011; January 1, 2005, Carolyn Phelan, review of *Silly Chicken,* p. 879.

Horn Book, March-April, 2003, Susan P. Bloom, review of *Ruler of the Courtyard,* p. 204; March-April, 2005, Kitty Flynn, review of *Silly Chicken,* p. 190.

Kirkus Reviews, June 15, 1998, review of *Bedtime Ba-a-a-lk,* p. 896; February 1, 2002, review of *Muslim Child,* p. 182; December 15, 2002, review of *Ruler of the Courtyard,* p. 1851; February 15, 2005, review of *Silly Chicken,* p. 230.

Publishers Weekly, October 5, 1998, review of *The Roses in My Carpets,* p. 90; February 11, 2002, review of *Muslim Child,* p. 189; January 6, 2003, review of *Ruler of the Courtyard,* p. 59; April 4, 2005, review of *Silly Chicken,* p. 59.

Quill & Quire, March, 1998, Patty Lawlor, review of *Bedtime Ba-a-a-lk,* pp. 71-72.

Resource Links, December, 2001, Kathryn McNaughton, review of *King of the Skies,* p. 6.

School Library Journal, November, 1998, pp. 87-88; February, 2002, Coop Renner, review of *Muslim Child,* p. 122; February, 2003, Dona Ratterree, review of *Ruler of the Courtyard,* p. 114; January, 2005, Ann W. Moore, review of *Muslim Child,* p. 55; April, 2005, Joy Fleishhacker, review of *Silly Chicken,* p. 105.

Toronto Star, April 18, 1999, Deirdre Baker, review of *Dahling if You Luv, Me Would You Please, Please Smile,* p. D31.

ONLINE

Canadian Review of Materials Online, http://www.umanitoba.ca/outreach/cm/ (September 24, 1999), David Jenkinson, interview with Khan; (February 4, 2000) David Jenkinson, review of *Muslim Child;* (November 2, 2001) review of *King of the Skies;* (April 29, 2005) Valerie Nielsen, review of *Silly Chicken.*

Canadian Society of Children's Authors, Illustrators, and Performers Web site, http://www.canscaip.org/ (May 28, 2005), "Rukhsana Khan."

Rukhsana Khan Home Page, http://www.rukhsanakhan.com (June 10, 2005).*

*   *   *

KOONTZ, Dean R. 1945-
(David Axton, Brian Coffey, Deanna Dwyer, K.R. Dwyer, John Hill, Leigh Nichols, Anthony North, Richard Paige, Owen West)

Personal

Born July 9, 1945, in Everett, PA; son of Ray and Florence Koontz; married Gerda Ann Cerra, October 15, 1966.

Addresses

Home—Southern CA. *Agent*—Robert Gottlieb, Trident Media Group, 488 Madison Ave., 17th Fl., New York, NY 10022.

Career

Teacher-counselor with Appalachian Poverty Program, 1966-67; high school English teacher, 1967-69; writer, 1969—.

Awards, Honors

Atlantic Monthly college creative writing award, 1966, for story "The Kittens"; Hugo Award nomination, World Science Fiction Convention, 1971, for novella *Beastchild;* Litt.D., Shippensburg State College, 1989.

Writings

FOR CHILDREN

Oddkins: A Fable for All Ages, illustrated by Phil Parks, Warner (New York, NY), 1988.

Santa's Twin, illustrated by Phil Parks, HarperPrism (New York, NY), 1996.

The Paper Doorway: Funny Verse and Nothing Worse, illustrated by Phil Parks, HarperCollins (New York, NY), 2001.

Dean R. Koontz

Every Day's a Holiday, illustrated by Phil Parks, Harper-Collins (New York, NY), 2003.

Robot Santa: The Further Adventures of Santa's Twin, HarperCollins (New York, NY), 2004.

NOVELS

Star Quest, Ace Books (New York, NY), 1968.

The Fall of the Dream Machine, Ace Books (New York, NY), 1969.

Fear That Man, Ace Books (New York, NY), 1969.

Anti-Man, Paperback Library (New York, NY), 1970.

Beastchild, Lancer Books (New York, NY), 1970.

Dark of the Woods, Ace Books (New York, NY), 1970.

The Dark Symphony, Lancer Books (New York, NY), 1970.

Hell's Gate, Lancer Books (New York, NY), 1970.

The Crimson Witch, Curtis Books (New York, NY), 1971.

A Darkness in My Soul, DAW Books (New York, NY), 1972.

The Flesh in the Furnace, Bantam (New York, NY), 1972.

Starblood, Lancer Books (New York, NY), 1972.

Time Thieves, Ace Books (New York, NY), 1972.

Warlock, Lancer Books (New York, NY), 1972.

A Werewolf among Us, Ballantine (New York, NY), 1973.

Hanging On, M. Evans (New York, NY), 1973.

The Haunted Earth, Lancer Books (New York, NY), 1973.

Demon Seed, Bantam (New York, NY), 1973.

(Under pseudonym Anthony North) *Strike Deep,* Dial (New York, NY), 1974.

After the Last Race, Atheneum (New York, NY), 1974.

Nightmare Journey, Putnam (New York, NY), 1975.

(Under pseudonym John Hill) *The Long Sleep,* Popular Library (New York, NY), 1975.

Night Chills, Atheneum (New York, NY), 1976.

(Under pseudonym David Axton) *Prison of Ice,* Lippincott (Philadelphia), 1976, revised edition under name Dean R. Koontz published as *Icebound* (also see below), Ballantine (New York, NY), 1995.

The Vision (also see below), Putnam (New York, NY), 1977.

Whispers (also see below), Putnam (New York, NY), 1980.

Phantoms (also see below), Putnam (New York, NY), 1983.

Darkfall (also see below), Berkley (New York, NY), 1984, published as *Darkness Comes,* W. H. Allen (London, England), 1984.

Twilight Eyes, Land of Enchantment (Westland, MI), 1985.

(Under pseudonym Richard Paige) *The Door to December,* New American Library (New York, NY), 1985.

Strangers (also see below), Putnam (New York, NY), 1986.

Watchers (also see below), Putnam (New York, NY), 1987, reprinted, Berkley Books (New York, NY), 2003.

Lightning (also see below), Putnam (New York, NY), 1988, reprinted, Berkley Books (New York, NY), 2003.

Midnight, Putnam (New York, NY), 1989, reprinted, Berkley Books (New York, NY), 2004.

The Bad Place (also see below), Putnam (New York, NY), 1990, with a new afterword, 2004.

Cold Fire (also see below), Putnam (New York, NY), 1991, with a new afterword, 2004.

Three Complete Novels: Dean R. Koontz: The Servants of Twilight; Darkfall; Phantoms, Wings Books (New York, NY), 1991.

Hideaway (also see below), Putnam (New York, NY), 1992.

Dragon Tears (also see below), Berkley (New York, NY), 1992, published in a limited edition, Putnam (New York, NY), 1993.

Dean R. Koontz: A New Collection (contains *Watchers, Whispers,* and *Shattered* [originally published under pseudonym K.R. Dwyer; also see below]), Wings Books (New York, NY), 1992.

Mr. Murder (also see below), Putnam (New York, NY), 1993.

Winter Moon, Ballantine (New York, NY), 1993.

Three Complete Novels: Lightning; The Face of Fear; The Vision (*The Face of Fear* originally published under pseudonym Brian Coffey), Putnam (New York, NY), 1993.

Three Complete Novels: Dean Koontz: Strangers; The Voice of the Night; The Mask (*The Voice of the Night* originally published under pseudonym Brian Coffey; *The Mask* originally published under pseudonym Owen West), Putnam (New York, NY), 1994.

Dark Rivers of the Heart (also see below), Knopf (New York, NY), 1994.

Strange Highways (also see below), Warner Books (New York, NY), 1995.

Intensity (also see below), Knopf (New York, NY), 1995.

TickTock, Ballantine (New York, NY), 1996.

Three Complete Novels (contains *The House of Thunder, Shadowfires,* and *Midnight*), Putnam (New York, NY), 1996.

Sole Survivor, Ballantine (New York, NY), 1997.

Fear Nothing, Bantam (New York, NY), 1998.

Seize the Night (sequel to *Fear Nothing),* Bantam Double-
day Dell (New York, NY), 1999.
False Memory, Bantam (New York, NY), 2000.
From the Corner of His Eye, Bantam (New York, NY),
2000.
The Book of Counted Sorrows (e-book), bn.com, 2001.
One Door away from Heaven, Bantam (New York, NY),
2002.
By the Light of the Moon, Bantam (New York, NY), 2003.
The Face, Bantam (New York, NY), 2003.
Odd Thomas, Bantam (New York, NY), 2004.
The Taking, Bantam (New York, NY), 2004.
Life Expectancy, Bantam (New York, NY), 2004.
Velocity, Bantam (New York, NY), 2005.
(With Kevin J. Anderson) *Dean Koontz's Frankenstein:
Prodigal Son,* Bantam (New York, NY), 2005.

UNDER PSEUDONYM BRIAN COFFEY

Blood Risk, Bobbs-Merrill (Indianapolis, IN), 1973.
Surrounded, Bobbs-Merrill (Indianapolis, IN), 1974.
The Wall of Masks, Bobbs-Merrill Indianapolis, IN), 1975.
The Face of Fear, Bobbs-Merrill (Indianapolis, IN), 1977.
The Voice of the Night, Doubleday (New York, NY), 1981.

Also author of script for *CHiPS* television series, 1978.

UNDER PSEUDONYM DEANNA DWYER

The Demon Child, Lancer Books (New York, NY), 1971.
Legacy of Terror, Lancer Books (New York, NY), 1971.
Children of the Storm, Lancer Books (New York, NY),
1972.
The Dark of Summer, Lancer Books (New York, NY),
1972.
Dance with the Devil, Lancer Books (New York, NY),
1973.

UNDER PSEUDONYM K.R. DWYER

Chase (also see below), Random House (New York, NY),
1972.
Shattered (also see below), Random House (New York,
NY), 1973.
Dragonfly, Random House (New York, NY), 1975.

UNDER PSEUDONYM LEIGH NICHOLS

The Key to Midnight, Pocket Books (New York, NY),
1979.
The Eyes of Darkness, Pocket Books (New York, NY),
1981.
The House of Thunder, Pocket Books (New York, NY),
1982.
Twilight, Pocket Books, 1984, revised edition published
under name Dean R. Koontz as *The Servants of Twilight,* Berkley (New York, NY), 1990.
Shadowfires, Avon (New York, NY), 1987.

UNDER PSEUDONYM OWEN WEST

(With wife, Gerda Koontz) *The Pig Society* (nonfiction),
Aware Press (Granada Hills, CA), 1970.
(With Gerda Koontz) *The Underground Lifestyles Hand-
book,* Aware Press (Granada Hills, CA), 1970.
Soft Come the Dragons (story collection), Ace Books (New
York, NY), 1970.
Writing Popular Fiction, Writer's Digest (Cincinnati, OH),
1973.
The Funhouse (novelization of screenplay), Jove (New
York, NY), 1980.
The Mask, Jove (New York, NY), 1981.
How to Write Best-selling Fiction, Writer's Digest (Cin-
cinnati, OH), 1981.

OTHER

(Author of text) David Robinson, *Beautiful Death: Art of
the Cemetery,* Penguin Studio (New York, NY), 1996.
("Editor") *Life Is Good!: Lessons in Joyful Living, by
Trixie Koontz, Dog,* Yorkville Press (New York, NY),
2004.

Contributor to books, including *Infinity 3,* edited by
Robert Haskins, Lancer Books, 1972; *Again, Danger-
ous Visions,* edited by Harlan Ellison, Doubleday, 1972;
Final Stage, edited by Edward L. Ferman and Barry N.
Malzberg, Charterhouse, 1974; *Night Visions IV,* Dark
Harvest, 1987; *Stalkers: All New Tales of Terror and
Suspense,* edited by Ed Gorman and Martin H. Green-
berg, illustrated by Paul Sonju, Dark Harvest, 1989; and
Night Visions VI: The Bone Yard, Berkley, 1991.

Adaptations

Demon Seed was filmed by Metro-Goldwyn-Mayer/
Warner Bros., 1977; *Shattered* was filmed by Warner
Bros., 1977; *Watchers* was filmed by Universal, 1988;
Hideaway was filmed by Tri-Star, starring Jeff Gold-
blum, 1994; *Mr. Murder* was filmed by Patchett Kauf-
man Entertainment/Elephant Walk Entertainment, 1999.
Many of Koontz's works were recorded unabridged on
audiocassette, including *Cold Fire, Hideaway,* and *The
Bad Place,* Reader's Chair (Hollister, CA), 1991; *Mr.
Murder* and *Dragon Tears,* Simon and Schuster Audio;
Dark Rivers of the Heart, Icebound, and *Intensity,* Ran-
dom House Audio; and *Strange Highways* and *Chase,*
Warner Audio.

Work in Progress

More novels in the "Frankenstein" series.

Sidelights

Popular among both adult and teen readers, Dean R.
Koontz is an acknowledged master of a hybrid class of
books that combine suspense, horror, romance, and science fiction. His more than seventy books have sold in
the millions and have been adapted for such successful

movies as *Demon Seed, Watchers,* and *Shattered.* Though often dubbed a horror novelist, Koontz himself rejects such labels and views his own work as basically optimistic, showing hard-fought battles between good and evil. A favorite Koontz theme is the conflict between emotion and reason, and the emotional level of his books—a step beyond the usual plot-heavy nature of much of the genre—has gained him the respect of many critics. According to Charles de Lint, writing in the *Magazine of Fantasy and Science Fiction,* Koontz consistently succeeds at "telling a harrowing, highly suspenseful story featuring quick-witted protagonists who face the world with a positive attitude and exchange rapid-fire dialogue." "I have attempted, book by book, to speak to the reader's intellect and emotions as well as to his desire for a 'good read'," the author himself once stated. "I believe the best fiction does three things well: tells an involving story, makes the reader think, and makes the reader feel."

An only child, Koontz grew up in Pennsylvania. "I began writing when I was a child," he once explained, noting that "reading and writing provided much needed escape from the poverty in which we lived and from my father's frequent fits of alcohol-induced violence." While still in college, he started publishing his short stories and won an *Atlantic Monthly* fiction contest. Marrying his fiancée, Gerda, and graduating from Shippensburg State College in 1966, Koontz taught for a while in the Appalachian Poverty Program and in Pennsylvania schools, while also continuing to write and sell stories. In 1968 his first novel, *Star Quest,* was published, and Koontz quickly followed it with a second science-fiction novel.

In the early 1970s, determined to make a try at full-time writing, Koontz was aided by his wife, who agreed to support the family for five years while her husband followed his dream. He adopted an assortment of pseudonyms and tackled various genres, including science fiction, mystery, and thrillers. "The curse lies in the fact that much of the early work is of lower quality that what came after," Koontz remarked, "both because I was so young and unself-critical and because the low earnings from each book forced me to write a lot of them in order to keep financially afloat." Koontz marks *Chase,* a suspense novel written under the pseudonym K.R. Dwyer about the after-effects of Vietnam on a veteran, as "the beginning of my *real* career as a writer." He moved from science fiction to suspense with that book, and never looked back.

Writing in several genres aided Koontz in developing his own unique form of dark suspense, and his addition of humor, romance, and occult elements have created a distinctive body of work. Considered his breakthrough novel, 1980's *Whispers* is a dark and violent story of childhood cruelty, rape, and murder. Hilary Thomas is a survivor of abusive alcoholic parents who has become a successful screenwriter; she is attacked by millionaire Bruno Frye, whom she subsequently stabs to death.

When Bruno returns from the grave to stalk her, it is left to Hilary's police officer boyfriend to help her unravel the twisted tale of Bruno's childhood and reveal the powers at work in this "slick tale of horror," as Rex E. Klett described the book in *Library Journal.* A *Publishers Weekly* reviewer noted that the "psychological portrait of the sick, sick Bruno makes skin crawl."

Koontz considers the horror novels *Phantoms* and *Darkfall* "sidesteps in my career." 1986's *Strangers* adheres to what would become characteristic Koontz form: it tells the story of a group of people connected only by a weekend each spent at a motel in Nevada two years prior—a weekend none of them remember. Soon the characters begin to experience nightmares, intense fears, and even supernormal powers that drive each toward uncovering the mystery and conspiracy that binds them. Deborah Kirk, writing in the *New York Times Book Review,* found some characters unconvincing but concluded that *Strangers* is "an engaging, often chilling, book," while *Library Journal* critic Eric W. Johnson dubbed the novel an "almost unbearably suspenseful page-turner." A *Booklist* reviewer deemed Koontz a "true master," and found *Strangers* to be "a rich brew of gothic horror and science fiction, filled with delectable turns of the imagination."

The misuse of science is at the heart of *Watchers,* which was chosen one of the American Library Association's best books for young adults in 1987. Recombinant DNA experiments go wrong at a government lab, and suddenly two mutants—one with human intelligence to be used for spying and the other a killer—are on the loose in Southern California. The intelligent mutant, a golden retriever, is pursued by the killer mutant, a blend of ape and dog that is named Outsider. Soon two humans, Travis and Nora, become involved helping the dog, nicknamed Einstein, as well as themselves, escape the wrath of Outsider. While Audrey B. Eaglen described *Watchers* in a review for *School Library Journal* as "about as horrifying as warm milk toast," others disagreed; *New York Times Book Review* contributor Katherine Weber had special praise for Einstein, whom she described as "the most richly drawn character in the book."

Koontz's works reflect a vivid imagination when it comes to plot and setting, and also an affinity for creating likeable protagonists. In *Intensity* he introduces Chyna Shepherd, a psychology student who must combat Edgler Vess, a killer obsessed with intensity of sensation, be it pleasure or pain. A *Publishers Weekly* reviewer found *Intensity* "masterful, if ultimately predictable," and lauded Koontz's racing narrative, calling it a contender for the most "viscerally exciting thriller of the year." A companion novel, *Velocity* finds novelist/bartender Billy Wiles facing a brutal killer in a game where an innocent victim loses their life due to Billy's inaction and inability to play by the rules. Soon, the game extends beyond Billy's control and he may become its next victim in a novel that a *Kirkus Reviews* critic cited for its "brilliant plotting" and suspense. In *Publishers Weekly* a critic wrote that the "graphic, fast-paced action, well-developed characters and relentless, nail-biting scenes" in *Velocity* "show Koontz at the top of his game."

Taking place in the coastal town of Moonlight Bay, California, *Fear Nothing* and *Seize the Night* also share the same protagonist: poet-surfer Christopher Snow, a man possessing a genetic mutation that makes him sensitive to light. In *Fear Nothing* the body of Snow's recently deceased father has vanished and been replaced by that of a murdered hitchhiker. Along with his Labrador-mix dog Orson, surfer-friend Bobby, and local disc jockey Sasha, Snow attempts to recover his father's corpse. Seven children abducted from their homes serves as the central mystery in *Seize the Night,* and Snow follows the trail of the kidnappers, joined by Orson, Bobby, Sasha, a mind-reading cat, and a biker. The chase leads to a supposedly abandoned military base, Fort Wyvern, where genetic experiments are actually being conducted. Among the strange, mutated creatures Snow and his companions uncover are wormlike crea-

tures that can devour almost anything; in addition, Snow becomes trapped by a malfunctioning "temporal locator" and goes on time-travel journeys into both the future and the past.

Commenting on *Fear Nothing* in the *New York Times Book Review,* Maggie Garb characterized the novel as an "overwrought narrative," maintaining that Koontz's detective trio "seem more like the stuff of adolescent fantasy than fully believable sleuths." Garb also criticized Koontz's "surfer lingo and literary pretension," as detrimental to the suspense of the book. Regarding *Seize the Night,* an *Entertainment Weekly* contributor dubbed the book "either an utterly zany thriller or the first really cool young-adult novel of 1999," and "Koontz without tears, sadism, or even much bloodshed." An *Entertainment Weekly* reviewer noted that *Seize the Night* is "that holy-cow kind of novel—park your brains, don't ask why, tighten your seat belt." In the *New York Times Book Review,* David Walton characterized the novel as "a bros-and-brew backslapper in which characters refer to Coleridge and T.S. Eliot as often as to genetic mutation."

Described by a *Publishers Weekly* critic as "less thematically ambitious but more viscerally exciting" than the "Snow" novels, *False Memory* focuses on a woman who suffers from the mental disorder autophobia, or fear of self. Marty Rhodes, successful at work and in her marriage, takes her agoraphobic friend Susan to therapy sessions with psychiatrist Mark Ahriman twice each week. Suddenly, Marty begins to develop a fear that she will inflict harm upon herself or her loved ones. Meanwhile, Marty's husband, Dusty, a painting contractor, courageously saves his half-brother Skeet from taking a suicidal leap off a rooftop. After Dusty places Skeet in rehab, he returns home to find that Marty has removed all the sharp objects from the house. Soon Dusty begins to develop signs of paranoia, a clue that the troubles of all four disturbed protagonists are somehow linked. Ray Olsen, writing in *Booklist,* called *False Memory* "remarkably engaging, despite having so many pages and so little plot." While noting that the book "could have been trimmed by 200 pages and not lost any impact," David Olsen wrote in *Library Journal* that Koontz's "characters are rich, and the main story compelling." A *Publishers Weekly* reviewer comments that with "the amazing fertility of its prose, the novel feels like one of Koontz's earlier tales, with a simple core plot, strong everyman heroes (plus one deliciously malevolent villain) and pacing that starts at a gallop and gets only faster."

This suspense-filled installment in the Koontz oeuvre finds a hardworking bartender guilty of murder by extension when a mysterious killer begin sending him demands: follow the killer's orders and one innocent person will die; don't follow them and the death of another will be the result. (Cover illustration by Ashton Franklin.)

In *The Taking* Koontz draws on his science-fiction roots and weaves a "gripping, blood-curdling, thought-provoking parable," according to Ray Olson in *Booklist.* At the home of novelist Molly Sloan and her husband Neil in California's San Bernardino Mountains, it seems like everything is suddenly starting to come apart. In addition to a mysterious, glowing acid rain, the power appears to be off, but somehow appliances run and soon clocks start spinning out of control. Before long the couple realizes their true dilemma: the nation is under attack by a malevolent alien race. "Mixing a hair-raising plot with masterly story telling and a subtle network of well-placed literary allusions, this deservedly popular author has written a tour de force," stated Nancy McNicol in *Library Journal,* while a reviewer for *Publishers Weekly* commented that "Koontz remains one of the most fascinating of contemporary popular novelists."

Koontz based his novel *Prodigal Son* on *Frankenstein,* by eighteenth-century writer Mary Shelley. In Koontz's update—written with Kevin J. Anderson as part of a multi-volume series—two centuries have passed and the perennially forty-something Dr. Victor Frankenstein is now living under the assumed name of Helios in pre-Hurricane Katrina New Orleans. Continuing his macabre experiments, he is gradually letting pod-grown creatures, members of a "New Race" of perfect humans, live as humans within the city, his ultimate intention to eventually replace all actual humans. Meanwhile, Deucalion, the doctor's original "monster," is also still living in seclusion at a remote Tibetan monastery. When he learns of Helios's existence, and discovers that one of the doctor's perfect beings has become a serial murderer, the "monstrous" Deucalion becomes a force for good in Koontz's characteristic battle of good against evil. Noting the novel's "cliffhanger" ending, a *Publishers Weekly* reviewer wrote that Koontz's "odd juxtaposition of a police procedural with a neo-gothic, mad scientist plot gives the novel a wickedly unusual and intriguing feel."

In addition to his adult fiction, Koontz has also aimed several books specifically at the juvenile market. In *Oddkins: A Fable for All Ages* magical toys have been created for the many children who, for many reasons, need a special secret friend. Called Oddkins, these toys can come alive and possess the power of speech although they look and feel like ordinary stuffed toys; when the child no longer needs emotional support, the caretaking toy returns to its inanimate state. When evil toys created by an equally evil toymaker escape from the cellar of their toy factory, the Oddkins must stop them. Once again, Koontz sends an optimistic message in this clearly told battle of good against evil. A *Publishers Weekly* commentator noted that *Oddkins* has "enough excitement and humor to hold a child's attention" although it might not appeal as much to adult readers.

Koontz has produced several picture books for very young children, among them *Every Day's a Holiday* and two books about the Christmas season. Borrowing the "unbirthday" concept from Lewis Carroll's *Alice in Wonderland,* Koontz creates a host of humorous holidays, both real and imagined. Illustrations by Phil Parks bring to life "Lost-Tooth Day," "Cinco de Mayo," and "Up-Is-Down Day," among others, creating a book that *Childhood Education* reviewer Angela Pitamber called "funny, easy to read, and informative." *Santa's Twin* presents the story of Father Christmas as he tries to save the holiday season from his evil double. Also illustrated by artist Parks and containing Koontz's light-hearted verse, *Robot Santa* finds Santa's brother Bob caught up in even more problematic activities. *Robot Santa* was described by de Lint in the *Magazine of Fantasy and Science Fiction* as "light-hearted and fun."

From serial killers to out-of-control technology and social decay, Koontz often surveys the darker regions of life, but within his stories he "gives readers bright hope in a dark world," according to a *Publishers Weekly* critic. As Edward Bryant noted in *Locus,* "Koontz successfully does what most editors warn their writers not to do. He crosses genre boundaries with impunity. . . . He simply does pretty much what he wants, and the novels are then categorized as "Dean R. Koontz books."" Koontz also admittedly peppers his books with upbeat messages. As he once remarked, he finds "the human species—and Western culture—to be primarily noble, honorable, and admirable. In an age when doomsayers are to be heard in every corner of the land, I find great hope in our species and in the future we will surely make for ourselves. . . . I think we live in a time of marvels, not a time of disaster, and I believe we can solve every problem that confronts us if we keep our perspectives and our freedom."

Biographical and Critical Sources

BOOKS

Kotker, Joan G., *Dean Koontz: A Critical Companion,* Greenwood Press (Westport, CT), 1996.
Munster, Bill, editor, *Sudden Fear: The Horror and Dark Suspense Fiction of Dean R. Koontz,* Starmont House, 1988.
Munster, Bill, *Discovering Dean Koontz: Essays on America's Best-selling Writer of Suspense and Horror Fiction,* Borgo Press (San Bernardino, CA), 1998.
Ramsland, Katherine M., *Dean Koontz: A Writer's Biography,* HarperPrism (New York, NY), 1997.
St. James Guide to Young-Adult Writers, St. James Press (Detroit, MI), 1999.

PERIODICALS

Analog, January, 1984.
Armchair Detective, summer, 1995, p. 329.
Booklist, March 1, 1986, p. 914; September 15, 1994, Ray Olson, review of *Dark Rivers of the Heart,* p. 84; April 15, 1995, p. 1452; December 15, 1999, Ray Olsen, review of *False Memory,* p. 739; May 1, 2004, Ray Olsen, review of *The Taking,* p. 1483; November 1, 2004, Ray Olsen, review of *Life Expectancy,* p. 444; January 1, 2005, Ray Olsen, review of *Prodigal Son,* p. 784.
Childhood Education, winter, 2004, Angela Pitamber, review of *Every Day's a Holiday,* p. 108.

Entertainment Weekly, January 12, 1996, p. 50; January 15, 1999, "'Night' Stalker," p. 56.

Kirkus Reviews, November 1, 1992, review of *Dragon Tears,* p. 1327; May 1, 2004, review of *The Taking,* p. 416; November 15, 2004, review of *Life Expectancy,* p. 1063; May 1, 2005, review of *Velocity,* p. 498.

Library Journal, May 15, 1980, Rex E. Klett, review of *Whispers,* p. 1187; April 15, 1986, p. 95; January, 2000, Jeff Ayers, review of *False Memory,* p. 160; April 15, 2004, Kristen L. Smith, review of *The Face,* p. 146; June 15, 2004, Nancy McNicol, review of *The Taking,* p. 58; December 1, 2004, Nancy McNicol, review of *Life Expectancy,* p. 101; February 1, 2005, Jeff Ayers, review of *Prodigal Son,* p. 68.

Locus, February, 1989, p. 21; March, 1990, Edward Bryant, review of *The Bad Place,* pp. 67-68; March, 1992, p. 62; September, 1994, p. 29; October, 1994, p. 21; December, 1994, p. 58; January, 1995, p. 49; February, 1995, p. 39.

Los Angeles Times, March 12, 1986.

Los Angeles Times Book Review, January 31, 1988, Dick Lochte, "The Perils of Little Laura," p. 8; March 8, 1987, Paul Wilner, review of *Watchers,* p. 6; January 21, 1990, Don G. Campbell, review of *The Bad Place,* p. 12; November 13, 1994, p. 14; May 21, 1995, p. 10.

Magazine of Fantasy and Science Fiction, June, 2004, p. Charles de Lint, review of *Odd Thomas,* p. 33; June, 2005, Charles de Lint, review of *Life Expectancy,* p. 29, *The Taking,* p. 30, and *Robot Santa,* p. 32.

New York Times Book Review, January 12, 1975; February 29, 1976; May 22, 1977; September 11, 1977; June 15, 1986, p. 20; March 15, 1987, Katherine Weber, review of *Watchers,* p. 16; November 13, 1994, Jay E. Rosen, review of *Dark Rivers of the Heart,* p. 58; February 25, 1996, p. 9; April 20, 1997, Charles Salzberg, review of *Sole Survivor;* February 8, 1998, Maggie Garb, review of *Fear Nothing;* February 7, 1999, David Walton, review of *Seize the Night.*

Observer (London, England), February 12, 1995, p. 22.

People, April 13, 1987; April 24, 1989; January 19, 2004, Rob Taub, review of *Odd Thomas,* p. 45.

Publishers Weekly, September 10, 1973, review of *Hanging On,* p. 41; April 4, 1980, review of *Whispers,* p. 61; March 7, 1986, p. 82; December 18, 1987; September 2, 1988, review of *Oddkins,* pp. 87-88; January 10, 1994, review of *Winter Moon,* pp. 56-57; December 19, 1994, p. 52; April 24, 1995, p. 60; November 6, 1995, p. 81; February 5, 1996, p. 41; December 13, 1999, review of *False Memory,* p. 67; December 22, 2003, review of *Odd Thomas,* p. 13; May 10, 2004, review of *The Taking,* p. 37; November 15, 2004, review of *Life Expectancy,* p. 41; January 17, 2005, review of *Prodigal Son,* p. 40; April 25, 2005, review of *Velocity,* p. 39.

Punch, July 15, 1981, p. 109.

Rapport, April, 1994, p. 27.

School Library Journal, April, 1988, Audrey B. Eaglen, "Stunners to Stinkers: The '87 BBYA List," p. 54; May, 2004, Katherine Fitch, review of *Odd Thomas,* p. 175.

Science Fiction Chronicle, March, 1995, p. 39.

Time, January 8, 1996.

Times Literary Supplement, September 11, 1981.

Tribune Books (Chicago, IL), April 12, 1981.

Voice of Youth Advocates, October, 1993, Christy Tyson, review of *Dragon's Tears,* p. 230.

Washington Post Book World, December 11, 1994, p. 8.

Writer's Digest, November, 1989, Stanley Wiater, interview with Koontz, pp. 34-38.

ONLINE

Bookreporter.com, http://www.bookreporter.com/ (March 2, 2001), "Dean Koontz."

Books@Random, www.randomhouse.com/ (October 20, 2004), "Dean Koontz: The Official Web Site."*

L

LEWIN, Ted 1935-

Personal

Born May 6, 1935, in Buffalo, NY; son of Sidney (a retail jeweler) and Berenece (a homemaker; maiden name, Klehn) Lewin; married Betsy Reilly (an author and illustrator of children's books), 1963. *Education:* Pratt Institute of Art, B.F.A., 1956. *Hobbies and other interests:* Photography, painting, and watching birds.

Addresses

Home—152 Willoughby Ave., Brooklyn, NY 11205. *Agent*—c/o Author Mail, HarperCollins Children's, 1350 Avenue of the Americas, New York, NY 10019. *E-mail*—betsyandted@aol.com.

Career

Professional wrestler, 1952-65; artist and freelance illustrator, 1956—. *Exhibitions:* Solo exhibit at Laboratory of Ornithology, Cornell University, 1978, and Central Park 200 Gallery, New York, NY, 1994; joint exhibition with Betsy Lewin at National Center for Children's Illustrated Literature, Abilene, TX, 2002. *Military service:* U.S. Army, 1958.

Ted Lewin

Awards, Honors

Mark Twain Award, 1981, for *Soup for President;* Sandburg Award, 1985, for *The Search for Grissi;* Book Can Develop Empathy award, 1990, for *Faithful Elephants;* Great Stone Face award, 1991, for *The Secret of the Indian;* Boston Globe/Horn Book Award, 1991, for *Judy Scuppernong;* Hungry Mind Award, 1993, for *Sami and the Time of the Troubles;* Caldecott Honor Book, American Library Association (ALA), 1993, for *Peppe the Lamplighter;* Notable Children's Trade Book in the Field of Social Studies designation, National Council for the Social Studies (NCSS)/Children's Book Council (CBC), 1997, for *American Too;* Best Books of the Year selection, Bank Street College, and Notable Chil-

dren's Trade Book in the Field of Social Studies designation, NCSS/CBC, 1998, both for *Fair!;* Best Books of the Year selection, Bank Street College, and Notable Children's Trade Book in the Field of Social Studies designation, NCSS/CBC, 1998, both for *Ali, Child of the Desert;* Big Crit award for excellence in design, *Critique* magazine, 1998, for signage at Central Park Children's Zoo; Parents' Choice Award, 1999, for *Nilo and the Tortoise;* Top-of-the-List Youth picture book honor, *Booklist,* 1999, for *Barn Savers;* Notable Children's Trade Book in the Field of Social Studies designation, NCSS/CBC, 1999, for *The Storytellers;* Notable Book for Children designation, *Smithsonian* magazine, 1999, and Outstanding Science Trade Books for Children designation, National Science Teachers Association (NSTA)/CBC, 2000, both for *Gorilla Walk;* Alumni Achievement Award, Pratt Institute, 2000; John Burroughs Award, American Museum of Natural History, and Outstanding Trade Books for Children Award designation, NSTA/CBC, both 2000, both for *Elephant Quest.*

Writings

SELF-ILLUSTRATED

World within a World—Everglades, Dodd (New York, NY), 1976.

World within a World—Baja, Dodd (New York, NY), 1978.

World within a World—Pribilofs, Dodd (New York, NY), 1980.

Tiger Trek, Macmillan (New York, NY), 1990.

When the Rivers Go Home, Macmillan (New York, NY), 1992.

Amazon Boy, Macmillan (New York, NY), 1993.

I Was a Teenage Professional Wrestler (memoir), Orchard Books (New York, NY), 1993.

The Reindeer People, Macmillan (New York, NY), 1994.

Sacred River, Houghton (Boston, MA), 1995.

Market!, Lothrop, Lee (New York, NY), 1996.

Fair!, Lothrop, Lee (New York, NY), 1997.

The Storytellers, Lothrop, Lee (New York, NY), 1998.

Touch and Go: Travels of a Children's Book Illustrator, Lothrop, Lee (New York, NY), 1999.

(With wife, Betsy Lewin) *Gorilla Walk,* Lothrop, Lee (New York, NY), 1999.

Nilo and the Tortoise, Scholastic (New York, NY), 1999.

(With Betsy Lewin) *Elephant Quest,* Morrow (New York, NY), 2000.

Red Legs: A Drummer Boy of the Civil War, HarperCollins (New York, NY), 2001.

Big Jimmy's Kum Kau Chinese Take-Out, HarperCollins (New York, NY), 2001.

The Girl on the High Diving Horse, Penguin Putnam (New York, NY), 2002.

Tooth and Claw: Animal Adventures in the Wild, HarperCollins (New York, NY), 2003.

Lost City: The Discovery of Machu Picchu, Philomel Books (New York, NY), 2003.

(With Betsy Lewin) *Top to Bottom Down Under,* HarperCollins (New York, NY), 2005.

How Much?: Visiting Markets around the World, HarperCollins (New York, NY), 2006.

ILLUSTRATOR

Jack McClellan, Millard Black, and Sid Norris, adapters, *A Blind Man Can!,* Houghton Mifflin (Boston, MA), 1968.

Wyatt Blassingame, *The Look-It-up Book of Presidents,* Random House (New York, NY), 1968.

Jack McClellan, Millard Black, and Sheila Flume Taylor, *Up, out, and Over!,* Houghton Mifflin (Boston, MA), 1969.

George S. Trow, *Meet Robert E. Lee,* Random House (New York, NY), 1969.

Margaret T. Burroughs, *Jasper, the Drummin' Boy,* Follett (New York, NY), 1970.

Janet H. Ervin, *More than Half Way There,* Follett (New York, NY), 1970.

Donald W. Cox, *Pioneers of Ecology,* Hammond, 1971.

Nellie Burchardt, *A Surprise for Carlotta,* Franklin Watts (New York, NY), 1971.

Darrell A. Rolerson, *Mr. Big Britches,* Dodd (New York, NY), 1971.

Gene Smith, *The Visitor,* Cowles, 1971.

Betty Horvath, *Not Enough Indians,* Franklin Watts (New York, NY), 1971.

Maurine H. Gee, *Chicano, Amigo,* Morrow (New York, NY), 1972.

Rose Blue, *Grandma Didn't Wave Back,* Franklin Watts (New York, NY), 1972.

Michael Capizzi, *Getting It All Together,* Delacorte (New York, NY), 1972.

Rose Blue, *A Month of Sundays,* Franklin Watts (New York, NY), 1972.

Rita Micklish, *Sugar Bee,* Delacorte (New York, NY), 1972.

Darrell A. Rolerson, *In Sheep's Clothing,* Dodd (New York, NY), 1972.

Rose Blue, *Nikki 108,* Franklin Watts (New York, NY), 1972.

Charlotte Gantz, *Boy with Three Names,* Houghton Mifflin (Boston, MA), 1973.

William MacKellar, *The Ghost of Grannoch Moor,* Dodd (New York, NY), 1973.

Marjorie M. Prince, *The Cheese Stands Alone,* Houghton Mifflin (Boston, MA), 1973.

Marian Rumsey, *Lion on the Run,* Morrow (New York, NY), 1973.

Darrell A. Rolerson, *A Boy Called Plum,* Dodd (New York, NY), 1974.

Jean Slaughter Doty, *Gabriel,* Macmillan (New York, NY), 1974.

Gene Smith, *The Hayburners,* Delacorte (New York, NY), 1974.

Matt Christopher, *Earthquake,* Little, Brown (Boston, MA), 1975.

Patricia Beatty, *Rufus, Red Rufus,* Morrow (New York, NY), 1975.

Charles Ferry, *Up in Sister Bay,* Houghton Mifflin (Boston, MA), 1975.

Jean Slaughter Doty, *Winter Pony,* Macmillan (New York, NY), 1975.

S.T. Tung, *One Small Dog,* Dodd (New York, NY), 1975.

Rose Blue, *The Preacher's Kid,* Franklin Watts (New York, NY), 1975.

Scott O'Dell, *Zia,* Houghton Mifflin (Boston, MA), 1976.

Lynne Martin, *Puffin, Bird of the Open Seas,* Morrow (New York, NY), 1976.

Laurence Pringle, *Listen to the Crows,* Crowell (New York, NY), 1976.

Patricia Edwards Clyne, *Ghostly Animals of America,* Dodd (New York, NY), 1977.

Mildred Teal, *Bird of Passage,* Little, Brown (Boston, MA), 1977.

Marian Rumsey, *Carolina Hurricane,* Morrow (New York, NY), 1977.

Nigel Gray, *The Deserter,* Harper (New York, NY), 1977.

Robert Newton Peck, *Patooie,* Knopf (New York, NY), 1977.

Philippa Pearce, *The Shadow-Cage, and Other Tales of the Supernatural,* Crowell (New York, NY), 1977.

Helen Hill, Agnes Perkins, and Alethea Helbig, editors, *Straight on till Morning: Poems of the Imaginary World,* Crowell (New York, NY), 1977.

Rose Blue, *The Thirteenth Year: A Bar Mitzvah Story,* Franklin Watts (New York, NY), 1977.

Leslie Norris, *Merlin and the Snake's Egg: Poems,* Viking (New York, NY), 1978.

William MacKellar, *The Silent Bells,* Dodd (New York, NY), 1978.

Robert Newton Peck, *Soup for President,* Knopf (New York, NY), 1978.

William MacKellar, *The Witch of Glen Gowrie,* Dodd (New York, NY), 1978.

Anne E. Crompton, *A Woman's Place,* Little, Brown (Boston, MA), 1978.

Margaret Goff Clark, *Barney and the UFO,* Dodd (New York, NY), 1979.

Patricia Edwards Clyne, *Strange and Supernatural Animals,* Dodd (New York, NY), 1979.

Robert Newton Peck, *Hub,* Knopf (New York, NY), 1979.

David Stemple, *High Ridge Gobbler: A Story of the American Wild Turkey,* Collins (New York, NY), 1979.

Jean Slaughter Doty, *Can I Get There by Candlelight?,* Macmillan (New York, NY), 1980.

Rose Blue, *My Mother, the Witch,* McGraw (New York, NY), 1980.

Margaret Goff Clark, *Barney in Space,* Dodd (New York, NY), 1981.

Francine Jacobs, *Bermuda Petrel: The Bird That Would Not Die,* Morrow (New York, NY), 1981.

Mark Twain, *The Adventures of Tom Sawyer,* Wanderer Books, 1982.

Margaret Goff Clark, *Barney on Mars,* Dodd (New York, NY), 1983.

Eleanor Clymer, *The Horse in the Attic,* Bradbury Press (New York, NY), 1983.

Priscilla Homola, *The Willow Whistle,* Dodd (New York, NY), 1983.

Enid Bagnold, *National Velvet,* Morrow (New York, NY), 1985.

R.R. Knudson, *Babe Didrikson, Athlete of the Century,* Viking Kestrel (New York, NY), 1985.

Mary Francis Shura, *The Search for Grissi,* Dodd (New York, NY), 1985.

Frances Wosmek, *A Brown Bird Singing,* Lothrop, Lee (New York, NY), 1986.

Patricia Reilly Giff, *Mother Teresa, Sister to the Poor,* Viking Kestrel (New York, NY), 1986.

Elizabeth Simpson Smith, *A Dolphin Goes to School: The Story of Squirt, a Trained Dolphin,* Morrow (New York, NY), 1986.

Scott O'Dell, *The Serpent Never Sleeps: A Novel of Jamestown and Pocahontas,* Houghton Mifflin (Boston, MA), 1987.

Susan Saunders, *Margaret Mead: The World Was Her Family,* Viking Kestrel (New York, NY), 1987.

Kathleen V. Kudlinski, *Rachel Carson: Pioneer of Ecology,* Viking Kestrel (New York, NY), 1988.

Yukio Tsuchiya, *Faithful Elephants: A True Story of Animals, People, and War,* translated by Tomoko Tsuchiya Dykes, Houghton Mifflin (Boston, MA), 1988.

Lynne Reid Banks, *The Secret of the Indian,* Doubleday (New York, NY), 1989.

Bruce Coville, editor, *Herds of Thunder, Manes of Gold: A Collection of Horse Stories and Poems,* Doubleday (New York, NY), 1989.

Leon Garfield, *Young Nick and Jubilee,* Delacorte (New York, NY), 1989.

Florence Parry Heide and Judith Heide Gilliland, *The Day of Ahmed's Secret,* Lothrop, Lee (New York, NY), 1990.

Scott O'Dell, *Island of the Blue Dolphins,* Houghton Mifflin (Boston, MA), 1990.

Gregory Patent, *Shanghai Passage,* Clarion (New York, NY), 1990.

Brenda Seabrooke, *Judy Scuppernong,* Cobblehill Books (New York, NY), 1990.

Jane Yolen, *Bird Watch: A Book of Poetry,* Philomel Books (New York, NY), 1990.

Margaret Hodges, *Brother Francis and the Friendly Beasts,* Scribner (New York, NY), 1991.

Megan McDonald, *The Potato Man,* Orchard Books (New York, NY), 1991.

Frances Ward Weller, *I Wonder If I'll See a Whale,* Philomel Books (New York, NY), 1991.

Corinne Demas Bliss, *Matthew's Meadow,* Harcourt (San Diego, CA), 1992.

Florence Parry Heide and Judith Heide Gilliland, *Sami and the Time of the Troubles,* Clarion (New York, NY), 1992.

Megan McDonald, *The Great Pumpkin Switch,* Orchard Books (New York, NY), 1992.

Frances Ward Weller, *Matthew Wheelock's Wall,* Macmillan (New York, NY), 1992.

Elisa Bartone, *Peppe the Lamplighter,* Lothrop, Lee (New York, NY), 1993.

Ann Herbert Scott, *Cowboy Country,* Clarion (New York, NY), 1993.

Sheldon Oberman, *The Always Prayer Shawl,* Boyds Mills Press (Honesdale, PA), 1993.

Louise Borden, *Just in Time for Christmas,* Scholastic (New York, NY), 1994.

Jan Slepian, *Lost Moose,* Putnam (New York, NY), 1995.

Mary Kay Kroeger and Louise Borden, *Paperboy,* Houghton Mifflin (Boston, MA), 1996.

Jane Yolen, *Sea Watch: A Book of Poetry,* Putnam (New York, NY), 1996.

Megan McDonald, *The Great Pumpkin Switch,* Orchard Books (New York, NY), 1996.

Elisa Bartone, *American Too,* Lothrop, Lee (New York, NY), 1996.

Jonathan London, *Ali, Child of the Desert,* Lothrop, Lee (New York, NY), 1997.

Jane Yolen, *The Originals,* Putnam (New York, NY), 1997.

Sheldon Oberman, *The Always Prayer Shawl,* Puffin Books (New York, NY), 1997.

Linda Oatman High, *Barn Savers,* Boyds Mills Press (Honesdale, PA), 1999.

Louise Borden, *A. Lincoln and Me,* Scholastic (New York, NY), 1999.

Faith McNulty, *How Whales Walked into the Sea,* Scholastic (New York, NY), 1999.

Corinne Demas Bliss, *The Disappearing Island,* Simon and Schuster (New York, NY), 2000.

Edward Grimm, *The Doorman,* Orchard Books (New York, NY), 2000.

Linda Oatman High, *Winter Shoes for Shadow Horse,* Boyds Mills Press (Honesdale, PA), 2001.

Tony Johnston, *Sunsets of the West,* Putnam (New York, NY), 2002.

Linda Oatman High, *The Girl on the High-diving Board,* Philomel Books (New York, NY), 2003.

T.A. Barron, *High as a Hawk: A Brave Girl's Historic Climb,* Philomel Books (New York, NY), 2004.

Ralph Helfer, *The World's Greatest Elephant,* Philomel Books (New York, NY), 2006.

Eve Bunting, *One Green Apple,* Clarion (New York, NY), 2006.

Illustrations have also appeared in periodicals, including *Boy's Life, Ladies' Home Journal, Seventeen,* and *Reader's Digest.*

Sidelights

Author and illustrator Ted Lewin was inspired in his career by his lifelong love of nature. "I am a deeply concerned environmentalist and conservationist," Lewin once noted, adding that he travels "to wilderness areas around the world for both graphic and literary material." Married to fellow author/illustrator and sometime collaborator Betsy Lewin, Ted Lewin has written and illustrated many books for children and young adults, among them *Gorilla Walk, Tiger Trek,* and *Lost City: The Discovery of Machu Picchu.* As an author, he has been praised for the poetic quality he brings to his texts, and his plots draw from his extensive knowledge of and concern for wildlife and its habitats throughout the world. As an illustrator, Lewin's work is characterized by its realistic detail, and his award-winning paintings have enhanced the texts of a wide variety of writers. Praising Lewin's watercolor art for Tony Johnston's *Sunsets of the West,* a *Kirkus Reviews* writer noted that the illustrator's paintings feature "characters and scenery . . . infused with life," while *School Library Journal* writer Rosalyn Pierini wrote that "prairie and mountain vistas are well served by Lewin's majestic, detailed paintings."

As a young boy growing up in upstate New York, Lewin always had dreams of becoming an artist. "Not a policeman, fireman, or doctor—an artist," he recalled in his autobiography, *I Was a Teenage Professional Wres-* *tler.* "I remember working first with a metal-armed copying toy I got for Christmas, then the Magic-Pad, on which you could pull up a flap and make whatever you'd drawn disappear." With the encouragement of his family, Lewin practiced drawing by copying photographs, illustrations from children's books, and even a portrait of President Harry S Truman, for which he received a personal letter from the White House.

By the time Lewin graduated from high school, he had made plans to study art at Pratt Institute in Brooklyn. Because paying for school and living expenses would be expensive, Lewin established the secondary career that would help support him for almost fifteen years: professional wrestling. He had attended professional matches with his family for many years, and his older brother Donn had become a wrestler after serving in the U.S. Marines during World War II. With the aid of his brother and the many contacts his family had made in the sport over the years, Lewin began wrestling at age seventeen during summers and at night during the school year. In his autobiography, Lewin recalled his dual life, alternating between art classes and wrestling matches: "Every day I had classes in two-dimensional design, three-dimensional design, and figure drawing. Around me, the light-filled, high-ceilinged studio would be electric with concentrated effort. . . . I would see a great play of light and shadow—in a sense, not so different from what I'd seen in the charged, dramatic atmosphere of a wrestling arena. The medium was different, that's all."

"More a series of vignettes than an autobiography," as *Bulletin of the Center for Children's Books* writer Deborah Stevenson described it, *I Was a Teenage Professional Wrestler* details Lewin's involvement with the sport and provides portraits—written and painted—of the many wrestlers he met during his career. "It is a fascinating story that leaves the reader wanting to learn more about both Lewin and the other wrestlers," noted Patrick Jones in the *Voice of Youth Advocates.* In recreating a different era, Lewin describes the wrestlers "quite masterfully in words, then he brings them to life with old black and white photographs, drawings and paintings." *School Library Journal* contributor Todd Morning likewise praised Lewin's "surprisingly funny and affectionate" remembrances, as well as the author's combination of "vivid" artwork and human stories. "The artist's sensibility and eye for detail are always in evidence," the critic concluded. "His talent in this realm is truly formidable."

After earning his bachelor of fine arts degree, Lewin continued wrestling as he slowly built a career as a freelance artist. He began with magazine work, and by the late 1960s obtained his first assignments illustrating children's books. In 1976 Lewin debuted his series, "World within a World," which focuses on wildlife in several regions visited by the author; the series has received high praise for both Lewin's text and the illustrations. The first volume in the series, concerning the Everglades, is based on observations of the plant and animal life in the area made by Lewin over a five-year period. The volume on Baja, California, describes elephant seals and details the annual migration of the California gray whales. Of the volume on the Pribilof Islands, which highlights the precarious fate of the seals who bear and raise their young on these Alaskan coastal islands, a reviewer from *Booklist* called Lewin's prose "elegant and uncompromising," adding that "the evocation of this small corner of the world is strong."

Many of Lewin's self-authored books are inspired by the many trips he has made while exploring planet Earth. He depicts a trip made on the back of an elephant through one of India's national parks in *Tiger Trek,* while other travel books include *The Reindeer People, Sacred River,* and *Tooth and Claw: Animal Adventures in the Wild.* Joan McGrath, reviewing *Tiger Trek* for *School Library Journal,* found the book "gorgeous" and "far above the ordinary." A similar journey is documented in *When the Rivers Go Home,* which describes Lewin's trip through a large swamp in central Brazil called the Pantanal. *When the Rivers Go Home* also received praise for its watercolor paintings, a *Kirkus Reviews* writer describing Lewin's work as "lovely" and "evocative." In *Amazon Boy* Lewin's "light-filled pictures, dense with detail, reinforce the theme that the riches of the rain forest must be protected," according to *School Library Journal* contributor Kathleen Odean.

The Reindeer People introduces readers to Ola, a Sami reindeer herdsman from Lapland, a remote area north of the Arctic Circle. In addition to describing Ola's unique line of work—herding reindeer, the book also describes favorite pastimes of the Sami people—racing reindeer—and a traditional wedding blended with some twentieth-century flavor. "The author's highly descriptive prose is as luxurious as a reindeer coat, and his finely detailed, snapshot-style watercolors will engage readers of any age," enthused a *Publishers Weekly* reviewer. Describing *Sacred River,* based on a trip Lewin made to India, *Horn Book* contributor Maria B. Salvadore wrote that the author's "descriptive, fluid, and straightforward text combines with richly detailed full-color illustrations to describe a pilgrimage to the Ganges River in the Indian city of Benares."

Together with his wife, Lewin has traveled the world, and in a series of books the couple recount their many adventures. *Gorilla Walk,* a recounting of a 1997 trip to Uganda to view the mountain gorillas, was praised for its "handsome paintings and carefully focused text" by *Horn Book* critic Margaret A. Bush, the critic adding that the Lewins "offer . . . intriguing glimpses of both the rarely seen animals and the ambiguities of ecotourism." *Elephant Quest* also take the couple to Africa, while in *Top to Bottom Down Under* they explore the vast continent of Australia, ranging from Kakadu National Park to Australia's Kangaroo Island. Illustrated

Lewin reveals the more unusual parts of his career-track to becoming a well-known author and illustrator in his self-illustrated 1993 autobiography I Was a Teenage Professional Wrestler.

with Lewin's paintings and his wife's field sketches, *Top to Bottom Down Under* was praised by *School Library Journal* contributor Patricia Manning as an "eye-catching and informative . . . treat for animal lovers and adventurers alike." Citing Lewin's "striking, realistic" watercolors and noting the inclusion of animal facts, *Booklist* reviewer Karin Snelson also lauded the work, noting that *Top to Bottom Down Under* allows readers to accompany the creative couple on a "contagiously cheerful Aussie expedition."

A perusal of the adventurous author/illustrator's *Tooth and Claw* prompted *Horn Book* critic Danielle J. Ford to exclaim: "Thank goodness Ted Lewin has survived" his travels. Calling Lewin a "gifted storyteller," Ford praised the author's presentation of fourteen "suspenseful, often terrifying, and sometimes quite funny experiences" Lewin and his fellow travelers have had during a life of globe-hopping. Lewin comes face to face with North American grizzly bears, Bengal tigers, African snakes and other grassland creatures, Florida bull sharks, and many other creatures, all told in a travelogue format. Ford praised the work as "outstanding nature storytelling," while in *Kirkus Reviews* a critic explained that, by hauling a rucksack full of drawing supplies with him, Lewin was able to highlight his "fascinating" stories with his "typically wonderful drawings" and "on-site photographs." Echoing other praise, *School Library Journal* critic Pam Spencer Holley noted that *Tooth and Claw* will serve children as "a great read-aloud" for budding naturalists or "simply as a good adventure story."

In addition to narrative accounts, Lewin sometimes weaves his experiences into picture-book texts, such as *Market!* and *Fair!* In *Market!* he creates "paintings so vivid you can almost smell the market scents," according to Susan Dove Lempke in *Booklist.* In the book Lewin describes the various people, products, and atmosphere of six markets—from New York City to Nepal. Similar in focus, *Fair!* presents the many scenes and flavors of a typical country fair, including animal and food contests, games, rides, and fireworks. A *Kirkus Reviews* critic described *Fair!* as a "pulsing, panoramic examination of a summertime ritual," and a *Publishers Weekly* reviewer asserted that "this visit to the fair [is] worth the price of admission." Lewin's fascination with the Galapagos Islands provided him with the setting for his fictional tale *Nilo and the Tortoise,* about a young boy who is stranded on one of the islands. In *Booklist* Stephanie Zvirin noted that Lewin's pictures once again are the main attraction of the book, capturing "the remoteness and beauty of the exotic place and some of its distinctive wildlife."

Several of Lewin's books focus on history, among them *Red Legs: A Drummer Boy of the Civil War* and *Lost City: The Discovery of Machu Picchu.* In *Red Legs* a nine-year-old boy accompanies his father to the reenactment of a U.S. Civil War battle, and plays the part of Stephen Benjamin Bertow, a young drummer boy who died during the fight. Noting Lewin's "brief yet stirring text" and evocative watercolors, a *Publishers Weekly* reviewer wrote that the book expresses a "true passion for history" that might inspire similar enthusiasm in young readers. The fascinating story of the discovery of an ancient Incan city also proves arresting in Lewin's book about Hiram Bingham's 1911 jungle adventure. Based on Bingham's account, *Lost City* follows the explorer through the Andes, linking his tale to the dreams of a young Quechua boy that anticipate Bingham's arrival. Lewin "balances a compelling visual chronicle with sure storytelling," according to a *Publishers Weekly* critic, while in *Horn Book* Bush called Bingham's "tortuous journey richly rewarded is a good adventure story" brought to life by Lewin's "evocative" watercolor art.

Working from photos he shoots during his travels and then projects onto a screen in his studio, Lewin manages to retain much of the original realism and force of scenes he has witnessed firsthand. A steady producer, he maintains a disciplined work regimen as well. His day begins at eight in the morning and continues without break into the afternoon. While he is at work in the upstairs of his New York brownstone, his wife, Betsy, works in her studio downstairs. In addition to creating the artwork for his own books, Lewin has also illustrated the texts of numerous other writers, among them

Peppe the Lamplighter by Elisa Bartone, *Paperboy* by Mary Kay Kroeger, and Louise Borden, and *Sea Watch: A Book of Poetry* by Jane Yolen.

A Caldecott Honor Book, *Peppe the Lamplighter* focuses on a young Italian immigrant living in New York City who takes a job lighting gas lamps to help support his family. "Lewin's masterly watercolors express the swirling energy of the crowded streets as well as the intimate feelings and interactions of individual people," Hazel Rochman observed in *Booklist.* Lewin also illustrated *American Too,* in which Bartone continues the young immigrant's adventures in his new country. *Paperboy,* "filled with carefully detailed watercolors," according to *Horn Book* contributor Elizabeth S. Watson, features Willie Brinkman, a young paperboy living in Cincinnati in 1927. After boxing hero Jack Dempsey loses a major prizefight, Willie honors his commitment to sell newspapers despite his and the neighborhood's shock and disappointment. Hazel Rochman, writing in *Booklist,* declared that the artist's watercolor illustrations are "more exuberant than the artwork in Lewin's Caldecott Honor Book, *Peppe the Lamplighter.*" For his contribution to *Sea Watch, Booklist* reviewer Lauren Peterson noted that "Lewin's trademark watercolors, fresh, realistic, and beautifully rendered, nicely complement the poetry."

About his career, Lewin once commented, "There are still so many stories out there waiting to be found and so many manuscripts by wonderful authors to take me on journeys I might never have made myself."

Biographical and Critical Sources

BOOKS

Lewin, Ted, *I Was a Teenage Professional Wrestler,* Orchard Books (New York, NY), 1993.

Seventh Book of Junior Authors and Illustrators, H.W. Wilson (Bronx, NY), 1996.

Silvey, Anita, editor, *Children's Books and Their Creators,* Houghton (Boston, MA), 1995.

Something about the Author Autobiography Series, Volume 25, Thomson Gale (Detroit, MI), 1998.

PERIODICALS

Booklist, January 1, 1981, review of *World within a World—Pribilofs,* p. 625; April 15, 1993, Hazel Rochman, review of *Peppe the Lamplighter,* p. 1522; December 15, 1993, Stephanie Zvirin, review of *The Always Prayer Shawl,* p. 750; October 1, 1994, Julie Corsaro, review of *The Reindeer People,* p. 322; March 1, 1995, p. 1250; June 1, 1995, Hazel Rochman, review of *Sacred River,* p. 1778; March 15, 1996, Hazel Rochman, review of *Paperboy,* p. 1269; April

15, 1996, Susan Dove Lempke, review of *Market!*, p. 1444; June 1, 1996, Lauren Peterson, review of *Sea Watch: A Book of Poetry*, p. 1716; August, 1996, Hazel Rochman, review of *American Too*, p. 1903; February 1, 1998, Hazel Rochman, review of *The Originals*, p. 917; April, 1998, Susan Dove Lempke, review of *The Storytellers*, p. 1332; May 31, 1999, Stephanie Zvirin, review of *Nilo and the Tortoise*, p. 93; November 1, 1999, p. 524; November 15, 1999, p. 622; January 1, 2000, p. 824; January 1, 2002, Cynthia Turnquest, *Big Jimmy's Kum Kau Chinese Take Out*, p. 866; June 1, 2002, Carolyn Phelan, review of *Sunsets of the West*, p. 1738; January 1, 2003, Carolyn Phelan, review of *Tooth and Claw: Animal Adventures in the West*, p. 882; July, 2003, Gillian Engberg, review of *Lost City: The Discovery of Machu Picchu*, p. 1895; January 1, 2005, Karin Snelson, review of *Top to Bottom Down Under*, p. 866.

Bulletin of the Center for Children's Books, May, 1993, p. 277; June, 1993, Deborah Stevenson, review of *I Was a Teenage Professional Wrestler*, pp. 321-322; April, 1998, Betsy Hearne, review of *The Storytellers*, p. 286; July, 1999, p. 393; January, 2002, review of *Big Jimmy's Kum Kau Chinese Take Out*, p. 177; September, 2003, Elizabeth Bush, review of *Lost City*, p. 23.

Horn Book, May-June, 1993, Margaret A. Bush, review of *Amazon Boy*, pp. 320-321; January-February 1996, Maria B. Salvadore, review of *Sacred River*, p. 99; July-August, 1996, pp. 481-482; September-October, 1996, Elizabeth S. Watson, review of *Paperboy*, p. 581; November-December, 1999, Margaret A. Bush, review of *Gorilla Walk*, p. 758; January 2001, review of *Elephant Quest*, p. 111; March-April, Danielle J. Ford, review of *Tooth and Claw*, p. 226; September-October, 2003, Margaret A. Bush, review of *Lost City*, p. 631.

Kirkus Reviews, February 15, 1992, review of *When the Rivers Go Home*, pp. 257-258; July 1, 1997, review of *Fair!*, p. 1031; May 15, 1999, review of *Touch and Go*, p. 803; May 15, 2002, review of *Sunsets of the West*, p. 734; February 2, 2003, review of *Tooth and Claw*, p. 235; March 15, 2003, review of *The Girl on the High-flying Horse*, p. 468; June 1, 2003, review of *Lost City*, p. 807; February 15, 2005, review of *Top to Bottom Down Under*, p. 231.

Publishers Weekly, August 10, 1990, review of *The Day of Ahmed's Secret*, p. 444; October 26, 1990, review of *Bird Watch*, p. 71; April 17, 1993, review of *Peppe the Lamplighter*, p. 61; April 26, 1993, review of *Amazon Boy*, p. 78; October 24, 1994, review of *The Reindeer People*, p. 61; August 7, 1995, review of *Sacred River*, p. 460; February 26, 1996, p. 81; April 29, 1996, review of *Market!*, p. 72; June 9, 1997, review of *Fair!*, p. 45; August 2, 1999, p. 84; November 1, 1999, p. 83; February 21, 2000, p. 89; June 19, 2000, review of *The Disappearing Island*, p. 79; September 4, 2000, review of *The Doorman*, p. 107; December 11, 2000, review of *A. Lincoln and Me*, p. 86; March 19, 2001, review of *Paperboy*, p. 102; June 18, 2001, review of *Red Legs: A Drummer Boy of the Civil War*, p. 81; February 25, 2002, review of *Big Jimmy's Kum Kau Chinese Take Out*, p. 68; May 13, 2002, review of *Sunsets of the West*, p. 70; January 13, 2003, review of *The Girl on the High-diving Horse*, p. 60; June 2, 2003, review of *Lost City*, p. 51.

School Library Journal, March, 1990, Joan McGrath, review of *Tiger Trek*, p. 208; June, 1993, Kathleen Odean, review of *Amazon Boy*, pp. 80, 83; July, 1993, Barbara Peklo Abrahams, review of *Peppe the Lamplighter*, p. 56; July, 1993, Todd Morning, review of *I Was a Teenage Professional Wrestler*, p. 108; March, 1994, p. 206; October, 1994, p. 37; July, 1997, Jackie Hechtkopf, review of *Fair!*, p. 85; April, 1999, p. 102; July, 1999, p. 110; July 2000, Kate McClelland, review of *The Disappearing Island*, p. 70; October 2000, Marianne Saccardi, review of *The Doorman*, p. 126; April, 2002, John Peters, review of *Big Jimmy's Kum Kau Chinese Take Out*, p. 114; July, 2002, Rosalyn Pierini, review of *Sunsets of the West*, p. 94; February, 2003, Carol Schene, review of *The Girl on the High-diving Horse*, p. 112; May, 2003, Pam Spencer Holley, review of *Tooth and Claw*, p. 173; June, 2003, Daryl Grabarek, review of *Lost City*, p. 163; November, 2003, Carol Fazioli, review of *I Was a Teenage Professional Wrestler*, p. 83; March, 2005, Patricia Manning, review of *Top to Bottom Down Under*, p. 196.

Social Education, January, 2001, Barbara J. Holt, review of *Faithful Elephants: A True Story of Animals, People, and War*, p. S9.

Voice of Youth Advocates, October, 1993, Patrick Jones, review of *I Was a Teenage Professional Wrestler*, p. 247.

ONLINE

Ted Lewin Web site, http://www.tedlewin.com (November 21, 2005).*

*   *   *

LO, Ginnie
(Virginia M. Lo)

Personal

Born in West Lafayette, IN. *Education:* University of Illinois at Urbana-Champaign, Ph.D., 1983. *Hobbies and other interests:* Origami, mahjong, ethnic music, foreign films, bicycling, hiking, soccer.

Addresses

Home—Eugene, OR. *Office*—Department of Computer and Information Science, University of Oregon, Eugene, OR 97403-1202. *E-mail*—lo@cs.uoregon.edu.

Career

Educator. University of Oregon, Eugene, assistant professor, then associate professor of computer and information science, 1985—.

A collaboration between Lo and her sister, artist Beth Lo, Mahjong All Day Long *follows a family tradition of gathering together to play a popular Chinese game while younger family members keep busy and good food is served.*

Writings

Mahjong All Day Long, illustrations by Beth Lo, Walker & Co. (New York, NY), 2005.

Also author of technical papers. Contributor to professional journals, including *Network Journal, IEEE Transactions on Parallel and Distributed Systems,* and *Journal of Telecommunication Systems.*

Sidelights

Ginnie Lo took time out from her job as associate professor of computer and information science at the University of Oregon to collaborate with her sister, ceramicist and educator Beth Lo, on a children's book. In *Mahjong All Day Long* Lo draws on memories from her childhood to create the story of a Chinese-American family enjoying an all-day game of mahjong. Her text, paired with Beth Lo's illustrations created by staining and glazing images onto porcelain plates, finds the elders in the family intent on their game while JieJie and her little brother watch. Not understanding the game, the children toy with the set-aside mahjong tiles, but as the years pass they grow older and come to understand the game, ultimately sharing it with their own children.

A *Kirkus Reviews* critic commented that Beth Lo's use of "alternating red and black pages" creates a book that is "visually arresting," and noted Lo's inclusion of several Chinese words and their meanings. In *Booklist* Jennifer Mattson maintained that the Lo sisters' work, while less sophisticated than some picture-book efforts, "speaks directly to kids," and praised the work for its usefulness in school classrooms and its "intergenerational themes." Josephine Bridges noted in the *Asian Reporter* that "early readers and their grown-ups can share this story whether or not they play mahjong."

Biographical and Critical Sources

PERIODICALS

Asian Reporter, June 7, 2005, Josephine Bridges, "Mahjong Runs in the Family," p. 16.
Booklist, February 15, 2005, Jennifer Mattson, review of *Mahjong All Day Long,* p. 1079.
Kirkus Reviews, March 1, 2005, review of *Mahjong All Day Long,* p. 290.
School Library Journal, May, 2005, Margaret R. Tassia, review of *Mahjong All Day Long,* p. 89.

ONLINE

Inside Oregon Online (University of Oregon), http:// duckhenge.uoregon.edu/io/ (October 7, 2005), "Children's Book on Mahjong Is Computer Expert's First Work."

Mahjong All Day Long Web site, http://www.mahjong alldaylong.com/ (October 7, 2005).

University of Oregon Department of Computer and Information Science Web site, http://www.cs.uoregon.edu/ (January 15, 2004), "Virginia M. Lo."

*   *   *

LO, Virginia M.
See LO, Ginnie

M

MACDONALD, James D. 1954-

(Nicholas Adams, a joint pseudonym, Victor Appleton, a joint pseudonym, Martin Delrio, a joint pseudonym, Douglas Morgan, a joint pseudonym, Robyn Tallis, a joint pseudonym)

Personal

Born 1954, in White Plains, NY; son of a chemical engineer and an artist; married Debra Doyle (a writer and teacher); children: Katherine, Brendan, Peregrine, Alexander. *Education:* Attended University of Rochester; University of the State of New York, B.A. (English literature). *Hobbies and other interests:* Science fiction, cats, computers, cryptography, fencing.

Addresses

Home—127 Main St., Colebrook, NH 03576. *Agent*—Valerie Smith, 1746 Route 44-55, Modena, NY 12548. *E-mail*—doylemacdonald@sff.net.

Career

Journalist and science-fiction/fantasy author. *Military service:* U.S. Navy; served fifteen-year tour of duty; attained rank of officer.

Awards, Honors

Mythopoetic Aslan Fantasy Award for Young-Adult literature, 1992, and New York Public Library Books for the Teen Age list, 1993, both for *Knight's Wyrd;* Best Young-Adult Science Fiction Award, *Science Fiction Chronicle,* 1997, for *Groogleman.*

Writings

NOVELS

The Apocalypse Door, Tor (New York, NY), 2002.

NOVELS, UNLESS OTHERWISE NOTED; WITH WIFE DEBRA DOYLE

(Under pseudonym Robyn Tallis) *Night of Ghosts and Lightning* ("Planet Builders" series), Ivy, 1989.
(Under pseudonym Robyn Tallis) *Zero-Sum Games* ("Planet Builders" series), Ivy, 1989.
(Under pseudonym Nicholas Adams) *Pep Rally* ("Horror High" series), Harper (New York, NY), 1991.
(Under pseudonym Victor Appleton) *Monster Machine* ("Tom Swift" series), Pocket Books (New York, NY), 1991.
(Under pseudonym Victor Appleton) *Aquatech Warriors* ("Tom Swift" series), Pocket Books (New York, NY), 1991.
Timecrime, Inc. ("Robert Silverberg's 'Time Tours'" series), Harper (New York, NY), 1991.
Night of the Living Rat ("Daniel Pinkwater's 'Melvinge of the Megaverse'" series), Ace Books (New York, NY), 1992.
Knight's Wyrd, Harcourt, Brace (New York, NY), 1992.
Groogleman, Harcourt, Brace (New York, NY), 1996.
Requiem for Boone (based on the television series *Gene Roddenberry's Earth—Final Conflict*), Tor (New York, NY), 2000.
(As Douglas Morgan) *Tiger Cruise,* Forge (New York, NY), 2001.
(As Douglas Morgan) *What Do You with a Drunken Sailor?* (nonfiction), Swordsmith, 2002.

NOVELS; "CIRCLE OF MAGIC" SERIES; WITH DEBRA DOYLE

School of Wizardry, Troll (Metuchen, NJ), 1990.
Tournament and Tower, Troll (Metuchen, NJ), 1990.
City by the Sea, Troll (Metuchen, NJ), 1990.
The Prince's Players, Troll (Metuchen, NJ), 1990.
The Prisoners of Bell Castle, Troll (Metuchen, NJ), 1990.
The High King's Daughter, Troll (Metuchen, NJ), 1990.

NOVELS; "MAGEWORLD" SERIES; WITH DEBRA DOYLE

The Price of the Stars, Tor Books (New York, NY), 1992.
Starpilot's Grave, Tor (New York, NY), 1993.
By Honor Betray'd, Tor (New York, NY), 1994.

The Gathering Flame, Tor (New York, NY), 1995.
The Long Hunt, Tor (New York, NY) 1996.
The Stars Asunder, Tor (New York, NY) 1999.
A Working of Stars, Tor (New York, NY), 2002.

NOVELS; "BAD BLOOD" SERIES; WITH DEBRA DOYLE

Bad Blood, Berkley (New York, NY), 1993.
Hunters' Moon, Berkley (New York, NY), 1994.
Judgment Night, Berkley (New York, NY), 1995.

NOVELS; UNDER JOINT PSEUDONYM MARTIN DELRIO; WITH DEBRA DOYLE

Mortal Kombat (movie novelization), Tor (New York, NY), 1995.
Midnight Justice ("Spider-Man Super-Thriller" series), Byron Preiss (New York, NY), 1996.
Global War ("Spider-Man Super-Thriller" series), Byron Preiss (New York, NY), 1996.
Harold R. Foster's Prince Valiant (movie novelization), Avon (New York, NY), 1998.
The Loch Ness Monster (nonfiction), Rosen Publishing (New York, NY), 2002.
Truth and Shadows (novel; "MechWarrior: Dark Age" series), Roc (New York, NY), 2003.

OTHER

Contributor (with Debra Doyle) of short stories to anthologies, including *Werewolves,* edited by Jane Yolen and Martin Greenberg, Harper Junior Books, 1988; *Vampires,* edited by Yolen and Greenberg, HarperCollins, 1991; *Newer York,* edited by Lawrence Watt-Evans, Roc, 1991; *Alternate Kennedys,* edited by Mike Resnick and Greenberg, Tor, 1992; *Bruce Coville's Book of Monsters,* edited by Bruce Coville, Scholastic, 1993; *Swashbuckling Editor Stories,* edited by John Betancourt, Wildside Press, 1993; *Bruce Coville's Book of Ghosts,* edited by Coville, Scholastic, 1994; *A Wizard's Dozen,* edited by Michael Stearns, Harcourt, Brace, 1995; *A Starfarer's Dozen,* edited by Stearns, Harcourt, Brace, 1995; *Witch Fantastic,* edited by Mike Resnick and Greenberg, DAW Books, 1995; *Camelot,* edited by Yolen, Philomel, 1995; *The Book of Kings,* edited by Richard Gilliam and Greenberg, Roc, 1995; *Tales of the Knights Templar,* edited by Katherine Kurtz, Warner, 1995; *Otherwere,* edited by Laura Anne Gilman and Keith R. A. DeCandido, Berkley/Ace, 1996; *A Nightmare's Dozen,* edited by Stearns, Harcourt, Brace, 1996; *Bruce Coville's Book of Spine Tinglers,* edited by Coville, Scholastic, 1996; *High-Tech Wars #2,* edited by Jerry Pournelle and John H. Carr; *On Crusade: More Tales of the Knights Templar,* edited by Kurz, Warner, 1998; and *Not of Woman Born,* edited by Constance Ash, Roc, 1999. Contributor to *Timewalker* comic-book series, Valiant Comics, 1995.

Sidelights

In close collaboration with his wife, Debra Doyle, James D. Macdonald writes science fiction and fantasy for children, young adults, and adults. Acknowledging both sides of their productive collaboration, Macdonald explained: "I have final say on the plot and characters, she has final say on the words and descriptions." This division of creative duties has produced dozens of novels, including the award-winning young-adult titles *Knight's Wyrd* and *Groogleman* as well as the popular "Mageworld" fantasy/sci-fi series.

Macdonald and Doyle's first series, the six-novel "Circle of Magic," is intended for an elementary and middle-school audience. The series focuses on Randal, an apprentice wizard whom readers meet as he begins wizard school at age twelve in the aptly titled *School of Wizardry.* In *Tournament and Tower* Randal graduates from the School of Wizardry although he must refrain from using his magic until Master Wizard Balpesh forgives him for breaking a pledge not to use a weapon. While working as a squire for his cousin Walter, Walter becomes seriously hurt, and Randal must seek out Balpesh and regain his magical powers in order to heal the injured man. Randall reaches age fifteen in *City by the Sea,* and as a journeyman wizard embarks on a hazardous journey as a result of a deathbed promise. *The Prince's Players* finds Randal and friend Lys visiting the court of Prince Vespian, where they encounter a corrupt master wizard and a dangerous adversary who seeks to overthrow the prince. Randal confronts an old enemy in *The Prisoner of Bell Castle,* while *The High King's Daughter* follows Randal and company as they journey into Elfland to rescue the High King's daughter, and restore her to her rightful throne. Praising the first volume of the series, *School Library Journal* reviewer Paul M. Kienlen dubbed the "Circle of Magic" series "masterfully rendered."

Geared for slightly older readers, the fantasy novel *Knight's Wyrd* combines a realistic story of knighthood with fantasy elements such as magic, dragons, and wizards. Just as young Will Odosson is about to be knighted, the castle wizard predicts his wyrd, or fate: Will is not destined to inherit his father's title and lands and will soon meet death. Although the wizard's prophecy comes to pass, it does not occur in the manner the boy expects. A young man of strong character, Will ignores his fate and becomes a knight. Leaving home to seek adventure, he rescues Isobel, his betrothed, is double-crossed by a duke, and becomes entangled in high magic as his destiny is fulfilled. A *Kirkus Reviews* critic praised *Knight's Wyrd* for its "strong sense of time, place, and code of honor." A *Horn Book* reviewer called *Knight's Wyrd* "a lively story," and a *School Library Journal* critic recommended it as "suspenseful" with a lively tempo.

Groogleman centers around thirteen-year-old Dan Henchard, a student healer who must save his teacher, Leezie, a natural healer, from her abductor. Dan, believing the kidnapper is the Groogleman, travels to the Dead Lands in search of Leezie, knowing that failure means certain death for him. Along the way he receives

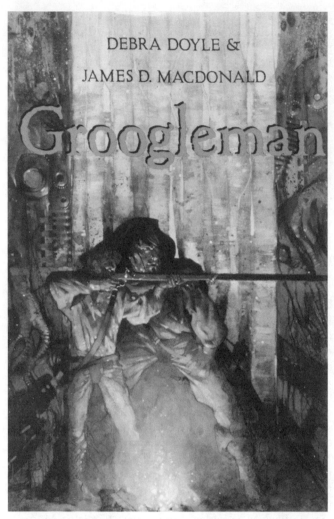

DEBRA DOYLE &

JAMES D. MACDONALD

Groogleman

A collaboration between Macdonald and wife Debra Doyle, this sci-fi fantasy follows a young teen as he aids a local healer during a plague that also brings forth the dreaded grooglemen, who behead plague victims and burn their homes.

help from a hunter named Joshua and in the process learns much more about himself. Selections from "historical documents" introduce each chapter and provide clues to the secret purpose of the Groogleman. A reviewer for *Realms of Fantasy* magazine wrote that *Groogleman* is "filled with adventure and action—a must read," and a *Science Fiction Chronicle* writer praised it as "an old fashioned post-collapse adventure."

In *Bad Blood,* the first installment of the spine-tingling series that shares its name, Macdonald and Doyle focus on a group of friends sharing hair-raising tales around a campfire. Valerie Sherwood and her friends do not for a minute believe any of the stories they hear are based in fact; after all, Jay's strange tale of moonlight and werewolves is just make believe. Right? But that night, when they hear a large creature prowling around the campsite, they remember Jay's words: "By morning, you'll all be dead." In *Hunters' Moon* Valerie attempts to live like a normal teen despite the fact that she is now a werewolf, but when her town is threatened by a group of vampires, she harnesses her new powers to protect

her home town. *Judgement Night* finds the teen werewolf haunted by the Wendigo, an ancient force that calls to her from the nearby mountains and thrives on her fear.

Macdonald and Doyle's most popular series, "Mageworld," was begun in 1992 and features a mix of science fiction and high fantasy. The long-running saga focuses on a five-centuries-long conflict between the human population of Entibor, a planet in the Republic galaxy, and the residents of the mysterious Mageworld in the Eraasian system, civilizations that share a common ancestry but have long been separated by a vast insterstellar gap. In series opener *The Price of the Stars* Beka Rosselin-Metadi is tired of constantly hearing about her parents' heroic roles in the Republic' history. When her mother is murdered on the Senate floor, however, the brave young woman experiences a newfound pride in her heritage and vows to bring the assassin to justice. Her father offers her *Warhammer,* his cherished ship, for her use in capturing the murderer. As the plot develops, Beka plans her own demise so that she can, with a new identity, do battle with the dangerous enemies plotting to harm her world.

As Beka continues the search for the man who arranged her mother's murder in *Starpilot's Grave,* it is revealed that a group of Magelords have breached the Republic's stronghold. Beka infiltrates the Magezone and learns that the Republic is far more vulnerable than she ever imagined. Despite her efforts, the Magelords have triumphed over the Republic by the third book of the series, *By Honor Betray'd.* Confronted with betrayal and surrounded by enemies, Beka now strives to reclaim what she can from the wreckage of her formal world.

With *The Gathering Flame,* the fourth installment in the "Mageworld" series, readers begin to cycle back through time. *The Gathering Flame* describes Beka's parents' contributions to the Republic's ongoing struggle against the Magelords, and also chronicles the attempts by these powerful Eraasian wizards to ravage the rival Repubic galaxy, planet by planet. However, the Magelords must take on several individuals to succeed in their plans: Perada Rosselin, Domina of Entibor; Jos Metadi, a notorious privateer who prefers to battle Mage ships one on one; and Errec Ransome, a man acquainted with the customs of the Magelords but with confidences he will not reveal. When the Magelords attack Entibor, the three are forced to unite and work together. *The Long Hunt,* which takes place after the second Magewar, finds Entibor facing a renewed attack by the Magelords. Meanwhile, on planet Khesat, a crisis unfolds and suddenly all depends on young Jens Metadi-Jessan D'Rosselin, the unwilling heir to the Khesat. Warring factions and criminal guilds know that control of the heir means control of Khesat and the galaxy, but young Jens avoids intrigue and instead sets off with his cousin Faral in search of off-planet adventure elsewhere.

Moving back to the beginning of the "Magewar" history, *The Stars Asunder* explores the root of the five-century conflict by introducing apprentice mage Arekhon Khreseio sus Khalgath and Garrod, a wizard who gathers together a mage circle in order to fuel his transport to the other side of the interstellar void. Before others can follow, the mage circle is shattered by the villainous Kief Diasul, and as Arekhon moves into a leadership role the die is cast: two parallel mage-run civilizations now begin their separate paths toward ultimate future conflict. *A Working of Stars* continues the saga, as Arekhon is haunted by prophecies that push him to attempt to reform the mage circle and locate Garrad. Now living quietly on Entibor, Arekhon learns that if he does not return to the Eraasian galaxy and join the efforts to close the great gap and reunite the two galaxies, the consequences will be tragic.

Reviews of the "Mageworld" novels have been positive, many reviewers noting the "swashbuckling space opera" quality of the series, as *Library Journal* contributor Jackie Cassasa termed it. While writing that "high technologies such as spaceships and robots interact seamlessly with what appear to be magical powers," *SFSite.com* reviewer Rich Horton added in a review of *The Stars Asunder* that Macdonald and Doyle's "rigorous approach to the use of the magical system, as well as . . . the space-going setting," makes the series more science fiction than fantasy. Reviewing *The Long Hunt* for *Locus,* Carolyn Cushman called the "Mageworld" series "a space opera with unusual depth, and some wonderful characters," while *Booklist* critic Roland Green described Macdonald and Doyle's books as "imaginative, intelligent, [and] fast-paced."

In addition to collaborating with his wife, Macdonald is also the author of *The Apocalypse Door,* which features what *Library Journal* contributor Cassada described as a "bare-bones style." Macdonald's "fast-paced tale" mixes supernatural powers, modern military intrigue, and a rivalry between two medieval orders: the Knights Templar and the Teutonic Knights. One of the thirty-three priests of the Knights' Templar, Peter Crossman works with fellow Templars Maggie and Simon to track down a U.N. peacekeeping force that has mysteriously disappeared from its assignment in Jerusalem. When the trio stumble on a barrel of demonic fungi, they find themselves embroiled in a Satanist plot that threatens to bring on the end of days. A *Publishers Weekly* reviewer praised Macdonald's solo outing, describing *The Apocalypse Door* as an "inventive melange of hard-boiled thriller and speculative fantasy," while in *Kirkus Reviews* a critic deemed the work a "breezy spy spoof" in which the author "sweetens his farce with puns, comic asides, references to *The Man from U.N.C.L.E.,* and . . . wonderfully bad Hemingway." Noting that other novels "have blended mysticism, mystery, and fantasy," the *Publishers Weekly* contributor concluded that "few have done it as smartly or succinctly as this one."

Biographical and Critical Sources

BOOKS

Macdonald, James D., and Debra Doyle, *Bad Blood,* Berkley (New York, NY), 1993.

PERIODICALS

Analog Science Fiction and Fact, February, 1999, Tom Easton, review of *The Stars Asunder,* p. 132; October, 2002, Tom Easton, review of *A Working of Stars,* p. 311; April, 2003, Tom Easton, review of *The Apocalypse Door,* p. 134.
Booklist, November 15, 1992, pp. 589-590; August, 2000, Roland Green, review of *Requiem for Boone,* p. 2124; April 15, 2002, Roland Green, review of *A Working of Stars,* p. 1387.
Bulletin of the Center for Children's Books, February, 1993, pp. 173-174; December, 1996, Janice M. Del Negro, review of *Groogleman,* p. 132.
Horn Book, January-February, 1993, review of *Knight's Wyrd,* pp. 89-90; March-April, 1996, p. 202.
Kirkus Reviews, October 1, 1992, review of *Knight's Wyrd,* p. 1253; March 1, 2002, review of *A Working of Stars,* p. 297; October 1, 2002, review of *The Apocalypse Door,* p. 1434.
Library Journal, November 15, 2002, Jackie Cassada, review of *The Apocalypse Door,* p. 105.
Locus, August, 1995.
Publishers Weekly, May 31, 2000, review of *The Stars Asunder,* p. 72; August 7, 2000, review of *Requiem for Boone,* p. 80; March 11, 2002, review of *A Working of Stars,* p. 56; October 14, 2002, review of *The Apocalypse Door,* p. 68.
Realms of Fantasy, April, 1997, review of *Groogleman.*
School Library Journal, November, 1992, p. 90; December, 1996, Susan L. Rogers, review of *Groogleman,* pp. 120, 122; April 2002, Paul M. Kienlen, review of *School of Wizardry,* p. 63; November, 2002, review of *A Working of Stars,* p. 194.
Science Fiction Chronicle, April-May, 1997, review of *Groogleman.*
Voice of Youth Advocates, June, 1993, Jennifer A. Long, review of *Knight's Wyrd,* p. 102; June, 2001, review of *Requiem of Boone,* p. 132.

ONLINE

BookLoons, http://www.bookloons.com/ (October 20, 2005), Wesley Williamson, review of *A Working of Stars.*
Doyle and Macdonald Web site, http://www.sff.net/people/doylemacdonald (October 20, 2005).
SFSite.com, http://www.sfsite.com/ (October 20, 2005), Rich Horton, review of *The Stars Asunder.**

*   *   *

MAYO, Margaret 1935-

Personal

Born May 10, 1935, in London, England; daughter of William John and Anna (Macleod) Cumming; married

Margaret Mayo

Peter Robin Mayo (a university lecturer), July 28, 1958; children: Roderick, Katrina, Andrew. *Education:* University of Southampton, B.Sc. (with honors), 1956, certificate in education, 1957.

Addresses

Home—85 Peacock Lane, Brighton, Sussex BN1 6WA, England. *Agent*—c/o Author Mail, Orchard Books, Hachette Children's Books, 338 Euston Rd., London NW1 3BH, England.

Career

Writer, 1974—. Teacher at numerous schools in England, 1957-61, 1969-71, 1973-75, and 1975-80.

Awards, Honors

Aesop Accolade, Children's Folklore Society/American Folklore Society, 1996, for *When the World Was Young: Creation and Pourquois Tales.*

Writings

(Compiler) *If You Should Meet a Crocodile, and Other Verse,* illustrated by Carol Barker, Kaye & Ward (London, England), 1974.

(Reteller) *The Book of Magical Horses,* illustrated by Victor Ambrus, Kaye & Ward (London, England), 1976, Hastings House (New York, NY), 1977.

(Reteller) *The Book of Magical Birds,* illustrated by Fiona French, Kaye & Ward (London, England), 1977.

(Reteller) *The Book of Magical Cats,* illustrated by Victor Ambrus, Kaye & Ward (London, England), 1978.

Saints, Birds, and Beasts, illustrated by Cara Lockhart Smith, Kaye & Ward (London, England), 1980.

The Italian Fairy Book, illustrated by Cara Lockhart Smith, Kaye & Ward (London, England), 1981.

Fairy Tales from France, illustrated by Cara Lockhart Smith, Kaye & Ward (London, England), 1983.

Little Mouse Twitchy Whiskers, illustrated by Penny Dann, Orchard (London, England), 1992.

(Reteller) *The Orchard Book of Magical Tales,* illustrated by Jane Ray, Orchard (London, England), 1993, published as *Magical Tales from Many Lands,* Dutton (New York, NY), 1993.

(Reteller) *How to Count Crocodiles,* illustrated by Emily Bolam, Orion (London, England), 1994, published as *Tortoise's Flying Lesson: Animal Stories,* Harcourt Brace (New York, NY), 1995.

(Reteller) *First Fairy Tales,* illustrated by Selina Young, Orchard (London, England), 1994, Barnes and Noble Books (New York, NY), 1996.

(Reteller) *The Orchard Book of Creation Stories,* illustrated by Louise Brierley, Orchard (London, England), 1995, published as *When the World Was Young: Creation and Pourquois Tales,* Simon & Schuster (New York, NY), 1996.

(Reteller) *How the Earth Was Made; Why People Shouldn't Be So Greedy,* illustrated by Tony Ross, Orchard (London, England), 1998.

(Reteller) *How Men and Women Were Mad: Why People Do Not Live Forever; Why the Sun Travels Slowly,* illustrated by Tony Ross, Orchard (London, England), 1998.

(Reteller) *The Orchard Book of Mythical Birds and Beasts,* illustrated by Jane Ray, Orchard (London, England), 1996, published as *Mythical Birds and Beasts from Many Lands,* Dutton (New York, NY), 1997, published as *The Orchard Book of the Unicorn and Other Magical Animals,* illustrated by Jane Ray, Orchard (London, England), 2001.

(Reteller) *How the Sun Was Made; Why the Moon Appears at Night; How People Were Given Fire,* illustrated by Tony Ross, Orchard (London, England), 1998.

(Reteller) *First Bible Stories,* illustrated by Nicola Smee, Barron's Educational (Hauppauge, NY), 1998.

(Reteller) *Why the Sea Is Salt; Why People Come in Different Colors,* illustrated by Tony Ross, Orchard (London, England), 1998.

Brother Sun, Sister Moon: The Story of St. Francis, illustrated by Peter Malone, Orion (London, England), 1999, Little Brown (Boston, MA), 2000.

Sleepytime Stories, illustrated by Penny Dann, Orchard (London, England), 1999.

Plum Pudding, Orchard (London, England), 2000, published as *Wiggle Waggle Fun: Stories and Rhymes for the Very, Very Young,* Knopf (New York, NY), 2002, published as *The Orchard Book of Favourite Stories and Poems,* 2003.

Hoddley Poddley, 2001, published as *The Orchard Book of Favourite Rhymes and Verse,* Orchard (London, England), 2003.

Dig Dig Digging, illustrated by Alex Ayliffe, Orchard (London, England), 2001, Holt (New York, NY), 2002.

(Reteller) *Cinderella,* illustrated by Philip Norman, Orchard (London, England), 2002.

(Reteller) *Hansel and Gretel,* illustrated by Philip Norman, Orchard (London, England), 2002.

(Reteller) *Sleeping Beauty,* illustrated by Philip Norman, Orchard (London, England), 2002.

(Reteller) *Snow White and the Seven Dwarves,* illustrated by Philip Norman, Orchard (London, England), 2002.

(Reteller) *Jack and the Beanstalk,* illustrated by Philip Norman, Orchard (London, England), 2002.

Emergency!, illustrated by Alex Ayliffe, Carolrhoda (Minneapolis, MN), 2002.

(Reteller) *Rumplestiltskin,* illustrated by Philip Norman, Orchard (London, England), 2002.

(Reteller) *Unanana and the Enormous Elephant; and, The Feathered Snake,* illustrated by Peter Bailey, Orchard (London, England), 2003.

(Reteller) *The Incredible Thunderbird; and, Baba Yaga Bony-legs,* illustrated by Peter Bailey, Orchard (London, England), 2003.

(Reteller) *The Giant Sea Serpent; and, The Unicorn,* illustrated by Peter Bailey, Orchard (London, England), 2003.

(Reteller) *The Fiery Phoenix; and, The Lemon Princess,* illustrated by Peter Bailey, Orchard (London, England), 2003.

(Reteller) *The Man-eating Minotaur; and, The Magic Fruit,* illustrated by Peter Bailey, Orchard (London, England), 2003.

(Reteller) *The Magical Mermaid; and, Kate Crackernuts,* illustrated by Peter Bailey, Orchard (London, England), 2003.

(Reteller) *The Daring Dragon; and, The Kingdom under the Sea,* illustrated by Peter Bailey, Orchard (London, England), 2003.

(Reteller) *Pegasus the Proud Prince; and, The Flying Carpet,* illustrated by Peter Bailey, Orchard (London, England), 2003.

Choo Choo Clickety-Clack!, illustrated by Alex Ayliffe, Orchard (London, England), 2004, Carolrhoda (Minneapolis, MN), 2005.

Sidelights

Margaret Mayo is a reteller of fairy tales and the author of picture books for very young readers. Mayo's work is distinguished by her careful selection of little-known but delightful tales from around the world, by her talent for engaging narration, and by her passion for her work. As she once told *SATA,* she hopes to preserve the oral storytelling tradition as well as unique stories worthy of being passed down to new generations. Mayo selects "stories that have passed the most difficult of tests—the test of time," as she explained; tales that "can still entertain and satisfy emotionally like no others. They are a precious part of our common heritage, and if our children are also to share it, then the tales must be told afresh to them."

Mayo began her career as a writer in the mid-1970s with *If You Should Meet a Crocodile, and Other Verse,* a collection of short rhymes, poems, and limericks penned by both famous and anonymous poets. Her first book for older readers contains thirteen fairytales about horses. *The Book of Magical Horses* tells of an enchanted mule, a winged horse, and even a water horse. A reviewer for *Junior Bookshelf* described the stories as "typically vigorous and full of action," and a *Booklist* contributor wrote that they are "told in an assured, conventional style." Mayo has also assembled similar collections featuring magical birds and cats.

Magical Tales from Many Lands, which includes fourteen folktales and comes complete with endnotes citing origins and sources, focuses on the magic that works wonders for people around the world, from Arabians and Australians to Zulus. There is a story about a king from the Caribbean, a Baba Yaga tale from Russia, a Native American tale about the morning star, a story from Peru, and a tale from China. "The stories read aloud well," observed Carolyn Phelan in a *Booklist* review. A critic for *Kirkus Reviews* described the collection as "remarkably felicitous" and added: "Mayo has chosen splendidly." A *Publishers Weekly* contributor cited the volume's "lively vocabulary" and "fine sense of theater," and dubbed the collection "a winner" whether read story by story or all at one sitting. "Mayo's book will work its magic on all who open it," asserted Barbara Chatton in *School Library Journal.*

How to Count Crocodiles, like Mayo's *If You Should Meet a Crocodile, and Other Verses,* is a collection for young children. In the words of *Magpies* contributor Nola Allen, these eight stories are told with "exuberance." Containing tales drawn from the folklore of Africa, Indonesia, Japan, and other countries, the book features a monkey, an eagle, a tortoise, crocodiles, rabbits, elephants, a hippopotamus, bears, a lion, and other animals and as a *Junior Bookshelf* critic noted, casts these creatures in "many amusing incidents, animal noises, tricks and games." The collection—published in the United States as *Tortoise's Flying Lesson: Animal Stories*—"brims with both vigor and cheer," wrote a contributor to *Publishers Weekly.* "What an engaging collection!" exclaimed Harriett Fargnoli in a *School Library Journal* review.

When the World Was Young: Creation and Pourquois Tales provides ten retold tales which explain some familiar aspect of life on Earth. Like Mayo's other collections, the focus here is multicultural: A Native-American story explains how fire gets in trees, a Polynesian story centers on the sun, a tale from Ghana discusses human skin color, a tale from Iceland explains why salt is in the sea, and a story from Egypt tells how the moon came to the sky. The work comes with a foreword and source notes. According to Susan Hepler in a *School Library Journal* review, in *When the World Was Young* Mayo speaks to her audience and offers "connections for today's youngsters." A *Publishers Weekly* reviewer described the retellings as "lively" and "suspenseful" and called Mayo a "masterful" storyteller.

Mythical Birds and Beasts from Many Lands provides ten tales of fantastic creatures from dragons to unicorns. A Thunderbird from Native-American folklore and an ancient Aztec Quetzalcoatl are featured alongside mermaids, serpents, and other creatures from Greek mythology. Once again, Mayo's storytelling talents were praised by critics. "Mayo lends the oral cadence of a storyteller's voice to these tales of enchantment," wrote a *Kirkus Reviews* contributor, while in *Publishers Weekly* a critic stated that "Mayo's energetically paced versions possess a lively intensity that never fails to entertain."

In *Brother Sun, Sister Moon: The Life and Stories of St. Francis* Mayo combines the true history and biography of St. Francis with myths about the saint's life, drawing a distinction between life and legend. After recounting the saint's life, Mayo explains what happened after his death, including information regarding his canonization and the formation of the Franciscan Order. The book concludes with "The Canticle of Brother Sun," a poem written by St. Francis. "By the time readers find St. Francis's own 'Canticle of Brother Sun,' . . . they'll know how to appreciate it," commented a reviewer for *Publishers Weekly*. Wendy Lukehart, writing in *School Library Journal*, considered the picture book "a highly readable and aesthetically appealing portrait." *Booklist* contributor Carolyn Phelan called *Brother Sun, Sister Moon* a "most beautiful portrayal," adding that it is "written with simplicity and grace."

Wiggle Waggle Fun: Stories and Rhymes for the Very Very Young is a collection of thirty-four stories, poems, and songs, some as short as four lines and others long enough for bedtime reading. Included among the stories are counting exercises, original stories, and retellings of traditional tales. The collection is "an ideal showcase for twenty-four illustrators," commented a *Publishers Weekly* reviewer, while Melinda Piehler pointed out in *School Library Journal* that some of the illustrators, including Jane Ray, Tony Ross, and Lauren Child, are well known to young readers, while others may be encountered for the first time. Piehler noted that "children will likely want to turn again and again to their favorite sections." A *Kirkus Reviews* contributor stated that, of all the stories and poems included, there is "not a bad one in the bunch," and Gillian Engberg noted in *Booklist* that Mayo's selections "reverberate with noise-making nonsense and giggly fun [in] language just right for the very young." *Christian Parenting Today* contributor Carla Barnhill predicted that the book's "poems and songs will provide hours of cuddle time."

Mayo has collaborated with artist Alex Ayliffe on a series of picture books about vehicles, starting with *Dig Dig Digging*. Featuring construction trucks, rescue helicopters, and nine other work vehicles, the book ex-plains the purpose of each vehicle and includes the noises and actions each makes as it does its job. A contributor to *Kirkus Reviews* noted the pairing of "simple rhymes and bold illustrations," while a *Publishers Weekly* contributor cited Mayo's use of "plenty of colorful adjectives and terse verbs." Alice Casey Smith, writing in *School Library Journal*, viewed the text as "visual word poems about large trucks, tractors, and cranes," and *Booklist* critic Hazel Rochman deemed *Dig Dig Digging* "a bright, noisy book to connect words and pictures with the excitement of the building site and the vroom of the streets."

Mayo and Ayliffe's second collaboration, *Emergency!*, focuses on fire trucks, ambulances, life boats, and snow plows. A *Kirkus Reviews* contributor commented that "Children will practically hear the sirens wail" as they read and follow the pictures from one emergency to the next. "Eager listeners . . . will want to revisit the scenes," commented Lisa Dennis in her review for *School Library Journal*. Another title in the series, *Choo Choo Clickety-Clack!*, also focuses on the noises made by vehicles such as airplanes, race cars, and trains. Commenting on the love toddlers have for motion, Ilene Cooper wrote in *Booklist* that *Choo Choo Clickety-Clack!* "brilliantly captures that rush in raucous words and eye-popping art." Julie Roach, writing for *School Library Journal*, considered the book "a surefire selection" where "toddlers and preschoolers go 'Zippity-zip' or 'RoarrrRR!'," while a *Kirkus Reviews* contributor cited Mayo's "snappy text," which "abounds with verbs to savor."

Biographical and Critical Sources

PERIODICALS

Biography, winter, 2001, Kevin Kelly, review of *Brother Sun, Sister Moon: The Life and Stories of St. Francis*, p. 326.

Booklist, November 15, 1977, review of *The Book of Magical Horses*, p. 552; November 1, 1993, Carolyn Phelan, review of *Magical Tales from Many Lands*, p. 517; September 1, 1996, pp. 122-123; March 1, 2000, Carolyn Phelan, review of *Brother Sun, Sister Moon*, p. 1242; October 1, 2000, Ilene Cooper, review of *Brother Sun, Sister Moon*, p. 358; February 1, 2002, review of *Wiggle Waggle Fun: Stories and Rhymes for the Very Young*, p. 942; May 15, 2002, Hazel Rochman, review of *Dig Dig Digging*, p. 1598; August, 2002, Carolyn Phelan, review of *Emergency!*, p. 1974; February 15, 2002, Ilene Cooper, review of *Choo Choo Clickety-Clack!*, p. 1079.

Bulletin of the Center for Children's Books, March, 2000, review of *Brother Sun, Sister Moon*, p. 250.

Christian Parenting Today, March, 2002, Carla Barnhill, review of *Wiggle Waggle Fun*, p. 50.

Commonweal, November 20, 1998, review of *First Bible Stories*, p. 23.

Growing Point, April, 1975, review of *If You Should Meet a Crocodile, and Other Verse,* p. 2605; November, 1977, p. 3203.

Horn Book, January-February, 1994, pp. 77-78; May, 2000, Mary M. Burns, review of *Brother Sun, Sister Moon,* p. 336.

Junior Bookshelf, August, 1976, review of *The Book of Magical Horses,* p. 207; December, 1978, p. 302; February, 1981, review of *Saints, Birds, and Beasts,* p. 23; June, 1995, review of *How to Count Crocodiles,* p. 101.

Kirkus Reviews, September 1, 1993, review of *Magical Tales from Many Lands,* p. 1148; May 1, 1997, review of *Mythical Birds and Beasts from Many Lands,* p. 725; December 1, 2001, review of *Wiggle Waggle Fun,* p. 1687; April 15, 2002, review of *Dig Dig Digging,* p. 574; August 15, 2002, review of *Emergency!,* p. 1229; March 15, 2002, review of *Choo Choo Clickety-Clack!,* p. 354.

Magpies, May, 1995, Nola Allen, review of *How to Count Crocodiles,* p. 29.

Publishers Weekly, September 6, 1993, review of *Magical Tales from Many Lands,* p. 91; May 1, 1995, review of *Tortoise's Flying Lesson: Animal Stories,* pp. 58-59; October 21, 1996, review of *When the World Was Young,* p. 85; April 14, 1997, review of *Mythical Birds and Beasts from Many Lands,* p. 73; March 13, 2000, review of *Brother Sun, Sister Moon,* p. 82; December 10, 2001, review of *Wiggle Waggle Fun,* p. 68; April 8, 2002, review of *Dig Dig Digging,* p. 225; August 5, 2002, review of *Emergency!,* p. 71.

School Library Journal, May, 1993, p. 57; September, 1993, Barbara Chatton, review of *Magical Tales from Many Lands,* p. 226; May, 1995, Harriett Fargnoli, review of *Tortoise's Flying Lesson: Animal Stories,* p. 101; December, 1996, Susan Helper, review of *When the World Was Young,* p. 116; April, 2000, Wendy Lukehart, review of *Brother Sun, Sister Moon,* p. 123; January, 2002, Melinda Piehler, review of *Wiggle Waggle Fun,* p. 121; May, 2002, Alice Casey Smith, review of *Dig Dig Digging,* p. 141; October, 2002, Lisa Dennis, review of *Emergency!,* p. 120; May, 2005, Julie Roach, review of *Choo Choo Clickety-Clack!,* p. 92.

Times Educational Supplement, September 30, 1983, p. 48.

*   *   *

McKAY, Sharon E. 1954-

Personal

Born 1954, in Montreal, Quebec, Canada; married David MacLeod; children: two sons. *Education:* York University, B.A.

Addresses

Home and office—Box 729, Kilbride, Ontario L0P 1G0, Canada. *E-mail*—Dmcmac111@aol.com.

Career

Writer and journalist. Worked in radio and film; former television host. Member, Christian Jewish Dialogue.

Member

Writer's Union of Canada, International Board on Books for Young People, Canadian Society of Children's Authors, Illustrators, and Performers.

Awards, Honors

Govenor General's Award shortlist, 2000, Mr. Christie Award, IODE Violet Downey Book Award, and Geoffery Bilson Award for Historical Fiction, all 2001, and International Board on Books for Young People (IBBY) Award, Hackmatack Children's Choice Book Award, White Raven Award, UNESCO International Youth Library, and Our Choice Selection, Canadian Children's Book Centre, all 2002, all for *Charlie Wilcox;* IBBY honor list designation, 2002, for *Charlie Wilcox's Great War;* Governor General's Award shortlist, Notable Book of Jewish Content designation, Association of Jewish Libraries, Hamilton Literary Award, and Sydney Taylor Book Award, all 2004, all for *Esther.*

Writings

FOR CHILDREN

Chalk around the Block, Somerville House Publishing (Toronto, Ontario, Canada), 1993.

The Picky Eater: Recipes and Survival Tips for Parents of Fussy Eaters, HarperCollins Publishers (Toronto, Ontario, Canada), 1993.

The Halloween Book, Sommerville House Publishers (Toronto, Ontario, Canada), 1994.

The Official Kick-the-Can Games Book, Sommerville House Publishing (Toronto, Ontario, Canada), 1994.

Take a Hike, Scholastic (Richmond Hill, Ontario, Canada), 1995.

Pat-a-Cake Dough Book, illustrated by Marilyn Mets, Sommerville House Publishing (Toronto, Ontario, Canada), 1996.

Make-a-Face: Book and Body Painting Kit for Kids of All Ages, Sommerville House Publishers (Toronto, Ontario, Canada), 1996.

Time Capsule for the Twenty-first Century, illustrated by Donna Reynolds, Sommerville House Publishers (Toronto, Ontario, Canada), 1998.

Charlie Wilcox, Stoddart Kids (Toronto, Ontario, Canada), 2000.

Timothy Tweedle, the First Christmas Elf, illustrated by Stephanie Pyren Fortel, Blamur Publishers (Toronto, Ontario, Canada), 2000.

A Bee in Karley's Bonnet, Balmur (Toronto, Ontario, Canada), 2001.

Harley's Blue Day, Balmur (Toronto, Ontario, Canada), 2001.

What Are Friends For?, Balmur (Toronto, Ontario, Canada), 2001.

Rodney's Race, Balmur (Toronto, Ontario, Canada), 2001.

Charlie Wilcox's Great War, Penguin Canada (Toronto, Ontario, Canada), 2002.

Esther, Penguin Canada (Toronto, Ontario, Canada), 2004.

FOR CHILDREN; "OUR CANADIAN GIRL" SERIES

Penelope: Terror in the Harbour, Penguin Books (Toronto, Ontario, Canada), 2002.

Penelope: The Glass Castle, Penguin Canada (Toronto, Ontario, Canada), 2002.

Penelope: An Irish Penny, Penguin Canada (Toronto, Ontario, Canada), 2003.

Penelope: Christmas Reunion, Penguin Canada (Toronto, Ontario, Canada), 2004.

OTHER

The New Child Safety Handbook, Macmillan of Canada (Toronto, Ontario, Canada), 1988.

The New Parent Survival Handbook, Macmillan of Canada (Toronto, Ontario, Canada), 1990.

Sidelights

Sharon E. McKay's long career as a writer has found her working for a variety of mediums, including newspaper, magazines, radio, and film as well as penning both fiction and nonfiction books. At one point, she even worked as a host on Canadian television, but the experience, while an opportunity to try something new, held little appeal to the Canadian writer, who has since made a name for herself as a children's book author. Beginning with nonfiction, McKay has produced a number of novels for middle-grade readers, among them the award-winning *Esther*, based on the true story of Esther Brandeau, a Jewish teen who rejects an oppressive, ghettoized life in eighteenth-century France and bravely strikes out on her own for the New World, surviving by taking up the disguise and the skills of a young seaman. Other books include the sequential novels *Charlie Wilcox* and *Charlie Wilcox's Great War*, as well as several volumes in the "Our Canadian Girl" series.

Featuring an Irish-Canadian girl named Penelope Reid, McKay's "Penelope" books in the "Our Canadian Girl" series follow Penny as she deals with family, friends, and multicultural Montreal society during and after the years Canada fought alongside the British in World War I. Reviewing the fourth book in the series, *Penelope: Christmas Reunion*, David Ward wrote in *Resource Links* that the author "has skillfully captured the post-war sentiment in upper-class Canada," while in another *Resource Links* review Connie Forst dubbed Penny "a courageous and gutsy young girl."

The fourteen-year-old protagonist of *Charlie Wilcox* also finds himself living in the midst of World War I. Marked for failure by a clubfoot and unhappy with his life in Newfoundland, Charlie plans to become a stowaway on a sealing vessel, determined to become a seal hunter like his father. Instead, the teen finds himself on a ship full of Canadian troops making their way to France in 1916. Put to work as a stretcher bearer in a French hospital near the front lines, Charlie sees first-hand the brutal side of war, but when given the chance to go home he declines and passes the opportunity to a less-fortunate friend. Moving to the front lines, he witnesses the Battle of the Somme and saves a friend's life before being assigned to a French field hospital. Describing the work as a "riveting story of friendship, loyalty, bravery, and honor," *School Library Journal* reviewer Nancy P. Reeder praised *Charlie Wilcox* for its "finely drawn" characters, action-packed plot, and its focus on "ordinary people caught in extraordinary events doing what they believe to be right."

Charlie's story is continued in *Charlie Wilcox's Great War*, which recalls the final months of his war experiences through the narration of hometown friend Claire. Finally returned home after the armistice is called, Charlie tells Claire his story: his experiences being shot down behind enemy lines; his long wait in the trenches amid the dead and dying, waiting for the cover of night to make his escape; and his difficulties in readjusting to life in Newfoundland after witnessing such carnage. Noting the larger-than-life themes of the book, a *Books in Canada* contributor praised the novel as "an epic story that's also touchingly human in its graphic detail, fleeting friendships and innate responses to danger." According to Joan Marshall in *Resource Links*, *Charlie Wilcox's Great War* "is full of snappy dialogue and adventuresome plot twists that work because of the chaos of war, and will attract teenage boys."

Biographical and Critical Sources

PERIODICALS

Atlantic Books Today, summer, 2000, review of *Charlie Wilcox*.

Bookbird, annual, 2001, review of *Charlie Wilcox*, p. 59.

Books in Canada, September, 2001, review of *Penelope: Terror in the Harbour*, p. 35; summer, 2003, review of *Charlie Wilcox's Great War*, p. 47.

Canadian Book Review (annual), 2000, review of *Charlie Wilcox*, p. 494; 2001, review of *Penelope: Terror in the Harbour*, p. 504.

Canadian Children's Literature, spring, 2001, review of *Charlie Wilcox*, p. 184.

Canadian Review of Materials, September 22, 2000, review of *Charlie Wilcox*; June, 22, 2001, review of *Timothy Tweedle, the First Christmas Elf*; December 14, 2001, review of *Penelope: Terror in the Harbour*; April 25, 2003, review of *Penelope: The Glass Castle*; June 20, 2003, review of *Charlie Wilcox's Great War*.

Maclean's, April 30, 2001, review of *Charlie Wilcox*, p. 54.

Quill and Quire, July, 1990, review of *The New Parent Survival Handbook,* p. 58; June, 1993, review of *Picky Eater: Recipes and Survival Tips for Parents of Fussy Eaters,* p. 29; February, 2000, review of *Charlie Wilcox,* p. 48.

Resource Links, February, 1999, review of *Time Capsule for the Twenty-first Century,* p. 15; October, 2000, review of *Charlie Wilcox,* p. 28; October, 2001, review of *Penelope: Terror in the Harbour,* p. 18; February, 2003, Connie Frost, review of *Penelope: The Glass Castle,* p. 12; April, 2003, Joan Marshall, review of *Charlie Wilcox's Great War,* p. 35; December, 2004, Brendan White, review of *Esther,* p. 37; December, 2004, David Ward, review of *Penelope: Christmas Reunion,* p. 21.

School Library Journal, November, 2000, Nancy P. Reeder, review of *Charlie Wilcox,* p. 159.

ONLINE

Sharon McKay Home Page, http://www.sharonmckay.ca (October 7, 2005).

Writers Union of Canada Web site, http://www.writers union.ca/ (October 7, 2005), "Sharon E. McKay."

*   *   *

MILLER, Ruth White
See WHITE, Ruth C.

*   *   *

MORGAN, Douglas
See DOYLE, Debra

*   *   *

MORGAN, Douglas
See MACDONALD, James D.

*   *   *

MORRIS, Jill 1936-
(Jill Farrar)

Personal

Born March 28, 1936, in Brisbane, Queensland, Australia; daughter of Francis William (a clerk) and Jessie Isabel (a clerk; maiden name, McMurtrie) Farrar; married John Morris (a pharmacist), 1960 (marriage ended); married Richard Dent (an engineer), 1988; children: Katy, Belinda, John. *Education:* University of Queensland, B.A. and diploma in education; Trinity College, London, study in speech and drama. *Religion:* Church of England (Anglican).

Addresses

Home and office—Book Farm, 330 Reesville Rd., Maleny, Queensland 4552, Australia. *E-mail*—jillmorris@greaterglider.com.au.

Career

Writer. Bundaberg State High School, Bundaberg, Queensland, Australia, teacher; Australian Broadcasting Commission, 1957-78, began as radio programming producer, then television and film producer; freelance writer. Swinburne Institute, Melbourne, lecturer in graphic design, c. 1990; teacher at schools including University of Queensland, Victoria College, and Melbourne Council of Adult Education. Greater Glider Productions (publisher), Maleny, Queensland, Australia, co-founder and managing editor, 1983. Member, Australian Council Literature Board, 1976-79, Film Queensland advisory committee, 1994-96, and Sunshine Coast University College planning committee and council, 1993-99. Artist-in-Schools, 1985-88; participant in National Book Council tours, 1986 1990, 1994; writer-in-residence, Australia Council Literature Board, 1993.

Member

Australian Society of Authors (member of management committee, 1992-93), Australian Writers Guild, Society of Editors, Children's Book Council of Australia, Queensland Writers Centre (regional representative, 1993-94), Business and Tourism Association of Sunshine Coast, Blackall Range Tourism Association, Churchill Fellows Association, Peace of Green Multiple Artform Collective, Eco-Tourism Association of Australia.

Awards, Honors

Churchill fellow, 1972; Australia Council Literature Board grants, 1981, 1985; Arts Queensland publishing grant, 1994, and writing grants, 1995, 1996; senior fellow, University of Sunshine Coast, 2000; Dame Annabelle Rankin Award for children's literature, 2005.

Writings

Kolo the Bush Koala, illustrated by Rich Richardson, Golden (Sydney, New South Wales, Australia), 1973.

Rusty the Nimble Numbat, illustrated by Rich Richardson, Golden (Sydney, New South Wales, Australia), 1973.

Rufus the Red Kangaroo, illustrated by Rich Richardson, Golden (Sydney, New South Wales, Australia), 1973.

Percy the Peaceful Platypus, illustrated by Rich Richardson, Golden (Sydney, New South Wales, Australia), 1973.

Harry the Hairy-nosed Wombat (also see below), illustrated by Rich Richardson, Golden (Sydney, New South Wales, Australia), 1973.

Saturday Street, illustrated by Geoff Hocking, Viking/Puffin, 1983.

Monkey and the White Bone Demon, Penguin Putnam, 1984.

The Boy Who Painted the Sun, illustrated by Geoff Hocking, Kestrel, 1984.

Monkey Creates Havoc in Heaven, Penguin Putnam, 1989.

Australian Bats, illustrated by Lynne Tracey, Greater Glider (Maleny, Queensland, Australia), 1993.

Dido Has Diabetes, illustrated by Margie Chellew, Greater Glider (Maleny, Queensland, Australia), 1993.

Australian Owls, Frogmouths, and Nightjars, illustrated by Lynne Tracey, Greater Glider (Maleny, Queensland, Australia), 1993.

Australian Frogs, Amazing Amphibians, illustrated by Lynne Tracey, Greater Glider (Maleny, Queensland, Australia), 1996.

The Wombat Who Talked to the Stars: The Journal of a Northern Hairy-nosed Wombat, illustrated by Sharon Dye, Greater Glider (Maleny, Queensland, Australia), 1997.

Australian Kangaroos, Magnificent Macropods, illustrated by Lynne Muir, Greater Glider (Maleny, Queensland, Australia), 1998.

Mahogany the Mystery Glider (nonfiction), illustrated by Sharon Dye, Greater Glider (Maleny, Queensland, Australia), 1999.

Endangered! (stage plays), Greater Glider (Maleny, Queensland, Australia), 2000.

Kaleidoscope 2000: A Collection of Short Stories and Poems, Post Pressed (Flaxton, Queensland, Australia), 2000.

Frog Thunder, Greater Glider (Maleny, Queensland, Australia), 2001.

Kookaburra School, illustrated by Heather Gall, Greater Glider (Maleny, Queensland, Australia), 2002.

Silly Baby Magpie!, illustrated by Heather Gall, Greater Glider (Maleny, Queensland, Australia), 2003.

Harry the Hairy-nosed Wombat, and Other Australian Animal Tales, Greater Glider (Maleny, Queensland, Australia), 2003.

Golden Wombats, illustrated by Jane Burrell, Greater Glider (Maleny, Queensland, Australia), 2003.

The Environment Collection, Phoenix Education (Melbourne, Queensland, Australia), 2003.

Wombat down Below!, illustrated by Lucy Everitt, Greater Glider (Maleny, Queensland, Australia), 2004.

Koala Number One, illustrated by Heather Gall, Greater Glider (Maleny, Queensland, Australia), 2004.

Also author of numerous other books, including *Where Is Kangaroo?,* illustrated by Lynne Tracey, 1994; *Numbat, Run!; Dugong, Dive!; Golden Wombats,* illustrated by Tracey; and *Bunyip on the Obi Obi* (radio play), illustrated by Ian Steep, for Harcourt. Author of *Platypus Point,* illustrated by Tracey; and (with Belinda Nissen) *The Cod Hole,* photographs by Mark Nissen, for HarperCollins. Author of *Rainbow Warrior: Battle for the Planet* (nonfiction), for Omnibus; *Ghost of DropCroc* (novel), for Addison Wesley Longman; *Velvet the Flying Gecko,* illustrated by Bronwyn Searle, for Queensland Science Centre; *The Lady down the Road,* illustrated by Irena Sibley, for SilverGum/Allen & Unwin; *Almost a Dinosaur* (play), illustrated by Veronica Hol-

land, for Currency Press; and *Green Air,* illustrated by Lindsay Muir, *Who's in the Sky?,* illustrated by Jane Benson, *Whose Pouch?,* illustrated by Jane Burrell, and *Fraser Dingo,* illustrated by Sharon Dye. Contributed six volumes to "Aussie Triumphs" series; creator of coloring books and of book and audiotape sets, including *Clever Company, Sam's House, Sounds Spooky!,* and *Frogmouth Fax.* Contributor to periodicals; contributor of reviews to *Age,* 1979-87; columnist for *Weekender* and *Green Guide,* 1980-97.

Work in Progress

Warriors of the Green, a novel for eight-to twelve-year-old readers; research on the Pacific Ocean, including the Philippines.

Sidelights

Australian author and publisher Jill Morris wrote her first poem following the tragic death of her father during World War II. A young girl then, she grew up to become a producer for the Australian Broadcasting Corporation, where her writing skills extended to radio and film documentaries as well as educational books. Founding her own publishing company, Great Glider Productions, in the early 1980s, Morris also owns a six-acre rainforest that she calls Book Farm. In addition to opening her farm, located on the coast of Brisbane, Australia, to authors, illustrators, and musicians alike, she has also combined her love of nature and writing in numerous books for children, among them her first book, *Harry the Hairy-nosed Wombat,* as well as titles such as *Kookaburra School* and *Silly Baby Magpie.* Combining fun and learning, *Silly Baby Magpie* was praised for its "simple, lively verse" by *Aussie Reviews* online contributor Sally Murphy, and the critic also praised the "delightful illustrations of Heather Gall" in *Koala Number One,* a story about a young koala named Kolo who, forced to leave the koala colony of his father, must find a new territory of his own.

Morris once told *SATA:* "I am committed to the preservation of the natural environment, and all my writing reflects this. I have worked for children on all fronts— television and radio production, newspaper and magazine journalism, and as a publisher, editor, and author of more than eighty books." Discussing Greater Glider Productions on her home page, Morris explained that the publishing company produces an average of ten volumes yearly, "some of my own titles and a number by other authors and illustrators. Greater Glider Books have a reputation for being accurate, informative, and stunningly beautiful. They have a very strong leaning towards the preservation of the natural environment."

Biographical and Critical Sources

PERIODICALS

Australian Book Review, July, 1997, review of *The Wombat Who Talked to the Stars,* p. 62.

Christian Science Monitor, September 12, 1985, review of *The Boy Who Painted the Sun,* p. 31.

Emergency Librarian, September, 1983, review of *The Boy Who Painted the Sun,* p. 20; March, 1987, review of *Saturday Street,* p. 23.

Junior Bookshelf, October, 1984, review of *The Boy Who Painted the Sun,* p. 200.

Magpies, March, 1993, Margot Hillel, review of *Dido Has Diabetes,* p. 34, and Stephanie Owen Reeder, review of *Australian Bats,* p. 35; May, 1994, review of *Where Is Kangaroo?,* p. 25; July, 1994, Hugo McCann, review of *Australian Owls, Frogmouths, and Nightjars,* pp. 35-36; March, 1997, Annette Dale-Meiklejohn, review of *The Wombat Who Talked to the Stars,* p. 23; November, 1998, Jennifer Poulter, review of *Australian Kangaroos, Magnificent Macropods,* p. 42; July, 1999, review of *Mahogany the Mystery Glider,* p. 41; November, 2001, review of *Frog Thunder,* p. 35; May, 2002, review of *Kookaburra School,* p. 27; March, 2003, review of *Silly Baby Magpie!,* p. 28.

Nature Australia, autumn, 2000, Cheryl Hook, review of *Mahogany the Mystery Glider,* p. 72.

New York Times Book Review, September 16, 1984, review of *The Boy Who Painted the Sun,* p. 26.

Publishers Weekly, June 29, 1984, review of *The Boy Who Painted the Sun,* p. 105.

School Library Journal, October, 1984, Connie C. Rockman, review of *The Boy Who Painted the Sun,* p. 150; May, 1989, Denise A. Anton, review of *Monkey Creates Havoc in Heaven,* p. 102.

Times Literary Supplement, April 6, 1973, review of *Kolo the Bush Koala, Rusty the Nimble Numbat, Rufus the Red Kangaroo,* and *Percy the Peaceful Platypus,* p. 390.

Wildlife Australia, summer, 2000, Robert Ashdown, review of *Australian Kangaroos: Magnificent Macropods,* p. 46; summer, 2000, Robert Ashdown, review of *Fraser Dingo,* p. 46; spring, 2004, Caelyn Jones, review of *Silly Baby Magpie!,* p. 42; spring, 2004, Samantha John-Hore, review of *Harry the Hairy-nosed Wombat, and Other Australian Animal Tales,* p. 42.

ONLINE

Aussie Reviews Online, http://www.aussiereviews.com/ (October 7, 2005), Sally Murphy, review of *Kukaburra School, Koala Number One,* and *Silly Baby Magpie!*

Jill Morris Home Page, http://www.greaterglider.com (October 7, 2005).*

*   *   *

MURRAY, Kirsty 1960-

Personal

Born November 21, 1960, in Melbourne, Victoria, Australia; daughter of Guy Martin (a sculptor) and Phyllis (Nairn) Boyd; married John Murray, December 17, 1982 (divorced, 1994); married Ken Harper (a drama teacher), 1998; children: (first marriage) Ruby, William, Elwyn; stepchildren: (second marriage) Isobel, Romanie, Theodore. *Education:* Attended Royal Melbourne Institute of Technology. *Hobbies and other interests:* Cooking, catering, books, music, film.

Addresses

Home—Australia. *Agent*—c/o Author Mail, Allen & Unwin, 9 Atchinson St., Sidney, New South Wales 2065, Australia. *E-mail*—Kirsty@KirstyMurray.com.

Career

Children's book author. Worked variously as a forest ranger, secretary, caterer, life model, waitress, graphic artist, administrator, art teacher, craftsperson, laborer, barmaid, editor, and researcher. Served on various school councils in the United Kingdom and Australia; Victorian Premier's Reading Challenge, ambassador, 2005.

Member

Australian Society of Authors, Amnesty International, Children's Book Council of Australia.

Awards, Honors

Western Australian Premier's Book Award, 2000, for *Zarconi's Magic Flying Fish;* Children's Literature Choice listee, 2001, for *What Kids Are Made Of;* Aurealis Award shortlist, 2001, and Children's Book Council of Australia (CBCA) Notable Book designation, 2002, both for *Market Blues;* CBCA Notable Book designation, 2003, and West Australian Young Readers Book Award shortlist, 2004, both for *Walking Home with Marie-Claire;* CBCA Notable Book designation, and New South Wales Premier's History Awards Young People's History Prize shortlist, both 2004, both for *Bridie's Fire;* CBCA Notable Book designation, 2005, for *Becoming Billy Dare.*

Writings

FOR CHILDREN

Maneaters and Bloodsuckers, Allen & Unwin (Crows Nest, New South Wales, Australia), 1998.

Howard Florey: Miracle Maker, Allen & Unwin (Crows Nest, New South Wales, Australia), 1998.

Tough Stuff, Allen & Unwin (Crows Nest, New South Wales, Australia, 1999, published as *What Kids Are Made of: True Stories of Young Rescuers, Rulers, and Rebels,* Chicago Review Press (Chicago, IL), 2000.

Zarconi's Magic Flying Fish, Allen & Unwin (Crows Nest, New South Wales, Australia), 1999.

Circus of Secrets, Allen & Unwin (Crows Nest, New South Wales, Australia), 1999.

Market Blues, Allen & Unwin (Crows Nest, New South Wales, Australia), 2001.

Walking Home with Marie-Claire, Allen & Unwin (Crows Nest, New South Wales, Australia), 2002.

"CHILDREN OF THE WIND" SERIES

Bridie's Fire, Allen & Unwin (Crows Nest, New South Wales, Australia), 2003.
Becoming Billy Dare, Allen & Unwin (Crows Nest, New South Wales, Australia), 2004.
A Prayer for Blue Delaney, Allen & Unwin (Crows Nest, New South Wales, Australia), 2005.

Work in Progress

The Secret Life of Maeve Lee Kwong, the fourth book in the "Children of the Wind" series.

Biographical and Critical Sources

PERIODICALS

Kliatt, May, 2004, Jessica Swain, review of *Walking Home with Marie-Claire,* p. 21.
Magpies, September, 1998, review of *Howard Florey Miracle Maker,* p. 42; July, 1999, review of *Tough Stuff,* p. 42; March, 2000, review of *Zarconi's Magic Flying Fish,* p. 34; May, 2001, review of *Market Blues,* p. 35; March, 2003, review of *Walking Home with Marie-Claire,* p. 34; November, 2003, review of *Bridie's Fire,* p. 36; March, 2005, Anne Briggs, review of *Becoming Billy Dare,* p. 36.
School Librarian, spring, 2001, review of *Zarconi's Magic Flying Fish,* p. 35.
Times Educational Supplement, July 7, 2000, review of *Zarconi's Magic Flying Fish,* p. 23.

ONLINE

Allen and Unwin Web site, http://www.allenandunwin.com/ (October 7, 2005), "Kirsty Murray."
Kirsty Murray Home Page, http://www.kirstymurray.com (October 7, 2005).

*   *   *

MUTH, Jon J.

Personal

Born in Cincinnati, OH; children: Nikolai, Adelaine. *Education:* Studied stone sculpture and sho (brush calligraphy) in Japan; studied painting, printmaking, and drawing in England, Austria, and Germany.

Addresses

Home—Upstate NY. *Agent*—c/o AFSA, 221 Lobos Ave., Pacific Grove, CA 93950.

Career

Author, illustrator, and artist.

Awards, Honors

Eisner Award; Gold Medal, Society of Illustrators.

Writings

GRAPHIC NOVELS AND COMICS

Dracula: A Symphony in Moonlight and Nightmares (based on the story by Bram Stoker; originally published in comic-book format), Marvel Comics Group (New York, NY), 1986, second edition, Nantier, Beall, Minoustchine (New York, NY), 1992.
(Illustrator with others) J.M. DeMatteis, *Moonshadow* (originally published in comic-book format), Epic Comics (New York, NY), 1989.
(Illustrator) Walter Simonson, *Havok and Wolverine: Meltdown* (originally published in comic-book format), Epic Comics (New York, NY), 1990.
The Mythology of an Abandoned City (originally published in comic-book format, 1983-91), Tundra Publishing (Northampton, MA), 1992.
(Illustrator) Grant Morrison, *The Mystery Play* (originally published in comic-book format), Vertigo (New York, NY), 1994.
(Illustrator) J.M. DeMatteis, *The Compleat Moonshadow* (originally published in comic-book format), DC Comics (New York, NY), 1998.
Swamp Thing: Roots (originally published in comic-book format), DC Comics (New York, NY), 1998.

Contributor of artwork to comic-book series, including "Moonshadow," by J.M. DeMatteis, 1985-87, "Sandman" by Neil Gaiman, and others.

FOR CHILDREN; SELF-ILLUSTRATED

The Three Questions (based on a story by Leo Tolstoy), Scholastic (New York, NY), 2002.
(Reteller) *Stone Soup,*, Scholastic (New York, NY), 2003.
Zen Shorts, Scholastic (New York, NY), 2005.

ILLUSTRATOR

John Kuramoto, *Stonecutter,* Donald M. Grant (Hampton Falls, NH), 1995.
Kelley Puckett, *Batman's Dark Secret,* Scholastic (New York, NY), 1999.
Patrick Jennings, *Putnam and Pennyroyal,* Scholastic (New York, NY), 1999.
Karen Hesse, *Come on, Rain,* Scholastic (New York, NY), 1999.
Eric A. Kimmel, reteller, *Gerson's Monster: A Story for the Jewish New Year,* Scholastic (New York, NY), 2000.
Remy Charlip, *Why I Will Never Ever Ever Ever Have Enough Time to Read This Book,* Tricycle Press (Berkeley, CA), 2000.

Jacqueline Woodson, *Our Gracie Aunt,* Hyperion Books for Children (New York, NY), 2002.

Douglas Wood, *Old Turtle and the Broken Truth,* Scholastic (New York, NY), 2003.

Sonia Manzano, *No Dogs Allowed!,* Atheneum Books for Young Readers (New York, NY), 2004.

Amy Hest, *Mr. George Baker,* Candlewick Press (Cambridge, MA), 2004.

Linda Zuckerman, *I Will Hold You 'till You Sleep,* Arthur A. Levine Books (New York, NY), 2006.

OTHER

Vanitas: Paintings, Drawings, and Ideas, Tundra Publishing (Northampton, MA), 1991.

Sidelights

Author and illustrator Jon J. Muth inherited his passion for the graphic arts while growing up as the son of an art teacher. Encouraging his growing talent, Muth's mother took her son to museums across the United States, exposing him to the works of a wide variety of paintings, prints, drawings, and other art forms. Muth debuted his paintings and drawings in a one-man invitational exhibit at age eighteen at Wilmington College. Determined to expand his influences, Muth traveled throughout England, Austria, Germany, and Japan, studying not only drawing and painting, but also stone sculpture, sho—brush calligraphy—and printmaking in classes and as an apprentice.

Muth began his professional career working as a comic-book illustrator, and quickly established himself as a talent in that field. In addition to developing and illustrating the groundbreaking "Moonshadow" series written by J. M. DeMatteis and portions of Neil Gaiman's well-known "Sandman" comic-book epic, Muth also wrote and illustrated several original story arcs based

In Muth's self-illustrated **Zen Shorts,** *a storytelling panda named Stillwater moves into the neighborhood and teaches three siblings to look at life through more enlightened eyes.*

on existing characters and published in their entirety as graphic novels, among them *Dracula: A Symphony in Moonlight and Nightmares* for Marvel Comics and *Swamp Thing: Roots* for DC Comics. As Muth was quoted as saying on the *Candlewick Press Web site,* comic-book illustration is "a natural forum for expressions of angst and questioning one's place in the universe."

With the birth of his own children, Muth naturally began to turn toward children's literature, and took account of a new potential audience with the need to hear other messages. In addition to illustrating texts for a variety of children's-book authors, he has also created original texts to pair with his highly praised watercolor art. In *The Three Questions,* based on a story by noted Russian writer Leo Tolstoy, Muth encouraged young readers to consider the needs of others as well as oneself when making decisions. "When is the best time to do things? Who is the most important one?, and What is the right thing to do?" are the questions raised in the author/illustrator's gentle story about a boy named Nikolai who learns to find answers to his own questions by relying on the natural wisdom of animals, in this case a wise old turtle named Leo. Noting the Asian inspiration in Muth's art, *School Library Journal* critic Susan Hepler commented that the book's "languid watercolors, some sketchy and others fully developed, . . . become less dramatic and more ethereal as the story moves towards its thematic statement." In *Publishers Weekly* a reviewer praised Muth's "misty, evocative watercolors" as well as the text, which is "moral without being moralistic," while in *Kirkus Reviews* a critic dubbed *The Three Questions* "a soaring achievement."

Compared by several critics to *The Three Questions,* *Zen Shorts* contains another simple story that poses three thoughtful questions and imparts a resonant message based on Zen teachings. In this tale a giant panda named Stillwater appears at the home of three children. Over several days, Karl, Michael, and Addy each spend time alone with Stillwater as the bear shares both fun and Zen stories, while also posing a philosophical question to each child. Noting that the author includes a valuable commentary about Zen at the book's conclusion, *Booklist* contributor Gillian Engberg wrote that, for even young readers, "Stillwater's questions will linger . . . and the peaceful, uncluttered pictures . . . will encourage children to dream and fill in their own answers." Coop Renner noted the value of *Zen Shorts* as a teaching tool, commenting in his *School Library Journal* review that the "visually lovely" book draws on fa-

miliar images to "prod children to approach life and its circumstances in profoundly 'un-Western' ways," while a *Kirkus Reviews* contributor concluded: "Every word and image comes to make as perfect as picture book as can be."

Biographical and Critical Sources

PERIODICALS

Booklist, March 15, 2002, Hazel Rochman, review of *The Three Questions,* p. 1264; January 1, 2003, Stephanie Zvirin, review of *Stone Soup,* p. 900; March 1, 2005, Gillian Engberg, review of *Zen Shorts,* p. 1194.

Bulletin of the Center for Children's Books, March, 2003, review of *Stone Soup,* p. 282.

Horn Book, July, 1999, Leo Landry, review of *Come on, Rain!,* p. 454; January, 2000, review of *Putnam and Pennyroyal,* p. 77; March-April, 2003, Margaret A. Chang, review of *Stone Soup,* p. 221.

Kirkus Reviews, March 15, 2002, review of *The Three Questions,* p. 420; February 1, 2005, review of *Zen Shorts,* p. 179.

Magazine of Fantasy and Science Fiction, April, 1995, Charles de Lint, review of *Stonecutter,* p. 37.

Publishers Weekly, August 28, 2000, review of *Gerson's Monster: A Story for the Jewish New Year,* p. 78; September 11, 2000, review of *Why I Will Never Ever Ever Ever Have Enough Time to Read This Book,* p. 90; February 11, 2002, review of *The Three Questions,* p. 187; January 13, 2003, review of *Stone Soup,* p. 60; October 27, 2003, review of *Old Turtle and the Broken Truth,* p. 68; February 28, 2005, review of *Zen Shorts,* p. 66.

School Library Journal, June, 2002, Susan Hepler, review of *The Three Questions,* p. 104; December, 2002, Anna DeWind, review of *Our Gracie Aunt,* p. 114; February, 2003, Lee Bock, review of *The Three Questions,* p. 96; March, 2003, Grace Oliff, review of *Stone Soup,* p. 222; August, 2003, Teresa Bateman, review of *Come on, Rain,* p. 63; October, 2003, review of *Our Gracie Aunt,* p. 28; February, 2005, Coop Renner, review of *Zen Shorts,* p. 108.

ONLINE

Candlewick Press Web site, http://www.candlewick.com/ (October 7, 2005), "John J. Muth."

FireBlade Book Review Online, http://www.hoboes.com/ (July 10, 2001), Jerry Stratton, review of *Moonshadow.*

Lambiek Web site, http://www.lambiek.net/ (October 7, 2005), "John J. Muth."

N

NICHOLS, Leigh
See KOONTZ, Dean R.

*   *   *

NORTH, Anthony
See KOONTZ, Dean R.

*   *   *

NOVAK, Matt 1962-

Personal

Born October 23, 1962, in Trenton, NJ; son of Theresa (a factory worker; maiden name, Belfiore) Novak. *Education:* Attended Kutztown State University, 1980-81; attended School of Visual Arts (New York, NY). *Hobbies and other interests:* Reading, hiking, biking, gardening, cooking.

Addresses

Home—PA. *Agent*—c/o Author Mail, Roaring Brook Press, 143 West St., New Milford, CT 06776. *E-mail*—matt@mattnovak.com.

Career

Author and illustrator of children's books, and educator. Pegasus Players, Sheppton, PA, puppeteer, 1979-83; Walt Disney World, Orlando, FL, animator, 1983, 1989-91; St. Benedict's Preparatory School, Newark, NJ, art teacher, beginning 1986; Parsons School of Design, New York, NY, instructor, beginning 1986; Pennsylvania College of Art and Design, instructor, 2001—.

Member

Society of Children's Book Writers and Illustrators.

Awards, Honors

Parent's Choice Honor Book, for *Mouse TV;* Children's Choice designation, International Reading Association/ Children's Book Council, 1997, for *Newt.*

Writings

FOR CHILDREN; SELF-ILLUSTRATED

Rolling, Bradbury Press (New York, NY), 1986.
Claude and Sun, Bradbury Press (New York, NY), 1987.
Mr. Floop's Lunch, Orchard Books (New York, NY), 1990.
While the Shepherd Slept, Orchard Books (New York, NY), 1991.
Elmer Blunt's Open House, Orchard Books (New York, NY), 1992.
The Last Christmas Present, Orchard Books (New York, NY), 1993.
Mouse TV, Orchard Books (New York, NY), 1994.
Gertie and Gumbo, Orchard Books (New York, NY), 1995.
Newt, HarperCollins (New York, NY), 1996.
The Pillow War, Orchard Books (New York, NY), 1997.
The Robobots, DK Publishing (New York, NY), 1998.
Jazzbo Goes to School, Hyperion (New York, NY), 1999.
Jazzbo and Friends, Hyperion (New York, NY), 1999.
Little Wolf, Big Wolf, HarperCollins (New York, NY), 2000.
Jazzbo and Googy, Hyperion (New York, NY), 2000.
On Halloween Street (lift-the-flap book), Little Simon (New York, NY), 2001.
No Zombies Allowed, Atheneum (New York, NY), 2001.
Too Many Bunnies, Roaring Book Press (Brookfield, CT), 2005.
Flip Flop Bop, Roaring Book Press (New Milford, CT), 2005.

ILLUSTRATOR

Pat Upton, *Who Does This Job?,* Bell Books (Honesdale, PA), 1991.

Lee Bennett Hopkins, selector, *It's about Time: Poems,* Simon & Schuster (New York, NY), 1993.

Dayle Ann Dodds, *Ghost and Pete,* Random House (New York, NY), 1995.

Susan Hightower, *Twelve Snails to One Lizard: A Tale of Mischief and Measurement,* Simon & Schuster (New York, NY), 1997.

Heather Lowenberg, *Little Slugger,* Random House (New York, NY), 1997.

Jessica Nickelson, *Five Little Monsters: Glow-in-the-Dark Boogly Eyes!,* Little Simon (New York, NY), 2003.

Jessica Nickelson, *Dinosaur Sleep: Glow-in-the-Dark Boogly Eyes!,* Little Simon (New York, NY), 2003.

Sidelights

Matt Novak enjoyed entertaining his family and friends with puppet shows and homemade Super-8 movies as a kid, and his studies at New York City's School of Visual Arts honed these natural creative skills. As an adult Novak channels his quirky humor and artistic talents into creating lighthearted picture books for children that have been praised for their ability to combine humor with a useful message. Alligators, salamanders, mice, and a little bear named Jazzbo are the stars of several of his books, and Novak's wacky tales focus on everything from earthshaking thunderclaps and favorite television shows to plastic flip-flops and a raucous monster party. In addition to writing and illustrating his own books, Novak has also created pictures for stories by other writers, such as Susan Hightower's *Twelve Snails to One Lizard* and Heather Lowenberg's *Little Slugger.*

Novak's first self-illustrated book, *Rolling,* is a story about thunder. The author's illustrations take center stage in this work, which, as a reviewer in *Publishers Weekly* noted, "consists of two long sentences stretched out over twenty-seven pages." In the book, wrote *School Library Journal* contributor Virginia Opocensky, "thunder, the mysterious, overpowering sound that frightens nearly every child at one time or another, is depicted . . . as a visible cloud-like force." Novak's "lines are deft and true, displaying a fine sense of form," asserted Denise M. Wilms in her *Booklist* review, while "gentle pastel washes keep the mood light despite the windy bluster."

Claude and Sun depicts an entirely different weather phenomenon as Claude follows his best friend, the Sun, through the course of a day. Some reviewers suggested that "Claude" is actually Claude Monet, celebrated French impressionist artist known for his paintings of water lilies and gardens. "The book's theme itself," wrote Karen K. Radtke in *School Library Journal,* "expresses the basic tenet of Impressionistic art—that light reflecting off an object creates what our eyes see." Radtke noted references to other well-known artists, such as Georges Seurat, Vincent Van Gogh, and Auguste Renoir, and concluded that "within this very simple storyline is a multi-faceted art lesson."

Elmer Blunt's Open House features very little text, making it, in the opinion of some reviewers, a good book for preschoolers. In this story, Elmer Blunt hurriedly rushes off to work, leaving the door to his home wide open. During the day, all manner of animals as well as a burglar enter his home, and when Elmer returns that evening he thinks the mess his unseen visitors have created was the result of his hurried departure that morning. Liza Bliss concluded in *School Library Journal* that *Elmer Blunt's Open House* is "a book that's sure to add a lot of fun to family reading." Praising the book as "bursting with action and uninterrupted by narrative," Opocensky noted in *Five Owls* that Novak's illustrations "beg for one-on-one sharing with a preschooler." "Since Novak's . . . gleeful, high-spirited art tells the story so adeptly," a *Publishers Weekly* critic maintained, "this is a great one for preschoolers to 'read.'"

A typical family drama plays out in *Mouse TV,* as a family of ten, with only one television set and varying tastes, winds up in a conflict of an amusing kind. On successive pages, Novak portrays various family members' favorite programs, such as the game show *Get the Cheese* and the science program *It's a Frog's Life.* When the much-vied-for television goes on the blink, however, the mice are surprised to discover that they have plenty of other entertaining ways to spend their time: playing games, reading, and engaging in other healthy activities. "Nobody will miss the unapologetic dig at the [television] medium," wrote Stephanie Zvirin in *Booklist;* "Here's the perfect picture book for pint-size couch potatoes." "The cleverest aspect of the message," maintained *School Library Journal* contributor Steven Engelfried, "is that TV-watching is never condemned or criticized. . . . Instead, Novak gently, and quite successfully, shows that there are countless ways to enjoy oneself as an active participant rather than as a passive viewer." Roger Sutton commented in the *Bulletin of the Center for Children's Books* that "the jokes are hip (in a way that kids and adults can share)," and Novak's artwork—which Sutton compared to Maurice Sendak's illustrations in *A Hole Is to Dig*—"is clean and confident."

Gertie Goomba, the human heroine of *Gertie and Gumbo,* spends a lot of time alone at her swampy home even though she shares space with her father and five grown 'gators. Then she finds a friend in baby alligator Gumbo, and Gumbo helps Gertie's dad with the alligator-wrestling act the man stages for tourists in order to earn a living. A reviewer in *Publishers Weekly* praised Novak's "lighthearted" illustrations, adding that Gumbo is depicted performing appropriately alligator-like activities such as "devouring inedible objects" and "popping out of the toilet" as well as in such uncharacteristic undertakings as learning to dance. "Gumbo's body language and toothy grins are splendid," concluded Zvirin in *Booklist.*

In *The Pillow War* siblings Millie and Fred get into a disagreement over who should be allowed to sleep with

Witches, Wizzle, and Woddle want to throw another Halloween bash, but as the list of bad-mannered guests continues to grow, party plans start to fizzle in Novak's amusing **No Zombies Allowed.**

the family dog, Sam. A pillow fight ensues, and as the story continues the fight escalates down the stairs, out the door, and into the atreet, where others soon join in the fun. In *Booklist* Stephanie Zvirin observed that Novak's "rhyme is catchy, and the pictures are a riot of color and pattern," particularly double-page illustrations "that begs kids to pick their favorite characters out of the crowd." To *School Library Journal* contributor Julie Cummins the book's detailed crowd-scene illustration recalls the "Where's Waldo?" cartoon series, while a re-

After kicking off their toe-hugging socks, boots, clogs, and shoes, everyone gets ready for summer fun by dancing and singing to the tune of Novak's **Flip Flop Bop.**

viewer in *Publishers Weekly* pointed out that young pre-readers will enjoy scouting out the main characters "in each bustling spread and follow[ing] the amusing antics of a menagerie of animals caught up in the frenzy."

Novak introduces a likeable character in *Jazzbo Goes to School, Jazzbo and Googy,* and *Jazzbo and Friends.* In

what a *Publishers Weekly* critic dubbed "a surefire anxiety buster for children facing the prospect of a new school," *Jazzbo Goes to School* finds the short-statured young cub resisting his mother's efforts to find him an appropriate preschool. After checking out the Grumpity School with its terse teachers, and Willy Nilly School, where playtime lasts all day, both mother and son finally agree on Miss Boggle's Super School, where animals and books abound. Calling the series star a "charming little bear," *School Library Journal* contributor Sheilah Kosco praised the "goofiness" of Novak's illustrations in *Jazzbo and Googy.* In this book, schoolmate Googy the pig is a constant disruption, knocking things over, moving too fast, and generally making a mess. However, when the ungainly pig rescues Jazzbo's precious teddy bear from a mud puddle, the bear and pig forge an instant friendship. Noting the book's simple text and its use as a way to reassure young children finding it difficult to make new friends, Kosco cited *Jazzbo and Googy* as "a perfect read-aloud."

Novak has continued to dish out fun in picture books such as *No Zombies Allowed,* about two witches and their preparation for their annual monster bash. Deciding to eliminate some less-desirable guests from this year's festivities—such as werewolves who kept coughing up furballs, and leg-dragging zombies whose eyeballs occasionally fell into the punch—the witches eventually realize that the two most disruptive guests at last year's bash were actually the hosts themselves! "Novak's fondness for silliness is put to good use" in both the "engaging" text and "bright and eye-catching" illustrations, noted *School Library Journal* reviewer Carol L. MacKay, while in *Horn Book* Martha V. Parravano deemed *No Zombies Allowed* a fun read, describing Novak's witches as "appropriately warted and dentally challenged," but nonetheless unthreatening to young readers. "Novak skillfully balances the gruesome factor with a spoof on spookiness," concluded a *Publishers Weekly* critic, noting the book's subtle message about "acceptance and tolerance."

In what *School Library Journal* reviewer Catherine Callegari described as a "humorous tale great for small groups," *Too Many Bunnies* is an interactive counting book featuring five rabbits who realize that their current home is a bit too small for comfort. One by one, the bunnies—Chubby, Fuzzy, Floppy, Bob, and Whiskers—made a mad dash across the field to a new hole, only to find the new place too tight once the last bunny arrives. Featuring large die-cut bunny holes that allow the humorous characters to "jump" the page at each turn, Novak's book also features "cartoony illustrations" that "ramp up the humor," according to Paravanno, who praised *Too Many Bunnies* as "an unassuming package that toddlers and preschoolers should find endlessly entertaining." Equally full of fun, *Flip Flop Bop* also feature's Novak's characteristic over-the-top text, packed with what a *Kirkus* critic called "exuberant" rhyme and "onomatopoeia." In the book, summer means that shoes and socks are exchanged for snappy plastic flip-flops, as people young, old, and even older do a wacky thing called the flip-flop bop. In *School Library Journal,* Sally R. Dow noted Novak's use of "short, easy-to-read rhyming phrases," adding that, with its "frenzy of activity," *Flip Flop Bop* will captivate beginning readers.

Among the works Novak has illustrated for others is Lee Bennett Hopkins's poetry collection *It's about Time,*

about which a critic in *Publishers Weekly* wrote: "Novak's soft pastel pencil drawings do much to bring unity to the divergent writing styles represented" in Hopkins's selections. Regarding Novak's artistic contribution to *Twelve Snails to One Lizard* by Susan Hightower, a *Publishers Weekly* commentator maintained that the illustrator's "winsome earth-toned acrylics once again amuse, with lizards who juggle and hula, a beaver wearing a tool belt, and a pair of picnicking mice who cavort" through the pages.

Biographical and Critical Sources

PERIODICALS

Booklist, August, 1986, Denise M. Wilms, review of *Rolling,* p. 1692; April 15, 1987, p. 1293; September 1, 1994, Stephanie Zvirin, review of *Mouse TV,* p. 53; September 1, 1995, Stephanie Zvirin, review of *Gertie and Gumbo,* p. 89; February 15, 1998, Stephanie Zvirin, review of *The Pillow War,* p. 1020.

Bulletin of the Center for Children's Books, October, 1994, Roger Sutton, review of *Mouse TV,* p. 60; February, 1996, Roger Sutton, review of *Newt,* p. 198.

Five Owls, September-October, Virginia Opocensky, review of *Elmer Blunt's Open House,* 1992, p. 12.

Horn Book, May-June, 1991, p. 319; September-October, 2002, Martha V. Parravano, review of *No Zombies Allowed,* p. 556; March-April, 2005, Martha V. Parravano, review of *Too Many Bunnies,* p. 192.

Kirkus Reviews, August 15, 1992, p. 1066; September 1, 1993, review of *The Last Christmas Present,* p. 1149; July 15, 2002, review of *No Zombies Allowed,* p. 1040; February 15, 2005, review of *Too Many Bunnies,* p. 234; May 15, 2005, review of *Flip Flop Bop,* p. 594.

New York Times Book Review, February 26, 1995, p. 21.

Publishers Weekly, June 27, 1986, review of *Rolling,* p. 87; January 4, 1991, review of *While the Shepherd Slept,* p. 71; July 13, 1992, review of *Elmer Blunt's Open House,* p. 54; May 31, 1993, review of *It's about Time,* p. 54; September 20, 1993, p. 37; July 4, 1994, p. 60; August 7, 1995, review of *Gertie and Gumbo,* p. 460; January 22, 1996; March 24, 1997, review of *Twelve Snails to One Lizard,* p. 82; February 9, 1998, review of *The Pillow War,* p. 94; June 14, 1999, review of *Jazzbo Goes to School,* p. 68; April 24, 2000, review of *Jazzbo and Googy,* p. 93; September 23, 2002, review of *No Zombies Allowed,* p. 71; February 14, 2005, review of *Too Many Bunnies,* p. 75.

School Library Journal, September, 1986, Virginia Opocensky, review of *Rolling,* pp. 125-126; May, 1987, Karen Radtke, review of *Claude and Sun,* p. 91; March, 1990, p. 199; July, 1991, Carolyn Vang Schuler, review of *While the Shepherd Slept,* p. 62; October, 1992, Liza Bliss, review of *Elmer Blunt's Open House,* p. 94; October, 1993, Jane Marino, review of *The Last Christmas Present,* p. 46; October,

1994, Stephen Engelfried, review of *Mouse TV,* pp. 95-96; October, 1995, p. 110; July, 1996, Gale W. Sherman, review of *Newt,* p. 70; May, 1997, p. 100; March, 1998, Julie Cummins, review of *The Pillow War,* p. 185; January, 2000, Pat Leach, review of *Little Wolf, Big Wolf,* p. 108; June, 2000, Sheilah Kosco, review of *Jazzbo and Googy,* p. 123; August, 2002, Carol L. MacKay, review of *No Zombies Allowed,* p. 162; June, 2005, Catherine Callegari, review of *Too Many Bunnies,* p. 123; July, 2005, Sally R. Dow, review of *Flip Flop Bop,* p. 80.

ONLINE

Matt Novak Home Page, http://www.mattnovak.com (October 20, 2005).

P

PAIGE, Richard
See KOONTZ, Dean R.

* * *

PAUSEWANG, Gudrun 1928-

Personal

Born March 3, 1928, in Wichstadtl, Bohemia, Czechoslovakia (now Czech Republic); father a diplomat; immigrated to West Germany, c. 1948; married Peter Wilcke; children: one son. *Education:* Trained as a teacher in Germany. *Hobbies and other interests:* Travel, gardening.

Addresses

Home—Brueder-Grimm-Weg 11, 36110 Schlitz, Germany. *Agent*—c/o Author Mail, Ravensburger Buchverlag Otto Maier GmbH, Postbox 1860, 88188 Ravensburg, Germany.

Career

Author, 1959—. Also worked as a teacher in South America, 1956-63, and Germany, 1963-68.

Awards, Honors

La vach qui Lit prize, 1981, for *Ich habe Hunger, Ich habe Durst;* Deutschen Jugendliteraturpreis, 1988, and Kurd Laßwitz Preis, 1998, both for *Die Wolk;* Gustav-Heinemann-Friedenspreis; Buxtehuder Bulle, 1997, for *Die Not der Familie Caldera;* numerous other awards.

Writings

Rio Amargo, 1959.
Der Weg nach Tongay, 1965.
Plaza Fortuna, 1966.
Bolivianische Hochzeit, 1968.
Guadalupe, 1970.

Gudrun Pausewang

Hinterm Haus der Wassermann, 1972.
Aufstieg und Untergang der Insel Defina, 1973.
Und dann kommt Emilio, Ravensburger (Ravensburg, Germany), 1974.
Kunibert und Killewamba, Ravensburger (Ravensburg, Germany), 1976.
Die Not der Familie Caldera, Ravensburger (Ravensburg, Germany), 1977, reprinted, 1997.
Auf einem langen Weg, Ravensburger (Ravensburg, Germany), 1978, reprinted, 1996.
Der Streik der Dienstmädchen, Ravensburger (Ravensburg, Germany), 1979, reprinted, 2000.
Rosenkawiesen: Alternatives Leben von 50 Jahren, Ravensburger (Ravensburg, Germany), 1980.

Rosinkawiese, 1980.

Ich habe Hunger, Ich habe Durst, Ravensburger (Ravensburg, Germany), 1981, reprinted, 1998.

Die Prinzessin springt ins Heu, Ravensburger (Ravensburg, Germany), 1982.

Die letzten Kinder von Schewenborn, Ravensburger (Ravensburg, Germany), 1983, translated by Norman M. Watt as *The Last Children of Schevenborn,* Western Producer Prairie Books (Saskatoon, Saskatchewan, Canada), 1988, published as *The Last Children,* Mac-Rae, 1989.

Wer hat Angst vor Räuber Grapsch, Ravensburger (Ravensburg, Germany), 1983.

Kinderbesuch, 1984.

Etwas lässt sich doch bewirken, Ravensburger (Ravensburg, Germany), 1984.

Friedens: Geschichten (stories; includes *Frieden kommt nicht von allein*), Ravensburger (Ravensburg, Germany), 1985.

Pepe Amado, 1986.

Ein wilder Winter für Räuber Grapsch, Ravensburger (Ravensburg, Germany), 1986.

Ein Eigenheim für Räuber Grapsch, Ravensburger (Ravensburg, Germany), 1987.

Ich gebe Nicht Auf, 1987.

Die Wolke, Ravensburger (Ravensburg, Germany), 1987, reprinted, Süddeutsche, 2005, translated by Patricia Crampton as *Fall-Out,* edited with introduction, notes, and vocabulary by Susan Tebbutt, Manchester University Press (Manchester, England), 1992, Viking (New York, NY), 1994.

Die Kinder in der Erde, illustrated by Annengert Fuchshuber, Ravensburger (Ravensburg, Germany), 1988.

Kreuz und qür übers Meer, Ravensburger (Ravensburg, Germany), 1988.

Fern von der Rosinkawiese, Ravensburger (Ravensburg, Germany), 1989.

Geliebte Rosinkawiese, Ravensburger (Ravensburg, Germany), 1990.

Das Tor zum Garten der Zambranos, Ravensburger (Ravensburg, Germany), 1991.

Es ist doch alles grün, Ravensburger (Ravensburg, Germany), 1991.

Das große Buch vom Räber Grapsch, Ravensburger (Ravensburg, Germany), 1992.

Eine Reise im August, Ravensburger (Ravensburg, Germany), 1992, translated by Patricia Crampton as *The Final Journey,* Viking (New York, NY), 1998.

Der Schlund, Ravensburger (Ravensburg, Germany), 1993.

Der Weihnachtsmann im Kittchen, Ravensburger (Ravensburg, Germany), 1995.

Der Glücksbringer, 1995.

Die Verräterin, Ravensburger (Ravensburg, Germany), 1995, translated by Rachel Ward as *Traitor,* Random House (Toronto, Ontario, Canada), 2004.

Adi, Jugend eines Diktators, Ravensburger (Ravensburg, Germany), 1997.

Ich geb dir noch eine Chance, Gott!, illustrated by Uschi Schneider, Ravensburger (Ravensburg, Germany), 1997.

Ich habe einen Freund in Leningrad, Ravensburger (Ravensburg, Germany), 1998, published as *Warum eigentlich nicht,* c. 1998.

Hörst de den Fluss, Elin?, Nagel & Kimche (Zürich, Switzerland), 1998.

Hinterm Haus der Wassermann, Ravensburger (Ravensburg, Germany), 1998.

1996-1997 Germanistikstudium, Ravensburger (Ravensburg, Germany), 1998.

Barfuss durch die grösse Städt, illustrated by Verena Ballhaus, Nagel & Kimche (Zürich, Switzerland), 1999.

Die letzten Kinder von Schewenborn oder . . . sieht so unsere Zunkunft aus?, Ravensburger (Ravensburg, Germany), 2003.

Du darfst nicht schreien, Ravensburger (Ravensburg, Germany), 2003.

Der Spinatvampir, illustrated by Markus Grolik, Sauerländer (Düsseldorf, Germany), 2003.

Ich war dabei. Geschichten gene das Vergessen, Sauerländer (Düsseldorf, Germany), 2004.

Roller und Rosenkranz, Arena, 2004.

Überleben!, Ravensburger (Ravensburg, Germany), 2005.

Also author of many other books.

Adaptations

Several of Pausewang's books have been adapted for film.

Sidelights

German writer Gudrun Pausewang is a prolific author of books for children, young adults, and adult readers. Familiar with many of the world's social ills through her own experiences during World War II and her travels throughout South America and Asia, the Czech-born Pausewang often focuses on serious subjects, such as Third-world poverty, war, and the environmental threats posed by nuclear energy. While her books for young children are lighthearted, those for older readers tell more sobering tales. Three of her books translated for English-language readers center on grim events: *The Final Journey* and *Traitor* take place during the Holocaust while *The Last Children of Schevenborn* and Pausewang's most acclaimed and highly awarded novel, *Die Wolke*—translated as *Fall-Out*—focus on young protagonists coping with nuclear destruction.

The oldest of six siblings, Pausewang was born in 1928 in Wichstadtl, a town formerly part of East Bohemia that had by now united with Slovakia to form Czechoslovakia. After her father, a diplomat, was killed on the Russian front in 1943, her mother was forced to raise her children alone. At the end of World War II, seventeen-year-old Pausewang and her family fled communism and moved to West Germany, where she trained as a teacher. After teaching in Germany for a few years, from 1956 to 1963 she traveled to South America, living and teaching in Chile and Venezuela. Returning to Germany, she taught in Mainz-Kastel for four years, then returned with her husband, Peter Wilcke, to South America, this time living in Colombia, where her son was born. In 1972, when her son was two years old, Pausewang returned to Germany, where she has continued to make her home. She began her writing career in the 1950s, while working as a teacher.

First published in Germany in 1983, *The Last Children of Schevenborn* follows the survivors of a nuclear attack and is narrated by a boy named Roland. Describing his experiences in graphic detail, the boy witnesses the decay of his community and way of life as his friends and family perish and he also begins to suffer from radiation sickness. Reflecting her only fear of nuclear dangers, Pausewang offers a stern warning for humanity. "*Schevenborn* is a terrible, frightening, haunting story, all too convincing," declared *Canadian Review of Materials* contributor Joan McGrath, while *Books for Keeps* critic David Bennett dubbed the novel a "bleak but gripping read."

Fall-Out is also a warning against the dangers of nuclear power; in this case, a power-plant accident is the source of the tragedy. Ironically, the novel was published in 1987, a year after the nuclear disaster at the Chernobyl nuclear facility in the Soviet Ukraine terrified Europe due to the short-term casualties and the fact that little was then known about the long-term effects of such an event. As the novel opens, an accident occurs at a reactor near the home of siblings Janna and Uli. With their parents absent, the children try to escape on their own. Tragedy heaps upon tragedy as Uli is killed by a car, and an ever-sicker Janna learns that the rest of her family died in the power-plant accident. In her novel, Pausewang contrasts the typical beliefs then held by many Europeans: Janna stays at the homes of two different aunts, one of whom encourages the girl to cover her now-bald head and pretend that everything is fine, while the other aunt, an activist, attempts to force people to recognize the dangers they face. By the end of the story Janna has become a spokesperson for her fellow victims, who call themselves the "Hibakusha" after those who died at Hiroshima.

Many reviewers commented on the grimness of *Fall-Out*, Roger Sutton pointing out in the *Bulletin of the Center for Children's Books* that the novel ends with "no real hope, false or otherwise." Calling *Fall-Out* a "realistic psychological novel" in a *Voice for Youth Advocates* review, Francine Canfield praised Pausewang's "crisp and assertive language," adding that the author "explores the unspoken horror of the unknown long-term effects of exposure to radiation without overwhelming the plot." *Booklist* reviewer Janice Del Negro also noted the author's ability to create a swift-moving plot, dubbing the book "a grim, unflinching, but fast-paced disaster tale with a strong message that does not overwhelm either the story or the characters."

First published in German as *Reise im August*, *The Final Journey* takes place on a train bound for a concentration camp during World War II. Pausewang's story focuses on eleven-year-old Alice, who is torn from her comfortable middle-class life and herded with her grandfather aboard a train bound for an unknown destination. During the arduous journey, Alice befriends a fellow traveler, but suffers tragedies when her grandfather dies due to the poor conditions aboard the train and her young friend is subsequently killed during an escape attempt. Pausewang describes with unrelenting accuracy the horrific conditions Alice endures during her trip as corpses begin to pile up in the cattle cars full of human passengers. While *Horn Book* contributor Roger Sutton called the book "unsubtle, even crude," he nonetheless acknowledged that Pausewang's graphic approach is appropriate in getting this important message across. "Relentless is certainly an understatement for this horrific, claustrophobic story," added Sutton, "but you have to put the word honest in there as well."

Pausewang once again gained an English-language readership when her 1995 novel *Die Verräterin* was translated and published as *Traitor*. The novel draws readers back to the Sudentenland, an area near the border of Czechoslovakia and Germany that, in 1944, has not yet been touched by the brutality of war. Anna is the middle sister in a loyal Nazi home; her older brother is fighting for the German Army on the Russian front while her younger brother, Felix, is an enthusiastic member of the Hitler Youth whose loyalty is unwavering despite German's imminent defeat. Anna's own feelings are mixed toward the war, however, and when she discovers an escaped and injured Russian prisoner of war in her family's barn, she is moved to help the half-dead man. Hiding the soldier in an abandoned bunker, she manages to bring him a steady supply of food despite the fact that her actions would result in her arrest if discovered. When Felix becomes suspicious, Anna is forced into further deception; meanwhile, she realizes the irony of her situation: the Russian advance that will allow the young Russian to return safely to his comrades will also put her town in the path of the war. Praising *Traitor* as "an incredibly moving book" *WriteAway* online contributor Bridget Carrington noted that the novel is valuable for questioning "the popular perception that all Germans were Nazis . . . and knew of the atrocities being committed in the name of the Fatherland."

Biographical and Critical Sources

PERIODICALS

Booklist, September 15, 1995, Janice Del Negro, review of *Fall-Out,* p. 154.
Books for Keeps, January, 1991, David Bennett, review of *The Children of Schevenborn,* p. 9.
Bulletin of the Center for Children's Books, September, 1995, Roger Sutton, review of *Fall-Out,* p. 23.
Canadian Review of Materials, January, 1989, Joan McGrath, review of *The Children of Schevenborn,* p. 19.
Horn Book, January-February, 1997, Roger Sutton, review of *The Final Journey,* p. 66.
Publishers Weekly, May 29, 1995, p. 86.
School Librarian, August, 1995, Jane Inglis, review of *Fall-Out,* pp. 118-119; winter, 2004, D. Telford, review of *Traitor,* p. 216.
Voice of Youth Advocates, October, 1995, Francine Canfield, review of *Fall-Out,* pp. 222-223.

*   *   *

PERRY, Marie Fritz

Personal

Born in Northfield, MN; daughter of Henry and Do-
lores Fritz. *Education:* Smith College, B.A., 1992; Dominican University, M.A. (library and information science), 1999. *Hobbies and other interests:* English and
Western horseback riding.

Addresses

Home—Northfield, MN. *Agent*—Elizabeth Child, Buttonweed Press, 7625 110th St. East, Northfield, MN
55057. *E-mail*—perry775@msn.com.

Career

Author, artist, educator, and librarian.

Writings

(Self-illustrated) *A Gift for Sadia,* Buttonweed Press
(Northfield, MN), 2005.

Contributor, with Henry E. Fritz, to *Encyclopedia of the
American West.*

Work in Progress

A series of picture books about the immigrant experience in America.

Sidelights

Minnesota-based author, artist, librarian, and educator
Marie Fritz Perry was inspired to write *A Gift for Sadia*
while working with seven English-as-a-second-language
(ESL) students in 1998. Although her new students
came from drastically different backgrounds and had arrived in Minnesota from different countries, Perry soon
realized that their experiences assimilating into the culture of the United States were fairly similar, and equally
difficult.

Following her experiences with these seven special students, Perry began to weave a story, drawing upon her
own childhood memories of feeding Canadian geese as
well as on the immigrant stories her students had shared.
A Gift for Sadia focuses on a young Somali girl who
finds herself in the United States after losing much of

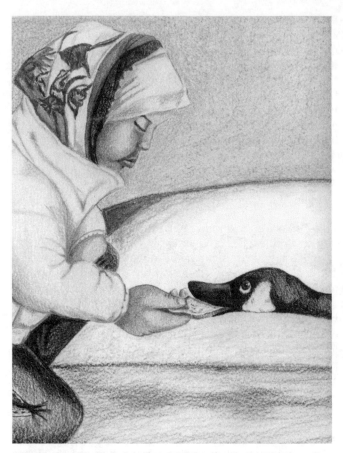

*When a Somali girl finds refuge with her family in Minnesota, her
feelings of isolation become less painful after she befriends another
transplant, a wounded Canada goose, in Perry's sensitive self-illustrated*
A Gift for Sadia.

her family. Lonely, cold, and feeling like an outcast, Sadia has difficulty communicating with the people who
try to help her. Ultimately, however, she makes a connection while caring for an injured Canadian goose that
helps her accept her new life yet honor her family's
memory by being proud of her cultural heritage. In the
opinion of a reviewer for *Small Press Bookwatch,* Perry's self-illustrated picture book is "beautifully drawn
and deftly told," while a *Kirkus Reviews* critic stated
that because Perry's artwork "captures Sadia's low spirits" at the beginning of the story, young listeners will
"come away from the episode . . . happy that, by the
end, she's feeling at least a bit more at home."

Biographical and Critical Sources

PERIODICALS

Kirkus Reviews, March 1, 2005, review of *A Gift for Sadia,* p. 293.
Rochester Post-Bulletin (Rochester, MN), February 8,
2005, Dawn Schuett, "Somali Woman Inspires Children's Book."
Small Press Bookwatch, May, 2005, review of *A Gift for
Sadia.*

Q-R

QUIN-HARKIN, Janet 1941-
(Rhys Bowen, Janetta Johns)

Personal

Born September 24, 1941, in Bath, England; immigrated to United States, 1966; daughter of Frank Newcombe (an engineer) and Margery (a teacher; maiden name, Rees) Lee; married John Quin-Harkin (a retired sales manager), November 26, 1966; children: Clare, Anne, Jane, Dominic. *Education:* University of London, B.A. (with honors), 1963; graduate study at University of Kiel and University of Freiburg. *Religion:* Roman Catholic. *Hobbies and other interests:* Tennis, travel, drama, music, sketching, hiking.

Addresses

Home and office—31 Tralee Way, San Rafael, CA 94903. *Agent*—Meg Ruley, Jan Rostrosen Agency, 318 E. 51st St., New York, NY 10011. *E-mail*—rhys@rhysbowen.com.

Career

British Broadcasting Corporation (BBC), London, England, studio manager in drama department, 1963-66; Australian Broadcasting Corporation, Sydney, member of staff; writer, 1971—teacher of dance and drama, 1971-76; teacher of writing at Dominican College, San Rafael, CA, 1988-95. Founder and former director of San Raphael's Children's Little Theater. Full-time writer, beginning 1980.

Member

Mystery Writers of America, Sisters in Crime, American Association of University Women.

Awards, Honors

Children's Book Showcase selection, Children's Book Council, Outstanding Books of the Year citation, *New York Times,* Children's Book Show citation, American Institute of Graphic Arts, and Best Books of the year citations, *School Library Journal, Washington Post,* and *Saturday Review,* all 1976, all for *Peter Penny's Dance;* Children's Choice citation, 1985, for *Wanted: Date for Saturday Night;* Barry Award nomination for Best Novel, 1998, for *Evan Help Us;* Agatha Award, *Romantic Times* Reviewer's Choice designation, and Herodotus Award, all 2002, all for *Murphy's Law;* Anthony Award for Best Historical Mystery, Bouchercon, 2004, for *For the Love of Mike;* Anthony Award for Best Short Story, 2004, for "Doppelganger"; Edgar Allan Poe Award finalist, Mystery Writers of America, 2004, for *Evan's Gate.*

Writings

FOR CHILDREN

Peter Penny's Dance, illustrated by Anita Lobel, Dial (New York, NY), 1976.

Benjamin's Balloon, Parents Magazine Press (New York, NY), 1979.

Septimus Bean and His Amazing Machine, illustrated by Art Cumings, Parents Magazine Press (New York, NY), 1980.

Magic Growing Powder, illustrated by Art Cumings, Parents Magazine Press (New York, NY), 1981.

Helpful Hattie, illustrated by Susanna Natti, Harcourt (New York, NY), 1983.

Three Impossible Things, Parents Magazine Press (New York, NY), 1991.

Billy and Ben: The Terrible Two, illustrated by Carol Newsom, Bantam (New York, NY), 1992.

YOUNG-ADULT NOVELS

Write Every Day, Scholastic (New York, NY), 1982.

(Under pseudonym Janetta Johns) *The Truth about Me and Bobby V.,* Bantam (New York, NY), 1983.

Tommy Loves Tina, Berkley/Ace (New York, NY), 1984.

Winner Takes All, Berkley/Ace (New York, NY), 1984.

Wanted: Date for Saturday Night, Putnam (New York, NY), 1985.

Summer Heat, Fawcett (New York, NY), 1990.

My Phantom Love ("Changes Romance" series), Harper-Collins (New York, NY), 1992.

On My Own ("Changes Romance" series), HarperCollins (New York, NY), 1992.

Getting Personal: Becky, Silhouette (New York, NY), 1994.

The Apartment, HarperCollins (New York, NY), 1994.

The Sutcliffe Diamonds, HarperCollins (New York, NY), 1994.

The Boy Next Door ("Love Stories" series), Bantam (New York, NY), 1995.

Who Do You Love? ("Love Stories" series), Bantam (New York, NY), 1996.

(With Thomas P. Taafe) *Fun, Sun, and Flamingos* ("Club Stephanie" series), Bantam (New York, NY), 1997.

(With Emily Costello and Emily Ecco) *Fireworks and Flamingoes* ("Club Stephanie" series), Bantam (New York, NY), 1997.

Flamingo Revenge ("Club Stephanie" series), Pocket (New York, NY), 1997.

King and I (adapted from the animated movie and the musical), Scholastic (New York, NY), 1999.

Torn Apart ("Love Stories" series), Bantam (New York, NY), 1999.

Love Potion ("Enchanted Hearts" series), Avon (New York, NY), 1999.

"SWEET DREAMS" SERIES

California Girl, Bantam (New York, NY), 1981.

Love Match, Bantam (New York, NY), 1982.

Ten-Boy Summer, Bantam (New York, NY), 1982.

Daydreamer, Bantam (New York, NY), 1983.

The Two of Us, Bantam (New York, NY), 1984.

Exchange of Hearts, Bantam (New York, NY), 1984.

Ghost of a Chance, Bantam (New York, NY), 1984.

Lovebirds, Bantam (New York, NY), 1984.

101 Ways to Meet Mr. Right, Bantam (New York, NY), 1985.

The Great Boy Chase, Bantam (New York, NY), 1985.

Follow That Boy, Bantam (New York, NY), 1985.

My Secret Love, Bantam (New York, NY), 1986.

My Best Enemy, Bantam (New York, NY), 1987.

Never Say Goodbye, Bantam (New York, NY), 1987.

"ON OUR OWN" SERIES

On Our Own, Bantam (New York, NY), 1986.

The Graduates, Bantam (New York, NY), 1986.

The Trouble with Toni, Bantam (New York, NY), 1986.

Out of Love, Bantam (New York, NY), 1986.

Old Friends, New Friends, Bantam (New York, NY), 1986.

Best Friends Forever, Bantam (New York, NY), 1986.

"SUGAR AND SPICE" SERIES

Flip Side, Ballantine (New York, NY), 1987.

Tug of War, Ballantine (New York, NY), 1987.

Surf's Up, Ballantine (New York, NY), 1987.

The Last Dance, Ballantine (New York, NY), 1987.

Nothing in Common, Ballantine (New York, NY), 1987.

Dear Cousin, Ballantine (New York, NY), 1987.

Two Girls, One Boy, Ballantine (New York, NY), 1987.

Trading Places, Ballantine (New York, NY), 1987.

Double Take, Ballantine (New York, NY), 1988.

Make Me a Star, Ballantine (New York, NY), 1988.

Big Sister, Ballantine (New York, NY), 1988.

Out in the Cold, Ballantine (New York, NY), 1988.

Blind Date, Ballantine (New York, NY), 1988.

It's My Turn, Ballantine (New York, NY), 1988.

"HEARTBREAK CAFE" SERIES

No Experience Required, Fawcett (New York, NY), 1990.

The Main Attraction, Fawcett (New York, NY), 1990.

At Your Service, Fawcett (New York, NY), 1990.

Catch of the Day, Fawcett (New York, NY), 1990.

Love to Go, Fawcett (New York, NY), 1990.

Just Desserts, Fawcett (New York, NY), 1990.

"FRIENDS" SERIES

Starring Tess and Ali, HarperCollins (New York, NY), 1991.

Tess and Ali and the Teeny Bikini, HarperCollins (New York, NY), 1991.

Boy Trouble for Tess and Ali, HarperCollins (New York, NY), 1991.

Tess and Ali, Going on Fifteen, HarperCollins (New York, NY), 1991.

"SENIOR YEAR" SERIES

Homecoming Dance, HarperCollins (New York, NY), 1991.

New Year's Eve, HarperCollins (New York, NY), 1991.

Night of the Prom, HarperCollins (New York, NY), 1992.

Graduation Day, HarperCollins (New York, NY), 1992.

"BOYFRIEND CLUB" SERIES

Ginger's First Kiss, Troll (Metuchen, NJ), 1994.

Roni's Dream Boy, Troll (Metuchen, NJ), 1994.

Karen's Perfect Match, Troll (Metuchen, NJ), 1994.

Ginger's New Crush, Troll (Metuchen, NJ), 1994.

Queen Justine, Troll (Metuchen, NJ), 1995.

Roni's Two-Boy Trouble, Troll (Metuchen, NJ), 1995.

No More Boys, Troll (Metuchen, NJ), 1995.

Karen's Lesson in Love, Troll (Metuchen, NJ), 1995.

Roni's Sweet Fifteen, Troll (Metuchen, NJ), 1995.

Justine's Babysitting, Troll (Metuchen, NJ), 1995.

The Boyfriend Wars, Troll (Metuchen, NJ), 1995.

"TGIF!" SERIES

Sleepover Madness, Pocket Books (New York, NY), 1995.
Friday Night Fright, Pocket Books (New York, NY), 1995.
Four's a Crowd, Pocket Books (New York, NY), 1995.
Forever Friday, Pocket Books (New York, NY), 1995.
Toe-Shoe Trouble, Pocket Books (New York, NY), 1996.
Secret Valentine, Pocket Books (New York, NY), 1996.

"SISTER, SISTER" SERIES

Cool in School, Pocket Books (New York, NY), 1996.
You Read My Mind, Pocket Books (New York, NY), 1996.
One Crazy Christmas, Pocket Books (New York, NY), 1996.
Homegirl on the Range, Pocket Books (New York, NY), 1997.
Star Quality, Pocket Books (New York, NY), 1997.
He's All That, Pocket Books (New York, NY), 1997.
Summer Days, Pocket Books (New York, NY), 1997.
All Rapped Up, Pocket Books (New York, NY), 1997.

FOR ADULTS; "CONSTABLE EVANS MYSTERY" SERIES; UNDER PSEUDONYM RHYS BOWEN

Evans Above, St. Martin's Press (New York, NY), 1997.
Evan Help Us, St. Martin's Press (New York, NY), 1998.
Evanly Choirs, St. Martin's Press (New York, NY), 1999.
Evan and Elle, St. Martin's Press (New York, NY), 2000.
Evan Can Late, St. Martin's Press (New York, NY), 2001.
Evans to Betsy, St. Martin's Press (New York, NY), 2002.
Evans Only Knows, St. Martin's Press (New York, NY), 2003.
Evans Gate, St. Martin's Press (New York, NY), 2003.
Evan Blessed, St. Martin's Press (New York, NY), 2005.

FOR ADULTS; "MOLLY MURPHY" SERIES; UNDER PSEUDONYM RHYS BOWEN

Murphy's Law, St. Martin's Press (New York, NY), 2001.
Death of Riley, St. Martin's Press (New York, NY), 2002.
For the Love of Mike, St. Martin's Press (New York, NY), 2003.
In like Flynn, St. Martin's Press (New York, NY), 2005.
Oh Danny Boy, St. Martin's Press (New York, NY), 2006.

OTHER

Madam Sarah (adult historical novel), Fawcett (New York, NY), 1990.
Fool's Gold (adult historical novel), HarperCollins (New York, NY), 1991.
Amazing Grace (adult historical fiction), HarperCollins (New York, NY), 1993.
The Secrets of Lake Success (based on the television miniseries created by David Stenn), Tor (New York, NY), 1993.
Trade Winds (based on the television miniseries created by Hugh Bush), Schoolfield/Caribbean Productions, 1993.

Contributor to *Chandler Reading Program,* five volumes, edited by Lawrence Carillo and Dorothy McKinley, Noble & Noble, 1967-72. Author of documentaries, radio plays, and scripts, including "Dandelion Hours," for British Broadcasting Corporation Radio, 1966. Contributor to periodicals, including *Scholastic* and *Mother's Journal,* and to anthologies, including *Blood on Their Hands,* 2004, and *Ungodly Orders.*

Author's works have been translated into other languages.

Sidelights

Janet Quin-Harkin's writing career has spanned numerous genres as well as two continents, several decades, and two names: her own and the pen name Rhys Bowen, under which she is the author of the popular "Constable Evans" and "Molly McGuire" mystery novels. Beginning her writing career in radio in her native England in the 1960s, Quin-Harkin soon to a new home in the United States, where she became known for her picture books and novels for teen readers. A prolific writer, Quin-Harkin's young-adult series include "Sweet Dreams," "Sugar and Spice," "Heartbreak Cafe," and "On Our Own," among others, and comprise novels featuring a group of characters involved in "the sort of lives that Middle America leads," as the author once described her work to *SATA.*

Born in Bath, England, Quin-Harkin published her first short story at age sixteen, and she eventually earned a bachelor's degree with honors from the University of London. Shortly after graduation, she worked for the British Broadcasting Corporation (BBC) as a studio manager and also as a writer of what she once dubbed "fairly highbrow" radio and television plays. Moving to Australia to work for the Australian Broadcasting Corporation, she met John Quin-Harkin. The couple married in 1966 and moved to the United States. Settling in the San Francisco Bay area, Quin-Harkin balanced the role of mother and writer, working first for a textbook company developing reading texts before writing her own books. Her first picture book, *Peter Penny's Dance,* was published in 1976, and set Quin-Harkin on a new career path: children's book author.

Inspired by the lyrics of a British folk song, *Peter Penny's Dance* features illustrations by Anita Lobel. Although the book earned critical praise and won numerous awards, it was followed by several years without sales as Quin-Harkin continued to raise her family while struggling to work at her craft. After she sold several titles to Parents Magazine Press, she began to establish her name in her new field, and in 1981 the chance to write a teen novel opened up even more opportunities. Her novel, *California Girl,* became the first installment in Bantam's "Sweet Dreams" series. The novel features a sixteen-year-old swimmer with Olympic aspirations. When Jenny's coach moves to Texas, the teen's family follows so that she can continue training. However,

Texas is a far cry from Jenny's former home state, and she is now viewed as strange due to her devotion to her sport. Fortunately, Jenny finds a new friend in injured football player Mark, who helps her train for her dream: a spot on the Olympic team. Ella B. Fossum, writing in *School Library Journal,* called *California Girl* "a cut above the usual teenage love story," while *Voice of Youth Advocates* contributor Becky Johnson gave the novel "high marks for readability," calling the plot "fast-moving and the main character . . . serious-minded and independent."

Quin-Harkin's "Sweet Dreams" series quickly gained a loyal readership as it expanded to include novels such as *Love Match, Daydreamer,* and the best-selling *Ten-Boy Summer,* all of which blend sympathetic and generally well-drawn main characters with a formulaic but entertaining plot. In *Love Match,* which also involves an athletic theme, Joanna refuses to ensure boyfriend Rick's affection by letting him beat her at tennis. *Ten-Boy Summer* finds Jill and Toni determined to liven up their junior-year summer by breaking up with their respective boyfriends and betting on who will be the first to have dated ten boys. Sally Estes, reviewing *Ten-Boy Summer* for *Booklist,* described the novel's premise "a bit farfetched, . . . but light and lively enough to attract nondemanding readers of teenage romances." Similarly, Susan Levine wrote in the *Voice of Youth Advocates* that *Ten-Boy Summer* "satisfies its requirements of a fast, uncomplicated, lightly romantic story with a happy ending."

The "Sweet Dreams" books sparked not just a new writing direction for Quin-Harkin, but also a major trend in young-adult publishing. Criticized by some as lacking in substance and praised by others as an encouragement to reading, teen books such as those Quin-Harkin produced became a staple of juvenile publishing, accounting for hundreds of thousands of sales annually. Writing to a tight schedule throughout the 1980s and well into the 1990s, she developed nine separate teen series, all of which focus on the concerns of contemporary teenage girls: what happens when a teen and her best friend break up, when a family moves, or when parents divorce? Most often there are young men involved: boys a girl wants to date, or love from afar, or beat at tennis. Other young-adult series from Quin-Harkin include "Sugar and Spice," "On Our Own," "Heartbreak Cafe," "Senior Year," "Boyfriend Club," "TGIF!," and "Sister, Sister," as well as "Friends," a series aimed at preteens that follows the relationship between two girls over summers spent together in a small resort town.

In between penning her many books for teen readers, Quin-Harkin also found time to author non-series fiction for adolescents. In her popular and award-winning novel *Wanted: Date for Saturday Night* the central problem is finding shy Julie a date for the freshman formal, while *Summer Heat* introduces teen protagonist Laurie Beth who, while on the verge of graduating from high school, must choose between two suitors and two completely different lifestyles. She has also penned the adult historical novels *Madam Sarah* and *Fool's Gold,* which deal with the "gold rush" eras in both California and Australia.

Beginning with *Evans Above* in 1997, Quin-Harkin started a new phase of her career, and began writing the type of books she most enjoys reading: mystery novels. Her "Constable Evans" series features Welsh policeman Evan Evans, and is set in the bucolic village of Llanfair, a town modeled on a small village the author loved as a child. For her "Constable Evans" books, as well as a second mystery series featuring young detective Molly Murphy, Quin-Harkin decided to use her Welsh grandfather's name, Rhys Bowen, as a way to keep her teen and adult writing separate.

In *Evans Above* young Evan Evans, a North Wales constable, is assigned to the village of Llanfair where he is known locally as Evans the Law due to the many residents sharing the name Evans. The town proves to be anything but tranquil, however; in one single day, two hikers presumably fall to their deaths on Mount Snowdon, while a third is discovered in a cave with his throat cut. Up to his ears in crime, the young constable also finds himself pursued by every eligible young lady in Llanfair. Reviewing *Evans Above* for *School Library Journal,* Judy McAloon cited the book's "well-crafted plot, nicely drawn characters, [and] strong sense of place," concluding that young-adult readers would enjoy both the book's setting and protagonist, "a hero who is young enough to feel self-conscious with women."

Constable Evans returns in *Evan Help Us, Evanly Choirs, Evan and Elle,* and *Evan Blessed.* An eligible bachelor, he is pursued by a woman who moves into the village with her daughter in *Evan Help Us,* until murder intrudes when a visitor from London claims to have found the ruins of Camelot near Llansfair, then loses his life. In *Evanly Choirs* the constable adds his voice to the local choir's preparations for an annual music festival, but things hit a sour note when a famous opera star vacationing in town winds up dead. Feminine wiles again come into play in *Evan and Elle* when an eligible widow opens a French restaurant and attempts to win the stomach—and heart—of the good constable away from his real sweetheart, the ever-true schoolmarm Bronwen Price. When Madame's restaurant burns to the ground, suspicion leads to Welsh extremists until a charred body turns the investigation into a homicide. And in *Evan Blessed* the search for a missing teen yields evidence of more grisly goings on, while on the home front Evan's parents prove themselves to be problematic in-laws. *Booklist* reviewer Jenny McLarin called *Evanly Choirs* a "charming tale" and a "perfect book to curl up with on a rainy day," while *Evan and Elle* was described as "a slight confection of a mystery" by a *Publishers Weekly* reviewer who added that the novel is "sweetened with the author's obvious affection for her characters, as well as for all things Welsh." Praising

Quin-Harken's "smooth, fast-paced" narrative, a *Publishers Weekly* contributor noted that in *Evan Blessed* she "keeps the suspense slowly building to a satisfying and tidy conclusion," and a *Kirkus* reviewer deemed Evan "likeable and resourceful."

Also published under Quin-Harkin's Bowen pseudonym, the "Molly Murphy" mystery series takes readers back to the turn of the twentieth century to introduce its spunky immigrant Irish sleuth in *Murphy's Law*. Recently arrived mystery in New York City after escaping from a rapist in her native Ireland, Murphy tackles a murder on Ellis Island, as well as navigating Hell's Kitchen and the city's Irish ghetto with two small children in tow, having promised their mother to reunite them with their father. In *Death of Riley*, against the urging of potential romantic interest Police Captain Daniel Sullivan, Murphy becomes an apprentice gumshoe, but winds up investigating the inconvenient death of her employer. The search for a killer soon expands to include a ring of anarchists and a plot to assassinate President William B. McKinley. At the helm of Riley's small detective agency in *For the Love of Mike*, Murphy finds herself embroiled in the theft of fashion designs, and going undercover in her investigation means working long hours in a New York garment district sweatshop. And as New York City is brought to a halt by the 1902 typhoid epidemic, Murphy escapes to points north, employed by an influential upstate politician to extricate his wife from the influences of a pair of suspicious spiritualists in *In like Flynn*.

Although noting that the "Molly Murphy" novels lack the lighthearted humor of Quin-Harkin's quaintly titled "Constable Evans" series, Rex E. Klett wrote in *Library Journal* that the award-winning series opener promises "a strong focus, great characters, and authentic period descriptions." "Molly is a smart, feisty, independent heroine," noted *Booklist* reviewer Sue O'Brien in a review of *Death of Riley*, while in *Publishers Weekly* a critic wrote that the author "nicely blends history and fiction" in a "light romantic mystery [that] should please most cozy fans." Praising *In like Flynn* as "absorbing" and "well-plotted," a reviewer for *Publishers Weekly* added that Quin-Harkin's energetic heroine bravely confronts both the mystery before her and a difficult issue in her own past in a "Molly Murphy" novel that "comes to a bittersweet and heartfelt conclusion."

Biographical and Critical Sources

PERIODICALS

Booklist, May 1, 1976, p. 1270; October 1, 1981, p. 189; January 15, 1982, p. 644; September 1, 1982, Sally Estes, review of *Ten-Boy Summer,* p. 37; May 15, 1983, Ilene Cooper, review of *Daydreamer,* p. 1221; February 1, 1984, p. 810; February 15, 1984, p. 862; June 15, 1984, p. 1474; October, 1998, GraceAnne A. DeCandido, review of *Evan Helps Us,* p. 224; April, 15, 1999, Jenny McLarin, review of *Evanly Choirs,* p. 1446; December 15, 1999, Jenny McLarin, review of *Evan and Elle,* p. 759; December 1, 2000, David Pitt, review of *Evan Can Wait,* p. 695; August, 2001, GraceAnne A. DeCandido, review of *Murphy's Law,* p. 2095; January 1, 2002, GraceAnne A. DeCandido, review of *Evans to Betsy,* p. 816; November 1, 2002, Sue O'Brien, review of *Death of Riley,* p. 476; March 15, 2004, Sue O'Brien, review of *Evan's Gate,* p. 1269; February 1, 2005, GraceAnne A. DeCandido, review of *In like Flynn,* p. 944.

Bulletin of the Center for Children's Books, October, 1976, Zena Sutherland, review of *Peter Penny's Dance,* p. 30; March, 1982, review of *Love Match,* p. 136; February, 1984, review of *Helpful Hattie,* p. 116; June, 1985, review of *Wanted: A Date for Saturday Night,* p. 192.

Horn Book, June, 1976, Ethel L. Heins, review of *Peter Penny's Dance,* p. 281; February, 1984, review of *Helpful Hattie,* p. 48.

Kirkus Reviews, November 15, 1997, review of *Evans Above;* April 28, 1999, review of *Evanly Choirs;* August 15, 2001, review of *Murphy's Law,* p. 1164; December 15, 2001, review of *Evans to Betsy,* p. 1723; October 1, 2002, review of *Death of Riley,* p. 1427; October 1, 2003, review of *For the Love of Mike,* p. 1201; February 1, 2005, review of *In like Flynn,* p. 149.

Kliatt, spring, 1982, p. 10; spring, 1983, p. 5; fall, 1985, Elaine Patterson, review of *101 Ways to Meet Mr. Right,* p. 16; May 15, 2005, review of *Evan Blessed,* p. 564.

Library Journal, December, 1997, Rex E. Klett, review of *Evans Above,* p. 159; March 1, 2000, Rex E. Klett, review of *Evan and Elle,* p. 128; January 1, 2001, Rex E. Klett, review of *Evan Can Wait,* p. 162; October 1, 2001, Rex E. Klett, review of *Murphy's Law,* p. 145; March 1, 2002, Rex E. Klett, review of *Evans to Betsy,* p. 144; December, 2003, Rex E. Klett, review of *For the Love of Mike,* p. 171; April 1, 2004, Rex E. Klett, review of *Evan's Gate,* p. 128; February 1, 2005, Rex E. Klett, review of *In like Flynn,* p. 57.

New York Times Book Review, May 9, 1976, p. 12; November 14, 1976, p. 53; April 1, 1979, p. 37; October 25, 1998, p. 43.

Publishers Weekly, January 20, 1984, review of *Helpful Hattie,* p. 89; July 25, 1986, review of *My Secret Love,* p. 192; December 22, 1989, review of *No Experience Required,* p. 57; June 29, 1990, review of *Summer Heat,* p. 103; May 24, 1991, review of *Starring Tess and Ali,* p. 58; August 17, 1998, review of *Evan Help Us,* p. 52; April 15, 1999, review of *Evanly Choirs,* p. 226; January 10, 2000, review of *Evan and Elle,* p. 48; November 13, 2000, review of *Evan Can Wait,* p. 88; September 3, 2001, review of *Murphy's Law,* p. 67; February 18, 2002, review of *Evans to Betsy,* p. 79; November 18, 2002, Sue O'Brien, review of *Death of Riley,* p. 476; February 3, 2003, review of *Evan Only Knows,* p. 58; November 3, 2003, review of *For the Love of Mike,* p. 57; March 29, 2004, review of *Evan's Gate,* p.42; February 28, 2005, review of *In like Flynn,* p. 45; May 30, 2005, review of *Evan Blessed,* p. 42; May 24, 1991, review of *Starring Tess and Ali,* p. 58.

School Library Journal, November, 1981, Ella B. Fossum, review of *California Girl,* p. 110; March, 1982, Joe McKenzie, review of *Love Match,* p. 160; October, 1982, review of *Ten-Boy Summer,* p. 158; May, 1983, review of *Daydreamer,* p. 84; September, 1986, Kathy Fritts, review of *The Graduates* and *The Trouble with Toni,* p. 148; January, 1987, Kathy Fritts, review of *Growing Pains,* p. 88; October, 1987, Kathy Fritts, review of *Two Girls, One Boy,* p. 150; January, 1988, Kathy Fritts, review of *Trading Places* and *Flip Side* and *Nothing in Common,* p. 95; January, 1989, Doris Fong, review of *It's My Turn,* p. 104; April, 1989, Doris Fong, review of *Campus Cousins* and *Home Sweet Home,* p. 127; October, 1989, Doris Fong, review of *One Step Too Far,* p. 144; May, 1998, Judy McAloon, review of *Evans Above,* p. 175; May, 2001, Pam Johnson, review of *Evan Can Wait,* p. 175.

Times Educational Supplement, April 21, 1995, p. 16.

Voice of Youth Advocates, December, 1981, Becky Johnson, review of *California Girl,* p. 34; December, 1982, Susan Levine, review of *Ten-Boy Summer,* p. 35; December, 1983, Maureen Ritter, review of *Daydreamer,* p. 281; December, 1986, review of *Old Friends, New Friends,* p. 228; December, 1987, review of *Two Girls, One Boy,* p. 241; April, 1988, Laurel Ibey, review of *Flip Side,* and Juli Lund, review of *The Last Dance,* p. 35; April, 1989, review of *It's My Turn,* p. 38; June, 1989, review of *Home Sweet Home,* p. 112; February, 1991, review of *Summer Heat,* p. 355; October, 1994, p. 215; December, 1994, p. 279.

ONLINE

Rhys Bowen Web site, http://www.jqh.home.netcom.com (October 20, 2005).

* * *

REID BANKS, Lynne 1929-

Personal

Born July 31, 1929, in London, England; daughter of James (a doctor) and Pat (an actress and writer; maiden name, Marsh) Reid Banks; married Chaim Stephenson (a sculptor), 1965; children: Adiel Mark, Gillon Adam, Omri Guy (sons). *Education:* Attended Italia Conte Stage School, 1946, and Royal Academy of Dramatic Art, 1947-49. *Politics:* "Socialist." *Hobbies and other interests:* Theater, gardening, teaching ESL abroad.

Addresses

Home—Bong-Roue Farmhouse, Beaminster, Dorset DT8 3SB, England. *Agent*—Sheila Watson, Watson, Little Ltd., 12 Egbert St., London NW1 8LJ, England.

Lynne Reid Banks

Career

Writer and journalist. Actress in English repertory companies, 1949-54; freelance journalist, London, England, 1954-55; Independent Television News, London, television news reporter, 1955-57, television news scriptwriter, 1958-62; taught English as a foreign language in Israel, 1963-71; writer, 1971—.

Member

British Society of Authors, PEN, Actors' Equity.

Awards, Honors

Yorkshire Arts Literary Award, 1976, and Best Books for Young Adults Award, American Library Association, 1977, both for *Dark Quartet;* West Australian Young Readers' Book Award, Library Association of Australia, 1980, for *My Darling Villain;* Outstanding Books of the Year Award, *New York Times,* 1981, Young Reader's Choice Award, Pacific Northwest Library Association, 1984, California Young Readers Medal, California Reading Association, 1985, Children's Books of the Year Award, Child Study Association, 1986, and Young Readers of Virginia Award, and Arizona Young Readers' Award, both 1988, all for *The Indian in the Cupboard;* Parents' Choice Award for Literature, Parents' Choice Foundation, and Notable Books Award, *New York Times,* both 1986, Children's Books of the Year Award, 1987, Rebecca Caudill Young Reader's Books Award, Illinois Association for Media in Education, 1988, and Indian Paintbrush Award, Wyoming Library Association, 1989, all for *The Return of the Indian;*

Great Stone Face (New Hampshire librarians) Award, 1991, for *Secret of the Indian;* Silver Award, Smarties Prize, 1996, for *Harry the Poisonous Centipede.*

Writings

FOR YOUNG PEOPLE

One More River, Simon & Schuster (New York, NY), 1973, revised edition, Morrow (New York, NY), 1992.

The Adventures of King Midas, illustrated by George Him, Dent (London, England), 1976, illustrated by Jos. A. Smith, Morrow (New York, NY), 1992.

The Farthest-Away Mountain, illustrated by Victor Ambrus, Abelard-Schuman (London, England), 1976, Doubleday (New York, NY), 1977, reprinted, 2003, illustrated by Dave Henderson, Doubleday (New York, NY), 1991.

My Darling Villain, Harper (New York, NY), 1977.

I Houdini: The Autobiography of a Self-Educated Hamster, illustrated by Terry Riley, Dent (London, England), 1978, Doubleday (New York, NY), 1988, reprinted, 2002.

Letters to My Israeli Sons: The Story of Jewish Survival, W. H. Allen (London, England), 1979, F. Watts (New York, NY), 1980.

The Writing on the Wall, Harper (New York, NY), 1981.

Maura's Angel, illustrated by Robin Jacques, Dent (London, England), 1984, Avon (New York, NY), 1998.

The Fairy Rebel, illustrated by William Geldart, Dent (London, England), 1985, Doubleday (New York, NY), 1988.

Melusine: A Mystery, Hamilton Children's Books (London, England), 1988, Harper (New York, NY), 1989.

The Magic Hare, illustrated by Hilda Offen, Collins (London, England), 1992, illustrated by Barry Moser, Morrow (New York, NY), 1993.

Broken Bridge (sequel to *One More River*), Morrow (New York, NY), 1994.

Harry the Poisonous Centipede: A Story to Make You Squirm, illustrated by Tony Ross, Collins (London, England), 1996, Morrow (New York, NY), 1997.

Angela and Diabola, illustrated by Klaas Verplancke, Avon (New York, NY), 1997.

Moses in Egypt (based on the film *Prince of Egypt*), Penguin (New York, NY), 1998.

Alice-by-Accident, illustrated by Tania Hurt-Newton, HarperCollins (New York, NY), 2000.

Harry the Poisonous Centipede's Big Adventure: Another Story to Make You Squirm, HarperCollins U.K. (London, England), 2000, HarperCollins (New York, NY), 2001.

The Dungeon, HarperCollins (New York, NY), 2002.

The Fairy Rebel, illustrated by William Geldart, Delacorte (New York, NY), 2003.

Stealing Stacey, Collins (London, England), 2004.

Tiger, Tiger, HarperCollins (London, England), 2004, Delacorte (New York, NY), 2005.

Harry the Poisonous Centipede Goes to Sea, illustrated by Tony Ross, HarperCollins (London, England), 2005, HarperCollins (New York, NY), 2006.

"INDIAN IN THE CUPBOARD" SERIES; FOR CHILDREN

The Indian in the Cupboard, illustrated by Robin Jacques, Doubleday (New York, NY), 1980.

Return of the Indian, illustrated by William Geldart, Dent (London, England), 1986, published as *The Return of the Indian,* Doubleday (New York, NY), 1986.

The Secret of the Indian, illustrated by Ted Lewin, Doubleday (New York, NY), 1989.

The Mystery of the Cupboard, illustrated by Piers Sanford, Collins (London, England), 1993, illustrated by Tom Newsom, Morrow (New York, NY), 1993.

The Indian Trilogy, Lions (London, England), 1993.

The Key to the Indian, illustrated by James Watling, Avon (New York, NY), 1998.

The Indian in the Cupboard and its sequels were translated into some twenty languages.

PLAYS

It Never Rains (produced by British Broadcasting Corporation [BBC], 1954), Deane (London, England), 1954.

All in a Row, Deane (London, England), 1956.

The Killer Dies Twice (three-act), Deane (London, England), 1956.

Already It's Tomorrow (produced by BBC, 1962), Samuel French (London, England), 1962.

The Unborn, produced in London, England, 1962.

The Wednesday Caller, produced by BBC (London, England), 1963.

Last Word on Julie, produced by ATV, 1964.

The Gift (three-act), produced in London, England, 1965.

The Stowaway (radio play), produced by BBC Radio (London, England), 1967.

The Eye of the Beholder, produced by ITV, 1977.

Lame Duck (radio play), produced by BBC Radio (London, England), 1978.

Purely from Principal (radio play), produced by BBC Radio (London, England), 1985.

The Travels of Yoshi and the Tea-Kettle (for children; produced in London, England, 1991), Thomas Nelson (London, England), 1993.

FOR ADULTS

The L-shaped Room (also see below), Chatto & Windus (London, England), 1960, Simon & Schuster (New York, NY), 1961, revised edition, Longman (London, England), 1976, reprinted, Vintage (London, England), 2004.

An End to Running, Chatto & Windus (London, England), 1962, published as *House of Hope,* Simon & Schuster (New York, NY), 1962.

Children at the Gate, Simon & Schuster (New York, NY), 1968.

The Backward Shadow (also see below), Simon & Schuster (New York, NY), 1970.

The Kibbutz: Some Personal Reflections, Anglo-Israel Association (London, England), 1972.

Two Is Lonely (also see below), Simon & Schuster (New York, NY), 1974.

Sarah and After: The Matriarchs, Bodley Head (London, England), 1975, published as *Sarah and After: Five Women Who Founded a Nation*, Doubleday (New York, NY), 1975.

Dark Quartet: The Story of the Brontës, Weidenfeld & Nicholson (London, England), 1976, Delacorte (New York, NY), 1977.

Path to the Silent Country: Charlotte Brontë's Years of Fame (sequel to *Dark Quartet*), Weidenfeld & Nicholson (London, England), 1976, Delacorte (New York, NY), 1977.

Defy the Wilderness, Chatto & Windus (London, England), 1981.

Torn Country: An Oral History of the Israeli War of Independence, F. Watts (New York, NY), 1982.

The Warning Bell, Hamish Hamilton (London, England), 1984, St. Martin's Press (New York, NY), 1987.

Casualties, Hamish Hamilton (London, England), 1986, St. Martin's Press (New York, NY), 1987.

Fair Exchange, Piatkus (London, England), 1998.

L-shaped Trilogy (contains *The Backward Shadow* and *Two Is Lonely*), Penguin U.K. (London, England), 2000.

Contributor to numerous periodicals, including *Ladies' Home Journal, Observer*, Manchester *Guardian*, London *Sunday Telegraph, Independent*, London *Sunday Times*, and *Saga*.

Adaptations

The L-shaped Room was adapted as a film starring Leslie Caron, Davis-Royal Films, 1962; all the "Indian in the Cupboard" books have been adapted as audiobooks; *The Indian in the Cupboard* was adapted as a major motion picture by Columbia Pictures, 1995; *The Farthest-Away Mountain, The Fairy Rebel, I, Houdini, The Adventures of King Midas, Harry the Poisonous Centipede, Harry the P.C.'s Big Adventures, Angela and Diabola, The Backward Shadow*, and other books have been adapted as audiobooks, read by Reid Banks, Listening Library, beginning 1994.

Sidelights

Best known to readers for her novel *The Indian in the Cupboard*, British author and former journalist Lynne Reid Banks is a versatile writer who has tackled complex subjects, such as single parenthood and the Middle East in books for both adults and children. Many of Reid Banks's titles for younger readers, such as the "Indian" books as well as standalone novels such as *The Adventures of King Midas* and *The Fairy Rebel*, feature magic as a central theme. Teen readers are attracted to more contemporary works such as *The Writing on the Wall*, in which Reid Banks deals with typical teenage problems like dating and family relationships. In many of her works, though not, perhaps in her juvenile fantasies, Reid Banks draws on a wealth of personal experiences.

Born in London in 1929, Reid Banks had her childhood interrupted by World War II, and she and her mother were evacuated to Saskatchewan, Canada, for five years. "Since my mother was evacuated with me, I was very happy, and though we were poor, I hardly noticed it, except that I couldn't have trendy clothes," the author once noted in an interview for *Authors and Artists for Young Adults* (*AAYA*). "I didn't really realize what the war meant, or the terrible things that had been happening, until I got back to England, at the very formative age of fifteen. I found my city in ruins, and learned what had been happening to my family, left behind, and in Europe, to the Jews. I felt like a deserter." Wartime experiences such as these have influenced much of Reid Banks' adult writing.

As a teen, Reid Banks's ambition was to be an actress like her mother. In order to prepare for this career, she attended the prestigious Royal Academy of Dramatic Art, and worked for five years in various repertory companies throughout Great Britain. Although she enjoyed the theatre, she eventually realized that she did not have the qualities needed to establish a successful career in acting, and in 1954 she left the stage to go to work as a television journalist. Her theatrical training came in useful, later, however, when she was working teaching English to Hebrew-speaking children in Israel beginning in the early 1960s. She treated each lesson as a performance, and was far more successful as a teacher than she had been as an actress.

Reid Banks's first literary success was the adult novel *The L-shaped Room*, which chronicles the life of unmarried, twenty-seven-year-old Jane Graham who goes to live in a run-down lodging house when she becomes pregnant. The book earned good reviews, *New Statesman* critic Janice Elliott calling it "touching and competent," as well as "ambitious and mature." Reid Banks eventually wrote two more novels featuring Graham: *The Backward Shadow* and *Two Is Lonely*.

The positive critical response to *The L-shaped Room* provided Reid Banks with the means to accomplish another dream. "Throughout my late teens and twenties, when Israel was going through its early traumas [as a newly formed modern nation], I had a great desire to go there," she explained in *AAYA*. In 1960 she traveled there, where she met the man who would become her husband, sculptor Chaim Stephenson. What had started as a series of visits now became a residency. "Living in a kibbutz, working the land, teaching and having my babies in that 'alien' country that I came to love so much, was a sublimation for my lingering feelings of guilt for having missed the War," the author explained.

In 1972 Reid Banks and her family moved to England and the following year she published her first young-adult book, *One More River*. Drawing on the author's life in Israel, the novel focuses on Lesley, a pampered Canadian girl attempting to adjust to life in an Israeli kibbutz. A sequel to *One More River, Broken Bridge* finds Lesley grown up, married, and raising her children in the kibbutz. The novel revolves around questions about Lesley's choice of lifestyle after her nephew is killed by an Arab terrorist during a visit to Jerusalem, a tragedy compounded by the fact that Lesley's daughter Nili witnessed the murder but will not divulge the terrorist's identity.

With her second children's book, *The Adventures of King Midas,* Reid Banks won over young readers and she has continued to win fans with her tales of magical kings, brave fairies, toys that come to life, and intrepid hamsters, hares, and centipedes. In *I, Houdini: The Autobiography of a Self-educated Hamster,* for example, she spins a yarn about a domesticated rodent that enjoys escaping from his cage to cause all manner of mischief in the house where his owners—three brothers—live. Part of a series, *Harry the Poisonous Centipede: A Story to Make You Squirm* finds a curious insect joining his friends on a forbidden trip to the "up side" world, where they avoid attacks by the treacherous two-legged, newspaper-swatting "homins" before making it back down into their cozy underground home. Written for older readers, *The Farthest-Away Mountain* introduces spunky, fourteen-year-old Dakin, who sets out to accomplish her three life goals: to reach the distant mountains, to meet a gargoyle, and to marry a prince. While tackling her first two goals, Dakin comes to realize that a prince need not have a princely character, and she ultimately abandons her search for royalty in favor of a trusted male friend. Within an imaginative plot and fantastic setting, Reid Banks "makes every character come alive, capturing the nuances of their natures, their pettiness, jealousy and fears," according to *School Library Journal* contributor Edith Ching.

Magic again appears in *Maura's Angel.* Eleven-year-old Maura lives in Belfast, Northern Ireland, where violence between Protestant and Catholic factions still persists. With her brother in jail and her father in hiding due to his affiliation with the terrorist Irish Republican Army, Maura and her mother try to keep the household together. During a bomb blast, Maura encounters a young girl who could be her twin and who goes by the name of Angela. In fact, Angela is no girl at all; she is Maura's angel. While Maura gets used to having an angel around, Angela must deal with the feelings of happiness and sorrow she had not experienced in heaven, but which come upon her in her human form. "It is [Angela's] desperate wish to make things right for Maura's family . . . that brings about terrible consequences," noted *School Library Journal* contributor Eva Mitnik, adding that Reid Banks' story will cause young readers to reflect on its message—about the value in life's hardships—"long after they turn the final page."

In *Angela and Diabola* Reid Banks plays up the fantasy elements of pure good and evil. Twin sisters Angela and Diabola are opposites; as their names would suggest, one is very, very good, while the other is absolutely awful. In fact, after Diabola kills the family cat and

gets her mother thrown into jail, the girls' parents decide that the best that can be done is to keep Diabola in a cage when she is not closely supervised. Unfortunately, steel bars do little to suppress the evil child, who turns to telekinesis as a way of spreading wickedness. In true storybook fashion, the two sisters ultimately do battle, with Angela coming out the victor, although slightly altered. Comparing the book to the work of British writer Roald Dahl, *School Library Journal* reviewer Anne Connor called *Angela and Diabola* "an absurd look at human nature [that] is often bitingly funny," while a *Publishers Weekly* contributor noted that Reid Banks's "expansive storytelling and comic exaggeration produce high kid appeal."

Among Reid Banks's most popular fantasy works for children are *The Indian in the Cupboard* and its sequels: *Return of the Indian, The Secret of the Indian, The Mystery of the Cupboard,* and *The Key to the Indian.* In each volume, a group of toy figurines belonging to a boy named Omri come to life when they are locked in a small metal cupboard with a lead key. Omri soon discovers that his favorite toy, a small plastic Indian figure named Little Bear, has, when brought to life, a taste for adventure—sometimes with near-

A homework assignment sparks a nine-year-old girl's decision to begin a secret diary in which she begins to make sense of her life and the people in it in this 2000 novel. (Cover illustration by Mark Elliott.)

disastrous results. Other characters, which *New York Times Book Review* contributor Michael Dorris described as "plucky, albeit creaky cultural stereotypes, ever predictable and true to the dictates of their sex, ethnic group, or time," include a cowboy, a British nurse, a soldier, a saloon-bar hostess, and a horse.

A reviewer for the *Times Literary Supplement* found *The Indian in the Cupboard* to contain "original, lively, compulsive writing" that "will well stand through repeated readings." In sequels to the first novel Omri discovers the history behind the cupboard, which has been in his family for many years. In *The Mystery of the Cupboard,* Omri and his family inherit an old house in the Dorset countryside. There the boy discovers an "account" written by his great aunt that reveals the cupboard's secret, and he also meets a host of new cupboard-sized characters. While questioning Reid Banks's inclusion of a "scientific" explanation for the workings of the cupboard, Dorris considered *The Mystery of the Cupboard* "a stunning, full-blown tale" and dubbed Omri's great-great aunt "a vivid, arresting personality, a woman consumed by jealousy and recrimination" whose own story will fascinate readers.

The final novel in the series, *The Key to the Indian,* finds Omri sharing his secret with his father, who joins his son in a trip back in time in an effort to help Little Bear and his Iroquois tribe survive the efforts of early American settlers to defeat them. "Readers will revel in all of the details of this book, from the intricate workings of the magic to the solutions Omri finds to [transportation] problems," wrote Eva Mitnik in *School Library Journal.*

Moving from fantasy to the real world, Reid Banks focuses on family conflict in *Alice-by-Accident,* a middle-grade novel about a ten-year-old girl who lives with her lawyer mother and has never met her father. In a series of diary entries, Alice describes her feelings as a child who came "by accident" to her mother and whose loving paternal grandmother, Gene, makes it clear she disapproves of Alice's out-of-wedlock birth. Although Gene does all she can to support her granddaughter— even loaning the use of a home for several months— tensions eventually develop between Alice's mom and Gene. Although adult issues remain a mystery, Alice realizes that she must chose between the few family members she has. A reviewer for *Horn Book* found Alice a "likable, well-developed character with an authentic voice," and a contributor to *Publishers Weekly* appreciated Reid Banks's "fresh" plotting and sensitivity to Alice's point of view.

Other middle-grade novels by Reid Banks include the historical novels *The Dungeon* and *Tiger, Tiger. The Dungeon* follows an ambitious Scottish laird as he constructs a fortress and then travels to China on the route taken by Marco Polo, his purpose to seek revenge and an outlet for his anger over the death of his wife and children. In the Orient MacLennan acquires a young tea

Provoked by grief over his dead family, a Scottish laird travels to China and acquires a young servant girl whose life turns to tragedy as a result of her master's pain and anger in Reid Banks' compelling novel **The Dungeon.**

slave named Peony, whom he brings back to Scotland. The young child's experiences in the service of a brutal master, as well as her friendship with MacLennan's stable boy, Fin, and her generous impressions of her new world show her to be an "agreeable" character in a novel resonant with passion and "the excitement of travel and battle," according to a *Kirkus* reviewer. Noting the novel's tragic end, *Booklist* critic John Peters described *The Dungeon* as a "brutal psychological character study," while in *Publishers Weekly* a critic called the novel a "riveting tale of reprisal and redemption" that "conveys a powerful message about the terrible price of unswerving revenge."

Taking readers back to ancient Rome in the days of Caesar, *Tiger, Tiger* focuses on twelve-year-old Aurelia, the daughter of the emperor. Given a small, de-fanged tiger club as a gift by her father, she names her new pet Boots, and cares for it with the help of a young slave named Julius. The girl does not realize that the cub's litter mate, Brute, is being brutally treated and half starved in preparation for his turn in the Coliseum, where he will battle gladiators to the death. Jealous that Aurelia cares more for her servant than she does him, cousin Marcus uses his knowledge of the two tigers to plot his revenge, but when the plot goes awry Aurelia must battle the implacable Caesar to save her beloved pet. While a *Kirkus* critic dubbed the novel "a melodramatic foray into an extremely fictional" Rome, in *Publishers Weekly* a contributor praised *Tiger, Tiger* as a "gripping, tantalizing examination of power, sacrifice, and mercy." Reid Banks "ably captures" the relationship between father and daughter, as well as revealing Aurelia's growing knowledge "that absolute power is a blunt instrument," and she brings to life an ancient world that "vibrates with life," according to *Horn Book* contributor Anita L. Burkham.

While Reid Banks enjoys writing for audiences of all ages, she brings a special enthusiasm to her works for younger readers. "Writing for young people is a much pleasanter, and easier, thing than writing for adults," she once commented. "I especially enjoy writing wish-fulfillment stories. . . . But in the end, one has to write what one wants to write, or what one is commissioned to write, and hope for the best. You can't win 'em all."

Biographical and Critical Sources

BOOKS

Authors and Artists for Young Adults, Volume 6, Thomson Gale (Detroit, MI), 1991.
Children's Literature Review, Volume 24, Thomson Gale (Detroit, MI), 1991.
Contemporary Novelists, Gale (Detroit, MI), 1988.
Drabble, Margaret, editor, *The Oxford Companion to Children's Literature,* 5th edition, Oxford University Press (New York, NY), 1995.
Parker, Peter, *A Reader's Guide to Twentieth-Century Writers,* Oxford University Press (New York, NY), 1996.
Science Fiction and Fantasy Literature, 1975-1991, Thomson Gale (Detroit, MI), 1992.
Silvey, Anita, editor, *Children's Books and Their Creators,* Houghton Mifflin (Boston, MA), 1995.
Twentieth-Century Young-Adult Writers, St. James Press (Detroit, MI), 1994.
Zipes, Jack, *The Oxford Companion to Fairy Tales,* Oxford University Press (New York, NY), 2000.

PERIODICALS

Booklist, March 15, 1995, Jeanne Triner, review of *Broken Bridge,* pp. 1321-1322; November 15, 1998, Kay Weisman, review of *The Key to the Indian,* p. 586; June 1, 2000, Kay Weisman, review of *Alice-by-Accident,* p. 1890; June 1, 2001, Kay Weisman, review of *Harry the Poisonous Centipede's Big Adventure,* p. 1878; October 1, 2002, review of *The Dungeon,* p. 311.
Carousel, spring, 1999, Chris Stephenson, interview with Reid Banks, p. 32.
Horn Book, September-October, 1993, p. 483; May 2000, review of *Alice-by-Accident,* p. 306; May, 2000, review of *Alice-by-Accident,* p. 306; July-August, 2005, Anita L. Burkam, review of *Tiger, Tiger,* p. 464.

Kirkus Reviews, September 1, 2002, review of *The Dungeon,* p. 1302; June 1, 2005, review of *Tiger, Tiger,* p. 633.
Kliatt, November, 2002, Paula Rohrlick, review of *The Dungeon,* p. 6; May, 2005, Janis Flint-Ferguson, review of *Tiger, Tiger,* p. 6.
Los Angeles Times Book Review, April 23, 1989, p. 10.
New Statesman, July 26, 1968, Janice Elliott, "Old Hat," p. 116.
New York Times Book Review, April 6, 1961, Otis Kidwell Burger, "Someone to Love," p. 38; April 16, 1989, p. 26; May 16, 1993, Michael Dorris, "A Boy and His Box, Batteries Not Needed"; May 16, 1993, Lawrie Mifflin, "Fairies and Elves All around Us" (interview), p. 36.
Publishers Weekly, October 27, 1989, Amanda Smith, interview with Reid Banks, p. 30; September 21, 1992, review of *The Adventures of King Midas;* February 22, 1993, review of *The Mystery of the Cupboard;* July 5, 1993, review of *The Magic Hare;* February 20, 1995, review of *Broken Bridge,* pp. 206-207; April 7, 1997, review of *Angela and Diabola;* June 9, 1997, review of *Harry the Poisonous Centipede,* p. 46; May 11, 1998, review of *Maura's Angel;* May 25, 1998, review of *Angela and Diabola,* p. 92; October 26, 1998, review of *The Key to the Indian,* p. 66; June 19, 2000, review of *Alice-by-Accident,* p. 80; October 28, 2002, review of *The Dragon,* p. 73; June 27, 2005, review of *Tiger, Tiger,* p. 65.
School Library Journal, June, 1993, p. 102; April, 1994, p. 88; April, 1995, p. 150; November, 1995, Linda W. Braun, "Good Conversation: A Talk with Lynn Reid Banks," p. 52; July, 1997, Edith Ching, review of *The Farthest-Away Mountain,* p. 56; July, 1997, Anne Connor, review of *Angela and Diabola,* p. 90; September, 1997, p. 172; August, 1998, Eva Mitnik, review of *Maura's Angel,* p. 160; December, 1998, Eva Mitnik, review of *The Key to the Indian,* p. 118; June, 2000, Darcy Schild, review of *Alice-by-Accident,* p. 138; May, 2001, Carrie Schadle, review of *Harry the Poisonous Centipede's Big Adventure,* p. 108; December, 2002, Daniel L. Dargon, review of *The Dungeon,* p. 132.
Times Literary Supplement, November 21, 1980 review of *The Indian in the Cupboard;* December 1, 1988.

ONLINE

Lynne Reid Banks Home Page, http://www.lynnereidbanks.com (November 23, 2005).*

*   *   *

RENSIE, Willis
See EISNER, Will

S

SENDAK, Maurice 1928-
(Maurice Bernard Sendak)

Personal

Born June 10, 1928, in Brooklyn, NY; son of Philip (a dressmaker) and Sarah (Schindler) Sendak. *Education:* Attended Art Students' League, New York, NY, 1949-51.

Addresses

Home—200 Chestnut Hill Rd., Ridgefield, CT 06877. *Agent*—c/o Author Mail, HarperCollins, 10 E. 53rd St., 7th Fl., New York, NY 10022.

Career

Writer and illustrator of children's books, 1951—. All American Comics, part-time artist, c. mid-1940s; Timely Service (window display house), New York, NY, window display artist, 1946; F.A.O. Schwartz, New York, NY, display artist, 1948-51. Co-founder and artistic director, The Night Kitchen (national children's theatre), 1990—. Instructor at Parsons School of Design and Yale University. Set and costume designer for numerous opera productions in the United States and Great Britain, including *The Magic Flute,* for Houston Grand Opera, 1980; *The Cunning Little Vixen,* for New York City Opera, 1981; *Love for Three Oranges,* for Glyndebourne Opera, 1982; *The Goose of Cairo,* for New York City Opera, c. 1984; *Idomeneo,* for Los Angeles Opera, 1988; and *L'Enfant et les sortilèges* and *L'Heure Espagnol,* both for New York City Opera, 1989; Designer for *The Nutcracker: The Motion Picture,* 1986. Appeared in "Mon Cher Papa" episode of *American Master Series,* PBS-TV, 1987. May Hill Arbuthnot Lecturer, 2003. *Exhibitions:* Sendak's illustrations have been displayed in one-man shows at School of Visual Arts, New York, NY, 1964, Rosenbach Foundation, Philadelphia, PA, 1970 and 1975, Trinity College, Hartford, CT, 1972, Galerie Daniel Keel, Zurich, Switzerland, 1974, Ashmolean Museum, Oxford University, 1975, American Cultural Center, Paris, France, 1978, and Pierpont Morgan Library, New York, NY, 1981.

Maurice Sendak

Member

Authors Guild, Authors League of America.

Awards, Honors

New York Times Best Illustrated Book award, 1952, for *A Hole Is to Dig,* 1954, for *I'll Be You and You Be Me,* 1956, for *I Want to Paint My Bathroom Blue,* 1957, for *The Birthday Party,* 1958, for *What Do You Say, Dear?,*

192

1959, for *Father Bear Comes Home,* 1960, for *Open House for Butterflies,* 1962, for *The Singing Hill,* 1963, for *Where the Wild Things Are,* 1964, for *The Bat-Poet,* 1965, for *The Animal Family,* 1966, for *Zlateh the Goat and Other Stories,* 1968, for *A Kiss for Little Bear,* 1969, for *The Light Princess,* 1970, for *In the Night Kitchen,* 1973, for *The Juniper Tree and Other Tales from Grimm* and *King Grisly-Beard,* 1976, for *Fly by Night,* 1981, for *Outside over There,* and 1984, for *The Nutcracker;* Caldecott Medal runner-up, American Library Association (ALA), 1954, for *A Very Special House,* 1959, for *What Do You Say, Dear?,* 1960, for *The Moon Jumpers,* 1962, for *Little Bear's Visit,* 1963, for *Mr. Rabbit and the Lovely Present,* 1971, for *In the Night Kitchen,* and 1982, for *Outside over There;* Spring Book Festival honor book, 1956, for *Kenny's Window;* Caldecott Medal, and Lewis Carroll Shelf award, both 1964, International Board on Books for Young People award, 1966, Art Books for Children awards, 1973, 1974, 1975, Best Young Picture Books Paperback Award, *Redbook,* 1984, and Children's Choice award, 1985, all for *Where the Wild Things Are;* Chandler Book Talk Reward of Merit, 1967; Hans Christian Andersen International Medal (first American to receive this award), 1970, for body of illustration work; Art Books for Children award, 1973, 1974, 1975, and *Redbook* award, 1985, all for *In the Night Kitchen;* American Book Award nomination, 1980, for *Higglety Pigglety Pop!; or, There Must Be More to Life;* Boston Globe/Horn Book award, and *New York Times* Outstanding Book, both 1981, and American Book Award, 1982, all for *Outside over There;* Laura Ingalls Wilder Award, Association for Library Service to Children, 1983, for lasting contribution to children's literature; National Medal of the Arts, 1997; Astrid Lindgren Memorial Prize (co-recipient), 2003. L.H.D., Boston University, 1977; honorary degrees from University of Southern Mississippi, 1981, and Keene State College, 1986.

Writings

FOR CHILDREN; SELF-ILLUSTRATED

Kenny's Window, Harper (New York, NY), 1956, reprinted, 2004.

Very Far Away, Harper (New York, NY), 1957.

The Acrobat, privately printed, 1959.

The Sign on Rosie's Door, Harper (New York, NY), 1960.

Nutshell Library (verse; contains *Chicken Soup with Rice: A Book of Months, One Was Johnny: A Counting Book, Alligators All Around: An Alphabet,* and *Pierre: A Cautionary Tale*), Harper (New York, NY), 1962.

Where the Wild Things Are, Harper (New York, NY), 1963, 25th anniversary edition, 1988.

Hector Protector, and As I Went over the Water: Two Nursery Rhymes, Harper (New York, NY), 1965.

Higglety Pigglety Pop!; or, There Must Be More to Life, Harper (New York, NY), 1967.

In the Night Kitchen, Harper (New York, NY), 1970.

Ten Little Rabbits: A Counting Book with Mino the Magician, Philip H. Rosenbach, 1970.

Pictures by Maurice Sendak, Harper (New York, NY), 1971.

Maurice Sendak's Really Rosie (based on the television program of the same title; also see below), Harper (New York, NY), 1975.

(With Matthew Margolis) *Some Swell Pup; or, Are You Sure You Want a Dog?,* Farrar, Straus (New York, NY), 1976.

Seven Little Monsters (verse), Harper (New York, NY), 1977.

Outside over There, Harper (New York, NY), 1981.

We Are All in the Dumps with Jack and Guy: Two Nursery Rhymes with Pictures, HarperCollins (New York, NY), 1993.

ILLUSTRATOR

M.L. Eidinoff and Hyman Ruchlis, *Atomics for the Millions* (for adults), McGraw (New York, NY), 1947.

Robert Garvey, *Good Shabbos, Everybody!,* United Synagogue Commission on Jewish Education, 1951.

Marcel Ayme, *The Wonderful Farm,* Harper (New York, NY), 1951.

Ruth Krauss, *A Hole Is to Dig: A First Book of Definitions,* Harper (New York, NY), 1952.

Ruth Sawyer, *Maggie Rose: Her Birthday Christmas,* Harper (New York, NY), 1952.

Beatrice S. de Regniers, *The Giant Story,* Harper (New York, NY), 1953.

Meindert De Jong, *Hurry Home, Candy,* Harper (New York, NY), 1953.

Meindert De Jong, *Shadrach,* Harper (New York, NY), 1953.

Ruth Krauss, *A Very Special House,* Harper (New York, NY), 1953.

Hyman Chanover, *Happy Hanukkah, Everybody,* United Synagogue Commission on Jewish Education, 1954.

Ruth Krauss, *I'll Be You and You Be Me,* Harper (New York, NY), 1954.

Edward Tripp, *The Tin Fiddle,* Oxford University Press (Oxford, England), 1954.

Marcel Ayme, *Magic Pictures,* Harper (New York, NY), 1954.

Betty MacDonald, *Mrs. Piggle-Wiggle's Farm,* Lippincott (Philadelphia, PA), 1954.

Meindert De Jong, *The Wheel on the School,* Harper (New York, NY), 1954.

Ruth Krauss, *Charlotte and the White Horse,* Harper (New York, NY), 1955.

Meindert De Jong, *The Little Cow and the Turtle,* Harper (New York, NY), 1955.

Jean Ritchie, *Singing Family of the Cumberlands,* Oxford University Press (Oxford, England), 1955.

Beatrice S. de Regniers, *What Can You Do with a Shoe?,* Harper (New York, NY), 1955, reprinted, Aladdin (New York, NY), 2001.

Jack Sendak (brother), *Happy Rain,* Harper (New York, NY), 1956.

Meindert De Jong, *The House of Sixty Fathers*, Harper (New York, NY), 1956.

Ruth Krauss, *I Want to Paint My Bathroom Blue*, Harper (New York, NY), 1956.

Ruth Krauss, *Birthday Party*, Harper (New York, NY), 1957.

Jack Sendak, *Circus Girl*, Harper (New York, NY), 1957.

Ogden Nash, *You Can't Get There from Here*, Little, Brown (Boston, MA), 1957.

Else Minarik, *Little Bear*, Harper (New York, NY), 1957.

Meindert De Jong, *Along Came a Dog*, Harper (New York, NY), 1958.

Else Minarik, *No Fighting, No Biting!*, Harper (New York, NY), 1958.

Ruth Krauss, *Somebody Else's Nut Tree*, Harper (New York, NY), 1958.

Sesyle Joslyn, *What Do You Say, Dear?: A Book of Manners for All Occasions*, W.R. Scott (New York, NY), 1958.

Else Minarik, *Father Bear Comes Home*, Harper (New York, NY), 1959.

Janice Udry, *The Moon Jumpers*, Harper (New York, NY), 1959.

Hans Christian Andersen, *Seven Tales*, Harper (New York, NY), 1959.

Wilhelm Hauff, *Dwarf Long-Nose*, Random House (New York, NY), 1960.

Else Minarik, *Little Bear's Friend*, Harper (New York, NY), 1960.

Ruth Krauss, *Open House for Butterflies*, Harper (New York, NY), 1960.

Janice Udry, *Let's Be Enemies*, Harper (New York, NY), 1961.

Clemens Brentano, *The Tale of Gockel, Hinkel, and Gackeliah*, Random House (New York, NY), 1961.

Else Minarik, *Little Bear's Visit*, Harper (New York, NY), 1961.

Sesyle Joslyn, *What Do You Do, Dear?*, Young Scott Books, 1961.

Clemens Brentano, *Schoolmaster Whackwell's Wonderful Sons*, Random House (New York, NY), 1962.

Charlotte Zolotow, *Mr. Rabbit and the Lovely Present*, Harper (New York, NY), 1962.

Meindert De Jong, *The Singing Hill*, Harper (New York, NY), 1962.

Leo Tolstoy, *Nikolenka's Childhood*, Harper (New York, NY), 1963.

Robert Keeshan, *She Loves Me, She Loves Me Not*, Harper (New York, NY), 1963.

Randall Jarrell, *The Bat-Poet*, Collier (New York, NY), 1964.

Amos Vogel, *How Little Lori Visited Times Square*, Harper (New York, NY), 1964.

Jan Wahl, *Pleasant Fieldmouse*, Harper (New York, NY), 1964.

William Engvick, editor, *Lullabies and Night Songs*, Pantheon (New York, NY), 1965.

Randall Jarrell, *The Animal Family*, Pantheon (New York, NY), 1965.

Isaac Bashevis Singer, *Zlateh the Goat and Other Stories*, Harper (New York, NY), 1966.

George Macdonald, *The Golden Key*, Harper (New York, NY), 1967, 2nd edition, Farrar, Straus (New York, NY), 1984.

William Blake, *Poems from William Blake's Songs of Innocence*, Bodley Head (London, England), 1967.

Robert Graves, *The Big Green Book*, Crowell (New York, NY), 1968.

Frank Stockton, *Griffin and the Minor Canon*, Collins (New York, NY), 1968.

Else Minarik, *A Kiss for Little Bear*, Harper (New York, NY), 1968.

George Macdonald, *The Light Princess*, Bodley Head (London, England), 1969, revised edition, Farrar, Straus (New York, NY), 1969.

Frank Stockton, *The Bee-Man of Orn*, Holt (New York, NY), 1971.

Doris Orgel, *Sarah's Room*, Bodley Head (London, England), 1971.

(And selector with Lore Segal) Jakob Grimm and Wilhelm Grimm, *The Juniper Tree, and Other Tales from Grimm*, translated by Segal and Randall Jarrell, Farrar, Straus (New York, NY), 1973, revised edition, 2003.

Marie Catherine Jumelle de Berneville Aulnoy, *Fortunia: A Tale by Mme. D'Aulnoy*, translated by Richard Schaubeck, Frank Hallman, 1974.

Randall Jarrell, *Fly by Night*, Farrar, Straus (New York, NY), 1976.

Jakob Grimm and Wilhelm Grimm, *King Grisly-Beard: A Tale from the Brothers Grimm*, Harper (New York, NY), 1978.

E.T.A. Hoffman, *The Nutcracker*, translated by Ralph Manheim, Crown (New York, NY), 1984, reprinted, 2001.

Philip Sendak (father), *In Grandpa's House*, translated and adapted by Seymour Barofsky, Harper (New York, NY), 1985.

Dear Mili: An Old Tale by Wilhelm Grimm, based on a letter by Wilhelm Grimm translated by Manheim, Michael Di Capua Books/Farrar, Straus (New York, NY), 1988, reprinted, HarperCollins (New York, NY), 2004.

(With Garth Williams) Jerome Griswold, *The Children's Books of Randall Jarrell*, University of Georgia Press (Athens, GA), 1988.

Lloyd Alexander, and others, *The Big Book for Peace*, edited by Marilyn Sachs and others, Dutton (New York, NY), 1990.

Iona Opie, *I Saw Esau*, Candlewick Press (Cambridge, MA), 1992.

Marcel Ayme, *The Wonderful Farm*, translated by Norman Denny, HarperCollins (New York, NY), 1994.

Herman Melville, *Pierre, or, The Ambiguities*, HarperCollins (New York, NY), 1995.

Arthur Yorinks, *The Miami Giant*, HarperCollins (New York, NY), 1995.

Heinrich von Kleist, *Penthesilea: A Tragic Drama*, translated and introduced by Joel Agee, HarperCollins (New York, NY), 1998.

James Marshall, *Swine Lake*, HarperCollins (New York, NY), 1999.

Else Minarik, *Present from Little Bear*, edited by Mark McVeigh, Harper Festival (New York, NY), 2002.

Else Minarik, *Little Bear and the Missing Pie,* edited by Mark McVeigh, Harper Festival (New York, NY), 2002.

Else Minarik, *Little Bear's Egg,* edited by Mark McVeigh, Harper Festival (New York, NY), 2002.

Else Minarik, *Little Bear's Flying Flapjack,* edited by Mark McVeigh, Harper Festival (New York, NY), 2002.

Else Minarik, *Little Bear's Wagon,* edited by Mark McVeigh, Harper Festival (New York, NY), 2002.

Tony Kushner, *Brundibar,* Hyperion (New York, NY), 2003.

Ruth Krauss, *Bears,* HarperCollins (New York, NY), 2005.

Also illustrator of *Little Stories* by Gladys B. Bond, Anti-Defamation League of B'nai B'rith.

OTHER

Fantasy Sketches (exhibition catalogue), Philip H. Rosenbach, 1970.

(Editor and author of introduction) *Maxfield Parrish Poster Book,* Crown (New York, NY), 1974.

(Author of appreciation) *The Publishing Archive of Lothar Meggendorfer,* Schiller, 1975.

(And director and lyricist) *Really Rosie, Starring the Nutshell Kids* (script for animated television special; based on characters from *The Nutshell Library* and *The Sign on Rosie's Door;* broadcast on Columbia Broadcasting System, 1975; also see below), music composed and performed by Carol King, Harper (New York, NY), 1975.

(Editor) *The Disney Poster Book,* illustrated by Walt Disney Studios, Harper (New York, NY), 1977.

(Lyricist and set designer) *Really Rosie* (musical play; revised from the television special of the same title), music by Carol King, produced in London and Washington, DC, 1978, produced off-Broadway, 1980.

(Lyricist and set and costume designer) *Where the Wild Things Are* (opera; based on his book of the same title), music by Oliver Knussen, produced in Belgium, 1980, produced at New York, NY, 1984.

(Author of introduction) Jean de Brunhoff, *Babar's Anniversary Album,* Random House (New York, NY), 1981.

Collection of Books, Posters and Original Drawings, Schiller, 1984.

(With Frank Corsaro) *The Love for Three Oranges: The Glyndebourne Version* (dialogue), Farrar, Straus (New York, NY), 1984.

(Librettist and set and costume designer) *Higglety, Pigglety, Pop!* (opera), produced in England, 1984.

(Author of commentary) Jonathan Cott, editor, *Masterworks of Children's Literature,* Volume 7, Chelsea House, 1984.

(Photographer) Rudolf Tesnohlidek, *The Cunning Little Vixen,* Farrar, Straus (New York, NY), 1985.

(Author of introduction) Jonathan Cott, *Victorian Color Picture Books,* Stonehill Publishing/Chelsea House, 1985.

Posters, Harmony Books (New York, NY), 1986.

(Author of foreword) John Canemaker, *Winsor McCay: His Life and Art,* Abbeville Press (New York, NY), 1987.

Caldecott & Co.: Notes on Books & Pictures, Michael Di Capua Books/Farrar, Straus (New York, NY), 1988.

(Author of introduction) *Mickey Mouse Movie Stories,* Abrams (New York, NY), 1988.

Maurice Sendak Book and Poster Package: Wild Things, Harper (New York, NY), 1991.

(Set and costume designer) *Frank and Joey Go to Work,* Harper Festival (New York, NY), 1996.

(Author of narration; with the Shirim Klezmer Orchestra) *Pincus and the Pig: A Klezmer Tale* (CD-ROM), Tzakik, 2004.

Contributor of illustrations to *McCall's* and *Ladies' Home Journal.* Contributor to *Worlds of Childhood: The Art and Craft of Writing for Children,* Houghton Mifflin (Boston, MA), 1998.

Sendak's books have been translated into numerous languages.

Sendak's manuscripts are collected at the Museum of the Philip H. and A.S.W. Rosenbach Foundation, Philadelphia, PA, and the Kerlan Collection, University of Minnesota, Minneapolis.

Adaptations

Film strips with cassettes have been produced by Weston Woods of *Where the Wild Things Are,* 1968, and *Pierre, Chicken Soup with Rice, Alligators All Around,* and *One Was Johnny,* all 1976. *Where the Wild Things Are* was recorded on cassette by Caedmon, 1988, and was adapted as an animated film, directed by Spike Jonze. *In the Night Kitchen* was adapted for film, Weston Woods, 1988, and as a talking book. The "Little Bear" books were the basis of an animated TV series. *Higglety Pigglety Pop!* was adapted as a Braille book and a record by Caedmon; Sendak's characters have inspired toy dolls and retellings including *Maurice Sendak's Seven Little Monsters,* by Arthur Yorinks, Hyperion, 2003.

Sidelights

The first American to win a Hans Christian Andersen International Medal and the first recipient of the Astrid Lindgren Memorial Prize, Maurice Sendak is credited as one of the most influential illustrators of late twentieth-century children's literature. With the Caldecott Medal-winning *Where the Wild Things Are,* Sendak led the way in creating more realistic child characters, moving away from the nostalgic models of innocence and sweetness portrayed in books published before the 1960s. By creating drawings inspired by the paintings of Degas and Cassatt as much as by nineteenth-century illustrators and modern cartoons, he also quickly demonstrated his unusual adaptability. Reflecting the view of many, critic John Rowe Townsend, in his *Written for*

Children: An Outline of English-Language Children's Literature, dubbed Sendak "the greatest creator of picture books in the hundred-odd years' history of the form."

Despite his popularity, Sendak has also been the subject of some controversy. "Critics of Sendak's work often argue that youngsters are not ready for the themes and images he presents," wrote Selma G. Lanes in her *The Art of Maurice Sendak.* "Sendak has forthrightly confronted such sensitive subject matters as childhood anger, sexuality, or the occasionally murderous impulses of raw sibling rivalry," This "honesty has troubled or frightened many who would wish to sentimentalize childhood—to shelter children from their own psychological complexity or to deny that this complexity exists," explained *Dictionary of Literary Biography* contributor John Cotham. For Sendak, this exploration of children's feelings has been more personal. As he revealed to Steven Heller in *Innovators of American Illustration,* "my work was an act of exorcism, an act of finding solutions so that I could have peace of mind and be an artist and function in the world as a human being and a man. My mind doesn't stray beyond my own need to survive."

The son of Jewish immigrants from Poland, Sendak grew up in a poor Brooklyn neighborhood with his older brother, Jack, and sister, Natalie. His family never stayed in one neighborhood for very long, moving from apartment to apartment every time their landlords painted because Sendak's mother could not stand the smell of fresh paint. Sendak was a sickly child, suffering from measles, double pneumonia, and scarlet fever between the ages of two and four, and because his parents did not like him playing outside for fear he would become sick, he also had difficulty making friends. Treated like a semi-invalid, the young boy became obsessed with the idea that he might not have long to live. "I was a miserable kid," he confessed to Lanes.

Sendak found escape from his childhood misery through drawing, reading, movies, music, and his imagination. His favorite reading included comic books featuring Mickey Mouse and other Disney characters, and some of his illustrations clearly reflect this early influence. He also loved musicals and comedy films starring Stan Laurel and Oliver Hardy, while in music his taste veered toward Mozart and the classics. Because his family could not afford piano lessons, he expressed his creativity by drawing and writing stories, and during his days spent sick in bed would sketch the people and houses in his neighborhood, dreaming up fantasies for them to be in. He learned to make up stories from his father, who amused the Sendak children with fantastic tales. At age seven, Sendak and his brother, Jack, started writing down stories on cardboard discarded from shirt wrappings. Jack would also become a children's author, and two of his books have been illustrated by Sendak.

In high school Sendak had a job creating backgrounds for the comic strips "Mutt and Jeff," "Tippy," and "Captain Stubbs"; he also wrote his own comic strip for his school newspaper and illustrated a physics book, *Atomics for the Millions,* for one of his teachers. After he graduated, he opted out of college. Instead, he worked for about two years in a warehouse in Manhattan. Leaving that job in 1948, he designed mechanical wooden toys with Jack that the brothers tried to sell to famous New York toy company, F.A.O. Schwartz. Although no sales were forthcoming, Sendak was hired to work on the store's window displays. One of his displays was seen by noted illustrator Leonard Weisgard, who offered Sendak a commission to illustrate *Good Shabbos, Everybody.*

While Sendak was working for Schwartz, he attended classes at the Art Student's League, and there his instructor, John Groth, told him that, because of his talent, his time would be better spent actively practiced his art in the real world. Taking Groth's advice, Sendak left art school and tried submitting his drawings to publishing houses. Editors felt his work was too old-fashioned, though, with its strong influences of nineteenth-century illustrators such as George Cruikshank, John Tenniel, Wilhelm Busch, and Louis Maurice Boutet de Monvel. The intricate, cross-hatching style Sendak had adopted from them was nothing like the simpler style preferred by book editors in the 1940s and 1950s.

Fortunately, F.A.O. Schwartz's children's book department head Frances Christie introduced Sendak to Harper and Brothers editor Ursula Nordstrom, who assigned him illustration projects that helped him develop his craft and reputation. "I loved her on first meeting," Sendak remembered in *The Art of Maurice Sendak.* "My happiest memories, in fact, are of my earliest career, when Ursula was my confidante and best friend. She really became my home and the person I trusted most." Nordstrom arranged for Sendak to be the illustrator for Ruth Krauss's *A Hole Is to Dig,* the book that first established Sendak as an important illustrator. *A Hole Is to Dig* was such a popular and critical success that Sendak was able to quit his job at F.A.O. Schwartz and work as a freelancer.

With Nordstrom's help, Sendak learned how to be flexible and adapt his drawings to the texts they accompanied. His illustrations show great variation, from the line drawings of *Kenny's Window* and *Where the Wild Things Are* to the cartoonish style of *In the Night Kitchen* to the highly detailed, cross-hatching style found in *Outside over There* and his drawings for the books by the Brothers Grimm. He also illustrated as many books as he could, adding to his recognition.

Many books featuring Sendak's illustrations have become popular and critical successes, among them the "Little Bear" series, written by Else Minarik, which proved so popular that four titles were added to the series in 2002, almost fifty years after *Little Bear* debuted in 1957. With the encouragement of Nordstrom, the illustrator also managed to find the time to write his own texts, and *Kenny's Window* and *Very Far Away* became his first published self-authored books. With *The Sign on Rosie's Door* he created his first hit with critics. Rosie is based on a real girl Sendak recalled from his Brooklyn childhood. The book draws from the sketches he once made of Rosie and her friends, and the story line uses actual events and quotes the real Rosie directly in some cases. *The Sign on Rosie's Door* focuses on a group of children with nothing to do on a long summer day in the city. Rosie, a somewhat bossy, but friendly and highly imaginative ten year old, shows her friends how to use fantasy to chase away their boredom. This book led to Sendak's first venture into live theater when he designed the sets and wrote lyrics for a stage version produced in 1980.

The Nutshell Library features some of the characters from *The Sign on Rosie's Door*. Comprised of an alphabet book, a counting book, a book about the seasons, and a cautionary tale—all measuring only two-and-one-half by four inches—*The Nutshell Library* books have been highly praised for Sendak's skill "at integrating text, design, and illustrations," according to Cotham. Today, they are still considered among the artist's most successful efforts.

After illustrating several picture books for other authors, Sendak decided to write several more picture books, and he considers *Where the Wild Things Are, In the Night Kitchen,* and *Outside over There* to form a loose-knit trilogy. Although the three stories seem unrelated, as the artist explained in *The Art of Maurice Sendak,* they "are all variations on the same theme: how children master various feelings—anger, boredom, fear, frustration, jealousy—and manage to come to grips with the realities of their lives." Each story involves the main character's voyaging into a fantasy world: In *Where the Wild Things Are* Max is sent to his room without supper after arguing with his mother and deals with his anger by imagining himself sailing to an island ruled by enormous, frightening monsters and becoming their king; *In the Night Kitchen* a boy named Mickey helps a group of all-night bakers make goodies in a strange city by scouting down the milk needed for the bakers' cake; and in *Outside over There* Oda, who is very jealous of her baby brother, neglects him, until one day goblins kidnap the baby and take him to another world "outside over there."

Parts of Sendak's books are inspired by the author/illustrator's personal memories. For example, the monsters in *Where the Wild Things Are* were inspired by the artist's hated Brooklyn relatives. "I wanted the wild things to be frightening," Sendak remarked in *The Art of Maurice Sendak.* "But why? It was probably at this point that I remembered how I detested my Brooklyn relatives as a small child. . . . They'd lean way over with their bad teeth and hairy noses, and say something threatening like 'You're so cute I could eat you up.'

And I knew if my mother didn't hurry up with the cooking, they probably would."

In the Night Kitchen was inspired by more recent memories. In 1967 Sendak suffered a heart attack, then lost his mother and beloved Sealyham terrier, Jennie, to cancer. Two years later, his father also died. After these tragic events, the artist left New York City and moved to Connecticut. *In the Night Kitchen* was his way "to . . . say goodbye to New York," as he told Martha Shirk in a *Chicago Tribune* article, "and say goodbye to my parents, and tell a little bit about the narrow squeak I had just been through." In the story, Mickey's brush with death when he is nearly baked in a cake symbolizes Sendak's own close call. *In the Night Kitchen,* the artist concluded in a *New York Times* article by Lisa Hammel, is about his "victory over death."

Sendak considers *Outside over There* his most personal work. "The book is obviously related to my own babyhood when my sister, Natalie, Ida's age, took care of me," he revealed to Jean F. Mercier in *Publishers Weekly.* The tale has its roots in the real-life story of the kidnapping of famous American pilot Charles Lindbergh's baby in 1932. Sendak recalled in his *New York Times Book Review* article how at the time he was "4 years old, sick in bed and somehow confusing myself with this baby. I had the superstitious feeling that if he came back I'd be O.K., too. Sadly, we all know the baby didn't come back. It left a peculiar mark in my mind." *Outside over There* "is really a homage to my sister, who is Ida," the artist later added.

Sendak became a controversial figure with the publication of *Where the Wild Things Are,* after critics and educators complained that the monsters are too frightening for small children. *In the Night Kitchen* was also attacked by some reviewers due to its use of cartoon-style illustrations, as well as a picture of Mickey with no clothing on. A more-recently censored book by Sendak is *Some Swell Pup; or, Are You Sure You Want a Dog?,* a realistic guide to taking care of puppies, which was censored because of an illustration showing a dog defecating. According to Sendak in a *New York Times* article by Bernard Holland, censoring books that portray some of the facts of life to children is more for the benefit of the adult than the child: "Children are willing to expose themselves to experiences. We aren't. Grown-ups always say they protect their children, but they're really protecting themselves. Besides, you can't protect children. They know everything."

In his new home in Connecticut, Sendak lived in virtual isolation during much of the 1970, enjoying the quiet of his ten-room stone and clapboard house located in a rural part of the state. Working ten to eleven hours a day in a room he converted into a studio, he illustrated picture books for other authors, and completed *Outside over There.* Sendak now felt that he needed a change from picture books, so, in 1980, he embarked on a new career in theatre.

A fan of classical music since childhood, Sendak had always wanted to get closer to the works of the masters, especially Mozart. Often, while writing and illustrating his books he would listen to Mozart for inspiration, and he consequently memorized many of Mozart's compositions. The image of Mozart has even entered into some of Sendak's illustrations, but this was never enough for the artist. Now he could "illustrate" the music he loved, in three dimensions no less! Designing the sets and costumes for Mozart's *The Magic Flute*, Sendak went on to create designs for such operas as *The Cunning Little Vixen* and *The Love of Three Oranges* as well as stage and film versions of Tchaikovsky's *The Nutcracker*. He also wrote the lyrics and did designs for his own musical based on *Where the Wild Things Are* and penned a libretto for *Higglety, Pigglety, Pop!* "That is why the operas are so important," Sendak told Ross, "because by costuming and setting them I have come as close to the music as I ever have in my life. I'm now literally on the stage, and I'm coloring Mozart, illustrating him in the way I used to illustrate people's stories." In 2004 he came even closer, putting aside the visual elements altogether to record a "Yinglish" adaptation of Peter Prokofiev's *Peter and the Wolf*, backed by the Shirim Klezmer Orchestra. Combining Yiddish and English, Sendak's "rumbly voice and humorous inflection of 'Yiddishisms'" creates an "entertaining" interpretation, according to a *Publishers Weekly* reviewer.

Speaking with *Horn Book* interviewer David E. White, Sendak explained that with his own theatre productions he hoped to correct what he had always disliked about stage productions geared for young audiences. "There are too many operas called children's operas," he noted. "Most of them suffer for this very reason. They are written down to children, as though children could not appreciate the full weight of good musical quality." In order to have complete freedom in creating the caliber of work he wanted to do for children, in 1990 Sendak and fellow writer Arthur Yorinks co-founded a national children's theater called The Night Kitchen. As artistic director, he intended to produce new versions of plays such as *Peter Pan* and *Hansel and Gretel* that will not talk down to children. "Our work is very peculiar, idiosyncratic," Sendak told *New York Times* contributor Eleanor Blau. "I don't believe in things literally *for* children. That's a reduction." Believing that children and adults should be treated with equal respect, he added: "Children are more open in their hearts and head[s] for what you're doing. . . . They're the best audience in town."

While moving into his stage work during the 1980s and 1990s Sendak has continued to illustrate books for other authors, including stories by the Brothers Grimm and *Pierre*, a tale by *Moby-Dick* author Herman Melville. In 1993, Sendak brought out a long-awaited author-illustrator title, *We Are All in the Dumps with Jack and Guy*, "an apocalyptic improvisation on two little-known English nursery rhymes," according to Lanes in the *St.*

James Guide to Children's Writers. Sendak hearkened back to *Hector Protector* with this title, again creating a fanciful extrapolation of a pair of nursery rhymes. A *Kirkus Reviews* writer commented that Sendak "penetrates deeply into society's ills in his elaborate visual extension of the words" and commended his "extraordinary art" and his expression of ideas in ways which have "never been more intricate, telling, or playful."

Other illustration projects have included the verse compilation *I Saw Esau: The Schoolchild's Pocket Book*, and *Swine Lake*, a tutu'd, tongue-in-cheek romp based on a story by the late children's author James Marshall. A tale of very cultured pigs whose world is invaded by a crass, philistine wolf, the humorous picture book "slyly reveal[s] the infectious pleasures of the performing arts," according to Peter Marks, writing in the *New York Times Book Review*. Sendak also blended his love of illustration with that of the theater in *Brundibar*, a collaboration with noted playwright Tony Kushner that is based on a 1942 opera about two siblings who attempt to sing for money to buy milk for their mother and are thwarted by a local bully. While the story ends on an up-note, the history of the opera's original production does not: it was originally performed at a Jewish boy's orphanage during World War II, and followed its cast to the Auschwitz concentration camp where most of the boys were eventually killed. Praising the book as a "stunning piece of art," a *Kirkus Reviews* writer also noted the "disturbing" qualities of the story, adding that "Sendak's incredible illustrations sprinkle in horrifying historical details" while also referencing some of his earlier art. Noting the collaboration, the reviewer summed up *Brundibar* as "a heartbreaking, hopeful masterpiece with powerful implications" for modern readers.

Sendak credits part of his ability to communicate with young children with the fact that he retains a vivid sense of what life was like from the viewpoint of a child. By maintaining contact with the young boy that still lives within him, he can easily relate to children, while his adult self is able to touch on subjects and feelings that can stir recognition in adults. "We've all passed the same places," he once noted. "Only I remember the geography, and most people forget it." This desire to maintain a connection with the fantasy world of childhood continues to inspire Sendak creatively. "The writing and the picture-making are merely a means to an end," he commented in *Down the Rabbit Hole*. "It has never been for me a graphic matter—or even, for that matter, a word matter!," he added "To discuss a children's book in terms of its pictorial beauty—or prose style—is not to the point. It is the particular nugget of magic it achieves—if it achieves. It has always only been a means—a handle with which I can swing myself into—somewhere or other—the place I'd rather be."

Biographical and Critical Sources

BOOKS

Arbuthnot, May Hill, and Zena Sutherland, *Children and Books,* 4th edition, Scott, Foresman (Glenview, IL), 1972.

Bader, Barbara, *American Picturebooks from Noah's Ark to the Beast Within,* Macmillan (New York, NY), 1976, pp. 495-524.

Bowman, John S., editor, *The Cambridge Dictionary of American Biography,* Cambridge University Press (Cambridge, England), 1995.

Carpenter, Humphrey, and Mari Prichard, *The Oxford Companion to Children's Literature,* Oxford University Press (Oxford, England), 1984.

Chevalier, Tracy, editor, *Twentieth-Century Children's Writers,* fifth edition edited by Sara Pendergast and Tom Pendergast, St. James Press (Detroit, MI), 1999.

Children's Literature: Annual of the Modern Language Association Seminar on Children's Literature and the Children's Literature Association, Volume 6, 1977, pp. 130-140; Volume 10, 1982, pp. 178-182; Volume 12, 1984, pp. 3-24; Volume 13, 1985, pp. 139-153; Volume 28, 2000, pp. 132-147.

Children's Literature Review, Thomson Gale (Detroit, MI), Volume 1, 1976, Volume 17, 1989.

Dictionary of Literary Biography, Volume 61: *American Writers for Children since 1960: Poets, Illustrators, and Nonfiction Authors,* Thomson Gale (Detroit, MI), 1987, pp. 258-272.

Encyclopedia of World Biography, second edition supplement, Volume 19, Thomson Gale (Detroit, MI), 2000.

Georgiou, Constantine, *Children and Their Literature,* Prentice-Hall (New York, NY), 1969.

Hart, James D., *The Oxford Companion to American Literature,* sixth edition, Oxford University Press (Oxford, England), 1995.

Heller, Steven, editor, *Innovators of American Illustration,* Van Nostrand (New York, NY), 1986, pp. 70-81.

Hopkins, Lee Bennett, *Books Are by People,* Citation Press (New York, NY), 1969.

Kingman, Lee, editor, *Newbery and Caldecott Medal Books: 1956-1965,* Horn Book (Boston, MA), 1965.

Kushner, Tony, *The Art of Maurice Sendak: 1980 to the Present,* Harry N. Abrams (New York, NY), 2003.

Lacy, Lyn Ellen, *Art and Design in Children's Picture Books: An Analysis of Caldecott Award-winning Illustrations,* American Library Association, 1986, pp. 104-143.

Lanes, Selma G., *The Art of Maurice Sendak,* H. Abrams (New York, NY), 1980.

Lanes, Selma G., *Down the Rabbit Hole: Adventures and Misadventures in the Realm of Children's Literature,* Atheneum (New York, NY), 1971, pp. 67-78.

Sendak, Maurice, *We Are All in the Dumps with Jack and Guy,* HarperCollins (New York, NY), 1993.

Shaw, John Mackay, *Childhood in Poetry,* third supplement, Thomson Gale (Detroit, MI), 1980.

Silvey, Anita, editor, *Children's Books and Their Creators,* Houghton Mifflin (Boston, MA), 1995.

Smith, Jeffrey Jon, *A Conversation with Maurice Sendak,* Smith (Elmhurst, IL), 1974.

Townsend, John Rowe, *Written for Children: An Outline of English Language Children's Literature,* revised edition, Lippincott (Philadelphia, PA), 1974, p. 310.

Ward, Martha, and others, *Authors of Books for Young People,* Scarecrow Press (Metuchen, NJ), 1990.

West, Mark I., *Trust Your Children: Writers against Censorship in Children's Literature,* Neal-Schuman (New York, NY), 1988, pp. 87-91.

Zipes, Jak, editor, *The Oxford Companion to Fairy Tales,* Oxford University Press (Oxford, England), 2000.

PERIODICALS

Appraisal, spring-summer, 1984, pp. 4-9.

Booklist, October 15, 1988, p. 347; December 15, 1988, p. 724; January 15, 1991, p. 1019; September 15, 1993, Carolyn Phelan, "Down and up with Jack," p. 156; May 1, 1997, p. 1507; July, 1998, p. 1889; May 1, 1999, Ilene Cooper, review of *Swine Lake,* p. 1590.

Books and Bookmen, June, 1969; December, 1974, pp. 74-75.

Chicago Tribune, July 17, 1980; January 29, 1990, Martha Shirk, "Relatively Monstrous: Maurice Sendak Says Nightmarish Kin Inspired His Famous 'Wild Things.'"

Chicago Tribune Book World, May 3, 1981.

Children's Book Review, June, 1971, p. 84.

Children's Literature (annual), 2004, Aparna Gollapudi, "Unraveling the Invisible Seam: Text and Image in Maurice Sendak's *Higglety Pigglety Pop!,*" pp. 112-133.

Children's Literature Association Quarterly, fall, 1985, pp. 122-127.

Children's Literature in Education, November, 1971, p. 48; spring, 1982, Eric A. Kimmel, "Children's Literature without Children," pp. 38-43; spring, 1982, pp. 38-43; summer, 1988, pp. 86-93.

Elementary English, February, 1971, Shelton L. Root, Jr., review of *In the Night Kitchen,* pp. 262-263; November, 1971, pp. 825-832, 856-864.

Entertainment Weekly, December 12, 2003, Troy Patterson, "Where the Wild King Is: Crowing a Career of Turning His Childhood Nightmares into Dreamy Kids' Books," p. 48.

Horn Book, December, 1970, Mary Agnes Taylor, "In Defense of the Wild Things," pp. 642-646; December, 1970, pp. 642-646; October, 1976, p. 495; June, 1977, p. 303; April, 1980, David E. White, "A Conversation with Maurice Sendak," pp. 145-155; August, 1983, pp. 474-477; May-June, 1986, pp. 305-313; May-June, 1987; March-April, 1989, p. 232; January-February, 1994, p. 92; March-April, 1997, p. 187; July, 1999, review of *Swine Lake,* p. 457; November-December, 2003, Gregory Maguire, "A Sendak Appreciation," p. 667, and Brian Anderson, "A View from the Island: Sendak in England," p. 717.

Junior Bookshelf, April, 1966, pp. 103-111; February, 1968, p. 30; August, 1970, pp. 205-206; June, 1971, C. Martin, review of *In the Night Kitchen,* pp. 165-166.

Kirkus Reviews, October 1, 1960, review of *The Sign on Rosie's Door,* p. 867; August 15, 1993, review of *We Are All in the Dumps with Jack and Guy,* p. 1080; November 1, 2003, review of *Brundibar,* p. 1312.

Ladies' Home Journal, March, 1969, Bruno Bettelheim, "The Care and Feeding of Monsters," p. 48.

Los Angeles Times, February 6, 1981; December 10, 1982; July 15, 1990, p. 14; October 3, 1993, p. 1.

National Observer, November 27, 1967.

Newsweek, May 18, 1981.

New Yorker, January 22, 1966.

New York Times, November 1, 1967; December 9, 1970; January 5, 1973, Lisa Hammel, "Maurice Sendak: Thriving on Quiet"; October 12, 1980, John Lahr, "The Playful Art of Maurice Sendak"; October 15, 1980; April 11, 1981; June 1, 1981; November 30, 1981; October 24, 1985; November 8, 1987, Bernard Holland, "The Paternal Pride of Maurice Sendak"; October 25, 1990, Eleanor Blau, "Sendak Is Forming Company for National Children's Theater."

New York Times Book Review, October 16, 1960, Alice Low, "Pretending," p. 40; October 22, 1967; November 1, 1970; February 29, 1976, p. 26; April 29, 1979; April 26, 1981, pp. 49, 64-65; October 9, 1983; May 17, 1987, Maurice Sendak, "Where the Wild Things Began"; November 14, 1993, Brian Alderson, "Children Who Live in Boxes," p. 17; November 16, 1997, p. 26; May 16, 1999, Peter Marks, "Pigs on Point."

New York Times Magazine, June 7, 1970.

Parabola, fall, 1981, pp. 88-91.

People, December 2, 1985, pp. 215-216; December 15, 2993, Mary Green, "Talk on the Wild Side," p. 115.

Publishers Weekly, April 10, 1981, Jean F. Mercier, "Sendak on Sendak," pp. 45-46; May 3, 1999, review of *Swine Lake,* p. 74; October 27, 2003, Sally Lodge, "Brundibar: A Collaboration with Remarkable Roots," p. 26; January 10, 2005, review of *Pincus and the Pig,* p. 25.

Quarterly Journal of the Library of Congress, Volume 28, number 4, 1971.

Rolling Stone, December 30, 1976.

Saturday Review, December 14, 1963.

School Library Journal, December, 1970; May, 1976, p. 54; September, 1985, p. 43; August, 1986, p. 22; August, 1988, p. 46; October, 1993, Kay E. Vandergrift, review of *We Are All in the Dumps with Jack and Guy,* p. 120; May, 1997, p. 154; July, 1999, Julie Cummins, review of *Swine Lake,* p. 77.

Signal, September, 1986, pp. 172-187.

Theatre Crafts, April, 1984, Ellenn Levene, "Illustrators Edward Gorey and Maurice Sendak Have New Careers as Scenic Artists," pp. 43-45, 75-78.

Time, July 6, 1981; July 28, 1986, p. 50.

Times Educational Supplement, May 19, 2000, Ted Dewan, review of *Swine Lake,* p. FRI23.

Times Literary Supplement, July 2, 1971; March 27, 1981.

Top of the News, June, 1970, pp. 366-369.

TV Guide, November 11, 1978.

Washington Post, November 1, 1978; November 20, 1981.

Washington Post Book World, May 10, 1981, Jonathan Cott, "When Ida Blew Her Magic Horn," pp. 1-2.

OTHER

The Lively Art of Picture Books (film), c. 1965.
Maurice Sendak (film), Weston Woods, 1986.*

*   *   *

SENDAK, Maurice Bernard
See SENDAK, Maurice

*   *   *

SHULEVITZ, Uri 1935-

Personal

Given name pronounced "*oo*-ree"; born February 27, 1935, in Warsaw, Poland; came to United States, 1959; naturalized U.S. citizen c. 1960s; son of Abraham and Szandla (Hermanstat) Shulevitz; married Helene Weiss (an artist), June 11, 1961 (divorced). *Education:* Teacher's College, Israel, teacher's degree, 1956; studied painting privately with Ezekiel Streichman, 1950-52; attended Tel-Aviv Art Institute, evenings, 1953-55, and Brooklyn Museum Art School, 1959-61; studied painting at Provincetown workshop with Leo Manso and Victor Candell, summer 1965; studied painting techniques of the High Renaissance with Peter Hopkins, 1977-83. *Religion:* Jewish. *Hobbies and other interests:* Art, music, travel, old tales and parables of Eastern traditions, movies, theatre, New York City, yoga, and tai-chi-chuan.

Addresses

Agent—c/o Author Mail, Farrar, Straus & Giroux, 19 Union Sq. W., New York, NY 10003.

Career

Kibbutz Ein-Geddi (collective farm), Israel, member, 1957-58; art director of youth magazine in Israel, 1958-59; illustrator of children's books, 1961—; author of children's books, 1962—; School of Visual Arts, New York, NY instructor in art, 1967-68; Pratt Institute, Brooklyn, NY, instructor in art, 1970-71; New School for Social Research (now New School University), New York, NY, instructor of writing and illustrating of children's books, 1970-86; Hartwick College, Oneonta, NY, director of summer workshop in writing and illustrating children's books, 1974. *Exhibitions:* Work included in American Institute of Graphic Arts Children's Books exhibitions, 1973-74 and 1980; Children's Book Exhibition, New York Public Library, 1967, 1968, 1969, 1972, 1973, and 1974; International Biennale of Illustrations (Bratislava, Czechoslovakia), 1969. *Military service:* Israeli Army, 1956-59.

Member

American Society of Contemporary Artists, Authors Guild, Authors League of America (member of children's books committee), New York Artists Equity Association.

Uri Shulevitz

Awards, Honors

Children's Book Awards, American Institute of Graphic Arts, 1963-64, for *Charley Sang a Song,* 1965-66, for *The Second Witch,* 1967-68, for *One Monday Morning,* and Certificates of Excellence, 1973-74, for *The Magician* and *The Fools of Chelm and Their History,* and 1979, for *The Treasure;* American Institute of Graphic Arts Children's Books citation, 1967-68, for *One Monday Morning;* Notable Book citations, American Library Association (ALA), 1967, for *One Monday Morning,* 1968, for *The Fool of the World and the Flying Ship,* 1969, for *Rain Rain Rivers,* 1974, for *Dawn,* and 1982, for *The Golem; Horn Book* honor list citations, 1967, for *One Monday Morning,* 1969, for *Rain Rain Rivers,* and 1979, for *The Treasure;* Certificate of Merit, Society of Illustrators (New York), 1965, for *Charley Sang a Song;* Caldecott Medal, ALA, 1969, for *The Fool of the World and the Flying Ship; The Fool of the World and the Flying Ship* was included in American Booksellers 1969 Gift to the Nation for the Library of the White House; Child Study Association of America's Children's Books of the Year citations, 1969, for *Rain Rain Rivers,* 1972, for *Soldier and Tsar in the Forest: A Russian Tale,* 1974, for *Dawn,* and 1976, for *The Touchstone;* Bronze Medal, Leipzig International Book Exhibition, 1970, for *Rain Rain Rivers; Book World* Children's Spring Book Festival Picture-Book honor, 1972, for *Soldier and Tsar in the Forest; Book World* Chil-

dren's Spring Book Festival Award for Younger Children, and *New York Times* Outstanding Books of the Year designation, both 1973, and Children's Book Showcase of the Children's Book Council (CBC) honor, 1974, all for *The Magician; New York Times* Outstanding Books of the Year designation, 1974, Christopher Award, and CBC Children's Book Showcase, both 1975, International Board of Books for Young People honor list citation, 1976, and Brooklyn Art Books for Children citations, 1976, 1977, and 1978, all for *Dawn; New York Times* Best Illustrated Books of the Year citations, 1978, for *Hanukah Money,* and 1979, for *The Treasure;* Caldecott Honor Book citation, 1980, for *The Treasure; New York Times* Outstanding Books of the Year citation, and *School Library Journal* Best Children's Books citation, both 1982, and Parents' Choice Foundation Award for Literature, 1983, all for *The Golem.*

Writings

SELF-ILLUSTRATED

The Moon in My Room, Harper (New York, NY), 1963, reprinted, Farrar, Straus (New York, NY), 2003.
One Monday Morning, Scribner (New York, NY), 1967, reprinted, Farrar, Straus (New York, NY), 2003.
Rain Rain Rivers, Farrar, Straus (New York, NY), 1969, reprinted, 1998.
(Adapter) *Oh What a Noise!* (text based on "A Big Noise" by William Brighty Rands), Macmillan (New York, NY), 1971.
(Adapter) *The Magician,* Macmillan (New York, NY), 1973.
Dawn, Farrar, Straus (New York, NY), 1974, reprinted, Econo-Clad Books (Minneapolis, MN), 1999.
The Treasure, Farrar, Straus (New York, NY), 1979.
Writing with Pictures: How to Write and Illustrate Children's Books, Watson-Guptill, 1985.
The Strange and Exciting Adventures of Jeremiah Hush, Farrar, Straus (New York, NY), 1986.
Toddlecreek Post Office, Farrar, Straus (New York, NY), 1990.
The Secret Room, Farrar, Straus (New York, NY), 1993.
(Reteller) *The Golden Goose,* Farrar, Straus (New York, NY), 1995.
Snow, Farrar, Straus (New York, NY), 1998.
What Is a Wise Bird like You Doing in a Silly Tale like This?, Farrar, Straus (New York, NY), 2000.
The Travels of Benjamin of Tudela: Through Three Continents in the Twelfth Century, Farrar, Straus (New York, NY), 2005.
SoSleepyStory, Farrar, Straus (New York, NY), 2006.

Author's works have been translated into Spanish.

ILLUSTRATOR

Charlotte Zolotow, *A Rose, a Bridge, and a Wild Black Horse,* Harper (New York, NY), 1964.

Mary Stolz, *The Mystery of the Woods,* Harper (New York, NY), 1964.

H.R. Hays and Daniel Hays, *Charley Sang a Song,* Harper (New York, NY), 1964.

Sulamith Ish-Kishore, *The Carpet of Solomon,* Pantheon (New York, NY), 1964.

Jack Sendak, *The Second Witch,* Harper (New York, NY), 1965.

Molly Cone, *Who Knows Ten? Children's Tales of the Ten Commandments,* Union of American Hebrew Congregations, 1965.

Jacob and Wilhelm Grimm, *The Twelve Dancing Princesses,* translated by Elizabeth Shub, Scribner (New York, NY), 1966.

Mary Stolz, *Maximilian's World,* Harper (New York, NY), 1966.

Jean Russell Larson, *The Silkspinners,* Scribner (New York, NY), 1967.

Dorothy Nathan, *The Month Brothers,* Dutton (New York, NY), 1967.

John Smith, editor, *My Kind of Verse,* Macmillan (New York, NY), 1968.

Jan Wahl, *Runaway Jonah and Other Tales,* Macmillan (New York, NY), 1968.

Arthur Ransome, adapter, *The Fool of the World and the Flying Ship: A Russian Tale,* Farrar, Straus (New York, NY), 1968, reprinted, Econo-Clad Books (Minneapolis, MN), 1999.

Jan Wahl, *The Wonderful Kite,* Delacorte (New York, NY), 1971.

Yehoash Biber, *Treasure of the Turkish Pasha,* translated from Hebrew by Naruch Hochman, Blue Star Book Club, 1971.

Alexander Afanasyev, *Soldier and Tsar in the Forest: A Russian Tale,* translated by Richard Lourie, Farrar, Straus (New York, NY), 1972.

Isaac Bashevis Singer, *The Fools of Chelm and Their History,* Farrar, Straus (New York, NY), 1973.

Robert Louis Stevenson, *The Touchstone,* Greenwillow (New York, NY), 1978.

(And translator and adapter, with Elizabeth Shub) Sholem Aleichem, *Hanukah Money,* Greenwillow (New York, NY), 1978.

Richard Kennedy, *The Lost Kingdom of Karnica,* Sierra Club, 1979.

Isaac Bashevis Singer, *The Golem,* Farrar, Straus (New York, NY), 1982.

Howard Schwartz, *Lilith's Cave: Jewish Tales of the Supernatural,* Harper (New York, NY), 1988.

Howard Schwartz and Barbara Rush, *The Diamond Tree: Jewish Tales from around the World,* HarperCollins (New York, NY), 1991.

Ehud Ben-Ezer, *Hosni the Dreamer: An Arabian Tale,* Farrar, Straus (New York, NY), 1997.

Fran Manushkin, *Daughters of Fire, Heroines of the Bible,* Silver Whistle/Harcourt Brace (San Diego, CA), 2001.

Contributor to periodicals, including *Horn Book.*

Adaptations

Weston Woods adapted *One Monday Morning* as a film, 1972, filmstrip, 1973; *The Treasure* as a film, 1980; and *Dawn* as a filmstrip with cassette, 1982. *The Fool of the World and the Flying Ship* was adapted as a filmstrip. *Snow* and *The Treasure* were adapted as audiobooks by Live Oak Media, 2000.

Sidelights

Embarking upon a career as an author and illustrator of children's books with his first published work, *The Moon in My Room,* award-winning author and illustrator Uri Shulevitz has also distinguished himself through his artwork for the texts by such celebrated writers as Arthur Ransome, Isaac Bashevis Singer, Fran Manushkin, Charlotte Zolotow, Robert Louis Stevenson, and the Brothers Grimm. Shulevitz's illustrations, which were characterized as "evocative" and "timeless" by a *Kirkus Reviews* critic, have garnered a host of accolades, including the 1969 Caldecott Medal for *The Fool of the World and the Flying Ship.* In addition, his self-illustrated works have been well regarded; his books *Rain Rain Rivers* and *The Treasure* have earned the author/illustrator both honors and critical acclaim. As *Horn Book* reviewer Mary M. Burns noted of the simply titled *Snow,* "through a minimalist text and carefully composed illustrations," *Snow* embodies Shulevitz's "belief that the true picture book, with its inevitable melding of words and art, is a distinct genre." Several of Shulevitz's early books have remained in print since their first publication in the mid-1960s.

Born in 1935, Shulevitz was drawing by age three. Unfortunately, during the next year bombs began falling on his family's home in Warsaw, Poland, and the Shulevitz's were ultimately forced to flee their country. As exiles, they wandered for eight years before settling in Paris, France, in 1947. Inspired by the illustrations he discovered in the book stalls scattered along the Seine, Shulevitz began drawing his own comic books, working from the stories a friend wrote. At age twelve he won a district-wide elementary-school drawing contest, furthering his creative ambitions. "The encouragement of my parents, who were both artistically talented, probably contributed to my early interest in drawing," he later recalled to Lee Bennett Hopkins, discussing the inspiration behind his career in *Books Are by People.*

After spending two years in Paris, the young artist's family moved to Israel. There, at age fifteen, Shulevitz became the youngest artist to have his drawings exhibited at the Tel Aviv Museum. To help support his family, he attended high school in the evenings and worked various jobs during the day, among them as apprentice to a rubber-stamp maker. At one point working at the dog-licensing desk in Tel Aviv City Hall, he occupied the time when business was slow by reading and writing stories. After graduating from high school, he studied literature and natural sciences at the Teachers' Institute and art at the Art Institute of Tel Aviv, while also taking private lessons with painter Ezekiel Streichman. In 1958, after two years' compulsory service in the Israeli Army, Shulevitz moved to Ein Geddi Kibbutz, a cooperative farm settlement formed by his friends and located near the Dead Sea.

After a year at Ein Geddi, the twenty-four-year-old Shulevitz traveled to New York City, and studied painting at the Brooklyn Museum Art School. His first work as an illustrator was for a publisher of Hebrew children's books. "I was strictly supervised and permitted only to work from sketches given to me," Shulevitz later recalled to *SATA.* "Still, this experience improved my pen and brush techniques." Interestingly, it was while working in this structured, controlled atmosphere that Shulevitz developed what would become his unique illustration style.

The young artist's first published book for children, *The Moon in My Room,* was released in 1963. Written and illustrated under the guidance of two editors at Harper & Row, the book allowed Shulevitz to come to terms with his own feelings of inadequacy as a speaker of English. "I eventually understood that my initial reaction, my fear that I could not write, was based on a preconception," he later explained. "A preconception that writing was strictly related to words and to spoken language. That it was essential to use many words in a skillful way. I was overlooking what was of primary importance—*what* I had to say; and I was caught in a secondary consideration—how to say it. That secondary concern has nothing to do with writing, but I was allowing it to take over the primary one." Shulevitz discusses his philosophy regarding the relationship between text and illustration in his 1985 book *Writing with Pictures.*

His life experiences in Poland, France, Israel, and New York City have provide Shulevitz with a wealth of first-

Shulevitz's award-winning picture book Snow *brings to life the transformational magic a winter's snowfall brings to a child's life.*

hand material for works that involve travel. Still, he will maintain, anyone with an imagination can be a traveler, much as the little boy in *The Moon in My Room* does as he explores the world without leaving his room. In creating his own original stories, Shulevitz begins by focusing on the action of the story, first visualizing it and then figuring out how to express it in words. He tries to express the action as simply as possible, using a pictorial approach. For example, the story about a young, imaginative boy who explores the world without leaving his room that is related in *The Moon in My Room* "unfolded in my head like a movie," he stated. "I was the camera seeing the action conveyed by pictures. The few words necessary to communicate the story fell into place on their own. It was all so simple and natural." Shulevitz has dubbed this technique "writing with pictures," maintaining that this method can also enhance the ability to visualize for writers who do not have a background in art. "Visual thinking can also avoid excessive wordiness in writing in general," the author/illustrator added. "In this way my visual approach evolved—an approach based on my writing and teaching experience."

Although Shulevitz became a U.S. citizen in the 1960s, his interests have continued to draw on many cultures. Finding an affinity with Chinese culture, he has studied picture-writing and practices tai-chi-chuan, a regimen of Chinese exercises that is thought to bring health to the body's internal organs. Not surprisingly, his interest in Oriental art and culture has influenced his work. "Realizing the excess of words in our culture," he once explained, "I [follow] an Oriental tradition, trying to say more with fewer words. *The Moon in My Room* contains very brief text and suggestive rather than descriptive illustrations, that have the purpose of awakening the child's imagination." Viewing such books, children are encouraged to picture in their own minds some of the events and characters described only by the text.

Reviewers have consistently praised Shulevitz's self-illustrated books for their thoughtful storylines and engaging illustrations. Reviewing his picture book *Toddlecreek Post Office*, *School Library Journal* contributor Carolyn Vang Schuler noted that "Shulevitz's fresh, orderly, yet angular, watercolors . . . are just right for group sharing," and *Booklist* critic Ilene Cooper commended his "as always, striking" artwork. The story centers on a small post office where everything from lamp-mending to button-sewing is performed by the helpful and under-worked local postmaster. Eventually, however, the regional postal inspector visits and decides to shut the office down. Writing in the *Bulletin of the Center for Children's Books*, Betsy Hearne called *Toddlecreek Post Office* a "fable about society's decline of humane concern."

Shulevitz's adaptation of a classic tale in *The Golden Goose* was dubbed "a fun version of a traditional tale" by *School Library Journal* contributor Donna L. Scanlon. The critic praised Shulevitz's use of contrast, as well as his "vibrant watercolor paintings, full of blocky angular characters and quirky off-kilter buildings" that "enhance the story." Characterizing the author's rhythmic text as a "challenging chant," *Bulletin of the Center for Children's Books* reviewer Elizabeth Bush opined that *The Golden Goose* "should attract a new generation of listeners." *Booklist* reviewer Susan Dove Lempke described Shulevitz's illustrations as "bursting with a bouncy vitality that fits the amusing story well."

One of several self-illustrated picture books Shulevitz has created, *Snow* has been widely praised for its spare text and its detailed illustrations, which capture "the transforming power of a snowstorm," as *Horn Book* contributor Mary M. Burns noted. A *Publishers Weekly* critic called the book "pure enchantment from start to finish," noting that Shulevitz "works a bit of visual alchemy as the tale progresses, gradually transforming the chilly gray watercolor washes with flecks of snow, until his cityscape is a frozen fairyland."

Another picture book, *What Is a Wise Bird like You Doing in a Silly Tale like This?*, spins a nonsensical tale about the twenty-six and one half (the one half being a half-invisible character who spoke using only half-words) residents of Pickleberry. Trouble brews when Lou, a wise talking bird who serves as counsel to the town's emperor, decides that he would be happier elsewhere. In a story within a story, the now-free Lou weaves Pickelberrians into a fantastic tale of escape. A reviewer for *Publishers Weekly* called the book an "engaging bit of frippery" and went on to noted that "The silliness referenced in the title reigns supreme here." As for the illustrations, the reviewer concluded, "Shulevitz's sunny watercolors range from beautifully detailed vignettes to puckish cartoons . . . ratcheting up the enjoyment factor." Commenting on the cartoon elements in the book, *School Library Journal* contributor Marie Orlando noted that "Shulevitz's wacky tale is told both through traditional text and dialogue balloons abounding in sly wit."

Turning from whimsy to world history, Shulevitz creates what *School Library Journal* contributor Margaret A. Chang dubbed "a picture book of epic proportions" in *The Travels of Benjamin of Tudela: Through Three Continents in the Twelfth Century*. In 1159 a Jewish traveler named Benjamin left his home town in Spain for a fourteen-year-long journey through Europe, Asia, and Africa. On this trip he was a witness to many of the medieval world's wonders, such as the Tower of Babel and the tombs of ancient Hebrew Kings, to Islamic processions, and the ancient wonders still standing to be marveled at in Rome and Egypt. While noting that the observations of a twelfth-century tourist "might not seem the stuff of picture books," Ilene Cooper added in *Booklist* that "outstanding execution can draw readers to almost any subject."The author/illustrator "outdoes himself here," Cooper added, praising illustrations that "capture the sweep of mysterious and far-away places."

Shulevitz recounts the journey of an actual twelfth-century traveler—a Spanish Jew—throughout much of Europe and the Middle East in his illuminating picture-book The Travels of Benjamin of Tuleda.

"Shulevitz keeps this lengthy tale's pace brisk," added a *Publishers Weekly* critic, "honing in on details sure to capture readers' imaginations."

In addition to his success at bringing his own story ideas to life by writing with pictures, Shulevitz has also received praise for his success in interpreting the works of other authors. Commenting on *The Diamond Tree: Jewish Tales from around the World*, *Horn Book* reviewer Hanna B. Zeiger hailed the illustrator's watercolor renderings, noting that these "add just the right touch of wit and fantasy" to the text by Howard Schwartz and Barbara Rush. "Shulevitz's illustrations evoke a strong sense of place," asserted Robin Tzannes in her review of Ehud Ben-Ezer's *Hosni the Dreamer* for the *New York Times*. "Pictures and text work together to create a portrait of a humble and compassionate hero that young readers should love." Commenting on his contribution to Fran Minushkin's *Daughters of Fire: Heroines of the Bible*, a *Publishers Weekly* re-

viewer noted that Shulevitz's watercolor and pen-and-ink "art, like the storytelling, startles the audience into fresh insights and appreciation."

Taking a visual approach to his craft, Shulevitz has noted that his books often "unfold" in his mind much "like a movie," and in the teaching he has done he encourages students to allow the art to evolve from the story itself. Using this technique, he urges his students, "all the parts of the book" are ultimately "coordinated into a coherent whole." This approach requires a measure of technical versatility on the part of the illustrator, and Shulevitz uses a variety of materials and artistic styles in his illustrations. "I am . . . constantly searching for a new way of illustrating," he once explained. "I use a lot of pen and ink and watercolor. I have used colored inks and tempera in full-color illustrations. In some black and white ones, I have also scratched with a razor blade the pen-and-ink line and then reworked for a long time to achieve a certain effect as in an etching

(*The Carpet of Solomon, The Month Brothers, Runaway Jonah,* and *Rain Rain Rivers*). I have used a Japanese reed pen (*Maximilian's World*) and a Chinese brush (*The Silkspinners*)."

Biographical and Critical Sources

BOOKS

Children's Literature Review, Thomson Gale (Detroit, MI), Volume 5, 1983, Volume 61, 2000.

Dictionary of Literary Biography, Volume 61: *American Writers for Children since 1960: Poets, Illustrators, and Nonfiction Authors,* Thomson Gale (Detroit, MI), 1987.

Hopkins, Lee Bennett, *Books Are by People: Interviews with 104 Authors and Illustrators of Books for Young Children,* Citation Press (New York, NY), 1969.

Kingman, Lee, editor, *The Illustrator's Notebook,* Horn Book (Boston, MA), 1978.

Lanes, Selma G., *Down the Rabbit Hole,* Atheneum (New York, NY), 1971.

St. James Guide to Children's Writers, 5th edition, St. James Press (Detroit, MI), 1999.

Shulevitz, Uri, *Writing with Pictures: How to Write and Illustrate Children's Books,* Watson-Guptil (New York, NY), 1985.

PERIODICALS

Booklist, November 15, 1990, Ilene Cooper, review of *Toddlecreek Post Office,* pp. 666-667; November 15, 1995, Susan Dove Lempke, review of *The Golden Goose,* p. 562; November 1, 1997, p. 478; January 1, 1999, p. 785; August, 2000, Michael Cart, review of *What Is a Wise Bird like You Doing in a Silly Tale like This?,* p. 2135; March 15, 2005, Ilene Cooper, review of *The Travels of Benjamin of Tudela,* p. 1293.

Bulletin of the Center for Children's Books, January, 1991, Betsy Hearne, review of *Toddlecreek Post Office,* p. 129; January, 1996, Elizabeth Bush, review of *The Golden Goose,* p. 171; January, 1999, review of *Snow,* p. 182.

Horn Book, February, 1982, Uri Shulevitz, "Writing with Pictures," pp. 17-22; January-February, 1992, Hanna B. Zeiger, review of *The Diamond Tree: Jewish Tales from around the World,* March-April, 1994, p. 211; January-February, 1999, Mary M. Burns, review of *Snow,* pp. 55-56; September, 2000, Joanna Rudge Long, review of *What Is a Wise Bird like You Doing in a Silly Tale like This?,* p. 557; March-April, 2005, Barbara Bader, review of *The Travels of Benjamin of Tudela,* p. 217.

Kirkus Reviews, October 1, 1995, p. 1428; October 15, 1998, review of *Snow,* p. 1537; March 1, 2005, review of *The Travels of Benjamin of Tudela,* p. 295.

New York Times, November 16, 1997, Robin Tzannes, review of *Hosni the Dreamer,* p. 42.

New York Times Book Review, January 17, 1999, Betsy Groban, review of *Snow,* p. 26.

Publishers Weekly, October 11, 1993, p. 85; November 6, 1995, review of *The Golden Goose,* August 31, 1998, review of *Snow,* p. 75; August 27, 2001, review of *daughters of Fire: Heroines of the Bible,* p. 81; July 17, 2000, review of *What Is a Wise Bird like You Doing in a Silly Tale like This?,* p. 193; August 27, review of *Daughters of Fire: Heroines of the Bible,* p. 81; March 28, 2005, review of *The Travels of Benjamin of Tudela,* p. 82.

School Library Journal, January, 1991, Carolyn Vang Schuler, review of *Toddlecreek Post Office,* March, 1992, p. 252; December, 1995, Donna L. Scanlon, review of *The Golden Goose,* p. 97; December, 1997, p. 81; December, 1998, p. 92; August, 2000, Marie Orlando, review of *What Is a Wise Bird like You Doing in a Silly Tale like This?,* p. 164; April, 2005, Margaret A. Chang, review of *The Travels of Benjamin of Tudela,* p. 142.

ONLINE

Farrar, Straus Web site, http://www.fsgkidsbooks.com/ (November 21, 2005), "Uri Shulevitz."

Horn Book Online, http://www.hbook.com/exhibit/ shulevitzradio (November 3, 2001), Anita Silvey, interview with Shulevitz.*

*   *   *

SILVERMAN, Erica 1955-

Personal

Born May 21, 1955, in Brooklyn, NY; daughter of Harold (in sales) and Gloria (Phillips) Silverman. *Education:* Attended State University of New York, Albany; University of California, Los Angeles, B.A. (magna cum laude), 1982. *Politics:* Democrat. *Religion:* Jewish. *Hobbies and other interests:* Psychology, politics, wildlife, ecology, social history, women's basketball.

Addresses

Agent—c/o Author Mail, Macmillan Publishing Co., 866 3rd Ave., New York, NY 10022.

Career

Freelance writer, 1982—. Teacher of English as second language, Los Angeles, CA, beginning 1982. Manuscript consultant and speaker.

Member

Society of Children's Book Writers and Illustrators, National Association for the Preservation and Perpetuation of Storytelling, Sierra Club, Southern California Council on Literature for Children and Young People.

Awards, Honors

North Carolina Children's Book Award nomination, Books for Children designation, Library of Congress, 1992, and Children's Choice designations, Children's Book Council and International Reading Association, both 1993, all for *Big Pumpkin.*

Writings

Warm in Winter, illustrated by M. Deraney, Macmillan (New York, NY), 1989.

On Grandma's Roof, illustrated by Deborah Kogan Ray, Macmillan (New York, NY), 1990.

Big Pumpkin, illustrated by S.D. Schindler, Macmillan (New York, NY), 1992.

Mrs. Peachtree and the Eighth Avenue Cat, illustrated by Ellen Beier, Macmillan (New York, NY), 1994.

Don't Fidget a Feather, illustrated by S.D. Schindler, Macmillan (New York, NY), 1994.

Fixing the Crack of Dawn, illustrated by Sandra Spiedel, Bridgewater Books (Mahwah, NJ), 1994.

Mrs. Peachtree's Bicycle, illustrated by Ellen Beier, Macmillan (New York, NY), 1996.

Gittel's Hands, illustrated by Deborah Nourse Lattimore, Bridgewater Books (Mahwah, NJ), 1996.

The Halloween House, illustrated by Jon Agee, Farrar Straus (New York, NY), 1997.

On the Morn of Mayfest, illustrated by Marla Frazee, Simon & Schuster (New York, NY), 1998.

Railel's Riddle, illustrated by Susan Gaber, Farrar Straus (New York, NY), 1999.

Follow the Leader, illustrated by G. Brian Karas, Farrar Straus (New York, NY), 2000.

(Adapter) Sholom Aleichem, *When the Chickens Went on Strike: A Rosh Hashanah Tale,* illustrated by Matthew Trueman, Dutton (New York, NY), 2003.

Sholom's Treasure: How Sholom Aleichem Became a Writer, illustrated by Mordicai Gerstein, Farrar, Straus (New York, NY), 2005.

Cowgirl Kate and Cocoa, illustrated by Betsy Lewin, Harcourt (Orlando, FL), 2005.

Cowgirl Kate and Cocoa: Partners, illustrated by Betsy Lewin, Harcourt (Orlando, FL), 2006.

Contributor of stories to periodicals, including *Scholastic Scope* and *Schofar.*

Sidelights

Erica Silverman is the author of picture books for young readers, most of which feature themes such as friendships and family relationships. In Silverman's first book, *Warm in Winter,* Rabbit tells her friend Badger that the best experience of warmth comes in winter. While Badger finds this difficult to believe on a sunny, summer day, she learns the truth of Rabbit's claim when she visits Rabbit during the winter's first snow. After Badger travels through the blustery storm and is offered a seat next to the fire, she agrees warmth is best appreciated during winter. Commenting on the relationship between Badger and Rabbit in a *Booklist* review, Julie Corsaro called *Warm in Winter* an "affectionate tale of friendship." In a *School Library Journal* review, Marianne Pilla found the "narration descriptive," and also complemented the witty conversations between the book's animal characters.

Silverman once described her work to *SATA:* "Without consciously deciding on it, my books seem to touch on the need to be connected; my characters seem to be concerned with the question of needing others and being needed. . . . In *Warm in Winter,* a lonely Badger must confront a blizzard in order to find the warmth of friendship."

On Grandma's Roof follows a young girl and her grandmother through a day's single activity: hanging laundry out to dry. Emily and her grandmother take a picnic basket along with the laundry, and spend the day on the roof of the grandmother's apartment building, where the chore is transformed into an expression of the loving relationship between the two. Mary M. Burns, writing in *Horn Book,* described the combination of text and illustrations as "superb," and went on to praise Silverman's "childlike celebration of life and love" as particularly suited for its intended audience. The story "vibrates with the delight the characters feel in each other," noted Virginia Opocensky in a *School Library Journal* review.

"My grandmother started me on the road to reading before I was in school," Silverman once told *SATA.* "She took me to the public library on 23rd Street in Manhattan, up the endless staircase to the children's room and let me pick out books to take home. I particularly loved folk tales. One of my favorites was an East European folk tale called 'The Turnip.' Years later, I walked into a library and heard a librarian reading 'The Turnip' to a group of children. I started wondering how I could adapt it in order to tell my own story."

In Silverman's version of the traditional tale, titled *Big Pumpkin,* a witch grows a pumpkin too large to move. After encounters with a cast of Halloween characters, none of whom can move the pumpkin, a little bat suggests that they all work together. "It is only by working together that the boastful characters finally have their pumpkin pie," the author explained. A *Publishers Weekly* reviewer felt that the dialogue creates "a pleasantly sinister mood that stops just short of being scary," while in *School Library Journal* Elizabeth Hanson called the book "rousing good fun for the Halloween season and far beyond."

"I didn't set out to write stories about teamwork or interdependence," Silverman recalled to *SATA.* "That would have resulted in an essay rather than a picture book. I generally start with a setting, the voices of characters, and an unidentified mood or feeling that I am trying to bring into focus. Part of the fun of starting a new book is finding out something new about myself along the way."

Critics often describe Silverman as a good storyteller. For example, Susan Scheps called *Gittel's Hands* "a charming tale . . . told in the careful words of a storyteller, with a bit of repetition thrown in for good measure," in her review for *School Library Journal. Booklist* contributor Ellen Mandel remarked that the book has "much to occupy the eyes as well as the hearts of story lovers" and holds a "satisfying conclusion." *Gittel's Hands* portrays the dilemma a young girl faces when her father brags about her sewing and cooking talents to the man who holds her father's debts. When Gittel is forced by the man into an impossible claim upon her handy talents in order to repay her father's debts, she unwittingly saves herself with an act of kindness to a stranger.

Silverman tells another good tale in *Mrs. Peachtree's Bicycle,* and also offers readers new ways to view people and their behavior by calling into question narrow patterns of thinking. According to a critic for *Kirkus Reviews,* "Silverman's story makes statements against sexism, ageism, and mindless adherence to convention." It's the turn of the twentieth century, and Mrs. Peachtree, white-haired and female to boot, takes on the established way of doing things with a show of open determination to ride a bicycle in order to make delivering food an easier job for herself. Silverman doesn't use heavy-handedness to tell her story but rather a "light, breezy tone throughout," according to a *Kirkus Reviews* critic. "Kids will relate to the intrepid, grandmotherly Mrs. Peachtree," predicted Carolyn Noah in a reviewer for *School Library Journal.*

With *The Halloween House* Silverman offers readers a humorous tale of two escaped convicts who seek shelter in a deserted house but find they are not alone on Halloween night. The escapees become the target of numerous creatures who make it their business to scare the living daylights out of these two criminals. And scare them they do, right out of the house and back to their prison cell where they find safety in "home sweet home." Susan Dove Lempke declared in *Booklist* that *The Halloween House* is a "very funny story" and predicted it will be a "story-hour hit all year round."

In *When the Chickens Went on Strike: A Rosh Hashanah Tale* Silverman borrows a story from Yiddish writer Sholom Aleichem, adapting it for a younger audience. The tradition of Kapores, a once-common way to honor the Jewish holiday of Rosh Hashanah, was practiced by holding a chicken over someone's head so that all of the person's misdeeds from the year would be passed along to the chicken. In the story, the chickens are tired of people using them in the ritual of Kapores, and they refuse to participate, "a scenario Silverman develops with great glee" in the words of a *Publishers Weekly* reviewer. No amount of pleading with the chickens will make them change their minds. Told through the perspective of a young boy witnessing the poultry rebellion, *When the Chickens Went on Strike* features "understated yet humorous text," making it a "perfect choice for holiday read-alouds" according to Kay Weisman of *Booklist.* Nancy Palmer of *School Library Journal* considered "Silverman's addition of a young narrator lends immediacy and empathy, and streamlines the story with no loss of flavor and point."

After adapting one of Aleichem's stories to picture-book form, Silverman wrote a picture-book biography of the author. *Sholom's Treasure: How Sholom Aleichem Became a Writer* tells the history of the Russian boy who grew up to be a great comedic writer. "Silverman's text combines a storyteller's narrative with dialogue based on Aleichem's own words," informed Teri Markson and Stephen Samuel Wise in a review for *School Library Journal.* A *Publishers Weekly* critic that "Silverman's accessible prose keeps a narrative dense with incidents and people moving along briskly." *Booklist* contributor Ilene Cooper observed that while Aleichem's biography takes place in a Russian shetl, "as in Aleichem's own stories, there's a universality here that transcends the borders of time and place."

Cowgirl Kate and Cocoa introduces readers to a girl and her talking horse and also initiated a series of chapter books about the friends. Cowgirl Kate takes care of Cocoa, but Cocoa worries about Kate's adventures when the horse isn't around to protect her. Written for beginning readers, *Cowgirl Kate and Cocoa* features characters with "enough star power to ride the range together in subsequent sequels," according to a *Kirkus Reviews* contributor. "Simple sentences and lots of repetition make these tales accessible, while occasional cowpoke vocabulary establishes the locale," noted Carol Ann Wilson in *School Library Journal.*

"As an only child, I spent a lot of time in pretend worlds, talking to imaginary animals and people," Silverman once told *SATA.* "Now, many years later, when

Adapted from a story by Sholom Aleichem, When the Chickens Went on Strike *finds a flock of wise chickens outsmarting the villagers who want to torment the birds in a local Rosh Hashanah custom. (Illustration by Matthew Trueman.)*

Silverman recounts the life of famed nineteenth-century Yiddish story-teller Sholom Aleichem, who wrote about life in his native Russia, in her picture-book biography **Sholom's Treasure.** *(Illustration by Mordi-cai Gerstein.)*

I am working on a story, I feel the same sense of total absorption as I create a world, fill it with characters and watch and listen to them interact.

"Mother Goose rhymes gave me my first awareness of the pleasure of language. My father had a big reel-to-reel tape recorder. Together we recited Mother Goose rhymes onto tape. As I grew older, our reciting material changed to include all kinds of poems and stories. Those hours of reciting onto tape nurtured in me a love for the sounds and rhythms of language."

Biographical and Critical Sources

PERIODICALS

Booklist, December 1, 1989, Julie Corsaro, review of *Warm in Winter*; March 1, 1990, p. 1349; April 1, 1995, p. 1409; May 15, 1996, Ellen Mandel, review of *Gittel's Hands,* p. 1594; September 1, 1997, Susan Dove Lempke, review of *The Halloween House,* p. 141; October 15, 2000, Connie Fletcher, review of *Follow the Leader,* p. 447; February 1, 2005, Ilene Cooper, review of *Sholom's Treasure: How Sholom Aleichem Became a Writer,* p. 960.

Horn Book, July, 1990, Mary M. Burns, review of *On Grandma's Roof,* p. 448; July-August, 2003, Lauren Adams, review of *When the Chickens Went on Strike,* p. 448; March-April, 2005, Susan P. Bloom, review of *Sholom's Treasure,* p. 218.

Kirkus Reviews, March, 15, 1996, p. 452; May 1, 1996, review of *Mrs. Peachtree's Bicycle,* p. 693; June 15, 2003, review of *When the Chickens Went on Strike,* p. 865; February 1, 2005, review of *Sholom's Treasure,* p. 182; April 1, 2005, review of *Cowgirl Kate and Cocoa,* p. 425.

Los Angeles Times Book Review, April, 14, 1996, p. 10; July 7, 1996, p. 11.

Publishers Weekly, July 20, 1992, review of *Big Pumpkin,* p. 248; August 25, 2003, review of *When the Chickens Went on Strike,* p. 61; January 31, 2005, review of *Sholom's Treasure,* p. 68.

School Library Journal, October, 1989, Marianne Pilla, review of *Warm in Winter,* p. 1332; March, 1990, Virginia Opocensky, review of *On Grandma's Roof,* p. 201; September, 1992, Elizabeth Hanson, review of *Big Pumpkin,* p. 211; November, 1994, p. 90; January, 1995, p. 93; June, 1996, Susan Scheps, review of *Gittel's Hands,* pp. 109-10; July, 1996, Carolyn Noah, review of *Mrs. Peachtree's Bicycle,* pp. 72-73; September, 2003, Nancy Palmer, review of *When the Chickens Went on Strike,* p. 191; March, 2005, Carol Ann Wilson, review of *Cowgirl Kate and Cocoa,* p. 188; April, 2005, Teri Markson and Stephen Samuel Wise, review of *Sholom's Treasure,* p. 127.

ONLINE

Farrar, Straus, and Giroux Books for Young Readers Web site, http://www.fsgkidsbooks.com/ (November 7, 2005), "Erica Silverman."*

*   *   *

SMALL, Mary 1932-

Personal

Born 1932, in Plymouth, England; immigrated to Australia, 1962. *Education:* London College of Speech and Drama, diploma (speech therapy), 1954.

Addresses

Home—Sydney, New South Wales, Australia. *Agent*—c/o Australian Socity of Authors Ltd., P.O. Box 1566, Strawberry Hills, New South Wales 2012, Australia.

Career

Children's book author and speech therapist.

Member

Australian Society of Authors, Childrens's Book Council of Australia (New South Wales branch), University of the Third Age, Riding for the Disabled Association of Australia (life member), Sutherland Shire Historical Society, Children's Writers Network.

Awards, Honors

Australian Publishing Association Award shortlist, and Australian Newspaper Award for Excellence in Educational Publishing Award shortlist, both 2003, both for *Simpson and Duffy;* Silver Logie award, 2003, for *Tracey McBean* television series;

Writings

FOR CHILDREN

A Bear in My Bedroom, illustrated by Ingrid van Dyk, Carroll's (Perth, Western Australia, Australia), 1976.

The Sea Dog, illustrated by I. Putu Santosa, Carroll's (Perth, Western Australia, Australia), 1978.

And Alice Did the Walking, photographs by Lionel Jensen, Oxford University Press (Melbourne, Victoria, Australia), 1978, published as *A Pony Named Shawney,* illustrated by Suçie Stevenson, Mondo Publishing (Greenvale, NY), 1997.

Night of the Muttonbirds, illustrated by Robert Ingpen, Methuen Australia (Sydney, New South Wales, Australia), 1981.

The Trouble with Peggetty, illustrated by Irena Sibley, Kangaroo Press (Kenthurst, New South Wales, Australia), 1984.

Rattletrap Rosie, photographs by Ron Ryan, Buttercup Books (Melboure, Victoria, Australia), 1984.

Jodie's BMX Wheelchair (with sound recording), illustrated by Neil Chenery, Harcourt Brace Jovanovich (Sydney, New South Wales, Australia), 1985.

Grandfather's Tiger, Methuen (North Ryde, New South Wales, Australia), 1985.

Peter Moss (with sound recording), illustrated by Neil Chenery, Harcourt Brace Jovanovich (Sydney, New South Wales, Australia), 1985, published as *Christmas and Peter Moss,* International Cultural Exchange (Great Neck, NY), 1987.

The Lizard of Oz, illustrated by Julia McLeish, J.M. Dent (Melbourne, Victoria, Australia), 1986.

Muddy Footprints, photographs by Sue McKinnon, J.M. Dent (Melbourne, Victoria, Australia), 1987.

Thack's Army, Methuen Australia (North Ryde, New South Wales, Australia), 1987.

Cat Crusoe, illustrated by Edward Crosby, Bookshelf Publishing, 1988.

What a Pest!, illustrated by Lynne Tracey, Curriculum Development Centre (Canberra, Australian Capital Territory, Australia), 1988.

The Enormous Hole, illustrations by Hal Slatter, Buttercup Books (Cheltenham, Victoria, Australia), 1989.

Tracey McBean's Stretching Machine, illustrated by Arthur Filloy, Collins Australia (Sydney, New South Wales, Australia), 1989, published as *Tracey McBean and the Stretching Machine,* ABC Books (Sydney, New South Wales, Australia, 2002.

Simpson and Duffy, illustrated by Ester Kasepuu, Harcourt Brace Jovanovich (Sydney, New South Wales, Australia), 1989.

Santa Claws, illustrated by Vicky Kitanov, Collins Australia (Sydney, New South Wales, Australia), 1989.

Broome Dog, illustrated by Arthur Boothroyd, Walter McVitty Books (Glebe, New South Wales, Australia), 1989.

Adam's Boat, illustrated by Heather Campbell, Harcourt Brace Jovanovich (Sydney, New South Wales, Australia), 1989.

Quiet Pony for Sale, illustrated by Heather Campbell, Harcourt Brace Jovanovich (Sydney, New South Wales, Australia), 1990.

Not Zackly, illustrated by Penny Azar, Harcourt Brace Jovanovich (Sydney, New South Wales, Australia), 1990.

Country Cousin, illustrated by Dee Huxley, Collins/Angus & Robertson (North Ryde, New South Wales, Australia), 1991.

(With Dianne Bates) *Who Pushed Humpty?,* illustrated by Craig Smith, Mimosa Publishing (Melbourne, Victoria, Australia), 1991.

Mr Thompson's Teddy, illustrated by Richard Collins, Angus & Robertson (Pymble, New South Wales, Australia), 1992.

Night of the Muttonbirds, illustrated by Ken Andrews, Harcourt Brace Jovanovich (Sydney, New South Wales, Australia), 1992.

(Compiler) *Saddle Up: A Collection of Australian Horse Stories,* Angus & Robertson (Pymble, New South Wales, Australia), 1994.

Lizard on the Loose, illustrated by Virginia Barrett, Angus & Robertson (Pymble, New South Wales, Australia), 1994.

A Wetland Home, illustrated by John Hurford, Pye Anderson Ltd., (New Zealand), 1994.

(Compiler) *Saddle up Again: More Australian Horse Tales,* Angus & Robertson (Pymble, New South Wales, Australia), 1995.

Knock Knock! Who's There?, illustrated by Cathy Lane, Koala Book Company (Redfern, New South Wales, Australia), 1996.

Trapped!, illustrated by Trish Hill, Longman Australia (Melbourne, Victoria, Australia), 1996, Sundance Publications (Littleton, MA), 1997.

Donald Bradman: Cricketing Hero (biography), Reed Library (Carlton, Victoria, Australia), 1997.

The $2 Scratchie, illustrated by Majory Gardner, Longman Australia (Melbourne, Victoria, Australia), 1997.

Simpson and Duffy (adapted from *Not Only a Hero: An Illustrated Life of Simpson, the Man with the Donkey*), illustrated by Ester Kasepuu, ANZAC Day Commemoration Committee (Aspley, Queensland, Australia), 2001.

The Unknown Australian Soldier, illustrated by Anne Langridge, ANZAC Day Commemoration Committee (Aspley, Queensland, Australia), 2001.

The Monster Hole, illustrated by Roland Harvey, Puffin (Camberwell, Victoria, Australia), 2003.

Catastrophe Cat, illustrations by Chantall Stewart, University of Western Australia Press (Crawley, Western Australia, Australia), 2004.

Ruff and Tumble, illustrated by Gus Gordon, Puffin (Camberwell, Victoria, Australia), 2004.

(With Vashti Farrer) *Feathered Soldiers,* ANZAC Day Commemoration Committee (Aspley, Queensland, Australia), 2005.

Author of television plays for children's programs *Storytime, Tracey McBean,* and *Let's Join in,* broadcast on Australian Broadcasting Corporation, 1977-88. Contributor to anthologies, including *Crutches Are Nothing,* Greenhouse, 1982; *Horse Australia,* Dorr/McLeod Publishing, 1982; *Funtastic Short Stories,* Jacaranda Press, 1993; and *Disaster and Survival,* Rigby Heinemann (Melbourne, Victoria, Australia), 1994; and to periodicals, including *School, Orana, This Australia,* and *Lu Rees Archives.* Editor, *Riding Free* (quarterly journal of Riding for the Disabled Association of Australia), 1979-91.

Adaptations

Several of Small's books have been adapted as audiobooks.

Biographical and Critical Sources

BOOKS

Dunkle, Margaret, *The Story Makers,* Oxford University Press (Melborne, Victoria, Australia), 1987.
McVitty, Walter, *Authors and Illustrators of Children's Books,* Hodder & Stoughton, 1989.

PERIODICALS

Children's Bookwatch, June, 2005, review of *Catastrophe Cat.*
Magpies, May, 1992, review of *Country Cousin,* p. 27; May, 2002, review of *Tracey McBean and the Stretching Machine,* p. 29; May, 2005, Lucinda Dodds, review of *Catastrophe Cat,* p. 38.

*   *   *

STANLEY, Mandy

Personal

Born in Lowestoft, Suffolk, England. *Education:* Attended Great Yarmouth College of Art and Design; Nottingham Trent Polytechnic, B.A. (fashion design). *Hobbies and other interests:* Theatre, ballet, cooking.

Addresses

Home—Suffolk, England. *Agent*—c/o Author Mail, Kingfisher Publications, New Penderel House, 283-288 High Holborn, London WC1V 7HP, England.

Career

Designer, illustrator, and writer.

Awards, Honors

Received *Mother and Baby* magazine award.

Writings

FOR CHILDREN: SELF-ILLUSTRATED

Lettice, the Dancing Rabbit, HarperCollins (London, England), 2001, Simon & Schuster Books for Young Readers (New York, NY), 2002.
Bloomer: The Dog You Can Play With!, Orchard Books (New York, NY), 2001.
What Do You Say?, HarperCollins (London, England), 2002, Simon & Schuster Books for Young Readers (New York, NY), 2003.
Busy Bugs, Kingfisher (Boston, MA), 2003.
Lettice, the Flying Rabbit, HarperCollins (London, England), 2003, Simon & Schuster Books for Young Readers (New York, NY), 2004.
A Christmas Wish, HarperCollins (London, England), 2004.
Who Tickled Tilly?, Chrysalis Children's (London, England), 2004.
The Bridesmaid, HarperCollins (London, England), 2005.
What Do You Do?, Simon & Schuster Books for Young Readers (New York, NY), 2005.

ILLUSTRATOR

Anna Nilsen, *I Can Count 1 to 10,* Kingfisher (New York, NY), 1999.
Anna Nilsen, *I Can Count 10 to 20,* Kingfisher (New York, NY), 1999.
Anna Nilsen, *I Can Subtract,* Kingfisher (New York, NY), 2000.
Anna Nilsen, *I Can Add,* Kingfisher (New York, NY), 2000.
Jane Kemp, *Tiny Trumpet,* Collins (London, England), 2000.
First Word Book, Kingfisher (New York, NY), 2000.
Patti Barber, *First Number Book,* Kingfisher (New York, NY), 2001.
Vanessa Gill-Brown, *Rufferella,* Scholastic (New York, NY), 2001.
Anna Nilsen, *I Can Multiply: Flip-Card Fun with Adding Groups and Multiplication,* Kingfisher (London, England), 2001.
On the Farm, Kingfisher (New York, NY), 2002.
Ann Montague-Smith, *First Shape Book,* Kingfisher (New York, NY), 2002.
At the Zoo, Kingfisher (New York, NY), 2002.
At the Beach, Kingfisher (New York, NY), 2002.
Shopping, Kingfisher (New York, NY), 2003.
Playtime, Kingfisher (Boston, MA), 2003.
Out and About, Kingfister (Boston, MA), 2003.
First Colour Book, Kingfisher (London, England), 2003.
Marie Birkinshaw, *Wipe Clean Read and Write: Read, Write, Wipe Clean, and Practice,* Ladybird (London, England), 2003.

Also illustrator of "Babe" board-book series. Several books illustrated by Stanley have been translated into Spanish.

Sidelights

British author, illustrator, and designer Mandy Stanley originally trained for a career in the fashion industry designing baby wear before discovering her passion for writing and illustrating children's books. Moving into book illustration, Stanley has also created original stories such as *What Do You Do?* and *Who Tickled Tilly?*, which she pairs with her whimsical illustrations. Popular with readers in both England and the United States is Stanley's picture-book series featuring a curious young rabbit named Lettice. This series has grown to include the books *Lettice, the Dancing Rabbit, The Bridesmaid,* and *A Christmas Wish,* all of which feature the author/illustrator's gentle, pastel-toned art.

Readers meet Lettice in *Lettice, the Dancing Rabbit* as the young bunny becomes frustrated by life as a rabbit and decides to become a ballerina instead. Bravely leaving home, she hops into town and finds a ballet school where they agree to give her lessons. After borrowing ballerina attire from a doll, Lettice quickly turns into the star of her class because she can jump so high. However, despite her love of dancing and stardom, the bunny misses the simple joys of the carefree rabbit lifestyle, and longs to let down her ears; she must now choose between dancing and her home and family. "This British import is charming: text, pictures, and design," commented Ilene Cooper in a *Booklist* review of *Lettice, the Dancing Rabbit.* Dorian Chong stated in *School Library Journal* that Stanley's "simple and sweet" story pairs well with "clear and clean illustrations [that] are prettily appealing."

In *Lettice, the Flying Rabbit* the spunky bunny takes on yet another challenge: flying. Inspired by the birds around her, Lettice becomes determined to fly, and when she sees a small pink motorized toy plane, she climbs inside. When the owner of the plane, a little girl, returns and begins to play with the toy, away goes Lettice into the sky, making her dreams a surprise reality, although when she lands far from her rabbit hole another, more fearsome challenge awaits. Other adventures include *A Christmas Wish,* which finds the ambitious bunny wishing she could be a Christmas fairy, and *The Bridesmaid,* in which an invitation to be a member of a wedding party fulfills yet another of the youngster's dreams. Noting that Stanley's storyline in *Lettice, the Flying Rabbit* is "just right" for preschoolers, *Booklist* reviewer Cooper also praised the illustrations, which she described as "sweet and simple and executed in candy colors that immediately attract." Judith Constantinides commented in *School Library Journal* that Lettice is "a lovable heroine with an expressive face and lots of bounce." *Lettice, the Flying Rabbit* is "a good read-aloud for one child or many," the critic added, noting "the added attraction of an essential life lesson as well."

Biographical and Critical Sources

PERIODICALS

Booklist, February 1, 2002, Ilene Cooper, review of *Lettice, the Dancing Rabbit,* p. 948; February 15, 2004, Ilene Cooper, review of *Lettice, the Flying Rabbit,* p. 1064.
Kirkus Reviews, December 1, 2001, review of *Lettice, the Dancing Rabbit,* p. 1690; June 1, 2005, review of *What Do You Do?,* p. 644.
Publishers Weekly, February 14, 2000, "In a Word," p. 203; February 26, 2001, review of *Rufferella,* p. 86; February 9, 2004, review of *Lettice, the Flying Rabbit,* p. 83.
School Library Journal, August, 2000, Christine Lindsey, review of *First World Book* p. 175; July, 2001, Melinda Piehler, review of *First Number Book,* p. 93; December 24, 2001, review of *Lettice, the Dancing Rabbit,* p. 63; April, 2002, Dorian Chong, review of *Lettice, the Dancing Rabbit,* p. 124; June, 2003, Olga R. Kuharets, review of *What Do You Say?,* p. 120; February, 2004, Judith Constantinides, review of *Lettice, the Flying Rabbit,* p. 124.

ONLINE

HarperCollins Children's Web site, http://www.harper collinschildrensbooks.co.uk/ (October 7, 2005), "Mandy Stanley."
World Book Day Web site, http://www.worldbookday.com/ (October 7, 2005), "Mandy Stanley."

*   *   *

STINE, Catherine

Personal

Born in Philadelphia, PA; father a college professor, mother a law editor. *Education:* Boston Museum School of Fine Arts, B.F.A.; New School of Social Research (now New School University), M.F.A. (creative writing), 2003. *Hobbies and other interests:* Painting, traveling, listening to world music.

Addresses

Agent—c/o Transatlantic Literary Agency, 72 Glengowan Rd., Toronto, Ontario M4N 1G4, Canada. *E-mail*—info@catherinestine.com.

Career

Author and educator. Has worked as a textile designer. New School University, writing instructor in continuing education division; teacher in elementary-and secondary-school writing workshops. *Exhibitions:* Work exhibited at Sunnen Gallery, 1993-94, and Margaret Bodell Gallery, New York, NY, 2000-01.

Catherine Stine

Awards, Honors
Winner, New School University Chapbook Contest in Writing for Children, 2004, for *Refugees*.

Writings

FOR CHILDREN

Refugees, Delacorte (New York, NY), 2005.

Also author of books for series published by Pleasant Company.

ILLUSTRATOR

Kate Heroman and Diane Dodge, *Building Your Baby's Brain: A Parent's Guide to the First Five Years,* Learning Strategies (Washington, DC), 1999.
Norris Chumley, *The Joy of Weight Loss,* Lantern Books (New York, NY), 1999.

Work in Progress
From Chapter Book to Teen Fiction, 2006.

Sidelights
Writer and artist Catherine Stine has penned series books published by Pleasant Company. Her first young-adult novel, *Refugees,* was described as an "earnest first

novel [that] follows the fate of two teens after Sept. 11, 2001," according to a *Publishers Weekly* contributor. In Stine's novel, sixteen-year-old Dawn runs away to New York City in the late summer of 2001, escaping her third foster home in San Francisco shortly after her foster mother, Louise, leaves to work for the Red Cross in Pakistan. At the same time, across the world in Afghanistan, fifteen-year-old Johar has fled his own family in order to avoid pressures to join the terrorist Taliban. Johar becomes Louise's translator, and when Dawn phones her foster mom Johar is the one who answers the calls. The friendship that forms between the two teens is shaken on September 11th, as terrorists kill thousands of Americans in New York City, Washington, D.C., and Pennsylvania.

Noting the book's organization into alternating narratives between Johar and Dawn, *Booklist* critic Gillian Engberg wrote that "Stine follows the teens' flights and tense struggles to cope with the tragedies of the attacks," deeming *Refugees* a "powerful first novel." A *Kirkus Reviews* reviewer also praised Stine's book, noting that "memorable characters and sudden rare beauty

While telephoning the Afghan refugee camp in Pakistan where her physician foster-mother works, runaway teen Dawn finds she has much in common with Johar, the young Afghani who helps field the camp doctors' calls. (Cover illustration by Kim McGillivroy.)

make it impossible not to care about Dawn and Johar's world." As Stine explained to Engberg, she wrote the novel as a way to deal with her upset following 9/11: "I wanted to create a dialogue, and I thought, Who better to speak about it than teenagers, who have a very ethical sensibility and an urge to create a better world?"

Stine told *SATA:* "In my booktalks, I speak on what led me to write my historical fiction, *Refugees,* about the unusual friendship between an American girl and an Afghan boy, during the fall of 2001. . . . I also describe my rather visual style of writing. As an artist, I strive to inspire reluctant as well as prolific student writers to 'write as if they are painting scenes with words.'"

Biographical and Critical Sources

PERIODICALS

Artforum International, November, 1993, Ronny Cohen "Catherine Stine," p. 110.
Art in America, December, 2001, Gerrit Henry, "Catherine Stine at Margaret Bodell," p. 120.
Booklist, March 1, 2005, Gillian Engberg, "Teens across Cultures" (interview), and review of *Refugees,* p. 1183.
Faces: People, Places, and Cultures, March, 2005, review of *Refugees,* p. 46.
Kirkus Reviews, January 1, 2005, review of *Refugees,* p. 57.
Publishers Weekly, March 28, 2005, review of *Refugees,* p. 80.
School Library Journal, March, 2005, Alison Follos, review of *Refugees,* p. 220.

ONLINE

Catherine Stine Home Page, http://www.catherinestine. com (October 7, 2005).
Teenreads, http://www.teenreads.com/ (March 15, 2005), interview with Stine.
Transatlantic Literary Agency Web site, http://www.tla1. com/ (October 7, 2005), "Catherine Stine."

*   *   *

STROUD, Bettye 1939-

Personal

Born July 17, 1939, in Athens, GA; daughter of Robert Lee (an Amtrak worker) and Luna Veal Moore; married Howard B. Stroud (an associate school superintendent), December, 1989. *Education:* Fort Valley State University, B.S. (English and library science), 1960; University of Georgia, M.Ed., 1972, Ed.S. (library media specialist), 1974. *Hobbies and other interests:* Travel, photography, gardening, reading, puzzles.

Bettye Stroud

Addresses

Home—243 Deerhill Dr., Bogart, GA 30622. *Agent*— Jennie Dunham, Russell and Volkening, 50 W. 29 St., New York, NY 10001. *E-mail*—bjstroud@bellsouth.net.

Career

Writer. Winder Middle Grade Schools, Winder, GA, media specialist, 1960-72; Barnett Shoals School, Athens, GA, media specialist, 1972-92; University of Georgia, Athens, lecturer in writing for children. Georgia Student Media Festivals, judge; Georgia Children's Book Awards, member of selection committee, 1985; Georgia Department of Education, member of instructional television panel, 1985; Georgia Library Association, member of committee for standards, 1986; Georgia Library Media Association, state president elect, 1989. Also member of Georgia Teacher Education Council, 1981-86, and President's White House Conference on Libraries, 1985.

Member

International Reading Association, Travel Writers International Network, National Education Association, Society of Children's Book Writers, and Illustrators (contact person and workshop presenter), Cassell Network of Writers, Four at Five Writers, Georgia Association of Educators, Library Board of Athens-Clarke county, Delta Kappa Gamma.

Awards, Honors

Sandhills Writers Workshop honor, 1994, for *Keep Running, Lizzie;* grants from Southeastern Advocates of Literature for Children, 1984, and Georgia Council for the Arts, 1995; University of Chicago Classic Children's Book selection, 1996, for *Down Home at Miss Dessa's;* Oppenheim Toy Portfolio Gold Award, 2004, for *The Patchwork Path.*

Writings

Down Home at Miss Dessa's, illustrated by Felicia Marshall, Lee and Low (New York, NY), 1996.

Dance Y'All, illustrated by Cornelius Van Wright and Ying-Hwa Hu, Marshall Cavendish (New York, NY), 2001.

A Personal Tour of Tuskegee Institute, Lerner Publications (Minneapolis, MN), 2001.

The Leaving, illustrated by Cedric Lucas, Marshall Cavendish (New York, NY), 2001.

(Editor) *The World's Wide Open* (poetry collection), illustrated by Pat Cummings, Simon & Schuster (New York, NY), 2003.

The Patchwork Path: A Quilt Map to Freedom, illustrated by Erin Susanne Bennett, Candlewick Press (Cambridge, MA), 2005.

Contributor of articles and book reviews to *Country America, Multicultural Review, Athens* magazine, *Georgia Journal,* and *Multicultural Resource Guide.* Author of unpublished manuscript *Keep Running, Lizzie.*

Sidelights

Bettye Stroud worked as a library media specialist for elementary schools in Atlanta, Georgia, for over thirty years before beginning her second career as a children's book author. Dedicated to inspiring an interest in reading among very young children throughout both her careers, Stroud has authored several picture books that feature inspiring stories geared toward African-American children. In addition to picture books, such as *Down Home at Miss Dessa's, The Leaving,* and *The Patchwork Path: A Quilt Map to Freedom,* Stroud has authored *A Personal Tour of Tuskegee Institute,* a nonfiction work profiling the school established in Alabama by Booker T. Washington, and has edited the poetry collection *The World's Wide Open.*

Taking place in the American South during the 1940s, *Down Home at Miss Dessa's* focuses on two sisters who spend a warm summer day visiting and tending to an elderly woman who lives nearby and is recovering from a minor injury. Also featuring likeable young characters, *Dance Y'All* finds young Jack Henry excited about the arrival of friends and family for the annual harvest celebration, but also worried that he and his cousin will have to spend the night in the barn, where a snake-like coach whip also "resides." Praising *Down*

Home at Miss Dessa's, Booklist reviewer Hazel Rochman called the book a "warm, autobiographical account of caring across generations," while Catherine Threadgill, reviewing *Dance Y'All* for *School Library Journal,* wrote that Stroud transforms her "realistic vignette of a boy who conquers a big fear" into a "quietly realistic story."

The flight of slaves to freedom via the Underground Railroad during the mid-nineteenth century is the backdrop to both *The Leaving* and *The Patchwork Path. The Leaving* takes place five years after slavery has been declared illegal by the Emancipation Proclamation, and finds a nine-year-old girl risking danger to lead her family's flight from their former master, who keeps control of them by claiming indebtedness. Praising the story as "suspenseful and episodic," *Booklist* reviewer Gillian Engberg also cited the "exceptional" pastel illustrations by Cedric Lucas. Taking readers back a few years, *The Patchwork Path* finds Hannah and her father living on a plantation in Georgia, where freedom is still only a dream. In their free time, Hannah and her mother stitch a beautiful quilt, patterning a secret key to freedom within the colorful patches. When Mama dies, Hannah and her father make a break for Canada, using the map sewn into the handstitched quilt as their guide. An Oppenheim Toy Portfolio Gold Award winner, *The Patchwork Path* was praised by *School Library Journal* reviewer Lauralyn Persson for its "first-person narrative [that] flows smoothly and lends immediacy to the dramatic events," while Rochman dubbed it an "exciting escape story" that is enhanced by Stroud's inclusion of an afterword that explains the history behind Hannah's tale.

Stroud once told *SATA:* "My writing landscape is the South, quite often the South of the past. My milieu is a mix of generations, chock full of grandparents, aunts, uncles, and extended families.

"After my mother died, I grew up with a great-aunt and uncle, but also had a father and his new family in another state. I spent a lot of time on trains, in the midst of the two families. It all made for a wonderful childhood!

"No wonder my stories are intergenerational. No wonder they swing between truck farms in the South and locomotives headed north. I hope they serve as evidence of the joy brought into the lives of young and old alike when generations come together to love, to share and to protect.

"But, present-day subjects find their way into my writing, too. More than thirty people died in my state in 1994 during the fury wrought by Tropical Storm Andrew. It was a setting I had to utilize, a subject I had to write about.

"Hopefully, in my writing, children meet the demons they have faced in their own lives and find they can be

The quilt Hannah and her mother stitched before Mama's death contains a secret map that helps guide the girl and her father to freedom in **The Patchwork Path.** *(Illustration by Erin Susanne Bennett.)*

banished. They get to know protagonists who come up against obstacles and problems and somehow find solutions.

"I want children to understand all is never lost. Fears can be conquered; lost friendships can be replaced by new ones and broken hearts can be mended in time. There's always tomorrow. There's always hope.

"Like any good writer, I want the echoes of my stories to reverberate through the reader's head long after the book is closed and the reader has gone on to something else." In addition to writing and visiting schools and libraries, Stroud also teaches a course in writing for children at the University of Georgia.

Biographical and Critical Sources

PERIODICALS

Booklist, December 15, 1996, Hazel Rochman, review of *Down Home at Miss Dessa's,* p. 734; February 15, 2001, Gillian Engberg, review of *The Leaving,* p. 1156; February 1, 2005, Hazel Rochman, review of *The Patchwork Path: A Quilt Map to Freedom,* p. 978.
Bulletin of the Center for Children's Books, December, 1996, review of *Down Home at Miss Dessa's,* p. 153; January, 2005, Timnah Card, review of *The Patchwork Path,* p. 229.
Kirkus Reviews, September 1, 1996, p. 1329; September 1, 2001, review of *Dance Y'All,* p. 1301; December 15, 2004, review of *The Patchwork Path,* p. 1209.
Publishers Weekly, September 16, 1996, review of *Down Home at Miss Dessa's,* p. 83; January 3, 2005, review of *The Patchwork Path,* p. 55.
School Library Journal, May, 2001, Susan Hepler, review of *The Leaving,* p. 136; November, 2001, Catherine Threadgill, review of *Dance Y'All,* p. 136; January, 2005, Lauralyn Persson, review of *The Patchwork Path,* p. 98.

ONLINE

Bettye Stroud Home Page, http://www.bettyestroud.com (October 20 2005).
Public Broadcasting Atlanta Web site, http://www.wabe.org/atlanta/community/ (October 20, 2005), *This Is Atlanta:* "Bettye Stroud."*

T

TALLIS, Robyn
See DOYLE, Debra

*   *   *

TALLIS, Robyn
See MACDONALD, James D.

*   *   *

TOEWS, Miriam 1964-

Personal
Surname pronounced "Taves"; born 1964, in Steinbach, Manitoba, Canada; daughter of Melvin C. Toews (a teacher); married; children: two. *Education:* University of Manitoba, B.A. (film studies); University of King's College, bachelor's degree (journalism). *Religion:* Mennonite.

Addresses
Home—Winnipeg, Manitoba, Canada. *Agent*—c/o Author Mail, Random House of Canada Ltd., 1 Toronto St., Unit 300, Toronto, Ontario M5C 2V6, Canada.

Career
Writer and journalist.

Awards, Honors
John Hirsch Award for Most Promising Manitoba Writer, Stephen Leacock Award for Humour shortlist, and McNally Robinson Book of the Year Award shortlist, all 1996, all for *Summer of My Amazing Luck;* McNally Robinson Book of the Year Award, 1998, for *Boy of Good Breeding;* National Magazine Award Gold Medal for Humour, 1999; McNally Robinson Book of the Year Award, and Alexander Kennedy Isbister Award for Nonfiction, both 2000, both for *Swing Low;* Giller Prize finalist, and Governor General's Award, both 2004, both for *A Complicated Kindness.*

Writings

Summer of My Amazing Luck, Turnstone Press (Winnipeg, Manitoba, Canada), 1996.
A Boy of Good Breeding, Stoddart (Toronto, Ontario, Canada), 1998, Arcade (New York, NY), 2001.
Swing Low: A Life (memoir), Stoddart (Toronto, Ontario, Canada), 2000.
A Complicated Kindness, Counterpoint (New York, NY), 2004.

Author of freelance documentaries for Canadian Broadcasting Corporation radio. Contributor to periodicals, including *New York Times Magazine, Geist, Prairie Fire, Saturday Night,* and *This American Life.*

Adaptations
A Complicated Kindness was adapted as an audiobook, BTC Audiobooks (Fredericton, New Brunswick, Canada), 2005.

Sidelights
Canadian novelist and journalist Miriam Toews is the author of the critically acclaimed novels *Summer of My Amazing Luck, A Boy of Good Breeding,* and *A Complicated Kindness,* the last the winner of Canada's 2004 Governor General's award. In addition, she has authored a moving memoir of her father, a teacher who suffered from manic depression throughout his life and ultimately committed suicide in 1998. The winner of several awards, *Swing Low: A Life* "engages" readers due to what a *Publishers Weekly* reviewer described as Toews's ability to present "a strong and realistic sense of a man who chose to use the little energy he had to construct a safe world for his family."

Born in Steinbach, Manitoba, Toews was raised in a Mennonite family where her parents valued education, both having earned master's degree. While her parents were not restrictive, the family church was very conservative; in fact, Toews only saw one movie—*Swiss Family Robinson*—as a child because she was allowed to go with a friend. As the author later told *Powells.com* interviewer Dave Weich, the film "magically changed my life. . . . Movies are as important to me as books. I love them. I would see three movies a day if I could." Leaving home at age eighteen, she studied French, and then lived in Montreal before spending time touring Europe. Returning to Manitoba, she earned her bachelor's degree in film studies. In addition to starting a family, Toews also moved to Halifax, Nova Scotia, and earned a second bachelor's degree, this time in journalism before starting her career as a freelance writer. She started her first novel after her youngest daughter began nursery school, stealing enough time to complete the manuscript for *Summer of My Amazing Luck,* which was published in 1996.

Published two years after her fiction debut, *A Boy of Good Breeding* is a humorous novel that focuses on a mother and daughter living in a small town in Canada. Knute and her daughter move back to Knute's parents house in Algren, Manitoba, after life in Winnipeg does not go according to plan. Working for Algren's mayor, Hosea Funk, Knute soon joins Funk in his efforts to prevent further population growth so that Algren can win the distinction of being Canada's smallest town—and Mayor Funk can achieve his lifelong dream of meeting Canada's prime minister on Canada Day. Noting that the tone of Toews's prose echoes the work of popular Minnesota writer and radio commentator Garrison Keillor, *Quill and Quire* contributor Mary Soderstrom praised the author's humor as well as her "short sentences, colourful characters, and a lot of charm in the timing of the telling."

In *A Complicated Kindness* Toews takes on a more serious topic: religious fundamentalism. In this novel, which takes place during the 1980s, sixteen-year-old Nomi Nickel lives in East Village, Manitoba. Part of a Mennonite clan, Nomi finds her family shrinking as her mother Trudie and older sister Natasha seemingly flee from their small home town. Nomi's father reacts with lethargy, leaving his daughter to deal with day-to-day matters; meanwhile the teen's only other source of emotional support, her best friend, is currently sidelined due to a strange illness that has put her in the hospital. Reacting to her strict Mennonite community, which is economically bankrupt and intellectually oppressive, Nomi begins to experiment with drugs and starts hanging around with other disaffected teens, "smoking dope, reading hipster novels, and listening to Lou Reed, dreaming of city people and city pleasures as distant as satellites," according to *Quill and Quire* contributor Adair Brouwer. As Nomi begins to reflect on the reasons for the flight of her mother and sister, she gains perspective on her own personality: as "a girl fated to overturn rocks, uncovering hissing toads," according to Brouwer.

Praising Toews's portrait of growing up in small-town Canada, Brouwer described *A Complicated Kindness* as similar to "waking up in a crazy Bible camp, or witnessing an adolescent tour guide tear off her uniform and make a break for the highway." Nomi is also compassionate, however; as *Catholic New Times* reviewer Colleen Crawley noted, "Even in a town that misunderstands and condemns her, Nomi sees 'a complicated kindness' in the eyes of her neighbours." In *School Library Journal,* Susan H. Woodcock noted that Toews's story "is a metaphor for those torn between a present lack of fulfullment and the fear of moving toward the unfamiliar—in other words, growing up."

Biographical and Critical Sources

PERIODICALS

Booklist, December 15, 2001, Marlene Chamberlain, review of *Swing Low,* p. 689; September 15, 2004, Michael Cart, review of *A Complicated Kindness,* p. 210.

a

complicated

kindness

a novel

MIRIAM TOEWS

Author of *Swing Low: A Life*

Drawing on the author's own Mennonite heritage, Toews's novel finds a teen abandoned by the older women in her family when the constraints imposed by a tradition-minded local minister force them to leave rather than have their spirit crushed.

Toews moves to the personal realm to tell the story of her father's life; a manic depressive, he was seen by those outside the family as a pillar of the community until his suicide. (Cover photograph by Charles Gullung/Photonica.)

Books in Canada, April 1997, review of *Summer of My Amazing Luck,* p. 37.

Canadian Book Review Annual, 1997, review of *Summer of My Amazing Luck,* p. 201; 1999, review of *A Boy of Good Breeding,* p. 188.

Catholic New Times, October 24, 2004, Colleen Crawley, "Perhaps a Canadian Holden Caulfield," p. 18.

Chatelaine, June, 2000, Buffy Childerhose, "Low Point," p. 14.

Kirkus Reviews, October 1, 2001, review of *Swing Low,* p. 1411; August 15, 2004, review of *A Complicated Kindness,* p. 775.

Maclean's, July 31, 2000, review of *Swing Low,* p. 21.

NeWest Review, April-May, 1999, review of *Boy of Good Breeding,* pp. 33-34.

People, October 11, 2004, Andrea L. Sachs, review of *A Complicated Kindness,* p. 56.

Publishers Weekly, October 8, 2001, review of *Swing Low,* p. 52; July 19, 2004, review of *A Complicated Kindness,* p. 141.

Quill and Quire, May, 1998, Mary Soderstrom, review of *A Boy of Good Breeding,* p. 27; April, 2000, review of

Swing Low, p. 39; May, 2004, Adair Brouwer, review of *A Complicated Kindness.*

School Library Journal, April, 2005, Susan H. Woodcock, review of *A Complicated Kindness,* p. 162.

ONLINE

Powells.com, http://www.powells.com/ (November 8, 2004), Dave Weich, interview with Toews.*

*   *   *

TOMLINSON, Theresa 1946-

Personal

Born August 14, 1946, in Crawley, Sussex, England; daughter of Alan (a vicar) and Joan (a teacher) Johnston; married Alan Tomlinson (an architect), 1967; children: Rosie, Joe, Sam. *Education:* Attended Hull College of Education. *Politics:* "Socialist." *Religion:* "Agnostic." *Hobbies and other interests:* Dancing, drawing, painting.

Addresses

Home—65 Hastings Rd., Sheffield, South Yorkshire S7 2GT, England. *Agent*—Caroline Walsh, David Higham Associates, 5-8 Lower John St., Golden Square, London W1R 4HA, England. *E-mail*—theresatomlinson@ talk21.com.

Career

Author, 1987—.

Member

National Association of Writers in Education, British Society of Authors.

Awards, Honors

Sheffield Children's Book Award shortlist, for *The Rope Carrier, The Herring Girls,* and *Dancing through the Shadows;* Carnegie Medal shortlist, British Library Association, 1991, for *Riding the Waves,* and 1998, for *Meet Me by the Steelmen;* America Library Association Notable Trade Book for Children designation, and *Booklist* Editor's Choice designation, both for *The Forestwife.*

Writings

FOR CHILDREN

The Flither Pickers, Walker Books (London, England), 1987.

Theresa Tomlinson

The Water Cat, Julia MacRae Books (London, England), 1988.

Summer Witches, Macmillan (New York, NY), 1989.

Riding the Waves, Walker Books (London, England), 1990, Macmillan (New York, NY), 1991.

The Rope Carrier, Red Fox (London, England), 1991.

The Herring Girls, Red Fox (London, England), 1994.

The Cellar Lad, Red Fox (London, England), 1995.

Haunted House Blues, Walker Books (London, England), 1996.

Dancing through the Shadows, DK Ink (New York, NY), 1997.

Little Stowaway (picture book), illustrated by Jane Browne, Julia MacRae Books (London, England), 1997.

Ironstone Valley, A. & C. Black (London, England), 1998.

(And illustrator) *The Lifeboat That Went by Land* (picture book), Bayfair Publications (Robin Hood's Bay, North Yorkshire, England), 1999.

The Voyage of the Silver Bream, A. & C. Black (London, England), 2001.

The Rope Carrier, Red Fox (London, England), 2001.

Beneath Burning Mountain, Red Fox (London, England), 2001.

The Moon Riders, Corgi (London, England), 2003.

Voyage of the Snake Lady, Corgi (London, England), 2004.

"TIME SLIP ADVENTURES" SERIES; FOR CHILDREN

Meet Me by the Steelmen, Walker Books (London, England), 1997.

Night of the Red Devil, illustrated by Anthony Lewis, Walker Books (London, England), 2001.

Errand Lass, illustrated by Anthony Lewis, Walker (London, England), 2003.

Scavenger Boy, illustrated by Anthony Lewis, Walker (London, England), 2003.

Blitz Baby, illustrated by Anthony Lewis, Orchard Books (London, England), 2004.

"FORESTWIFE" TRILOGY

The Forestwife, Red Fox (London, England), 1993, Orchard Books (New York, NY), 1995.

Child of the May, Orchard Books (New York, NY), 1998.

The Path of the She-Wolf, Red Fox (London, England) 2000.

The Forestwife Trilogy (contains *The Forestwife, Child of the May,* and *The Path of the She-Wolf*), Corgi (London, England), 2003.

Sidelights

British writer Theresa Tomlinson's novels, many of which are set in her native Yorkshire, are regional only in location, for their themes span borders and cross continents. While daily courage in the face of hardship is a major Tomlinson motif, her books are not overbearingly polemical. Character-driven, her high-action tales involve the reader in both historical and contemporary situations and generally feature assertive female protagonists. From the angst of a frustrated surfer to the exploits of Maid Marian in the forests of Sherwood, Tomlinson's novels engage young readers on several levels and generally end with an upbeat message. "I love writing about people who had a hard life but worked together and found ways to survive," Tomlinson once commented. "Resilience is what I admire most in human beings. I think that it is important to find exciting ways of passing a sense of history on to our children. A knowledge of the resilience of ordinary people who have lived before us can inspire modern children and help them with their own struggles and decisions."

Born in 1946, Tomlinson was raised in North Yorkshire and as a child had a strong desire to be a ballet dancer. Although she had no inclination to become a writer, her parents read to her and encouraged her love of books. "I started making little picture books for my own children when they were small," Tomlinson explained of her gradual transition to authorship. "As the children got older, the stories got longer, and I found that I enjoyed it very much." Tomlinson's first official literary ventures included stories inspired by the local history of North Yorkshire, including stories told by her grandparents, "about the fisherwomen who arrived on the train early in the morning and stories about storms, shipwrecks, and daring lifeboat rescues."

Tomlinson's first published novel was inspired by the hardships endured by the wives of Yorkshire fishermen at the turn of the twentieth century, who braved all sorts of weather to gather shellfish bait, or "flithers," for their husbands. *The Flither Pickers* tells the story of the daughter of one such family, Lisa, who has the opportunity to break away from this harsh life by pursuing an education. Lisa is torn between loyalty to her family and her desire to become a writer, however. Thoroughly researched, like all Tomlinson's books, *The Flither Pickers* is also illustrated by the period photographs by Frank Meadow Sutcliffe. In a *Junior Bookshelf* review, Marcus Crouch noted that Tomlinson "has written a most distinguished novel which is also a convincing piece of historical reconstruction." The critic also observed that Lisa's narrative has "a rough eloquence . . . which strikes exactly the right note." Writing in *Books for Keeps,* David Bennett commented that the community of women in the novel is realized "vividly and compassionately," while in a subsequent review the of the novel for the same publication he concluded that the "juxtaposition of story and pictures makes up one of the best produced and affecting paperbacks I've come across in the twelve years I've been reviewing fiction for young people."

The Water Cat, while also set in Yorkshire, takes place in the more recent past. Set in 1953 in a steel-working town, the novel focuses on a brother and sister who take in a stray cat. The bedraggled creature turns out to be anything but a garden-variety cat, however; in fact, it is a shape-changer, a merman whose access to the sea has been cut off by the steel plant. The children vow to help the merman return back to his rightful home in the ocean. In a *Growing Point* review, Margery Fisher noted that in "plain prose which is circumstantial enough to deny disbelief the author describes the practical contrivances by which Jane and Tom manage to carry the merman/cat past the metal barrier, helped by seagulls and pigeons which put up a diversion."

Other Tomlinson books that deal with social and economic history include *The Rope Carrier, The Herring Girls,* and *The Voyage of the Silver Bream,* the last about the battle between canals and railways. Tomlinson examines the forgotten craft of rope-making in the first title, which is set in a Derbyshire village. Minnie Dakin was born in the underground cottages in Peake Cavern, near Sheffield, England, and chances are that, like generations of rope workers before her, she will die there as well. When her sister Netty marries and then falls ill, Minnie is called from the caverns to help her. Witnessing the advances made during the growing Industrial Revolution, Minnie now wonders whether life would not be better above ground, amid Sheffield's bustling metal industries. "This is social and industrial history with a human face," observed Crouch, "and very convincing it is." Crouch went on to praise *The Rope Carrier* as "a most absorbing and attractive book, of great educational value but likely to be read with interest for its moving story and its vividly realized characters." Noting the book's descriptive passages, well-developed characters, and quickly paced plot, Geoff Dubber commented in *School Library Journal* that, "Clearly and carefully written, based loosely on real

people, and interspersed with some excellent contemporary lithographs of the area," Tomlinson's novel "will have wide appeal."

In *The Herring Girls,* Tomlinson once again uses Victorian-era photographs by Sutcliffe to illustrate the lives of the young nineteenth-century women who cleaned fish during the herring season. In this story thirteen-year-old Dory is among them, forced into the trade to save her family from the poor house. George Hunt, reviewing the novel in *Books for Keeps,* described Dory's narration as "a good, honest, unadorned voice reminiscent of that of Laura Ingalls Wilder," while S.M. Ashburner noted in *Junior Bookshelf* that Tomlinson "presents a world that has gone forever, vividly recreating the economic hardships which then faced the poor."

More social history is served up in *The Cellar Lad,* a novel that deals with the efforts to gain the right to vote for all men and unionization for workers in the steel industry in Sheffield. Young Ben Sterndale and his family are caught up in these fights in a story "full of detail and very convincing," according to Linda Saunders in *School Librarian.* Reviewing *The Cellar Lad* for the *Junior Bookshelf,* Crouch noted that "Tomlinson has made the fictional interpretation of the English industrial revolution her own." With all the difficulties facing the characters in this novel, Crouch added, it "would have been easy to lay on the suffering with a trowel, but here is a writer who sees her subject whole."

Tomlinson brings to life the culture of the Yorkshire coast for younger readers in her picture book *Little Stowaway,* based on the true story of a young boy who stowed away on his father's fishing boat. In the book, little John Robert desperately wants to accompany his father when the man takes his boat out on the North Sea. Hiding behind the coal box, John is finally discovered by the cook, and the frightened little boy, worried about punishment, is hugged by his father. Unable to turn back, the boat plows out into the fishing grounds, where John Robert brings the fishermen such luck that they quickly fill their holds and are able to return to shore early. "Children will enjoy the return home and the heartfelt portrait of family reunion as much as the exciting journey," predicted Hazel Rochman in a *Booklist* review of the illustrated volume.

A versatile story teller, Tomlinson has also written books with contemporary settings and themes, focusing on issues ranging from intergenerational relationships to fighting cancer in novels for older readers, while presenting middle graders with her entertaining "Time Slip Adventures" series. In the young-adult novel *Summer Witches* she addresses the misconceptions concerning powerful women. In the novel friends Sarah and Susanna decide to clean out a World War-II air-raid shelter uncovered in Sarah's backyard and use it as a clubhouse. In doing so, they discover evidence of earlier inhabitants of the shelter: Lily and Rose, the two older women who live nearby. The girls had branded Lily as

In Little Stowaway *a young boy determined to help his fisherman father hides out aboard ship, but soon realizes that life at sea is much more difficult than he had imagined. (Illustration by Jane Browne.)*

something of a witch due to the elderly woman's inability to speak and her knowledge of healing plants. Eventually Sarah and Susanna come to learn that Lily, far from being a witch, has a sad secret involving the shelter and a tragic incident fifty years before. "Gradually," a reviewer for *Junior Bookshelf* commented, "the two girls come to realize that many so-called witches of the past were really 'wise' women who knew much about the use of herbs and nature's secrets, and were seldom evil." A contributor to *Kirkus Reviews* noted that, "with admirable skill, Tomlinson weaves her serious theme into an appealing, accessible story with likable, well-individualized characters and a neatly satisfying conclusion." *Horn Book* reviewer Martha V. Parravano concluded that "middle-grade girls will be hooked immediately by the private hideaway with a sense of mystery surrounding it," as well as by Tomlinson's tale, which "unfolds, living up to its enticing premise."

Children from the present gain a new appreciation for the comforts of modern civilization in Tomlinson's

"Time Slip Adventures" books, which include *The Errand Lass, Night of the Red Devil,* and *Scavenger Boy.* In *The Errand Lass* young girl who is miserable in her new school setting is transported back into the past during a visit to a Sheffield museum, and finds herself one of many children employed in polishing silverware in a cutlery factory. The lives of nineteenth-century steelworkers is similarly brought to life through a modern preteen's eyes in *Meet Me by the Steelmen,* while in *Scavenger Boy* Michael learns that while cotton is soft, life in a cotton mill was nothing of the sort.

Steven Engelfried, writing in *School Library Journal,* described *Riding the Waves* as a "strong novel about the surprising relationship that evolves between a boy and an elderly woman." Set in a small English coastal town, the novel deals with the dreams of Matt, who desperately wants to be part of a group of surfers. Such membership is elusive until Matt is forced to visit an old family friend, Florrie, for a class project. A bond slowly forms between the two when Matt, an adoptee, learns that Florrie was long ago forced to give up her out-of-wedlock child. When Matt accompanies Florrie to the beach one day, their relationship is cemented: expecting to be embarrassed by the old woman, Matt is instead introduced through her to the surfers, who have a soft spot in their hearts for Florrie from the days when she ran a local restaurant. Deborah Abbott noted in *Booklist* that Tomlinson's "startlingly refreshing story about an intergenerational friendship" is "well-paced" and has "an upbeat and satisfying ending." Applauding the book for its well-crafted characters, Sheila Allen observed in *School Library Journal:* "There are so many aspects to this book to absorb and encourage the reader. . . . Surfing, history, adoption, care of and respect for the elderly, are all woven into this very readable tale."

Tomlinson's own struggle with breast cancer inspired her novel *Dancing through the Shadows.* "When faced with a long period of treatment," the author once commented, "I felt that it would be beneficial to try to keep writing, so I decided to use what was happening to me as the theme for a novel. I wrote as though I was the young daughter of a woman going through the experience. Once I'd decided to do this, I found that I felt much better. When I went to the hospital, suddenly I was a researcher, rather than a patient. It was very therapeutic. The story is quite upbeat and also suggests ways of giving help."

In the novel, Ellen's mother has breast cancer, and Ellen, along with the rest of the family, is trying to be supportive. Soon Ellen begins to find some solace at an abandoned spring that her teacher discovers near the school, one that was probably once sacred and had healing powers. Restoring the natural spring to a semblance of its former pristine condition parallels the chemotherapy Ellen's mother is receiving, until both are finally restored to health. "Gracefully avoiding didacticism, Tomlinson makes regular reference to the many sources of healing," noted a writer reviewing *Dancing through the Shadows* for *Kirkus Reviews.* "Readers will be borne along by the lively pace and the first-person, dialogue-heavy style." A contributor to *Publishers Weekly* noted the themes of "courage, survival and rebirth" and concluded: "Tomlinson addresses painful truths about the progression of cancer and at the same time celebrates the resiliency of body and spirit."

The author's personal experience has also inspired a trilogy focusing on Marian of Sherwood Forest. "As a child I loved Robin Hood stories," Tomlinson recalled, "but felt a little frustrated that Marian, the only woman that a girl could identify with, was usually locked up in a castle and needing to be rescued. I wanted to imagine Marian rushing through the forest like the men, having adventures and doing the rescuing herself." To satisfy this need for an exciting story, Tomlinson penned a series of three novels comprising the "Forestwife" trilogy: *The Forestwife, Child of the May,* and *The Path of the She-Wolf.* In *The Forestwife* Mary de Holt runs away

from an arranged marriage at age fifteen and flees into a nearby forest. Accompanied by her nurse, Agnes, she tries to find the local wise woman, the Forestwife, whom some believe is a witch. Discovering that the woman has died, Agnes takes on the role of forestwife, renaming her young charge Marian, and training the young woman as her assistant. The duo's adventures involve people on the run and a group of defrocked, renegade nuns. Romance enters Marian's life from an unlikely source: Agnes's offputting son, Robert, a local outlaw whom Marian grows to love as he becomes Robin Hood. Wen Agnes dies, however, Marian must forgo her plan to marry Robin due to her obligation to become the new forestwife. She enlist the many women of the forest to join together and aid in her fight against injustice. Reviewing *The Forestwife* in the *Bulletin of the Center for Children's Books,* Deborah Stevenson called it "an atmospheric read about a durable heroine," while *Booklist* reviewer Cooper deemed the novel a "rich, vibrant tale with an afterword that describes how various legends are braided into the story."

The second book in the "Forestwife" trilogy, *Child of the May* focuses on Magda, the daughter of John and an apprentice to Marian, now the forestwife. By the age of fifteen, Magda has grown bored with the drudgery and safety of Barnsdale forest and longs for adventures with her father and the rest of the band of outlaws. She gets her wish, and more, when she aids her father and Robin Hood in the rescue of Isabel and her mother, Lady Matilda, from the clutches of the sheriff of Nottingham. "Tomlinson does a fine job of juxtaposing the story's many exciting moments with history," noted Cooper, who also found Magda to be "strong and prickly, and tender when necessary." Anne Deifendeifer St. John, writing in *Horn Book,* also had praise for this installment in the trilogy, noting that, "although the plot is well constructed, the novel's strength is in its fully realized setting and cast of strong-willed characters." A contributor for *Kirkus Reviews* felt that "Tomlinson's language creates a powerful mood; readers will hope for more news of Magda, with her courage, strength, and skills."

Further news of Magda comes in the final novel in the "Forestwife" trilogy. In *The Path of the She-Wolf,* set in the time of the Magna Carta, it appears that King John may be about ready to repeal the hated Forest Laws. When the king reneges on his promise to implement the Magna Carta, however, Marian, Magda, and Robin Hood must band together for one last battle that ends in tragedy but preserves Marian's legacy for future generations. The three volumes of the series were combined into a single volume, *The Forestwife Trilogy,* and published in 2003.

Pulling up her literary stakes, Tomlinson moves her focus from Briton to ancient Troy in her book *The Moon Riders.* Dedicating her life to the service of Maa, goddess of the moon, thirteen-year-old Myrina joins a nomadic tribe of amazons, known as the Moon Riders.

Expert horsewomen, the Moon Riders range through Asia Minor and, under the leadership of Penthesilea, enter history through their involvement in the Trojan war. Tomlinson continues Myrina's story in *Voyage of the Snake Lady,* which references Myrina's chosen totem, the serpent, which is tattooed on her arms. Sometimes captured and enslaved, and living precariously off the land, Myrina endures storms, shipwreck, and other challenges in her effort to survive and reunite the Moon Riders following the fall of Troy.

Praising *The Moon Riders* in a London *Guardian* review, Adéle Geras noted that "Tomlinson has done her research," and praised her ability to "transport" readers into Myrina's world. Noting the author's skill in bringing to life "the texture of daily life" in the ancient world, Geras added of the novel: "there are terrible deaths, accounts of almost superhuman courage and hope of new birth at the end of the story." Andrea Deakin, writing in Okanagan College's *Deakin Newsletter Online,* noted that, "totally convincing, fast-moving, and often very moving," *Voyage of the Snake Lady* serves Tomlinson's first "Moon Riders" novel as "a very satisfying sequel."

Biographical and Critical Sources

BOOKS

Children's Literature Review, Volume 60, Thomson Gale (Detroit, MI), 1999.

PERIODICALS

Booklist, March 1, 1991, Ilene Cooper, review of *Summer Witches,* p. 1389; May 1, 1993, Deborah Abbott, review of *Riding the Waves,* p. 1593; March 1, 1995, Ilene Cooper, review of *The Forestwife,* p. 1241; November 1, 1997, Michael Cart, review of *Dancing through the Shadows,* p. 463; October 15, 1998, Ilene Cooper, review of *Child of the May,* p. 413; November 15, 1998, Hazel Rochman, review of *Little Stowaway,* p. 600; April 1, 2000, Ilene Cooper, review of *The Forestwife,* p. 1479.

Books for Keeps, May, 1992, David Bennett, review of *The Flither Pickers,* p. 20; July, 1993, David Bennett, "David Bennett on the Novels of Theresa Tomlinson," p. 32; May, 1996, George Hunt, review of *The Herring Girls,* p. 13.

Bulletin of the Center for Children's Books, March, 1995, Deborah Stevenson, review of *The Forestwife,* p. 252.

Growing Point, January, 1989, Margery Fisher, review of *The Water Cat,* p. 5087; January, 1992, Margery Fisher, review of *The Rope Carrier,* p. 5641.

Guardian (London, England), February 8, 2003, Adéle Geras, review of *The Moon Riders.*

Horn Book, May-June, 1991, Martha V. Parravano, review of *Summer Witches,* p. 332; November-December, 1998, Anne Deifendeifer St. John, review of *Child of the May,* p. 742; November, 1998, Anne Deifendeifer St. John, review of *Child of the May,* p. 742.

Junior Bookshelf, August, 1989, review of *Summer Witches,* p. 181; December, 1990, Marcus Crouch, review of *The Flither Pickers,* p. 302; June, 1991, A.R. Williams, review of *Riding the Waves,* p. 123; December, 1991, Marcus Crouch, review of *The Rope Carrier,* p. 269; June, 1995, Marcus Crouch, review of *The Cellar Lad,* p. 110; June, 1996, S.M. Ashburner, review of *The Herring Girls,* p. 126.

Kirkus Reviews, April 15, 1991, review of *Summer Witches,* p. 540; May 1, 1993, review of *Riding the Waves,* p. 605; September 15, 1997, review of *Dancing through the Shadows,* p. 1464; October 1, 1998, review of *Child of the May,* p. 1465.

Magpies, May, 1989, review of *The Water Cat,* p. 28; March, 1998, review of *Little Stowaway,* p. 31; May, 2003, review of *The Moon Riders,* p. 42.

Publishers Weekly, May 10, 1993, review of *Riding the Waves,* p. 72; February 13, 1995, review of *The Forestwife,* p. 79; November 3, 1997, review of *Dancing through the Shadows,* p. 86; October 26, 1998, review of *Child of the May,* p. 68.

School Librarian, August, 1995, Linda Saunders, review of *The Cellar Lad,* p. 119; spring, 1998, Cliff Moon, review of *Little Stowaway,* p. 37; autumn, 1998, Kay Ecclestone, review of *Child of the May,* p. 159; autumn, 2000, review of *The Path of the She-Wolf,* p. 159; autumn, 2001, review of *Beneath Burning Mountain,* p. 161; spring, 2002, review of *The Voyage of the Silver Bream,* p. 34; autumn, 2004, Sarah McNicol, review of *Voyage of the Snake Lady,* p. 163.

School Library Journal, February, 1991, Sheila Allen, review of *Riding the Waves,* p. 33; May, 1991, Virginia Golodetz, review of *Summer Witches,* p. 95; February, 1992, Geoff Dubber, review of *The Rope Carrier,* p. 33; May, 1993, Steven Engelfried, review of *Riding the Waves,* p. 110; March, 1995, Susan L. Rogers, review of *The Forestwife,* p. 225; November, 1997, Rosalyn Pierini, review of *Dancing through the Shadows,* p. 124; November, 1998, Cheri Estes, review of *Child of the May,* p. 131; November 1, 1998, Cheri Estes, review of *Child of the May,* p. 131.

Times Educational Supplement, December 7, 1990, Sandra Kemp, review of *The Flither Pickers,* p. 30; August 11, 1995, David Buckley, review of *The Cellar Lad,* p. 17.

Times Literary Supplement, February, 1988, Deborah Singmaster, review of *The Water Cat,* p. 120.

Voice of Youth Advocates, June, 1995, Mary L. Adams, review of *The Forestwife,* p. 100; Nancy Thackaberry, February, 1998, review of *Dancing through the Shadows,* p. 391; October, 1998, review of *Child of the May,* p. 290; April, 1999, review of *Child of the May,* p. 16.

ONLINE

Okanagan College Deakin Newsletter Online, http://www.okanagan.bc.ca/ (March, 2005), Andrea Deakin, review of *Voyage of the Snake Lady.*

Theresa Tomlinson Web site, http://www.theresatomlinson.com (November 21, 2005).*

V

van GENECHTEN, Guido 1957-

Personal

Born August 19, 1957, in Mol, Belgium. *Education:* Attended Academy of Graphic Arts (Mol, Belgium).

Addresses

Home—Belgium. *Agent*—c/o Author Mail, Clavis Uitgeverij BVBA, Vooruitzichtstraat 42, 3500 Hasselt, Belgium. *E-mail*—fa312962@skynet.be.

Career

Author and illustrator.

Writings

SELF-ILLUSTRATED

Kom maar binnen, Clavis (Hasselt, Belgium), 1999.
Mijn papa, Clavis (Hasselt, Belgium), 1999.
Het grote billen-boek, Clavis (Hasselt, Belgium), 2000.
Blackie, Clavis (Hasselt, Belgium), 2001.
Het grote slap-boek, Clavis (Hasselt, Belgium), 2001.
Ono eet, Clavis (Hasselt, Belgium), 2001.
Ono kleedt zich aan, Clavis (Hasselt, Belgium), 2001.
Ono speelt, Clavis (Hasselt, Belgium), 2001.
Rikki, Clavis (Hasselt, Belgium), 2001.
Rikki durft, Clavis (Hasselt, Belgium), 2001.
Flop-Ear, Barron's Educational Series (Hauppauge, NY), 2001.
Potty Time, Simon & Schuster (New York, NY), 2001.
Bij opa en oma, Clavis (Hasselt, Belgium), 2002.
Hoe Tito zinj neus kwijtspeeide, Clavis (Hasselt, Belgium), 2002.
Piep, zei Bruno, Clavis (Hasselt, Belgium), 2002.
Rikki en Anni, Clavis (Hasselt, Belgium), 2002.
Rikki: knuffel en mini-boekje, Clavis (Hasselt, Belgium), 2002.

Het grote knuffel-boek, Clavis (Hasselt, Belgium), 2003, translated as *The Cuddle Book,* HarperCollins (New York, NY), 2005.
Omdat ik zoveel van je hou, Clavis (Hasselt, Belgium), 2003, translated as *Because I Love You So Much,* Tiger Tales (Wilton, CT), 2004.
Rikki durft, Clavis (Hasselt, Belgium), 2003.
Rikki en zijn vriendjes, Clavis (Hasselt, Belgium), 2003.
Het geheim van IJsje, Clavis (Hasselt, Belgium), 2004, translated as *Snowy's Special Secret,* Tiger Tales (Wilton, CT), 2005.
Het grote billen-boek, Clavis (Hasselt, Belgium), 2004.
Jonnie, Clavis (Hasselt, Belgium), 2004.
Klein wit visje, Clavis (Hasselt, Belgium), 2004.
Klein wit visje is zo blij, Clavis (Hasselt, Belgium), 2004.
Klein wit visje telt tot elf, Clavis (Hasselt, Belgium), 2004.
Nieuwe laarzen, Clavis (Hasselt, Belgium), 2004.
Rikki wile en kerstboom, Clavis (Hasselt, Belgium), 2004.
Familie Vanderknor, Clavis (Hasselt, Belgium), 2004, translated as *The Von Hamm Family: Alex and the Tart,* Tiger Tales (Wilton, CT), 2005.
Klein wit visje wordt groot, Clavis (Hasselt, Belgium), 2005.
Kleine Kangoeroe, Clavis (Hasselt, Belgium), 2005, translated as *Kangaroo Christine,* Tiger Tales (Wilton, CT), 2006.
Lieve mama, Clavis (Hasselt, Belgium), 2005.
Tito tovenaar, Clavis (Hasselt, Belgium), 2005.

OTHER

Kermis, het spiegelpaleis van het volk: tentoonstelling, Centrum voor Kunst en Cultuur, St.-Pietersabjij, Gent, 28 februari-13 april 1986 (catalog), Kritak (Louvain, Belgium), 1986.

Sidelights

Popular with young children in his native Belgium, author and illustrator Guido van Genechten engages toddlers with his many book series featuring boldly drawn characters that range from smiling children to wide-eyed zebras to cuddly, flop-eared rabbits. In van

A popular and prolific children's author and illustrator in his native Belgium, van Genechten has won new fans with English translations of picture books like this 2003 work.

Genechten's books, animals often take the place of human children, with humorous results; in *Potty Time,* for example, a lanky young giraffe, a roly-poly polar bear, and a young boy each take turns testing out a bright red potty chair. Turning the pages of *The Cuddle Book*

young children discover that animals and humans are also very different, and that animals express feeling in a variety of ways. While pigs rub noses to show affection, monkeys hug gently and turtles slowly, elephants hug with their trunks, and cats grapple playfully. Van Genechten "embraces just the right amount of sentiment" in his text and illustrations, noted a *Kirkus Reviews* critic, while Ilene Cooper wrote in *Booklist* that *The Cuddle Book* is a good story-hour choice, as well as excellent for sharing "one on one, where after the reading, cuddling can ensue."

Biographical and Critical Sources

PERIODICALS

Booklist, October 1, 2001, Kathy Broderick, review of *Potty Time,* p. 315; December 1, 2004, Ilene Cooper, review of *The Cuddle Book,* p. 663.
Bulletin of the Center for Children's Books, January, 2005, Deborah Stevenson, review of *The Cuddle Book,* p. 231.
Kirkus Reviews, November 15, 2004, review of *The Cuddle Book,* p. 1094.
Publishers Weekly, November 26, 2001, review of *Shhh!,* p. 63.
School Library Journal, June, 2001, Jane Marino, review of *Flop-Ear,* p. 131; December, 2001, JoAnn Jonas, review of *Potty Time,* p. 114.

ONLINE

Clavis Publishers Web site, http://www.clavis.be/ (October 7, 2005), "Guido van Genechten."
Guido van Genechten Home Page, http://www.guidovan-genechten.be (October 7, 2005).*

W

WALKER, Diane Marie Catherine
  See WALKER, Kate

*   *   *

WALKER, Kate 1950-
  (Diane Marie Catherine Walker)

Personal

Born January 10, 1950, in Newcastle, New South Wales, Australia; daughter of William Walter (a salesperson) and Eileen Maisie (a homemaker; maiden name, Appleyard) Sruhan; married Roger Edwin Walker (a mechanic), January 24, 1975 (divorced August 8, 1980); children: Josie. *Politics:* "Independent." *Hobbies and other interests:* Reading, gardening, film, Tai Chi.

Addresses

Agent—c/o Author Mail, Allen & Unwin, 9 Atchinson St., Sidney, New South Wales 2065, Australia. *E-mail*—kw_writer@hunterlink.net.au.

Career

Writer and house sitter. Writing teacher at workshops for primary and high-school teachers, beginning 1987. Has worked variously as a waitress, cook, restaurant manager, clerk, cleaner, and offset printer.

Awards, Honors

Highly Commended designation, Picture Book Section, Australian Children's Book of the Year, 1981, for *Marty Moves to the Country;* Australian Children's Book of the Year Honour Book designation, Junior section, 1990, for *The Dragon of Mith;* Mary Grant Bruce award, 1991, for "Running away to Sea"; highly commended designation, Australian Human Rights Award, New South Wales Premier's Literary Award shortlist, South Australian Literary Award, and Australian Children's

Book of the Year Honour designation, Young-Adult section, all 1991, Talking Book of the Year Award, 1992, and American Library Association Notable Book, Best Book for Young Adults, and Best Book for Reluctant Young-Adult Readers designations, all 2003, all for *Peter;* grants from Literature Board of the Australia Council; several awards for short fiction.

Writings

FOR CHILDREN

Marty Moves to the Country (picture book), illustrated by Bruce Treloar, Methuen Australia (North Ryde, New South Wales, Australia), 1980.

The Alien Challenger (beginning reader), illustrated by Peter Lewis, Methuen Australia (North Ryde, New South Wales, Australia), 1983.

Suzie and the Pencil-Case Genie (beginning reader), illustrated by Trish Hill, Ashton/Bookshelf, 1988.

The Letters of Rosie O'Brien: A Convict in the Colony of New South Wales, 1804 (beginning reader), illustrated by Paul Borg, Ashton/Bookshelf, 1988.

Tales from the Good Land (beginning reader), illustrated by Gillian Campbell, Ashton/Bookshelf, 1988.

Burying Aunt Renie, (beginning reader), illustrated by Margie Chellew, Nelson, 1989.

The Dragon of Mith (beginning reader), illustrated by Laurie Sharpe, Allen & Unwin (Crows Nest, New South Wales, Australia), 1989.

The Frog Who Would Be King (picture book), illustrated by David Cox, Ashton/Bookshelf, 1989.

King Joe of Bogpeat Castle (picture book), illustrated by Margie Chellew, Ashton/Bookshelf, 1989.

The First Easter Rabbit (picture book), illustrated by Marina McAllan, Martin Educational, 1989.

Peter (young-adult novel), Ashton/Omnibus (Norwood, New South Wales, Australia), 1991, Houghton (Boston, MA), 1993.

Our Excursion (picture book), illustrated by David Cox, Ashton/Omnibus (Norwood, South Australia, Australia), 1994.

The Flying Pieman (picture book), Moondrake, 1994.

I Hate Books! (beginning reader), illustrated by David Cox, Omnibus Books (Norwood, New South Wales, Australia), 1995.

Changes, and Other Stories (young adult), Omnibus Books (Norwood, New South Wales, Australia), 1995.

A Pride of Noses (picture book), Houghton Mifflin (Boston, MA), 1996.

Elephant's Lunch (beginning reader), illustrated by Ann James, Omnibus Books (Norwood, New South Wales, Australia), 1998.

Sticky Stuff (beginning reader), illustrated by Craig Smith, Omnibus Books (Norwood, New South Wales, Australia), 2000.

Mitch 2 Sue (young-adult novel), Omnibus Books (Norwood, New South Wales, Australia), 2003.

Recycle, Reduce, Reuse, Rethink, Macmillan Education (South Yarra, Victoria, Australia), 2004.

"SPIES AND SPYING" SERIES; NONFICTION FOR CHILDREN

(With Elaine Argaet) *Super Spies of World War I,* Macmillan Education (South Yarra, Victoria, Australia), 2003.

(With Elaine Argaet) *Super Spies of World War II,* Macmillan Education (South Yarra, Victoria, Australia), 2003.

(With Elaine Argaet) *Spies in History,* Macmillan Education (South Yarra, Victoria, Australia), 2003.

(With Elaine Argaet) *Spies and Their Gadgets,* Macmillan Education (South Yarra, Victoria, Australia), 2003.

(With Elaine Argaet) *So You Want to Be a Spy,* Macmillan Education (South Yarra, Australia), 2003.

(With Elaine Argaet) *Famous Spy Cases,* Macmillan Education (South Yarra, Victoria, Australia), 2003.

OTHER

Writing Games, Kate Walker Ink, 1991.

Step by Step Stories, Kate Walker Ink, 1991.

Story Writing the Low Stress Way: A Manual for Primary and High School Teachers, Kate Walker Ink, 1992.

Creativity and Story Writing, Kate Walker Ink, 1993.

Story Writing: Teaching and Tapping Your Subconscious Mind, (manual; for adults), Kate Walker Ink, 1993.

Writing Enrichment, Kate Walker Ink, 1994.

Journal Writing, Kate Walker Ink, 1994.

Bridging the Realms, Walker Publishing (Fish Creek, Victoria, Australia), 2004.

Contributor to numerous anthologies and magazines.

Sidelights

Australian writer Kate Walker held a number of odd jobs before becoming a professional writer, and her varied experiences and imagination had contributed greatly to her stories for children. Among Walker's many books for children are picture books such as *The Frog Who Would Be King* and *A Pride of Noses,* and young-adult novels *Peter* and *Mitch 2 Sue.* For beginning readers,

When a fifteen year old finds his attention shifting from dirt-biking to a gay friend of his older brother, he begins to deal with questions regarding his sexuality in Australian writer Walker's sensitive coming-of-age novel. (Cover photographs by Masakatsu Yamazaki and Shinichiro Okajama/Photonica.)

she has also contributed a list of entertaining stories, such as *Burying Aunt Renie, I Hate Books,* and *Sticky Stuff. Sticky Stuff,* which recounts the efforts of young Sophie to unstick herself from the sidewalk after stepping in yellow chewing gum, was praised by *Resource Links* critic Evette Berry as "very engaging and imaginative." In addition to children's fiction, Walker has collaborated with fellow writer Elaine Argaet on the "Spies and Spying" series of nonfiction titles.

Walker once told *SATA:* "I began writing after a campervan tour of Australia with my husband and daughter, during which I started making up bedtime stories for her. When I came home, I began writing them down and realized I loved it! That was it, I wanted to be a writer.

"I have breakfast, walk the dog, do some Tai Chi, read, and *then* finally start writing and work from nine in the morning till four in the afternoon. I write my stories in longhand first and will do another three or four drafts in longhand, literally cut-and-pasting the story with a pair of scissors and a roll of sticky tape.

"After four drafts, it's a great mess of paper, written in various colored pens with lots of scratchings-out, and it is almost unreadable. At this point I key it into the computer, get a printout, and start over again—rewriting passages, sticking in new bits, cutting out old ones, until I've turned a neat manuscript into another multi-colored mess. I go back to the computer and key in the changes, run off a clean printout, and begin all over again with my scissors, sticky tape, and colored pens. Some stories write themselves in six drafts. Others I chase and change and do battle with over a hundred drafts or more. And I always work on three stories at once so I can skip from one to the other.

"My main interest is people. The crazy things they do, their foolishness, their vulnerability, their great strength and courage, their determination to discover who and what they are. When I teach writing, I feel that's what I'm doing also, showing people a means by which they can take a small part of themselves and project it out and get a glimpse of themselves, maybe even of their spirit."

Biographical and Critical Sources

PERIODICALS

Booklist, October 15, 1988, p. 424; April 15, 1993, p. 1505; March 15, 1994, pp. 1355, 1359, 1361; June 1, 1999, review of *Peter,* p. 1811; March 1, 2004, Hazel Rochman, review of *Famous Spy Cases,* p. 1187.
Horn Book, July, 1993, p. 467; September, 1993, p. 571.
Junior Bookshelf, October, 1982, p. 180.
Magpies, July, 1995, review of *I Hate Books!,* p. 23; September, 1995, review of *Changes, and Other Stories,* p. 35; November, 1998, review of *Elephant's Lunch,* p. 32; July, 2000, review of *Sticky Stuff,* p. 37; November, 2003, review of *Mitch 2 Sue,* p. 45.
Resource Links, February, 2004, Evette Berry, review of *Sticky Stuff,* p. 6.
School Library Journal, March, 1987, p. 168; September, 1987, p. 133; June, 1993, p. 132.
Times Literary Supplement, July 23, 1982, p. 792.
Voice of Youth Advocates, June, 1993, p. 96.

ONLINE

Kate Walker Home Page, http://www.katewalker.com.au (November 20, 2005).

*   *   *

WEST, Owen
See KOONTZ, Dean R.

*   *   *

WHITE, Ruth C. 1942-
(Ruth White Miller)

Personal

Born March 15, 1942, in Whitewood, VA; daughter of John Edward (a coal miner) and Olive (a hospital food server; maiden name, Compton) White; divorced; children: Dee Olivia. *Education:* Montreat-Anderson College, A.A., 1962; Pfeiffer College, A.B., 1966; Queens College (Charlotte, NC), library media specialist certification, 1976. *Politics:* "Independent." *Hobbies and other interests:* Yoga, exercising, walking with her golden retriever.

Addresses

Home—Virginia Beach, VA. *Agent*—c/o Author Mail, Farrar, Straus & Giroux, 19 Union Square W., New York, NY 10001.

Career

Mt. Pleasant Middle School, Mt. Pleasant, NC, English teacher, 1966-76; Boys Town, Pineville, NC, house mother, 1976-77; Harleyville-Ridgeville High School, Dorchester, SC, librarian, 1977-81; Dougherty Junior High School, Albany, GA, librarian, 1981-85; Association for Research and Enlightenment Foundation, Virginia Beach, VA, librarian, 1986-97.

Awards, Honors

Best Children's Book by a North Carolinian designation, North Carolina chapter of the American Association of University Women, 1977, and Georgia Children's Book Award nomination, both for *The City Rose;* Newbery Honor Book designation, 1997, for *Belle Prater's Boy;* Notable Book designation, American Library Association (ALA), for *Sweet Creek Holler;* ALA Best Book for Young Adults designation, New York Public Library 100 Titles for Reading and Sharing selection, both for *Weeping Willow;* ALA Best Book for Young Adults, 2000, for *Memories of Summer.*

Writings

(Under name Ruth White Miller) *The City Rose,* McGraw (New York, NY), 1977.
Sweet Creek Holler, Farrar, Straus (New York, NY), 1988.
Weeping Willow, Farrar, Straus (New York, NY), 1992.
Belle Prater's Boy, Farrar, Straus (New York, NY), 1996.
Memories of Summer, Farrar, Straus (New York, NY), 2000.
Tadpole, Farrar, Straus (New York, NY), 2003.
Buttermilk Hill, Farrar, Straus (New York, NY), 2004.
The Search for Belle Prater, Farrar, Straus (New York, NY), 2005.

Contributor to *Venture Inward.*

White's works have been translated into German, Dutch, Chinese, Indonesian, French, Polish, Africaans, and Japanese.

After his mother disappears, gawky Woodrow comes to live with his grandparents in a coal-mining Virginia town, and finds a new friend in popular next-door-neighbor Gypsy. (Cover illustration by John Kachik.)

Adaptations

Many of White's books have been adapted as audiobooks.

Sidelights

Ruth C. White is the author of several award-winning novels for middle-grade and young-adult readers, and her works include *Sweet Creek Holler, Weeping Willow, Belle Prater's Boy* and its sequel, *The Search for Belle Prater,* and *Tadpole*. Prater's stories are set in the South, in particular in the coal-mining region of western Virginia where the author grew up. Commentators have praised White for her characterizations, depiction of locale, and sensitive treatment of such difficult experiences as the death of a parent, divorce, abandonment, and rape. In 1997 White's much-acclaimed novel *Belle Prater's Boy* was named a Newbery Honor Book.

In her works, White focuses primarily on teenage girls, and the action in many of her novels takes place in the 1950s, when she herself was a girl. "I work with and write for adolescent girls because that was the time in my life when I was most confused and unhappy," she

once explained. "I can relate to these girls now because I remember the pain of trying to grow up, trying to find my identity, and trying to be an individual in a conformist's world. Adolescents today have basically the same problems, only more of them. It is a very hard time in which to grow up."

Growing up in a poor western Virginian family during the 1950s provided White with both incentive and fodder for her later writing career. "Born in the poverty-stricken coal mining region of Virginia, I was the fourth daughter of a coal miner who died when I was six," she once told *SATA*. Although her family had no television, it was probably for the best: they read aloud and performed music together. In this setting, White developed her imagination and "managed to get the most out of the public school system and go on to a better life," building a career as a school teacher and librarian, and also gaining respect as a writer.

Although White published her first novel, *The City Rose,* in 1977, it was over a decade before her second book appeared. In *Sweet Creek Holler* six-year-old Ginny and older sister June must deal with the rumors that swirl around them when they move to a new town. The girls are actually the object of these rumors because their father was shot to death, leaving them and their beautiful mother to fend for themselves. During the six years they live in the small mining town of Sweet Creek Holler, the sisters witness the tragic effect gossip can have on sensitive souls. *Voice of Youth Advocates* Joanne Johnson praised White's "carefully drawn characters" and "well-thought out and presented" relationship between Ginny and a young friend. In *Horn Book,* critic Nancy Vasilakis judged the novel to be "stronger in its delineation of character and in its evocation of time and place than in its narrative development," yet she praised White's obvious "affection for the indigent folk of its Appalachian locale."

In *Weeping Willow,* set in 1956, White tells the story of fourteen-year-old Tiny, who is the eldest child in her family. As she grows into adulthood, Tiny must deal with her stepfather's unwanted sexual advances, as well as the typical challenges of high-school life. Writing in *Voice of Youth Advocates,* Myrna Feldman praised the novel's characters, setting, and details, deeming *Weeping Willow* an "exceptionally fine book" that is "honestly written and difficult to put down." "While the sweep of the novel is admirable," *New York Times Book Review* critic Linda Lee commented, the critic took issue with White's novel's message: that "incest is a bad thing, but it can be lived with." While praising the story's detailed setting and "strong" voice, Alice Casey Smith contended in a *School Library Journal* review that *Weeping Willow* "has too, too many threads that don't weave together." Betsy Hearne viewed the novel more favorably, however, writing in the *Bulletin of the Center for Children's Books* that White's second novel contains "vividly rendered" characters and a "plot following variably but believably from their [the characters'] patterns of action."

In *Belle Prater's Boy,* which takes place in the fall of 1953, White explores the nature of friendship, loss, and love. Despite its title, the novel revolves around twelve-year-old Gypsy, who is known in Coal Station, Virginia, for her beautiful long hair and for having a father who died tragically seven years earlier. When her cousin Woodrow Prater moves in next door following the mysterious disappearance of his mother, Belle, he and Gypsy develop a close friendship that, according to a *Publishers Weekly* reviewer, allows both of them to "face tragedy and transcend it—and the ability to pass along that gift to the reader."

Reviewers praised *Belle Prater's Boy* highly. Writing in *Kliatt,* Jana Whitesel deemed White's novel a "rare" book that "transcends age with its timeless story." In the *New York Times Book Review,* Meg Wolitzer declared that "it takes a writer of real lyricism and energy to tell a good young-adult story, and Ruth White is one." Several critics cited the author for her well-drawn

When two sisters and their father move from Appalachia north to the booming economy and better life to be found in Michigan, older sister Summer slowly descends into madness in White's sensitive young-adult novel. (Cover illustration by Julie Monks.)

In this sequel to White's acclaimed Bell Prater's Boy, *Woodrow and Gypsy join a psychic friend on a search for Woodrow's missing mother after a mysterious phone call on his birthday signals someone's intent to contact him. (Cover illustration by Allen Garns.)*

characterizations and vivid depiction of locale, Wolitzer remarking: "The author's vivid and accurate eye has helped her fashion an ideal backdrop for the story and its element of suspense." "White's characters are strong . . . and her storytelling is rich in detail and emotion," asserted Maeve Visser Knoth in a *Horn Book* review, while *Booklist* reviewer Stephanie Zvirin praised the book's "humor and insight," "solid picture of small-town life," "unpretentious, moving story," and "strongly depicted characters." *Belle Prater's Boy* "balances disturbing emotional issues with the writer's light touch," summed up a critic in *Voice of Youth Advocates.*

The curiosity of many readers was sparked by the central mystery of *Belle Prater's Boy:* namely, what happened to Woodrow's Prater's mom? White serves up an answer in *The Search for Belle Prater,* which was published over nine years after the first book. In what a *Kirkus Reviews* contributor praised as an "elegantly conceived sequel" containing "tiny glints of magic," thirteen-year-old Gypsy narrates the adventures of the two seventh graders who, joined by friend Cassie Daul-

When Piper Berry's parents break up and her father moves out, she feels lost until she finds a way to deal with her feelings by writing poetry in this 2004 novel. (Cover illustration by Nancy Carpenter.)

Summer, gradually declines mentally, becoming a stranger with schizophrenia; meanwhile, the young teen must also deal with a new culture as the family moves north to Flint, Michigan where her widowed father finds work in an automobile plant. Praising White's novel as "affecting," *Kliatt* contributor Paula Rohrlick noted that the story is based on White's experiences with her own sister, and added that in *Memories of Summer* the author includes "gentle humor . . . as well as pathos, and the tale is simply but movingly told."

1955 is the year thirteen-year-old music-loving Tadpole shows up at the Kentucky home of ten-year-old cousin Carolina Collins, guitar in hand and fleeing from an abusive uncle. Carolina's mother, Serilda, is usually docile, but she fights to protect the troubled young boy in White's novel *Tadpole,* which a *Publishers Weekly* reviewer praised for its "homespun language" and "evocation of ordinary people as they stumble into enduring truths about human strength and vulnerability." Another ten year old is the focus of *Buttermilk Hill,* which finds wise and self-reliant Piper Berry weathering her parents' divorce by focusing on her own dreams and gaining insights and strength from both her friends and her poetry. Praising White's "down-home, approachable style," *Horn Book* contributor Christine M. Heppermann noted that *Tadpole* is full of "appealing characters" and "eloquently crafted images of . . . life in the Kentucky hills." A *Kirkus Reviews* critic also had praise for *Buttermilk Hill,* dubbing it a "poignant, compassionate exploration of the hopes and dreams that burn in the hearts of a small-town community in 1970s America," while in *Booklist* Ilene Cooper praised White for maintaining "a good balance of happiness and hard knocks."

Biographical and Critical Sources

PERIODICALS

ALAN Review, winter, 1995, Pam B. Cole, review with White.

Booklist, June 1, 1993, p. 1865; April 15, 1996, Stephanie Zvirin, review of *Belle Prater's Boy,* p. 1434; May 1, 2003, Gillian Engberg, review of *Tadpole,* p. 1598; August, 2004, Ilene Cooper, review of *Buttermilk Hill,* p. 1937; February 15, 2005, Cindy Dobrez, review of *The Search for Belle Prater,* p. 1079.

Bulletin of the Center for Children's Books, June, 1992, Betsy Hearne, review of *Weeping Willow,* p. 284; April, 2003, review of *Tadpole,* p. 336.

English Journal, November, 1993, p. 79.

Horn Book, November-December, 1988, Nancy Vasilakis, review of *Sweet Creek Holler,* p. 785; September-October, 1996, Maeve Visser Knoth, review of *Belle Prater's Boy,* p. 601; May, 2001, Kristi Beavin, review of *Memories of Summer,* p. 362; May-June, 2003, Christine M. Hepperman, review of *Tadpole,* p. 358; September-October, 2004, Betty Carter, review of *Buttermilk Hill,* p. 600; May-June, 2005, Betty Carter, review of *The Search for Belle Prater,* p. 334.

borne, who claims to have second sight, as well as by a teen runaway named Joseph, attempt to track down Woodrow's missing mother. After receiving a mysterious phone call on the exact hour of his birth, Woodrow decides that his mother wishes to reestablish contact. Traveling to West Virginia, the group encounters racial prejudice, reunites Joseph with his family, and ultimately brings an answer to the question posed by the novel's title.

Calling *The Search for Belle Prater* a "worthy sequel" to the award-winning *Belle Prater's Boy,* Marie Orlando added in *School Library Journal* that White's sequel shares "the warmth, love, and humor" of the first book. Noting the deepening friendship between Woodrow and Gypsy, *Horn Book* contributor Cindy Dobrez added: "Characterization, dialogue, and setting are among White's many literary strengths, and she doesn't disappoint here."

Other novels by White have continued to focus on young characters coming to terms with their personal reality during the 1950s. In *Memories of Summer* thirteen-year-old Lyric witnesses as her older sister,

Kirkus Reviews, August 1, 2004, review of *Buttermilk Hill,* p. 750; April 1, 2005, review of *The Search for Belle Prater,* p. 428.

Kliatt, May, 1998, Jana Whitesel, review of *Belle Prater's Boy,* p. 42; July, 2002, Paula Rohrlick, review of *Memories of Summer,* p. 25; March, 2005, Janis Flint-Ferguson, review of *The Search for Belle Prater,* p. 16.

New York Times Book Review, November 13, 1988, p. 20; August 23, 1992, Linda Lee, review of *Weeping Willow,* p. 26; October 27, 1996, Meg Wolitzer, review of *Belle Prater's Boy,* p. 44.

Publishers Weekly, January 6, 1989, p. 52; November 4, 1996, p. 49; March 11, 1996, review of *Bell Prater's Boy,* pp. 65-66; February 9, 1998, p. 26; December 23, 2002, review of *Tadpole,* p. 71; November 8, 2004, review of *Buttermilk Hill,* p. 56.

School Library Journal, October, 1988, p. 165; July, 1992, Alice Casey Smith, review of *Weeping Willow,* p. 91; March, 2003, Connie Tyrrell Burns, review of *Tadpole,* p. 242; September, 2004, Miriam Lang Budin, review of *Buttermilk Hill,* p. 219; April, 2005, Marie Orlando, review of *The Search for Belle Prater,* p. 143.

Tribune Books (Chicago, IL), July 27, 2003, review of *Tadpole,* p. 5.

Voice of Youth Advocates, December, 1988, Joanne Johnson, review of *Sweet Creek Holler,* p. 244; October, 1992, Myrna Feldman, review of *Weeping Willow,* p. 234; June, 1997, review of *Belle Prater's Boy,* p. 87.*

*   *   *

WINCH, John 1944-

Personal

Born May 25, 1944, in Sydney, New South Wales, Australia; son of Jack and Jean (Cook) Winch; married August 26, 1967; wife's name Madeleine (an illustrator); children: Martina, Jessie. *Education:* Attended Sydney Teachers College; National Art School, diploma in design; Alexander Mackie C.A.E., graduate diploma. *Hobbies and other interests:* Classical music.

Addresses

Home—36 Merton St., Rozelle, New South Wales 2034, Australia. *Office*—P.O. Box 7, Stuart Town, 2820, New South Wales, Australia.

Career

Self-employed artist, illustrator, and writer since c. 1967. Kings School, Cambridgeshire, England, Art Master, 1968-70; guest lecturer, *S.S. Canberra. Exhibitions:* Numerous one-man shows; work exhibited at National Gallery of Australia; Bibliotheque Nationale, Paris, France; British Council, London, England; Art Gallery of New South Wales; and Guggenheim Museum, New York, NY.

Awards, Honors

International Board on Books for Young People Honour Book, Australia, for *The Old Woman Who Loved to Read;* Mary Gibbs fellow, University of Canberra, 2002; numerous prizes for painting in Australia.

Writings

SELF-ILLUSTRATED

One Sunday, Angus & Robertson (Sydney, New South Wales, Australia), 1988.

One Saturday, Walter McVitty Books (Sydney, New South Wales, Australia), 1989.

The Old Man Who Loved to Sing, Scholastic (Sydney, New South Wales, Australia), 1993.

The Old Woman Who Loved to Read, Holiday House (New York, NY), 1997.

Millennium Book of Myth and Story, Millennium (Alexandria, New South Wales, Australia), 1997.

Keeping up with Grandma, Holiday House (New York, NY), 2000.

The Folly, 2000.

The Boatman, 2000.

Two by Two, Holiday House (New York, NY), 2004.

Run, Hare, Run!: The Story of a Drawing, Little Hare Books (Surry Hills, New South Wales, Australia), 2005.

The Deluge, in press.

ILLUSTRATOR

Ian Hansen, *Leonardo Pigeon of Siena,* Margaret Hamilton (Sydney, New South Wales, Australia), 1998.

Ursula Duborasky, *The Game of the Goose,* Viking (Ringwood, Victoria, Australia), 2000.

Patricia Hooper, *Where Do You Sleep, Little One?,* Holiday House (New York, NY), 2001.

Marni McGee, *The Colt and the King,* Holiday House (New York, NY), 2002.

Laurie Lawlor, *Old Crump: The True Story of a Trip West,* Holiday House (New York, NY), 2002.

Eric Kimmel, *Brother Wolf, Sister Sparrow: Stories about Saints and Animals,* Holiday House (New York, NY), 2003.

Sidelights

Artist and writer John Winch creates picture books that celebrate the joys of the Australian "bush" where he lives. Both *The Old Man Who Loved to Sing* and *The Old Woman Who Loved to Read* feature main characters who, like the author/illustrator, moved to a rural area to enjoy the natural silence only to be found there. In *The Old Man Who Loved to Sing* an elderly man loves the sound of music—and of his own singing voice—so much that he moves to the country, where he can listen to both undisturbed by the noises of the city. At first his music disturbs the animals in his care, and they are later disturbed by its absence, when the old man becomes so elderly that he forgets to sing, whistle, or play his gramophone records while he performs his chores. The animals decide to remind the man of music by beating their tails, croaking, or trilling, thus making their own variety of noise. Their plan works, and the man bursts into song. "Winch's beautifully detailed paintings give this slight tale tremendous charm," observed Janice Del Negro in *Booklist*. Ellen Fader, writing in *Horn Book*, similarly observed that while Winch's

story "possesses a simple elegance," the illustrations "command the most attention." Executed in gouache and watercolor on paper made to look like it has been torn from an old book, the illustrations for *The Old Man Who Loved to Sing* are distinguished by unusual perspectives and animals with human expressions.

In *The Old Woman Who Loved to Read* the main character leaves the city behind and rents a farm in search of the peace and quiet she needs to be able to read all the books she owns. Living on a farm entails numerous

Combining an original text with his detailed oil paintings, Winch tells a very old and very familiar story about a man named Noah and a great flood in the 2004 picture book Two by Two.

chores, however, and every season brings its own emergency, from a newborn lamb that needs bottle feeding in the spring to bush fires in the summer to autumnal rains that bring a flood. The old woman never has enough time to read until the middle of winter, which finds her sitting before a fire with a book in her lap—falling asleep! Reviewers noted that Winch keeps his text to a minimum, as he did in *The Old Man Who Loved to Sing,* and lets the pictures extend the narrative thread. *Booklist* contributor Ellen Mandel remarked of *The Old Woman Who Loved to Read* that "it's a simple story line that finds rich and humorous embellishment in Winch's engagingly detailed watercolors." In his illustrations, which again feature animal portraits, Winch allows the realism of the basic story to expand to include some elements of fantasy without abandoning what a reviewer in *Publishers Weekly* called the book's "core of recognizable feelings." A *Kirkus Reviews* contributor concluded: "All of it—house and inhabitants—are cunningly, winsomely painted by Winch, who makes his story gently wry."

Keeping up with Grandma again features an elderly woman and an elderly man. Grandma is an adventurous sort, and although Grandpa, a painter, is not as enthusiastic, Grandma persuades him to go on journeys and try out adventure sports. Grandpa cannot keep up, however, and eventually the couple come home and return to their normal lives. Although Grandpa returns to his paints, the journeys have a surprising result: new material for his paintings. "The action-filled text and eye-catching art make this book a winner for group sharing," observed Carolyn Stacey in *School Library Journal.* Shelle Rosenfeld, reviewing *Keeping up with Grandma* for *Booklist,* noted that Winch's "wonderfully detailed, richly hued illustrations, with folk-art flavor, are filled with subtle wit."

Winch turns to the Bible for his self-illustrated *Two by Two.* Telling the story of Noah's ark from the perspective of the animals, Winch shows the animals trying to evade the rain and finding shelter on a large boat. While the animals may not have realized the un-named Noah working to getting ready for the flood, "all along, keen-eyed readers have observed the ark being built in the background of Winch's dramatic oil paintings," pointed out a *Publishers Weekly* contributor. *Booklist* critic Gillian Engberg also commented on *Two by Two,* praising its "simple, poetic sentences" and "lush, detailed paintings."

Beyond his self-illustrated titles, Winch has also provided illustrations for several picture books by other writers, including a story of animals finding places to sleep in Patricia Hooper's *Where Do You Sleep, Little One?,* a Palm Sunday tale in Marni McGee's *The Colt and the King,* an excursion through the Old West in Laurie Lawlor's *Old Crump: The Story of a Trip West,* and a collection of stories about the lives of saints in Eric Kimmel's *Brother Wolf, Sister Sparrow: Stories about Saints and Animals.* Of his illustrations for *Where*

Do You Sleep, Little One?, a *Publishers Weekly* contributor noted, "his brush strokes are so delicate that individual feathers can be discerned." *School Library Journal* reviewer Patricia Pearl Dole noted that the paintings in *The Colt and the King,* "inspired by Renaissance frescoes, delineate every hair, blade of grass, and wisp of straw in intricate detail." In a *Publishers Weekly* review of *Old Crump,* the critic commented, "The illustrations set the artist's characteristic folk-art-style against photographs of the Valley's lunar rocks and sands." Reviewing *Brother Wolf, Sister Sparrow* for *School Library Journal,* Harriett Fargnoli wrote that "Winch's dramatic, full-page paintings are filled with deep colors and images that highlight each saint's identity and significance."

Winch once told *SATA:* "I live in the 'bush' five hours west of Sydney in an old mining town of the gold rush era. Nothing has changed much, except the steam train is now a flash silver streak. With the help of the other four or five artists that have fled here from the city, we are trying to keep the town in the last century. Here most of my work is based on simple country life—the struggles with the seasons, drought, fire, floods, clinging onto old values.

"Apart from writing children's books, I am also an artist and my work encompasses printmaking, sculpture, painting, and ceramics. I have had exhibitions in Paris at the Bibliotheque National, and my work is in major museums throughout the world. I often feel I am spreading myself too thin over so many activities instead of concentrating on one media—but I'm having fun—which after all is more important that having a glowing reputation."

Biographical and Critical Sources

PERIODICALS

Booklist, April 15, 1996, Janice Del Negro, review of *The Old Man Who Loved to Sing,* p. 1447; March 1, 1997, Ellen Mandel, review of *The Old Woman Who Loved to Read,* p. 1175; November 15, 2000, Shelle Rosenfeld, review of *Keeping up with Grandma,* p. 651; September 1, 2001, Marta Segal, review of *Where Do You Sleep, Little One?,* p. 115; April 1, 2002, Kathy Broderick, review of *The Colt and the King,* p. 1334; October 1, 2004, Gillian Engberg, review of *Two by Two,* p. 346.

Children's Bookwatch, December, 2004, review of *Two by Two.*

Five Owls, January, 2001, review of *Keeping up with Grandma,* p. 67.

Horn Book, July-August, 1996, Ellen Fader, review of *The Old Man Who Loved to Sing,* p. 458; March-April, 2002, Mary M. Burns, review of *The Colt and the King,* p. 202.

Kirkus Reviews, February 15, 1997, review of *The Old Woman Who Loved to Read,* p. 308; March 1, 2002, review of *The Colt and the King,* p. 340; August 15, 2004, review of *Two by Two,* p. 814.

Magpies, July, 2000, review of *Keeping up with Grandma,* p. 44; May, 2005, review of *Run, Hare, Run!,* p. 29.

Publishers Weekly, February 10, 1997, review of *The Old Woman Who Loved to Read,* p. 84; August 27, 2001, review of *Where Do You Sleep, Little One?,* p. 83; February 11, 2002, review of *Old Crump: The True Story of a Trip West,* p. 185; February 18, 2002, review of *The Colt and the King,* p. 65; October 25, 2004, review of *Two by Two,* p. 46.

School Library Journal, April, 1996, pp. 121-122; May, 1997, p. 117; November, 2000, Carolyn Stacey, review of *Keeping up with Grandma,* p. 138; April, 2002, Patricia Pearl Dole, review of *The Colt and the King,* p. 116; June, 2002, review of *Old Crump,* p. 98; May, 2003, Harriett Fargnoli, review of *Brother Wolf, Sister Sparrow,* p. 137; October, 2004, Kathy Piehl, review of *Two by Two,* p. 152.

ONLINE

Scholastic Australia Web site, http://www.scholastic.com.au/ (November 7, 2005), "John Winch."

University of Canberra Mary Gibbs Fellowship Program Web site, http://www.canberra.edu.au/marygibbs/ (November 7, 2005), "John Winch.*"

*   *   *

WINDAWI, Thura al- 1983(?)-
(Thura al-Windawi)

Personal

Born c. 1983. *Education:* Attended University of Baghdad and University of Pennsylvania.

Addresses

Agent—c/o Author Mail, Viking/Penguin Group, 375 Hudson St., New York, NY 10014.

Writings

Thura's Diary: My Life in Wartime Iraq (young adult), translation by Robin Bray, Viking (New York, NY), 2004.

Sidelights

Thura al-Windawi, the daughter of a British-educated father and a middle-class Iraqi mother, is the author of *Thura's Diary: My Life in Wartime Iraq,* a memoir of the time leading up to and including the U.S. invasion that began in March of 2003. A British journalist who

Iraqi teen al-Windawi (right), who was living in Bagdad the night U.S. bombs began to fall on that city, is photographed with school friends prior to the events she outlines in **Thura's Diary: My Life in Wartime in Iraq.**

saw al-Windawi's diary helped get it translated and published. The book contains the thoughts and observations of a young woman whose life changed after her country came under attack. Al-Windawi writes of family moments, including baking bread with her mother and listening to her sister's protestations over the wearing of a head scarf. Most of the details involve the U.S war on Iraqi dictator Saddam Hussein's government and that conflict's aftermath, including how a childhood friend died trying to help others in his Baghdad neighborhood.

Al-Windawi expresses mixed feelings toward both Hussein and the country's U.S. liberators. As Elizabeth Bush pointed out in the *Bulletin of the Center for Children's Books,* "Readers are not required to sort out a political position on the Iraqi conflict." Alison Follos wrote in *School Library Journal,* that al-Windawi's "focus is on explicitly and calmly exposing the ravages of war on the vulnerable members of society."

Al-Windawi studied pharmacology in Baghdad, and when her story reached the admissions department of the University of Pennsylvania, she was offered a four-year scholarship to continue her studies there. She told Rebecca Bellville of *Citypaper.net* that "the message that I want from my diary is that I want peace. After I came here, people are different and everyone has a good heart inside their hearts, and I want to take this message back to Iraq."

Biographical and Critical Sources

BOOKS

Al-Windawi, Thura, *Thura's Diary: My Life in Wartime Iraq* (young adult), translation by Robin Bray, Viking (New York, NY), 2004.

PERIODICALS

Booklist, May 15, 2004, John Green, review of *Thura's Diary,* p. 1613.

Bulletin of the Center for Children's Books, July-August, 2004, Elizabeth Bush, review of *Thura's Diary,* p. 452.

Horn Book, July-August, 2004, Christine M. Heppermann, review of *Thura's Diary,* p. 464.

School Library Journal, July, 2004, Alison Follos, review of *Thura's Diary,* p. 114.

ONLINE

Citypaper.net, http://citypaper.net/ (April 8, 2004), Rebecca Bellville, interview with al-Windawi.*

*   *   *

WINFIELD, Julia
See ARMSTRONG, Jennifer

*   *   *

WOLFE, Gene 1931-

Personal

Born May 7, 1931, in Brooklyn, NY; son of Roy Emerson (a salesman) and Mary Olivia (Ayers) Wolfe; married Rosemary Frances Dietsch, November 3, 1956; children: Roy II, Madeleine, Therese, Matthew. *Education:* Attended Texas A & M University, 1949-52; University of Houston, B.S.M.E., 1956. *Religion:* Roman Catholic.

Addresses

Home—P.O. Box 69, Barrington, IL 60011. *Agent*—Virginia Kidd Agency, Box 278, Milford, PA 18337.

Career

Writer. Project engineer with Procter & Gamble, 1956-72; *Plant Engineering* magazine, Barrington, IL, senior editor, 1972-84. *Military service:* U.S. Army, 1952-54; received Combat Infantry badge.

Member

Science Fiction Writers of America.

Awards, Honors

Nebula Award, Science Fiction Writers of America (SFWA), 1973, for novella *The Death of Doctor Island;* Chicago Foundation for Literature Award, 1977, for *Peace;* Rhysling Award, 1978, for poem "The Computer Iterates the Greater Trumps"; Nebula Award nomination, 1979, for novella *Seven American Nights,* and 1993, for *Nightside the Long Sun;* Illinois Arts Council award, 1981, for short story "In Looking-Glass Castle"; World Fantasy Award, 1981, for *The Shadow of the Torturer,* 1989, for collection *Storeys from the Old Hotel,* and 1996, for Lifetime Achievement; Nebula Award, and *Locus* Award, both 1982, both for *The Claw of the Conciliator;* British Science Fiction Award, 1982; British Fantasy Award, 1983; *Locus* Award, 1983, for *The Sword of the Lictor;* John W. Campbell Memorial Award, University of Kansas Center for the Study of Science Fiction, 1984, for *The Citadel of the Autarch;* World Fantasy Award for Lifetime Achievement.

Writings

SCIENCE FICTION AND FANTASY

Operation ARES, Berkley Publishing (New York, NY), 1970.

The Fifth Head of Cerberus (three novellas), Scribner (New York, NY), 1972, reprinted, Orb (New York, NY), 1994.

(With Ursula K. LeGuin and James Tiptree, Jr.) *The New Atlantis and Other Novellas of Science Fiction,* edited by Robert L. Silverberg, Hawthorn (New York, NY), 1975.

The Devil in a Forest (juvenile), Follett (New York, NY), 1976, reprinted, Orb (New York, NY), 1996.

Plan(e)t Engineering, New England Science Fiction Association (Framingham, MA), 1984.

Free Live Free, Ziesing Bros. (Willimantic, CT), 1984, new edition, Tor Books (New York, NY), 1985.

Soldier of the Mist, Tor (New York, NY), 1986.

There Are Doors, Tor (New York, NY), 1988.

Seven American Nights (bound with *Sailing to Byzantium* by Robert L. Silverberg), Tor (New York, NY), 1989.

Soldier of Arete (sequel to *Soldier of the Mist*), St. Martin's Press (New York, NY), 1989.

Pandora by Holly Hollander, Tor (New York, NY), 1990.

Castleview, Tor (New York, NY), 1991.

Castle of Days, Tor (New York, NY), 1992.

Latro in the Mist (contains *Soldier of the Mist* and *Soldier of Arete*), Orb (New York, NY), 2003.

The Knight (book one of "Wizard Knight" series), Tor (New York, NY), 2004.

The Wizard (book two of "Wizard Knight" series), Tor (New York, NY), 2004.

SHORT STORIES

The Island of Doctor Death, and Other Stories, Pocket Books (New York, NY), 1980, reprinted, Orb (New York, NY), 1997.
Gene Wolfe's Book of Days, Doubleday (New York, NY), 1981.
The Wolfe Archipelago, Ziesing Bros. (Willimantic, CT), 1983.
Storeys from the Old Hotel, Kerosina (Worcester Park, England), 1988, Orb (New York, NY), 1995.
Endangered Species, Tor (New York, NY), 1989.
Strange Travelers, Tor (New York, NY), 2000.
Innocents Abroad: New Fantasy Stories, Tor (New York, NY), 2004.
Starwater Strains, Tor (New York, NY), 2005.

"BOOK OF THE NEW SUN" SERIES

The Shadow of the Torturer, Simon & Schuster (New York, NY), 1980.
The Claw of the Conciliator, Simon & Schuster, 1981.
The Sword of the Lictor, Simon & Schuster, 1982.
The Citadel of the Autarch, Simon & Schuster, 1983.
The Urth of the New Sun, Tor (New York, NY), 1987.
Shadow and Claw (contains *The Shadow of the Torturer* and *The Claw of the Conciliator*), Orb (New York, NY), 1994.
Sword and Citadel (contains *The Sword of the Lictor* and *The Citadel of the Autarch*), Orb (New York, NY), 1994.

"BOOK OF THE LONG SUN" SERIES

Nightside the Long Sun, Tor (New York, NY), 1993.
Lake of the Long Sun, Tor (New York, NY), 1993.
Calde of the Long Sun, Tor (New York, NY), 1994.
Exodus from the Long Sun, Tor (New York, NY), 1995.

"BOOK OF THE SHORT SUN" TRILOGY

On Blue's Waters, Tor (New York, NY), 1999.
In Green's Jungle, Tor (New York, NY), 2000.
Return to the Whorl, Tor (New York, NY), 2001.

OTHER

Peace (novel), Harper (New York, NY), 1975, reprinted, Tor, 1995.
The Castle of the Otter (essays), Ziesing Bros. (Willimantic, CT), 1982.
Bibliomen, Cheap Street (New Castle, VA), 1984.
Empires of Foliage and Flower, Cheap Street (New Castle, VA), 1987.
For Rosemary (poetry), Kerosina (Worcester Park, England), 1988.

Contributor of stories to anthologies, including awards anthologies *Best SF: 70,* 1970, *Nebula Award Stories 9, The Best SF of the Year No. 3,* and *Best SF: '73,* all 1974. Contributor of short stories to *Omni, New Yorker, Isaac Asimov's Science Fiction Magazine,* and other publications. Collaborator with Neil Gaiman on *A Walking Tour of the Shambles: Little Walks for Sightseers £16,* published for World Horror Convention, 2002.

Work in Progress

Soldier of Sidon, a sequel to *Soldier of the Mist* and *Soldier of Arete.*

Sidelights

With his five-volume "Book of the New Sun" series, American science-fiction writer Gene Wolfe "entered the ranks of the major contemporary writers of science fiction," Pamela Sargent asserted in *Twentieth-Century Science-Fiction Writers.* The series, which was published between 1980 and 1987, takes place far in the future in a society reminiscent of medieval Europe in its social structure but where long-forgotten technologies appear magical. When Severian, an apprentice torturer, is exiled from his guild for aiding the suicide of a prisoner he loves, a journey of discovery is inaugurated that culminates in Severian's elevation to autarch, ruler of Urth. "The far-future world of Urth through which Wolfe's characters move is a world of beauty and horror, one in which humanity's great accomplishments are not only past, but also nearly forgotten, and in which the lack of resources makes the knowledge that remains nearly useless," noted Sargent. Thomas D. Clareson, discussing Wolf's writings in the *Dictionary of Literary Biography,* called the "Book of the New Sun" series "one of the high accomplishments of modern science fiction."

Wolfe was born in Brooklyn, New York, and developed an early love of reading, and his fascination with science fiction branded him as an outcast in high school. Although he excelled at English, he chose to purse engineering in college, taking a few years out to serve overseas in the Korean War. After finishing college, Wolfe found work as an engineer, and married childhood friend Rosemary Dietsch. Early in their marriage, the couple looked for extra income, and Wolfe hoped to write a novel to earn additional money; it took him eight years before his first story, "The Dead Man" was bought by *Sir!* for eighty dollars.

A second tale, "Mountains like Mice," when published in Frederik Pohl's *If,* cemented Wolfe's desire to write. From then on, although he worked primarily as an engineer, his writing career began to grow. He joined the Science Fiction Writers of America, and his stories were published regularly in *Orbit.* Damon Knight, *Orbit's* editor (whom Wolfe has called "the greatest influence on my career"), convinced the author to develop one short work titled "The Laughter Outside at Night" into a longer tale; this he did, and *Operation Ares* became Wolfe's first novel.

After publishing *The Fifth Head of Cerberus,* his second novel, Wolfe quit his engineering job and became an editor at a technical magazine. His fiction, well received by critics, was soon sold in Great Britain, France, Germany, Italy, and Sweden. It was at this point in his career that Wolfe began the story that evolved into the "Book of the New Sun," his most successful series of books.

The "Book of the New Sun" tetralogy takes place in the far future. The original volumes include *The Shadow of the Torturer, The Claw of the Conciliator, The Sword of the Lictor,* and *The Citadel of the Autarch;* Wolfe subsequently added a one-volume sequel, *The Urth of the New Sun.* The first four titles were described by Wolfe in an essay for the *Contemporary Authors Autobiography Series* (*CAAS*) as "the autobiography of the Autarch Severian, who began life as an orphaned apprentice in the Order of the Seekers for Truth and Penitence (known unofficially as the torturers guild), was exiled for showing mercy, and rose to the throne of the Commonwealth, a peculiar monarchy occupying the South America of a world remote in time from our own." Wolf considers *The Shadow of the Torturer* to be his most successful novel.

In the *Washington Post Book World,* James Gunn called *The Shadow of the Torturer* "an engrossing narrative and perhaps a book in which wisdom can be found." Discussing the entire series, *Los Angeles Times Book Review* critic David N. Samuelson dubbed "Book of the New Sun" "a monumental achievement in the oft-despised genre of science fantasy. Well written, vividly imaged, symbolically united and internally consistent, it has the dubious distinction of dwarfing what mediocre competition there is." *Magazine of Fantasy and Science Fiction* book critic Algis Budrys wrote that "Wolfe is, I think, without peer at his own kind of story, and has a particular gift for the depiction of cataclysmic events through the eyes of a naive central character."

As the series continues in *The Urth of the New Sun,* Severian attempts to revive Urth's dying sun. Colin Greenland, writing in the *Times Literary Supplement,* stated that, "if this book is less brilliant than its predecessor, the flaw is one that is hard to spot with the unaided eye." According to Fred Lerner in *Voice of Youth Advocates,* "Wolfe employs a richness of language unmatched in science fiction, and his imagination is equally unfettered by the traditions of the genre."

After taking some time away from his "New Sun" universe, Wolfe released *Nightside the Long Sun,* the first of a new four-volume epic called "Book of the Long Sun" which takes place in the same future as his original tetralogy. *Lake of the Long Sun, Calde of the Long Sun,* and *Exodus from the Long Sun* rounded out the sequence. The action takes place inside the Whorl, a massive cylindrical starship whose inhabitants have long forgotten what mission, if any, the ship is on. Lit by a central "long sun," the culture of the vast ship is a cross

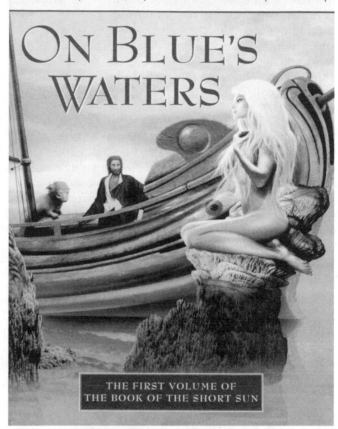

A sequel to Wolfe's "Book of the Long Sun" series, this 1999 novel finds narrator Horn on a quest to seek Patera Silk, a legendary leader who has long since abandoned the planet Blue and the human colonies he helped establish there for a new home beyond the end of the known world.

between modern science and medieval superstition. The main character, Patera Silk, is a schoolmaster and priest who has a vision of the Outsider, a god who transcends the Whorl, that changes his life. While attempting to ransom his parish house from unsavory creditors, Silk uncovers the starting truth about the Whorl. Of the "Book of the Long Sun" series, *New York Times Book Review* critic Gerald Jonas wrote that "Wolfe loves his characters, and it is not possible to accompany them on their long and strange journey without sharing that feeling."

In 1999 Wolfe published the first of three books in a third series, "Book of the Short Sun." The action begins decades after the last of the "Book of the Long Sun" novels. Narrated by the character Horn, series opener *On Blue's Waters* follows Horn's quest to find Silk, the original leader of the colonies on the planet Blue, in an effort to save the decaying human cities. "Wolfe's prose is masterful and his main characters are well developed," wrote a critic in *Publishers Weekly.* As Horn searches for Silk across Blue, through the jungles of the planet of Green, and even to the original ship the Whorl, he begins to resemble the sainted figure he seeks, so much that even his wife and sons no longer recognize him. Through his journeys, Horn also comes to terms with the race of blood-drinking inhumu, and finds that his initial hatred for the species turns to a loving acceptance. "Longtime fans of Wolfe's complex plotting and ornate literary style will find much to cheer," wrote a *Publishers Weekly* reviewer of the third volume, *Return to the Whorl.* The same novel led *Booklist* critic Jackie Cassada to call Wolfe "one of the genre's most brilliant contributors."

Although Wolfe's series are divided into separate parts, many readers have grouped the books together as a single, drawn-out tale. "This huge twelve-volume cathedral of worlds is of infinite fascination, one of the most complex religious allegories ever set to paper," wrote Nick Gevers on the *Infinity Plus Web site.* In a review of *Return to the Whorl* for the *Magazine of Fantasy and Science Fiction,* Robert K.J. Killheffer commented: "I don't know if anything can outdo *The Shadow of the Torturer* for sheer wonderment and strangeness. . . .

A prolific author of short fiction as well as novels, acclaimed storyteller Wolfe collects fantasy as well as horror and ghost stories in this 2004 collection. (Cover illustration by René Magritte/C. Herscovici.)

But Horn is an adult, where Servian is a boy, and Horn's story plumbs caverns of sorrow, hope, grief, and guilt." Killheffer concluded, "'The Book of the Short Sun' is a tale of personal redemption, not cosmic, and as such, it is not so fine an sf novel as 'The Book of the New Sun.' But it may be the finer novel overall."

Although they remain his prime contributions to the sci-fi genre, Wolfe's writing has extended far beyond the universe of the "New Sun" books. His stand-alone novel *Soldier of the Mist* is innovative in its account of Latro, a soldier of ancient Greece whose memory is wiped clean every time he sleeps—payment for having seen the gods; Latro's condition necessitates the keeping of a journal in which he records each day's events—with each new day he must read the journal and relearn his life. Guided by his text and various gods, Latro journeys to regain his memory. Wolfe continues Latro's story in *Soldier of Arete,* in which the soldier becomes embroiled in the political and military rivalry between Greece and Sparta. John Calvin Batchelor observed in the *Washington Post Book World* that *Soldier of the Mist,* while difficult reading, is "a work of consequence." The author "is a master of science fiction," Batchelor concluded, "and for the best of all reasons, vaulting ambition." As Killheffer explained in the *Magazine of Fantasy and Science Fiction,* "Wolfe set himself to the arduous task of recounting a story through the eyes of a narrator who cannot recall events from one day to the next, and he stayed true to his conceit with astounding fidelity."

Wolfe's literary reputation is also bolstered by his short fiction, notably the collections *Storeys from the Old Hotel,* a highly accessible gathering of imaginative fiction, and a somewhat more challenging volume of philosophically inclined tales titled *Endangered Species.* As Sargent stated, "Wolfe is a writer for the thinking reader; he will reward anyone searching for intelligence, crafted prose, involving stories, and atmospheric detail. He is the heir of many literary traditions—pulp stories, fantasy, adventure stories of all kinds, and serious literature—and he makes use of all of them." Wolfe has continued writing short stories throughout his career, and his collections continue to garner praise from critics. In a review of *Innocents Abroad,* a *Publishers Weekly* reviewer commented that the stories in the collection stand as "further proof that Wolfe ranks with the finest writers of this or any other day." Roland Green, reviewing the same title for *Booklist,* maintained that "Short fiction doesn't often get better than this."

Although much of Wolfe's science fiction has been known to teen readers for decades, in 2004, a duo of fantasy novels brought his books to a wider young-adult audience. *The Knight* and its sequel, *The Wizard,* feature a teen named Able who wanders into a mythical realm and becomes trapped in the heroic body of Sir Able of the High Heart by an elf queen. While trying to retain some of his own identity, much of which the elf queen has stolen from him, the teen finds himself slowly

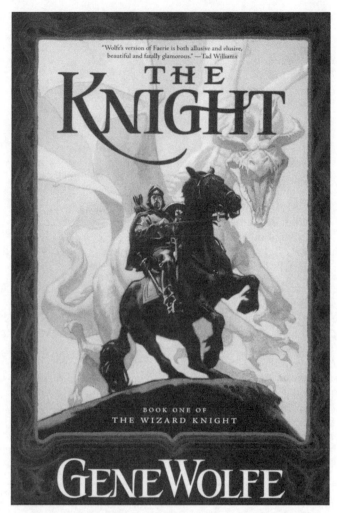

The first volume of Wolfe's two-part series finds a modern teen transported to a multi-level world where, magically given the body of a brawny knight, he begins a quest to find the special sword that will make him a true knight. (Cover illustration by Gregory Manchess.)

transforming into the knight he pretends to be. A *Publishers Weekly* critic called *The Knight* "a compelling, breathtaking achievement." In *The Wizard,* after leaving the world for a time, Able must return to try to resolve a conflict between the realm of King Arnthor and his enemies the Frost Giants, who seek to raid Arnthor's lands and capture human slaves. "This is fantasy at its best: revelatory and inspirational," wrote a *Publishers Weekly* reviewer of *The Wizard.* Of the "Wizard Knight" series, *Booklist* critic Green considered it "one of the few fantasies that can justly be compared with" J.R.R. Tolkien's *Lord of the Rings.*

When asked by James Jordan in an online interview for *Infinity Plus* where he came up with the idea for the "Wizard Knight" books, Wolfe explained: "I met a nice little boy named Nick. . . . He was very, very bright, and crazy about knights and the whole medieval scene. I tried to figure out what attracted him to it so much, and began to write a book." Wolfe explained to Gevers in another *Infinity Plus* interview about his decision to combine chivalry with Teutonic mythology in the two books. "I started thinking about knighthood, and won-

dering why that period has an eternal fascination for us," Wolfe stated. "Greek myth is laid in the Golden Age. The Dark Ages are our Golden Age; most fairy tales, and all the best ones, are laid there."

A writer who enjoys his craft, Wolfe explained to Brendan Baber in an interview for the *Lupine Nuncio Web site:* "I've tried to do things that seemed to me should be done and nobody had done yet. But everybody who's worth reading is trying to do exactly that." Talking with British writer Neil Gaiman in a *Locus* interview about fiction's most important qualities, Wolfe responded, "The most important thing is that it assures the reader that things need not be as they are now. In other words, the most important thing is hope."

Biographical and Critical Sources

BOOKS

Andre-Driussi, Michael, *Lexicon Urthus: A Dictionary for the Urth Cycle,* Sirius Fiction (San Francisco, CA), 1994.
Contemporary Authors Autobiography Series, Volume 9, Thomson Gale (Detroit, MI), 1989.
Contemporary Literary Criticism, Volume 25, Thomson Gale (Detroit, MI), 1983.
Dictionary of Literary Biography, Volume 8: *Twentieth-Century American Science-Fiction Writers,* Thomson Gale (Detroit, MI), 1981.
Gordon, Joan, *Gene Wolfe,* Borgo Press (San Bernadino, CA), 1986.
Lane, Daryl, William Vernon, and David Carson, editors, *The Sound of Wonder: Interviews from "The Science Fiction Radio Show,"* Volume 2, Oryx (Phoenix, AZ), 1985.
Twentieth-Century Science-Fiction Writers, St. James Press (Detroit, MI), 1986.

PERIODICALS

Analog Science Fiction/Science Fact, August, 1990, p. 143; June, 1991, p. 178; June, 1994, p. 161; February, 1995, p. 159; November, 2000, review of *In Green's Jungles,* p. 131.
Booklist, July 1, 1975; November 1, 1982; August, 1989; November 15, 1992; September 15, 1994, p. 118; August, 2000, Roberta Johnson, review of *In Green's Jungles,* p. 2126; February 15, 2001, Roberta Johnson, review of *Return to the Whorl*; December 15, 2003, Roland Green, review of *The Knight,* p. 735; July, 2004, Roland Green, review of *Innocents Abroad,* p. 1830; November 1, 2004, Roland Green, review of *The Wizard,* p. 472.
Chicago Tribune Book World, June 8, 1980; June 14, 1981.
Chronicle, February, 2004, Don D'Ammassa, review of *The Knight,* p. 30.
Extrapolation, summer, 1981; fall, 1982.

Kansas Quarterly, summer, 1984.

Kirkus Reviews, December 1, 1999, p. 1854; October 15, 2004, review of *The Wizard,* p. 990.

Library Journal, November 15, 1990, p. 95; December, 1992, p. 191; August, 1994, p. 139; September 15, 1994, p. 94; December, 2003, Jackie Cassada, review of *The Knight,* p. 173.

Locus, February, 1990; December, 1993; August, 1994; September, 2002, "The Wolfe and Gaiman Show."

London Tribune, April 24, 1981, article by Martin Hillman.

Los Angeles Times Book Review, April 3, 1983, David N. Samuelson, review of *The Citadel of the Autarch,* p. 4; June 6, 1993, James Sallis, review of *Nightside the Long Sun.*

Magazine of Fantasy and Science Fiction, April, 1971; May, 1978; May, 1980, Algis Budrys, review of *The Shadow of the Torturer,* p. 23; June, 1981; September, 1994, p. 16; October, 2001, Robert K.J. Killheffer, review of *Return to the Whorl,* p. 49.

New York Times Book Review, July 13, 1975; September 12, 1976; May 22, 1983; November 24, 1985; July 2, 1989; May 13, 1990; May 9, 1993, p. 20; January 2, 1994, p. 22; September 11, 1994, Gerald Jonas, review of *Calde of the Long Sun,* p. 46.

Publishers Weekly, September 8, 1989; November 9, 1992; September 13, 1999, review of *On Blue's Waters,* p. 65; December 20, 1999, p. 61; January 22, 2001, review of *Return to the Whorl,* p. 307; December 1, 2003, review of *The Knight,* p. 45; June 14, 2004, review of *Innocents Abroad,* p. 48; October 11, 2004, review of *The Wizard,* p. 61; June 27, 2005, review of *Starwater Strains,* p. 46.

Science Fiction Review, summer, 1981.

Times (London, England), April 2, 1981.

Times Literary Supplement, May 18, 1973; January 15, 1988; January 15, 1988, Colin Greenland, "Miracles Recollected in Tranquility," p. 69.

Voice of Youth Advocates, April, 1988, Fred Lerner, review of *The Urth of the New Sun,* p. 42; February, 2001, review of *In Green's Jungles,* p. 437.

Washington Post Book World, May 25, 1980, James Gunn, review of *The Shadow of the Torturer,* p. 8; March 22, 1981; July 26, 1981; January 24, 1982; January 30, 1983; November 24, 1985; October 26, 1986, John Calvin Batchelor, "Warriors, Gods, and Kings"; October 27, 1987; August 28, 1988; April 30, 1989; January 31, 1993; December 26, 1993; October 23, 1994.

ONLINE

Gene Wolfe Home Page, http://www.urth.org/~gac/Wolfe (November 6, 2005).

Infinity Plus Web site, http://www.infinityplus.co.uk/ (October, 2003), Nick Gevers, Michael Andre-Driussi, and James Jordan, "Some Moments with the Magus: An Interview with Gene Wolfe."

Lupine Nuncio Web site, http://mysite.verizon.net/~vze2tmhh/wolfe.html (March 20, 1994), Brendan Baber, interview with Wolfe.

Illustrations Index

(In the following index, the number of the *volume* in which an illustrator's work appears is given *before* the colon, and the *page number* on which it appears is given *after* the colon. For example, a drawing by Adams, Adrienne appears in Volume 2 on page 6, another drawing by her appears in Volume 3 on page 80, another drawing in Volume 8 on page 1, and so on and so on. . . .)

YABC

Index references to *YABC* refer to listings appearing in the two-volume *Yesterday's Authors of Books for Children,* also published by Thomson Gale. *YABC* covers prominent authors and illustrators who died prior to 1960.

A

Aas, Ulf *5:* 174
Abbe, S. van
  See van Abbe, S.
Abel, Raymond *6:* 122; *7:* 195; *12:* 3; *21:* 86; *25:* 119
Abelliera, Aldo *71:* 120
Abolafia, Yossi *60:* 2; *93:* 163; *152:* 202
Abrahams, Hilary *26:* 205; *29:* 24-25; *53:* 61
Abrams, Kathie *36:* 170
Abrams, Lester *49:* 26
Abulafia, Yossi *154:* 67
Accorsi, William *11:* 198
Acs, Laszlo *14:* 156; *42:* 22
Adams, Adrienne *2:* 6; *3:* 80; *8:* 1; *15:* 107; *16:* 180; *20:* 65; *22:* 134-135; *33:* 75; *36:* 103, 112; *39:* 74; *86:* 54; *90:* 2, 3
Adams, Connie J. *129:* 68
Adams, John Wolcott *17:* 162
Adams, Lynn *96:* 44
Adams, Norman *55:* 82
Adams, Pam *112:* 1, 2
Adams, Sarah *98:* 126
Adamson, George *30:* 23, 24; *69:* 64
Addams, Charles *55:* 5
Ade, Rene *76:* 198
Adinolfi, JoAnn *115:* 42
Adkins, Alta *22:* 250
Adkins, Jan *8:* 3; *69:* 4; *144:* 2, 3, 4
Adler, Peggy *22:* 6; *29:* 31
Adler, Ruth *29:* 29
Adlerman, Daniel *163:* 2
Adragna, Robert *47:* 145
Agard, Nadema *18:* 1
Agee, Jon *116:* 8, 9, 10; *157:* 4
Agre, Patricia *47:* 195
Aguirre, Alfredo *152:* 218
Ahl, Anna Maria *32:* 24
Ahlberg, Allan *68:* 6-7, 9; *165:* 5
Ahlberg, Janet *68:* 6-7, 9
Aicher-Scholl, Inge *63:* 127
Aichinger, Helga *4:* 5, 45
Aitken, Amy *31:* 34
Akaba, Suekichi *46:* 23; *53:* 127
Akasaka, Miyoshi *YABC 2:* 261
Akino, Fuku *6:* 144
Alain *40:* 41
Alajalov *2:* 226
Alborough, Jez *86:* 1, 2, 3; *149:* 3

Albrecht, Jan *37:* 176
Albright, Donn *1:* 91
Alcala, Alfredo *91:* 128
Alcorn, John *3:* 159; *7:* 165; *31:* 22; *44:* 127; *46:* 23, 170
Alcorn, Stephen *110:* 4; *125:* 106; *128:* 172; *150:* 97; *160:* 188; *165:* 48
Alcott, May *100:* 3
Alda, Arlene *44:* 24; *158:* 2
Alden, Albert *11:* 103
Aldridge, Andy *27:* 131
Aldridge, George *105:* 125
Alex, Ben *45:* 25, 26
Alexander, Ellen *91:* 3
Alexander, Lloyd *49:* 34
Alexander, Martha *3:* 206; *11:* 103; *13:* 109; *25:* 100; *36:* 131; *70:* 6, 7; *136:* 3, 4, 5
Alexander, Paul *85:* 57; *90:* 9
Alexeieff, Alexander *14:* 6; *26:* 199
Alfano, Wayne *80:* 69
Aliki
  See Brandenberg, Aliki
Allamand, Pascale *12:* 9
Allan, Judith *38:* 166
Alland, Alexandra *16:* 255
Allen, Gertrude *9:* 6
Allen, Graham *31:* 145
Allen, Jonathan B. *131:* 3, 4
Allen, Pamela *50:* 25, 26-27, 28; *81:* 9, 10; *123:* 4-5
Allen, Rowena *47:* 75
Allen, Thomas B. *81:* 101; *82:* 248; *89:* 37; *104:* 9
Allen, Tom *85:* 176
Allender, David *73:* 223
Alley, R. W. *80:* 183; *95:* 187; *156:* 100, 153
Allison, Linda *43:* 27
Allon, Jeffrey *119:* 174
Allport, Mike *71:* 55
Almquist, Don *11:* 8; *12:* 128; *17:* 46; *22:* 110
Aloise, Frank *5:* 38; *10:* 133; *30:* 92
Althea
  See Braithwaite, Althea
Altschuler, Franz *11:* 185; *23:* 141; *40:* 48; *45:* 29; *57:* 181
Alvin, John *117:* 5
Ambrus, Victor G. *1:* 6-7, 194; *3:* 69; *5:* 15; *6:* 44; *7:* 36; *8:* 210; *12:* 227; *14:* 213; *15:* 213; *22:* 209; *24:* 36; *28:* 179; *30:* 178; *32:* 44,

46; *38:* 143; *41:* 25, 26, 27, 28, 29, 30, 31, 32; *42:* 87; *44:* 190; *55:* 172; *62:* 30, 144, 145, 148; *86:* 99, 100, 101; *87:* 66, 137; *89:* 162; *134:* 160
Ames, Lee J. *3:* 12; *9:* 130; *10:* 69; *17:* 214; *22:* 124; *151:* 13
Amon, Aline *9:* 9
Amoss, Berthe *5:* 5
Amstutz, Andre *152:* 102
Amundsen, Dick *7:* 77
Amundsen, Richard E. *5:* 10; *24:* 122
Ancona, George *12:* 11; *55:* 144; *145:* 7
Andersen, Bethanne *116:* 167; *162:* 189
Anderson, Alasdair *18:* 122
Anderson, Bob *139:* 16
Anderson, Brad *33:* 28
Anderson, C. W. *11:* 10
Anderson, Carl *7:* 4
Anderson, Catherine Corley *72:* 2
Anderson, Cecil *127:* 152
Anderson, David Lee *118:* 176
Anderson, Doug *40:* 111
Anderson, Erica *23:* 65
Anderson, Laurie *12:* 153, 155
Anderson, Lena *99:* 26
Anderson, Scoular *138:* 13
Anderson, Susan *90:* 12
Anderson, Wayne *23:* 119; *41:* 239; *56:* 7; *62:* 26; *147:* 6
Andreasen, Daniel *86:* 157; *87:* 104; *103:* 201, 202; *159:* 75
Andrew, Ian *111:* 37; *116:* 12
Andrew, John *22:* 4
Andrews, Benny *14:* 251; *31:* 24; *57:* 6, 7
Anelay, Henry *57:* 173
Angel, Marie *47:* 22
Angelo, Valenti *14:* 8; *18:* 100; *20:* 232; *32:* 70
Anglund, Joan Walsh *2:* 7, 250-251; *37:* 198, 199, 200
Anholt, Catherine *74:* 8; *131:* 7; *141:* 5
Anholt, Laurence *141:* 4
Anno, Mitsumasa *5:* 7; *38:* 25, 26-27, 28, 29, 30, 31, 32; *77:* 3, 4; *157:* 10, 11
Antal, Andrew *1:* 124; *30:* 145
Antram, David *152:* 133
Apostolou, Christy Hale
  See Hale, Christy

I

J

Author Index

The following index gives the number of the volume in which an author's biographical sketch, Autobiography Feature, Brief Entry, or Obituary appears.

This index includes references to all entries in the following series, which are also published by The Gale Group.

YABC—*Yesterday's Authors of Books for Children: Facts and Pictures about Authors and Illustrators of Books for Young People from Early Times to 1960*
CLR—*Children's Literature Review: Excerpts from Reviews, Criticism, and Commentary on Books for Children*
SAAS—*Something about the Author Autobiography Series*

Author Index

Author Index

Author Index

Author Index